Baltimore's Loyola, Loyola's Baltimore

Father John Early, S.J., founder of Loyola College and president, 1852–1858, 1866–1870

Baltimore's Loyola, Loyola's Baltimore

1851–1986

NICHOLAS VARGA

The Maryland Historical Society
Baltimore, Maryland

LIBRARY OF CONGRESS CATALOGING-IN-PUBLICATION DATA

Varga, Nicholas, 1925–
  Baltimore's Loyola, Loyola's Baltimore, 1851–1986/Nicholas
Varga.
      p.   cm.
  Includes bibliographical references.
  ISBN 0-938420-34-8: $29.95
  1. Loyola College in Maryland—History.   I. Title.
LD3131.L62V37   1989
378.752'6—dc20   89-48249 CIP

Contents

Illustrations

Tables

Preface

When he learned that I had begun work on the history of Loyola College, a friend instantly asked, "What's the matter? Are you ill?" He knew that such projects are often assigned to or taken up by infirm or elderly faculty members. Too often they laud everything associated with their schools and point to distinctions or innovations that have supposedly been ignored. Old glories are recounted in fulsome tones and old feuds are fought again, with justice predictably on the side of alma mater. Examples of such institutional glorification are numerous, and they explain in large measure the suspicion attached to the genre.

A more telling criticism, especially of the histories of Catholic schools, is that too often they are told with little or no reference to what was happening at other American colleges. Changes in curriculum, structure, administrative practice, and so on have been described entirely from within the ivied walls of a particular college or university. As a result, readers have the uncomfortable feeling that they are studying a disembodied "being in itself" instead of a group of humans trying to work out their institutional and individual destinies.

If college histories have such a dubious reputation, why would a scholar undertake to write a college history? More precisely, why did I decide to write the history of Loyola? There was, of course, the hope to add another volume to the small but growing shelf of worthwhile institutional histories. But pride and ambition might have been as well or better satisfied with some other project. The actual process was more involved than this answer might suggest. In the end, the main reason was the obvious need.

Memory is a major element in maintaining an individual's sense of identity. We recognize who we are by recalling what we have done and how we have reacted to our experiences. This function of memory is even more vital to a group, because the arrival and departure of members constantly changes the group's memory of itself and, consequently, its sense of self. For Loyola, there was not much available beyond Father John Ryan's *Historical Sketch of Loyola College*, published around 1902, after the college's fiftieth anniversary. For many years, more pressing concerns and a touch of diffidence militated against such a project. Loyola, after all, was a very small school until quite recently. What use could such a history serve?

As the centennial of Loyola's founding approached, some thought was given to producing a history for the occasion. Father Francis Talbot, an able author and historian who served as Loyola's president and rector from 1947 to 1950, started preliminary research and uncovered a larger corpus of original documents than previously had been supposed to exist. But for various reasons, including the relative brevity of Talbot's term, this effort produced nothing for publication.

Several years later, the project was revived and assigned to a Jesuit who had served honorably in the classrooms of several institutions, including Loyola College. In obedience he started research, and completed ten long chapters that covered only the first four decades. On review, the projected length of the final work and the idiosyncratic form of documentation were questioned. The author shared with Hilaire Belloc a disdain for footnotes and similar devices. He preferred to quote original documents, sometimes at length, or to incorporate bibliographical information directly into his narrative. Disconcerting as this approach might sound, the author was in fact marvelously inventive and smooth in the ways he introduced his references. He told stories leisurely, his style exemplifying the virtues of the old liberal arts curriculum. History is more than citing and verifying documents. The sources themselves reveal much about how things were done and what the authors thought about their experiences. The direct use of sources in a historical account has in the past been an acceptable narrative technique, but it has gradually been abandoned because it increases bulk and slows the pace. The author might have been willing to condense the narrative, but the prospect of recovering all the references and reforming them into what is called scholarly apparatus was daunting. And then his health took a bad turn.

My entrance into this field came in response to a request from *The New Catholic Encyclopedia* in the early 1960s for an article on Loyola College. This I prepared from Ryan's *Historical Sketch* and other publications. Upon completing the article, I discussed the need for a book-length history with the incumbent president, Father Vincent Beatty, who responded with encouragement. The Jesuit author of the unfinished manuscript gave it to me on condition that his name not appear anywhere in my work. His injunction is scrupulously observed, but the fruits of his labors are here. He was generous with his suggestions, especially of sources within the Society of Jesus that might not be familiar to an outsider.

To prepare for the task, I read a number of institutional histories. Their general tendency was toward a slow-moving narrative recounted in a heavy, impersonal tone, or, alternatively, a mechanical listing of marginally pertinent names and events. These conditions, it seemed to me, arose from a conscientious desire to be thorough in some, and in others from strictures against personal ascriptions inherent in the religious life and from a narrow view of the potential audience. The authors seemed to believe that only alumni could be expected to read histories of educational institutions. Thus, much could be assumed and little effort was needed to engage the interest of the reader. Both the writing *and* the reading, therefore, were acts of piety rather than of scholarship, of learning, or of general interest.

My intention has been to write a brisk account of how and why Loyola College was founded and grew. I thought short sentences and paragraphs would set the appropriate pace. I also thought that explaining Loyola's development required attention to more than presidential directives, committee reports, and the *Ratio Studiorum*. Any school except Mark Hopkins on his log is a group enterprise. Leadership in any group there must be, but what is finally accomplished is mediated through a process that involves a number of participants. This includes students, whose attitudes and roles have changed radically over more than a century but who of necessity have always been the center of the educational enterprise. No vital philosophy of education, and especially not that of the Jesuits, considers students passive receptacles into which masters pour the accumulated knowledge and wisdom of the ages. Popular exposition and even practice may appear at variance with this assertion, but education at its best has always been a process intended to create autonomous persons and not merely to produce identical replacements for preceding generations.

As noted above, this history aims to provide the Loyola College community with a true and useful past—with a memory—and thus with a sense of historical identity. As in a healthy person, this sense of self is not unchangeable, nor does it narrowly circumscribe future development. It serves as a schematic map to afford congruity and balance to discussions of when the next step should be taken and in what direction. Within the Roman Catholic ethos, tradition is a useful and adaptable resource, but it is not necessarily a straitjacket. For a philosopher, there might be several ways to define the reality covered by the phrase *Loyola College*. For the historian, however, there is essentially only one: the meaning of these words is defined by what all the citizens in the community have done.

I have chosen to describe many more things, and in more detail, than is customary in such works. The schedule of classes, financing, tuition, administrative practices, student attitudes, and similar matters in the life of Loyola College have been included for two reasons. The first is a personal conviction that fallacies, falsehoods, and what is now called hype are easily hidden in swift but plausible generalities; truth is discovered (if at all) in detail. The second reason is that I thought it better to show the characters in action rather than to call each in turn to center stage, where his virtues and accomplishments could be spotlighted. This latter method, like the awarding of honorary degrees, allows for little subtlety or rounded judgment. There is indeed something to be learned from inspecting a dried butterfly impaled on a pin, but even more can be discerned by watching its behavior over the course of its life. All this is complicated by the fact that Loyola College is not a single specimen but a group whose membership changes regularly.

To introduce and describe the main players and auxiliaries in a way that can be understood by almost anyone has required attention to historical events and processes beyond the bounds of the college campus. At various times prevailing attitudes toward higher education, toward Catholicism, and toward the Jesuits impinged on the way things were done. External changes for better or worse were registered in the activity at Loyola. Economic prosperity usually meant rising enrollments, and financial panic or depression normally was followed by declines. We humans are largely creatures of habit and imitation, and as a result the society in which we live largely defines our means and ends. For these reasons, developments at Loyola are described in the context of what was simultaneously happening in Baltimore, in Maryland, and in the United States.

One special concern was to show how developments and attitudes at Loyola College were similar to or differed from those at other institutions. Although several general histories of American higher education are cited, it has not been possible to make consistent or detailed comparisons among schools. Too often data have been incorporated in these (and in the histories of particular schools) in a post-holing fashion, with gaps between and variations in the size and shape of the fragmentary information offered. When suitable and sufficient information about other Jesuit schools and other American colleges was available, comparisons have been included.

The title, *Baltimore's Loyola, Loyola's Baltimore,* emphasizes the relation between the college and the city. It also identifies the first of the four Jesuit schools in America to be given the name of the founder of the Society of Jesus, Saint Ignatius Loyola.

Over 130 years ago the college began to function in two small houses on Holliday Street with a faculty and staff of 9 Jesuits and a layman, and a student body of 95. Tuition was $60 a year. Today Loyola College occupies over sixty acres radiating north, east, and west of the Charles Street–Cold Spring intersection, with satellite locations in Howard and Baltimore counties. Over 300 full-time and part-time faculty, some Jesuits, teach more than 6,000 undergraduate and graduate students. Tuition is more than a hundred times as much as at the college's founding.

How and why Loyola College developed as it has are the foci of this narrative. For convenience, the history may be divided into three unequal segments. Until 1921, Loyola was a traditional liberal arts college offering both the secondary and collegiate levels of instruction. The move to the Evergreen campus in 1921 and the desire for accreditation by the Middle States Association severed the connection to high-school instruction and resulted in the conversion of Loyola into a small commuter college. After World War II economic and demographic changes impelled Loyola into its third incarnation, caught and pushed successfully by Father Joseph Sellinger, who has been Loyola's president since 1964. These dates provide landmarks to help us navigate through the varied currents, eddies, and waves that have affected the college's life. Nevertheless, many of the antecedents and consequences of these developments cannot be squeezed into this neat periodic scheme.

This description of the historic sweep offers, I believe, a fuller answer to the question "Why write a college history?" Such a history provides entrance into the social, cultural, and intellectual history of a much larger community. It offers information about ideas and practices that helps explain the mores and ideals of other times. It explicates the long and phenomenal, but by no means preordained, development of

Loyola College. The doing has been rewarding—even fun—and so, I hope, will be the reading.

The standards of scholarly documentation were fully applied in the preparation of the original manuscript. More than one episode was saved from error or distortion by the discipline imposed by the need to use reliable sources accurately. Nevertheless, the narrative as might be expected relies heavily on sources available nowhere else but at Evergreen, and that effectively precludes any independent review of the evidence. The probative value of the documentation that cannot be studied is minimal. Where a direct quotation appears in the text, its source whether extramural or from the college archives has been cited, but otherwise citations of purely local sources—house and deans' diaries, minutes of the meetings of the board of trustees and of the faculty, financial statements, student and alumni publications, and personal interviews—have been kept to a minimum in the final version. Numbers in parentheses following names of alumni indicate the year the alumnus graduated or would have graduated if he had not left the college before graduation.

The reader will find several references to myself in the narrative. However it may seem, these have been kept to a minimum, but I have been an active participant in the life of Loyola College since September of 1955. My memory, chastened by documentation, was I thought a suitable historical resource. To have effaced these episodes would have diminished the narrative and distorted the record, and not to have identified myself as a participant would have been unduly coy. Please ascribe such references more to professional duty than to personal pride.

Acknowledgments

Having engaged in the research and writing of this book over a good many years, I have incurred numerous personal debts. These acknowledgments are merely public notices of an indebtedness I can never fully discharge. They are arranged in convenient categories rather than according to the proportion of my obligation.

Archives are fundamental to historical research, and the archivists I met have invariably been courteous and helpful. Among these were Brother Joseph Ramspacher, who made the Maryland Province Archives an open book; Father Vincent Bellwoar and Jon Reynolds did the same for me at Georgetown; Father William Lucey showed me the treasures of Holy Cross; Baltimore and race relations in the 1950s and 1960s would have been murky and thin without the resources of the Josephite Archives and the cheerful guidance of Father Peter Hogan; for the circumstances that led to the founding of Loyola I had the help of Fathers Vincent Eaton and John Bowen of the Sulpician Archives; Phebe Jacobsen guided me through the Maryland State Archives, and Richard Cox performed the same service at the Baltimore City Archives. Fathers William Michaelman and Jerry McAndrews are not archivists but they graciously gave me access to the holdings at Saint Ignatius Church and Loyola High School. When he served as minister, Father Joe Drane was equally helpful with the records of the Evergreen Jesuit community. Finally, the librarians in the Maryland Room at the Enoch Pratt Library answered my questions and requests with attention and dispatch.

There are too many people who have endured interviews or who answered specific questions to be enumerated; my thanks to each of you for your patience and candor.

I have been blessed with generous readers who willingly studied the evolving text and politely suggested improvements. The early chapters were read by Ed Kaltenbach, Father Bill Davish, and Father Joseph Sellinger. In 1976 at the request of college administrators I sent the manuscript—then about half-finished—to Father Joe Durkin of Georgetown and Phil Gleason of Notre Dame. They offered suggestions and general encouragement.

Through a department colleague I began a long and fruitful association with Bill Wolfe of Middle Tennessee State University about the same time. Bill became my confidante and a kindly, if also demanding, editor. To his guidance I attribute the basic consistency of tone and whatever felicity of language or graciousness of thought may be detected in the text.

The later chapters were read by Jack Breihan and Chuck Cheape of the history department and Tom Scheye, Michael Goff, and Paul Melanson of the administration of Loyola College. Each indicated some personal views but none involved any unacceptable prompting.

Father Bill Davish offered to read the galleys from the very beginning but when it dawned on me that the manuscript would be going to the compositor on a diskette I thought it better to enlist his assistance earlier. His sharp editorial eye and pencil further burnished the text, and his enthusiasm was balm for my soul.

I am grateful to the Publications Committee of the Maryland Historical Society for recommending that this book be published under its auspices and especially to its chair, George Callcott, whose patience and savvy were critical to the success of this project.

Jackie Eckhart Wehmueller, an editor, Martha Farlow, a designer, and Therese Boyd, a production editor, each imbued with a personal warmth and with a high professionalism, took the typed manuscript and converted it into this book.

Gen Rafferty, when secretary in the history department, typed and retyped various versions of all of these chapters. Her indefatigability, good cheer, and skill made our collaboration a pleasure. I developed a similar, if more recent, relationship with the persons in our word-processing center, especially Melia Peisinger.

Being biased if not blind, I can detect no serious blemishes in the text but if any are discovered they are the responsibility not of my helpers and associates but of myself alone.

The college has supported this effort with one and a half sabbaticals and in other ways. The Maryland Historical Society contributed a most useful grant.

By far the most patient have been my wife, Joan, and our family. I am grateful that their endurance proved to be inexhaustible and that their encouragement, if occasionally jocular, has been unfailing.

Part One

1851–1885

Foundation and Early Development

1

New Arrivals

As the sun rose over Baltimore on October 10, 1851, Jonathan Mullan, sexton at the Catholic cathedral, was startled as he entered the sacristy to find Francis Patrick Kenrick preparing to celebrate Mass. Mullan recognized Kenrick because the latter had visited Baltimore many times. That spring, Kenrick had straightened out the affairs of the archdiocese after the death of Samuel Eccleston. Since Archbishop Eccleston's burial, there had been speculation that Kenrick might be translated from Philadelphia to America's premier see, though other, more familiar, names had also been mentioned. Bishop Kenrick's presence startled the sexton only because Mullan had not been informed of the change. With characteristic dispatch, Kenrick identified himself as the new archbishop of Baltimore. He was the spiritual leader of about one hundred thousand Catholics, who composed approximately 17 percent of the population of Maryland.

• •

Kenrick's arrival in Baltimore marked the beginning of a new era in the American Catholic church. It signalled a shift in dominance from American and French influence to immigrant Irish and Roman influence. The unconscionable muddling of the British government and the potato blight had combined to force able Irish men and women to seek new homes and new hope in America. Their rapidly increasing numbers and their steadfast devotion to Catholicism were naturally reflected in the structure of the American church. Archbishop Kenrick's elevation to the see of Baltimore brought closer relations between the American hierarchy and Rome, because he was then one of the few American bishops who had completed his studies for the priesthood in the Eternal City. Furthermore, he had arrived not merely as the new ordinary but also as the apostolic delegate, the pope's personal representative and the presiding officer of the forthcoming first plenary council of the American church.

Education would be one of the most important subjects treated at this congress of the Catholic hierarchy, and educational concerns were evident in a decision made within a few days after Archbishop Kenrick's arrival. On October 13, he directed the Sulpician superior to close Saint Mary's College, a respected Baltimore institution conducted by the Sulpicians for almost half a century. The head of the Maryland province of Jesuits, the provincial, promised to establish another school to fill the void created by the closing of Saint Mary's.[1] The details of timing, of location, and even of what kind of school the Jesuits would open had to be left to later elaboration, but the essential step had been taken.

The rapidity and smoothness of this sequence of events reflected not only Kenrick's leadership but an important movement within the American church. The Catholic bishops, certain that higher education was inherent in their cultural traditions, had observed what other denominations were achieving and sensed a threat in the rapid development of sectarian colleges. They urgently besought the Society of Jesus to establish schools in the country's major cities. By 1851 the Jesuits were already active in New York and New Orleans. Less than a month before Kenrick left Philadelphia, the Jesuits there had inaugurated Saint Joseph's College (now University). Similar foundations were being considered for Charleston and Boston, but only the Boston school proved successful.[2] In such circumstances it would have been a practical blunder and a historic anomaly if a Jesuit college was not established in Baltimore. The importance of the city and its port, as well as the city's historical associations with the Jesuit order, cried out for a Jesuit school in Baltimore.

· ·

Kenrick's swift decision and the agreement between the Sulpicians and the Jesuits were the products of much previous thought. In Philadelphia, Kenrick had scotched a plan to couple a regular college with a seminary (the situation at Saint Mary's). The Sulpicians had always considered such an arrangement an unwelcome adaptation to practical necessity. Their primary mission is the training of candidates for the priesthood, and at the beginning of the century they had reluctantly opened Saint Mary's College as a temporary means of support. In 1806 the Maryland legislature permitted the college to conduct a lottery to raise needed funds, on condition that it remain open for another thirty years. In 1837 (the legislature's condition having been met) Archbishop Eccleston asked the Jesuits to staff Saint Mary's College but to leave the associated seminary under the direction of the Sulpicians. The plan was attractive, particularly to the Jesuits, but it would have taken a stronger hand than Eccleston's to harness so high-spirited a team.

Nevertheless, the Jesuits welcomed Archbishop Eccleston's proposal, because it would reestablish them in the city. After an association that went back to colonial times, the Jesuits had been unseen in Baltimore, save as pilgrims, since 1829; the strength of their desire can be measured by their willingness to accept an entanglement with the Sulpicians. (To those unfamiliar with the general history of such relations in the church, this attitude may seem strange, but there are records of more than a few instances when an alliance between religious communities resulted in difficulty and grief for both. A whole-souled commitment to one group tends to make people wary of cooperation with other groups.) Contingent on approval from the Jesuit general in Rome, the Maryland provincial agreed to the proposal, as well as to paying the valuation of $170,000 placed on the college's buildings and grounds. Eccleston was pleased with this response, although he expressed some qualms about whether the Sulpicians would agree. They were reluctant to act until Saint Charles College, a preparatory school for Saint Mary's Seminary, was in full operation.[3]

There were other obstacles to Eccleston's plan. The year 1837 was a bad one for launching new and expensive enterprises. There was a bank panic—something unknown to most living Americans, but a periodic phenomenon of the nineteenth century. A bank panic meant, among other things, the closing of insolvent institutions, restriction of credit, and a rise in the cost of borrowing, as well as disorientation and stagnation of the economy. In these circumstances, the manpower and financial resources of the Jesuits would have been strained under the burden of their existing responsibilities. Financial and other kinds of prudence forced them to discontinue the negotiations in 1837.

Archbishop Eccleston did not forget the project, however, and sought to revive it eleven years later, after Saint Charles College opened. The Jesuits, still without a base in Baltimore, indicated a willingness to discuss a number of possibilities. The Sulpician superior, however, "after much prayer and mature reflection," gave up "the notion *entirely*."[4] This impasse marked the end of Eccleston's direct efforts to transfer Saint Mary's College to the Jesuits.

. .

In 1849, however, the Jesuits were able to resume their ministration to the people of Baltimore through less formal channels. This break-through resulted from an offer made by the Reverend Edward Damphoux, who formerly had been a member of the Sulpician community and who served for a time as president of Saint Mary's. Father Damphoux, after resigning from the Sulpicians, built Saint Joseph's Church at Howard and Barre streets. The title to ownership of this church was vested in him because the applicable law at the time did not recognize the concept of a Catholic bishop as a corporation sole. Title to church property was held by individual priests rather than by the ordinary. By 1849, Damphoux was feeling the burdens of age and ill health. With the concurrence of Archbishop Eccleston, he offered Saint Joseph's to the Society of Jesus on condition that the Society assume responsibility for the church's debts and pay him an annuity of $400 until his death. Despite these encumbrances the offer was accepted, and William Clarke was sent to accept the transfer.[5] The hiatus in the association of Baltimore and the Society of Jesus was closed with the arrival of Father Clarke. With regard to the stymied plan for a college, he would become the Jesuit on the spot and would play an important role in the foundation of Loyola College.

When Eccleston died in the spring of 1851, Kenrick immediately set out for Baltimore, where, with no warrant more specific than obvious necessity, he established a temporary administration and reported what he had done. Kenrick had acted decisively and with no little courage. His effectiveness and responsibility would not be forgotten when it came time to decide who might best fill the vacant chair. As the senior suffragan, Kenrick presided over the obsequies for Samuel Eccleston.

The vacancy at Baltimore prompted a variety of nominations. The suffragans next senior to Kenrick, Bishop Michael O'Connor of Pittsburgh and Bishop John McGill of Richmond, added to the number by submitting the name of Kenrick himself. He was, they wrote to Rome, a man "versed in all ecclesiastical disciplines, as well as pious, zealous, prudent, and eminent in handling affairs."[6] What they failed to note was that Francis Patrick Kenrick was much more diplomat than popular leader, more scholar than preacher, more lawgiver than pastor. His gracious manners made some Americans see him as somewhat aloof and even effeminate. Americans, if crude by European standards, proudly identified their own lack of polish with honesty and manliness. And Kenrick's ready tendency to laughter roused frowns on more solemn faces.

· ·

Later, Bishop O'Connor had some additional thoughts on the matter. He had no doubts about Kenrick's ability, but Kenrick was not a native American. To appoint a native American, O'Connor believed, would help blunt the increasing attacks on Catholicism as an alien force.[7] The recent influx of Germans and Irish so alarmed "native" Americans that they were organizing to stem the flow of immigrants. Because of their secrecy, these superpatriots came to be called Know-Nothings. Their political influence would be important throughout most of the 1850s—nowhere more so, as it later proved, than in Baltimore.

Archbishop Eccleston, himself a native, had apparently anticipated this development. In the bewildering disarray of his papers the names of two American-born candidates appeared. The first was Oliver Lawrence Jenkins, scion of a distinguished Maryland family and at that moment the president of Saint Mary's College. Some of Jenkins's Sulpician confreres worked quietly for his candidacy. On another of Eccleston's lists was found the name of John Chanche, bishop of Natchez. He seemed the most likely successor, at least to Father James Dolan, unofficial chieftain of Baltimore's Irish, who wrote in his diary: "I would not be surprised if we would [?] have Chanche here. He is an American and a Baltimorean. I am sure his appointment would give general satisfaction."[8] In addition to these, there were undoubtedly other names submitted to Rome.

Around mid-August the matter was settled. Francis Patrick Kenrick's loyalty and his demonstrated ability apparently outweighed local misgivings about his ancestry. The papal bulls naming him archbishop of Baltimore and apostolic delegate to the plenary council were signed, sealed, and dispatched to Philadelphia, where they arrived on October 9. In a rented coach Kenrick left that night for Baltimore. "I had to flee," he later explained to his friends, "in order to spare you as well as myself."[9] Thus it was that early the next morning the sexton, Jonathan Mullan, found him in the sacristy of the Baltimore cathedral preparing to celebrate Mass and to take on his new responsibilities.

· ·

The October 13 meeting between Archbishop Kenrick and the local superiors of both the Jesuits and the Sulpicians resulted in a decision to open a Jesuit school in Baltimore. At the October 13 conference there was some consideration of site. The Jesuit provincial apparently revived the original proposal of Kenrick's predecessor: some of the buildings at Saint Mary's would be reserved for the new school until more suitable quarters could be found. This had much to recommend it from the point of view of both the Jesuits and the archbishop. The Sulpicians, on the other hand, could hardly object, and in ecclesiastical circles "silence gives consent." The Jesuits did not, however, attempt to take immediate advantage of this turn.

The most serious difference had arisen about whether or not a full collegiate course would be offered at the new school. The Jesuit provincial, Ignatius Brocard, could not make a commitment on this point. A small but critical group of his teachers were refugees from recent revolutionary upheavals and persecutions in Italy, Switzerland, and other countries in Europe. These Jesuits were among the best educated and most experienced priests in the Maryland province. Father Brocard's superiors had only recently admonished him that a change for the better in Europe would necessitate recalling these men to the Continent. If this occurred, the faculties of the province's existing schools would be depleted, and Father Brocard thought he could not guarantee the final two years of college at the proposed school for Baltimore. This distressed Archbishop Kenrick. He wanted a smooth transition, with no student at Saint Mary's abandoned a year or two short of his diploma.[10] The initiative on questions of site and curricular scope now rested with the Jesuits.

. .

Because the effort to resolve these issues involved William Clarke, and because he became so closely associated with Loyola College after its establishment, his life requires attention here. In him, several honorable lines and heritages were fused. He could, on his father's side, claim descent from Robert Clarke, one of Maryland's earliest settlers and a member of the colonial assembly that voted the renowned Act of Religious Toleration. On his mother's side he came from the venturesome Boone family that spread to North Carolina, Tennessee, and Kentucky. Washington was his birthplace (in 1816), and after graduating from Georgetown he entered the Society of Jesus in 1833. Ten years later William Clarke was ordained a priest on the Fourth of July, a combination of religion and patriotism that helps define him.

His was an independent, though not rebellious, spirit. As the first Jesuit pastor of Saint Joseph's he started services in Italian for immigrants who could not speak English. Remarkably, he was equally solicitous for the black people in his parish and tried to open a school for their children. The teachers he secured were a small group of Oblate Sisters of Providence, an order of nuns founded in Baltimore about a decade earlier that accepted free black women into full membership. On the day the Oblate Sisters took up residence in the house provided by Father Clarke, rowdies terrorized them by twice smashing down the front door.[11] Sadly, this violent demonstration convinced all that the project was premature. What Father Clarke had tried to do was just too much too soon for the putative guardians of the neighborhood.

He demonstrated his initiative and the American roots of his spirit in another way. When the Catholic bishops began the movement to establish parochial schools, he did what was expected of him but would not raise the needed funds merely by pastoral fiat. Instead, he circularized his parishioners to seek consent from a "majority of the pewholders."[12] He may not have been the only Catholic pastor to solicit such support, but few other examples come to mind—especially in the 1850s or for many years to come.

His connection with Loyola College began early (indeed, before the college came into existence) and continued over three decades. He was Loyola's second president, serving from 1858 to 1860. After a year away he returned to Baltimore and worked in the pastoral ministry at Saint Ignatius Church and occasionally taught in the college. One of his students remembered Father Clarke as a "slender, wiry figure . . . [with] drawn brows and . . . penetrating eyes . . . [He was] a man of ascetic life and of much learning."[13] From his reading of the Bible, Shakespeare, and Burke (a noteworthy addition), he developed a literary and oratorical style that impressed several generations of Baltimoreans as well as a wider audience. Surviving photographs convey an impression of assurance—testimony to his lineage and his Jesuit training—and the hint of a smile.

• •

Immediately after the October 13, 1851, meeting with Archbishop Kenrick, Father Brocard began actively to seek a new site for Baltimore's new Jesuit school. A temporary location at Saint Mary's was now weighed against opening the college in combination with a parish church—Saint Joseph's, for instance. It was a familiar arrangement, but Pastor Clarke quickly registered dissent. Not wishing to appear in opposition to his religious superior, he suggested another location— Saint Vincent's Church at Front and Fayette streets— primarily because it was nearer the college's prospective clientele. However, Clarke was not confident in this suggestion, because Archbishop Kenrick, despite an evident affection for the Jesuits, had already been heard to say that he "was not in favour of trusting parishes to Regular Clergy."[14]

Kenrick's attitude had its roots in the medieval disputes between regulars (members of religious orders) and seculars (as clerics in the ordinary pastoral ministry were called). This attitude would affect the development of Loyola College even many years later. Just before Christmas of 1851, Father Clarke recommended two other sites, but these recommendations, however sound, apparently evoked no reply and did not figure in later deliberations.

As the winter yielded to spring, a new and unexpected prospect arose. Frederick Crey, a master paver and a banker, suggested to Father Clarke that the Jesuits buy the three-story Carmelite convent and academy at Aisquith Street. Crey apparently made his suggestion without any knowledge of plans to open a Jesuit college. He had heard only of Archbishop Kenrick's order that the Carmelites relocate to a more secluded area—a desideratum in the days before Vatican II. The new archbishop apparently intended to demonstrate that new brooms sweep clean during his first year in Baltimore. Crey must have learned of Kenrick's decision through Father Damphoux; despite the latter's retirement from the active ministry, he still celebrated Mass at a chapel maintained by Crey. This chapel (at Madison Street) would later play a small but not insignificant role in the selection of a permanent site for Loyola College.

Father Clarke for one favored Crey's proposal. The Carmelite convent, he reported, was nearer the residential center of Baltimore than Saint Vincent's Church. Its well-established congregation could easily be increased with some additions to the church, and that would attract more benefactors and revenues— though Clarke felt no need to make so obvious a point. On Aisquith Street, too, there were already classrooms and living quarters for a religious community. "In the rear," Clarke wrote to Brocard, "is a fine garden which would contribute to the recreation and health of the Teachers."[15] The convent seemed ideal.

On April 1, 1852, however, Father Ignatius Brocard died, and the office of provincial was filled ad interim by Joseph Aschwanden. He could not be certain how long he would occupy this post, but he had to concern himself with essential matters; and the question of school sites in Baltimore was not among them. Without undue haste, Father Clarke urged Aschwanden to act on the school for Baltimore. Clarke's letter to Aschwanden of April 15, 1852, dealt primarily with the need for a full college curriculum. This could be had, Clarke wrote, if what he considered the "unfortunate" school at Frederick that had recently suffered a disastrous student "rebellion" were closed and its faculty transferred to Baltimore. He even suggested recalling additional priests from the new missions in Erie and Maine. Although he did not use the phrase *carpe diem*, Clarke conveyed a clear message of opportunity and urgency— with all due deference.

In late April Father Clarke made one last effort to resolve the remaining questions. He abandoned the Crey project as too expensive (and premature, as it happened, since the Carmelites remained at Aisquith Street for twenty years). Clarke now proposed the purchase of a lot at Eutaw and Paca streets, where he thought a college could be built for about $12,000. He detailed the distances from this spot to the cathedral, Saint Vincent's, Saint Joseph's, and other churches, to establish the centrality of the location. On the following day he added a long postscript again urging the closing of Saint John's in Frederick.[16] He did not presume to urge explicitly, but Father Clarke was clearly saying again that time was awasting.

Father Aschwanden, after receiving Clarke's reports, outlined the problems and alternatives to the Jesuit general in Rome. Although Aschwanden did not overtly urge a course on "His Paternity," Aschwanden's emphasis on the need to act quickly to accommodate the desires of Archbishop Kenrick, as well as on the "miserable condition" of the school at Frederick, made clear which approach he thought the more advantageous. He duly noted that he had made no commitments and would take no action until the general replied. Propriety and deference had been maintained, despite the clear implications of his message.

• •

The waiting period coincided with the first plenary council of America's Catholic bishops. Rome convoked this council to bring greater uniformity to ecclesiastical discipline and practice in America. This objective guided the decrees enacted by the bishops, especially decrees on the administration of church property—a subject that would later directly impinge on the development of Loyola College.

Other regulations were aimed at defending against various threats to the faith, but the most significant was an injunction to establish and support schools in every parish.[17] It would not have seemed appropriate for the bishops themselves to reduce their decree to a slogan, but others formulated the phrase "Catholic Education for Catholics!" This concept, conceived mainly as a hedge against the absolute monopoly of education claimed by revolutionary statists in Europe, triggered a nationwide campaign to secure public funds for parochial schools.

Whatever the justice or wisdom of such an effort on this side of the Atlantic, some Americans saw it as a threat to the principle of separation of church and state posed at a time when the number of Catholics was rapidly increasing. The question of public aid to the Catholic schools immediately became an issue in Cincinnati's mayoral election and the cause of bitter wrangling among the councilmen of Jersey City. In the newest state (California) the legislature proved sympathetic to the claims made by Catholics.

In Maryland this effort found its spokesman in Martin Kerney. (A graduate of Mount Saint Mary's College in Emmitsburg, Kerney thought of becoming a lawyer but instead wrote widely used textbooks in American history, arithmetic, and English grammar before entering politics.) Kerney was elected to the House of Delegates, where, on the eve of the plenary council, he submitted a bill aimed primarily at establishing a statewide system of public schools but also providing public support for students attending private institutions, including parochial schools. The Kerney school bill, as it was called, instantly roused fierce opposition. It would, opponents claimed, sound the death-knell for public education. Others denounced it as the opening shot in a campaign to exclude Bible reading from public schools. Still others rejected it as the first step toward a union of church and state.[18]

One Catholic observer had anticipated the furor that attended the Kerney bill. Indeed, Father James Dolan confided in his diary, "I should be sorry to see it pass in its present form." He thought the change of a few teachers and the establishment of nondiscriminatory hiring practices would prove sufficient and be more generally acceptable.[19] Unfortunately, his irenic approach—so reminiscent of Archbishop John Carroll—was disappearing from American public life.

Readers in Baltimore and throughout the country were disturbed by an even more rousing subject. In 1852 Harriet Beecher Stowe published her antislavery novel, *Uncle Tom's Cabin.* In less than a year, two hundred thousand copies were sold, and the story was adapted to the stage, where its emotional impact was even greater. Soon traveling companies brought the affecting spectacle of "life among the lowly" (as the book was subtitled) to rural, unlettered audiences.

This phenomenal success required attention in *Metropolitan,* a Catholic magazine published in Baltimore. A year after publication of

Uncle Tom's Cabin an anonymous critic (probably Martin Kerney, the editor) conceded literary artistry to the author but objected to Mrs. Stowe's "fanatical and extreme views." He thought the novel flawed by a "false philanthropy" that sought to gratify its "selfishness even at the risk of the public peace and the Union."[20] The reviewer was particularly apprehensive that *Uncle Tom's Cabin* would "rekindle the flame of civil strife." And in some degree it evidently did, for President Abraham Lincoln in the midst of the Civil War would welcome Harriet Beecher Stowe to the White House with a mock-serious statement that she had instigated the war.

• •

It was during the furor roused by the Kerney school bill that the Jesuit general responded in 1852 to Father Aschwanden's report. Clarke, attending what was to be Saint Mary's last college graduation, informed the Sulpicians on June 12 that the necessary authorizations had arrived. No public announcement was made until the end of July. Then President Oliver Lawrence Jenkins merely declared that Saint Mary's College would close so the Sulpicians could, in accordance with their distinctive vocation, devote themselves "exclusively to the education of candidates for the sacred ministry." Father Jenkins gratefully acknowledged "the liberal encouragement" the people of Baltimore and of the nation had given Saint Mary's College.[21] He vaguely assured the lay students about the completion of their courses, but he made no reference to plans for opening a new Jesuit institution.

Jenkins could not be more explicit because there were a number of loose ends on the Jesuit side of the process. These loose ends were tied up with dizzying dispatch, and partly by an "ill wind." Initially Aschwanden appointed Francis Knackstedt superior of the inchoate Jesuit community, because he was already on the scene (serving as assistant to Father Clarke at Saint Joseph's) and because he was persona grata to Archbishop Kenrick. When Charles Stonestreet took office on August 15 as provincial of the Maryland Jesuits, however, he named Father John Early the very same day to open the college in Baltimore.

One factor in the change from Knackstedt to Early was a fire that on July 14 burned Holy Cross College in Worcester, Massachusetts, to the ground. This disaster left the staff at Holy Cross without employment, and Archbishop Kenrick, seeing the event as providential, insisted that these Jesuits be transferred to Baltimore's new school.[22] Because Father Early had already completed a term as president and rector of Holy Cross, he knew the men who would be coming to Baltimore; he had, in addition, endured his long training as a Jesuit in the company of the new provincial, Stonestreet. Chance may be excluded from more logically ordered processes but it cannot be ignored in life or history.

Indeed, the close association of Stonestreet and Early would be of critical importance to the establishment of Loyola College. Their collaboration also was symbolic of the general development that the Catholic church in America was then experiencing. Stonestreet was descended from an old southern Maryland family, and John Early was an Irish immigrant. He was, in fact, a member of what a knowledgeable historian of Georgetown and things Jesuit identified as the "Irish Trio." The trio—James Ryder, Bernard Maguire, and John Early—served as presidents of Georgetown and in various other important offices within the Maryland province of the Society of Jesus during the middle decades of the nineteenth century.

• •

Although the general spirit of Loyola College is a compound of many elements, it has been enriched by admixture from several individuals. The most critically important at the start was the person, character, and ideas of Father John Early. He was Loyola's president and rector from 1852 to 1858 and again from 1866 to 1870, and in the years between these terms he was a trustee.

By all accounts he was an amiable and prudent gentleman. Doctor Edward Milholland (class of 1856), who transferred to Loyola from Saint Mary's College, recalled Father Early's "benevolent countenance" and how "kind, fatherly and approachable" he was. Over the years, photographs of Early record changes in his face. It gradually got rounder and broader. Throughout, however, there was evidence of a patient reserve that is more than the effect of having to hold very still for the camera. He was a quiet, sensitive man who nonetheless could laugh at a joke. The obituary in Baltimore's *Catholic Mirror* shows that his contemporaries thought him "old school"—generous, discreet—and "not a brilliant man but one of breadth and soundness of views." Among his Jesuit colleagues, John Early was considered "a man of most estimable and winning manners," of surpassing executive ability, and of unbounded charity.[23] These qualities served him well in a life climaxed by successive appointments to the presidencies of Holy Cross, Loyola, and Georgetown.

From northern Ireland, Early's road to Baltimore had been long and unpredictable. His father (for whom he was named) farmed a few acres near Maguiresbridge, a small market town in County Fermanagh. The year of John Early's birth, 1814, was marked by the downfall of Napoleon, the restoration of the Society of Jesus, and the end of Ireland's brief, war-related prosperity. There were at least three other children in the Early family—an older sister, Mary, and two younger brothers. They all emigrated to America, but only the circumstance of John's departure was recorded.

He left Ireland when, at age 19, the door to his hopes was barred. Early's parents had strained their meager resources to secure a good education for him. Beyond the care and instruction of his family, he was (like many of his fellows) tutored in a "hedge school." This was a common but extralegal arrangement necessitated by penal laws imposed on Ireland. An itinerant teacher (often himself a needy student) received food and shelter for a winter or two while his host's children and others in the neighborhood were drilled in the rudiments of arithmetic and languages. From this informal classroom, John Early secured admission to the Armagh Academy—a school conducted under Protestant auspices—where he won five prizes during his first year. What this was leading to became clearer when in July of 1833 he presented himself at Maynooth, the most important Catholic seminary in Ireland. Unfortunately, the number of candidates admitted each year was severely limited, and at that moment there were no vacancies. So John Early left for America.

• •

The wide sea worked no change in John Early's objectives. In October he was admitted as a third-year college student at Mount Saint Mary's, conducted by the Sulpicians in Emmitsburg, Maryland. "The Mount" was both a college for lay students and a seminary. Indeed, the seminarians were often assigned to teach the younger lay students. During Early's brief stay he taught a class in elementary Latin and a class in slightly more advanced Greek. This arrangement might have permitted him to continue his preparation for the priesthood at a school that already numbered bishops among its alumni, and there was more than one bishop on the Early family tree. Shortly after the second semester began, however, Early left Emmitsburg for Georgetown, where he continued his studies—and also sought admission to the Society of Jesus.

Early's late admission to Mount Saint Mary's, his short stay, and the sequel strongly suggest that sometime after his arrival from Ireland he met John McElroy. Father McElroy, a legend among the Jesuits, also was from County Fermanagh, and the Earlys numbered McElroys among their cousins. It seems likely that, in the traditional manner of immigrants, Early had arrived in America with an introduction to a well-situated relative. If they did not meet under these circumstances, McElroy and Early certainly became acquainted during Early's two-year noviceship at Frederick, where Father McElroy served as pastor of Saint John's Church and principal of the academy. Not only did McElroy encourage his younger countryman during the rigors of this testing period, but he provided a link with someone else who later would be of assistance. Among Father McElroy's congregation was the family of Enoch Louis Lowe, governor of the state of Maryland at the time Loyola College was chartered.[24] After being transferred to Boston, John McElroy became the founder of the Jesuit college established in that city in 1863.

• •

Having survived noviceship, John Early went back to Georgetown College, then the headquarters of the Maryland province and the Jesuit scholasticate. Here, Mister Early—as students traditionally address scholastics, who are Jesuits not yet ordained as priests—completed most of his training. He pursued the long, required study of philosophy and theology and at the same time, like other scholastics, taught some lower classes. The preferred practice among Jesuits has been to alternate periods of study with periods of teaching, but pressing needs then forced rectors to exact double duty from their younger brethren.

Mister Early, as prefect, became responsible for maintaining order among the students. With notable understatement, Early reported to an older and knowing friend, "The Students behave as well as ever they did." From other sources, however, we know the 1830s and 1840s were years of frequent student riots. In that period, one apprehensive colleague of Early's carried a poker under his cassock whenever he was assigned to the recreation yard. Another young Jesuit had been forced to establish his claim to respect by accepting a student's challenge to a fist fight. Though not officially condoned, such bouts were generally ignored by rectors—especially if the scholastic subdued his student challenger.

John Early spent these years at Georgetown under the attentive direction of William McSherry, Thomas Mulledy, and James Ryder. For almost twenty years these able men alternately served in the offices of Jesuit provincial and president of Georgetown College. After entering the Society, all of them had been sent to Rome in 1820 to finish their studies and to become thoroughly imbued with the spirit of the order. Association with Italians had a maturing effect on Father Ryder. His

Dublin birth would always be evident in his vehement eloquence, but he displayed tact and finesse of a distinctly Italian nature. Ryder believed that to deal effectively with humankind—scholastics and students included—he should be "to their virtues ever kind, and to their faults a little blind."[25]

• •

A similar disposition would be evident in John Early. From whom could he have learned this lesson more directly than from Father Ryder? Not only was Ryder one of Early's superiors but along with Thomas Mulledy he preceded Early as president of Holy Cross College. In 1843 Father Mulledy went to Worcester, to supervise the college when the Jesuits were asked by Bishop Benedict Joseph Fenwick (himself a member of the Society) to accept responsibility for its continuance. Two years later Ryder took up this task while Mulledy spelled him as president of Georgetown. In 1848, when it became necessary to appoint a new rector and president, the lot fell to John Early, then 34 years old. Although he had by then been ordained a priest, the demands of the manpower of the province had postponed his completion of the period known as "tertianship"—a time when, in the words of a gentleman who knew by experience, "a Jesuit's long training is given, let us say, its hard finish." That Early was appointed to so exacting a post before he had finished his training, or for that matter before he had taken his final vows, bespeaks both the pressing circumstances and the confidence already vested in him.

What the new president and rector of Holy Cross found on his arrival in August 1848 was a tidy little community. There were eight Jesuits to teach and direct the students, and there were about 125 students, all boarders. The largest contingent came from Massachusetts, but there were lads from New York, Maryland, Pennsylvania, the District of Columbia, and other states, and even a few from abroad. Among Father Early's charges were sons of Orestes Brownson, a distinguished writer and convert, as well as the brothers Healy. The latter, from Georgia, were sons of a prosperous Irish planter and a slave mother. Of the four Healys, James, the eldest, later became bishop of Portland, while Patrick, the third son, joined the Society of Jesus and two decades later served as Father Early's assistant at Georgetown.

Holy Cross, like other Jesuit schools, was then in the educational mainstream. It offered a standard liberal arts program, available at any respectable college in America. An integrated study of language, literature (modern and classical), mathematics, science, and philosophy was then thought to lay a solid basis for a lifetime of eloquence and leadership. No less essential was character training and religious practice; there was no difference on these basic principles among America's schoolmasters, whatever their preferences in theology. The curriculum at Holy Cross was the same as the one that John Early had himself pursued and had taught at Georgetown.

Brief glimpses of him in the occasional comments of his colleagues and students reveal Early in the familiar role of community father. If he was "very angry and impatient" when reading marks to the assembled college exposed the recalcitrance of too many students, he did not, on the other hand, frown on ice skating, fishing, or hunting by either the Jesuit scholastics or their young charges. Nor did he discourage the effort of a teacher and his class to make friends with their peers at a nearby Baptist institution. Then, as later, he readily granted a holiday when a deputation of students formally asked for it.[26]

· ·

To his dismay, President Early discovered shortly after his arrival in Worcester that the college suffered under two disabilities. Technically still a proprietary institution, it was liable for several hundred dollars in taxes each year; and it could not confer degrees. Both difficulties resulted from lack of a charter. A number of students were near completion of the full course (among them a son of Orestes Brownson), but they might leave their alma mater empty-handed unless a charter was obtained. Furthermore, Holy Cross could not claim tax-exempt status until it was incorporated.

President Early sought help from people knowledgeable in the public affairs of Massachusetts. It was easy to engage Orestes Brownson, because he was a notable promoter of causes and was the father of a Holy Cross senior. Early also consulted the bishop of Boston, John Fitzpatrick, who was equally forthcoming with advice and support. Together Early, Brownson, and Fitzpatrick prepared the necessary documents. It fell to Brownson to draw up the petition; he got Daniel Webster's law partner to present it to the legislature.

According to the petition, six Jesuits (not including John Early, probably because he had not fulfilled a residence requirement or because he was not yet an American citizen) were to be constituted a body corporate with all the usual privileges. One stipulation, however, proved disastrous: the restriction of enrollment to Catholics. This was included because Bishop Fitzpatrick insisted, despite Father Early's prudently expressed doubts. The bishop thought himself obliged to follow this course by the stated (though not binding) wish of the college's patron, Bishop Fenwick, and against his better judgment, Early acquiesced. The Holy Cross charter bill provoked several weeks of wrangling in the Massachusetts legislature, only to be rejected. The restriction had enabled the nativists to characterize the college as "exclusively Catholic" at a time when any special privilege was suspect and the fevers of anti-Catholicism were rising again.

A minority in the Massachusetts legislature (including the historian John Lothrop Motley) thought the rejection of the Holy Cross charter violated the civil and religious rights of all, not merely of Catholics. However, the attempt to find an acceptable compromise foundered on the conscience of Bishop Fitzpatrick. Weakening the restriction would violate Bishop Fenwick's wish, he thought. As a result, Holy Cross remained unchartered for another sixteen years, but its graduates were granted their diplomas by arrangement with the federally chartered institution at Georgetown.[27] This affair taught John Early a valuable lesson. A few years later, when he sought incorporation for Loyola College from the Maryland legislature, the charter was free of anything that might serve as an obvious stumbling block.

Because three years was the canonical term for a rector, and Early had not yet undergone his tertianship, it was to be expected that a replacement would be appointed in 1851. The day before the third anniversary of his arrival, Father Early yielded his post to Anthony Ciampi, who, as it turned out, would follow him as a president of Loyola. It was Father Ciampi's fate to watch helplessly when, in July of 1852, Holy Cross College was reduced to ashes.

• •

Meanwhile, Early was engaged for the most part in completing his training as a Jesuit. His master at Frederick for this period of tertianship was Father Felix Sopranis, an Italian exile who had been a member of the Holy Cross community when Early was its rector. Such reversals are common practice among Jesuits, to remind them of the transitory nature of any office. (Furthermore, colleagues must be treated with a sobering recognition that today's subordinate might be tomorrow's superior.) Sopranis later earned the intramural sobriquet "felix culpa" (happy fault—an allusion to the famous hymn from the Easter Vigil) for taking actions that proved serendipitous. On the eve of the Civil War, for instance, he had provincial headquarters transferred from Georgetown to Loyola. Father Sopranis was apparently a gentle taskmaster, for he permitted John Early to go to Baltimore on several occasions, sometimes to visit his sister at the Carmelite convent, other times to exercise his priestly ministry.

On these occasions Father Early stayed as a guest of James Dolan, pastor of old Saint Patrick's Church at Fells Point. Early first appeared in "Good Father" Dolan's diary on Sunday, September 21, 1851. The full entry reads "Early preached today. It was a prepared sermon. He too has a name and if this is his best he has one without deserving it."[28] Despite this harsh judgment (not shared by others), Father Dolan invited his countryman back to preach a pre-lenten mission for his parish beginning in mid-February. This is a much surer measure of Dolan's opinion. In mid-April, Father Early stopped by again, about the time that Clarke was urging Aschwanden, the interim provincial, to reconsider plans for the Baltimore school. Thereafter, Early did not appear in Dolan's diary until after the task of opening the new college fell to him.

• •

Early had not, of course, been the first choice for this assignment. He had been slated by Father Aschwanden for southern Maryland, and he had responded by noting some problem about his health. When Aschwanden graciously substituted a term in a Washington parish, Early, on August 8, remorsefully wrote:

> I now regret exceedingly having made any difficulty and pray your Reverence most earnestly to adhere to your first arrangement. I prefer to go to the counties at any risk, because otherwise I fear I would be resisting the will of God expressed through you and of course could not feel happy.[29]

He was then in Emmitsburg, giving a retreat for the seminarians at Mount Saint Mary's. This chore was completed on August 15—the day on which Father Charles Stonestreet became provincial—and John Early was forthwith posted to Baltimore.

There was hardly a month left before the new school was scheduled to open its doors, and so Father Early quickly returned to the city. On August 23 he dined with Father Dolan. About the same time he leased two adjoining houses on the east side of Holliday Street, numbers 29 and 31, which had until recently served as the city dispensary for the area. The Jesuits were to live at number 29, in the upper stories, while classes were conducted in the lower part and in the other house. These twin dwellings had three stories with three windows on each of the upper floors; both were topped by high gabled roofs. The only visual record of Loyola's first home appears in a photograph taken from the porch of City Hall during dedication ceremonies almost a quarter of a century later. Nearby was the city's high school for boys, only a door away was the famous Holliday Street Theater, and just around the corner was the birthplace of James Cardinal Gibbons. The approximate site is now marked by a plaque in the plaza opposite City Hall.

The new Jesuit school having acquired an address, it was possible to announce its opening. The Baltimore *Sun*, on Friday, September 3, contained the following notice:

> COLLEGE OF LOYOLA HOLLIDAY STREET CORNER OF ORANGE ALLEY BALTIMORE
>
> This Institution, which is designed to supply the vacancy occasioned by the discontinuation of St. Mary's College, so long and so favorably known to the citizens of Baltimore, and to the Union at large, will be opened for the reception of students on Wednesday, September 15, 1852. To insure the success in their undertaking, the Directors of Loyola College have secured the services of professors of known ability, and of many years experience. The course of studies will differ little from that heretofore pursued in St. Mary's, and will be essentially the same as that now followed in Georgetown College, D.C., embracing the Latin, Greek, French, and Spanish languages, and a complete course of Mathematics, Mental and Natural Philosophy and Chemistry will also be taught as soon as a class for these studies can be formed. The College is intended for Day scholars only. Terms of tuition will be precisely the same as at St. Mary's viz:-$60 per annum, payable quarterly.
>
> JOHN EARLY, PRESIDENT

It was a succinct advertisement and tasteful in its *ave atque vale* to Saint Mary's College.

Furthermore, Father Early had not flaunted what was otherwise obvious. Loyola was to be a Jesuit college conducted in accordance with the order's plan of studies, but Early did not use any titles, initials, or phraseology that might unduly annoy or alarm anyone. The tuition was comparable to that charged by other schools, private or public. Sixty dollars then was the equivalent of two months' rent for a well-appointed six-room apartment or the railroad fare from New York City to Council Bluffs, Iowa—or a year's wages for an Irish serving girl.

By the time the notice appeared in the *Sun*, Father Early and a few of his associates had already taken up their residence at Holliday Street.

Samuel Lilly came in on the tenth, but it would not be until September 14, 1852—the day before Loyola College opened its doors—that the rest of the Jesuits arrived.[30] On schedule, if barely so, Baltimore's new school was ready to begin its long service to the community.

2

At Holliday Street

Sometimes colleges are extensions of the personality and ideas of one man. This can be true of a Jesuit school only in a limited sense; the strong community ethos and, until a few decades ago, the short tenure of the chief officers militated against a one-man show. As a result, the order and the college's plan of studies—the *Ratio Studiorum*—have naturally provided the focus for older institutional histories. However, no system is self-executing, and it takes individual men to apply general principles to particular circumstances. The founding and development of a college, even a Jesuit college, is not an inevitable unfolding of pre-determined events. It was individuals, working together under specific conditions, taking one decision after another, and dealing with a certain group of students, who gave life to Loyola College.

. .

Before the opening of Loyola College on September 15, there was not time enough to publish a detailed prospectus, even if it had been thought necessary. President Early's announcement in the *Sun* covered the essential points. He offered an experienced faculty. Three Jesuit priests on Loyola's original faculty had taught at Holy Cross: Samuel Lilly, Anthony Maraschi, and Augustine Kennedy. They were in their thirties and had been members of the order for ten, eleven, and eighteen years respectively.

Father Sam Lilly served as Early's principal assistant; he was the treasurer of the college and "minister" of the Jesuit community. The presence of Fathers Maraschi and Kennedy was essential to the initiation of classes for the college seniors. Father Maraschi guided his small but intrepid band through the tangle of syllogistic forms to the mysteries of "being"—and to the determination of a rational norm for distinguishing good actions from bad; teacher and students worked through logic, metaphysics, and ethics. Father Kennedy inducted the seniors into chemistry. After only two years in Baltimore, Maraschi left for California, where he founded the institution that became the University of San Francisco. His companion, Father Kennedy, departed after only two months, his transfer to the cooler and less humid clime of Maine suggesting a reason.

Chemistry was continued by Father James Ward, who was hurriedly transferred to Baltimore and who remained at Loyola through most of President Early's term. His scientific interests were not merely pedagogical. In November of 1853 he addressed an inquiry about an obscure physical phenomenon to Joseph Henry, secretary of the Smithsonian Institution, and received a prompt, thorough reply.

Father Ward was a Philadelphian who entered the Society of Jesus in 1832 and spent his first years in the order at Georgetown, in the company of William Clarke and John Early. To his students Father Ward appeared "gentle as a dove, wise as a serpent"; he was "a tender-hearted, sympathetic, affectionate" man who also had a "caustic humor."[1] These elements were in contrast, as was his broad, calm face, with a "hoarse, broken voice." At the death of Sam Lilly only two years after Loyola opened, Ward became the treasurer. In fact, the earliest financial accounts of the college are written in his small, neat hand.

Ward's responsibilities extended to the parish, which grew along with the college. In 1856 Father Ward organized the confraternity of Bona Mors, a traditional association in Jesuit parishes. He would also find time to prepare a textbook of Greek grammar, "arranged," as the subtitle declared, "for the students of Loyola College, Baltimore." In 1859 the book was in its fifth edition, but Ward had returned to his native Philadelphia to serve as rector of Saint Joseph's.[2]

• •

The remainder of Loyola's original faculty consisted of five Jesuit scholastics: Robert Fulton, Edward McNerhany, Thomas Sheerin, Patrick Forhan, and Edmund Young. These "Misters" had been members of the order for an average of five years and had taught mostly at Georgetown. They were a group of zealous young men—their ages ranged from 21 to 31 years. Mister McNerhany got the task of organizing the most pious students into the sodality, a traditional feature of Jesuit colleges whose purpose was promoting religious fervor. He recruited a small group who according to tradition began their initiation on December 8, 1852. Two months later, thirteen were formally inducted into this extracurricular activity and another group began postulancy.

It was no easy thing to gain admission or to remain a member: not every applicant was admitted to membership, and each year one or two less fervent sodalists were expelled. General conduct, the punctual observance of the sodality's religious program, and regular attendance at meetings were carefully monitored by a council of twelve students and a Jesuit director. Together the council and director made all the decisions but, to ensure a free expression of student opinion, voting was by ballot, with the student-prefect and the director counting the votes. This concession to democratic procedure was balanced by the fact that the Jesuit director could cast three votes and break any ties. When vacancies occurred in the sodality council, they were filled with students selected by the remaining councillors, not with students chosen by the general membership. In the sodality, at least, government was the prerogative of a self-perpetuating student elite, leavened with Jesuit authority.

The new sodality's name was prescient, if not unique. It was dedicated to Mary under her title as the Immaculate Conception several years before the formal definition of this dogma. It was primarily from the sodality that vocations to the priesthood and to the order were anticipated. Edward McNerhany was eventually ordained and would again be numbered among Loyola's faculty after the Civil War, during Father Early's second term. "Father Mac," as he was affectionately remembered by his students, was after that lost to the records of the college and to those of the Society of Jesus, as well, suggesting that he may have left the order.

• •

As Father Early had noted in his announcement, Loyola's course of studies was similar to that offered elsewhere. He restricted his comparison to Saint Mary's and Georgetown, but had he wished to be redundant the list could easily have been lengthened. It was not until after the Civil War that the Jesuit *Ratio Studiorum* had to be explained or justified among American educators.

Like its sister colleges, Loyola offered an integrated curriculum "to sublime the heart and purify the mind." Study of the ancient classics and philosophy was then considered essential to creating the liberally educated gentleman. Some people were demanding a more "practical" form of education— but they had been answered earlier by the faculty of Yale. Latin, Greek, and a full course of philosophy, the faculty said, would produce eloquent, dignified leaders. Because social leadership was the ultimate aim, character training and religious practice also were integral elements of "the college way." It was at this point that a difference between Catholic and other educators arose. The former insisted that only within the Catholic church could the aim of education be fully realized.[3] The latter, naturally, were loath to concede either the argument or its historicity.

Nevertheless, the discussion was carried on among men who shared basic premises. Father Early put the matter succinctly when he admonished graduates, "It will be your part not [to] receive your tone from but to give tone to public feeling; not to learn those lessons of morality which the world will inculcate, but to inculcate on the world those lessons which you have elsewhere learned."[4] Similar sentiments might have been uttered by the president of any American college in the 1850s and earlier.

Because there were other schools in Baltimore, a local comparison can be made. The Baltimore College (at Mulberry and Cathedral) was affiliated in 1830 with the University of Maryland, and Newton University (hardly a block away from Loyola, at Lexington between Calvert and present-day Guilford) was incorporated in 1845. Both schools numbered Protestant clergymen among their trustees, administrators, and faculty, although Newton's charter required strict nonpartisanship in both religion and politics. These schools, like Loyola, accepted youngsters at both the secondary and collegiate levels. This was common practice in America, because colleges were founded before enough secondary schools were established. What proportion of college students to high schoolers obtained at these institutions is not determinable, but at Loyola it was one to six, or about 15 percent college students.

The situation at Newton University and Baltimore College was replicated at Male Central High School, later known as Baltimore City College. It, too, was a neighbor of Loyola's, and numbered clergymen on its staff. Teaching would not become a discrete, lifelong profession until the second half of the nineteenth century. Before then, teaching tended to be a sometime occupation for clerics between appointments, for lawyers not yet established, and for students in need of funds to continue their own education.

All these Baltimore institutions offered the same curriculum. Classical languages, mathematics, science, and philosophy were listed in their catalogues. Newton University supplemented these with "divisions" aimed toward careers in business or a machine shop or the merchant marine. To accommodate students who were unfamiliar with Latin and Greek, Baltimore's high school for boys had an "English" course. Such programs, however, did not have a good reputation, and this one was dropped at the end of the Civil War.

It was not easy to keep a school going in the mid-nineteenth century. Survival depended on obtaining the support of a well-established social institution. For the Male Central High School this was the city government. Despite turnover in its administration and faculty, this school continued to develop. Baltimore College and Newton University, on the other hand, lacked such patronage. They were unable to engage the general support of Baltimoreans and produced only a couple of dozen graduates before they ceased operations, Newton in 1859 and the Baltimore College a few years later.[5]

Such losses were not peculiar to Baltimore. Steiner's *History of Education in Maryland* (1894) listed nearly a score of "colleges no longer in existence." A similar record could probably be found in other states. Throughout America nearly half the Catholic colleges established between 1850 and 1866 failed during the same interval. Few tears were shed at their demise, because the prevailing attitude was Darwinian: "Time alone can determine whether a college has the right to live."[6] Survival in those days was assumed to be a function of basic fitness and adaptability.

• •

No one thought to record an eyewitness account of that Wednesday in mid-September of 1852 when nearly sixty boys and young men responded to Father Early's announcement. Records indicate that on succeeding days, other students enrolled, so that by Christmastide there were nearly eighty students. The register was not closed even then, for the enrollment reached ninety-five, with the last fellow entered on May 14 of the following year. There was, it appears, always "room for one more."

What this practice lacked in administrative regularity it made up for with flexibility regarding personal circumstance. Because there was no urgency about enrolling on the first day, even after classes had begun there would be "reluctant schoolboys" added to the rolls. By the early years of the twentieth century, this straggling was reduced to the month of September—in the main. It should be noted that the faculty to student ratio at Loyola's start was one to ten, whereas the national average was one to twenty.[7]

Almost half the first registrants at Loyola came from Saint Mary's. No religious test for admission had been applied there, and none would

ever be at Loyola. In fact, one of every four students first admitted to
Loyola was not Catholic, and this ratio remained constant throughout
the ensuing decades. Not membership in a specific church, but merely
the notation of "P" or "Prot." was usually listed in the register. For some
few, however, the note was "no religion," and others were identified
as Jewish. These latter two groups were small, but their presence was
significant.

Openness to persons of other religious persuasions was not characteristic of other colleges in this era. The denominational interests that
founded most American colleges tended to make them more or less in-
hospitable places for persons of other faiths. Church affiliation different
from that of the school might not prevent admission, but attendance at
the chapel services of the founding denomination was required of all
students, regardless of their preferences. What was true at the Methodist, Presbyterian, Baptist, Episcopalian, and other colleges was even developing at some Catholic schools. The proclamation in 1851 of a rule
restricting admission to Catholics at another Maryland institution was
not decried but "caused much favorable comment."[8] At the least this
restriction made it possible to avoid the questionable practice of requiring all students to attend denominational services—something that
had been done even at a few Catholic institutions.

Loyola was indeed a Catholic college, but it did not conceive this
association in a restrictive sense. No one was excluded on religious
grounds and none but Catholics have ever been required to attend religious services. This policy Loyola owed to the experience and wisdom
of John Early and to the Jesuit practice of vesting broad authority in
such men.

• •

The students Father Early first admitted to Loyola might seem
young by today's standards. Fifteen then was the generally accepted age
for admission to collegiate studies, and 10 years of age was the norm for
entrance into high school. The median age at Loyola's first enrollment
was 14, with more than two thirds between 12 and 16 years old. The
youngest two were only 9, but one was the son of the doctor who attended the Jesuits and the other was already somewhat advanced in his
studies. The oldest two were in their early twenties. This age pattern
persisted during the next four decades and was similar to the pattern in
schools along the eastern seaboard.

From the college registers and *Matchett's Baltimore Director*, it is possible to locate where Loyola students lived and to discover something

about their social and economic status. More than half of the first en-
rollees lived within walking distance of the college at Holliday Street;
this area was then a rather substantial neighborhood. About 20 percent
were sons of lawyers and doctors. Others were members of families in
which the breadwinner operated a small shop, and the next smaller
group was composed of sons of wholesale or commission merchants. For
almost 14 percent, only mothers' names were listed in the college register, probably widows. The occupations of the parents of the remaining
30 percent varied: lottery vendors, customs officers, contractors, stock
and bill brokers, clerks and bookkeepers, a ship's captain, and the officer of a newspaper (the Baltimore *Patriot*). These first students were,
therefore, children of well-established elements in Baltimore. Poor immigrants there may have been, but the average socioeconomic level of
the student body at Loyola was higher than that and thus was similar to
that at many other American colleges.[9]

There were scions of several prominent Maryland families in the
first enrollment. The best known were the Carrolls of Doughregan
Manor: Albert Henry Carroll (age 17) and his brother Robert Goodloe
Harper Carroll (13) transferred to Loyola from Saint Mary's College.
This association, however, proved to be rather short-lived.

More continuous and more intimate was the connection with the
Jenkins family. It was not as widely known as the Carroll family but its
lineage was hardly less distinguished. In 1784 William Jenkins had led
three brothers up from Saint Mary's County to Baltimore. He built a
large tannery on York Road and became "the father of the leather trade"
in Baltimore. From this base, the Jenkins brothers expanded into banking, insurance, finance, real estate, and probably other fields as well.
The family could boast several Jesuits, a larger number of nuns, and
Oliver Lawrence Jenkins, a Sulpician and the last president of Saint
Mary's College.[10]

Though Loyola's connection with this family involved several
branches, it was the descendants of William Jenkins with whom the
closest and most significant association was established. One of his
grandsons, Joseph W. Jenkins (1862), enrolled on September 15, 1852.
The following year an older brother of Joseph's, George Carrell Jenkins,
briefly had his name entered on the Loyola register, but it was almost
immediately crossed out and he went to Mount Saint Mary's in Emmitsburg instead. Nevertheless, George Jenkins would become Loyola's
most magnanimous benefactor when it moved in 1921 to the Evergreen
campus.

There were other noteworthy names to be found among the earliest registrants. Two of them were Moales, from a family that had a trading post at the confluence of Gwynn's Falls and the Middle Branch before the town of Baltimore was chartered. The earliest picture of Baltimore is a 1752 sketch by John Moale; it shows only twenty-five houses, "all of them small and insignificant." The Moales had been cool to the idea of chartering Baltimore but later came to be considered one of the city's "founding families." Through various members they were prominent in the Masonic fraternity and in the United States Army. Edward Moale and his older brother Henry both entered Loyola on September 15; Edward went on to a military career and Henry became a merchant.[11]

In the first registry book, which covered about a decade, various names of historical note appear. There were several Goldsboroughs; the son of Solomon Hillen (a former mayor of Baltimore); Frederick May, whose father, Henry, served in Congress; an Appold; several McKims; Walter Abell and his brother Charles, sons of A. S. Abell; an heir of the Prussian envoy, Baron Friedrich von Gerolt; a ward, a nephew, and a son of Zenus Barnum, proprietor of the city's best hotel; and August Shutt, whose father managed a different kind of hostelry—the city jail.

After a second, a third, and later generations had sons, the posterity of these early registrants appeared as students at Loyola. To trace these connections here would be impractical. Suffice it to note that the registers of Loyola College list Tormeys, Heuislers, Chatards, Cooks, Milhollands, Boones, Hoens, Shrivers, and Storcks—"to mention a few of Baltimore's finest families."[12]

The first register also provides an index to a different status and to a different concern of the college. "Gratis," "nothing," "1/2 price," "$10 per quarter," were written after some entries to indicate that the tuition of $60 was to be completely or partly remitted. These students obviously could not afford even that modest charge. The exact number of these students can not be derived from the records, and even a rough estimate would be misleading, because there were also persons who defaulted entirely or in part on their payments.

Subsidizing the student body was a common practice at American colleges. At some institutions it meant that professors, some of whom had families, were forced to underwrite the education of their students by taking lower salaries. Remitting tuition, however, did not force any Jesuit teacher to a level of poverty he had not already accepted willingly.

Traditionally, Jesuit institutions did not charge tuition, and in Europe they could operate without it because of endowments. In America, however, such financing was not available, and the Catholic bishops who wanted institutions of higher education petitioned Rome to permit the Jesuits to charge tuition; the necessary dispensations were granted decades before the founding of Loyola.[13] Nevertheless, the Jesuit ideal remained unchanged and would surface in periodic but unsuccessful efforts to secure an endowment large enough to eliminate all tuition charges.

. .

As students were registered at Loyola they were tested for proficiency in various subjects. They were assigned accordingly to a basic class, which combined a number of humanistic subjects and which was conducted during the morning hours. In ascending order these were listed in the catalogue as: second rudiments, rudiments; third, second, first humanities; poetry; rhetoric; and philosophy. Over the years some of these terms would be changed but, putting aside the disputes among historians of education, the first four were equivalent to the freshman, sophomore, junior, and senior years of high school. First humanities was the equivalent of college freshman, poetry of sophomore, rhetoric of junior, and philosophy of the senior class at the college level.

Although not listed in the catalogue, there was an even higher level of study available at Loyola from the very beginning. A graduate could, after completing the full course, engage in an additional year or so of directed studies, usually with a senior faculty member who taught philosophy. On finishing the schedule of readings and discussions, the candidate was examined orally by a board of professors who would (if his performance warranted) certify him as a master of arts *in course*. This additional phrase distinguished its recipient from the lawyers, doctors, and clergymen who embellished their names with an honorary M.A. Not many students chose to extend their studies at Loyola through this higher level.

More than half the first registrants at Loyola were assigned to the two sections of the lowest class, the rudiments. Their instructors were two scholastics, Patrick Forhan and Edmund Young. These men would guide their charges through English grammar, the history of the Bible, geography, Latin grammar, tales of Roman heroes, and Cicero's letters, and would drill them in both Latin and English. The seventeen who were assigned to third humanities had Mister Thomas Sheerin who, in addition to the subjects in rudiments, instructed in Greek grammar and readings as well as in the geography of North America. In second humanities, English, Latin, and Greek were supplemented with the history of ancient Greece and the geography of South America and Europe. This completed the high-school curriculum.

• •

The basic college subjects were pursued by about 20 percent of the entering class—higher by 4 percent than the average proportion of entering Loyola classes doing so over the next twenty years. In 1852, first humanities had nine members and their studies were differentiated from high-school studies by a change in geography: they studied Asia and Africa. Robert Fulton taught a combined class of poetry and rhetoric. Here grammar and translation yielded to a consideration of style and composition, Mister Fulton's forte. The rhetoricians also studied English and American history. Father Anthony Maraschi taught logic, metaphysics, and ethics (in Latin) to his three seniors. The morning hours at Loyola were spent on subjects that were the focus of attention during the same period at most American colleges.

At registration the students were tested for proficiency in mathematics. In the catalogue, certain levels of mathematics were associated with designated classes: analytical geometry and calculus, for instance, were the mathematics courses assigned for poetry. In practice, however, students were assigned to all their courses, including mathematics, on the basis of skill.

A similar flexibility was evident in the language assignments. The afternoon session was reserved for the study of French and Spanish. Normally the "poets," or higher-level students, were engaged at this time in the study of the natural sciences. Five of them, it was thought, would find the study of French or Spanish more profitable than the study of chemistry. Furthermore, the same French section held a college freshman, a high-school senior, four juniors, and twenty-seven from rudiments. Father Maraschi and Misters Forhan and McNerhany taught the French classes.

The Spanish section, even more of a scholastic melting pot, was taught by the only layman on Loyola's faculty, Joseph Pizarro. However slight Pizarro's role may have been, his presence deserves to be noted. As a young officer in the Spanish army he fought the Napoleonic invasion and was wounded at the siege of Cadiz. Sometime before 1830 he came to Baltimore as Spain's vice-consul. This was a responsible position, because Cuba was still under Spanish rule and the city's trade in sugar and copper ore was measured in millions of dollars. In addition to performing his consular duties, Pizarro gave private lessons in Spanish, wrote a "phrase book and self-instructor," and became a member of the faculty at Saint Mary's College. There he established a warm, lifelong association with one of his pupils, Severn Teackle Wallis, who became a leader of civic reform in Baltimore. Many years later Wallis gave testimony of his regard by providing a grave for Pizarro in his own family plot.[14]

• •

Within the framework of this generally accepted curriculum, the Jesuits at Baltimore's new college paid attention to individual differences. The students were placed in different sections for the literary core, for mathematics, and for modern languages. The variety of these assignments must have necessitated moving from one classroom to another. Furthermore, a Loyola student was taught by several instructors. Eugene Didier (1859), for instance, spent the mornings studying Latin, English, and other core subjects with Mister Forhan; Father Sam Lilly taught him arithmetic; in the afternoon, Edward McNerhany taught him French.[15] There was, therefore, movement and variety for both students and teachers. This, along with a brief mid-morning recess and a longer respite after the math class, provided new starts and spurs to keep the day from lagging. Varied class assignments also meant that Loyola's students associated with their fellows from different classes and age groups. Their teachers, in turn, became acquainted with more than one section of pupils. In such circumstances it was possible to build a sense of cohesion—even of community.

Such adaptations might be accepted by the Jesuits as necessary, but they were not considered ideal. In the optimum arrangement a student was taught by one instructor, not three or more. Students and teachers normally progressed together, so that last year's instructor of second rudiments taught the next higher class this year, and so on. This created a personal bond between students and a particular instructor and provided a simple means of training teachers for a variety of later assignments. Moreover, having students walking the hallways from one classroom to another was considered an invitation to disorder. With so many comings and goings the prefect of discipline could not distinguish truants and other miscreants from dutiful students. The importance attached to these points was evident in the first decisions made after Fordham was turned over to the Jesuits in 1846. They immediately eliminated all these practices.[16] Such cleansing was never possible at Loyola, because few faculty members stayed for longer than two years; thus, the pattern of moving up with the class was constantly disrupted.

One other standard Jesuit practice, however, was followed at Loyola from its beginning. After midterm examinations came the announcement of promotions and, be it noted, demotions. Eugene Didier proudly recalled a half-century later that in February he was passed from the class of rudiments to third humanities.[17] From one remaining report and the record of promotions in the college catalogues, it is evident that advancement was not automatic. Students were judged individually and either promoted or demoted as their teachers considered justified. Nor was it merely a matter of dropping or advancing one class at a time. A student might be vaulted ahead by two or three classes; no less possible was a fall of similar magnitude. Virtue was rewarded and sloth punished, and not according to some pre-set schedule or curve of normal distribution. Some other traditional Jesuit practices could not be inaugurated at Holliday Street because of limited facilities.

• •

The houses on Holliday Street, for all the nostalgia they later evoked, could not serve Loyola long. They lacked "the space and convenience for a very large number of students; the rooms were small, and poorly furnished; there was no playground, no gymnasium, no stage, no hall, no library."[18] Another site was obviously needed. Legal incorporation would facilitate this move as well as the general development of the college, because incorporation would formally establish the college's rights, especially to tax-exempt status.

Father Early delayed taking action on these matters until there was evidence of the reaction of Baltimoreans to the new school. There were signs of a lingering attachment to Saint Mary's, but before Christmas this seems to have faded. Father Early was more concerned about a campaign, encouraged by several ministers, urging the incautious members of their congregations to withdraw their sons from Loyola. By mid-February of 1853 this crusade failed; indeed, it had a contrary effect: it made the existence of Loyola more widely known. Parents were prompted to investigate and compare its faculty and teaching methods with those of other schools. Loyola College, Father Early reported, "gained in the comparison."[19]

Before winter loosed its grip on Baltimore, Father Early had sufficient evidence that his college was gaining public acceptance. Indeed, the Jesuits were being asked when they planned to begin building not only a school but a church. Some inquiries undoubtedly came from substantial members of the community, because it was at Crey's Chapel at East Madison Street that Fathers Early, Ward, and Maraschi were celebrating Mass, baptizing infants, and witnessing marriages. These occasions provided the Loyola teachers with opportunities to talk to Crey and other men active in civic life.

Three sites were considered, all within a few blocks of one another and just a bit above the Washington Monument. The westernmost was in the neighborhood of Cathedral and Richmond streets, only a few blocks from Saint Mary's and the convent of the Oblate Sisters of Providence. The second, the northernmost site, was at the corner of Saint Paul and Chase. It was 104 feet above tide level, above the point to which water could be delivered by ordinary means; this would mean an additional expense. Calvert and Madison, the third and easternmost site, was below this level, and was owned by the Baltimore Water Company. The prospect of being relieved of a costlier "water rent" proved decisive, despite the proximity of the Calvert Street location to a railroad line and the penitentiary. A sequel indicated that other considerations were involved.

With a site selected, Father Early had an audience with Archbishop Kenrick in February. "His Grace" appeared pleased, Early reported, "& without difficulty allowed us to build a church." A week later, Father Charles Stonestreet, the Jesuit provincial, visited Baltimore and gave permission to purchase the plot.[20] The ease with which these approvals were secured may be taken as a measure of John Early's prudence.

• •

A similar quality was evident when he turned his attention to the civil aspects of the process. On March 18, 1853, the Reverend John Early presented himself in a Baltimore court to declare his intention of becoming a citizen of the United States. Father Early swore to uphold the Constitution and abjured forever "all allegiance and fidelity to the Queen of the United Kingdom and Ireland."[21]

With this brief ceremony completed, John Early, like many another immigrant, got his first papers. The motives for seeking citizenship now were clear enough. Rising threats from the Know-Nothings prompted Father Stonestreet to change the too obviously Irish names of members of the Maryland province; one Father O'Toole, for instance, was carried in the catalogues as "Toale." Jefferson Davis, then secretary of war, even asked the provincial to answer the charge that Jesuits took an oath to subvert "all Republican Institutions and bring them under subjection to the Pope." Stonestreet replied patiently, but words could not convince where two hundred years of contact were not reassuring enough.

Three days after Early's appearance in court, a petition was submitted to the Maryland legislature "from Rev. John Early, Samuel Knight, and others, for an Act of Incorporation." This petition was presented to the House of Delegates by Bolivar Danels, a member from Baltimore City. He was an alumnus of Saint Mary's College and a lawyer, and would be listed among the pewholders at Saint Ignatius Church when it was organized a year or two hence. Knight, the only other petitioner mentioned by name, was a respected Baltimore doctor and not a Catholic—adding a politic touch. Knight's sons later enrolled at the college and, still later, the older, Louis, would be proudly numbered among its benefactors.

After the petition was read to the House it was referred to a select committee. Danels, acting for this group, quickly reported the draft of a bill to incorporate "the Associated Professors of Loyola College in the City of Baltimore." A copy of the original draft has survived and it defines the mission of the new school. The preamble asserts: "Education of Youth is . . . a sure means of securing good and useful citizens and an important aid in the perpetuation of our free institutions." These were the public purposes for which Loyola was incorporated. Because this objective was so commonplace, the preamble was stricken from the final version of the bill.

The breadth of purpose was safeguarded instead by the extensive nature of the degrees the college was empowered to grant. Loyola College was vested with the power "to confer any degree or degrees in any of the faculties arts & sciences and liberal professions which are usually permitted to be conferred in any colleges or universities in America."[22] The intent was identical to that in the provisions in the charter of Saint Mary's College. Today we distinguish between colleges and universities but that was not the case before the Civil War. The legal effect of this terminology was to make Loyola a university from the sealing of its charter.

Few restrictions were intended by either Loyola's founders or the state legislature. The only one worth noting was the deletion by the Senate of a clause that would have permitted the corporation to receive "any gifts, bequests, and devises of any money stocks or other property." Perhaps the Senate's action arose from nothing more than a desire to apply the section of the Maryland Constitution that restricted the right of ministers and religious corporations to accept gifts, especially of land and real estate.

Excision of this clause, however, required the concurrence of the lower house, and at first the delegates "respectfully requested" the Senate to recede from its amendment, but without success. If the lower house remained adamant, Loyola would suffer the fate that a few years earlier had befallen Holy Cross (though for other reasons). The impasse was decisively resolved in a manner that suggests that a strong influence—possibly that of Governor Enoch Louis Lowe—had been applied. All the delegates except one agreed to the Senate's amendment.

The charter that remained clearly would allow Loyola College to operate comfortably. "An act to incorporate the associated professors of Loyola College in the City of Baltimore" was finally passed on April 13, 1853.[23] The lawmaking process in that period did not require the governor's signature, but there was no doubt that Governor Lowe would have willingly assented.

How chancy this whole process was can be deduced from the fate of another piece of legislation. A few days before Father Early submitted his petition, Martin Kerney renewed his efforts to establish a statewide system of education, and his new bill, like the previous one, contained a provision allocating public monies to private schools. The uproar against the new Kerney school bill was so great that it was not even reported out of committee.

In such a climate of opinion, insistence by the college on the retention of the gifts and bequests clause that had been excised by the Senate would certainly have killed the Loyola charter. Another bill granting the right to gifts and bequests was quietly sought almost three decades later. What had been denied in 1853 was, without objection, granted by the state legislature in 1880.[24]

• •

Even before the formalities of incorporation were completed, Father Early was arranging for the acquisition of a permanent site. On April 17 the Maryland provincial agreed "to pay the ground rent of the lot purchased for the erection of a church College & dwelling of the Society of Jesus on Calvert & Madison Streets, Baltimore."[25] This was no trifling subsidy (it was continued for only a few years). The Baltimore Water Company, owner of the 200- by 124-foot lot, was asking $23,333.33 for it, and outright purchase would have totally absorbed the loan that had been advanced to Loyola from the province. By leasing the land for a ground rent of only $1,400.00 a year, Father Early was able to use the loan for construction instead. The lease was to run for ninety-nine years, although the college retained the right to purchase at the stated price within eight years, and there were indications that outright purchase was intended. The first payment of the ground rent was postponed until April a year later. This generosity indicates how desirable the new college was in the view of the company's officers, who were among the city's leading citizens.

Ground rent is a distinctive Baltimore institution. Throughout the rest of the United States, at least since the Revolution, land and buildings have been sold together—in fee simple, according to legal terminology. In Baltimore, however, a building may be sold without transfer of title to the land. This allows the purchaser to avoid paying the price of the land but at the cost of an annual rent to the holder of the land title. This practice is a survival from the colonial period that creates a symbiotic relationship between homeowners and investors in ground rents. It helps explain the consistently higher rate of home ownership in Baltimore than elsewhere.

The formal inauguration of the new corporation was recorded in its minute book on Sunday, May 1. After the full text of the act of incorporation and its acceptance by the trustees, there follows a series of by-laws. These provided for the election and removal of officers and as-signed duties to the various authorities. The president was given the power "to receive and dismiss students" and to act for the corporation in financial transactions. The adoption of a seal whose main features were the badge of the Society of Jesus and a Jesuit figure holding a book com-pleted the inaugural process.

The business of the corporation's third meeting was purely aca-demic. On July 10 a resolution to authorize the conferring of honorary and earned degrees at the graduation two days hence was passed. The program of orations and dialogue had undoubtedly been in rehearsal for several weeks. With two young men (albeit transferees from Saint Mary's) having completed their collegiate studies, Baltimore's new Jesuit school could end its first year with a flourish.

• •

There was a different aura to college commencements a century ago. It was a more sentimental age, a time when people were more ad-dicted to oratory. More than today, these were civic festivals, and com-peting events were fewer. Commencement was a time when a school put its finished and developing products on display. Only a small percentage of the American population was ever formally presented to the commu-nity in this manner.

Commencement, on July 12, 1853, was an important occasion for Loyola College, and appropriate preparations had been made. The new-est and most elegant hall in Baltimore, the New Assembly Rooms at

Hanover and Lombard streets, served as the location. Archbishop Kenrick was invited; the diplomas were, in Father Early's judgment, "very prettily done."[26] These were large parchment-like sheets printed in elegant Latin with blanks left for the name of the recipient, the degree, the date, and the signatures of the president and all the professors. The seal and a light blue ribbon were attached to the diploma. Later, when the development of athletics required a choice of school colors, Loyola's emblems (while it remained on Calvert Street) were light blue and gold—the same colors used on the cover of Ryan's *Historical Sketch.*

The rest of the graduation exercises in 1853 were similarly stylish. The best band in the city, the Independent Blues, would start the proceedings and provide appropriate musical interludes. Weeks before, Father Early could confidently report, "Our boys are well prepared & will, I feel sure, make a good impression."[27] Programs were printed, listing the subjects for the fifteen orations and the names of the participants; these must have persuaded a few more friends, relatives, and leisured curious to attend. Only the weather could not be managed. That July, like so many others in Baltimore, was "intolerably hot."

Nevertheless, students, faculty, honored guests, and proud parents were seated around nine o'clock to hear the Independent Blues strike up the opening number. There followed (for how long can only be imagined) declamations on such varied subjects as the pathetic Mary Queen of Scots, the fiery Attila, the grandeur of Rome, the honor due Maryland, and the future of America. A dialogue on Greek "furnished the *school boys* argument against the study of that language with the reasons of the *riper scholar* in its favor."

Later in the program, a dialogue on disappointments provided comic relief. One of the orators essayed the role of a "hungry office-seeker, who had failed in his efforts to fatten on the spoils." The second was a pupil "who was tired of 'College rules and slavery' "—a familiar pout—and longed to join the gold rush to California. The third was a disappointed forty-niner who had learned from experience how illusory that pursuit was; to him was given the task of drawing the lesson that "honest industry" was the only sure warrant against disappointment. These presentations were separated by band interludes.

Reports in the *Sun* and another report (which survives only as an unidentified clipping, but for the reason cited below probably appeared in the *Patriot*) noted general approval by the audience. The frequent rounds of applause were "quite profuse." A few of the orators garnered bouquets of flowers from "fair listeners" moved by eloquence (and possibly by a reminding nudge from a doting mother). The gentleman from the *Sun* gave the palm to John Curlett (1854), but his rival thought more highly of the "inimitable Joshua Jones." Master Jones's father was an officer on the *Patriot*, and any sensible reporter from that paper had reason enough to describe him as "a lad scarcely yet in his teens, but with the action, the emphases and dignity of a man!" The anonymous writer rose to the occasion with a notice of "long and loud applause by his fellow-students, with whom he was evidently in high favor." The more sophisticated writer from the *Sun* did not report in such detail; he merely noted that "all the addresses were written expressly for the occasion, and delivered in that style of oratory which would have conferred credit upon older heads." Twenty years later on a similar occasion, the house diarist would put the matter more succinctly. He wrote, "The Baltimore boy seems most efficient in declamation."[28]

The climax, of course, was a valedictory delivered by one of the graduates. George Warner, "a young gentleman of great promise," feelingly expressed appreciation for the "self-sacrificing spirit of the Jesuit fathers, his instructors." His brother, the other graduate, had already delivered himself "with becoming dignity" of "many fine sentiments" on the subject of education. Their eloquence was noted in both newspaper accounts. Though most of their collegiate training had been completed at Saint Mary's, their final polish bore a familiar sheen.

After another rousing band number the student-orators yielded stage center to Archbishop Kenrick, who presided over the final act. His Grace gave George and William Warner their diplomas as bachelors of arts. Three other gentlemen received warrants for the more honorific title of master of arts. They were a lawyer and two doctors who had qualified not by taking additional courses but merely by being practitioners in a learned profession for two years or more. Giving the M.A. degree under such circumstances was a common and ancient practice, but some thought it more accurate to say that the degree "customarily went to all college men who three years after graduation were not in jail."[29]

There was still one scene to play. The archbishop began reading the names of students who had distinguished themselves in the basic literature classes, in arithmetic, in languages, or in regular attendance and deportment. Each marched up (with audience applauding) to receive a premium, an inscribed book. These awards were issued with a generous hand so that a third or more of the students received at least one distinction; some got multiple laurels. A few came away with no more than a mention of their improvement in recitation, composition, or conduct. The contrast between their situation and the recognition given others was meant to incite competition, and probably did. Competition was "one of the prominent factors" in the Jesuit system of education. Funded medals did not become part of a Loyola commencement until the 1880s.

• •

Observers thought this first commencement quite creditable. The *Sun* reporter, as cited above, was restrained but generally favorable in his judgment of the students and of the new school. His counterpart from the *Patriot* said about the same thing in more words and thought it proper to do his bit against Know-Nothings by referring to the orations as evidence that Jesuits inculcated "a due regard for the Institutions of our country . . . and the importance of preserving them." It was, how-ever, a time when such assurances were not enough. The tide of anti-Catholicism and mob violence had begun to rise in Baltimore and in the rest of the nation.

In such circumstances, the appearance of one name on the program for the next commencement is remarkable. In 1854, Martin Kerney was honored with a master of arts degree, but there were not the usual grounds for such an award. He was by training a lawyer but had at best only briefly practiced that learned profession. Furthermore, as a mem-ber of the House of Delegates, Kerney had voted for the bill incorporat-ing Loyola, but others had been more diligent on its behalf.

To honor Kerney after he had become the center of political contro-versy was a singular gesture for so conciliatory a man as John Early. Per-haps there was a little more pepper in that gentle Jesuit than appears in his formal portraits. Father Early and Kerney could claim the same alma mater, Mount Saint Mary's, and Kerney had produced a set of textbooks that had the endorsement (until recently) of the Baltimore public school authorities. From all this one could readily piece together cre-dentials for an honorary M.A. degree.

• •

In 1858 Early added a new element to Loyola commencements, an address. That year, Severn Teackle Wallis spoke for about an hour on how young men entering business life might ensure "the respect of their fellowmen and happiness to themselves." He cautioned them "against a greed for gain before all things else."[30] It was (and still is) sound and generally acceptable doctrine (whatever the actual practice), but Wallis demonstrated the idealism he professed by leading a civic reform move-ment that broke the Know-Nothing grip on Baltimore a year later.

This address and those at the next two annual exercises were spon-sored by the Loyola Literary Society, organized in September of 1857. Its resident members (as identified in the catalogues) were the senior class. There were in addition honorary members, mainly graduates (thus a proto-alumni association) and such notables as Wallis, Gover-nor Lowe, Orestes Brownson, Congressman Henry May, Doctor L. Sil-liman Ives, and James Ryder Randall. These men had been granted honorary status on the expectation that they would eventually give a commencement address under the auspices of the literary society, and so it happened with Wallis, Brownson, and Ives.

In establishing its literary society, Loyola was abreast of a general movement in American education. Such organizations were then ap-pearing on other campuses, but there they served a different function. They provided a vehicle to supplement the emphasis on character train-ing and classics with access to newer intellectual, cultural, and scien-tific pursuits. These literary societies also invited speakers whose views were considered too novel to be presented under the formal auspices of the school.

Neither of these functions was apparent at Loyola. Addresses by such well-known figures as Wallis, Brownson, and Ives were meant to provide models of educated thought and eloquence and to counter the Know-Nothing propaganda that the Roman Catholic faith was an alien force. Wallis's sound performance was followed in 1859 by Brownson's address on patriotism. The subject was timely and appropriate. The speaker, according to the *Sun*'s reporter, treated the matter "in a half literary and half political manner, but [to] the infinite interest and amusement of his audience, who were profuse in their applause."[31] Brownson, a native American, convert to Catholicism, and close friend of Father Early's, seemed an ideal choice for a commencement speaker at Loyola. The invitation also served to assure Brownson that he had not lost all his Jesuit friends after being rebuked by Archbishop John Hughes during a recent Fordham graduation. At the next year's ex-ercises, the address was given by another noteworthy, Silliman Ives, who had served as bishop of the Protestant Episcopal church in North Carolina before he became a convert in 1852.

This short series ended with the outbreak of the Civil War and dis-sipation of the Know-Nothing movement. The latter development made the original function of the literary society as sponsor of such addresses superfluous. The society continued, but only as a student debating club. Its function as a bridge to the alumni was quietly forgotten. Occasionally a local dignitary or alumnus was invited to address the graduates, but after the Civil War this was no longer a regular feature of Loyola's commencements.

3

"The College"

The day after Loyola's first commencement Father Early received permission to begin building. It was not customary then to make a ceremonial occasion of breaking ground, and none of the sparse correspondence refers to the start of construction. However, Early would not have begun work without the provincial's permission, and the feast day of Saint Ignatius Loyola was near. Under the circumstances it would have been especially fitting to turn the first shovelful of earth on that occasion.

. .

By 1853 the city of Baltimore had reached its pre–Civil War peak of development. It was ranked in the guidebooks of the period "amongst the most important commercial cities in the Union" and as "the great commercial centre of the South." The combined value of the varied products that passed through the sea and rail terminals of Baltimore totaled more than eighty million dollars a year. Swift sailing ships, steamboats, and trains connected Baltimore with major ports around the globe, to the financial centers of the north, and to markets in the southern and western states.

Baltimore could also boast of being the "third city in the Union." The 1850 census found over 140,000 whites, about 25,000 free black persons, and nearly 3,000 slaves within the bounds of Baltimore. The population had grown by almost one-third since the previous decennial census, with part of the increase due to an influx of German and Irish immigrants. The 1850 census disclosed that nearly one fourth of the city's inhabitants were foreign-born.

The increase of foreigners disturbed some Baltimoreans (notably those who supported the intimidating terrorism of the Know-Nothings) but generally Baltimore society was still considered "the most warm-hearted, generous, and hospitable" in America. The city's people, visitors said, had the attractive features of inhabitants of both North and South but avoided the vices characteristic of people in each section. The ladies of Baltimore were admired as "exquisitely beautiful" and much more modest than those of Boston and New York. The city was publicly acclaimed "the gastronomic metropolis of the union," and its inhabitants relished a distinctive addiction to oysters and canvasbacks. Horse racing, of course, was not so much a pastime in Baltimore as a way of life.

In geographical terms, the boundaries of Baltimore encompassed ten thousand acres in a shape that was almost a square. There were many hills, but some of the low-lying acres were marshy—a breeding place for insistent mosquitoes. Jones Falls, then a rapid, unruly stream, divided the city lengthwise into nearly equal parts. Occasional flooding from the Falls posed a threat to life, property, and the bridges that stapled together the halves of Baltimore. The city's streets were wide by the standards of that day and lined with well-built red brick houses whose white marble steps conveyed a note of elegance.[1]

. .

For nearly seven decades (almost a lifetime as reckoned in the Bible) Loyola College operated from the west side of the 700 block of Calvert Street. The college site, for most of that time, occupied only three-fifths of the block; private houses fronting on Monument Street filled the remainder until the late 1890s. The northern limit was Madison Street, and Hargrove Alley marked Loyola's western bound. The campus was just around the corner from the Washington Monument—the landmark that earned Baltimore its nickname "the Monumental City."

This location promoted a sense of assurance. Mount Vernon Place, after all, was proclaimed Baltimore's "parlour" by the novelist Henry James. It was also "the most fashionable, the most elegant, and probably the most expensive" residential area in the city. Among its distinguished inhabitants were the Garretts, John Pendleton Kennedy (civic leader and author), and Henry May, who represented the district in Congress. One of its quadrants would eventually be graced by the Peabody Institute's library and Conservatory of Music.

Just south of Monument Street on the west side of Calvert stood the unique group of houses known as Waterloo Row. These twelve handsome brick houses were designed by Robert Mills, who supervised construction of the Washington Monument. Both their style (Classic Revival) and their location (so far north from where sensible Baltimoreans lived in 1816) made them and their builder objects of derision. These houses would prove to be Mills's Waterloo, said skeptical Baltimoreans.

More than propinquity linked Loyola to the row, because Thomas Courtney Jenkins, head of that noteworthy clan, lived at 608 North Calvert Street. When the pace of building around Mount Vernon Place increased, Jenkins and his family moved to the 700 block of Saint Paul Street, where their neighbors across Hargrove Alley were the Jesuits. Although the Jenkins residence is still standing (it is operated as a hotel), Waterloo Row finally succumbed to urban renewal—as the process is euphemistically called. What little has survived from it may be seen in the American Wing of the Baltimore Museum of Art.

Across Calvert Street from Waterloo Row was the Hippodrome Lot. On this "wide and vacant plain" traveling circuses pitched their tents each spring. Between engagements, the "picturesque Bedouins of the amusement world" left their performing ring on the lot as a reminder and as a pledge of their return. There, during the interim, more than one Loyola schoolboy "beguiled away . . . many a thoughtless hour."[2] Eventually, this lot was filled by houses.

For a time the block opposite the college was empty. The boys could chase one another down the steep hill to Jones Falls. From the intersection of Calvert and Madison there was a good view down into the yard of the penitentiary located on the other side of the watercourse. One day, when four murderers were scheduled to hang, an "immense crowd" gathered along Calvert Street to watch the stark drama.

Development of the surrounding neighborhood was promoted by construction of "the College." This term signified not merely the area of the structure used for classes, but the whole structure. One wing housed Saint Ignatius Church, and the longer section facing Calvert Street was used for classrooms, a Jesuit residence, and community activities. The building was constructed in an architectural style different from the one dominant in Baltimore. Instead of fashionable Gothic brownstone, it was Ionian and brick. The Roman Temple of Concord provided the basic pattern—a choice not only of an architectural model but of a significant ideal.

Louis L. Long was the supervising architect, but the concept and much of the design was probably the work of Henry Hamilton Pittar, who had recently arrived from England after touring the Continent and studying the architecture of Rome. (Long was more adept at the Gothic style, as may be seen in the tower he designed for Saint Alphonsus

Church.) There are several surviving examples of Long's work, but no structure in Baltimore is ascribed to Pittar; indeed, he does not appear to have stayed in town longer than it took to sketch "The College."[3]

Entrances of "the College" were designed with attention to unpleasant realities. The path of virtue is said to be steep and narrow; both characteristics are evident in the stairway to the classroom wing of the structure. There was not much space available for a church, so two small doorways at either end of the facade provide access to the narrow vestibule. Only one central door, however, admits worshippers and others to the nave of the church. Limitations of space may partly explain these arrangements, which would also tend to obstruct a mob. Such a consideration, fantastic to a later generation, could not be ignored in the 1850s.

• •

Most of the construction was handled by local artisans. Michael Roche was responsible for general supervision of the carpentry, with the masonry subcontracted to George Callis. This combine, which was working on various projects in the neighborhood, was supplemented by other contractors, all duly noted in the newspapers. Notices also credited the heating, gaslight fixtures, furniture, tinning, stuccowork, plastering, and glazing to various firms. It was good business for the city and its newspapers to take note of such matters; futhermore, the elaborate descriptions of the architectural features of this and every new building were an expression of municipal pride.

Actual building had a slow start. Little more than the foundations were completed by Christmas Eve of 1853. The Associated Professors were by then indebted to Roche for a total of only $1,500. Because he was the general supervisor, this sum may be taken as a measure of how much progress had been made before the snows began to fall. Through the winter months entries of a few hundred dollars were periodically added to his account.[4]

Father Early's winter correspondence contains no reference to the new building. With the coming of March, however, he noted the resumption of work. "If the weather only continues favorable," he wrote, "we hope to hope to move into the new College next September."[5] The redundant aspiration may serve as a clue to his anxiety—and his distraction.

To complete construction, additional funds were necessary, and these were secured from local creditors, both private and institutional, and from the Maryland province. The total raised from extramural sources was over $75,000. The loans from the province included the original $22,000 plus later sums raised by the sales of the original homestead of the Jenkins family near White Plains and of forty or more acres at Goshenhoppen, Pennsylvania.[6] All these loans would eventually have to be repaid—with interest—but, in the interim, work on "the College" could continue.

In 1854 Father Early had hoped that his third September in Baltimore would find the college in its new home. This hope proved illusory, although after the rush of registration he reported, "The plastering of the new College is progressing rapidly & will be done next month. The Church will be roofed about the same time."[7] Entries in Roche's ledger were regularly made, even during the ensuing winter.

By the start of 1855 Father Early's list of accomplishments was impressive. Loyola College had been legally incorporated with a minimum of difficulty, and a handsome new building was being completed. There was no likelihood of Early being replaced, even though his first term as rector was nearly over. He remained head of the Jesuit community for another three years.

• •

During the remainder of his time at Loyola, John Early presided over a number of beginnings. These included the formal opening of classes at "the College" as well as the consecration of Saint Ignatius Church. A series of steps was taken to ensure that the Jesuit formative process—the *paideia*—was fully instituted at Loyola College.

By mid-February of 1855 the classroom wing of the college was ready for use. Classes at Holliday Street were interrupted for two days while desks, chairs, and other furnishings were carted to the new location. The scholastics (who probably did most of the hauling) were described at the end of the move as being "in good health, good humor, and in good little rooms, a thing they long desired."[8] Prominent members of the Maryland province and other distinguished guests were invited to the formal opening of Loyola's new home. Teachers and students polished their presentations as they rehearsed the inaugural program, scheduled for February 22.

Nowadays we celebrate George Washington's birthday in ways unheard of by earlier generations, some of the ways better left unmentioned: the anniversary has become a legal holiday and a commercial orgy. In 1855, what notice was taken of the day came from private initiative. That year in Baltimore, the local militia led by the Baltimore

City Guards paraded to the beat and blare of the Independent Blues, and a rival ensemble, the Independent Grays, sponsored a ball in the evening. Other companies gave witness to their patriotism and cheerful sociability in ways prompted by their imagination and permitted by their means.

"One of the most attractive features" of February 22, 1855, according to the *Sun*, was the formal opening of Loyola College. It was an auspicious day. Winter briefly slackened its grip on the city, and a warm breeze raised the temperature to the mid-sixties. The main hall was already filled when at ten o'clock a lively band started the proceedings. Fifteen young men in turn recited prose pieces and verse in English, Latin, and French. The first half of the program was devoted to the life and character of George Washington, and the second extolled the virtues of Saint Ignatius Loyola. This combination was obviously intended to assuage suspicions against the school's Americanism without concealing its dedication to the memory of the founder of the Jesuit order. The main address, entitled "Patriotism," was delivered by William George Read, the grandson of hero of the American Revolution and promoter of Baltimore John Eager Howard. Read was a prominent civic leader and a Catholic, and he was wealthy enough to loan funds to Loyola on occasion. A final band number dismissed the invited guests to a repast in "the dining saloon" below the main hall.

• •

While these guests were enjoying their food, others toured the new building. They were duly impressed with what they saw. The main hall or exhibition room, where the inaugural ceremonies had taken place, was described as "small but handsome." Its dimensions were approximately thirty-one feet broad by fifty-five feet long, extending from the Calvert Street face of the building to the yard in the rear and rising upward from the second through the third story. There was a raised platform at the yard end of the hall and "a very comfortable gallery" around the other three sides. The main floor and gallery could seat about six hundred people, and was used until near the end of the century, when a more commodious auditorium replaced it.[9]

Father Early intended to generate a congregation by celebrating Mass in this hall until the church was completed. By May he was pleased to note that "the passages were filled with people. . . . The choir is first rate. Mrs. Curley, formerly Miss Walters, is the prima donna."[10] On school days, the same hall served for the monthly reading of marks, class exhibitions, discourses by the president or other members of the faculty or visiting speakers, and, later, for dramatic presentations.

There were other essential facilities in the new building. A student library and classrooms were located on the second floor, and above these were living quarters for the Jesuits. Similar accommodations were available on the fourth floor, which also contained a faculty library, shelved in mahogany, for five thousand volumes. About one-fifth of the shelf space was already filled by donations from Father James Dolan, Edward Jenkins, and other benefactors, and by purchases. On the first floor was the dining room; the remainder of the floor was probably occupied by reception parlors, meeting rooms, and the like. These facilities were optimistically thought ample to accommodate five hundred students and thirty or so Jesuits. Though this ideal provides a measure of Father Early's intention, enrollment never equalled the capacity of the structure.

The school was described later by John J. Ryan (1861), a student and later a member of the faculty. This structure, he wrote, was "bright and airy, well supplied with gas and water and other modern conveniences, but lacking everything sumptuous and luxurious; it had spotlessly clean, uncarpeted floors, glittering white, unpapered, undecorated walls, rooms furnished without superfluity."[11] There were apparently few distractions, of opulence or of poverty. These are of course relative terms, but deeply ingrained in Jesuit practice is the aversion of Saint Ignatius to an ostentatious display of either extreme. "The manner is ordinary" summarizes the fundamental principle of the Jesuit life style.

• •

No immediate changes were made in the operation of the college after the transfer to Calvert Street. The remainder of the 1855 spring semester was spent mainly in anticipation of September. In his expense ledger, Father Ward was recording necessary acquisitions: two dozen chairs and tables, crockery, gas fixtures, tables and washstands, a special desk for the provincial's room—and more. There were also the monthly bills for bread and milk (lunch for the students enrolled as half-boarders), newspaper subscriptions, watches mended, shirts made, and pictures framed. Special books in analytical geometry and rhetoric were bought for one student, and unnamed Baltimoreans received varying sums of money to ease their needs. Among the other notations were old loans repaid, new ones contracted, and regular payments of interest—usually at 6 percent.

President Early could not be other than satisfied with the preparations when classes resumed in September. Registered students numbered 130, and several more could be expected to straggle in during the year. There were also new faces among the faculty. Father Charles King, for one, served both as professor of college juniors and as prefect of studies—the dean in today's parlance. There were also two new scholastics: Edward Henchy (who became Father Clarke's protégé) and Martin Morris, who after leaving the Society became a notable member of the federal judiciary. Henchy later served as president of the college, but in 1855 he was prefect of discipline. In this office he became an awesome figure to new students, because they were told by their more knowledgeable betters that Henchy had "custody of the cat-o'-nine-tails, with special authority delegated by the Pope . . . to use them on necessary occasions."[12]

A stellar addition to the faculty was Father Edward Holker Welch. Of an honored Massachusetts family, he had studied at Harvard under the poet Henry Wadsworth Longfellow and the eminent jurist Joseph Story. He went to Heidelberg after graduation and traveled extensively in Europe, joining the Catholic church in the course of his wandering. There was at the time a veritable tide of conversions, with that of John Henry Newman possibly the most conspicious. After Welch entered the Society of Jesus, he retained the friendship of Longfellow and was not excluded from Boston society. Father Welch was described as an "earnest and painstaking" teacher—not very imaginative but always clear and careful. "The Philosophers" (college seniors), reported Father Early, "seemed to be very much pleased with Welch."[13] After a time he left Baltimore to return to "the Hub," where he became one of the incorporators of Boston College. Father Welch spent his last years at Georgetown lecturing on ethics and constitutional law.

• •

The new facilities permitted Father Early to introduce much of the routine that was characteristic of Jesuit schools. On the first Monday morning of October, at half past eleven, the students and teachers gathered for a reading of marks. There was no escaping this assize. Father Early concluded the exposure of student diligence or sloth "by giving a general pardon to the condemned, provided they would promise amendment."[14] On the following evening before supper, he called the teachers to his room to announce that specimens would be given monthly in each class. A specimen was a demonstration, before the president and faculty, of a class's proficiency in its studies. For the "philosophers" a specimen might take the form of a disputation in which one student defended certain theses against objections raised by a peer. In the natural sciences the demonstration might be a carefully prepared lecture or experiment. These gradually acquired the requisite polish and were presented to the entire student body.

Such exhibitions might take another form. In 1856 the classes of second and first humanities (the equivalent of high-school seniors and college freshmen) exchanged challenges for a test of their skills in Latin and Greek grammar. The classes were paired so that a student from each was questioned and could in turn question his inquisitor. Of course, this was a contest not only among the students but among their instructors. At the next reading of marks a majority of the honors went to the lower class, but the college freshmen and their teacher were not bereft of their share. Such competitions were intended to spur the participants and their audience to greater effort. The reading of marks at the end of October 1855 was encouraging. Several students were promoted, and the whole student body was given a holiday "to visit the Agricultural Exhibition." Although no other reason was stated, this largesse may have been a way to disperse the students and thus discourage Halloween pranks.

A month later Father Charles Stonestreet, the provincial, made a formal inspection of the new school. He listened carefully as Father Welch presided over the questioning of the college seniors by Early, Ward, and King. The provincial judged the students' skill in philosophy good enough to warrant an afternoon's holiday. Thereupon, President Early delicately absented himself on some business in southern Maryland while Stonestreet visited all the other classes. Among the Jesuits, the provincial formally instituted ascetic practices shared by the order and monastic communities: reading at meals, exhortations, penances, and the like. The Jesuits were, after all, men striving "to perfect themselves in virtue and in learning" and thereby "to procure the same blessings for the youth committed to their charge."[15]

Tradition does not permit Jesuits to draw attention to the ascetic side of their communal lives. As a result, many occasions arise when strict practice may be adapted to circumstance. For example, it would have been ungracious to have silence and reading at table when Bishops McGill of Richmond and O'Reilly of Hartford visited the new school.

And wine was served at an evening meal for an Italian Jesuit in transit to California. Nothing but gracious hospitality was evident when Governor Lowe and Baron von Gerolt, the Prussian envoy, came for a quiet evening. Even a Dominican was welcomed at Loyola's table—for one meal at least. Asceticism was maintained, but out of public view and never at the expense of other responsibilities. Among American Jesuits, the Maryland province has always enjoyed a reputation for being the most hospitable.

Loyola's Jesuits were not mere spectators; they participated in the varied life of the city. Father Early and some scholastics listened to a Miss Edmonde give a reading of American and Irish poets. Banvard's "panorama of the Holy Land" must have been particularly interesting, because several groups of priests and scholastics went to see it. During Christmas vacation the scholastics topped off a little celebration by attending a lecture by Silliman Ives, the convert and former Episcopalian bishop. A couple of weeks later Father Early and several others heard a discourse by Archbishop John Hughes of New York at the Maryland Institute. In later years Loyola presidents received similar invitations from the Institute and took their turn at its podium. Scholastics and priests regularly attended the lectures and concerts offered by the Peabody Conservatory and the Johns Hopkins University.

The Jesuits were involved also in a broad range of church activities. Father Early, for instance, served as a consultor to Archbishop Kenrick. Early and his colleagues celebrated Mass and heard confessions at various churches, convents, and hospitals around the city. Eventually a member of the Loyola community became chaplain at the nearby penitentiary. Quickly and in various ways Loyola's Jesuits extended their service to Baltimore's Catholics.

• •

Work on the church continued during the eighteen months that followed the opening of the school section. Entries in Roche's ledger rose more in amount than in number because the church wing was roofed and funds were being expended for interior decoration. Over the main altar was a work by Brumidi, the artist who spent his life decorating the Capitol in Washington, depicting Saint Ignatius Loyola in ecstasy.

The conditions of the site made it difficult to achieve harmonious proportions in the church, built to accommodate fifteen hundred people. Space was gained by making the nave somewhat wider than appropriate. The church's interior dimensions were approximately sixty-eight by ninety feet, with a recessed sanctuary at the western end balanced at the east by a choir gallery and entrance. Floor to ceiling measured about fifty feet. Viewing this interior shortly before the consecration of the church, one reporter was transported into exclamations about its "elegance and grandeur." The uncluttered ceiling, he wrote, "adds a lightness and elegance to the whole design, justly rivalling the more elaborate Gothic."[16]

In order for Saint Ignatius Church to be consecrated, certain legal matters had to be settled. Who owned it and was it free of debt? According to ecclesiastical law, title to a church must be vested in the bishop unless the church is the responsibility of a religious order. At least one archbishop in California claimed that the exception for religious orders had no practical effect, and that title to a local church should be formally vested in him. Religious orders viewed this legal doctrine as a threat to their traditional exemptions from the powers of the local ordinary. In addition, the Loyola College charter could be interpreted to restrict the college from owning property except such as could be used directly in pursuance of its educational purpose. The college might have sought passage of clarifying legislation, but the rising power of the Know-Nothings and the earlier difficulty with the Maryland Senate made such a course seem imprudent.

For some obscure reason (doubt about the legalities involved seems the most probable) Archbishop Kenrick suggested in 1855 that title to both the college and the church be vested in the Jesuit provincial. Such a transfer would undoubtedly have settled matters under both canon and civil law. But a less drastic solution was chosen by the Associated Professors, a solution that avoided the centralizing tendency of Archbishop Kenrick's suggestion. Title to the whole property was vested in the college corporation, not in the provincial, and the debt from the construction of Saint Ignatius Church was assigned entirely to the Associated Professors. This made impractical any attempt to separate the church from the college and to transfer the former to the care of the archdiocesan clergy. Farfetched as this possibility might seem to others, it was obviously a concern for the Jesuits, and the argument of the California archbishop made it seem worthy of attention.[17] The arrangement they chose allowed the Jesuits to avoid both a possible, if remote, threat and saying no to an archbishop.

Since the church technically was free of debt, it could be consecrated. The date for this event was not the patronal feast, July 31, but

August 15, which in the Roman calendar is dedicated to the Assumption of the Blessed Virgin Mary. This date was probably chosen long before, and it fit the subject of the large central fresco in the church ceiling.

• •

Scant attention had been paid to the church basement. Newspaper reports indicated merely that it was well appointed and intended for scholastic purposes. And so it was used, for the most part, but it also served for about six years as the Chapel of Blessed Peter Claver, in honor of a Catalan Jesuit missionary priest whose sanctity was eventually recognized by canonization. About a year after consecration of the church, "colored people" were "earnestly invited" to attend Mass and other services in the chapel.

Providing separate facilities for blacks had not previously been common practice for Catholics; until the 1850s, black and white Catholics generally attended Mass in the same church. This practice aroused suspicions in non-Catholic Marylanders and differentiated "Papists" from other Christians. By the 1850s, most major Protestant churches had established separate facilities for their black members, and so, desiring to appear fully American, the Catholic laity began to indicate a preference for similar arrangements.

The desire of white Catholics to accommodate themselves and their church to prevailing practice had resulted in the establishment of the Peter Claver chapel. Even the Jesuits were finally yielding to what could be opposed only at the price of what they then saw as greater harm. Initially this ministry to blacks was conducted by Fathers Edward Sourin and James Tehan, a much younger Jesuit. Father Sourin was a saintly priest, generous almost to a fault. He had served as Kenrick's vicar general in Philadelphia before seeking admission to the Society of Jesus, and he lived out the rest of his life at Loyola.

Fathers Sourin and Tehan alternated conducting service in the Claver chapel until 1858. In that year Father Peter Miller (familiarly known as Pap) arrived, and the chapel's subsequent history is associated with him. He was a native of Belgium baptized with a name much longer and harder to pronounce, which had been shortened and Anglicized, probably for reasons like those which prompted name changes for other Jesuits in the Maryland province. He is often mistakenly credited with founding the Claver chapel. Father Miller did establish the first distinct parish for black Catholics in America, Saint Francis Xavier

Church, in the midst of the Civil War. He was aided in this endeavor by Michael O'Connor, a quondam bishop turned Jesuit who also lived at "the College."[18]

· ·

After the graduation in July of 1856, President Early issued Loyola's first catalogue. Like him, it was terse, neat, and practical. The catalogue was always published after the end of the school year, and besides the commencement program, offered a prospectus of the following year's work. Father Early listed the faculty and reprinted the 1852 advertisement as a statement of purpose. To counter antipathy to Latin and Greek literature, he italicized the assertion *"During the whole course, great attention is paid to Composition, particularly English."* Loyola was willing to offer Italian and German, but at an additional fee. Early's general tone and format were reproduced until the 1890s, although changes in student regulations and curriculum were from time to time incorporated in the catalogue.

President Early, unlike his counterparts at Yale, Harvard, Princeton, and Columbia, did not believe in burdening the operations of the college with numerous detailed regulations. Fifteen short sentences in the catalogue covered all the important rules for student conduct. The lawgivers at other American schools listed precisely what was permitted and forbidden, with the result that "eight pages of fine print" did not suffice. This contrast may indicate that many schools felt the need to legislate for residents; the contrast may also be attributed to a difference in philosophy.

Loyola's regulatory tradition was derived from Rome, which laid down a few general rules to be applied in particular cases by an official with broad powers of interpretation. Puritans viewed such governance as too imprecise and fraught with opportunities for what they considered tyranny. The conduct of school authorities, no less than that of the students, was given precise definition, and the limitations on both were supposed to be scrupulously observed. The difference in regulatory philosophy should not distract from the basic similarity of purpose of these institutions, however. The liberal arts philosophy of education, whether in the Jesuit or the Puritan tradition, emphasized character training. Furthermore, many of the students were quite young, and as a result, in loco parentis was a reasonable approach to faculty-student relations.[19]

The first few regulations in the Loyola catalogue specified the schedule. Classes began promptly at 9:00 (but all Catholic students had to arrive half an hour earlier to attend daily Mass). The morning session ended at 12:00 and classes did not resume until 2:30; dismissal was at 5:00. This schedule was practically identical with the one followed at nearby Male Central High School. It was observed until the outbreak of the Civil War, when the long noon respite was eliminated.

The other regulations dealt with conduct and attendance. "Every student" was expected to be "clean and becoming in apparel." What exactly was meant by this and other general phrases was left to the decision of "the officers and Professors of the College." Wrestling, improper language, and disorderly conduct were prohibited; general behavior and attendance were reported frequently to parents.

Formal examinations were given in February and July. Senior members of the faculty served as examiners—no class was tested by its own instructor. For the February testing in 1856, Father Ward took third humanities in small groups to his room for a quizzing on Latin and Greek grammar, geography, Bible history, and so on. Father Welch interrogated the members of second humanities individually in one of the parlors. Rudiments were arranged in groups of four for Father King's questioning. When this was completed, Father Ward reviewed the progress of the various mathematics sections. Afterward he joined Welch and King in listening to how well the students had mastered their French lessons. Such oral examinations demonstrated (maybe too forcefully) that learning was a social, human process and not merely an encounter between a student and a book and a blank sheet of paper. The result, according to the catalogue, was a series of promotions. Mercifully, no other result was published, although at least a few demotions are likely to have occurred.

In 1858 there was little else that President John Early could add to Loyola's immediate development. Still, at the very end of his tenure, he introduced regular courses in the German language and literature. It was a prudent addition, because Germans constituted the largest immigrant group in the city. Furthermore, Germans were so devoted to their language and customs that they supported private schools and eventually secured establishment of seven bilingual schools within the public system.

By any standards, Father Early had for six years presided over a solid and successful beginning. The time had come for a change in leadership at Loyola College and a sign of the order's approval of John Early.

4

Time of Troubles

In Jesuit houses the installation of a new rector is handled matter-of-factly—the minister reads the formal announcement at dinner—but there was in this period a touch of ceremony. The new head took the seat at the dining table designated by a napkin ring. Napkins for all the other members of the Jesuit community were placed in a hutch of small boxes near the entrance. The boxes, assigned to individual members of the community, were used also as receptacles for mail or messages. The rector's napkin was not returned to the communal hutch but was folded and placed in a ring.

· ·

Thus, on October 5, 1858, Father William Clarke inherited the napkin ring. John Early had departed discreetly on the previous day for his new assignment. He had served at Loyola for over six years, and a longer tenure, though possible, would have been unprecedented. Other officers in the Maryland province—the incumbent president of Georgetown, for one—had completed their terms, and so it was a generally fitting moment to rotate responsibilities. Father Early became the new rector and president of Georgetown.

This system of short terms has much to recommend it as regards the Jesuit community, but it militates against steady development of schools. In the history of Loyola the periods of most significant growth coincide with presidential terms extended beyond the customary limit of six years. Other Catholic colleges suffered in the same fashion from joining the presidency of a school with the office of superior to the religious community. Nevertheless, the practice continued into the twentieth century; the first experiment in dividing these responsibilities among the Jesuits occurred during World War II.

Father Clarke seemed an apt choice as Loyola's second rector and president. He had been active in the process of establishing the new college and had been pressing for a full collegiate curriculum. He was familiar with the people and ways of Baltimore, having lived in the city for nearly ten years, and was on friendly terms with Archbishop Kenrick. Temperamentally, he was a strict moralist and disciplinarian who could be expected to tighten whatever ends had been left loose during the initiation of Loyola.

For the record, a notation of the change was entered in the corporation's minute book. Father Early's resignation, as well as Clarke's election to membership and elevation to the presidency, were duly, if summarily, recorded. The decision, of course, had ultimately been made by the Jesuit general.

It seems to have taken some time for the students at Loyola to recover from the shock of Early's departure. The officers of the Literary Society—William Tyson (1859), John Coonan (1864), and John Daly (1860)—composed an appropriate memorial three weeks after they were told of the change. In the name of the student body of and "the community at large," they opined that Father Early's departure was "a loss which cannot well be repaired." Nevertheless, they offered him their "best wishes" for his "future welfare and success."[1] Father Early, already busy with the affairs of Georgetown, cherished the message enough to preserve it. He maintained a tie with Loyola as a member of the college's board of trustees. Early's Baltimore connection was strengthened on the eve of his return to the city in 1866 when his name was included among the incorporators of the new Jesuit seminary at Woodstock.[2] This action may be taken as a symbol of the esteem in which he was held by his superiors, because Jesuits have always been most careful in choosing those associated with the houses where Jesuits are taught theology.

• •

Father Clarke's accession marked a shift in the college's tone and emphasis. Though his predecessor had been an Irish immigrant and he was a native American, Clarke proved to be more militant in asserting the Catholic character of the college and more insistent on specific exercises of piety by the students. Where Early had been discreet, even conciliatory, Father Clarke was headlong and assertive. He was a scrupulous man, tending to a rigorous morality, with a touch of hauteur that gained for him the intramural moniker Sir William.

The impact of his temperament and thought was soon evident. "Catholic students," the catalogue now proclaimed, "are carefully and frequently instructed in their holy Religion." Concretely, this referred to the catechism class that Father Clarke himself conducted each Friday for all Catholic students and Jesuit lay brothers. This was in fact where his essential talent lay.

Father Clarke made changes in the schedule that reflected his concerns. He extended the school day by a half-hour for Catholic students so they could end their work with recitation of the rosary. Clarke added a proscription against "the use of tobacco" to the rules that applied to all students. The inspiration for this new rule was an identical rule at Georgetown. Twentieth-century readers might mistakenly assume that the object of the prohibition was cigarettes, but the "coffin nail" would not make its appearance in the United States until after the Civil War. Nor was it likely aimed at cigars, because smoking cigars (later to become the common emblem of big business) was then considered a laboring-class vice. Father Clarke's new proscription was aimed at tobacco chewing. This form of indulgence was most prevalent in America (to the disgust of European travelers); it was the accepted test of manhood on these shores.[3]

. .

Father Clarke's term coincided with several significant changes in Baltimore's public life. First there was the emergence of the Civic Reform Association, led by Severn Teackle Wallis. Wallis's aim was to provide an alternative force to the two parties then contending for control of the city: the new American (Know-Nothing) party and the Democrats. The struggle between these two was not confined to the ballot box. Election riots had become so dangerous that Father Clarke, soon after he became Loyola's president, called classes off so that none of his charges would be caught in a Know-Nothing–Democrat crossfire on election day. The reformers soon wrested control of Baltimore's police force from the Know-Nothings and had it placed under state direction. In 1860 reformers and Democrats captured the mayoralty and both houses of the city council, but further progress was halted by the Civil War and the military government it brought to the city.

Before merging into an even newer party (the Republican), the Know-Nothings established a magnificent monument, Druid Hill (or *Droodle* in the local patois) Park. This greensward near what later became the geographical center of Baltimore was obtained through the foresight of an American party administration. Just before they lost control of Baltimore the Know-Nothings granted franchises for horse-drawn streetcar lines. This new public utility was required to return a portion of its profits to the municipal government, and these revenues were assigned to the purchase of park land.[4]

An unforeseen result of the establishment of streetcar lines was a gradual sorting out of the socioeconomic classes and ethnic groups in Baltimore. Until then people of all sorts lived together rather indiscriminately within walking distance of the places where they worked. Now they could flock together in economically and ethnically distinct neighborhoods and take the streetcar to their offices or shops. One of the early routes, the Blue Line, soon had cars rumbling up Calvert Street on a regular schedule. Students and parishioners from far away could now easily reach Loyola College and Saint Ignatius Church.

Streetcars made it easier for casual visitors in Baltimore to drop by Loyola. These included, as one might expect, Jesuits passing through to New England or returning to Georgetown. So constant was this flow that one diarist took special note of a rare day. "No arrivals or departures today!!!" he wrote. "The gadabouts seem to have settled down. Thank God. We'll have a breathing spell."[5] Because he was responsible for putting up the visitors, his relief was heartfelt indeed.

• •

This bustle was notably increased by the transfer of the provincial headquarters from Georgetown to Baltimore shortly after Father Felix Sopranis's official visit between November of 1859 and March of 1860. Periodically, the head of the Jesuit order dispatches a "visitor," an inspector general with plenary authority, to observe and reform. The last such visitation to America had occurred thirty years before.

Sopranis's visit produced no more startling effect than moving the Maryland provincial seat to Loyola. Jesuits are credited, by their enemies at least, with uncanny powers of foresight, and some have judged this move as proof that they anticipated the outbreak of civil war. The truth is that the decision was made well before the nominations and election campaign of 1860. To have anticipated the eruption of hostilities so early would have required occult powers of the highest (or lowest) order, and only the worst enemies of the Jesuits would entertain the possibility that the Jesuits possessed such powers.

The seat of Jesuit provincial authority was transferred for other, more prosaic reasons: Father Sopranis considered Loyola College more centrally located in relation to the other Jesuit houses. Furthermore, Jesuits conducted most of their financial transactions with Baltimore banks and agencies. Finally, living at Georgetown made it awkward for members of the Corporation of Roman Catholic Clergymen of Maryland (the trust for the old Jesuit properties in southern Maryland) to fulfill the legal requirement of maintaining residence in the state.[6]

This shift must have been viewed by the Jesuits teaching at Loyola as a mixed blessing at best. It created a delicate situation for rectors, because they had to exercise their authority under scrutiny of their immediate superior. They were in the position of a captain of a flagship with the admiral and his staff on board. Presence of the provincial, on the other hand, made it less likely that civil authorities or an archbishop would question Loyola's title to Saint Ignatius Church. When this issue was later resolved by an amendment to the college charter, the provincial's residence was moved again, in 1880, this time to New York City. For twenty years, however, the buildings on Calvert Street were the center of authority among Maryland Jesuits.

• •

Maybe it was anticipation of Father Felix Sopranis's visit or a change in the office of provincial that led to an acerb and revealing exchange between Fathers Clarke and Stonestreet. By the time it occurred Stonestreet had yielded office to Burchard Villiger, a Jesuit refugee from Switzerland. How the affair began is unclear. Father Clarke apparently applied to his new superior for $1,400 to pay the ground rent, an arrangement that been in effect for the previous five years. When he received a negative response, Clarke appealed to his old classmate Stonestreet, who was now president of Gonzaga College in the District of Columbia. Instead of corroboration he got a curt reply: "The Prov[incia]l . . . has only an agents power to administer & not a lordly power to dispose of the goods of the Province. . . . It was always urged that Loyola w[oul]d soon pay off all advances made for it & liquidate interest and principal—a prophecy your Rev[eren]ce will no doubt fulfill."[7] In the margin next to this passage, an unknown hand (but likely Clarke's) wrote "A lie."

This situation was not unique. The first president of Saint Joseph's College thought his provincial had given a gift to help the new foundation, but he eventually learned to his dismay that it was only a loan.[8] Misunderstandings of this kind happen, but in intramural circumstances there is no effective recourse except for the unfortunate rector to shoulder the unexpected burden. Beginning in 1859, Loyola's presidents had to raise $1,400 more each year to pay the ground rent and to keep the college open.

During President Clarke's two-year tenure, enrollments dropped from almost 160 to just below 115. This disappointing turn cannot be ascribed to Clarke's stewardship but was merely the result of an economic depression that gripped the still-United States from 1857 till the outbreak of the Civil War. Baltimore's commerce had fallen into the doldrums, and more than one family retrenched its expenditures by withdrawing its sons from school or by postponing their registration until times got better.

The signs were clear that President Clarke's days at Loyola were numbered. In June of 1860 Father Burchard Villiger moved into the provincial's room, and in another month Clarke was transferred to Gonzaga College. This and the fact that he had been permitted to preside over a particularly elaborate commencement indicate clearly that he had not been judged at fault. A year later he returned to Calvert Street, where he lived out the rest of his life in the service of the college and Saint Ignatius Church.

. .

Near the end of July in 1860, the rector's napkin ring passed to Joseph O'Callaghan, a man different in background and temperament from Father Clarke. O'Callaghan was born in New England of Irish immigrant parents. He was a small, gentle, nervous man with an extraordinary hooked nose and rather sad eyes. To an old-time physiognomist, that nose (like Cyrano's) bespoke nobility of spirit, and the eyes carried a hint of tragedy. O'Callaghan entered the Society in 1844 and briefly taught at Holy Cross while Father Early was its rector. Although Joseph O'Callaghan's record might by itself have recommended him for greater responsibilities, it is not improbable that his appointment to Loyola was promoted by Early—however quietly.

Father O'Callaghan was the kind of man and priest who made a deep impression on others. At Georgetown, where he had taught, he was remembered as an outstanding Latin scholar who was devoted to Shakespeare, and as "the most universally beloved man" on the faculty. What was especially remembered by others was his self-effacing manner. One student at Loyola later recalled how, when Father O'Callaghan entered a room and the class stood up, he would entreat them with a "deprecating smile" to be seated.[9]

There was another side to Father O'Callaghan. His natural shyness did not disable him to the point of keeping him from lecturing at the Maryland Institute. He inaugurated the practice, continued well into the twentieth century, of inviting certain members of the archdiocesan clergy to the college on the feast of Saint Ignatius Loyola, July 31. He was trying to recommend the college to the attention of influential pastors and to lessen any estrangement between other priests and Jesuits.

Father O'Callaghan's efforts to improve Loyola's public relations were coupled with similar attempts to remedy its financial plight. In February of 1861, just before expiration of the option, he filed formal notice of his intention to purchase the land on which Loyola College and Saint Ignatius Church were erected. On the face of it, this required raising over $23,000 at a time when the corporation's debt was already around $90,000. Actually he was trying to prompt action by a gentleman who at the inauguration of the college had informally promised to donate the purchase price. Business conditions, particularly the depression in the late 1850s, had forced delay, and then the putative donor died suddenly.[10] Anxiously, Father O'Callaghan organized a groundrent association, but when this produced little he appealed directly for generosity from the parishioners of Saint Ignatius Church.

Although their help eased the burden, he was unable to shed the liability, and so O'Callaghan sought additional revenues. He organized a fair to be held at the New Assembly Rooms, the most popular gathering place in the city. Though the program of this fair has not survived, like innumerable others before and since, the fair must have offered various inducements to buy and to take a chance. To ensure the attendance of crowds, Father O'Callaghan petitioned the mayor for permission to place a "transparency" advertising the fair over the gaslights near the busiest intersection in Baltimore[11]—hardly Madison Avenue but no doubt of some effect. The absence of any further mention suggests that this first fair was neither an overwhelming success nor a singular failure. At least, as they say, a very good time was had by all.

• •

Loyola's third president tried to make the college more attractive to prospective students. He shortened the school day by eliminating the long break for lunch; dismissal for students now came two hours earlier, at 2:30. Father O'Callaghan maintained the religious emphasis of his immediate predecessor by continuing the daily recitation of the rosary and by adding a retreat several days in length for the Catholic students. While their peers attended regular classes, the Catholics participated in a concentrated course of religious instruction, meditation, and various liturgical and pious exercises. Such retreats were a regular feature of the life at Jesuit and other Catholic schools.

President O'Callaghan's most important decision to attract more students was the introduction of an "English," or "commercial," course, offered in response to persistent complaints that Latin and Greek were useless to youth who had to make their living in America. Uniformly, this alternate program was deprecated in academe. Students who completed the commercial course received only a "certificate of proficiency" rather than the customary diploma. Among Jesuits, the English course was flatly described (in confidential correspondence) as "humbugging."[12] From Loyola's point of view, however, something had to be done; and the Male Central High School, a few blocks away, had already established its English department.

During the first year of operation this new course did not entirely halt the decline in enrollments, but its absence might well have resulted in even greater losses. Registrations fell to a low of 108, almost one-third of them in the new English department. A few students at Loyola shifted to the new program. If this option had not been available, these students might well have gone elsewhere. The remainder (about three fourths) of the total enrolled in English were new students who might not otherwise have come to Loyola. In the following year registrations rose to 127, with more listed in the new course than before. The upward trend might be partly attributable to the English course, but it must also have been caused by the general recovery of the nation's and of Baltimore's economy. The economic depression was finally relenting under the stimulus of civil war. Later, when enrollments at Loyola had stabilized, the English course was quietly but summarily dropped.

• •

The reaction of Marylanders and Baltimoreans to the outbreak of hostilities is hard to describe. Many accept the view that most people in the state were unwilling captives of an oppressive federal government. This often repeated belief does not square with the best historical evidence. In 1901, George Radcliffe, who later represented Maryland in the United States Senate, took note of the division and instability of opinions among Marylanders when the issue of secession was raised. More telling, however, was the general support Governor Thomas Hicks received for not yielding to pressure to convene the state legislature at a time when that body might have voted to join the Confederacy.

Using modern historical methods of analysis and documentation, Charles Wagandt made explicit what Radcliffe judiciously left unsaid.

Division there was; Marylanders would have preferred peace and were active in the efforts to find a compromise. No workable agreement could be achieved, however, because "the secessionists could envision no plan assuring their old dominance, and the Republicans could find no settlement that would not destroy the power they had just gained." Wagandt demonstrates from the elections held before federal troops became a factor in Maryland politics that a majority freely favored the Union.[13]

No less than their fellow citizens, Catholics were divided on the issues raised by the Civil War. Some, like Orestes Brownson, General Philip Sheridan, and Thomas Francis Meagher (to name only the most famous), worked ardently for a Union victory. There were others, like Generals Pierre Beauregard and James Longstreet, who strove with equal determination for the independence of the Confederacy. In Maryland, Archbishop Kenrick was strongly pro-Union, but Congressman Henry May, Judge Parkin Scott, and Police Marshal George Kane were so obviously sympathetic to the Confederate cause that they were arrested by federal authorities. Chief Justice Roger Brooke Taney was spared this particular indignity by reason of his office, but he suffered a scoring by the Republican press as an "apologist of treason."

A dramatic expression of the strong pro-Confederate sentiment among Catholics occurred within the Baltimore cathedral. Early in the war Archbishop Kenrick asked priests to read a prayer composed by John Carroll, founder of the archdiocese. All offered excuses to avoid this chore because the prayer included a petition for preserving the Union. Kenrick therefore decided to recite the prayer himself. When he came to the offensive passage, however, "many people got up and left the Cathedral and those who remained expressed their dissent," as James Cardinal Gibbons later recalled, "by a great rustling of papers and silks"[14]

The division among Maryland Catholics can be given definite form using the records of Georgetown alumni. Four times as many volunteered for service under the Stars and Bars as remained loyal to Old Glory. That college had, of course, drawn many of its students from the Southern states, but a similar ratio showed among its alumni from Maryland alone. In fact, several of these had been students at Loyola before transferring to Georgetown. Only one alumnus of both colleges, William Marye, served in the Union forces, but joint alumni Albert, Daniel, and Robert Carroll, William Bolton Fitzgerald, Richard McSherry, Charles Morfit, Eustace and Wilfred Neale, John Daniel

Smith, and Samuel Raborg joined Confederate units.[15] These were not the only Loyolans in uniform, but the tendency to favor the Confederate cause is apparent from even this brief accounting.

Why were Catholics so sympathetic to the Confederacy? They may have felt some residual attraction for the agrarian, hierarchical, relatively static Southern society, which was believed to represent the natural order. Also, it was easy to romanticize a distant milieu when conditions near at hand were strange, harsh, and threatening. Industrialization in the Northern states was being achieved through the sweat and humiliation of the Irish. Furthermore, after the demise of their organization, the Know-Nothings had joined the Republican party and worked eagerly for the election of Abraham Lincoln. The Baltimore Irish, in particular, could not forget the blows they had suffered from these ultrapatriots. In reaction to such immediate dangers and irritants, the Confederacy appeared at least as the lesser evil, if not an actual ally.

• •

The Jesuit general specifically enjoined American Jesuits in 1862 "to keep themselves free from all party spirit." He directed provincials to correct any Jesuit "who should so far forget himself as to speak with too much warmth in favor of, or against, either party." In Maryland the provincial was even more explicit. No one was to repeat any news or rumors, lest they be traced back to the Jesuits and so compromise the Society.[16] It was a difficult regimen in a divided community located so close to the sites of several crucial battles.

On the eighty-sixth anniversary of the battle of Lexington and Concord, one week after Confederate forces fired on Fort Sumter, a skirmish of the Civil War was fought in Baltimore. On April 19, 1861, a Massachusetts regiment had to march through the streets of Baltimore to entrain for Washington. Federal officials, victims of their own suspicions, failed to give adequate notice of the troop movement to the municipal authorities, and as a result police protection was not available during the initial phase of the march. When jeering, harassment, and shots finally provoked the soldiers to open fire on the mob, Marshal George Kane quickly rushed his force into position between the populace and the soldiery. Kane's heroic action permitted the troops to continue their journey to the capital. Baltimore's streets, however, were crimsoned with the "patriotic gore" of twelve citizens and four soldiers killed. The number of Baltimoreans wounded is unknown, but thirty-six soldiers suffered injury.[17]

• •

The riot had a ludicrous sequel in the yard behind the college. City authorities were arming the populace and organizing a defense force to prevent the movement of troops through Baltimore, and the boys at Loyola decided to imitate their elders. August Shutt (1868) organized his schoolmates into drill companies. He was qualified by virtue of having enlisted in the "Dandy Fifth" Regiment of Maryland Volunteers and having his father as its commanding officer. The elder Shutt, before he reached this eminence, had accepted the dangerous task of running for mayor against a Know-Nothing. He was unsuccessful, but none could doubt the courage and integrity of the Shutts.

At first the "civilian" students were amused by the commands of young Shutt and by the awkward maneuvers of the cadets with their wooden guns. Amusement soon gave way to impatience, because "Colonel" Shutt's squads were monopolizing the play area. As the drilling continued, some of the bolder spirits began running around the yard, in and out of the orderly ranks. Bumping into the cadets was considered great sport, and it distressed the drillmaster.

Finally the "civilians" decided to take direct action. On a prearranged day they gathered at one end of the yard and, like the mob on April 19, hooted at the "sojers." Then they picked up the coarse gravel that covered the play yard and began pelting the cadets. "Colonel" Shutt shouted an order to form a line of battle and then led a charge on the rabble. The resultant din brought Father Joseph O'Callaghan, Loyola's tiny president, rushing to the second-floor gallery, which overlooked the yard. He remonstrated with the boys to end the ruction, but he was no Marshal Kane. The bruising of bodies, bloodying of noses, and blackening of eyes continued for almost an hour, until all the wooden guns were smashed. When quiet was restored the president and Loyola's faculty prudently agreed that both sides had suffered so much that no additional penalties were to be exacted from either.

What makes the incident particularly ironic is that the elder Shutt, though trusted by federal authorities, was known to be a Southern sympathizer. His son's politics were probably the same, and thus the sentiments of the "sojers" and the "mob" were reversed in the Loyola melee. The irony would have been lost on the boys. They acted as boys must— and had a good story to tell years later. The crestfallen Shutt completed the year but did not return to Loyola College. He does not appear to have borne it any enmity; in later years he made a point of including his education at Loyola in an autobiographical notice.

Two days after the riot, Sunday morning services were interrupted by the ringing of bells throughout the city. Men and boys shouldered their weapons and rushed to the ramparts to prevent the passage of more federal troops. The alarm proved false, because the troops came only as far as Cockeysville and turned back. By the following morning there was a still uneasy but calmer atmosphere in Baltimore. A few weeks later, on May 13, federal troops commanded by General Benjamin ("Beast") Butler occupied the city without opposition. Thereafter no serious incidents upset the orderly regime in Baltimore. There were occasional outrages, some committed by the authorities, others by mobs; but the feverish early months of 1861 were at an end—to everyone's relief.

• •

Drafting soldiers was especially distasteful to Americans, because the practice was identified with the oppressive governments of the Old World, but appalling casualties finally forced both sides to conscription after two years of bloody battles. First the Confederacy and then the Union enacted draft laws early in 1863. Under the Union law a board was established in each congressional district to make the actual choices. None but the physically, mentally, or morally incapacitated was exempt, although an unwilling and affluent draftee could buy his exemption by paying for a substitute.

In July 1863, on the three days preceding the holiday on which Americans celebrate their Declaration of Independence, the battle of Gettysburg was fought. Gettysburg was the point farthest north reached by Confederate armies; at the end of the battle they retreated across Maryland to their base in Virginia. Shortly after the battle, on July 7, one tired gentleman remarked as he lay down to rest, "I hope we shall soon have peace."[18] Francis Patrick Kenrick, sixth archbishop of Baltimore, was found dead the next morning. The prelate who had impelled the founding of Loyola College left Baltimore as suddenly as he had arrived.

The federal draft law, as might be expected, was not popular in Maryland. Neither it nor repeated appeals from federal and state officials could raise the assigned quota of troops. These circumstances led, toward the end of the war, to a shadowy affair involving a Jesuit scholastic, John Abell Morgan, who later served as president of Loyola College (1891–1900). On June 25, 1864, Mister Morgan was notified by the provost marshal that he had been "legally drafted." He was to report five days hence "or be deemed a deserter and be subject to the penalty prescribed by the Rules and Articles Of War."[19]

In person or otherwise, Morgan appealed for an extension and was given an additional day. The draft notice meanwhile was hurriedly carried to Washington, where Father Early (*persona gratissima* to the federal government) persuaded his friend Secretary of War Edwin Stanton to delay its execution until Morgan received further notice from Stanton himself. "Further notice" was never given. This action effectively saved Morgan from military service; left unanswered is the question of why he had been drafted in the first place.

A month after the Morgan draft affair, a last desperate cavalry raid on Baltimore prompted military authorities to muster Jesuit priests and scholastics for the defense of the city. Confederate troopers penetrated to Govans and burned the governor's mansion on Charles Street before quickly retreating. By the time of the raid, the Jesuits had long since been relieved of militia duty; this treatment of clergymen, obviously, was resented in some quarters.

. .

The period following Abraham Lincoln's assassination in 1865 was difficult for the nation as a whole, more difficult in some regions than in others. Contrary to the conventional myth that was accepted by many Baltimoreans after the Civil War, repression by the federal government and the devastation of the former Confederacy did not bring the city and its people to the edge of bankruptcy. Hamilton Owens, writing in the 1940s, dismissed any local long-term negative effects of the war. "Despite sentimental chroniclers," he opined, "Baltimore was not ruined by the Civil War."[20] Baltimore still enjoyed major geographical advantages over its rivals New York and Philadelphia in regard to western markets, and in the postwar era Maryland exploited the same advantages in regard to Virginia, the Carolinas, and Georgia. The port city became the chief source of and transfer point for new capital and manufactured goods moving southward, particularly clothing, hats, and canned vegetables.

The Reconstruction era did bring a significant alteration in the life of Baltimore, however. The civic-mindedness, energy, and drive so evident before the Civil War was now muted. Despite economic prosperity, the physical development and maintenance of the city were neglected. Owens ascribes this to a threefold migration into the city. Baltimore was in the first place a preferred refuge for many whites from states of the former Confederacy. Richard Malcolm Johnston (a white teacher and writer), for instance, saw a more congenial society and climate for himself and his family in Baltimore than in his native—and now reconstructing—Georgia.[21] At the same time there was an influx into Baltimore of newly freed blacks as well as new waves of immigrants from eastern and southern Europe. Baltimore's location made it the favored landfall for these newcomers. Because no section of the nation was willing to welcome the newly freed blacks, cheap labor for proliferating factories was sought in Italy, Russia, Poland, Bohemia, and neighboring regions of Europe.

These people, many not thoroughly schooled in the methods of urban living, strained the resources of the city. Then it was that upper-class native whites and their emigrant cousins from the South talked themselves into the belief "that all urban problems were equally insoluble." This attitude, born in part from racial and ethnic prejudice, also demanded less from whites in taxes and effort. So, says Hamilton Owens, Baltimore's leaders after the Civil War did little to maintain (let alone develop) the physical fabric of the city.[22]

• •

During the Civil War there was a change of leadership at Loyola. Father Joseph O'Callaghan was replaced on September 3, 1863, when Anthony Ciampi, an elegant Roman, became Loyola's president and rector. Ciampi was a handsome man with finely molded features and long black curly hair, and his speech always retained a delicate trace of his native Italy. Almost thirty years earlier, as a student at the Roman College, he had volunteered to come to the United States. After completing his training at Georgetown he was ordained, and he served as rector of several small Jesuit communities. In 1851 he was named Father Early's successor at Holy Cross. There Father Ciampi almost immediately faced a disaster when the college was destroyed by fire. (The effect of this event on Loyola College has already been described.)

In comparison with then current standards, Ciampi's religious attitudes were quite sophisticated. He and other Italian Jesuits who came to America helped to leaven the moral earnestness of their Irish and American colleagues. Although Father Clarke, for instance, insisted that the church's ban on round dancing (the waltz) had to be enforced with full rigor, his Italian confreres took a more indulgent view of this diversion. For his part, Father Ciampi encouraged one of his female converts to accompany her husband (not a Catholic) to his church for the sake of association and to hear the eloquence of the preacher. "Discretion," he wrote her, "is a virtue which has to control even our religious exercises."[23] Ciampi came to Baltimore at age 47. This made him the oldest of Loyola's presidents (Father Early's second term excepted) until 1891.

Father Ciampi's approach to education was less pietistic than that of his immediate predecessors. He discontinued the daily recitation of the rosary instituted by Father Clarke. To encourage greater effort in the classroom Loyola, under Ciampi, began to offer a new annual award, "the Cross of Honor," to the most proficient student in each of the basic classes. These and other changes during President Ciampi's three-year term increased enrollments from 108 to 167, the highest number yet reached.

Ciampi, who would eventually demonstrate his taste for drama (albeit religious drama), gave impulse to formation of the Dramatic Club. There had been earlier hints of such a development in the commencement programs, but in April 1865 the students, probably led by Fred Hack (1868) and Walter McCann (1868) and possibly primed by Daniel Ford, a Jesuit scholastic from New England, petitioned the president for the establishment of a dramatic club. Father Ciampi readily agreed. Mister Ford impressed one of the founding members of the club as "tall and pallid, with a sensitive, intellectual face and a special enthusiasm for the stage."[24]

Ford proceeded methodically to experiment with his human and literary materials and, like a good showman, to rouse anticipation in his audience. For one of the regular school assemblies he had coached Richard Hamilton (1868) in reciting Gloucester's opening speech from *Richard II*. Hamilton, who transferred to Loyola in 1863, had become the school comedian; he was described as being "very earnest . . . and unsuspicious." He prepared himself by watching Edwin Forrest, the leading Shakespearean actor of the day, perform the role of Gloucester at one of Baltimore's theaters. Forrest made a point of speaking the first two lines,

Now is the winter of our discontent
Made glorious by this sun of York,

offstage and then rushing onstage to complete the soliloquy. When Hamilton explained Forrest's technique to his classmates, they urged him to imitate this best of models.

On the fateful noon Hamilton took his customary place among his peers, while Mister Ford anxiously waited on the stage with the rest of the faculty. When Hamilton's name was called to recite, he stood up and launched into the speech where he stood. "The boys and professors were transfixed with astonishment at this abrupt outburst." Striding up the aisle to the platform, Hamilton continued "in a voice even more enthusiastic and high pitched." It was too much—laughter broke out —but the hapless Hamilton redoubled his straining for dramatic effect as he mounted the steps. More laughter and slaps. At stage-center, he fairly yelled

Our stern alarums changed to merry meetings,
Our dreaded marches to delightful measures!

The aptness of these lines produced such convulsions that the prefect (dean) restored decorum by firmly ordering Hamilton "to desist."[25] Neither the prefect nor Ford left a record of their reactions, but no one could doubt the élan of the new Dramatic Club.

The experience did not crush Richard Hamilton, who performed important roles in both presentations for commencement on July 5. The first was Nicholas Cardinal Wiseman's *The Hidden Gem*, and the other was the trial scene from *The Merchant of Venice*. The part of Portia was played not by a girl but by one of the club's stars, Fred Hack. Casting of males in female roles was customary in the Shakespearean and Jesuit theaters and would be the rule in Baltimore until well into the twentieth century. Shylock was performed by the other luminary, Walter McCann. This inaugural performance was made even grander by the presence of the Holliday Street Theatre orchestra.

Reaction to the debut of Loyola's Dramatic Club was favorable. Newspaper notices and those of *Southern Society*, a literary magazine, praised the productions, casting, direction, and acting. Fred Hack regularly got rave reviews. In fact, Edwin Booth, who accepted an honorary membership in the Loyola club, even suggested that Hack adopt acting as his career. More sober counsel prevailed, and after graduation Hack became a lawyer. Hamilton too eventually was graduated and even received a master's degree in 1871. McCann left before he became eligible for a diploma but served over forty years as drama editor of the *Baltimore News*.

The study and performance of drama has always held an honorable place in Jesuit schools. In America, Holy Cross seems to have been the first college, save Harvard with its Hasty Pudding Club, to organize a dramatic club. This occurred during Father Early's presidency. Three years later, in 1852, Georgetown followed suit, and 1855 saw the establishment of a similar association at Fordham.

Though the study of dramatic literature was part of the curriculum at other institutions, it is doubtful that clubs for performing dramatic works were being formed. General histories of higher education, although noting the foundation of literary societies and debating clubs, are silent on a similar development of dramatic clubs. The emergence of theatricals at these colleges would have to await a general decline in the prevailing Puritan attitude, which associated the theater with pagan mummery and immorality. Loyola College and the other Jesuit schools, if no less opposed to sin, were culturally more fortunate.

As president of Loyola College, Father Ciampi made an even more significant contribution to the musical life of Baltimore. Near the end of his term at Loyola he managed a spectacular religious production. "For the first time in these regions," Ciampi noted, "I had the Exercises in honor of the three hour Agony of Our Lord. It was so imposing, and so deeply impressive, Protestants as well as Catholics still speak of it."[26] In Saint Ignatius Church a small string orchestra and piano performed Saverio Mercadante's musical setting for "The Seven Last Words"; sermons preached by Father Ciampi on Jesus' utterances from the cross were interspersed among musical pieces. This production was indeed the climactic event of Father Ciampi's service in Baltimore and helped establish the reputation for fine music that Saint Ignatius Church enjoyed into the twentieth century.

After leaving Loyola in 1866, Father Ciampi was named to several important offices. He was president of Saint Joseph's College for a time and later returned to direct Holy Cross. He finally settled at Gonzaga College in the District of Columbia, where he ministered quietly until his death twenty years later.

The Civil War and its aftermath produced a fundamental realignment in national and state politics. At the national level, the Republican party managed the government without interruption for two decades. After a great deal of difficulty the Democrats in Maryland recovered control of the state government that was about as successful as the Republicans' control on the national level. One of the leaders of this effort was A. Leo Knott, who established a close bond with the college. From the postwar years until his death in 1918 he appeared at Loyola as a commencement speaker, as a judge of debates, and in similar roles. In his will Leo Knott endowed a history professorship in memory of his wife, and Loyola College continues to number members of the Knott family among its most generous benefactors.

• •

The departure of Ciampi from Loyola in 1866 was followed by the reappointment of John Early, now 52 years old. Though his appointment was dated July, Father Early did not arrive in Baltimore until September. Trustees seem to have been confused, but with aplomb and no explanation they recorded Father Ciampi's resignation as dated September 20, and then proceeded to note and ratify Early's election as of July 16.

However casually, Father John Early was again head of the institution he had founded. His appointment was meant to reverse the decline in the number of students who continued their education through the full course. Though Fathers O'Callaghan and Ciampi had succeeded in raising registrations, only nine graduates received A.B. degrees between 1860 and 1866. The return of Father Early immediately attracted 192 registrants, and he had the pleasure of handing diplomas to twenty graduates during a term of only four years.

Father Early's first recorded action on his return to Loyola was a very curious one. On September 26 he asked his four consultors whether Protestants should be required to attend catechetical instructions with their Catholic schoolmates. On the basis of his previous policy one must assume that he could not have been asking for an affirmative answer, and he did not receive one. The consultors unanimously agreed that Protestants should remain exempt from the catechism class—but they prudently left the discussion of incidental religious points in regular classes to the discretion of teachers.[27]

The whole affair is tantalizingly vague. Father Early was not likely to require instruction in the Catholic faith for all. Why then had he raised the question? If someone else, say Father Clarke, who enjoyed teaching catechism, were pressing for something like this, Early's consultation effectively quashed the notion and its proponents. None could doubt his authority or the continuing policy of Loyola in regard to religion. Loyola was not going to become exclusively Catholic.

In October of 1866, Baltimore was again the site of an assemblage of Catholic bishops. Their number and that of the faithful had grown during the fourteen years since the first council, so that Catholics now totalled four million and composed 13 percent of the population. This second plenary council was held between October 7 and October 22, 1866. It had a number of major objectives. The most obvious was to demonstrate the unity and vitality of the American Catholic church. Immediately after the Civil War the nation was exhausted and was laboring under the double weight of the memory of the past and the anticipation of a future that to many seemed hopeless. More quickly than any of the other churches, the Catholic church was able to resume its cor-

porate life. Bishops from all parts of the country were observed march-
ing together in public procession and transacting business without
rancor. [28] Continuing differences unfortunately still prevented such harmony in several other denominations.

Another objective to be treated most circumspectly was countering
the effect of Pope Pius IX's 1864 *Syllabus of Errors,* which was a listing
"of the chief tenets of 19th-century liberalism" accompanied by a firm
papal condemnation of them all. This tract aroused great indignation
in the American press because it appeared that the pope was condemning the Constitution, separation of church and state, and freedom of
conscience.

Shortly after the appearance of the *Syllabus,* Martin Spalding, the
new archbishop of Baltimore, issued a pastoral letter in which he attempted to limit its effect on American opinion. He noted that Pius
IX's concerns, though stated in general terms, were directly aimed
against "European radicals and infidels" and had little or no bearing on
the American constitutional settlement. This was at best a polemical
stopgap. Spalding, who organized and presided at the second plenary
council, had the council issue a positive statement of the Catholic faith
in a tone that would be acceptable to American ears. There were no
anathemas or condemnations, and the collegial authority of the bishops
was emphasized. [29] The papal position was in no way contradicted, but
the bishops presented a posture more congenial to American sensibilities. The immediate effectiveness of this performance on the general
public may be doubted but it was of some reassurance to American
Catholics.

Historically, the most important matter considered by the Catholic
bishops was how to respond to the situation created by the abolition of
slavery. A number of freedmen, especially those in Louisiana and
southern Maryland, had been baptized as Catholics, and these and
their brothers and sisters elsewhere were in need of an active—possibly
distinct—ministry. A preliminary suggestion to the council favored establishment of an official of episcopal rank to coordinate the work
among blacks. This was rejected by the bishops because it would have
divided the jurisdiction within each diocese. At the suggestion of
Bishop Richard Whelan, the council agreed instead to solicit support in
personnel and funds from Europe. [30]

From whom did Whelan get this idea? One very likely source is
Father Michael O'Connor, formerly bishop of Pittsburgh but then a
Jesuit living at Loyola. As bishop he had been solicitous about the

blacks in his diocese. He maintained this concern after he joined the Society of Jesus and in wartime Baltimore helped establish Saint Francis Xavier Church, the first black Catholic parish in the United States. O'Connor had an entree with Bishop Whelan through Father Early, who was attending the council as Whelan's theologian.

The council's choice of O'Connor as its agent for implementing the decision points even more strongly to his authorship. He went to London and soon returned with two members of the Mill Hill Fathers, an organization of English priests engaged in the urban apostolate. The two stayed at Loyola until formalities were completed for transferring the responsibility for Saint Francis Xavier Church to them. O'Connor lived only a year after successfully completing his mission.[31] The Mill Hill Fathers would in time generate the Society of Saint Joseph (Josephites), which by the turn of the century had become the Catholic church's main arm of service to blacks.

· ·

During Father Early's second term the students at Loyola engaged in surreptitious journalism. Someone in the class of poetry began issuing the *Voice of the Muses*. No action was taken against this underground paper; indeed, notice of it appeared in the regularly printed programs of the Dramatic Club. After a few issues (none of which seems to have survived), the deliciously secret task of editing the paper was taken over by someone who reportedly preferred the comic muse and titled his handwritten sheet the *Brick Bat Journal*. One issue of this paper would reappear a quarter of a century later when, in 1900, Father Frank Barnum, a "poet" of this era and quite likely the author, deposited a copy in the Georgetown archives.

Such secret publications were not unique to Loyola. They seem, in fact, to have been a feature at Jesuit schools and probably at others during this era. Fordham, for instance, was kept informed and amused for a time by the *Goose Quill*. Georgetown's risibilities were tickled by such anonymous productions as *Paddy's Complaint*, a doggerel pasquinade defending the honor of the Irish.[32] At Loyola the underground press periodically issued broadsides even later, after the appearance of regular school publications. This activity may be considered a traditional rite of passage for the bolder (but not overly bold) students.

Father Early's second term was marked by another modest development—in finances. Tuition was raised from the original $60 per annum to $80, and a graduation fee of $10 was added. This was a small increase in view of wartime inflation and the college's debt, now risen to

$120,000. At best the tuition increase was meant to cover current expenses rather than to reduce the debt. That would have to await a different rector, because John Early was reluctant to "talk money," even to relieve Loyola of its formidable debt.

By 1870 time was exacting its toll both on Father Early's friends and on his energies. Joseph O'Callaghan, Loyola's third president, was killed during a violent storm at sea, and his body was consigned to the waves. His sudden, tragic death had a profound effect on both his Jesuit brethren and his former students. In January the Reverend James Dolan of old Saint Patrick's Church died, leaving his library to Loyola. After the July commencement Early was once again transferred to Georgetown. There he was assisted by Patrick Healy, who with his brother (later the bishop of Portland) had been a student at Holy Cross when Early was first its president. In fact, Father Healy was running the show at Georgetown. The transfer was meant to provide Early with a dignified but none too strenuous position. Nevertheless, his health declined, and on May 23, 1873, a few months short of 59, he died.[33]

With quiet dignity and heartfelt sorrow, they buried John Early in the cemetery at Georgetown. His friends attempted to perpetuate his memory in various ways. The obituary was long, noting, among other things, "He left everywhere the impress of his kind and generous heart, no less than of his talents and executive abilities."[34]

5

A New Generation

With the turn into the 1870s a new cycle in the life of Loyola College got a jolting start during the brief presidency of Father Edward Henchy. He was installed at Calvert Street on July 13, 1870, and was replaced by the end of the following January—the shortest term of any of Loyola's presidents and rectors. Nevertheless, he made a number of significant changes during his six months in command.

• •

Of Henchy only a few things are known. He was a native of Ireland and had been a scholastic at Loyola during the mid-1850s. In that period he acquired a fearsome reputation as a disciplinarian. The image of Father Henchy as an austere, formidable person makes it understandable that he alone among the scholastics ever evoked a favorable recommendation from William Clarke. He was also a person of considerable courage and independence. In 1859 at Holy Cross he acted as spokeman for his fellow scholastics in appealing to the provincial for permission to organize a military drill company even though their rector was opposed.[1]

This energy and decision would be evident when Father Henchy returned to Loyola and later in his career. To increase enrollments that had fallen to 108, Loyola's new president reestablished the commercial course. Tuition for college students was reduced from $80 to $75, and for high-school students to $50 a year. These measures and probably other factors brought 50 more students to Loyola College in 1870–71.

Why Henchy served so brief a time at Loyola cannot be satisfactorily explained. The official reason offered for his sudden departure was "on account of ill health," but no hint of this appears in the house diary. Instead, within two weeks of Henchy's arrival, the diarist ceased making entries. Apparently, the new broom meant to sweep very clean and very swiftly, and the diarist thought it better to let the dust settle before he recorded anything—but also better to draw attention of the inquisitive, because two pages were left blank when entries in the house diary were resumed on February 11, 1871. By this time Edward Henchy was gone and Father Stephen Kelly was in charge. Maybe Henchy had proven too rigorous in his demands on his fellow Jesuits. Maybe there was a direct personal clash with the provincial, who lived under the same roof. In any case, some sudden storm arose, and when it was over Father Edward Henchy was on his way to the Eastern Shore of Maryland. He had failed spectacularly and no one felt his departure more acutely than his mentor, Father Clarke.

Whatever occurred at Loyola may have been incompatible with Father Henchy's continuing as a Jesuit, but not with his status as a priest. Soon after he left Baltimore, he was accepted into the diocese of Wilmington. Like the shrewd steward in the gospels, he appears to have made provision for his future by diverting an inheritance from his former confreres to the Wilmington diocese. For the next quarter of a century he was active in restoring old, nearly abandoned churches in Queenstown, Cambridge, and Wye Mills; he ministered honorably and well to the Catholics of Dorchester County. In 1886 his bishop transferred him to yet another parish that needed refurbishing and revitalization. Thinking himself deserving of something better, Henchy refused to accept the new assignment. Instead he returned to the Queenstown area to live in retirement with a well-to-do and respected Catholic family until his death in 1895.[2]

• •

This was a time of major changes in American higher education generally. Under various pressures, the old-time "college way," symbolized by Mark Hopkins and his log, was inexorably being displaced by a German style of scholarship. There was a demand for technological and scientific education and for less emphasis on character training. This would eventually prompt such educational leaders as Charles Eliot of Harvard to champion the principle of free election of courses instead of the prescribed classical curriculum. Women were being admitted to existing institutions, and colleges were being founded to educate them. Humanities—the cultural courses—were being yielded to the ladies while gentlemen were engrossed in the newer scientific fields. The result of these postwar reforms was the shattering of "the old unity, the old sameness," and the devaluation of liberal studies.[3]

One of the integral elements of humanistic education has always been historical literature, and it did not undergo the relative decline during the nineteenth century suffered by other branches of the classical curriculum. The works of Caesar, Livy, Tacitus, Suetonius, Saint Augustine, Plutarch, Herodotus, Thucydides, Xenophon, and other ancient historians had always been read by students of the liberal arts. As a distinct subject, however, history did not emerge until the Renaissance and then mainly as the study of biblical and ancient times. In the seventeenth century a group of Jesuits known as the Bollandists began to refine historical methodology, and in the following century Jean Mabillon, a Benedictine, discovered means for verifying the age and origin of medieval documents. At the University of Berlin, Leopold van Ranke further developed the historian's craft in the early nineteenth century through close attention to and analysis of documents. He also advanced the study and teaching of history by introducing the seminar method.

No general interest in history was evident in America until after the War of 1812. The patriotic fervor aroused during the war later expressed itself in the organization of state and other historical societies and the publication of early documents and the correspondence of America's revolutionary leaders. History, especially of the founding and development of the nation, entered the curriculum of the common schools as a means of promoting the Americanization of youngsters.

The emergence of history as a separate discipline up to this point was due largely to dedicated people with only a rudimentary understanding of scholarly methods. The newly established state historical societies and historical magazines kept alive this avocational interest. Scholarly work in this field began among Americans with George Bancroft (1800–1891), who studied in Germany and brought back more systematic methods developed there. Bancroft demonstrated the new methodology in his multivolume classic, *The History of the United States*. To promote the growing professional interest in the subject, the American Historical Association was founded in 1884, and about the same time universities such as Johns Hopkins, Columbia, Chicago, and Harvard were introducing the seminar method in their graduate programs for historians.

Loyola's curriculum was affected by the development both of history and of the natural sciences. Until 1871 the formal study of history had been limited to that established during the Renaissance. Courses in biblical and ancient history were major elements of the secondary and early college years. Now these were displaced by study of the history of the United States and of the modern world. Ancient history became a subject taught only to college sophomores. Natural philosophy—as the sciences were then known—had been reserved until 1871 for the final year of college, but now physics and chemistry were taught across each of the last three years of the curriculum.

At other American schools increased attention to the sciences was being resisted as an unwelcome innovation, but at Loyola the tilt toward the sciences was considered neither improper nor disruptive. This may in part have been because of the corresponding increase in attention to history; the study of the interaction of humans was not being sacrificed for that of the properties and interaction of inanimate things. In any case, the two most important intellectual concerns of the nineteenth century, history and science, were expanded in the Loyola curriculum without the fuss that accompanied such changes in other American schools.

Similar developments may well have been occurring at other Jesuit colleges, since it is unlikely that Loyola would have departed significantly from the general norm. Unfortunately, the histories of these colleges give scant attention to specific reforms, thus by omission confirming the impression that Jesuit education was cast in a rigid, uniform mold. From the data at Loyola College it is clear that curricular adaptations were being made, but with little fanfare and always on the basis of a religiously integrated view of mankind. If more conservative and more humane, this seemed to some a less exciting approach than was being embraced by other college authorities.

• •

Although some changes at Loyola in 1870–71 may be difficult to attribute, it is clear that Father Stephen Kelly was responsible for hiring more laymen. There had always been a non-Jesuit or two on the Loyola roster, but the hiring of four in one year was unusual. This was done so the province's scholastics could continue their education without interruptions. One of the new teachers, Charles LeLoup, got an additional hundred dollars, probably because his was a college-level class, possibly because he was over 60 years old. Loyola's salaries were not high even by the standards of the day, but were comparable to those offered at several other schools, Baltimore City College excepted. These new lay teachers were paid $300 a year—about what was being sought as an endowment to maintain one scholastic at Woodstock.

Of these lay teachers, LeLoup was by far the most interesting. The Civil War roused in him a deep dedication to the cause of the Confederacy. Indeed, he was so unreconstructed a rebel that even long after the war his students could easily entice him into yet another defense of "the Lost Cause." At Loyola he was known to waive regular lessons so he could consider current topics of the day—like the trial of Mrs. Elizabeth Wharton, a stunningly attractive matron of 50 who was accused of poisoning General W. S. Ketchum at her Baltimore residence.

LeLoup was judged a "polite, punctilious gentleman" and was generally liked by his students. Like all schoolboys, however, they were not above baiting the white-haired, rotund old man. One day someone scribbled "Shad-Belly LeLoup" on the blackboard. When he entered the classroom and espied the epithet, he threw off his coat and challenged the "blackguard" to declare himself—with no takers. This display of temper (and possibly LeLoup's digressions) prompted Father Kelly to offer LeLoup employment not for a whole year but at $40 per month. Although the monetary terms were the same as in the previous year, this was too short a leash for LeLoup so he left for Emmitsburg, where at Mount Saint Mary's he taught with equal verve until his death twenty years later.[4]

Throughout Father Kelly's nearly seven-year term, there were between four and six laymen on the faculty each year. The students readily accepted them and once expressed their affection by giving each a gold-headed cane. These laymen, however, were not equally valued by the Jesuits. In a report sent to the general in Rome (the annual letter for 1876), the unidentified author complained that the lay teachers "had done nothing for the reputation of our school." They had "neither pleased the parents nor attracted students; in fact they have done so much positive harm that we have cause to worry about the future of the school."[5] This attitude toward lay teachers was common at Catholic schools until the 1960s.[6]

President Kelly's main problem was, of course, not the faculty but money —or lack of it. He organized a church debt association, whose membership included parishioners of Saint Ignatius Church, patrons of the college, and friends of the Jesuit order. Within a week Father Kelly enrolled over five hundred members, and their contributions over two years amounted to more than $17,000. In the late spring of 1873 he organized a bazaar and festival that became an annual affair. The first one brought in $2,000, and over the next ten years the income from the fair more than trebled. When Kelly took office there was a two-year tuition arrearage of over $2,300. This informal and unilateral remission of tuition could not prudently be continued. Kelly instructed an attorney to dun these and other debtors. Although this action was not immediately successful, it did eventually end the disparity between tuition due and tuition paid. By these methods Father Kelly reduced the debt of $130,000 that he found at his arrival to about $118,000.[7]

The Civil War and its aftermath wrought changes in the fabric of American society. Wartime profiteering and that of the Reconstruction era provided an enticing example for imitation. Furthermore, the customary social restraints were made less effective by wartime dislocations, increasing mobility within America, arrival of more immigrants, and the population flow toward the cities. This combination of circumstances made the prewar social hierarchy and set of values less compelling for certain persons. One effect was the emergence of criminals organized in persistent gangs.

The tendencies toward criminality and profiteering were intensified when in 1873 America suffered another bank panic. With banks refusing to cash checks, currency was at a premium and even the notorious greenbacks commanded an extra charge of 4 percent. Father Kelly responded to the situation by liquidating the college's account at one of the Baltimore banking houses and sending the treasurer daily on a diligent hunt for additional cash. Eventually this panic died out and business gradually resumed its normal pace.

. .

For all his attention to management, President Stephen Kelly did not slight the academic development of Loyola. At commencement in June 1871, the graduating class—all three students—put on a scientific exhibition. One student discussed the physical properties of air, another dealt with its chemical properties, and the last explained the wonders of hydrogen and carbon. On the following day these same seniors spoke confidently on such subjects as society, human destiny, and war and its influences. This combination of science and humanities remained a regular feature of Loyola's commencement exercises for a number of years.

The college's attention to contemporary advances was evident in other areas, as well. In the house diary the entry for May 22, 1872, notes that a scholastic "brought back the magic lantern all safe from Woodstock." The writer unfortunately felt no need to be more specific as to what kind of instrument it was; nor does any other record indicate how the lantern was being used. But, clearly, an instrument used to project images on a screen was owned by the college.

The growing opinion that sports are a valuable adjunct to education was reflected in developments at the college. One notation of expenses for 1872 listed $4.38 for bats and balls. By then the boys were also beginning to play football—not the game of disciplined teams and careful strategy, but a game consisting of kicking the ball around the yard in a general melee. By the mid-1880s a committee on sports had been formed (mainly to raise money to buy a new football), but it was still another decade before Loyola students engaged in interscholastic athletics.

Sports were gaining acceptance in American college life as a remedy for underdeveloped physiques and for secret vices, both associated with intellectual pursuits. The caricature of the intellectual as a "puny exotic" (that is still with us) served to motivate students and teachers alike to engage in sports.[8] This attitude was having its effect at Loyola as well as at other American colleges.

Another venerable institution had undoubtedly existed before Father Kelly's time, but it was first described in the recollections of a man who was a student in this period. In 1909, Matthew Brenan (1879), then president of the Mutual Life Insurance Company of Baltimore, remembered that when he was a student at Loyola fractious members were sent to the jug. About two o'clock each day the prefect of discipline sent the jug-book round to each classroom. In it the instructor inscribed the names and delinquencies of culprits. When classes ended the students assembled in the corridor, where the prefect read out the names of those deserving of jug. These marched to the largest classroom, where one of the scholastics had to sit for an hour while the boys completed their expiations.

Jug was a familiar ordeal at Georgetown and at other American colleges. They still regarded character training as an essential ingredient in the educational process and had to deal with many young and obstreperous adolescents. Mount Saint Mary's tariff of punishments for this era listed some specific offenses and punishments. Laughing in class, for instance, merited writing 250 lines of Caesar. Shooting stones through a study hall window (presumably opened) resulted in a similar penance. Running down the stairs warranted only 100 lines of Sallust.[9] That assigning as punishment passages from the classics—the matter to be learned—was a sound procedure seems not to have been questioned.

Associated with jug was another tradition. Brenan remembered a peer who not only had been consigned to stay after school but had proven so unregenerate that the presiding scholastic ordered him to sit on the edge of the platform near him. To the amazement and interest of the other penitents, the student "deftly placed a strap around the leg of the professor and the leg of the desk" so that "getting up suddenly the professor and the desk rolled together on the floor." The student was vigorously cuffed and suffered "intense pain." Almost every class left Loyola with at least one story in which the students scored on the faculty.

It was under Father Kelly that greater precision was introduced into the grading system. Up to this time the catalogues assured parents only that they would receive regular reports on the academic progress of their sons, and these were formulated in appropriate adjectives. From 1871 on, marks were defined in numerical terms. A grade of a hundred units (not percent) indicated perfection, and one of less than fifty units meant "that all the Exercises or Recitations" for that subject "have been, on an average, unsatisfactory, and classed—*Neglected* Lessons." Furthermore, "lateness, inattention, talking, and other violations of the Rules of the College" meant demerits that lowered the test and recitation grades. This concatenation of grades for intellectual effort with demerits for disciplinary failings might be faulted today but should be judged by the standards of that day. Although some educators may have divided intellectual from other values, those following tradition did not; and it was the customary view that still obtained at Loyola.

• •

From incidents already described and others yet to come it may be possible for the reader to infer the nature of the formative process at Loyola. This *paideia,* however, is too basic an element to be left to inference but, unlike the curriculum, cannot be simply listed or outlined. There was an abiding personal and psychological impress that Loyola made on its students by the whole manner in which the enterprise was conducted and in which the faculty related to the students.

Recollections of student days were especially eloquent in their testimonials to the faculty. Decades after graduation or departure, Loyola alumni remembered specific scholastics and priests affectionately by name—and the ability they possessed for "winning the confidence" of their pupils. For these students, the word *Jesuit* meant "earnest, erudite Mentors" who on the play yard became "unconstrained sharers" in the games. They were "as the parents of the younger boys, and the elder brothers of the more advanced."

The faculty could rouse an attachment that not even forty years or the width of the continent could dim. The poet Isaac Reiman Baxley (1868) wrote:

Many many times I have thought of the old place and the old people, and they both shape themselves in my mind in an atmosphere of extreme affection. Time after time in this far country [California] when persons ask me where I was educated (or even if they don't), I claim my old privilege of your scholar. . . . The old letters "A.M.D.G." affect me strangely and in a manner very sweet.[10]

Baxley's contemporaries said much the same thing in different words, but his testimony is particularly interesting because he did not share the Catholic faith of his former teachers.

Such affection was not, of course, unique to Loyolans. It was a sentimental age and many men lavished endearing words on their alma maters and the great teachers who guided them: this was evident in the testimonials to Loyola. There was also an esprit de corps that arose merely from having attended a Jesuit school. Elements of distinction in both the curriculum and the educational process made the alumni feel they had acquired a special character.

In Baltimore the process began each year on the first Monday of September, when both the public schools and Loyola resumed regular sessions. On that day a crowd of new and returning boys would begin to collect around the college by eight o'clock. The few who had not yet been registered were called in to be enrolled and quickly tested for placement. Meanwhile returning students continued to gather in the yard, telling the usual end of summer stories and engaging in the customary start of the school year horseplay.

At half past nine or so, when youthful impatience could no longer be contained (or the mounting din ignored), the doors were opened and the mob was admitted to the main hall. There the students were formally greeted by the president with a "few pleasant and appropriate remarks . . . about their future behaviour and about their success in their studies."[11] The comments led directly to the prefect's task of reading the results of the previous year's final exams (a rather realistic introduction for the new boys). This was followed by announcing the coming year's class assignments and the schedule. When all this was finished, teachers and students filed out to their designated rooms.

There the instructors continued the process. They drew up their class rolls and briefly outlined the work for the coming year. As textbooks were listed in the catalogue, these may already have been obtained by some of the students. (In 1884, references to a bookstore began appearing and these necessary transactions had likely become centralized.) By eleven o'clock or thereabouts, the teachers dismissed their charges. Thus ended the familiar ritual of *schola brevis*.

It was followed sometimes by a small celebration for the teachers. The minister, the assistant for internal administration of the Jesuit community, once invited the scholastics "to the Refectory and signalized his joy at the large attendance by opening a few. . . ." At this point, the diarist's pen skipped across the page; "Reader," he slyly continued "supply what your imagination suggests."[12] The teasing blank was filled elsewhere with a reference to some boxes of cigars.

. .

The presence of Loyola's president at the opening exercises was symbolic of his importance to the educational process. As the teachers and pupils together constituted a large family, so the president was supposed to be its loving, just, and prudent father. Teaching was then considered a parental obligation, and authority in schools was therefore exercised in loco parentis.

This conception of the role of the president as the source of authority was in fact shared by most American colleges. At Loyola, however, there was an added dimension because the head of the college was also rector of the Jesuit community and pastor of Saint Ignatius Church. He enjoyed a plenary authority vested in him by virtue of the state charter and the consequent bylaws—and by virtue of a still common authoritarian conception of education, the Jesuit constitutions and traditions, and the habitual deference that Catholics then gave priests. His function was to adapt the general directives of the Society of Jesus to the practical circumstances found in Baltimore.

Loyola's presidents were young enough to be energetic, usually in their late thirties or early forties at the time of their appointment. They were nevertheless older and more experienced than all but one or two of the teachers serving under them. The presidential term from 1852 to 1891 averaged four years (similar to the terms of presidents at Fordham) and, surprisingly, this meant that presidents were at Loyola longer than most individual faculty members. The turnover of Jesuits occurred because of the exigent needs of the province, and because college teaching was not then considered a lifetime profession for a layman. Thus, the presidency was not only a powerful office but an office held by a man who enjoyed seniority over many if not all of the teachers.

For students, the president was the very image of a paterfamilias. Like his ancient counterpart, he finally decided who would be accepted to membership and who was to be dismissed. His was a ubiquitous presence in the college. He was regularly seen at assemblies and celebrating Mass. He was no stranger to the classroom, where he might drop in to observe both the students and the instructor. He might even take a turn at teaching if illness suddenly created a vacancy that could not otherwise be filled. He appeared more often, however, as an examiner, or at least as the audience for a specially prepared demonstration or contest between classes.

There were formal, reciprocal gestures of affection between him and the students. His name day was celebrated with a release from classes, and on the last day before the Christmas vacation there was a program of poems, greetings, and declamations in his honor. If respectfully petitioned, he could (and often did) declare a holiday. His judgment of when such a release might be appropriate was not always shared by the faculty. Across one entry recounting how the boys had gotten time off to watch a circus parade, someone had written: "Foolish idea. Hope it will not be repeated." It was nonetheless repeated, to the delight of the students. Understandably, then, the presidents of Loyola were warmly and well remembered by their erstwhile charges.

• •

Loyola's *paideia* emphasized the intellectual element—not merely in the subjects or texts but in what was actually expected of the students. Much of this emphasis can be found in test ledgers in which the questions and assignments for the semiannual examinations were listed.

As one might expect, there was a good deal of matter to translate. The college sophomores of 1878, for instance, were required to convert a paragraph from their modern history text into Latin. They also had to render into English and parse thirteen lines from Horace's *Ars Poetica* and eight from Virgil's *Georgics*. Similarly, nine lines of Homer were to be translated and analyzed.

When these assignments had been completed, there was an essay to be written in English on a historical subject. Apparently, four hours were allotted to this part of the testing. And well it might be, since the question was "What was the origin of dissension between Marius and Sulla? What modern parties might best show their manner of thinking and governing? What is your judgment regarding them and their administration of public affairs?" In another exam, the question was more brief, but one can only wonder at the length of the answer. "What," the students were asked, "do you think of the conquest of Mexico by H.

Cortez?"[13] Nor were contemporaneous subjects slighted. In 1885 the college juniors were required to write an oration in the style of Cicero on Grover Cleveland's election to the presidency.

In one instance the question was followed by an outline of the expected answer. The college sophomores were instructed to "write an essay on the Fine Arts as manifested in the external worship of the Catholic Church." The arts they were expected to discuss were architecture, sculpture, music, painting, and poetry. These were to be considered with reference to Saint Peter's, Saint Mark's in Venice, and "Michael Angelo, Fra Angelico, Mozart, Palestrina, Dante, etc." Part of the composition was to be devoted to explaining the influence of such "splendor" on the human heart and how "it elevates the moral tone of society." At the end the essayists were to respond to the question "Is Christian art superior to the productions of the great Greek artists?"[14] Perhaps it would have been shocking had any of the students preferred the Greeks. Still, these teachers anticipated a broad familiarity with historical matters and aesthetic concerns that can no longer be taken for granted—indeed, that may now seem exotic.

Fairness requires a notation that some of these wide rivers of discussion ran rather shallow. The emphasis was on rhetoric and a fluent style of expression, but required also was a demonstration of systematic knowledge and diligent study in all the fields covered by the questions. The product of a liberal education was a cultured gentleman who knew something about a lot of things but who did not normally study any subject exhaustively. The very breadth of the questions was an invitation to invention, a skill that is at the very heart of rhetoric.

There were less formidable exercises for the lower grades. The students in second rudiments, for instance, were required merely to translate a few phrases into Latin: "a good book—a great treasure—a free citizen—an industrious boy—a short lesson." In the reverse exercise (from Latin into English) the boys listed all the nouns in an assigned selection, then gave the declension and case of each. Similarly, verbs were to be written down with their conjugations, parts, tenses, and persons. The geography portion of the test called for an essay on the natural features of Maryland or, in another instance, on the peculiar advantages of Texas. Spelling, punctuation, and penmanship were tested by taking dictation of a passage from a book. This part of the test was made to do further service by having the pupils parse two of the sentences.

There were, of course, more gradations in the questions than are cited here. Nevertheless, the emphasis on the student's formation and expression of an opinion should be noted. How much variety was accepted cannot be determined, because the test papers have not survived and there are no anecdotes of a student expelled or punished for the novelty of his views. Silence gives support neither to the supposition that wide variances in judgment were expressed by Loyola students nor to the assumption that all difference had been effectively suppressed. All that can be substantiated is that the Jesuits expected their pupils to think and to take a stand on the basis of their considered opinions. It is clear that the test assignments required the students to synthesize historical data and to make comparisons between the past and what was happening in their contemporary world. There was no encouragement of melancholy retreat, like Miniver Cheevy's, into a fantastic past. From virtually all the disciplines, lessons in public morals were derived for appropriate application in the future. The recent divorce between content and methodology produced not a notably more productive approach.

Embedded in these exercises were ideas and attitudes that the students were expected to incorporate into their own thinking. One passage for translation expressed doubt whether boys should be openly praised, "for boys seek for glory with excessive joy, and are so much inclined to approve plans that bring injury." The duties of a citizen were inculcated during the effort to convert the following into Latin: "When you obey the laws of the state you obey God, for he tells you that you owe honor to superiors and justice points out the truth that we should give everyone what is due him." There was strategy to be learned in the exploits of a commander who "sent a large troop to occupy the mountain, and terrify the enemy from the rear, while he renewed the battle on the plain." And a vision of courtroom drama was evoked while rendering into Greek a passage beginning: "Those who are obliged by the laws & their oath to give an impartial hearing both to prosecutor & defendant will not deprive me of their good will on account of the calumnies of this traitor who has so often been corrupted by the bribes of our enemy."[15]

These test items provide a glimpse of more personal attitudes on the part of the questioners. What might be learned if the context could be discovered for this phrase to be translated: "I am secretly supporting the boys"? And there was more than merely an exercise in translation involved in the choice of these sentences: "Both you and I are ignorant of many things" and "We differ from each other in manner and taste." Surely there was a heartfelt cry in: "O prudent men! O lazy boys!" And finally, there must have been a fine irony in having the students convert into Latin couplets of elegiacal meter lines starting:

Happy who hath grown callous by suffering,

And learned by suffering much to suffer more.[16]

Unfortunately, no instrument has yet been constructed that can measure how much more was implied by these phrases than appears on their surface.

More apparent were the intent, mood, and preachments of another passage to be metamorphosed into Greek. The Jesuit teacher, after summarizing the classical curriculum, was described in the passage as instructing his pupils "to restrain themselves so that the praises of these boys are sung by all foreigners except the English" (an understandable exclusion among Irish Catholics and Baltimoreans after 1814). He noted that the students brought their own lunch consisting of "bread & a little meat and often an apple or a pear as seasoning."

The Jesuit affirmed that he had been formed in the same system of education. He also had loved his teacher "for in all his conversations he was most agreeable." The lesson he had learned (and probably wanted to impart) was "that if we wished to speak well we ought to keep silence." Although his charges were to become men of fewer words, they were also enjoined "to give a reason for everything." They were not to be credulous but "always questioning those around us how such & such things are."[17] It was an engaging portrayal that had the students working over a description of what ostensibly was their teacher's experience but what was also in fact a summary of what they themselves were undergoing.

No printed notice was taken of the fact that Thursday rather than Saturday served as the weekly holiday at Loyola. Thursday was the traditional respite in the European school week, but in America only Catholic colleges and seminaries followed this arrangement. It was as distinctive and noticeable as the traditional prohibition against eating meat on Friday.

This similarity of schedule may help in some measure to explain why casual observers confused Catholic colleges with seminaries. This was particularly ironic because location of preparations for the Catholic priesthood had been restricted at the Council of Trent to the seminaries. Unlike other American schools, which made clerical education a major objective, Catholic colleges could not directly prepare candidates for the sacred ministry. Indeed, they might serve as a channel through which some young men were recruited for the priesthood—few though they might be—but a diploma from a Catholic college would not be accepted as a warrant for ordination.[18]

This distinctive schedule and the confusion with ecclesiastical seminaries served to differentiate the students at Catholic institutions from their peers. Students at Loyola increasingly resented having to attend classes on Saturday when their friends at other schools were free on that day. In the mid-1890s President Morgan changed the weekly schedule to a Saturday holiday but his successor reverted to the traditional schedule, which was maintained until the transfer to Evergreen.

• •

There was, as noted above, an esprit de corps among the Loyola students that was not merely directed vertically, so to speak, toward the Jesuits; it also had a horizontal sweep. College chums, after all, have a way of becoming lifelong friends. The distinctive element at Loyola, as one alumnus put it, was the association with "schoolmates as opposed to classmates."[19] The whole student body, rather than some smaller "in" group, made up the pool of acquaintances.

In so small a number (100 to 150 students), only the most inattentive could fail to learn the names of most of his fellows. Together the classes made up what today would be only a few busloads. It would have taken a very determined person to achieve the kind of anonymity that is readily available in a larger group. The association of students at Loyola was promoted by their assignment to different sections for the basic course, for math, and for languages. As a result they had to mingle with their older and younger fellows. Furthermore, every month the whole company assembled in the main hall for reading of marks. Under these circumstances, there was no way to hide one's skills or lack of them.

It must also be noted that the education offered by Loyola reinforced some of the characteristics generally attributed to Baltimoreans. Loyola's alumni tended to be modest rather than aggressive, to cultivate a small circle of sociability, to be dependable, and to avoid flashiness. Their ideas, like those of their neighbors, tended toward the conventional not so much from fear as from delight in what is comfortable. One perceptive social commentator of the time asserted that "the enjoying principle" is the root of conservatism, and if evidence were required to support this it would be readily available from the experience of Loyola and Baltimore in this period.

Most Loyola students were, after all, inhabitants of a city with a solid sense of social restraint and cohesion. This arose from a number of interconnected factors. There was the high percentage of home ownership, due partly to the institution of ground rent. Ground rents made it profitable for builders and conservative investors to pack as many houses as possible on a given tract, and so the row house was adopted as the characteristic domicile in Baltimore. In this form separate homes along one block are built with side walls shared so that there is no alley or yard between them. Such closeness to one's neighbors induces a habitual rejection of what is new, strange, or big. Closeness also produces a strong desire for privacy and a corresponding reluctance to invade another's domain. Baltimoreans, as a result, are renowned for their tolerance of peaceful eccentricity. Because ground rents were paid to the more substantial members of the community, a connection was created between a class of small homeowners and the wealthier sort. This relationship found expression in a manly, not servile, deference to "the powers that be."

In sum, the formative process at Loyola was a combination of principles and circumstances, of people and procedures. It produced a fellow rather like his Georgetown brother who "was a poor rebel . . . rarely rating a genius and . . . at his best as a citizen and head of a family.[20]

• •

In the autumn of 1877, when Father Edward McGurk arrived at Loyola College, what most people first noted about the new president was his youth. Indeed, when he made a courtesy call on the mint-new and nearly as young archbishop, James Gibbons, Father McGurk was mock-seriously upbraided for his paucity of years.[21] It was a shared defect that both the gentle chider, aged 43, and his guest, aged 36, knew was being remedied with each passing day.

The joviality of this exchange revealed not only Gibbons's ready wit but what proved to be the warmth of his relationship with Loyola. More than a few of the college's commencements, exhibitions, and student entertainments during the next forty-four years were graced by his presence, and the house diary records innumerable private visits with the Jesuit community. Although McGurk and Gibbons had come to Baltimore almost simultaneously, Father McGurk's stay proved to be hardly one-fifth the length of that of the great churchman and great American.

The year of their arrival was memorable for the nation. In early 1877, the United States was brought again to the brink of civil war over the election dispute between Rutherford B. Hayes, Republican, and Samuel J. Tilden, Democrat. Corruption and intimidation marred the 1876 campaigns of both parties. Congress established an electoral commission to resolve the dispute, but it was dominated by Republicans and awarded the presidency to Hayes. Still wanting was Democratic acquiescence, and this was purchased with an agreement that left the control of race relations in the former Confederate states to local (Southern Democratic) determination. For the next half-century the main business of America was to be business. Civil rights and social justice were less important than industrialization.

The emergence of this new age was heralded with appropriate noise and fury. In July, the Baltimore and Ohio Railroad Company suddenly cut wages by 10 percent, and workers responded by walking off their jobs. Soon sabotage and rioting hit the yards along the B&O right-of-way. By July 20 these disorders reached Baltimore, where after a few days of hesitation state authorities ordered the militia, aided by regular troops, to quell the strike. Eleven lives were lost in the ensuing operation, but soon trains were again running on schedule while workers and their families had to make do with lower wages.[22] The strikes of 1877 were only one round in what proved to be a continuing struggle between workers and employers in the course of the drive to industrialize America. In this turmoil, one of the significant ameliorative influences would be James Gibbons.

He had returned to the city of his birth in late October of 1877 after an absence of almost a decade. Gibbons had spent that time in the service of the church as vicar apostolic of North Carolina and later as bishop of Richmond. The city to which Archbishop Gibbons returned had changed significantly. Despite its growth (its population was then 330,000), however, Baltimore, which before the Civil War had ranked third among the nation's metropolitan centers, was now only sixth. Other cities were growing more rapidly.

In the 1870s education was still not a matter of much concern in commercial Baltimore. Another quarter of a century would pass before a compulsory school attendance law was enacted. It was not surprising, therefore, that in this era fewer than one-third of the city's young people between the ages of 5 and 19 were in school. With such a narrow base, the difficulty of maintaining an institution like Loyola College may be inferred. Nonetheless, Father McGurk was able to raise enrollment (perched at a little over one hundred at the beginning of his term) by almost 40 percent in eight years. At this statistical eminence (small as it seems by today's standards), Loyola's registration approximated the national average for colleges then reported by the federal commissioner of education.[23]

. .

Beyond his youthful appearance, there were other qualities for which Edward McGurk was noted. In particular, he was described as high-strung, "deeply religious . . . energetic, kindhearted." He inherited his earnestness from his father, a tradesman who had moved to Philadelphia after his son's birth because he believed "that no one could save his soul in N.Y." In Philadelphia, the younger McGurk attended public schools until 1854, when he was old enough to be enrolled at the recently opened Jesuit school, Saint Joseph's. There his association flowered into a religious vocation, so that he entered the novitiate at Frederick several years before the Civil War. Thereafter, he was sent to teach at Holy Cross and at Boston College. The next rotation of Jesuits returned McGurk to Holy Cross, where in addition to teaching he served as vice-president. Just before he was ordered to Baltimore in 1877, he was ordained to the priesthood.[24]

Athough Father McGurk would be remembered primarily as an educator par excellence, his record as an administrator is even more impressive, if somewhat mysterious. The college's debt stood at $116,000 a few months after he became president. Despite declining income from tuition and church collections, the debt was halved during the next seven years, to a low figure of $57,500. How Father McGurk managed this feat is nowhere explained. How marvelous it was can be gauged by the financial difficulties of another Catholic institution in Maryland, which for a time operated under the control of a court-appointed receiver.

One of the most annoying expenses for him and his predecessors was the ground rent attached to the land on which the college had been erected. This annual $1,400 was a constant drain on Loyola. One way to be rid of this particular burden was to move to another site, and serious thought was given to relocation northward to a tract near the present site of Saints Philip and James Church on Charles Street. In the end, however, Father McGurk chose the more conservative course of staying at Calvert Street and buying the land outright. Originally the land had been priced at $23,300, and during the intervening three decades its value had appreciated to $32,000.[25] Though the purchase at this price added to Loyola's debt, it ended forever a persistent drain on the college's resources.

The name *Edward* means "guardian of property," and Father McGurk lived up to his name. He had the facade of the college building refurbished and the inside of Saint Ignatius Church renovated. This redecoration was accompanied by installation of additional gaslights in the church. These were connected to a wet-cell battery and spark-coil arrangement in the sacristy so that by merely pushing a switch one operator could instantly illuminate the interior. About the same time this very modern convenience was installed at the new Academy of Music on North Howard Street, whose auditorium was the site of Loyola's commencements in the era.

Greater wonders were in the offing. Electric arc lamps were installed along a few of Baltimore's streets during the summer of 1882, and later that same year the Sun Iron Building would sport 170 Edison incandescent electric bulbs.[26] Such lights would be installed at Calvert Street at the next major renovation.

In 1880 Loyola College ceased to be the headquarters of the Maryland province. The Jesuit provincials had been a not unwelcome presence on Calvert Street for twenty years, but one that required great tact from both them and the college rectors. The move was made as a result of a merger between the New York mission and the Maryland province. Obviously this placed the Jesuit headquarters in America's leading city, but it also meant a wider circulation of personnel. An important but unanticipated effect was an extension of the influence of the New York Board of Regents, an agency that was becoming more active in setting educational standards within the state of New York. The authorities and teachers of the new Maryland–New York province had to pay close attention to directives from the regents, and they could not fully isolate their response in New York alone, even if they wanted to.[27]

Important as the provincial's departure from Calvert Street was, it passed unnoted in the Loyola house diary. The omission suggests a very quiet sigh of relief.

• •

Father McGurk's achievements at the college were not all financial and administrative. His students remembered him as "an educating force magnetic and inspiring, . . . one of the noblest and truest of men."[28] Among his innovations was a reorganization of the Loyola Literary Society. Previously it had been, in the main, a passive audience for outstanding commencement orators, but it now became an association in which the students provided the performers, criticism, and audience. The purpose of the society, as described in its new constitution, was "to promote Eloquence and to acquire an accurate knowledge of History." This was done at weekly meetings outside the regular school hours. One member read a piece he had selected, another recited some-

thing from memory, and four others debated the affirmative and negative of some momentous question. The presiding officer was a Jesuit
scholastic who, if the Georgetown custom was followed (and likely it
was), was chosen by the society's student members—subject, of course,
to the president's veto. Members of the revitalized Literary Society
tended to be leading lights of the school.

The society's most important officer was "the critic," who was
chosen each month by the faculty moderator. His duty was to write a
commentary on the merits and defects of all the performers and their
presentations and to read his criticism at the beginning of the next
meeting. To ensure that he would perform this "kindly-intentioned duty
without fear or favor" he could not be required to explain his strictures
by anyone but the moderator. An even more significant limitation on
the critic was the fact that the office rotated monthly, and any unfair
blow could soon be returned with interest. The critic's problem, of
course, was how to be critical and still be civil. This is an art perfected
only in reference to specifics; once learned, it can be generally applied.

Surviving reports make it clear that critics took their responsibilities very seriously. They commented on both the content and the
manner of presentation in detail, with an obvious effort made to report
in an incisive and a graceful style. Greater variety in choosing set pieces
to read or recite was urged. Tennyson was being heard too regularly for
the taste of some critics. They were equally tired of yet another recitation of Fitz-Greene Halleck's "Marco Bozzaris." Speakers were warned
to modulate their voices to avoid monotony. Others were denounced for
timidity. One debater was chided for casting a blot on his whole argument through a gratuitous slur on the state of Maine. "We are sure," the
critic asserted, "he got no credit for it from the Literary Society."[29] If
they were diamonds in the rough, their grit was being used to polish the
edges of one another.

Members of the Literary Society were eligible to participate in an
annual prize debate, another McGurk innovation. Among the questions proposed were that the American Indians have a right to the soil;
that Monopolies are injurious to the state; that centralization of power is
hostile to the spirit of the American Constitution. These efforts were
judged by gentlemen of note in Baltimore. Some, like Judge William
Fischer (1855), were alumni; others like Leo Knott, the state's attorney
for Baltimore, were familiar public figures. In 1881, Knott led his fellow
judges in congratulating the winner but also in delivering an encomium
on the "effectiveness and high excellence of the Institution." Father

McGurk thought so highly of this testimonial that he had it reprinted in the next issue of the catalogue.

Father McGurk tried to encourage more student effort and competition by securing the establishment of funded medals—"six valuable gold medals" for the college-level classes, as he announced it on June 25, 1879. These medals were named for the donors: Hillen, Jenkins, Knott, MacTavish, Murphy, and Whelan. The first medal was endowed by the widow of a former mayor of Baltimore; the second was the gift of Austin Jenkins, a member of an honorable and numerous clan. Knott has already been identified, and Maria MacTavish, the donor of the fourth medal, was a descendant of Charles Carroll of Carrollton. The Murphy Medal was the gift of John Murphy, quite likely though not certainly the well-known Baltimore publisher. The legal counsel to the college, Thomas Whelan, endowed the sixth. His was for general excellence in studies and deportment, and the Jenkins Medal became the prize for the Literary Society's annual debate. Otherwise these awards seem to have been distributed by what is now an unfathomable rule. One year the Knott Medal was given for debating and another year to the student most proficient in philosophy. These examples could be multiplied, but to no purpose other than to indicate the insouciance with which these forefathers handled such matters.

The next addition to this group of medals was identified with Father Abram J. Ryan, "the poet-priest of the South." Though associated with the Deep South, Father Ryan was a Marylander by birth. Late in November of 1880, he came to Baltimore to promote a book of verses that a local house had recently published. He stayed at Loyola for nearly three weeks. Someone, probably Father McGurk, suggested that he give a poetry reading at the Academy of Music, with the proceeds to fund a medal for the most proficient student in the class of poetry (college sophomores). The program was a success, and a year later Austin Fink (1883) became the first recipient of the Ryan Medal.[30]

What Father McGurk was attempting to do at Loyola with the Ryan Medal and the others was similar to what his fellow presidents were doing at many American colleges. Schools like Bowdoin and Williams tried to stimulate interest in intellectual endeavors by offering various medals and prizes. At Emory the effort resulted in such a profusion that this period in its history has been called the "Age of Medals."

Students were engaged in an intercollegiate competition established by the Jesuit provincial, Robert Fulton, who as a scholastic had been one of the incorporators of Loyola College. For the best essay on an assigned subject in Christian doctrine, Father Fulton offered a prize of $100—a princely sum, enough to pay tuition for more than a year. The first run of the contest, which included all but two schools of the Maryland–New York province, was won by a Loyola student, Oscar Quinlan (1890). The following year, with all seven schools competing, Alfred Jenkins Shriver (1889), another Loyola student, was the winner. Both went on to respectable careers as lawyers, and Shriver would four decades later list "Won Intercollegiate Prize $100 over 2500 rivals" as the first of his many distinctions.[31]

Another participant in the contest was Bart Randolph (1888), who did not win a prize but achieved an even flashier distinction. Shortly after Grover Cleveland's inauguration, young Randolph translated the president's address into Latin. Father McGurk was so proud of the translation that he brought it to the attention of Leo Knott, who had just been appointed assistant postmaster general. Knott arranged for young Randolph to present the translation to President Cleveland in person. On June 19, 1885, Randolph, Father McGurk, and Knott all went to the White House for a pleasant little interview.[32] Later, Randolph joined the Vincentians and became a noted figure on the faculty of Saint John's College (now University) in Brooklyn.

Shortly after he took office, Father McGurk sought to add to the cultural life of the city by offering a regular series of lectures. Discussions of Dante's *Paradiso*, the early phases of Christian art, volcanoes, glaciers, the solar system, the antiquity of man, Charlemagne, Peter the Great, and Egyptian hieroglyphics, as well as various entertainments by the students, were offered to the public.

What Loyola was offering was in no way competitive with the lectures at the recently established Johns Hopkins University. With the inauguration of its first president, Daniel Coit Gilman, on February 22, 1876, the new institution began presenting lectures of the most advanced scientific content and highest scholarly quality. The scholastics and priests at Loyola were regular auditors of these disquisitions, and they took pleasure at being "cordially received" by President Gilman himself.

• •

The city had time also for less serious matters. For a number of years in the early 1880s the anniversary of the British attack on Baltimore was celebrated with appropriate pageantry. To organize these fetes, the Mystic Order of the Oriole was formed, with Robert Garrett, Baltimore's leading financier, as its president. (The Baltimore Oriole was adopted as the state bird in 1882.) These festivals were climaxed by torchlight parades up Calvert Street. On such occasions the students were invited to watch from the library windows, but the best view—from the class-room for the high-school juniors—was reserved for guests. The porch in front of the rector's room accommodated the Jesuits. In plumes and pomp, the glories of Maryland and Baltimore were proclaimed on these municipal holidays.

A less formal flourish of civic pride appeared in the establishment of the baseball team named the Orioles. It would be some time before this new institution was fully accepted, but meanwhile it inspired tentative imitation. At Loyola, for instance, two baseball nines were organized in some unrecorded fashion, and a game arranged with Saint Joseph's Academy (today's Mount Saint Joseph). At the end of May 1885, "the first nine," as noted in the prefect's diary, "went to Catonsville. . . . Our boys were beaten, the score being 25 to 24. . . . What a game! Such an umpire!" For the following day, the scribe recorded "rain— temperature of nature & boys low & cloudy."[33] Undaunted, Loyola's "second nine" traveled all the way to Catonsville on the next Saturday, only to find that a scheduling mistake had been made. It would be some time before arranging such events became systematic.

With such an inauspicious beginning it is not surprising to find sports deemphasized the following spring. "Base Ball batting [was] for-bidden in yard—too many windows broken." Another four years would pass before this unfortunate memory receded enough to allow formation of the Loyola Athletic Association.

In 1880 Baltimore celebrated the sesquicentennial of its founding, and the college joined its neighbors in marking the anniversary. For the main anniversary parade Father McGurk received tickets from Mayor Ferdinand Latrobe so that he and other members of the faculty could join officials on the reviewing stand. Three days later the president and associated professors were participants in another grand procession, this time in the company of other religious, social, medical, temperance, and "colored" organizations of Baltimore.[34]

• •

It was a somewhat more dignified but no less festive gathering that Father McGurk addressed in the spring of 1884. The occasion was the annual remembrance of the state's original settlement. This commem-oration had been started at Georgetown in 1842 by the Philodemic So-ciety, but it had gradually come under the sponsorship of the Maryland Pilgrim's Association. This 250th anniversary bore a distinctively

Loyola character. Father McGurk celebrated the Mass and was one of the principal speakers. The other was Judge Richard T. Merrick, who in 1854 had received a master's degree from the college and had become a distinguished member of the federal judiciary.

One May afternoon, they led a hundred and fifty pilgrims onto the *Eastern Shore,* the steamboat that was to carry them along the Bay and up the Potomac. "The trip down was exceedingly pleasant. Fine music by Charles' band was followed by vocal selections by members of the choir, and it was past midnight when all had retired," reported one of the participants. The next morning found them at Saint Inigoes, where Mass was celebrated with éclat—the choir was still "in excellent voice, and rendered Hadyn's Second Mass . . . in fine style." After some sightseeing they boarded the steamboat for the journey to Saint Mary's City, meanwhile inviting the people at Saint Inigoes Church that morning to accompany them. At least fifty did, and most of them were black.

At Saint Mary's City the rest of the program was presented, with President McGurk and Judge Merrick delivering their addresses. Both stressed the heritage of religious pluralism and "how the tolerant spirit of Maryland fostered strength." Between their orations two other recitations were given by Loyola students. The first was a poem declaimed by Charles Bouchet (1887), the other a Latin ode delivered by Francis Coad (1886). All these speeches were given in the shade of the mulberry tree "against whose trunk the [first] Jesuits erected a temporary chapel."

The holiday crowd wandered about looking at the remains of the governor's palace and other relics. One can imagine that at five o'clock the impatient captain blew the whistle, waited for one last straggler, and gave orders to cast off the lines. A brief stop was made at Saint Inigoes to return those passengers, and then it was a clear night's ride back to Baltimore. The resolutions adopted by the participants made clear how pleased they were with the speakers and the arrangements.[35]

The house diarist was summarizing more than a particular moment when he commented on 1885. "On the whole," he wrote, "it must be acknowledged that this has been a brilliant year for Loyola."[36] Enrollments were up; a student had won an intercollegiate prize; young Randolph had been invited to the White House. It was a remarkable record for any year, and Father McGurk's whole term must be characterized with the same adjective.

Part Two

New Directions

6

Second Spring

Normally the departure of one president-rector was followed almost immediately by the installation of a successor. This sequence was not observed in 1885. Father McGurk left Loyola on July 31, but it would be another year before Francis Smith was formally recognized as president of the college and rector of its Jesuit community. The delay suggests that the change had come earlier than expected.

· ·

There was, however, no interregnum in 1885–86, because Father Smith had been in charge for some time at Calvert Street. He had been assigned to the college during McGurk's final year, in the triple capacity of vice-president, treasurer, and minister of the Jesuit house. Such a combination of offices made it plausible that Smith would soon be bearing greater responsibilities. Why was there a delay in the usual formalities after Father McGurk's departure? For one thing, there was a technical difficulty: Father Smith would not take his final vows until February 2, 1886. Upon making his final profession, he was named vice-rector by the provincial, but it took longer to secure his full commission from the Jesuit general in Rome.

Father Smith's biography, like that of most Jesuits, survives as little more than an austere list of basic facts. He was the son of an Irishman who in 1840, in middle age, had emigrated to New York, where he established some unspecified business. Whether the elder Smith brought over a family or started one in America is unknown, but a son, Francis, was born in 1844. The Smiths lived for a time near the gate of Saint John's College (today's Fordham), so it was only natural that young Smith enter that school.

As a student he was remembered as an "earnest worker and great lover of every sport," especially baseball. He may indeed have been left-fielder on the Fordham club that played the first intercollegiate game under rules that are basically those of today's game. In any case, he was graduated during the Civil War and spent an additional year at the school in both advanced studies and teaching.

What Smith had on his mind became evident at the end of that year. He journeyed to the novitiate near Montreal, where he joined the Society of Jesus. There he demonstrated his zeal as well as "his talent for making himself all to all." Upon completion of his noviceship, Smith underwent a typical *cursus honorum* for a young Jesuit of this era. He returned to New York, where by turns he taught at Fordham and the in-town college, Saint Francis Xavier's. For most of the 1870s he continued his studies at Woodstock College, where he was ordained to the priest-hood. He spent the early 1880s teaching at Saint Peter's College in Jersey City, from which he was sent in 1884 to Frederick for his final year of preparation. It was from there that Father Smith came to Loyola College. By then, he was 41 years old.

Beyond biography, some things can be learned by studying a person's portrait. Francis Smith looks a vigorous man—calm, serious, de-termined. His face does not convey the high-strung sensitivity of his predecessor, Edward McGurk, or the bonhomie of Father John Morgan, his successor. Unlike both his peers, Smith does not seem to have made endearing contact with either the students or his colleagues at Loyola. Nevertheless, all would recall his term as marked by significant initia-tives, so that President Smith might easily be called "the New York operator."

• •

His desire to promote the reputation of Loyola College was evident from the beginning. Commencements again became noteworthy occa-sions, with programs of student declamations and music augmented by well-known speakers. Even as he remained in a titular limbo, Father Smith invited both the governor of Maryland and the mayor of Balti-more to grace the June 1886 graduation exercises. Though these digni-taries regularly appeared on the platforms at other schools, this was the first evident attempt to secure their glamor for Loyola. Unfortunately both declined the honor, but an even more spectacular alternative pre-sented itself. True, the featured speaker was only a local notable (Judge Daniel Gans), but the presiding eminence was a papal emissary who was in Baltimore to deliver a red hat and other cardinalatial insignia to Archbishop Gibbons.[1]

Nothing quite equal to this could be expected another time, and yet the featured speaker for the following year, Charles Joseph Bonaparte, carried his own note of distinction. He was a rising celebrity because he had recently launched a national crusade for civil service reform. In addition, his name assured the attention of Baltimoreans because he was the grandson of Betsy Patterson, a local belle who in 1803 married Napoleon's brother in proper Catholic ceremonies, only to be brutally jilted at the emperor's command a few years later. Furthermore, he strikingly combined the virtues of a liberally educated gentleman with a growing public fame and a solid devotion to the Catholic church.

Bonaparte's address, as reported in the *Sun*, contained the mixture of warning and advice customary on such occasions. He cautioned the students against becoming "human phonographs," mindlessly recording what others say and then broadcasting these opinions at a convenient turn of the crank. (The phonograph, one of the mechanical wonders then regularly emerging from the laboratories of Thomas Edison, had been on the market for about ten years and must have graced the parlors of more than a few of those in the audience.) Bonaparte coupled his call for independent thought with equal praise for "very strong party feeling." He was not using the occasion to recruit for the Republicans (his own political persuasion), but like Edmund Burke and James Madison he was urging party affiliation as an effective means of influencing public policy.[2]

In 1890 high-school commencement ceremonies were held separately and on an earlier date than the grander ritual for the new bachelors and masters of arts. The division certainly gave better focus to the separate programs, but it also marked the beginning of a process to establish the high school and the college as distinct bodies, a process that would not be completed for another thirty-five years.

Father Smith expended his effort to bring greater dignity and notice to the college's exhibitions in other directions, as well. Cremation was the subject chosen for an annual prize debate; one of the judges was president of Baltimore's newly organized Cremation Society. Another judge was chancellor of the archdiocese, and the third was a professor at the Johns Hopkins University. At a later forensic encounter, the proposition asserted that a national system of education was opposed to the interest of the American people. The Jenkins Gold Medal—the prize for this debate—was awarded to Albert Brown (1887) by the president of City College; Herbert Baxter Adams, professor of history at Johns Hopkins; Severn Teackle Wallis, still Baltimore's civic conscience; and Thomas Lanahan, the éminence grise of Maryland politics in that era.

• •

President Smith's promotion of Loyola to favorable notice also centered on more substantive concerns. Two months after McGurk's departure, the remaining lots fronting on Calvert Street were purchased for $35,000. This action was contrary to Father McGurk's program of liquidating the college's debt and perhaps helps explain the sudden change in leadership at Loyola. A year later, at the first meeting with his consultors after he was formally named rector, Father Smith proposed buying the six houses on Monument Street that abutted on the college's now extended property. This too would increase the debt. The degree of Smith's determination can be estimated by the fact that the trend among institutions in the Maryland–New York province was to bring down their debts—some entirely.[3]

The consultors, however, could not see the value of the purchase. Father Peter Fitzpatrick, the faculty elder, thought the addition would merely increase the "encumbrance" of the college corporation. Superficially at least, this objection would seem to be aimed at the debt. But this, at the moment, totalled only $48,000, and Fitzpatrick may have had something more in mind. His opposition was seconded by Francis Ryan, who was generally accounted among Father Smith's closest collaborators. Father Ryan favored delay because it would save money, since the property in question was steadily declining in value. Was this the encumbrance to which Father Fitzpatrick alluded? Was it prudent for the college to acquire more property in a neighborhood that, however fashionable in the past, had evidently passed its economic prime? Only the dean, David Daly, agreed to Father Smith's proposition, and Father Henry Shandelle, an alumnus and instructor of college freshmen, abstained. In the face of such division, it was prudent to postpone action, at least until it could be reconsidered in more favorable circumstances.

Smith, for one, seemed to attach much importance to the remaining burden of debt. By 1886 the debt was reduced by 37 percent, and a year later it stood at only $14,000.[4] Smith's methods for achieving these results are as obscure as those of his predecessor but are even more remarkable because enrollment (and tuition) dropped during his five years from 148 to 109. It was no doubt a matter of good management. For the time being, McGurk's policy of debt reduction continued, even though Father Smith clearly had other things in mind.

Smith turned his attention to a related matter. He sought to remedy a major defect in the college charter. It could be argued that the state, in its 1853 grant, had intended only to create an educational body and had not authorized it to own a church. Embarrassing questions on this score had been forestalled for almost a quarter of a century by establishing the provincial headquarters at Loyola and by the assumption of the church debt by the college corporation. By 1888, however, both these circumstances had disappeared, because the provincial's residence had been moved to New York and the debt was well on the way to liquidation.

Some thought therefore had to be given to what might happen if by mischance the issue of the legality of the college's ownership of the church was raised. The formal solution was another amendment to the Loyola charter. Quietly Father Smith secured the requisite legislation during the winter of 1888.[5]

• •

Although the legislature had not been disturbed by passage of the Loyola charter amendment, "out of doors" there arose a furious blizzard—literally. It was in fact while the amending bill was passing through the legislative mill that the famous blizzard of 1888 struck Maryland and the eastern seaboard. In a few hours Baltimore was enveloped by howling winds and snow. The delicate network of transport and public utilities was ripped into virtual uselessness. The winds were so fierce and the tides so low that the bottom of Baltimore harbor was exposed for several days. Many lives were lost to the fury of the storm. Eventually the blizzard blew itself out to sea. Gradually the people of Baltimore and the other areas hit by the storm resumed their daily round of activities and so restored the life of the community.[6]

As already noted, diaries were kept by various officers of the college and of the Jesuit community. Although notations in these journals tend to be laconic, they occasionally include references to the weather. One might therefore expect some mention of this untimely March blizzard—some elegant allusion to a classical storm, or at least meteorological data—but no such entry appears. As the winds blew and the snowdrifts piled higher, the diarists at Loyola wrote only *"de more,"* "order as usual."

Perhaps it was due to a change of scribes that a later siege of winter distresses was duly recorded. For Saturday, January 4, 1890, the entry reads: "Reg[ular] order Twenty-eight (28) absences. This poor attendance is owing to the prevalence in the city of the epidemic 'La Grippe.'"

During the ensuing fortnight, about a quarter of the student body stayed home, suffering from the miseries of the fever and from home remedies. The favored panacea appears to have been

Little grains of quinine, little drops of rye,

Make La Grippe that's got you

Drop its hold and fly.

This will quickly help you, if you'll only try,

But when you take the quinine,

Don't forget the rye.[7]

On Friday, January 17, the Loyola diarist was relieved to record "10 absences 'La Grippe' losing its hold." As intimated in the verse, this pun seemed to fascinate Baltimoreans of the era. The house diarist at least buried it in a source meant only for the eyes of other Jesuits.

The blizzard year was notable in Baltimore for a more pleasant development: the city's size was enlarged in June of 1888 by the annexation of a one-and-a-half-mile belt along its western and northern boundaries. This more than doubled the area of the city and converted 36,000 rustics into bona fide Baltimoreans; the city's population now exceeded 416,000. Included in this newest part of the Monumental City were the villages of Homestead and Waverly, the estates of such prominent families as the Abells, Wymans, and Browns, the milltowns of Hampden and Woodberry, Druid Hill Park, and the suburbs of Peabody Heights, Walbook, and Calverton. No expansion eastward occurred because the densely packed residents along that boundary refused to be annexed and formally urbanized. They preferred the lower tax rate of Baltimore County.[8]

• •

The following year, 1889, was aglitter with centennial celebrations. The whole nation joined in heartfelt thanks for the Constitution, which had successfully weathered the changes and violence of a difficult century. Several other commemorations were associated with the church, and in February the Jesuits marked the hundredth anniversary of Georgetown's establishment. Toward the end of the year, Cardinal Gibbons presided over solemnities to honor the hundredth anniversary of the Roman Catholic hierarchy in America.

To enhance this final event several prominent Catholics decided to convene a national congress of the laity. A leading role in this movement was played by Henry Brownson, son of Orestes Brownson and a sometime student of Father John Early. He was aided by a prominent local figure, Charles Bonaparte. Initially Cardinal Gibbons thought such a lay congress might be premature, but seeing that it was going to be held anyway, he gave his approval. In early November American Catholic leaders—lay and clerical—converged on Baltimore.

Most of what happened at this convention can here be passed over, but there were several points of contact between the Catholic congress of 1889 and Loyola. For one thing, almost a dozen alumni or men closely associated with the college were among the delegates. President Smith's presence was prominently noted in the official program.[9] He had attracted notice because of his spectacular proposal for the organization of the alumni of Jesuit colleges and universities into one nationwide association. From the listing of Loyola's graduates in the 1887–88 catalogue it is evident that he had been interested in the subject even before the congress was conceived. With the energy of a New Yorker, he seized the opportunity to invite all the Jesuit alumni at the congress to meet at the college.

Michael Mullin (1859), acting in the name of Father Smith and Loyola, greeted over one hundred delegates representing thirty Jesuit institutions. Among the honored guests were various prelates and the head of the Maryland–New York province of Jesuits. The concerns of the meeting reached well beyond the borders of the United States. Honoré Mercier, premier of Quebec, and a representative of Mexico were present.

All agreed on the formation of a fraternal union of Jesuit alumni, in which membership in the association of one institution made a man eligible to join that of any other. A temporary steering committee was established with a president from Fordham, a secretary from Georgetown, and vice-presidents from each of the other institutions. The ease with which all this was done and the presence of the provincial suggest sufficient preparation for what appeared a timely conception. Although no deadline was set for inaugurating the proposed association, it seems likely that the Chicago World's Fair, three years later, figured in the planning.

In 1893 a congress of lay Catholics was held in the Windy City, but no mention of the proposed Jesuit alumni association was made. The plan (however sound) ran afoul of a strong Jesuit preference for maintaining the separate identity of their institutions. A decade later, when Loyola College was planning to celebrate its fiftieth anniversary, some thought was given to reviving Father Smith's idea, but again nothing came of it. The Jesuit connection, such as it was, continued to rely on flexibility rather than centralization.

The 1889 lay congress endorsed a resolution requested by Indian chiefs who were present. The resolution protested government policies that endangered Catholic schools, and appealed for action to prohibit the sale of alcoholic beverages. Instead of composing a separate resolution applying only to Indian reservations, the congress condemned saloons, drunkenness, and the lax enforcement of Sunday-closing laws. If these sentiments seem incongruous today, it should be recalled that they were identical to what many other Americans were feeling and saying several decades before the "noble experiment" of Prohibition. In fact, the immediate aftermath of the congress saw the active presence of Catholics, including Cardinal Gibbons and President Smith, in the local movement for strict saloon-licensing and liquor-dispensing laws.[10] Alcohol abuse was so pervasive a social problem that it required general cooperation—though Catholic churchmen remained wary of public action with leaders of other denominations.

· ·

Smith had prepared for the lay Catholic congress by forming the Loyola College Alumni Association. A few days before the national meeting was convened, he called together a small group of graduates. Sixteen "old boys," ranging from students of the first class to the most recent, attended. Michael Mullin was elected temporary chairman, the secretarial chore fell to Charles Tiernan (1858), and a five-man committee on organization was formed. Their work was completed late in April of the following year, when Mullin and Tiernan were given permanent rank and Edward Milholland (1856) was designated vice-president. This was only three years after formation of a similar organization at the Johns Hopkins University.

However it may seem in these days, the Loyola Alumni Association was not originally formed to raise funds. It tended instead during its early decades to promote social ties and bonds of affection with the college. The focus of its life was an annual banquet at one of Baltimore's best hotels, where old comrades were greeted heartily, new friends made, familiar anecdotes laughed at, and an esprit de corps maintained. Of course, some of the "old Padres" who unfailingly remembered names and faces were in attendance.

The menu and program for these gatherings conformed to the elegant standards of Baltimore. There were, de rigueur, seven courses. With soup an appropriate wine (sauterne seemed favored) was served, and another wine was poured to accompany the main course. After dessert came café noir, cigars, and speeches. The speeches were mercifully restricted in number and brief in duration, and usually took the form of toasts.

At the 1905 reunion, for instance, a bright young attorney, James Kearney (1896), was toastmaster. The first salute came from Walter Mc-Cann, drama critic for the *Baltimore News*, and was addressed to "the press." The district attorney for Prince George's County, Hampton Magruder (1896), offered some thoughts on "the state," and Doctor Charles O'Donovan (1877) toasted "our sister alumni." (The choice of his subject was particularly apt, since Loyola shared the doctor with Georgetown.) The final toast was reserved for the Reverend Father President, who quite naturally honored "our alma mater." It was with such silken cords that the alumni bound themselves to Loyola and to one another. Much the same tone and program was then evident in the alumni associations of other Jesuit schools.

Elsewhere, however, the relations of alumni and their colleges was developing differently into what was becoming, in the view of one eminent historian, a substitute religion. The presidents of many American colleges and universities were looking for ways to raise funds and found they could do better with the services of alumni secretaries and similar administrators. These in turn discovered that a prodigious fervor could be induced among the former students by getting them together periodically to watch and cheer at intercollegiate sporting events.

Previously, decorous presentations of oratory or music had been sparsely attended and resulted in small, if any, additions to the institutional coffers. Football, baseball, track, boxing, crew, and the like provided a meeting ground for the alumni (among whom were included non-graduates), ministering functionaries, enthusiastic students, and some of the faculty. Varsity sports provided these new congregations with a ritual drama of presumably cosmic significance—virtue and vice struggling for victory. The alumni began donating more and demanding more occasions on which they could express their communal devotion. The rise of college alumni associations thus meant the growth of intercollegiate athletics and increased confusion about the nature and purpose of American higher education at some of our leading institutions.[11]

In the aftermath of the Baltimore congress of 1889, Father Smith formed several other organizations warranted by the resolutions of that conclave. The congress had called for, among other things, associations that would promote Catholic literature. This resulted in what was first called the men's "reading circle"; it quickly shifted focus to an intelligent discussion of practical questions of the day. For the 1890–91 meetings of the Loyola League the subject chosen was most timely and significant: the growing conflict in America between industrial owners (popularly known as robber barons) and workers. The Loyola program was balanced to ensure a critical analysis of the rights and duties of both capital and labor. Not surprisingly, religion (especially the church) was offered as an essential ingredient in solving the menacing struggle between economic classes.

These bimonthly meetings at Loyola evoked favorable notice and editorial comment from the local press. Although the views expressed were quite mild by today's standards, one fellow indicated some doubts about the orthodoxy of the enterprise. He loudly queried the Jesuit moderator whether a copy of the group's program had been sent to the pope. The Jesuit's instant reply was that he soon hoped to receive a letter from "His Holiness endorsing the principles . . . and plan of the Loyola League."

The chuckles roused by this sally soon turned to wonder. On May 15, 1891, Pope Leo XIII issued his encyclical letter *Rerum Novarum,* in which he applied Christian principles to the relations of the working and possessing classes. This event certainly boosted the moderator's prestige as well as the general reputation of Jesuits for "being in the know." Unfortunately the seed fell on relatively barren ground. Catholics lacked the tools and methodology to adapt the abstract principles enunciated in *Rerum Novarum* to American circumstances.[12] Only after another forty years and the Great Depression would a serious hearing for these papal pronouncements, even among Catholics, be gained. Meanwhile the Loyola League underwent several permutations until the mid-1890s, when it merged with another group that had been using the facilities of Loyola College.

• •

Father Smith's efforts to enlarge Loyola's service to the surrounding community had not diverted him from his main concern, the college itself and its students. He modified the old practice of remitting tuition with a new system of scholarships. At his first commencement in 1886 he announced the endowment of two scholarships to be awarded by competitive examination. Although a circular notice was sent to Catholic pastors in and around Baltimore, not one candidate presented himself on the appointed day. Reasons for this lack of response can only be conjectured but it is indicative of the prevailing opinion of education.[13]

Father Smith, in typically Jesuit fashion, was not discouraged but sought prudent means to gain his end. He succeeded in increasing the number of scholarships to six with such patrons as Cardinal Gibbons, Maria MacTavish, Thomas Lanahan, George Jenkins, Mary Abell, Sara Johnson, and the Misses Andrews. No specific figures were recorded for these endowments, but they likely amounted to at least two thousand dollars each. Furthermore, Father Smith publicized the opportunities more widely. Although he continued to send notices to the pastors, he also advertised in all the major Baltimore newspapers. The success of his efforts can be measured by contrasting the lack of response in 1886 with the application of sixty candidates in 1890.

These scholarships had several purposes. They were meant to induce a sense of distinction in the recipients as a motive to maintain their eminence. Candidates were to be inspired either to emulation or to competitive determination to excel, and the scholarships were devices to recruit more and more able students. Families of promising but unsuccessful scholarship candidates were visited by Father Smith to see if some means could be found to secure the candidates matriculation at Loyola. Here would likely reappear the old partial or full remission of tuition.

Smith's search for endowments brought in another funded medal in 1888. The Whiteford family, who had been and would continue to be generous benefactors of Loyola and of Saint Ignatius Church, donated a sum for a gold medal to be awarded annually for the best essay on an assigned historical subject. Over the years these topics have included a varied assortment of perennial and contemporary interests. Among the Whiteford medalists were students who would become outstanding alumni, including George Melville Bolling (1891), a world-renowned scholar of Greek and Sanskrit; Eugene Saxton (1904), editor "extraordinaire" for Doubleday; Herman Storck (1897), who alone won this competition twice and who lived out a gentle and productive life as a Jesuit; and Vincent de P. Fitzpatrick (1907), for many years the editor of the *Catholic Review* (the archdiocesan newspaper). There were, of course, other recipients of more modest accomplishments, but at least once their names glistened with distinction.

• •

President Smith was not merely bustle and administration. He was also concerned about the educational program. At the opening of his first school year in September of 1885 he finally abolished the English, or commercial, course. It had attracted only eight students that year and had always been an embarrassment to the Jesuits' sense of academic propriety. The students from the defunct program were apportioned to various regular classes but were exempted from the rigors of Latin and Greek. Their erstwhile instructor was better utilized in a subdivision of the large first rudiments class. A year later, a similar program was discontinued at Baltimore City College.[14] From then on, young Baltimoreans had to resign themselves (for the time being) to the study of ancient classics if they wanted a college education.

At that moment, however, secondary and college education in America was beginning a major reform. Charles Eliot, president of Harvard, inaugurated a nationwide campaign against the uniform traditional curriculum and for student election of a wider variety of courses. Reform and progress were in the air; indeed, Eliot's educational program may quite properly be viewed as one aspect of the rising Progressive movement, which would deeply affect American politics, law, and society. In that connection President Eliot's educational reforms were (in the judgment of one historian) a "self-conscious tactic" of the older American social stock to prevent its displacement by newer elements rapidly increasing in numbers. The devotion of these "lesser breeds" (as the newer immigrants came to be called) to their cherished traditions and institutions was to be dissolved by ridicule and by the invocation of such slogan-ideals of Eliot and the other Progressives as "efficiency," "progress," and "democracy."[15] Probably aware of this trend and unwilling to conform, the Jesuits chose at this juncture to reemphasize Latin and the *Ratio Studiorum* in contrast to the general trend toward modernization. This increased the differentiation between Jesuit and other American colleges.

Early in 1890 there appeared a significant, if tentative, addition to the extracurricular program at Loyola. The sodalities, Literary Society, Dramatic Club, and Choir were joined on September 22, 1890, by the Loyola Athletic Association. Its originators were undoubtedly Francis Homer (1892) and Cluskey Mullin (1892), who served as the association's first officers. They may have been encouraged not only by the development of athletics at other institutions but by Father Smith's well-known enthusiasm for sports. About this same time references to an athletic association appear in the records of the Johns Hopkins University.

The aim of this new organization was "to promote physical development and foster the college spirit." Its wherewithal came from voluntary contributions and was probably assigned for the purchase of balls, bats, and the like rather than major capital resources—gymnasiums or playing fields. What Homer and Mullin scheduled in the way of practice sessions and contests is lost, except for the notation that "athletic games" were conducted in the yard on Thanksgiving Day of 1891. The graduation of Homer and Mullin in the following year dampened the spirits of Loyola's athletes for a time, but sporting events would soon again be regularly recorded in the college diaries and Baltimore newspapers. The development of sports at Johns Hopkins was similarly tentative and sporadic during these years.[16]

• •

All this did not distract President Smith from something that had gone unnoted for several years. He had not forgotten the plan to extend the college property. In May of 1890 he again put the question to his consultors—who included none of those he had queried four years earlier. In the new group the name of Thomas Sheerin, one of the pioneer scholastics at Loyola, reappears. He had been ordained and now was teaching logic, metaphysics, and ethics to the seniors.

Smith was nothing if not direct during a meeting with his consultors early in 1890. He proposed to erect a new building. One of the consultors distinguished this proposal into basic questions: whether or not new facilities were needed and then whether the new building should merely fill the land currently held by the corporation or be extended along Monument Street. On each of these subpropositions the consultors divided, so Father Smith took no action. It was probably just as well, because the provincial soon made clear that he did not favor any additional purchase of land.[17]

Francis Smith, however, was not easily deterred from the goal he had set. The college's debt hung like the sword of Damocles over his plans, and so he worked diligently to reduce this threat. In the fall of 1890, Father John Ryan, Loyola's premier historian, recorded (on a typewriter, be it noted): "By good management, he [Smith] has reduced the debt to small figures."[18]

A few months later the house diarist wrote: "It is said that the debt, formerly about $150,000, is now liquidated."[19] Possibly the passage of a few months accounts for the relative finality of the second accounting, but the use of indirect discourse raises a small question. Financial reports (at least at Fordham in this era) were a marvel of contradiction and inconsistency—pleasantly wondrous to the eyes of a latter-day president.

On this basis the question was again put to the consultors, but not by Father Smith. He was excused from the November 21 meeting, where the visiting provincial presided. This ensured the freest possible discussion and a probing inquiry by the provincial; the consultors now unanimously recommended what only a few months earlier had divided them. Furthermore, the consultors were united for extending the college along Monument Street.[20] Father Smith had finally succeeded. It would be years before this resounding "yes" was embodied in brick, steel, glass, and wood, but the essential decision to remain at Calvert Street and to expand had been made. The question of whether or not this was the better course would be asked again shortly after the project was completed. As is evident in this turn of events, Jesuit obedience does not inhibit practical reasoning.

In the provincial catalogue for 1891 Francis Smith's name came to the top of the list of superiors, an event followed often enough by a transfer. Normally, appointments were changed during the summer months—after commencements and after the loose ends of the academic year had been tidied up. Nevertheless, Father Smith was transferred to the New England mission band late in May of 1891.[21] There was no evidence that the change was prompted by any fault. Its suddenness served as a reminder that the ways of God and superiors cannot be fathomed.

7

Full Bloom

The keynote of Father Smith's term had been *fortiter in re;* that of his successor, John Abell Morgan, was *suaviter in modo.* Loyola's ninth president was a native of Maryland who, though no less determined and energetic than his predecessor, was a more effective communicator and unfailingly courteous. Father Morgan's personality was marked, a colleague wrote, by that "old time Maryland geniality and *bonhomie,"* which won for him (and for the college) "a large circle of friends in Baltimore."[1] The pace of activity at Loyola continued to increase under President Morgan, but his personality gave the college a buoyant, even relaxed, air.

• •

Morgan was no stranger to Baltimore or Loyola. As a scholastic he had taught freshman and sophomore classes during the last years of the Civil War. He was reputed to be a competent instructor, although perhaps too mild in his dealings with recalcitrant students. He was noted for his love of books, not so much those of ancient Latin or Greek writers, but the works of Dickens, Lamb, and Thomas Hood. The most noteworthy event of Morgan's first stint at Loyola was the attempt in June of 1864 to draft him into the Union army. This bizarre episode, as noted in an earlier chapter, was curtly ended on order from Secretary of War Edwin Stanton.

The quarter-century between this earlier tour of duty and Morgan's return to Baltimore was spent in various pastoral and administrative engagements. He was ordained to the priesthood in 1872 by James Gibbons under circumstances which strongly suggest that these two native sons had met in wartime Baltimore and had formed a close bond of affection. For the next eight years John Morgan served in the Jesuit mission band as a preacher and retreat director. Then this itinerant life gave way to a short respite at Woodstock College, where he edited the *Woodstock Letters*, which kept Jesuits of the New York–Maryland province informed about the doings of their brethren.

There followed a period at Saint Joseph's Church in Philadelphia after which Father John Morgan was sent to Saint Thomas Manor in Charles County, where he was again in his native habitat. Here and in neighboring Saint Mary's County (his birthplace) the map is sprinkled with names like Morganza, Abell, and Morgantown—testimonies to the early presence of his progenitors. Here he would play host to Cardinal Gibbons in late May 1891, when he received news of his appointment to the presidency of Loyola College. The congratulations of his old friend must have been warm indeed.

Morgan's arrival at Calvert Street produced hopeful expectations among the Jesuits. "It is generally thought," wrote the house diarist, "that the College will under his guidance take a new course of prosperity."[2] This anticipation must be understood in its context. Although the college had served Baltimore almost forty years, its development had been slow, to say the least. It was embarrassing for its Jesuits to compare their current enrollment of nearly 130 students with that of Boston College, which, although founded later than Loyola, boasted three times that number. Was Boston to best Baltimore on this too? The competitive spirit that Jesuits sought to instill in their students also resonated among them, and under their new leader Baltimore's Jesuits anticipated campaigning more successfully.

Their expectations were at least partially realized. Enrollments surpassed the seemingly unattainable level of two hundred during six of the nine academic years for which Father Morgan was responsible. This was a particularly remarkable achievement, because his tenure coincided with the financial panic of 1893 and the resulting period of economic stringency. In the past such an economic climate had usually meant declining enrollments, but this proved not to be the case for Loyola and many other American colleges, although other Jesuit schools were suffering declines in enrollment.[3]

One factor in this development was an expansion of the scholarship program. To the six funded grants Father Morgan added two new categories. In the first, the "medal boy" (the one with the highest grades) from each parochial school would pay no tuition. The second group was composed of lads chosen by their pastors for financial assistance, a bit of patronage that may have been intended to secure the good will of these priests.

The scope of the college's largesse can be gauged by the fact that there were thirty-six churches in Baltimore and fifteen outside listed on the scholarship registers. A few of the recipients were Leo Scheurich (1903), whose career as a physician eventually took him to Tomah, Wisconsin; Eugene Jendrek (1905), who became a bookkeeper; Thomas Toolen (1906), a latter-day archbishop of Mobile; and Edward Burke (1906), a lawyer who would defend a president of Loyola College in a unique court suit. There were many others, some who left after only a brief bout with Jesuit education. Father Morgan's intention was larger than merely increased enrollments. He planned ultimately to eliminate all tuition payments at Loyola—in accord with the basic policy of the Jesuit order.

What he did not do, however, was increase enrollments by lowering standards. Indeed, where previous diarists had discreetly recorded only the total number admitted, under Morgan appeared such notations as "8 received, 19 rejected." The mere recording of such figures represented a change, although the casualty figures were not always so large. Nor was it only at the portals that excellence was required. After the mid-1892 examinations the house diarist noted the rule that any student who failed to achieve a grade of 60 would be demoted to next lower class. It is clear from the consultors' minutes that this policy was enforced.[4]

As often happens, rising expectation was met by more successful effort. There had been years in the past, sometimes several in a row, when no one persisted to graduation. From this point on, however, every year would end with the awarding of at least several baccalaureates.

• •

Basic to Loyola's development was the distinctive style of operation that Father John Morgan instituted. One might expect a man aged 53 merely to deepen well-worn grooves. On the other hand, it is precisely a person of Morgan's age and experience who could give less heed to the cautions that afflict younger men who have a lifetime to lose if they make a grave mistake. Within the church it was the age of Gibbons and Pope Leo XIII—a period notable for significant initiatives. In American educational circles there was a vehement and detailed review under way that was fully reported in the press and in professional journals. All these factors contributed to the way President Morgan operated at Loyola.

Morgan chose to act unlike any of his predecessors or immediate successors. He persistently sought to involve the trustees, consultors, and faculty in the decision-making process, where previously these individuals had been restricted to minimal functions or ignored for years at a time. President Morgan left no doubt who was boss, but he convened the trustees and consultors often. He gave them substantive business to consider, recorded their formal recommendations, and did not act against their expressed views. This was not the way things had been done.

It had not been *de more* even for the faculty to meet regularly. Before the Morgan era, occasional references to faculty meetings appeared in the records, but neither what was discussed at these gatherings nor the procedure was ever specified. The faculty, it should be recalled, consisted of only nine or ten with about half of them scholastics, and there was no need to keep minutes in so small a group. Now, every Thursday evening the teachers met in the scholastics' recreation room. The chore of presiding at these meetings Father Morgan yielded to the prefect of studies. The first five minutes were reserved for discussion of the prefect's concerns and the next ten minutes were controlled by the faculty. There was a preliminary go-round during which each raised whatever question was bothering him. Presumably the more urgent matters or problems mentioned by several members were given priority, and discussion was then in order. Mercifully, attendance was obligatory only during these first fifteen minutes.

More important than these procedural regulations was the spirit in which they were applied. Father Morgan's general attitude was reflected in the musings of the prefect, Francis Powers. Powers was convinced that merely bringing up a subject, "whatever it may be," was worthwhile because doing so provided notice that such a matter was under consideration. This left each faculty member "free, at his leisure, to express to the Prefect, or his fellow-teachers his opinions."[5] The emphasis obviously was on free and unhurried dialogue—something quite feasible in the small, homogeneous faculty of Loyola at that time—rather than on the imperatives of parliamentary procedure. It would be anachronistic to use the word *collegial* as it is understood today, but one can discern the lineaments of the concept in President Morgan's mode of operation. Whether he was an original or was applying the example of someone else cannot be ascertained. Whatever their source, his departures from the common impression of how authority was exercised among the Jesuits are worthy of notice.

The first scheduled faculty meeting, at least, ended with a "haustus," a familiar though loosely defined institution in Jesuit houses. Its meaning varies according to the liberality of the host and the balance in the contingency account. At a minimum it indicated that the prefect had provided such refreshments as would ensure that the participants would rejoin the rest of the community in good humor. That each faculty meeting ended with such éclat can be doubted—nowhere later in the prefect's diary does that cheering word appear.

This change of general style did not presage the eruption of democracy at Loyola. Father Morgan acted in accordance with a familiar and basic principle on matters he considered of critical importance. When the plans for the new wing of the college were being studied early in 1897, he stipulated that each of the consultors was to examine the architect's drawings.[6] He wanted their views—*plural*—and did not propose to face a single, concerted position. In this he was acting on the old Roman principle that authority is weakened to the extent that any connection among subordinates is strengthened.

· ·

No one outside the Jesuit community would have been aware of all these intramural developments. Nevertheless, signals that a new era had begun at Loyola were quickly displayed. At Father Morgan's first commencement (which occurred less than a month after his return to Baltimore), the college awarded its first honorary doctorates. Three well-known public figures—Leo Knott, Michael Mullin, and Thomas Whelan—were invested as Doctors of Laws, *honoris causa.* Other colleges and universities (including some of the most esteemed) were lavish in granting honorary doctorates. To maintain its value, this new accolade from Loyola was awarded only three more times during President Morgan's term—mostly to distinguished alumni.[7] Father Morgan's successors have been almost as restrained as he in the exercise of this pleasant but undefined public function.

The direction and momentum of change were apparent in the new edition of the catalogue. Customarily the text, with amendments and the latest data, was delivered to the printer shortly after graduation. So it may have been with the 1891 edition, although the doubled length and thorough revision suggest that Father Morgan took the task with him to Saint Thomas Manor, where he vacationed that summer with a group of Loyola students.

Under his editorial pen, much remained unchanged. Much, however, was added by way of elaborating Loyola's educational philosophy and justifying the limitation of its offerings to the classical curriculum. The ideas were familiar enough, but the presentation was smooth—

almost conversational in tone. No aspersions were cast at institutions that differed from Loyola. Morgan's aim obviously was to make a positive, attractive offer to prospective clients rather than to seek support by way of a more aggressive or denunciatory strategy.

Father Morgan's irenic approach was evident in a small change in terminology. Until then, the catalogue had consistently referred to Loyola as a university, in accordance with the broad powers granted in its charter. This passage was now modified to state only that the Maryland government had granted Loyola "full *collegiate* powers and privileges" (emphasis added). The change of words was legally insignificant and the college would, under President Morgan, experiment with several graduate programs. The character of these programs, however, differed from those pursued at the Johns Hopkins University, which all Baltimore now simply called "the University." John Morgan saw reason for accommodating that local convention.

Morgan's determination to attract more students was evident in all editions of the catalogue during his years at Loyola. Course outlines, required textbooks, and even subjects were modified with an unaccustomed rapidity. Whether other Jesuit schools were similarly engaged is not recorded in their histories. To detail all these permutations would be tedious. Suffice it to note that the interest in history and the natural sciences was continued. According to the course descriptions of the 1891 catalogue, for instance, college sophomores would be discussing the United States Constitution on the basis of their readings of Bryce, Story, Tocqueville, and Fiske. This last author has since lost his academic cachet, but the others have remained intellectually respectable. The sophomores would be studying chemistry from a text equally solid, and Ira Remsen's *Introduction* was named in more than a few catalogues of the era.

• •

Another sequence required even more attention to history. In fact, the subject, arranged by epochs, was included in each of the four collegiate years. The focus was on the significance of the period rather than mere chronological sequence, however. Freshmen were exposed to a general review of the development of Western civilization. The historical attention of the sophomores was directed to the church as a generally conservative force with a sympathy for the poor. The students in the third year wrestled with the philosophy of history. The texts for this course were Schlegel, Saint Augustine's *City of God,* and Bossuet's *Universal History.* These certainly have a Christian and Catholic tendency, but they could be included in any such course. The final year was a history of philosophy. Aristotle and Saint Bernard were the terminals of the first semester's sequence, and the second began with Abelard and came up to the present day.

The heavy dosage of history was not administered at the expense of either philosophy or the natural sciences. In fact philosophy, previously restricted to the senior year, was now expanded to the junior year. The juniors acquired skills in dialectics and major logic that they then used in the study of ontology and cosmology. The seniors were guided through natural theology, psychology, and ethics. The sophomores took general chemistry, and in the next year physics. Seniors were scheduled for "physiological psychology," which was described in the catalogue as "lectures on the anatomy and physiology of the nervous system; localization of the cerebral function; connection of the nervous mechanism and mental conditions and actions." These curricular changes, in the main, came at the expense of modern languages and mathematics.

Among the leading faculty lights during the Morgan years were Father John Ryan (1861) and Doctor William Tonry, the Maryland state chemist. For Father Ryan there was no gap between the literary and scientific cultures. He maintained a more or less extracurricular interest in history while teaching classes in mechanics and astronomy. To deepen interest in the natural sciences Father Ryan in 1893 organized the Secchi Scientific Society. Tonry offered a more intensive study of the sciences. Tonry's life before he came to teach at Loyola was quite fascinating and will be described below.

The new extracurricular activity was named for Angelo Secchi, a Jesuit astronomer who pioneered the classification of stars by their spectra. Briefly in the late 1840s he taught at Georgetown. The new society's program consisted in the main of field trips and visits to industrial sites where members observed what had been described in general terms during class and students presented formal papers. One of the early programs of the Secchi Society was a student symposium on astronomy. Observers on this occasion included Cardinal Gibbons, William Pardow (the Jesuit provincial), Havens Richards, who was president of Georgetown, and Daniel Coit Gilman. So formidable an audience would not have been risked unless the student presentations demonstrated a high level of scientific knowledge. Similar confidence is evident in the distribution of these student presentations in pamphlet form. The explicit theme of the presentations was that despite the urgings of some, there was no real conflict between science and religion.

Nor was this a one-shot affair. Throughout the 1890s scientific exhibitions were presented regularly by the students. One of the most notable was a demonstration of X-rays only two years after their discovery. The scene was recorded in a formal portrait of the students, the apparatus, and Francis Tondorf, a Jesuit scholastic who undoubtedly was the originator of the project. Some of the X-ray pictures taken with the apparatus have survived in an album preserved in the archives of Saint Ignatius Church. A year later, the subject of a similar program was "wireless telegraphy," then also on the world's technical and scientific frontier.

Probably the most lasting effect of the scientific emphasis during the Morgan era was in the lives of two students. J. Albert Chatard (1898) went on to become a protégé of Sir William Osler, one of the "Four Doctors" at the Johns Hopkins Medical School. Doctor Chatard's distinguished career in Baltimore spanned the first half of the twentieth century.[8] From the same class Joseph Didusch took a different route. He became a Jesuit and for nearly three decades served as a demanding taskmaster who taught biology to Loyola's premedical students. Verbal adroitness might suffice in other classes; in Father Didusch's there was no substitute for accurate knowledge, detailed observation, and logical reasoning. In the lives of both these men the discipline of science was combined with genuine service to fellow humans and a devotion to religion.

During the Morgan years explicit attention was paid to religious exercises. Now the day's work began in the classrooms with a joint recital of an Our Father and a Hail Mary, but only the latter was said before dismissal in the afternoon. Time spent in formal instruction in religion, previously only a half-hour per week, was raised to a full hour. Even at that such instruction represented a relatively small investment of effort and time and must have presupposed a greater involvement of the home, the parish, and other institutions than today appears adequate. No change was made in the policy established at Loyola's foundation: students who were not Catholic continued to be exempt from formal instruction in religion.

• •

Father Morgan's approach to explaining the purpose of Jesuit education was equally latitudinarian. In the catalogue he argued that the classical curriculum produced men better able to master the details of business or any other special training than someone instructed in a more narrowly focused course or one significantly modified by the elective principle. When he addressed the students at the start of an academic year, these generalities were given practical formulation. The headings for his remarks on one such occasion stressed pleasure in learning, in responsibility, and in self-culture. His peroration was framed between the rubrics of "Eye to the main chance" and "Be Some Body."[9] This appeal to self-interest and activity, rather than to an otherworldly idealism and passive acceptance, was characteristic of the spirit of the Jesuit order and was quite congenial to an American audience.

The accession of Father Morgan to Loyola's presidency quickly resulted in tangible improvements at the college. On their return in September 1891 the students and "other gentlemen" were duly impressed by the general repairs and renovations completed during the summer. Morgan's words sounded so clear and attractive that 140 students were enrolled on opening day, 10 more than at the end of the previous year. By December registrations had risen above 190. Riding this momentum, President Morgan purchased the six houses on Monument street. An intervening brick wall was knocked down, and soon the buildings were being used both for classes and for the meetings of various affiliated organizations. Additional gymnastic equipment (punching bags and a springboard) was placed in the enlarged yard for the exercise and mild exhaustion of youthful spirits.

The improvements included additions to the faculty, as noted above. By far the most significant was William Tonry, who provided a recognized competence in things scientific, especially in chemistry. In his governmental capacity, he was the guardian of Baltimore's water and milk supplies. More glamorous, however, had been the occasions when his testimony proved crucial in various murder trials. Indeed, it was his analysis and work in the early 1870s that laid the basis for acquitting Mrs. Wharton of the charge that she had poisoned General Ketchum. At various times Tonry had taught at the Maryland and Peabody institutes, as well as at the Baltimore Medical College. He appeared among the Baltimore City councilmen and briefly served on the board of school commissioners. He was indeed a public figure.

More fascinating than his professional life, however, was Tonry's personal history. After graduating from Georgetown in 1865 he briefly became a member of the Society of Jesus, but his predilection for going on unauthorized picnics prompted the suggestion that he might find life outside the order more to his liking. What resulted was employment at a chemistry laboratory attached to the surgeon general's office. This interlude of several years ended abruptly when he became engaged to Anna Surratt, daughter of the woman who was hanged for her supposed complicity in the plot to assassinate Abraham Lincoln. Tonry's superiors threatened him with immediate dismissal if he went through with the marriage. Within days after the nuptials, William Tonry was discharged from the employ of the United States.

Washington's loss, however, proved to be Baltimore's and eventually Loyola's gain. Doctor Tonry joined the faculty in 1892 and was given space in the Monument Street houses for his classrooms and laboratories. Despite his fame, Tonry does not figure prominently in student recollections or in the various diaries kept at the college. Two of his sons graduated from Loyola; one, his namesake, would occasionally spell his father in the classroom.[10] The elder Tonry's employment at Loyola ended about the same time Father Morgan was transferred to another post. Five years later Tonry died.

• •

A more cheering addition to the faculty was Father Patrick Quill. He was well over six feet tall and red haired. He had a competence in several languages, including Sanskrit, that duly impressed his students. More to the point was his quick tongue. When introduced to one sly gentleman who thought the name Quill might be a nom de plume, Patt (for so he ordinarily signed his name) retorted, "Well, that's a matter of o-pinion." Father Quill loved his native land, and his students could easily divert him from "the glory that was Greece and the grandeur that was Rome" by asking him about the oppression of Ireland.

Once, boastfully, he told the class that a new chef for the Jesuit community had formerly been sovereign of the kitchens at Delmonico's—that legend among American restaurants. Murmurs of disbelief prompted Quill to assert excitedly that the chef could bake the best pies in the world. One knight-errant defended the honor of Baltimore's womanhood by claiming greater culinary skill for his own mother. Father Quill vowed to convert all doubters.

Some days later he walked into his classroom and smilingly placed a pie on his desk. Just as he was about to slice through the crust, one fellow objected that none could eat it because the filling was mincemeat and the day was Friday. "Begorra," said Quill, "I thought it was Monday" and proceeded to cut and distribute wedges of the pie. Even the scrupulous fellow had at least a nibble and all agreed that it was indeed the best pie they had ever eaten.[11]

Among other additions to the college in this era was Father F. X.

Brady, who arrived in 1893. Although his titles and specific responsibilities changed often, he remained an administrative sparkplug at Loyola for almost two decades. His Irish and Pennsylvania Dutch ancestry combined to produce a man of personal magnetism and persistent effort whose talents lay mainly in the field of public relations. It became his constant aim to keep the name of Loyola in the consciousness of Baltimoreans by a stream of almost daily notices to the press. Furthermore, Brady was probably the decisive influence for listing Loyola in the *American College and Public School Directory* well before a number of the leading Maryland and Jesuit institutions were so advertised.

To his diligence, in part, must be attributed the growing enrollment at Loyola, although his aggressive style contrasted with the smoother tone of his immediate superior. The difference between them was summarized in the couplet recalled by Gower Lawrence (1898):

Morgan played the organ

Brady beat the drum.

Nevertheless, they worked well together. In fact, Father Morgan was soon heard to predict that Brady would some day serve as president and rector of Loyola College.

Father Brady's talents and energy were made evident in a number of ways. Within a year after his arrival he began publishing a journal for the parishioners. At the time only two other Jesuit parishes in America issued such a periodical. Its immediate object then was to provide direct and regular communication. Its monthly schedule of services and events, of notices, announcements, comments, and observations now provides data on the life of the college until after World War I.

In the penumbra beyond the faculty were other stalwarts associated with Loyola. William Lapsley, who briefly attended the school in 1870, returned later to take up the post of porter. Until a decade ago, any person who rang the bell at a Jesuit school was likely to be greeted by someone like him. The porter was a tactful but firm guardian of the doorway to the cloister, saving the inmates from needless scurrying. For nearly three decades Lapsley, as he was known to students and Jesuits, was an abiding, friendly presence in the college community.

Another such assistant was Madison Fenwick, a black man who worked in the kitchen. He had less occasion to meet the students, so there are fewer references to him in publications and reminiscences. Still, the house diary contains notations attesting to the affection in which he was held by the Jesuits. On March 6, 1899, his brother-in-law was buried from Saint Ignatius Church—certainly the doing of Fathers

Morgan and Brady. A quarter of a century later, a solemn requiem mass was offered at the same altar for Madison Fenwick.[12] Although the mores of Baltimore, which required racial segregation, were not overtly challenged, the older attitudes of the Jesuits found continuing, if limited, expression.

• •

During President Morgan's term the college inaugurated something entitled the university extension. This was a broad administrative device for offering courses, some in continuing education but others organized into undergraduate and graduate degree programs. Classes were offered mainly in the evenings, but the graduate courses in particular had the character of tutorials and were scheduled at the convenience of teacher and student. The extension program tended to focus on philosophy and ethics, although courses in languages and other subjects were occasionally offered in the Monument Street houses. The instructors, especially for the philosophical subjects, included faculty stars such as Fathers Thomas Sheerin, Anton Mandalari, William Brett, and John Morgan.

From 1893 to 1900, fifty-eight men secured the bachelor's degree, thirty-two the master's, and five the doctorate. In the doctorate program men were tutored in preparation for a comprehensive examination, rather then being participants in regular classes or research. A special science and philosophy course, unattached to any degree program, enrolled seventy-six members including David Streett, dean of the Baltimore Medical College. Three years later a postgraduate course of unspecified subject matter attracted thirty-eight registrants.

What is interesting, however, is that in both the degree and other courses there were men whose signatures already sported M.D.s, LL.B.s, D.D.S.s, A.B.s, M.A.s, and other degrees. Remarkably, a number of Baltimore's professional men were willing to invest their time, effort, and money in the Loyola programs. Why? For most, it was probably the congenial, stimulating, and distinctive atmosphere generated by the Jesuits and their students. A few, like Frank Boland, had been regularly enrolled at Loyola but for one reason or another had dropped out before graduation. Boland for a time fancied the glamorous life of the New York theater but eventually decided there was more of a future in the law and hotel management. He therefore arranged to complete his studies through Loyola's extension and secured his bachelor's degree in 1894.

The experience of Charles Cohn was different. Already admitted to the bar, he felt the need for a liberal education and enrolled in the evening undergraduate program. In 1897 he was awarded his A.B. diploma. The following year found him a member of a nondegree course for which he received a gold medal at commencement. Finally, in 1899, he successfully completed the requirements for a master of arts degree. Cohn was already employed by the Consolidated Gas Company (precursor of today's Baltimore Gas and Electric Company) and would eventually rise to become its president and chairman of the board. This connection must have played some role in the tendency of the company to favor recruiting its managers from among Loyola graduates.[13] Both Boland and Cohn would later be numbered among the college's generous benefactors; they and many of their fellows from the extension joined the alumni association. The undercroft of the alumni chapel is named Cohn Hall for Charles Cohn.

. .

The inventiveness and energy of Father Morgan were not exhausted in formally academic enterprises. He converted the Loyola League, which his predecessors had founded, into the Catholic Association of Baltimore. His characteristic approach to such matters was evident in the fact that despite its title the association was open to "*all* gentlemen." John Morgan apparently thought it better to start something potentially productive than to ponder and carefully define what he was doing—a common and pragmatic trait among Jesuits.

The only formative principle of the Catholic Association was to involve prominent Baltimoreans and thus to connect them with Loyola. The first president was Richard McSherry (1860), whose lineage included a mayor of Baltimore and otherwise entitled him to membership and even high office in the Society of Cincinnati. McSherry had attended Loyola for all but the final year of his college course, when he transferred to Georgetown. His successor as the association's president was Colonel Richard Malcolm Johnston, a writer of considerable celebrity. His work was identified with the dialect and bracing humor of the Old South. The other officers and members of the board of directors included such familiars as Leo Knott, Charles Bonaparte, Edgar Gans, Thomas Whelan, and Alfred Shriver.

The association met in one of the Monument Street houses. A large room served as an auditorium and other rooms provided space for classes or small gatherings. The members took lessons in conversational German and French, listened to debate on the merits of the gold and bimetallic standards, heard a Johns Hopkins student from Japan explain the causes of the current Sino-Japanese War, were roused to outrage when a lecturer from Catholic University described the horrors being suffered by the Armenians. On one occasion they were informed on the subject of "flying machines" by the secretary of the Aeronautic Congress, and at another time Father René Holaind, professor of ethics at Woodstock, held forth against those who asserted that state officials had a proper role in education. The object of his attack was a professor at Catholic University who held the opposite view. Scattered across the schedule of the association were occasional reminiscences about the Confederate soldier and service on the staff of General Robert E. Lee.[14] In a word, the program was a mixed bag of culture, information, and public discussion from which the members could choose at will. The association does not seem to have survived the deaths of McSherry and Johnston and the remodeling of its Monument Street headquarters, all of which occurred about the turn of the century.

Despite his tendency to positive thought and action, President Morgan could sound a negative note on occasion. Shortly after his installation he sought to dissociate the college from a private enterprise that for more than a decade had operated out of the basement of the college. During Father McGurk's tenure a group of parishioners had organized a savings and loan association. The Loyola Perpetual Building Association was eminently sound, but for this very reason rumors circulated that the college was becoming wealthy from the connection. Father Morgan wanted a physical separation.

The association accepted the decision, but until better facilities could be secured it merely moved to the other side of Calvert Street. The bothersome rumor persisted, and Father Morgan asked the association to issue a public statement denying any connection between it and the college.[15] In good time this was done, and eventually the enterprise found a more suitable location at North Charles and Preston streets. It has grown to be the largest such financial institution in the state, its name changed to the Loyola Federal Savings and Loan Association.

• •

Athletics, which had previously received only sporadic attention, became a permanent, if subordinate, part of the college's life during the Morgan era. The source of the decision cannot be accurately traced. No anecdote connects the portly Father Morgan with the playing field, and it was Brady who made the first announcement of plans for a sports program. The decision reflected the fact that intercollegiate sports were becoming a national craze. Equally important was the swell of Baltimore's pride with each triumph of its professional baseball team, the Orioles. Other Catholic schools might view such developments with alarm, but Jesuit institutions such as Georgetown, Fordham, and Boston College had teams on the playing fields.

In September of 1894 Father Brady inserted a brief notice in the newspapers that Loyola would have a football team as soon as a suitable practice space could be secured, but it was not until the start of the school year in 1896 that the necessary foundation was established. The athletic association was revived and a practice field at North Avenue and Washington Street (a good distance from the school) was acquired. No trace of this first season's endeavors has survived except for the names of winners at an October "field day." Though lightly regarded nowadays, such events were then common features at American colleges. Some anonymous archivist clipped newspaper notices of field days at Princeton, Cornell, Yale, Harvard, and Mount Saint Mary's and pasted them alongside the news from Loyola. The last recorded only a modest performance, but it was a beginning.

Spring brought new plans, and a regular uniformed baseball team was organized. Officially it played eleven games, with no eligibility rules and only rudimentary scheduling practices. Loyola's opponents included the Calverts (presumably the Calvert Hall nine), the Crescents, and the North Avenue Athletic Club. The opening game, against the Calverts, was a 25 to 15 triumph, but the next, with the North Avenue Athletics, resulted in a 0 to 8 shellacking. This was soon redressed when the Loyolas and North Avenue met again, this time with an 11 to 9 Loyola victory. On the final tally the Loyola team won eight of its eleven games—a respectable record for a start. Why the one-run loss to Rock Hill College was not included in that first year's record must remain mystery.[16]

The ensuing seasons in both football and baseball might better be passed over. Much character may have been pounded into the Loyola athletes in these years, but the scores reflected an inglorious reality. Only after several years of bleak experiences did the pattern change. The turn into the next century brought a new gymnasium and a coach for the Loyola teams: "Prof." John Doyle of the Baltimore Athletic Club. Even these developments, necessary as they were, did not bespangle the sports record at Loyola with many wins. They meant, however, that Loyola athletes could now give a better account of themselves.

· ·

The crowning physical achievement of John Abell Morgan was erection of the buildings that completed the structure on Calvert Street. Others might doubt or demur, but he decided and built. In the first issue of the *Journal of Saint Ignatius' Church* (February 1894), he appealed for contributions from the parishioners. This became a regular feature of the publication. How much was collected in response to this appeal is nowhere listed, but beyond the sum what was important was evidence of broad interest and support—and these Fathers Morgan and Brady obtained in full measure. Despite Brady's wholehearted support of this effort, he was convinced that Loyola would soon have to move to another location north of the city.

By January of 1897 Thomas Kennedy, an architect specializing in churches and school buildings, submitted plans for approval, which Father Morgan referred to his consultors. There were two phases in the project. The lesser was a remodelling of the old hall and library into six additional classrooms. The more impressive was the building of a five-story "Monument Street wing," joined to the existing structure by a four-story "link building."

Kennedy succeeded in maintaining the balance and harmony of the Calvert Street façade without resorting to a merely symmetrical reproduction of the features of the older structure. "The frontage of our buildings" exclaimed Father Edward Devitt from Georgetown, "is one of the sights of the City, and must certainly impress on the minds of numerous passers-by on this most busy thoroughfare, the presence of Catholic education in their midst. The new college building is of massive proportions."[17]

Incorporated in the new structure were a magnificent hall ("pronounced by competent judges perhaps the finest in the Province," Devitt reported), a gymnasium (of unique character, one that was most helpful to Loyola's basketball teams), a student chapel, more classrooms, and chemistry laboratories. The cost for completing these plans was estimated at over one hundred thousand dollars. At one stroke, President Morgan had the Associated Professors assume a new burden nearly equal to the one they had recently discharged.

Among the Jesuits there was some difference about how to raise the money. Father Morgan preferred to rely on a private appeal to affluent friends of the college. He, like Father Early, was reluctant "to talk money from the pulpit." The house consultors urged a public campaign. As often happens on such occasions, the differing views were combined into one general program. Loans from within the Society of Jesus, private donations, and the net proceeds from the fund appeal and a fair accounted for nearly half the cost. The remaining $56,000 was covered by a promissory note from the college to George Blake, the contractor.[18]

The process of building was rapid enough, despite the usual delays. Demolition of the Monument Street houses began in the spring of 1898. In the rubble a cherished landmark disappeared, the little store in the basement of the corner house where for years Loyola students "at noon 'feasted' on the penny bun." Trouble arose when the foundation was dug, creating a delay and raising the cost. The roof was supposed to be on by Christmas of 1898, but bad weather postponed closure until the following March. By June the new hall was the site successively for the high-school and the college commencements.

• •

It was not until fall of 1899 that the formal dedication took place. On Thursday, October 5, books and chalk were hurriedly put away at ten o'clock, and classes adjourned to the hall. There a formal procession brought Father Morgan, the Loyola faculty, visiting clergy, and Cardinal Gibbons on stage. The ceremonies opened with Gounod's "Viva Cardinale" and a few words of welcome from Father Morgan. After a series of orations, all joined in singing the "Te Deum" and Cardinal Gibbons blessed the new building. He had the final word, for when young Eugene Saxton (1904) made the customary request for a holiday the cardinal granted three. Whether decorum was rent by any boyish whoops was not noted, but the prefect in his diary recorded the scrupulous execution of the cardinal's largesse.

More quietly, Saint Ignatius Church and the rest of the old college building were renovated. The most noteworthy change was the installation of electric lighting. Here, as in the new wing, gaslights were still attached to the fixtures in case of a power failure, but it was evident that the past was yielding to the future. Various other additions and refurbishings added almost another $50,000 to a grand total of $150,000 on the debit side of Loyola's ledgers—a sum that would not be repaid for twenty years.

Long before then, John Abell Morgan had been relieved of that responsibility. Given his impressive achievements, it might have seemed fitting to leave Father Morgan at Loyola for still another term, even though he had already served nine years and such a lengthy appointment as rector then was rare. Had he been reappointed, Father Morgan would have presided at the celebration of Loyola's fiftieth anniversary; next to the college's founder, who had a better title to such consideration? Nevertheless, on August 29, 1900, after nine years and three months as Loyola's president and rector, Father Morgan resigned.

The transfer came none too soon, for within a year he suffered a stroke. He was still able to get about and was eventually assigned to the community at Gonzaga College in the District of Columbia. In these surroundings he whiled away his remaining days, reportedly writing his reminiscences; but no trace of these writings can be found. In 1906, another stroke ended his mortal life. Of John Abell Morgan, the Baltimore *News* wrote that "with all his push and enterprise, he was never a hurried man; he had time to spare and a handshake for every person who came to him, and this unfailing courtesy and kindness of heart gave him a warm place in the thoughts of thousands."[19] With his departure, one of the most innovative periods in the history of Loyola College came to an end.

8

Jubilee

E ven under the most favorable circumstances it would have been
difficult to maintain the momentum of the Morgan era, and Loyola's development in the next few years was restrained by the new debt.
Furthermore, the stability of leadership that the college had enjoyed
and under which it had prospered for nine years was not continued.
Noticeable in the immediate post-Morgan years was a distinctly Bostonian influence at Loyola.

. .

Father Morgan's immediate successor was William Brett, an erudite
Jesuit who taught philosophy during Morgan's final year. He was elected
president by the board of trustees but was only the vice-rector of the
Jesuit community. Everyone assumed that in due time Brett would be
confirmed with full authority, but on the eve of graduation in 1901 the
dean noted in his diary: "June 22. Saturday. A new rector announced
today; house taken by surprise—Rev. John F. Quirk—Fr. Brett made
rector of Woodstock."[1] Brett officiated at commencement but shortly
thereafter left for Woodstock, where for six years he directed the education and spiritual development of many young Jesuits.

Brett's term at Woodstock nearly coincided with Father Quirk's at
Loyola. Quirk, like Brett, was a Bostonian. Quirk was a former student
of Father Robert Fulton, one of Loyola's original incorporators. For several years Father Quirk had served as prefect of studies at Boston College. He was 42 years old when he picked up the rector's napkin ring.
His manner was formal, even a bit stiff; he was considered "a man of
very great dignity and precision." A eulogist would sum up his matured
purpose: "The more perfect was John Quirk's hourly intent."[2]

His earnest character is demonstrated in the one anecdote regularly
associated with his name. Quirk's reputation as a Latinist prompted an

eminent non-Jesuit institution of higher learning to invite him to give a discourse on Virgil. The occasion required, he thought, some more elegant ending than the customary "I thank you"; after his peroration, Quirk paused and gravely uttered the Latin word *Dixi* ("I have spoken"). A befuddled orchestra conductor took that as a cue. He jumped to the podium, grabbed his baton, and waved the ensemble into Dan Emmett's stirring tune with homophonous title.[3] What then flashed through Father Quirk's mind is not recorded (possibly for the better), but the glee of his Jesuit brethren is evident in the relish with which they have repeated the story. However, they have discreetly obscured just where the incident occurred.

• •

Quirk's sense of style was well suited to the earliest major public event of his term, the 1902 celebration of Loyola College's fiftieth anniversary. In February of that year the Johns Hopkins University marked its first quarter-century, with Loyola's president among those attending. Father Quirk avoided the exact anniversary of Loyola's founding, and chose to associate the ceremonies with an apposite holiday— Thanksgiving.

The college's week-long festivities began on Monday with a solemn requiem mass for all graduates, "old students," and benefactors. The following evening was brightened by a banquet in the Club Room of the Hotel Rennert, then still one of Baltimore's finest hostelries. Although the menu and speeches drew their attention, reporters also remarked on the fact that the banquet hall was decorated with bunting in the Loyola College colors—light blue and gold.

When these colors were chosen, by whom, and why, went casually unrecorded (as did so much else about the school). The blue ribbon by which the seal was attached to the diploma in 1853 may have provided the inspiration. The only firm record is a 1901 reply to an inquiry from Georgetown wherein the Loyola colors are identified. Presumably the growth of varsity athletics and the example of other institutions had prompted the decision. From then until the move to Evergreen, the teams, events, and pomps of Loyola College were marked with blazons of blue and gold—however and whenever the colors had been selected.

The program of the alumni banquet certainly met Baltimore's standards. With black coffee and cigars came the inevitable round of toasts and speeches. The special guest of the evening, Ira Remsen, the new president of Johns Hopkins, gave the main address. Naturally he paid tribute to the American Jesuits and their "various colleges and universities." He ridiculed young men who preferred to go abroad for an education when equally good facilities were available in America. Remsen derided those who attended American schools that offered such innovative degrees as an "M.W.W." Searching through the catalogue in which he found this cryptic notation, Doctor Remsen said, he concluded that the letters meant "made of wax work"—a pleasantry likely to evoke laughter from such an audience.

After more oratory and a poem, President John Quirk proposed the final toast. It was entitled "Loyola: The Home-Harvesting." On this theme he cited the biblical warrant that made every fiftieth year a jubilee and enjoined men to renew contacts with their origins. To Loyola's sons, said Father Quirk, this applied also in a spiritual sense. Their roots lay not in a certain building or location, but in the principles for which the college stood; these he summarized as obedience to God and to lawful authority, charity for "God's special children"—the poor—precedence of the spiritual in human life, acceptance of the resulting alienation from "the world at large," recognition of life as a probation where "success waits on effort and toil." Living by these precepts was the means to secure true happiness and peace.

These brief remarks led to the toast proper. Noting that it was the eve of our unique national holiday, Thanksgiving, John Quirk asked the company to join him in "this prospering pledge and sentiment": "Loyola: the home-harvesting! Strong truths well lived; pure hearts well fired with love of God and man,—such be the sheaves of her spiritual reaping."[4] The resonance of that aspiration would be caught and fixed when later the key phrase "Strong truths well lived" was adopted as the college's motto. It summarizes Loyola's informing purpose.

• •

The last part of Loyola's jubilee was a presentation of *Macbeth*. As he entered the great hall, Father Patrick Dooley, the prefect of studies, was pleased to see all the seats occupied and even a hundred or more spectators standing. He surely fussed at the delay in starting the program, but something held up the orchestra. After its arrival and the performance of specially written music, James Kearney delivered a brief curtain-raising speech in which he noted the advantages of drama as an educational instrument and its historical cultivation at Jesuit institutions.

When the curtain finally went up, what proved most startling was the absence of Lady Macbeth. Her speeches, adapted to a change of gender, were delivered by William Storck (1905), identified in the pro-

gram as "Lulach, stepson of Macbeth." The author of this "glaring in-
congruity," as it was described by an otherwise sympathetic observer,
was nowhere given credit—or blame. Fortunately, this bold (if ill-
advised) experiment was not repeated; instead, the ancient convention
of using males for female roles was continued in the Loyola College dramatic productions as it was elsewhere in Baltimore and nationally for
many more decades.

William Kean, the scholastic-impresario who directed the play, was
more than moderately pleased with the review in the *News*. The anonymous critic took exception to the "Lady Macbeth–Lulach" experiment
but otherwise thought the production "really worth seeing, . . . costumes . . . all appropriate, . . . scenic effects surprisingly good." The
scenery was better, he said, than that featured in a play then being
offered at one of Baltimore's professional theaters. "Music . . . well selected and rendered," continued the writer, "the whole stage management . . . remarkably good." The actors, if appropriate allowances
were made, "did very well indeed."[5]

The triumph was repeated on Friday night for "an audience," Father
Dooley wrote proudly, "that some declared even larger" than at the first
performance. After the final bows, Kean rewarded his actors and stage
crew with "an excellent supper." Saturday was busy with students taking
down the decorations and tidying up. For Sunday Father Dooley con-
tentedly wrote: "Time to reflect on the tired feeling—and that the Jubilee was a success."[6]

Although Father Dooley was obviously referring to the events of
that week, his focus and judgment might properly be expanded to cover
the whole period for which the celebration served as a climax. In fifty
years the Jesuits, their school, and Saint Ignatius Church had become
familiar and integral parts of the life of Baltimore. The press coverage,
as well as the participation of representative community leaders, made
this evident.

• •

A school, however, should be judged by the quality of its alumni.
The most complete list indicates that about 2,600 boys and young men
had enrolled at Loyola during its first half-century. Only about 15 percent continued to the college level, and more than half of these completed the full course to graduation. Some of those who did not graduate
from Loyola transferred to other schools, such as Georgetown, from
which they received their diplomas, and they properly are numbered
among Loyola's "old students." A larger number left the college to enter

regular employment. During the latter half of the nineteenth century, Baltimoreans still tended to think it rather impractical, if not spend-thrift, to finish a college course unless one were preparing to enter a learned profession. And how many more doctors, lawyers, and clergy-men did the city need?

The small proportion of graduates to registrants should, however, be viewed in a broader, contemporaneous context. Even Georgetown, with its larger, more varied constituency and better facilities, was grad-uating only one out of seven, and the ratio for all twenty-three Jesuit colleges was less than one in twenty-five.[7] The high attrition rate was not peculiar to Jesuit colleges, and in the face of such discouraging sta-tistics the dedication of teachers was marvelous.

Loyola's product might be judged from Father John Ryan's *Historical Sketch.* Shortly after the anniversary celebration he printed what he ac-knowledged to be little more than a compilation of graduation lists, newspaper clippings, and reminiscences. Included, however, were no-tations of names, occupations, and other data on graduates, as well as on 350 or so "old students." These obviously were the ones with the closest ties to Loyola. Together they account for almost a quarter of the total number that had ever registered at the college.

Table 8.1 provides the information that a respectable proportion of alumni were in the learned professions. But the largest category in the table is business. This was probably the result of the relatively smaller proportion of entrants who stayed the full course. A college degree was not then considered necessary for a career in business, but one out of five business-connected alumni had secured a diploma. Two among the teachers were university professors. Among the miscellaneous were two chemists, several architects, an artist, a farmer, and a theatrical entre-preneur. Although Father Ryan did not summarize his data in statistical form, his citations and references adequately documented the college's claim that its program of studies served as a base for virtually any career a young man might envision.

Numbers are convenient tools, but measuring quality—especially of a school's alumni—requires attention to individual persons. So far, references to the later careers of Loyola students have been widely scat-tered in this narrative. Now, like Cornelia, the legendary Roman ma-tron, this alma mater has the occasion to display a few of her family jewels. The selection is small, spread across the five decades, and chosen for the distinctive color or brilliance of the individual mentioned.

Among Baltimore's physicians could be numbered such Loyolans as

TABLE 8.1   Careers of Selected Loyola Alumni, c. 1902

	Numbers	Percentages
Doctors	105	19
Lawyers	74	13
Clergymen	80	14
(Jesuits)	(34)	(6)
Businessmen	164	30
Government officers	10	2
Teachers	7	1
Accountants	11	2
Graduate students	17	3
Engineers	8	1
Writers	11	2
Miscellaneous	68	12
Total	555	99

Charles Morfit (1859), who served as a surgeon in the Confederate navy; Ernest Neale (1879), later regent and professor of medicine at the University of Maryland; and Albert Chatard (1898), whose brilliant career has already been noted. Raphael Espin (1855) returned to Cuba, and Jacob Arnold (1873) went to California.

Loyola's proudest claim on the local bench was William Fisher (1855), who led a civic reform movement during the 1870s. In addition, Maynard McPherson (1856), wandered to Brooklyn, and his classmate William Gleeson served as a judge in the Dakota Territory. Harry Clabaugh (1876) settled in the District of Columbia and there served honorably on the bench. Their brethren at the bar included Oscar Wolff (1879), Austin Fink (1883), who evoked Father Ryan's accolade as "an esteemed attorney, and leading Catholic," and Mark Shriver (1902). For the sacred ministry Loyola had helped prepare Randolph McKim (1858), who later became rector of Washington's Protestant Episcopal Church of the Epiphany; Jerome Daugherty (1869), president of Georgetown (1902–5); and John McNamara (1897), later auxiliary bishop of Washington.

This brief sampling indicates that Loyola contributed effectively to the professions traditionally associated with the old collegiate curriculum. The literary emphasis in the classical course was evident in the life work of other alumni. Eugene Didier (1859) became the first sympathetic expositor of Edgar Allan Poe's art and produced a number of books about him. This would earn him notice in the *Dictionary of*

American Biography. The literary impulse, however, tended among Loyola's alumni to express itself in work on the Baltimore newspapers. The contributions to journalism of a few drew recognition and honor. John Roche (1882) was at the time of the jubilee president of the Journalists' Club. More significantly, Joe Callaghan (1891; longtime city editor of the *Herald*) was credited by H. L. Mencken with cleansing the Baltimore press corps of "boozy," roustabout reporters and bringing in a newer, cleaner, more self-respecting breed. Mencken said that Callaghan "discovered some of the best" of Baltimore's journalists. Later, Edwin Murphy (1893) became managing editor of the *Evening Sun* where, with Hamilton Owens, he shared the honor of discovering some of the brightest writing talent of the twentieth century. William Unduch (1893) joined the Sunpapers' staff in 1897 and became business manager.[8]

In richly panelled boardrooms, too, there could be found former students and graduates of the college. Henry Judik (1865) and Thornton Rollins (1863) successively served as president of the old Maryland National Bank (no connection to the same name institution of today). At Metropolitan Savings, there was Francis Dammann (1863), whose namesake graduated from Loyola in 1900 and chose to pursue a legal career in Chicago. Father Ryan proudly claimed Frank Hambleton (1875) for the college and duly noted his "recent" bid to buy the Western Maryland Railroad. At the B&O, Vansant McNeal (1866) was treasurer; his son Preston was graduated a few years before the jubilee. On the staff of the Pennsy was Bernard Courlaender (1881), and managing the United Railway and Electric Company (later named Baltimore Transit Company) was William House (1879). The views of all these Loyolans on how they reconciled the competing claims of God and Mammon would be interesting, but in Baltimore fashion they chose to live quietly without prattling advice at later generations. Their careers enlarge a point made earlier in regard to the gas company: Loyola College was the school from which local enterprises recruited their managers.[9]

Loyolans were involved also in more modest enterprises. The Helldorfers (John, 1888; Francis, 1889) were noted brewers in a city where such a reputation was hard to achieve. Their equally skilled competitor was Henry A. Brehm (1887). Real estate claimed the endeavors of Frank Caughy (1881), Hammond J. Dugan (1885), and Paul Quinn (1895). Father Ryan identified Joseph Linsmeier (1881) as a "manufacturing pharmacist" without noting what panaceas he offered the public.

The Laroques (Emile, 1878; Regis, 1880) and Joseph Ayd (1881) were listed only as "druggists." Few years of the college registers were devoid of a Hoen from one or another branch of this well-known tribe. Many of its scions entered the family business of printing and lithographing and made it the nation's largest. Though fewer in numbers, the Baldwins enrolled in each succeeding generation at Loyola and went on to substantial careers in architecture. Among the alumni involved in construction were Francis Gibbons (1858), who erected many of the lighthouses along the Atlantic coast, and John Curley (1888), whose "monument" was a faculty endowment for Loyola College.

Not all chose such well-trodden vocational paths. James "Addie" Kernan (1860) became one of Baltimore's most flamboyant showmen. Six-day bike races, burlesque (then a family style of entertainment), vaudeville, light opera, and classical drama were all performed on the stage of one or another of Kernan's theaters and arenas. For a time he expanded his operations into the District of Columbia, and he built the Lafayette Square Theatre in Buffalo for the Pan-American Exposition of 1901. All this was preliminary to Kernan's "million dollar triple enterprise"—the combination of the Maryland and Auditorium theaters with his hotel. The building, at the corner of Franklin and Howard streets, drew those who wanted to see "the highest class vaudeville" or who wanted to be seen in a lobby finished in the most opulent decor. Meredith Janvier, reminiscing about turn-of-the-century Baltimore, took special delight in recalling the marvels to be seen and savored at Kernan's.[10] James Lawrence Kernan endowed the hospital in northwest Baltimore that still bears his name.

Another of the city's benefactors, Henry Walters (1870), briefly attended Loyola. He entered during Father Early's second term but transferred to Georgetown about the time Loyola's founder was again appointed as that school's president-rector. In 1903 Walters remembered his Loyola interlude with a small gift. He would eventually endow his native city with a magnificent art gallery at the southeast corner of Mount Vernon Square.

The endowment of Charles Ghequiere Fenwick (1898) was neither financial nor limited to Baltimore. He lived a rich, useful life as a scholar of international law and as a diplomat. Doctor Fenwick was one of the founders of the Catholic Association for International Peace, which in its early days sought to rally support for the League of Nations. During the presidency of Franklin Roosevelt he was regularly included in American delegations to various conferences where the Good Neighbor policy was gradually embodied in treaties and protocols. Fenwick, throughout his career, wrote so copiously and effectively on international affairs that in a professional survey conducted in the 1960s he was identified by other scholars and writers as one of the most influential figures in this field.[11] The college joined in recognizing his achievements with an Andrew White Medal.

There is another perspective from which the college's product may be viewed. Since the late 1880s the social arbiters of the city have published the *Blue Book Baltimore Society Visiting List.* In 1902 educational affiliations were not included (as they are now), but a reasonably careful comparison of the alumni lists and the *Blue Book* yielded thirty names common to both among the several hundred in the *Blue Book.* These men were members of such clubs as Bachelor's Cotillion, Green Spring Valley, and Elkridge Fox Hunting Club. The college was well aware of this association with Baltimore's upper class and included note of it in the descriptions it contributed to a nationally distributed handbook of colleges and universities.

· ·

This point is important, especially in regard to the founding purpose of the school. It is commonly asserted that Jesuit colleges were established in America to provide the means by which the sons of recent and relatively poor immigrants could become upwardly mobile. Often it is assumed that this was the only objective, and that all Jesuit schools were particular instances of a single policy. Whatever may be true of other Jesuit institutions, the student body of Loyola College has throughout its history spread along a broader socioeconomic spectrum. Sons of later and poorer immigrants were certainly enrolled, and they studied side by side with descendants of "adventurers" who arrived much earlier in the *Ark* and the *Dove.* Most came from homes located at neither extreme.

Furthermore, the religious and ethnic mix at Loyola has always been richer than at a number of other American colleges. Its registers consistently list a student body in which at least 25 percent were not Catholic. Some were Jewish and others had no religious association. Although most names were Irish or German or "American," many others had a French, Italian, Spanish, Greek, Lithuanian, Polish, or other Slavic flavor.

Loyola College was in fact a meeting ground for young men and families unlikely to associate in the larger community. Although there was rising a still persistent myth that America's cities were a vast melting pot, we now know that there has been less contact and communication across ethnic and religious lines than was previously assumed. The prevailing ideology and social practice was not that of melting the ethnic strains into a new alloy, but rather of assimilation or Anglo conformity.[12] In this endeavor, educational institutions (public and private) were among the preferred instruments for Americanization.

On such a bleak social landscape, Loyola College appears as something of an outpost on an urban frontier. Here members of various tribes and societies met on friendly terms, as did their analogues at similar stations elsewhere. For Baltimore Catholics, however, Loyola never served as the social and cultural citadel that Boston College provided for that city's Catholics. No Loyola graduating class gave two-thirds of its members to the priesthood, as did the class of 1877 at Boston College. Futhermore, Loyola did not come close to the general average for American colleges of every church association; elsewhere it was to be expected that half the graduates would enter the sacred ministry. Only 14 percent of Loyola's alumni became clergymen, and a small but significant number of those entered Protestant ministries. Furthermore, Loyola's presidents and other Jesuits gave little evidence of conforming to the rigid cultural mold adhered to by their counterparts in Boston.[13]

Loyola College undoubtedly helped to perpetuate a certain subculture in Baltimore, but one that encompassed a notable presence of those who were neither Catholic nor Christian, and one that was responsive to the prevailing cultural currents in the city—such as they were. Loyola College was a place where Catholic, Protestant, Jewish, and other men and boys met and acquired a common and, as they felt, a distinctive citizenship through a shared experience of Jesuit education. Association at the college became the basis for many lifelong friendships. A similar process may well have been going on at other American colleges, and it might be possible to rehabilitate the melting-pot metaphor through a closer study of this aspect of college and university life. For the moment, however, there is not enough information for comparison or generalization.

· ·

Between the college's jubilee in 1902 and that of Saint Ignatius Church in 1907, President Quirk directed Loyola. The experimentation of the Morgan years gave way to adjustment of the curriculum, with a regular fourth year added to the high-school program. In other small but indicative ways, the high-school and college departments at Loyola were gradually being differentiated. A similar development, which originated at Saint Louis University in 1887, was occurring at other Jesuit institutions. They were slowly responding to one of the more generally accepted reforms championed by President Eliot of Harvard and to persistent complaints that Jesuit schools were losing their former prestige because of the continuing presence of small boys. This process would reach a climax at Loyola when in 1921 the college division moved to a new site.

Some interesting changes were made in the collegiate curriculum during Father Quirk's term. The overall workload was restored to nearly the level of ten years earlier, and all the major subjects were retained. This might create the illusion that no changes were occurring. In fact, a recent historian of Fordham insists that what curricular changes were made at that school between 1865 and 1916 "could not have been startling."[14] At Loyola, however, the relative weight of standard subjects was undergoing significant (maybe even startling) alterations.

Changes in the curriculum at the college have been summarized in table 8.2. The figures in table 8.2 belie abstract assumptions about the rigidity and focus of the Jesuit curriculum, at least as it was offered at Loyola.

It would be more satisfying if the pattern of changes at Loyola could be placed in a larger context through comparison with other Jesuit schools. Unfortunately, no comparable data have been made generally available, although curricular development at Boston College in 1900

TABLE 8.2   Loyola College Curriculum Changes, 1895–1912
(In Percentage of Curriculum Hours)

	1895–96		1901–2	1906–7	1911–12
Latin	22		17	15	16
Mathematics	21		5	4	4
Greek	15		12	13	10
English }	13	English	14	12	7
History }		History	10	8	7
Political Economy	0		1	2	0
Philosophy	12		18	17	23
Sciences	10		11	17	14
Languages	3		2	2	2
Religion	2		5	6	9
Elocution	2		5	2	2
Electives	0		0	2	6

appears similar.[15] This is a slim reed on which to rest a generalization, but the cohesiveness of the Society of Jesus suggests that, allowing for adjustments to local circumstance, such changes and reallocations were occurring at other Jesuit institutions, as well.

The appearance and growth of electives in the Loyola program may seem incongruous at a time when the Jesuits were denouncing Charles Eliot's electivism. Whereas Eliot dispensed with virtually all course requirements, however, at Loyola electives merely served to accommodate differences among the students. The response of the Johns Hopkins University to Eliot's ideas was to follow a distinct but middle course for its undergraduates. They could choose among seven groups, but courses were prescribed within the group.[16] Other colleges and universities groped for ways to change, but not too much or too fast.

Electives at Loyola included courses in various sciences, pedagogy, law, mathematics, languages, literature, and economics. The core of liberal studies, however, remained intact. In addition, students who wished to augment their program could add "optional studies" to the established course load. Whether any availed themselves of the opportunity to work harder and longer is not recorded.

What is obvious from the table is drastic changes in the time allotted for various courses. Mathematics was reduced most heavily, from nearly 25 percent of the college program to only 4 percent. Latin, esteemed the very heart of the *Ratio Studiorum*, was adjusted downward from 22 percent to 16; Greek suffered a comparable paring. English and history briefly enjoyed an increment in their total allocation of time, but they were eventually reduced to the earlier apportionment, with English the main loser. Presumably the various exercises and translations in Latin and Greek did double duty and so justified this constriction. The brief experiment with political economy was abandoned by 1912.

Although the natural sciences were afforded a modest increase in time, the main beneficiaries of these changes at Loyola were philosophy and religion. From occupying only 12 percent of the curriculum, philosophy virtually doubled its share and religion underwent a fourfold increase. Hereafter these two subjects provided the specific difference that distinguished Loyola College and comparable Jesuit schools within the genus institutions of higher learning. Philosophy and religion were being augmented as a prophylaxis against the materialism and skepticism that were seen to afflict the age. Pope Leo XIII in 1879 gave impetus to a renewed emphasis on the philosophy of Saint Thomas Aquinas in Catholic schools, and this provided them with a distinction they cultivated until the 1960s.

Now listed in the Loyola College catalogues were the major propositions to be proven "syllogistically and adequately" (according to the phrase that would appear on tests). Juniors in logic labored to establish that "universal skepticism, as a fact, is impossible; as a theory, it is self-contradictory." In ontology they proved that "every being is one, true and good; evil consists in the absence of some perfection due to a being." Senior cosmologists prepared to argue that "the origin of the world could not be explained by any theory of self-existent matter." In psychology they defended the free will of humans, and in natural theology they made an effort to demonstrate the existence of God "by metaphysical, physical, and moral arguments." In ethics they reasoned that "happiness" is "man's last end" and that it consists in "the perfect knowledge and love of God." They argued that murder, suicide, duelling, and lying were forbidden by the "natural law." This sample of theses should bring a flash of recognition to anyone who has studied scholastic philosophy under the Jesuits.

• •

During Father Quirk's term a rumor that Loyola would soon be moving from Calvert Street was published. With the announcement of the purchase of the Homewood site by the Johns Hopkins University, speculation seems to have risen that Loyola too was contemplating a relocation, and not far from the new home of the university. On August 11, 1905, the *American* headlined a story: LOYOLA COLLEGE SEEKS NEW SITE.

The item was created from two circumstances. First, James Cotter (1882) had recently acquired a tract of land in the Homewood-Guilford neighborhood; second, Father Brady had answered a reporter's questions somewhat ambiguously. Although he denied that the college was negotiating with Cotter, Brady alluded to intramural discussions about moving. He also observed that Calvert Street was becoming less desirable as a school location—among other reasons, the Pennsylvania Railroad was planning to expand its nearby freight yards.[17] From this, an enterprising reporter turned what otherwise was a pedestrian story into a scoop. Some unidentified hand wrote across the clipping preserved in the files at Saint Ignatius: "No truth to this." So indeed it may have been in regard to current negotiations with Cotter, but Father Brady had already predicted that Loyola would be moving. When a few years later planning began in earnest, it eventually came to center on Cotter's tract.

President Quirk's term was notable for some remarkable student displays. In the spring of 1904 Clarke Fitzpatrick, a freshman, volunteered to be examined on the whole text of Homer's *Odyssey.* He was prepared to translate any passage in those twelve thousand lines, analyze the grammatical aspects, scan the verse, and describe "the Homeric world, the heroes, and deities of the Odyssey and the nature and laws of epic poetry." That was quite a program—especially for a lad of 15. His examiners were two members of the Loyola faculty, a Jesuit scholastic from England who was attending Johns Hopkins after studying at Oxford, and Doctor Leslie Shears of the university.

"For more than an hour," wrote one reporter, "an uninterrupted volley of questions was hurled at the youthful scholar. . . . With charming modesty of manner, readiness and ease, . . . he invariably went to the heart of every question and grappled with each successive difficulty with extraordinary penetration and dispatch."[18] When the board of examiners finished, members of the audience were invited to continue the quizzing. The result was a triumph for Clarke Fitzpatrick and, of course, for his school. Informally, he was promised an instructorship at the Johns Hopkins University upon graduation from Loyola.

Because this Wunderkind repeated the performance in each of the ensuing three years (substituting the *Iliad,* the tragedies of Sophocles and Aeschylus, and Plato's *Republic,* in turn), it was assumed that he was destined for an academic career. Instead, Fitzpatrick joined the Sunpapers staff after graduation, and by 1920 occupied the city editor's desk. He then transferred to United States Fidelity and Guaranty Company, a locally headquartered firm, and soon became vice-president in charge of publicity and advertising. Eventually, he was named secretary of the company and a member of its board of directors, posts he retained until his retirement in 1956. He maintained a close connection with Loyola through its alumni association and service on various advisory committees.

He was not the only stellar performer during this era. Another Loyolan became the Maryland finalist for the newly established Rhodes Scholarship. To qualify for the empire builder's bounty, a candidate had to pass the entrance examination for Oxford and to have exhibited "fondness for and success in outdoor sports; the highest qualities of manhood . . . and moral forces of character."

In mid-April of 1904, twelve Marylanders from a variety of schools appeared at Johns Hopkins to take the academic tests. There were two hopefuls from Loyola—Hale Dineen (1904) and Elliott Ross (1902)—

of whom only the latter survived the written examination. Then it was for a committee made up of the presidents of Johns Hopkins, Saint John's, and Western Maryland to apply the other criteria specified by Rhodes, and they chose Loyola's Ross as the state finalist. The choice certainly attested to his personal qualities, and by association those of his alma mater. Though his candidacy did not survive the nationwide review, Ross's later life indicates that the Rhodes Scholarship board of Maryland had indeed been perceptive in their choice.[19]

• •

About the mid-point of President Quirk's term, Baltimore suffered a major disaster. On Sunday, February 7, 1904, a spark from a discarded cigar or a match ignited the stock of a downtown dry goods store. Quickly flames leaped up and engulfed building after building. The devouring monster outraced the efforts to contain it. The wind, blowing from the southwest, drove the fire northward along Charles and Calvert streets. From the attic of the Morgan building, the Jesuits anxiously watched as the wall of flame and smoke advanced toward the college. Some members of the community climbed on the roof to extinguish burning embers, and in the glow of the fire they patrolled the rooftop throughout the terrible night. At midnight the wind shifted to the northwest and drove the fire back along the harbor.

On Monday morning the fire was still raging out of control. Some Baltimoreans watched the smoke and flames that marked the expiration of still more business establishments, while other inhabitants tried as best they could to resume their regular work. Even though no trolleys were running, nearly half the student body reported for the first bell at Loyola. They were soon dismissed to rejoin the rest of the awe-struck spectators. By evening the fire was brought under control, but during the terrible days and night seventy blocks of Baltimore's business district had been reduced to ashes, rubble, and ruined walls.

For the next few days the inhabitants and officials of Baltimore surveyed the damage and thought of rebuilding. The trolleys were out of service for several days and some Loyola students walked four miles to get to school. On Tuesday as on Monday, at least half the students were in attendance, and now the regular schedule of classes was resumed. Among the absentees was Hale Dineen, a senior, who had "been summoned," the prefect noted in his diary, "by his militia company to guard the burnt district."[20]

By Friday the mayor of Baltimore had appointed a committee of civic leaders (including some Loyola alumni) to plan the reconstruction of the center of the city. Their initial discussions were aimed at a more attractive and more functional layout, but differences of opinion soon stymied these larger plans. What resulted was a rapid reconstruction in accordance with private interests. The general burden and the slighting of the public weal so depressed the mayor that he committed suicide, although the prevailing mores required avoidance of so obvious a verdict. The mayor's death prompted the Loyola house diarist to observe ruefully, "It would need Job's patience . . . to make a modern city."[21]

• •

President Quirk's term coincided with a nationwide recession. Although the American economy had entered a period of general prosperity, the years 1903 and 1907 were scarred by financial panics. As in the past, financial stringency affected Loyola by a decline in enrollment. Other Jesuit schools were suffering too, and some attributed the decline to the connection between college and high-school programs. In the nineteenth century, especially before the Civil War, the reputation of Jesuit schools towered above that of other institutions, but since then colleges in general had improved. The Jesuit schools now had many more Catholic competitors for what was still only a small proportion of the population, and other institutions were offering a greater variety of programs.[22]

The effect of this development along with the financial stringency is evident in the response Father Quirk made to a questionnaire from the new Federal Bureau of Education. After Father Morgan's departure, there occurred a precipitous decline in enrollments to the level that obtained before his presidency. During Quirk's six years, Loyola College suffered loss of almost a quarter of its student body, so that in June of 1907 enrollment totalled only 127. Fortunately, every school year was still climaxed by the awarding of baccalaureate degrees. Declining enrollments could hardly be blamed on the tuition, because this was now only $50—as Father Quirk reported in 1907. One can imagine the amazement of the person in the Bureau of Education who read Loyola's report. Was it possible to conduct a college on such a slender fiscal base? The Jesuits at Loyola were doing it.

The decline in enrollment at Loyola had local cause. Enrollments declined not because of the overall increase in the workload, or because the teachers at Loyola had become more demanding—though both were true—but rather because John Quirk proved insensitive. Very early in his term, just before the Christmas holidays, he issued a decree to this effect: "Students are hereby informed that the giving of class presents to Professor or Teachers is forbidden . . . by order of the Revd Father Rector."[23] The goodness of his motives cannot be doubted, nor the propriety of the ukase, but Quirk's brisk New England manner and rigor seemed inappropriate to men and boys raised in the warm climate of Baltimore. Many of them near the end of the 1907 school year in-formed the prefect that they did not intend to return in September. It took some time for the Jesuit provincial to recognize this threatening development, but when he did Quirk was transferred to Fordham.[24] In his stead, a Loyola alumnus (class of 1879) and former president of Boston College, Father William George Read Mullan, was appointed president and rector of Loyola.

9

New Starts

When Father Mullan returned to Baltimore late in August of 1907, he was something of a celebrity. He had been the protagonist in a famous confrontation with President Charles Eliot of Harvard over the merits of Jesuit education. Such an eruption was surprising in both men. Harvard had until then maintained generally cordial relations with Catholics (of Yankee ancestry, at least), and Eliot had by this time come to view the Irish even as a positive force in American democracy. Mullan, for his part, was something of an educational reformer among Jesuits and was notably even-tempered. They seemed an unlikely pair of opponents.

Nevertheless, in 1898, shortly after Read Mullan became president of Boston College, he had to know why Harvard Law School, after including Boston College for some time on its list of schools whose graduates were admitted unconditionally, chose to drop Boston College and two other, but not all, Jesuit schools. Thereafter, Boston College students who gained admission to the law school were required to take additional courses and to maintain a higher grade. To President Mullan's inquiry Doctor Eliot replied that the university's experience with a "considerable number" of Boston College graduates had been uniformly disappointing.

Quite naturally Father Mullan asked to discuss the matter with Harvard's reviewing authorities. In the course of this conference he discovered that they had not rated institutions, that there were in fact only a small number of applications to either Harvard College or the law school from Boston College alumni, and that the records of the few matriculating students provided no clear evidence one way or the other. When Mullan summarized the data for President Eliot's consideration, he received in reply a new charge, now leveled not merely at Boston College but at Jesuit colleges in general. They, "in the judgment of Harvard University," said Eliot, were "inferior to such schools as Dartmouth, Rutgers, or Connecticut's Wesleyan." Father Mullan asked what the basis for this adverse judgment might be, but obtained nothing from Eliot except an offer to provide a confidential statement for the Jesuit's private instruction. This President Mullan refused, because the condition hampered his ability to defend Boston College when Harvard's sudden disapproval was a matter of public knowledge.

The correspondence, still carried on privately, had reached a logical impasse. It was brought to an end when an exasperated Mullan (of whom it was said otherwise that none could "rouse his Irish") finally hurled back a bitter, and nowhere substantiated, charge at President Eliot. Harvard, he wrote, was attempting to discredit all Catholic education in order to increase its own registration. Although declining enrollments at Boston College and at other Jesuit schools might be noted to extenuate Mullan's outburst, obviously nothing informative from Eliot could be expected after that. The exchange followed what some might consider an archetypical pattern in dealings between Irish and WASP.

The Mullan-Eliot correspondence was published several months later, because the Boston College alumni association asked for a report. Father Mullan responded by giving the full text of the exchange to the Boston newspapers. His action was not prompted by the unfortunate way the discussion had ended, but had been stipulated in his early and more irenic letters to President Eliot.[1]

There the matter might have remained if Charles Eliot had not hoped to have the last word. In a magazine article promoting his elective system, he took a gratuitous swipe at Jesuit colleges. He described them as essentially changeless, offering only a "uniform prescription" for all students, ultimately "impossible and absurd" in an enlightened, democratic age. Warming to his theme, Eliot went on to lump the Jesuit curriculum with the study of the Koran in Moslem countries. Furthermore, he drew the attention of his readers to the fact that both these systems of education were under "ecclesiastical" direction.[2]

How were the Jesuits to deal with this new and even more public denunciation? The editor of the *Atlantic Monthly* (in which Eliot's essay had appeared) received a veritable blizzard of indignant letters—sixty or more from Jesuit school officers alone, he later recalled. One correspondent, Father Timothy Brosnahan (himself a former president of

Boston College, then a teacher at Woodstock, and eventually a member of the Loyola College faculty), offered to submit a suitable reply to President Eliot. The editor consulted Eliot and found him unwilling to participate in any further exchange on the subject; Brosnahan, moreover, was informed that it was the policy of the *Atlantic* to avoid controversies. The effect on Timothy Brosnahan can be imagined, because even his eulogist characterized him as "never politic or diplomatic."

Foreclosed from the most appropriate forum, he turned to less prestigious publications and reprinted some of his articles as pamphlets. He mounted a direct, trenchant attack on the logical inadequacies and factual errors in Eliot's description of Jesuit education. Nor did he avoid ad hominem jabs—such as declaring the president of Harvard to be "pathetically naive." That, Father Brosnahan thought, would certainly get a rise out of Eliot, and he gathered more data for the next round.

In particular, he set about collecting affidavits from Harvard graduates to prove that it was possible to receive the Harvard diploma with only a concatenation of snap courses. With these he planned to argue more concretely what he had already suggested through a close comparison of Harvard's elective curriculum and that of Boston College. However, weeks passed with no reply from Eliot. When the silence continued through many more months, Father Brosnahan turned his dialectical and rhetorical skills to other targets. For the president of Harvard that must have been a welcome diversion, because about this time there was laid on his desk an intramural report that concluded an undergraduate at Harvard could indeed maintain high grades with little or no study.

• •

Even without benefit of this decisive bit of evidence, the reaction to Brosnahan's polemics was favorable. The *New York Sun* and a Columbia University professor gave the palm to the Jesuit, especially for making Eliot's "alleged facts and iridescent theories" a laughingstock. Another educator from the University of Pennsylvania was grateful that someone had challenged the new imperative, namely "the way they do [things] at Harvard."

The one contrary note was struck, curiously enough, within the Jesuit household. Some of the allegedly "more sophisticated Catholics of the Buffalo area" were convinced that the development of their Canisius College was hampered because of the Brosnahan-Eliot controversy. In their view, the image projected by the Jesuit polemicist was not progressive, but seemed to justify a charge of obscurantism. By association, they thought, this unfavorable judgment was being applied to Canisius as well.[3]

The practical results of this affair were meager. There was no melioration of Harvard's policy toward Boston College graduates for many years. The cause célèbre, electivism, had peaked and was already in decline. Jesuit schools and other liberal arts colleges were moving toward programs that combined a core of required studies with various elective elements. This development should have made it possible for the Jesuit schools to reestablish themselves in the mainstream of American higher education. They, however, now preferred to emphasize their specific differences, especially in the requirement of Latin, philosophy, and religion, rather than the ways in which they continued to resemble other institutions. They contrasted their conserving of the liberal arts tradition with the innovations adopted by other American colleges and rallied the support of the faithful.

The long-term reactions to this affair have varied. When Henry James later published his two-volume biography of Eliot, he passed over this episode in silence. At Boston College, excerpts from Brosnahan's essays were used for a time to teach persuasive argumentation, but that passed many years ago. With the cooling of tempers and recollections, a less partial judgment has been registered by a historian generally favorable to Eliot. Hugh Hawkins is convinced that in this instance President Eliot's performance was "paternalistic and lacking true acquaintance" with either Jesuit schools or Catholic institutions in general.[4]

There are more than a few links between this controversy and Loyola College. Father Mullan, Eliot's initial protagonist, shortly afterwards returned to his alma mater. Father Brosnahan would join the Loyola faculty in 1909 and serve here with distinction until his death in 1915. The last ripple from the Mullan-Eliot exchange had been stilled many years before Harvard found occasion for awarding an honorary degree to an incumbent president of Boston College.

The most startling but not well-known connection, however, involved a Loyola graduate. Edward Hanlon (1909) applied to Harvard Law School and was immediately admitted without being forced to submit to the special conditions then required of Boston College graduates. From Cambridge, young Hanlon registered his favorable impressions of the university, but also his nostalgic remembrance of a school where the "Sources of Knowledge" (professors) and students enjoyed a real friendship, where one got to know the names of one's classmates. Harvard's larger size and the Harvard system shut "out much interest from the student and much chance for an influence for good from the professor," Hanlon opined.[5] Had Hanlon been statistically inclined he might have noted that there were over 4,000 students then at Harvard with almost half that number in the graduate and professional schools. He completed the course at the law school in the usual number of years and joined one of New York City's most respected legal firms.

Hanlon's admission to Harvard and Harvard's uninterrupted acceptance of Georgetown graduates may serve to narrow the issue in the controversy a bit. Harvard's new regulations did not discriminate against all Catholics, or all Irish, or all Jesuit-educated students. Its animus was aimed only at those who came from Boston College, Holy Cross, and Fordham. Why this particular combination?

•   •

By the time Father Read Mullan was appointed president of Loyola, the dispute between Harvard and Boston College had disappeared from the active attention of both participants and spectators. His problem now was how to reclaim the disaffected students who had warned at the end of the preceding school year that they would not return. As soon as he arrived in Baltimore he launched his campaign. Eager, personable young Jesuit scholastics under the direction of Father Michael Purtell visited the families of the recalcitrants and other prospects. What inducements (if any) they offered must be left to conjecture or be deduced from the changes instituted during Read Mullan's brief term.

When the roll was called two and a half weeks later, it was clear that Father Purtell and the scholastics had succeeded—modestly. There were 129 young men and boys registered on September 10, two more than at the end of the preceding year. By the following Monday, when Loyola's new president celebrated the traditional Mass of the Holy Ghost, the figure had risen to 149. There must have been an added heartfelt note to his opening prayer, "*Introibo ad altare Dei, ad Deum qui laetificat iuventutem meam*" (I will go unto the altar of God, to God who gives joy to my youth). The final tally for the year was 177, well above registrations in each of the previous five years.

This encouraging result was achieved through a combination of factors. About 60 percent of the enrollment consisted of students who were continuing their education at Loyola. Some of the recruits were assigned to a special classics section comprising transferees and others in need of additional tutoring before they could be introduced to the regular program of Latin and Greek.

What about those students who did not return in September of 1907? Some, in fact, did continue their education: Stanislaus Cook, for instance, returned a few years later and then transferred to the University of Maryland Law School; he was eventually admitted to the bar. Vincent Keelan, George Strohaver, and Henri Wiesel chose to enter the Jesuit novitiate. Their schoolmate, Leo Barley, preferred the local seminary and the archdiocesan priesthood. Most other absentees, however, are lost to Loyola's records and memory.

• •

A significant factor in attracting additional students to the college was certainly Father Mullan's deep roots in the Baltimore Catholic community. A great-great-aunt had been one of the first to join Mother (now Saint) Elizabeth Seton's new religious and teaching order. His grandfather, Jonathan Mullan, was sexton of the cathedral for over thirty years. It was he who had been startled that October morning in 1851 when Archbishop Kenrick made his unexpected appearance. The office passed to Read Mullan's father, but he soon resigned and turned instead to a marble-working enterprise.

Both Read and his younger brother, Alexius Elder Mullan, attended Loyola College for a few years before entering the Jesuit novitiate. Both inherited the Mullan traits of soft-spoken amiability, and Read in particular was judged a true "southern gentleman." In his brother this amiability was combined with an especially bright intelligence. Father Elder Mullan would be called to serve in the central administration of the Jesuit order in Rome.

For Read Mullan the years between his departure from Baltimore and his return to Loyola were marked by increasing responsibility. He was ordained in 1890 and served a stint as prefect of studies at Fordham. There followed five difficult years (1898–1903) as president of Boston College, where he continued the moderate program of curricular changes and reforms instituted under his predecessor, Father Timothy Brosnahan. Mullan even tried to rally the presidents of other Catholic colleges in America to this reform effort—with little noticeable effect. Unfortunately, the Brosnahan-Mullan amendments of the Boston College program did not arrest the decline in the college's enrollment.[6]

Having surmounted that immediate problem at Loyola, President Mullan turned his attention to winning the allegiance of the students and to promoting the school's development. For both these objectives he could count on the able and energetic assistance of Father Joseph

Mulry, who had served under him at Boston College. At the earliest opportunity, Mulry made a number of important announcements at a meeting of the college students. Required attendance at daily Mass was abolished, although students still were to be present for a community Mass on Saturday mornings and on the first Friday of the month. He then solicited their advice on how to improve their lunch counter. Although no startling solutions were offered for this perennial problem, the students must have been flattered by this evidence of the new prefect's attitude. Finally, "college men" (as Father Mulry now called them) would no longer have to line up in the yard and march in ranks with their younger brethren; they could enter like the adults they were. In the very structure of that meeting the policy to promote a differentiation between the college and secondary students was being implemented.

The policy of separating the college from the high school was even more evident in the assembly Father Mulry held with the younger students. He repeated, on the following day, the announcement about daily Mass and added that thereafter the "Acad[emic] Dep[artmen]t [would] hold its own graduation exercises and give diplomas." (This was soon extended to dramatic productions and other extracurricular activities.) Father Mulry ended his more gracious announcements with a previously unknown proscription: "No cigarette smoking in or near college premises."[7]

By this new rule, Loyola authorities were taking notice of a change that had occurred in the larger community. At the time of the school's founding, chewing tobacco was the commonly accepted sign of manhood; by the early twentieth century, however, it had become the more sanitary and genteel smoking of "coffin nails"—and the college looked with disfavor on this no less than on the previously fashionable vice. The reason most parents and social authorities gave for banning cigarettes was that they stunted growth, but many of their sons and charges were quite prepared to risk that deformity.

• •

The first month of the new school year ended on a joyful note. Father John Ryan, an alumnus and long a faculty member, celebrated the fiftieth anniversary of his entrance into the Society of Jesus. Such celebrations (by their very nature uncommon) had occurred before and certainly reinforced the sense of continuity that the general pattern of life at "the College" induced. On such occasions the honoree was indulged.

There was a special aura surrounding Father Ryan's jubilee, because he was a living link with the earliest period of Loyola's existence. Although he originally attended Calvert Hall, he transferred to Loyola in 1855 when it moved to its new home. Indeed, his is the clearest and most affectionate description of the college in that era. After a few years, young Ryan left for the Jesuit novitiate at Frederick. As a scholastic, he returned to teach for several years during Father Early's second term as president. There followed periods of service at other Jesuit schools until 1880, when he suffered a nervous breakdown. It took another decade for him to recover, and thereupon he returned to Loyola, where he was to remain.

His professional life reflected the breadth that was inherent in the Jesuit system. At Loyola, he organized the students into the Secchi Scientific Society. Father Ryan often was assigned to teach introductory classes in physics, and occasionally he also offered courses in astronomy. These scientific interests were balanced by several creditable publications in history and biography. He was the author of the *Historical Sketch of Loyola College, a Chronicle and Sketch of the Church of Saint Ignatius*, a biography of Father Burchard Villiger (a leading figure in the Maryland province during the latter half of the nineteenth century), and a history of the Catholic church in Maryland. Such versatility was a common result of the classical curriculum but it was becoming an anachronism in the drive for specialization.

Eventually age would take its natural toll and Father Ryan would relinquish the classroom to younger men. His was a striking figure—naturally tall and thin, but habitually stooped. It was said that he was as well known for his daily walks along Calvert Street as Cardinal Gibbons was for similar exercise along Charles Street. Passersby greeted each with smiles and a tip of the hat, and both responded with a word and a friendly gesture. [8]

• •

President Mullan, as a responsible administrator, surveyed the physical plant. For the good humor and well-being of the faculty, he renovated their dining room. The Calvert Street facade was refurbished; steel girders were inserted between the church ceiling and the outside roof; and the electrical system was completely rewired. Along with these repairs, a new convenience was quietly and tentatively introduced. The telephone lines in Baltimore had been extended beyond the central business district up to the section around Mount Vernon Square. A single unlisted instrument was installed in the minister's room, and within a few months a second telephone was acquired and both numbers (Mt. Vernon 1905 was the general number and Mt. Vernon 5171 served Father Mullan) were announced in the church *Journal.*

Sports facilities and varsity competition received renewed emphasis. Father Mulry had the gymnasium floor resurfaced and marked for both indoor baseball and basketball. The walls around the college yard were reinforced with concrete so that they could be used for a handball court. The athletic association was revived with the election of a new slate of officers: president, Frank O'Brien (1908); vice-president, Joseph Wozny (1909); secretary, John Hanson Briscoe (1910); and treasurer, Edward Hanlon. The last was the only one with any strong affinity with sports; he was the son of the manager of the Baltimore Orioles. As already noted, Hanlon went on to a substantial career in the law, and Briscoe became state's attorney for Saint Mary's County and served for a time in the Maryland legislature. After graduation from Loyola, Wozny became a contractor; Frank O'Brien went into advertising and, like Hanlon, ended in New York.

The reorganization of the athletic association quickly bore fruit when, over the Christmas holidays of 1907, Loyola's basketball team ("very light but developing speed") beat its first opponent, Rock Hill College, by a score of 29 to 10. (These tallies seem meager by comparison with more recent ones, but contemporary rules slowed the play.) More significantly, the victory was achieved on the opponent's court in Ellicott City. Had the game been played at Loyola, the Rock Hill five might have claimed that they had lost not to the Loyola five but to the six steel pillars that supported the large auditorium above the gym. For several decades losers would regularly grumble that Loyola teams enjoyed an unfair advantage because they had learned to maneuver around these posts in addition to the posts created by their teammates (a basic maneuver known to all basketball teams). Soon there began to appear in the Loyola diaries and publications references to "rooting practice," to won-and-lost records, and to the propriety of engaging teams like Yale.[9]

These and other promising developments continued after President Mullan became ill. Just before the Christmas holidays of 1907 he had been unable to deliver his weekly lecture to the assembled student body on Christian doctrine. He remained at the college and even began planning for a large alumni reunion, but before that was held he was forced to enter Saint Agnes Hospital. For the rest of the year he would retain formal responsibility, but in fact operations devolved on others.

• •

The spring semester of 1908 was marked by a happy event. A formal
student publication was founded, the *Loyola Annual*. It was a combination of literary magazine, yearbook (of both college and high school),
and alumni newsletter. The editorial board indicated in no uncertain
terms that the "debutante" was entirely a student enterprise—saving,
of course, an unnamed moderator appointed (in their words) "by the
'powers that be.'" The founding impulse came from the leaders of the
junior class, James Murphy and Edward Hanlon, and their anonymous
mentor was revealed some years later as Father Richard Fleming.

The inaugural issue appeared in blue-and-gold flexible covers and
contained about 120 pages. The price was twenty-five cents per copy,
but students could get five for a dollar and were encouraged to resell
them outside the college at the regular rate. For that quarter, the reader
got short stories, several with mystery-detective plots; one story recounted the agonizing struggle of a doctor against his addiction to mor-
phine (with virtue finally triumphing). There was a six-page essay on
the power of the media: "The newspaper is the seal," asserted C. C.
Rohr of the junior class, "this great country is the plastic wax." He
warned his readers to beware of the newspaper's imprint. In another
essay Cyril A. Keller (1910) offered a closely reasoned comparison of
Macbeth and Oedipus; a peer reviewed the recent performance of "the
only really great tragedian since . . . Edwin Booth." This nonesuch
was Richard Mantell—now known only by a brief notice in the *Oxford
Companion to the Theatre*.

There were, to be sure, other evidences of youth and enthusiasm.
Charles Lerch (1911) immortalized the battle of the freshman class pic-
nic at Gwynn Oak in mock-Homeric style. Scattered throughout the
Annual were knowing references to Budweiser, Schlitz, and Anheuser-
Busch.

These japeries spilled over into the way members of each class were
characterized. There were apparently more than a few punsters (fortunately, none quoted), several challengers of professors (obvious folk
heroes), smokers (as well as the inevitable moochers) of cigarettes, late
sleepers, early risers, "the Sport," "the Sphinx," a "pony" rider, a second Demosthenes, a katzenjammer, a "Beadle of beadles," the "Village
Beauty"—in a word, a gallery of familiar types. They had been collected from Saint Mary's and Harford counties, from Roland Park,
Melvale, Catonsville, Orangeville, and Govans. There was little apparent malice in these sketches, although the point or truth of some of

these jibes cannot now be deciphered. They were "in" jokes meant to provide a chuckle for the cognoscenti and to promote a sense of belonging to a friendly group of fellows.

Six pages were devoted to news about the alumni. Oldsters like Doctor Edward Milholland (1856), Charles Tiernan (1858), and Michael Mullin (1859) were felicitated on the length of their days or a recovery from a recent illness. Notice was given of J. B. Joujin-Roche's (class of 1889) transfer to "the West." Congratulations were offered to Doctor Charles O'Donovan for being elected president of the Medical and Chirurgical Society and to Doctor Chatard for being secretary of that body. The marriages, births, and other significant personal events of alumni were included to inform their confreres and to offer examples of what Loyola men were doing in the world. These notices became longer with each issue of the publication.

An interesting feature of this and succeeding issues was the photographs. Opposite page 33 in the first *Annual,* for instance, a view of the gym with the infamous six pillars was reprinted. There were other familiar scenes and portraits, all conveying visually the impression of a mature and relaxed group of men and boys. These pictures were supplemented by little sketches and art work from the pen of Cyril Keller, some of whose designs had a distinctly art noveau style, then very much the mode but hardly classical in form or feeling.

A regular element in the *Annual* was the verse. If eminently perishable, the poetry served to fill out the half-page or so at the end of a story or essay. Apparently Loyola's teachers regularly assigned the composition of triolets, a short but strict stanza, because examples were included in each issue.

The one historically noteworthy piece was the text of Loyola's first school song, probably written expressly for this *Annual.* Its author was a Jesuit scholastic, A. M. Fremgen, who used the melody from a composition entitled "The Old Brigade" for two aspiring verses and a chorus that read:

Then steadily unfurl Loyola's pennant,
Steadily with valiant hearts and true.
Lift it on high, her fame ne'er will die
While triumphs the Gold and Blue.[10]

Mister Fremgen (by then, Father) would return to Loyola during the 1930s to resume, among other things, the production of words and music to bestir school spirit.

The last significant student achievement for the academic year of

1908 was Loyola's first prom. It was already four years since such an event had been held at Georgetown, and again it was the leaders of the junior class— James Murphy and Edward Hanlon (with Joseph Tewes assisting)—who organized the affair. For Wednesday night (Thursday being the school holiday), May 13, they hired Lehmann's Hall and Harvey's Orchestra—both now forgotten but then quite fashionable. Father Mulry, although not opposed to the fete, had made it perfectly clear that Murphy and company—not the college—would be financially responsible. It was, reportedly, an "affair . . . long to be remembered by the friends of Loyola and the people of Baltimore."[11] Unfortunately, the sponsors awoke the next morning with a problem. Although three hundred people had attended (including parents and alumni), they had grossed much less than the bills that now came due. The members of the junior class covered the deficit but, as could be anticipated, years would pass before the experiment was repeated.

• •

This academic year, although shadowed by President Mullan's illness, ended on an upbeat note. Mullan, still confined to the hospital, submitted his resignation some time before the commencement exercises. The board of trustees accepted it but kept his name on the list of trustees. The new president, F. X. Brady, was elected on June 15, 1908, and thereby fulfilled Father Morgan's prediction.

President Brady's immediate concern was to complete arrangements for the graduation program, which he was determined to make memorable. Underclassmen (in formal dress) served as ushers. On each was pinned a length of ribbon in the school colors. The seniors in caps and gowns marched in and sat at center stage surrounded by nearly one hundred alumni (most capped and gowned) and the faculty.

Father Brady was particularly pleased that night, because he had got Maryland's new, energetic, and "unbossed" governor, Austin Crothers, to accept an honorary degree from Loyola. (Sixteen years before, President Smith had attempted such a coup but had been unsuccessful.) Father Brady's long acquaintance with the leading figures of the Democratic party apparently provided him the necessary entree.

Indeed Governor Crothers proved to be the star of the evening. Not only did he receive the degree of Doctor of Laws, honoris causa, but he awarded the diplomas to the graduates (among them a future auxiliary bishop of Washington, John McNamara) and the other honorees. Since the principal speaker, Judge Charles Heuisler, was ill, Governor Crothers also "graciously made the address." "It was very good," noted

Father Mulry. "About 1,000 people present," he added—enough to fill the college hall.[12] Loyola's new president and his aides had turned what might have been a subdued event into a joyous occasion—and there was the summer to plan for the coming year.

· ·

There were new faces at the college when *schola brevis* was conducted in September 1908. Father Peter O'Carroll came from Woodstock to take charge of Loyola's financial records and dealings. For the simpler and less useful method of listing all receipts and expenditures consecutively as they occurred, as was done in the ledgers that survived from the founding of the college, O'Carroll substituted the double-entry method of accounting; this had become standard in business practice.

O'Carroll appears to have introduced a vast new set of categories for recording revenues and expenditures so that the president could monthly identify when and where difficulties or new resources were making their appearance. He further subdivided certain items, especially such expenses as gas, electricity, and wages, so that an appropriate fraction was assigned to either the college, the church, or the house accounts. Because financial procedures are strictly regulated in a Jesuit community, it is safe to assume that O'Carroll was acting in accordance with directives from the province procurator or even higher authority. For more than twenty years Peter O'Carroll faithfully, even obsessively, kept the records of the college's financial transactions.

An intriguing addition in September of 1908 was a layman, J. B. E. Sainte-Seine, who had charge of the special classics section but also taught French. More interesting was the fact that Professor (for so teachers were now denominated) Sainte-Seine was the first to offer Baltimoreans lessons in the artificial language Esperanto. This language had been created by L. L. Zamenhof in 1887 to promote universal peace through a common language that was grammatically consistent and free of identification with any particular nation. It still holds the interest of many people around the world—there is an active group of Esperantists in Baltimore. What happened to Sainte-Seine is unknown, for after a few years his name merely drops from the Loyola records.

At the next opening of classes more significant additions were made to the Loyola community. Father Timothy Brosnahan transferred from Woodstock to Loyola; here, for his last six years, he served as professor of ethics, offered evening courses in philosophy and logic, and continued his polemics on educational and public issues. He obviously brought a special luster to the college, but his broad interests and busy life made him a figure remote from the students.

It was otherwise with Father Dick Fleming, who returned to Loyola in September of 1909. Successive issues of the *Annual* are replete with appreciations for the support and cooperation he gave to various student projects. He had a character that inspired "nobleness and determination to seek the heights of the ideals he so well proposed." And his long tenure as prefect provided additional continuity.

In mid-year, Father Joseph Zeigler (1873) returned to his alma mater. During the intervening decades he had studied at Harvard and taught at Boston College, Fordham, and Saint Peter's. Among his former students he counted Boston's William Cardinal O'Connell, Joseph Tumulty (who later became Woodrow Wilson's secretary), and the historian Will Durant. On various occasions these published personal tributes to Father Zeigler, with Durant recalling especially his "bubbling good humor."

On the Loyola faculty Father Zeigler served as a kind of utility infielder, being assigned at irregular intervals to teach this or that class. Shortly after his arrival he published a little guide to help the high-school students deal with regular Greek verbs. His main responsibility, however, was as moderator of the Loyola alumni association. During Father Zeigler's long term in that office, and despite his chronic ill health, his diligence saved the association from ever lapsing again, as it had periodically in the past, into dormancy.

· ·

President Brady's administrative style was faintly reminiscent of Father Morgan's. He had, for instance, submitted the assignment of teachers for 1909–10 to the board of trustees for their formal review. Normally this had been treated solely as the responsibility of a president, who acted under the direction of the provincial. There are references to faculty meetings: in one instance it is noted that a change of schedule was arrived at "with consensus of teachers," and at another time that a reading of rules produced "no general 'growls.'"[13] These actions hardly matched the systematic application of the techniques of his mentor, but Brady's presidency was much shorter than Morgan's.

While adding to the faculty, President Brady was raising enrollments. During his first full year (1908–9) registration rose 25 percent, to a total of 214—a figure matched only in Father Morgan's time. The increase resulted both from the confidence Baltimoreans had in Father Brady and the Loyola faculty and from the return of general prosperity.

Not even the recession of 1910–11 brought decline in enrollments. On the contrary, there was another 25 percent increase in Brady's second year, and a somewhat more modest rise in the following year, to a total of 284—a figure never before achieved (but one that would be consistently maintained or exceeded in the next decade). A few recruits were got in a new program aimed at Saint Casimir, Saint Stanislaus, and Holy Rosary parishes—loci of Polish working-class families. For them tuition was reduced by 30 to 40 percent. Other students were listed as "protégés" of one or another of the archdiocesan priests who paid their bills, and several more secured support from generous relatives or friends.

By this time, American society (Baltimore's included) was beginning to consider education an attractive investment, and in this new market Jesuit education was proving to be one of the leading gainers. It is well to recall, however, that only about 15 percent of those enrolled would reach the college level and that fewer still would stay the full course.

More than numbers was involved. It was during Father Brady's term that such Loyola luminaries as Edward Bunn, Herbert O'Conor, and Ferdinand Schoberg were admitted. Together they constituted the nucleus of the class of 1917, which developed a nonpareil reputation both during their years at the college and in their later lives. The constant admiring references to the class of 1917 by the faculty soon brought disapproving murmurs from the students who had to listen to these laudations.

Loyola's clientele was again significantly augmented by professional men and other adults who enrolled in the evening or extension courses. Since the Morgan era these courses had received less attention and had suffered a quiet decline in interest and attendance. Father Brady now refurbished the program with a full menu of languages, logic, ethics, and philosophy; these courses were not part of a curriculum that would lead to a degree, they were just continuing education. At a charge of $10 "for one or all" the courses offered, the program was obviously a community service rather than a break-even or profitable enterprise.

• •

Amid these developments, Loyola's new president turned to deal with that perennial headache—finances—and he acted with typical optimism and determination. The college's modest endowment (as best it can be deduced from the listing of professorships, scholarships, and funded medals) came to about $30,000 in 1904; by 1911 this figure had risen to $53,000.

There was, on the other hand, a debt of $160,000, most of it incurred during Father Morgan's term. Tuition at $50 per annum for about 130 students (as in 1907) could not begin to cover the operating cost of approximately $12,000, even if each student paid in full. In fact, however, hardly half the tuitions were paid for that year (admittedly a bad one). The rising enrollments under Father Brady, and the return of the sixty-dollar tuition, could probably have covered the operating cost after 1909, if all the students paid. That must have made the present and future seem bright.

There still was the heavy debt, however. Father Brady late in 1908 called together several alumni and they organized a new laymen's finance committee. This group was made up of prominent businessmen, lawyers, and physicians, most of whom were alumni. They were to recruit members, who would pledge an annual subscription of $10 or preferably more. To make payment of the pledges convenient, Shorb Neale (1886), an officer of the Metropolitan Savings Bank at Lexington and Calvert streets and the treasurer of the committee, was ready to receive any and all donations.

As far as can be determined, the returns on this first general fundraising effort were modest—a few thousand dollars per year. With that, however, plus money from other sources (such as bequests, which were now coming in more regularly), the debt began to decline. In a few years it was reduced to $129,000. Thereafter it would continue to diminish steadily.

In both creation of debts and their periodic reduction, church authorities (Catholic or whatever) had a vehicle to dramatize the development of their communities and to provide goals to mobilize the loyalty and effort of their constituencies. Other landowners and businessmen, by contrast, had come to accept debt, even debt that gradually increased, as merely a factor of production to be monitored carefully. Churchmen, however, preferred to alternate between plunging into debt and crusading to pay off the mortgage.

• •

From the start of his term President Brady had been especially solicitous of the alumni. On November 17, 1908, 600 (according to the church *Journal*; 700 to 800, reported the Baltimore *American*) attended a "reunion" at the college. The halls were lined with old photographs that inspired "many a laugh" when the earlier, callow incarnation of some "dignified and well known professional or business man of the city" was recognized. There were, of course, a "collation," cigars, and speeches ("three hours or more," noted the *American;* "short speeches which fired the enthusiasm of the assembly," said the church *Journal*). Edward Milholland, then Loyola's oldest grad but one, warmed the company with reminiscences of the first days at Holliday Street and of the founder, Father John Early. President Brady's remarks emphasized the continuing interest of the faculty in "whether the world has frowned or smiled on you." He quickly added notice of his pleasure at learning how well "most of you have succeeded in your chosen professions," and continued with other sentiments appropriate to the occasion.

An unexpected dividend resulted from this attention to the alumni. Doctor Louis Knight (1866), whose father had endorsed Loyola's original petition for incorporation, now offered his collection of medals and coins, and Father Brady accepted it. Although it was a large collection (containing a coin or medal for each of the popes from the early 1900s back nearly to the reign of the emperor Constantine), its market value was modest; nevertheless, it gave rise to recurrent whispers about the treasure of the college. More important, it bespoke a continuing association that was heartening and particularly cherished by the Jesuits. Most remarkable was that neither Doctor Knight nor his father was a member of the Catholic church. An honorary doctorate seemed the appropriate token of appreciation, and it was awarded to Louis Knight at the 1909 ceremonies.

President Brady paid close attention to the students and their education. He undertook no major changes in the curriculum, although the philosophy courses lost the historical component introduced about ten years earlier. Now that time was devoted to a close analysis of theses in logic, ontology, cosmology, psychology, natural theology, and ethics. Juniors and seniors could elect a few advanced courses in the social or natural sciences, mathematics, languages, or pedagogy. Loyola submitted its petition for registration with the Board of Regents of the State University of New York. Favorable action by that body meant that Loyola's graduates would be admitted to the schools of law, medicine, and dentistry of that region. After the customary delay, the college was accredited.

A number of academic practices emerged. Examinations may have been written in blue books before this era, but mention of these now appeared in the prefect's diary. According to this notation, the pamphlets in which students wrote their exams cost two cents each, or three for a nickel. They were brought from the bookstore by a member of the class appointed by the teacher to handle the transaction. Furthermore, final grades were derived in these years by a formula that weighted the monthly class marks more heavily (60 percent) than either the midyear or end-of-year exams, each 20 percent of the final average. In 1911 a grade of 60 was the dividing line between salvation and failure.

After midyear some students were conditioned, put on notice that they were in danger of failing. These were required to attend jug, where presumably the guardian-scholastic saw to it that they fulfilled a substantial part of the three hours of daily home study that was declared essential in the catalogue. Though sure to be deprecated these days, the technique benefited some students. "All but 6 or 7 hopeless ones are clear," noted the prefect.[14] As for the rest, Father Brady suggested to their parents that early withdrawal might be prudent, and most followed the president's advice.

. .

Varsity sports came in for renewed support and attention. A new field on Edmondson Avenue near Gwynn's Falls was acquired for baseball and track. Coaches for football and basketball were engaged—one of them with the indicative name of Meanwell—but none remained long. Football was suddenly abolished in November of 1909 after a Georgetown player died from injuries.`

Basketball enjoyed a brightening record in this period. The team's willingness to learn was evident in their traveling to Annapolis to watch the Middies play the team from Baltimore City College. Some of the plays they saw were quickly put to use. That plus their own developing skill resulted in a successful season. In fact, the students began demanding that Loyola schedule games with more formidable opponents. To this end Harry Noeth (1911) and Stan Cook (1910) attended a conference of southern colleges with instructions to "secure 'big' teams" for the basketball schedule.

The following season, presumably as a result, included games with a number of better-known opponents. Loyola won the match with the University of Maryland (played at the Richmond Market Armory) by a score of 33 to 29; Gallaudet also bowed. Georgetown needed two overtimes to squeak by with one decisive basket. Baltimore Medical College, "claimants [as it was said] to the intercollegiate championship of the South," won by an even narrower score: 29 to 28. The rest of the season was a series of easy victories. This level of competition and winning was maintained through several more seasons.

Another facet of student life emerges in the records of the Brady era. On March 14, 1910, Father Fleming thought it necessary (as he noted in his diary) to make "a warning, threatening speech on gambling" to the student body. The notation for the next day reads: "Five boys caught throwing dice for money—all upper college classes. Suspended to await decision of authorities. Great commotion."[15] There the record ends. Who were the culprits? What happened to them? Silence.

Their fate was probably similar to Herbert O'Conor's in a later incident. He too was caught shooting craps in the locker room, and was suspended. To assure his parents that nothing drastic was intended, Father Fleming decided to call on the O'Conors. Unfortunately, the visit exposed an even greater fall from grace; Herb had taken Father Fleming's notice of suspension out of the mailbox and disposed of it before his mother could see it. Some contrition undoubtedly was exacted by the school and by his mother, but O'Conor graduated with his class.[16] His career included service as state's attorney, governor, and United States senator. A reader might question this procedure but it was then an accepted way of maintaining proper order without exaggerating the offense by summary dismissal of a promising student.

More characteristic of the cycle of life at the college was the response of the faculty and students to a new scientific wonder. On November 7, 1910, the daring Hubert Latham was scheduled to fly an airplane over Baltimore City Hall. At the appointed time classes at Loyola were dismissed and everybody crowded onto the roof to get a glimpse of the flying machine. "What I would give to be with him, exclaimed many a Loyola student," according to an item in the *Sun*.[17]

This enthusiasm was soon turned into a more academic channel. During the following March the college physics class gave a specimen on aerial navigation. The student lectures were illustrated with models, some obtained from Woodstock College. The program ended with the flying of several of the models (motive power unspecified—probably just glided). One sailed from the balcony to the stage in the college hall. So spectacular a success deserved a repeat performance, delivered a few weeks later for the nuns and young ladies at Mount Saint Agnes College.

· ·

The intended high point of 1911 was a unique celebration of the silver jubilee of Father Brady's ordination. Such a commemoration was not customary among Jesuits, but many people were so persistent in pressing for the affair that the provincial granted permission. The organizers planned to give Brady a purse containing a thousand dollars in honor of each of his years in the priesthood. Planning continued while Father Brady went about performing his regular duties. Among these was his participation in the "Novena of Grace"—a series of devotional exercises in honoi of Saint Francis Xavier—that he had made a significant feature in the church life of Baltimore. In 1911 the novena began on Friday, March 4, and was scheduled to end on Sunday, March 12, the feast of the canonization of Saint Francis. Attendance, as always, was numbered in the thousands, and almost half the participants were men. To accommodate this multitude, the prescribed prayers and the discourses were had three times each day.

This year, as in every preceding year, Father Brady took his turn at the altar and in the pulpit. At the closing service he described "most vividly the lonely death of his patron saint." Later, walking down the corridor to his room, he met a colleague and exclaimed, "Well, thank God! I have given my last talk."[18] There followed a chat with his brother and a pastoral visit to a sick friend. The rest of the evening followed a familiar routine. However, in the morning when the bell to call the Jesuits to chapel was rung, Father Brady "did not answer the summons." The brother sacristan checked and found him lying across his bed still clothed in cassock and cincture—dead. He had been under treatment for a heart condition and that was assigned as the cause of death. The doctors judged the attack to have taken place before midnight, on his patron's feast day. On such occasions Jesuits repeat with a wry smile what is an ironic commonplace to them, that the Catholic least likely to receive the last rites is a priest living in a community surrounded by priests.

The depth and breadth of the resulting grief was both amazing and a testimony to the esteem in which Loyola's thirteenth president was generally held. The sad news quickly circled the city. Monday was reserved for prayers and farewells of the Jesuit community, but on the following day Father Brady's body was placed in the college parlor so the public could pay their last respects. They came despite the "most inclement weather." They came in a stream of humanity that started at ten in the morning and lasted until nine at night. "Children of tender years, . . . old men with tottering steps, the poor and lowly, and rich and exalted, the Catholic and non-Catholic, the Jew and Gentile" offered this last tribute to what Father Brady had come to mean to each of them.[19]

There were other evidences of the high regard in which he was held. The *Sun* printed a five-column obituary that included a statement from Cardinal Gibbons:

> As a priest, Father Brady was saintly and honored. . . .
> In his death, I lose not only a dear friend but an
> indefatigable worker of the Church. As a man, he was
> many sided and possessed all the qualities the world
> holds dear. His popularity was well deserved. . . . His
> friend's devotion was proverbial and I am glad to be
> among those who looked up to and respected him.[20]

The editor of the Baltimore *American* eulogized Brady as "a friend of the weak and erring, a liberal giver to the poor, a scholar of high merit, an administrator of exceptional value, a genial and kindly man."[21]

On Wednesday the formal obsequies were completed with great solemnity. Then the body of Father Brady was buried in the Jesuit cemetery at Woodstock. Nearby was the grave of his predecessor, William George Read Mullan, who little more than a year before had traveled the same route. Their various initiatives had opened a bright future for Loyola College, but the realization of that prospect was left to successors.

10

On to Guilford

The following weeks were marked by continuing tributes to Father Brady. Every few days from late March until the end of April 1911, one or another school or church organization gathered for a memorial mass. Brady's silver jubilee, originally scheduled for late summer, somewhat hurriedly became a commemorative fair at the end of April. Despite the haste, a substantial sum was realized and donated to the college.

• •

During the same period speculation grew about who would take Brady's place. As the interregnum stretched to two months, Father Brosnahan good-naturedly but urgently chided the "councillors of state" (the provincial consultors) to do their duty and give Loyola a new president. Some, including one local paper, were sure that the rector's napkin ring would pass to Father Mullan's brother. The erroneous report that Elder Mullan was en route from Rome appeared the day before Loyola's new president and rector, William Ennis, arrived from Philadelphia. Next morning, May 17, Baltimoreans got an official introduction to him through a long column and portrait in the *Sun*.

What stuck in their minds, and was repeated in all accounts of Father Ennis, was his geniality, determination, and competence. The *Sun* reporter described him as a man with "a contagious smile, a hearty laugh and a merry twinkle in his eye," but added that he had "a strong will and firm hand." A lay friend and longtime correspondent many years later recalled that Father Ennis "was always so jolly and joked so much."[1] This recollection was certified by the breezy tone that began to characterize announcements in the church *Journal*.

In the *Journal* notices there also appeared a militant, almost censorious, note. In some comments on extramural personalities, events, and institutions, there was a new assertiveness that was not peculiar to Ennis but was becoming common in the public utterances of other Catholic churchmen in the area. Many factors account for this development, but the growth in numbers and the gradually increasing prosperity of the church must have contributed. Between 1900 and 1920 the number of Catholics in American grew from twelve to eighteen million, and in the 1920 census they constituted almost 17 percent of the population.[2]

A simple but clear index to Ennis's abilities is his reduction of Loyola's debt. At his arrival it hung around $130,000, and at his departure seven years later it had been lightened by almost a quarter. As with those of his predecessors, Ennis's methods for achieving such results must be left to conjecture.

Even fewer biographical details survive than for most of his Jesuit brethen. This reticence arose from the commitment and general style of religious life. Entrance into the community is meant to be a severance from one's previous existence. Furthermore, the habitual practice is to ascribe what is accomplished to the animating spirit of the religious community rather than to the initiative of individuals. Acceptable as this attitude may be, it discouraged the recording of such data as can generally be found for persons who have not entered the religious life. Instead, what remain for many Jesuits are a few sketchy recollections, mostly of their life in the Society, with a testimonial of religious virtue and zeal. Fortunately, this austere style has been giving way in recent years to a more common and more humanly engaging practice.

At the time of Ennis's appointment to Loyola he was 49 years old. He was born in the Greenwich Village section of New York in 1862. Of his family no information has survived except that he had a sister who made her way in life as a department manager in a fashionable store. The history of his early education is sketchy, though one may assume some connection with either Saint Francis Xavier's or Fordham before he entered the Jesuit order in 1879. Thereafter, he followed the customary pattern of rigorous training and education.[3]

By the time he came to Baltimore, Father Ennis had filled a variety of positions. There was more than a decade of teaching on his record, including a year (1905–6) in a Loyola classroom. There was also a short stint as vice-president of Georgetown. For more than three years he was part of the mission band based in Philadelphia; Father Ennis and a companion had conducted a mission at Saint Ignatius Church in January of 1911. He would later recall Father Brady's telling him "that when a person became acquainted with Baltimore and its people, he never wanted to leave it." These words he repeated shortly after his arrival at Calvert Street, and added: "I hope to be able to say the same thing from experience."[4]

Along with everything else, President Ennis was paying close attention to fund raising for the college. He was, as already noted, largely successful. Some money came in response to direct appeals to parishioners of Saint Ignatius Church. These donations increased, but their total hardly matched the annual interest on the college's debt. Nevertheless, Ennis warmly thanked the givers and pledged that the Jesuits would not close their school, as the fund raisers for another local institution had recently threatened to do. Loyola's sons would persist in the Lord's work and be thankful for whatever support they got.

These sentiments by no means suggested that he and his confreres were about to lapse into presumptuous inactivity. To the contrary, and characteristically, the occasional money raisers were continued and new methods were developed. Father Zeigler inquired of his counterparts at Holy Cross and Saint Peter's what they were doing that made them so successful. They responded with an outline of procedures and with samples of the forms they were using. To this stock Zeigler added models from institutions closer at hand. In preparation for a campaign, he published a directory with names, addresses, and professions of more than eight hundred active alumni. To this he appended the text of the alumni association's constitution and other information about the college. He scoured old catalogues, registers, and other records for the name of anyone who had ever enrolled at Loyola up to 1916. In this way he produced another list, of more than thirty-five hundred names. The directory bolstered the pride and sense of cohesion of the alumni; along with the second list, it was useful for fund raising and for recruiting new alumni members.

The special target of the 1915 campaign was the alumni, and they responded rather well. First to answer was the ever-reliable Matthew Brenan (1879), who, while making a substantial contribution, cheered the effort on with the observation "The switch [a direct appeal from Father Ennis] does good work sometimes."[5] One letter that somehow strayed beyond the alumni circle fetched back a fifty-dollar check, but neither Ennis nor Zeigler seems to have acted on this hint; they continued to limit their appeals to the alumni and Catholics of Baltimore. This reticence must seem strange today, and no likely explanation offers except that was the way things were done in those days. The amount of money gained in this effort can only be guessed from the 25 percent drop in the college debt during Ennis's term.

• •

More significant to the fiscal health of Loyola was an extraordinary windfall in the Ennis era. Thomas O'Neill, one of Baltimore's leading Catholics and merchants, included the Associated Professors in his will with a bequest of half a million dollars to build a new church and school. An exasperatingly long and involved process finally resulted in receipt of the full sum in 1936, but from the summer of 1912 onward the Jesuits at Calvert Street enjoyed great expectations.

Thomas O'Neill provided Baltimoreans with their own Irish-immigrant-makes-good legend. O'Neill was born in 1849, after the worst of the potato famine had passed, to a dry goods merchant and his wife. His father urged him at the age of 15 to set out for Dublin to gain some business experience but young O'Neill chose to come to America, and to Baltimore. He clerked in various local establishments until 1881, when he formed a partnership to open a small shop at Charles and Lexington streets. The clientele and profits grew so rapidly that within a year O'Neill bought out his partner. He secured additional space, diversified his merchandise, and on the site of the original shop eventually built one of Baltimore's largest and best department stores. In time he opened branches in Dublin, London, and Paris. With success came invitations to serve on the boards of various local banks: Union Trust, National Exchange, and Fidelity Trust, among others.

Success raised thoughts of a family. In 1890, aged 41, he married Roberta Le Brou, whose brothers had attended Loyola College and later became parishioners of Saint Ignatius Church. The wedding took place in Corpus Christi Church, where O'Neill became a daily communicant. Some Sundays, in fact, he would stay on to serve one of the other masses. His piety was surpassed by that of his wife. On occasion he was heard to suggest jokingly that his wife might have done better by becoming a nun.

Thomas O'Neill's direct association with Loyola began in 1910. In that year he endowed a professorship in physics. Father Ennis probably took an early opportunity to meet one of Loyola's benefactors and one of Baltimore's leading citizens. The only tangible result was a small sum to fund a medal in mathematics.

Shortly thereafter Thomas O'Neill signed his remarkable will. Under its terms his employees would at his death have the opportunity to buy stock in the department store in proportion to the length of their service. This meant the continuation of O'Neill's department store as a publicly owned corporation and meanwhile provided for a loyal work force. In addition to generous provision for Loyola he allotted a substantial sum for a hospital, with ample and sensitive stipulations for service to the poor. The remaining millions were to be used to build a new cathedral. By these bequests O'Neill seems to have intended to provide Catholic equivalents to the magnificent gifts to Baltimore made by George Peabody, Johns Hopkins, Henry Walters, and Enoch Pratt. However, in his provision for a new cathedral and in offering his employees the opportunity to buy stock in the department store, his bequests had no equal.

His choice of monuments seems to have been made without consultation, even with those he meant to benefit. The silence of Gibbons's biographers on the O'Neill bequest is eloquent testimony to the dilemma that his generosity created for the aging cardinal. Few occupants of the see of Baltimore had given such warm and persistent expression to their love for the old cathedral as James Gibbons. Nevertheless, he had little choice but to accept the proffered gift, possibly in hopes that the donor might later be persuaded to allow a more suitable use.[6]

There was a further complication in the O'Neill will. Although he seemed inclined to start these projects as soon as possible, he provided that upon his death the estate would revert to the management of trustees who were to support his widow and relatives. Only upon the death of Mrs. O'Neill would the inheritance finally be divided among the residual beneficiaries. The arrangement securely protected the family but put a premium on completing any project (once begun) before Thomas O'Neill died. This encumbrance induced Father Ennis to move slowly on the plan to transfer the college and church to a new location.

• •

However, the matter became urgent when late in May of 1913 the Pennsylvania Railroad announced it would be expanding its freight yards and warehouses on Calvert Street. This threatened to bring even more smoke, noise, and traffic to the very door of the college. Ennis and his consultors quickly agreed on the need to relocate. Now the five hundred thousand dollars that O'Neill had allotted in his will was seen as the means to effect the transfer expeditiously, and the donor's health seemed robust enough so the chance of O'Neill's death and the transfer of his wealth into a trust for his family appeared remote.

O'Neill's will was not the only source of difficulties. The effort to find a suitable central location in a choice residential neighborhood involved several frustrating episodes. No thought seems to have been given by President Ennis to any site other than one associated with a suburban development known as the District. This was a tract of more than fifteen hundred acres encompassing the present-day sections of Roland Park, Guilford, and Homeland. Most of the land extended northward along Charles Street Avenue between the Jones Falls and York Road beyond the pre-1918 boundaries of Baltimore.

For over twenty years this prime real estate had been carefully developed by the Roland Park Company, which protected the general style and real estate values of the District by requiring that all building plans be approved by its architectural committee. The Roland Park Company, relying on private contracts, was aiming at much the same results as we now seek by means of zoning and "new town" restrictions.

The effort of Loyola's Jesuits to secure a base in the District was complicated by the fact that they had to deal not only with the Roland Park Company but with the people who actually owned the property. The first negotiation for a five-acre parcel on Charles Street, between Wendover and Highfield roads failed because the neighboring owners raised objections to having a church at such a prime location. In support of the Jesuits the Roland Park Company mounted a newspaper campaign with pictures and descriptions of the sort of buildings that were planned—to no avail. (A few years later the building of a church one block north and of another one block south of the Wendover-Highfield site appears not to have aroused the objection that the denizens of the District urged against the Jesuits.) The company then found a forty-acre tract located well away from Charles Street and the price was less than twice that of the first site. The putative sellers, after agreeing to the deal, significantly raised the price before the contract was signed. Father Ennis responded with objections on certain stipulations that the Roland Park Company was insisting on.

In May of 1914 a firm agreement was reached when the company had a suitable tract just outside the limits of the District and thus beyond the reach of its restrictions. (The tract extended northward from Thirty-fourth Street, between Saint Paul and Calvert streets to University Parkway with a smaller section on the other side between Greenway and Calvert—the site today of the Marylander and Carrollton apartment houses.) A friendly ghost hovered over the deal. The owner of the tract was James Cotter (1882), whose name in 1905 had figured in the short-lived rumor that Loyola College was about to move.

Written into the contract and later in the deed were a number of stipulations to ensure the general interests and standards that the Roland Park Company zealously guarded. There was a reversionary clause by which the company could, for twenty-five years, buy the land back if Loyola abandoned its plans. Furthermore, the Associated Professors were not permitted to install any "church or school bells or chimes or other bells of like character" without the company's written permission. This may indeed have been the overt issue raised against the earlier plan to locate in the District itself and would reappear a few years later in the negotiations for a section of Evergreen. The agreement provided for a closing in November 1914, but because of various delays the deal was not completed until a year later.[7]

A detailed site and architectural plan was attached to the contract. It was prepared by Charles Maginnis of Maginnis and Walsh, a rising new architectural firm headquartered in Boston. Thomas O'Neill, possibly at the suggestion of but certainly with the concurrence of Father Ennis, had engaged Maginnis to design and supervise the construction of the new Loyola. The choice indicated that the new college and church would be a variation on an English collegiate Gothic theme. Maginnis and Walsh had recently won a prize with a design in that style for the erection of a new Boston College; like Loyola and other American colleges and universities (Columbia and Johns Hopkins among them), Boston College was moving out of a congested downtown location to residential suburbs.[8] This was in fact part of an even larger population shift made possible (or required) by the automobile and the network of paved roads developed for it.

There were two obstacles to the acquisition of the Guilford tract: the Maryland Constitution did not permit ecclesiastical corporations to obtain land without specific legislative authorization, and Saint Ignatius Church could not be transferred without permission of the archdiocese. In due course and quietly, the necessary approval of the legislature was obtained. Discussions with the archdiocesan authorities were more involved. Although permission for moving the church was granted, it was conditioned on requirement that the new church in Guilford not be opened until the one on Calvert Street was sold—a rather distant prospect. The secular clergy were careful to protect their prerogatives against the possibility that the Jesuits might end with two parishes in Baltimore. This condition was relaxed after an ironclad guarantee that the Jesuits would operate only one parish was underwritten by the provincial.[9] Later there were difficulties over the boundaries for the new parish in Guilford that were never resolved.

The hope that this marked the end of the obstacle course was not realized, because at this point Thomas O'Neill introduced a new hurdle. Although he provided the funds for the Guilford tract ($80,000), he added a codicil to his will assigning the full $500,000 to building only a church. This meant that the Jesuits would have to abandon the plan to move the college or else raise additional funds. There was no question what they intended to do. In fact, an adjoining five-acre parcel was added to the Guilford site to allow adequate room for the school. The money for this came from Mrs. William Lanahan, George Carrell Jenkins, (a prominent banker and leader in the Baltimore Catholic community), and his sister. All obstacles overcome, the real estate transaction was completed in November of 1915.

· ·

While these plans and arrangements were maturing, President Ennis kept the alumni and students informed. He first publicly uttered the word *Guilford* at the alumni banquet of 1914. It was an eminently respectable address, having been the country residence of A. S. Abell and opened for development only two years before. During the next year's festivities, they were singing "It's a short, short way to Guilford Estate." In the 1915 *Annual* it was evident that visions of diamonds and gridirons danced in the heads of student athletes.

The sense of a new and grander beginning was symbolically conveyed by an original device that appeared on the cover of the 1915 *Annual*. Imprinted there was a new heraldic seal consisting of a circlet and shield. In the circlet was printed LOYOLA COLLEGE BALTIMORE MD. 1852, which directly translated the Latin legend on the old corporate seal. A distinctive element from the national, state, and city flags, in addition to the wolves and kettle from the standard of the House of Loyola, was placed in each of the quadrants of a quartered shield. The designer probably was Thomas Whelan, the legal adviser to the college. It had an elegant (if busy) style and would be used for unofficial purposes from 1915 to 1928. The original corporate seal would continue to be impressed on official records and diplomas until 1968.

Father Ennis gave thought to breaking ground immediately, but the Jesuit general required that the college wait until it had more capital. Throughout this period, relations with Thomas O'Neill developed to the point of chumminess. He regularly invited President Ennis and Father Fleming to join him for a few days in Atlantic City every spring. These presumably were occasions on which "Sir Thomas" (as he was now familiarly called) reviewed the progress of the Guilford project. In

1916 the Roland Park Company officers were alarmed to find that Mrs. O'Neill was urging her husband to delay the start of construction. Reportedly, she wanted a postponement because she feared completion was a death omen. Whether this was her real motive or merely a device for playing on her husband's sensibilities was not clear, but it worried the company officers.

The growing entanglement of the United States in the war then raging in Europe forced a real delay. The rising demand for steel and other construction materials inflated costs so much that in September of 1917 further planning was cancelled until the war ended. Meanwhile O'Neill periodically transferred additional funds and securities to the college corporation and, welcome as they were, they unintentionally became the source of later difficulty.[10]

Well after Ennis and the Jesuits had begun to avoid making allusions to Guilford, others continued to draw attention to it. Roger O'Leary (1916) still hopefully referred to "the spacious halls, the well-equipped lockers [and] the wide spread campus of Guilford" in the 1916 *Annual.* A year later the Roland Park Company included a map of the Guilford site in its advertisement. By then, however, the readers of the *Loyola Annual* as well as their neighbors were more interested in the war, which the United States had finally entered on April 6, 1917. Thus the vision of a new Loyola gradually faded—only for the duration, it was thought.

．．

There was in this era a development in church life that Father Ennis supported but that was primarily the work of Loyola alumni. Charles Conlon (1906), Boiseau Wiesel (1907), Mark Shriver (1902), and Frank O'Brien (1908) founded the Baltimore League for Laymen's Retreats in 1913. Thus they brought to this area a movement started in France late in the nineteenth century that reached New York City only in 1911. How Conlon and company heard of this development is unclear. It may have been through their close connection with the Loyola Alumni Association, in which they continually served as officers. Or it may have been from their work together at an east Baltimore settlement house sponsored by the Saint Vincent de Paul Society. At the beginning there was a close connection between the lay retreat movement and the church's effort to deal with the social and economic dislocations that accompanied industrialization. In any case, this group of Loyola alumni organized the league and persuaded Father Ennis to serve as its spiritual director.

Retreats, familiar as they have since become, were not then generally available to the Catholic laity in America. They were a regular element in the life of the clergy and religious and at Catholic colleges, but for most adult communicants the parish mission was the usual prod to spiritual reflection and renewal.

The parish mission was of value, but it suffered from a number of drawbacks. Preachers had to gain the attention and cooperation of participants still immersed in the pressures and distractions of their workaday lives. The audience probably shared little beyond geographical proximity. Thus, the mission preachers had to pitch their exhortations at the broadest possible level. They had to rely heavily on emotional rhetoric and appeals. An American Catholic was most likely to hear a sermon on damnation with terrifying evocations of hellfire and brimstone during a parish mission.

A retreat is organized and focused differently. Its exercises and devotions are concentrated during several days, usually a weekend, at a facility away from home and its pressing cares. It can be organized around occupational or professional interests, fraternal or religious associations, or age, sex, or other group characteristics. Although not entirely free of appeals to emotion, retreat directors (especially in the Jesuit tradition) rely on a logical and serious analysis of the great questions of life, religion, and morality. The occasion is meant to induce reflection on the fundamental values around which the participants have organized their lives and to review how well (or badly) they have managed to live according to these principles. It took the new Baltimore retreat league a year to arrange its first exercise at Georgetown. There were eighteen participants, and they found the overall experience appealing.[11]

• •

There were in the same period several notable faculty losses. First, in mid-December of 1913, came the death of Father John Ryan, whose life and work directly linked Loyola to the period of its foundation. This was followed in June of 1915 by the death of Timothy Brosnahan. His passing finally stilled his rushing stream of pamphlets and articles in defense of things Catholic. It was also a severe blow to the college. His course in ethics had been an attractive feature of the master's program. It was in fact so well received that his lecture notes were reprinted by a Baltimore publisher. At the time of his death, Father Brosnahan was reportedly compiling a code of Christian morals in which he intended to cover the whole field of human action. This magnum opus, like so many others, would never be reduced to print, although his notes were later published.

Fortunately there were compensating additions to the faculty. In 1911 Justin Ooghe came to Loyola after completing his tertianship at Saint Andrew-on-Hudson. He was from Belgium and in 1893 entered the Society of Jesus there. His early training was in India, where to waste no time he learned Sanskrit during his daily walks to the dining hall and while serving or waiting to be served. One hot day his instructor (an Indian who wanted to improve his English) was incensed when Ooghe automatically swatted a mosquito that had lighted on his hand. "That might have been my grandfather," objected the Hindu. "Oh no," said Ooghe, "surely your grandfather would return only as a lion."

Years later students could recall his manner of teaching in detail. Briskly he walked into a classroom, methodically arranged his materials, placed his notes on the reading stand, shuffled the cards on which he had written the students' names, chose one, and launched into the matter that had been assigned for that day. What followed was a probing conversation with the student whose card had been chosen. The aim of the dialogue was for the student and the class to learn to reason and to develop clear-cut, logically unassailable, and convincing answers to the philosophical questions Father Ooghe propounded. The subject—not his personality or those of the students— was the focus of the dialogue. Despite this teacher's impersonal method, the attractive character of Justin Ooghe was quickly discovered and long cherished.[12]

Ooghe attracted notice even among his fellow Jesuits—a much less impressionable audience. At a conference of philosophy teachers during the early 1920s he vigorously objected to the position espoused by Francis Connell, who was the leading figure in the province on pedagogy and educational theory and a Loyola alumnus, class of 1885. Father Connell asserted that "the main purpose in teaching philosophy to our students is to defend the faith, . . . to render our students immune from the infections of skepticism and materialism that are in the air we breathe." He even considered the teaching of philosophy to be "propaganda in the justifiable sense of the word."

What his forty or so other listeners thought of these dicta went unrecorded, but Father Ooghe insisted on the proper autonomy of his discipline. Philosophy, he objected, was "by no means a mere handmaid of theology; . . . a man will listen to reason and experiment, whatever his religious beliefs."

Ooghe's declaration was seconded by a Fordham colleague. The sage from Fordham sought to resolve the difference by first yielding to Connell on the "nature" of philosophy: it was indeed "a handmaid of theology." But, he noted, this did not determine the "proximate end" of an actual philosophy course. He went on to reinforce his support of Ooghe's position by citing his own experience that students were "most impressed . . . by the fact that reasons of the purely natural order can be given for the great facts of life."[13]

This exchange indicated a basic difference of opinion among Jesuits, and among other Catholic educators. The priority for many was the maintenance of orthodoxy and moral formation. Others saw these as functions of the church as a whole but thought the informing purpose of Catholic colleges and universities ought to be academic excellence and scholarship.[14] The struggle between these two visions continued until after Vatican II—and is still not completely resolved.

Justin Ooghe did not believe that philosophy could replace or preempt the function of other subjects in the curriculum. He opposed too early or too exclusive a concentration on it. Talking to one of his best students, he conceded that philosophy "makes you egotistic, literature makes you altruistic." If somewhat trite, his aphorism gives evidence both of his objectivity and of his broad approach to the aims of education.

Even more telling was his willingness to reconsider positions when faced with student challenges. One student raised a doubt in class and Father Ooghe (somewhat taken aback) offered to sleep on it; he believed all problems yielded to that remedy. When the class reconvened he announced that the student's objection was indeed valid and that he would be forced to revise his position. How many such student triumphs there were can only be guessed, but one is enough to reveal the logic and utter sincerity of the man.

An editorial writer for the *Sun* thought Ooghe's most engaging quality was an "unending and purposive curiosity." His students might have chosen various other qualities, and of no other Loyola teacher has it been said (or is it likely to be said) that he was a "darling." Short in stature, with a round, mobile face and clear blue eyes that gazed directly through round gold-rimmed glasses, Justin Ooghe had a high-pitched voice that never quite lost its piquant accent. In tribute to the custom of his native Belgium, his students called him "Père"—even as they improvised his surname (out of earshot) into the urgent sound of a Klaxon horn.[15]

Another addition to the faculty during the Ennis era was Father Henry McLoughlin, professor of chemistry, who provided a contrast to

Ooghe. The latter's classes were ruled by a recognizable (if sometimes disrupted) decorum, but McLoughlin captured the attention of his listeners by surprise attack. In the laboratory, if no immediate answer was forthcoming to his sudden "What are you doing there?" he facetiously threatened to exile the hesitant fellow to a sandpile in Druid Hill Park. Once, noting that Herbert O'Conor was about to apply a flame to a test tube containing a highly explosive compound, McLoughlin invited the rest of the class to leave both the laboratory and O'Conor to their certain fate.

McLoughlin's portrait, for many years a familiar fixture in the vestibule of Beatty Hall, carries the hint of a tolerantly amused smile that must have appeared quite often in life. One can imagine him at the moment each year when, after writing his name on the blackboard and carefully pronouncing it, he declaimed the lines from Goldsmith's *Deserted Village*: "And still they gazed, and still the wonder grew, / That one small head could carry all he knew." This couplet was meant to amuse and also to warn his listeners. The schoolmaster to whom he was alluding was described a few lines earlier as kindly enough but "if severe in aught / The love he bore to learning was in fault." Whether more than a few of the "gazing rustics ranged around" understood the message can be doubted, but all discovered its essential meaning through their experience with Father McLoughlin.

Any pedagogic style is hard to reproduce or to describe. It is proverbially easy to exaggerate one element or another and thus make an idiosyncratic style seem laughable or self-indulgent. The esteem expressed for him and the amused recollections of his sallies by those who saw him in action suggest that Henry McLoughlin had that crucial sense of balance that distinguishes the master teacher from the egoistic ham.[16] His students became aware eventually of the genuine interest and concern for them that animated his prodding wit.

• •

Under Father Ennis, Loyola students were involved in a number of new ventures. They imitated their peers at other American institutions of higher learning by recording their preferences and foibles for posterity. With only ten members in the class of 1916, at Loyola the data were quickly gathered. The recorders, Roger O'Leary and Joe Quinn, reported the average height of the members of the class as 5 feet 9 inches (about the same as for the class of 1958) and the average weight as 157 pounds. Law and medicine were the favored careers of these graduating seniors, and four became lawyers and two doctors.

A meeting of the class was used to secure more information. Half of them admitted to corresponding with young ladies, although none would acknowledge having kissed a member of the opposite sex who was not a family relation. Of course, in those days gentlemen did not tell, and the poll takers who duly recorded this demurrer added their own declaration of disbelief. Forty percent of their classmates claimed freedom from any addiction to tobacco and all but one indulged in some form of athletics—mainly basketball. That one member might have been accounted for had O'Leary and Quinn allowed playing the "ponies" among the accepted sports.

They held conventional views of good literature. Shakespeare was their unanimous choice as the world's master dramatist and they gave the palm for prose fiction to Charles Dickens. In poetry, however, the Loyola students exhibited their local loyalties and preferred Edgar Allan Poe. They chose Mae Marsh as their movie queen over America's sweetheart, Mary Pickford. They concluded this quaint collegiate ritual by naming sundry of their members as the most consistent student, the deepest thinker, the handsomest, and the like. Similar compilations would appear more or less regularly until the 1930s, when the Great Depression made such things seem trivial and callow.

For most of the Ennis years the roof of the college sported a new and noteworthy ornament. From 1912 until April 8, 1917, an antenna made it possible for Loyola's students and faculty to study the wonders of radio. The apparatus was assembled and erected by Joseph Kelley, a Jesuit scholastic who already had a federal license. He was, in addition to his other responsibilities, moderator of the Secchi Scientific Society, and in connection with it had started the Wireless Club.

In those days it was relatively easy to set up a radio station. A carefully measured arrangement of wires served as an antenna, which could both receive and transmit radio signals. The transmitting equipment consisted of little more than a telegraph key, an induction coil, and a condenser. Reception was managed through a crude predecessor of today's transistor. A stiff wire called a cat's whisker was moved across a carborundum or silicon crystal to locate a particularly sensitive spot. This was connected through another circuit to a telephone receiver. All this equipment was then readily available, and countless operators sat for hours probing their crystals for messages from beyond the horizon.

What is reported to have been the first such apparatus in Baltimore was set up at Loyola in 1898, only three years after Guglielmo Marconi's first successful demonstrations. It had a very limited range and was used primarily to demonstrate the basic scientific principles involved and that radio waves passed through solid walls. In 1912 Joseph Kelley, with funds from his family, boosted the power of the set so that it could broadcast and receive signals over long distances. This made it possible for Loyola students to contact others, including their peers at Jesuit schools around Philadelphia and New York, for undefined "experiments"—presumably, testing reception under various conditions.

All this came to an end on Sunday, April 8, 1917—two days after the United States declared war on Germany. The federal government, to shield its orders, directed that all radio transmitters and receivers *except its own* discontinue operations.[17] More than half the hundred or so installations in Baltimore (Loyola's among the number) were closed down that day. For the duration of the war the study of radio at the college and elsewhere was restricted to blackboard diagrams and theory.

• •

Athletics were not neglected during President Ennis's term. In 1912 William Schuerholz was engaged to coach the blue and gold basketball team. The personable young coach, aged 25, was a plumber by trade, but otherwise was dedicated to promoting the play of this relatively new sport. There followed a fourteen-year association during which Bill Schuerholz was readily identifiable by a talisman—a heavy, maroon cardigan sweater that he wore to every event connected with the game.

During these years basketball and Schuerholz came to be associated in the imagination of Baltimore fans. Not only did his Loyola teams amass a respectable record against increasingly formidable opponents, but he coached other teams—neighborhood, amateur, and professional. He taught the sport simply by watching the play or practice and then quietly offering remedial advice. He relied not on flash but on persistent attention to basics, as is evident in the rules his players were required to memorize.[18]

His first season ended with twelve wins and four losses. For this and the next three seasons, Loyola's squad could claim the state championship, although such matters were not then as well organized or defined as they have since become. Schuerholz's overall record for these four campaigns was a respectable thirty-seven wins against twenty-five losses. Some of each were collected during annual trips to Pennsylvania, New Jersey, and New York, against teams such as Saint Joseph's, Lehigh, Manhattan, and Fordham.

One loss was to a team with a national reputation. The blue and gold schedule was already full for the 1913–14 season (including George-town, the Naval Academy, and the University of Virginia). The team manager, August Bourbon (1914), however, responded quickly and af-firmatively to a request from Yale for a game in Baltimore during its southern excursion. Bourbon and his schoolmates were pleased when over a thousand fans came to the Richmond Market Armory that night, even though it was the Christmas holiday and vacation season. Less pleased were he and the Loyola rooters with the final score, 41 to 29 in favor of Yale.

Four years later Herbert O'Conor made a similar arrangement with a similar result. The January 1917 game, O'Conor reported, had been "nip and tuck throughout" till the final ten minutes, when the tiring Yale squad was replaced by a fresh crew. Under such circumstances, the result (47 to 33) might be viewed merely as misleading statistics. Re-dress of a sort was achieved in 1936 when the Loyola squad so domi-nated the game that the Elis lost not only the game but their New Eng-land composure.

Before the next basketball season began, the United States entered the world war, and student ranks were so depleted that Loyola could not (it was said) field a varsity team. Schuerholz took over the high-school squad and it too won the state championship. For the same period the record in other sports was not nearly as exciting. In 1913 Herbert O'Conor succeeded in reestablishing a football team, its precursor having been disbanded four years earlier, after the death of a player at Georgetown. Thereupon he managed and quarterbacked the small squad, which of necessity included both college and high-school students. During their first season the students played five games and lost only one. They played more games during the next season and again won more than they lost. In 1915 the team, bereft of college-level players, scheduled games only with high-school teams. The result for the next few years was a steady but not spectacular record of football victories for Loyola. Baseball was revived in this period, but with less positive results.

Despite this, the outstanding football and baseball players were given recognition equal to that of the basketball stars when in 1914 the practice of awarding varsity letters was begun. At the December school assembly, that season's standouts on the football team were awarded their blue and gold *L*. Was this Captain Herbert O'Conor's doing or some perceptive Jesuit's idea? The February meeting provided a like occasion for awards and applause for the basketball stars, and the assembly in May was brightened by appropriate homages to the baseball players.

• •

To inspire competitiveness and emulation, publicity was given to the success of Loyola students in a different kind of contest, the national oratorical competitions then sponsored by the Intercollegiate Peace Association. The contests for 1914, 1915, and 1916 among Maryland and District of Columbia institutions were won by Loyolans Jerome Joyce (1914), Leo Codd (1916), and William Sehlhorst (1917). They were awarded prizes of seventy-five dollars (more than a year's tuition) and their winning orations were reprinted in the *Loyola Annual*.

These speeches were unabashedly idealistic and hortatory; still, there is a discernible movement of ideas in them, and they parallel contemporary developments in American thought. Joyce defended arbitration as an alternative to war, as did America's incumbent secretary of state, William Jennings Bryan. Leo Codd, echoing Woodrow Wilson's "new freedom" and Theodore Roosevelt's "new nationalism," called for a "new patriotism" in his 1915 oration. Whereas the old patriotism meant dying for one's country, Codd's new patriotism would have his listeners "living for it and living rightly and being a credit to it." In the following year, Sehlhorst won with a plea for an "over-government"— an international agency with authority to legislate future conduct and settle disputes judicially after the fact.[19]

The same honors would no doubt have been heaped on the next in this series of orations, as Herbert O'Conor prepared for the 1917 contest. But the developing crisis, which resulted in the declaration of war, forced cancellation of the contest scheduled for that spring. In all likelihood the main ideas and form of O'Conor's entry appear in the oration that won him an intramural prize. The timeliness of his subject and the polished style of the oration—titled "A League to Enforce Peace"— mark it as a sure winner. He had to be satisfied with publication in the 1917 edition of the *Annual*.

In his speech O'Conor no longer merely exhorts to virtue. He persuasively offers a practical plan that already had the endorsement of President Woodrow Wilson and other world leaders. His vision, if too hopeful by our skeptical measure, realistically admits the possibility of war even after the establishment of the league. He argues, however, "that such a [world] federation would greatly reduce the probability of hostilities."[20] His peers (as evident in the *Annual*) saw Herbert

O'Conor as a talented politician, and his prize oration gives ample evidence of his skill and style. In 1917 no one (least of all a graduating senior) could have foreseen that the hopes embodied in the League of Nations would never be fully realized.

Although peace advocates were given a certain priority, theirs was not the only view that found expression among Loyola students. John Lardner (1915) doubted that any nation would willingly submit its grievance to an international arbiter after a "stinging insult" or a "measured blow." Man was a complicated being with stronger passions than reason could rule. War, Lardner insisted, was an integral part of the world's "working order." A year later George Loden (1916) argued for a big navy so America could defend its interests in the Caribbean, at the Panama Canal, and in China. Loden sought support even among the peace advocates by arguing that a strong American navy could serve as a counterweight to maintain equilibrium among the major nations of the world. In the same issue William Hodges (1917) made a general plea for military preparedness. This was a touchy topic in 1916, both for those who feared a rise in federal taxation and for President Wilson—it being an election year.

Hodges's concern and plea were evidently quite sincere. On April 9, 1917, the first working day after the declaration of war, he left Baltimore to volunteer for service in the navy. The prefect found out about it only four days later, when at the end of the Easter holiday Hodges did not report for classes. A month or so later, two other seniors, John Quinn and Michael Ryan (having taken their final examinations early), left for Fort Myer, Virginia, seeking commissions. Soon enough, Quinn was flying in France as a lieutenant in the Army Aviation Corps. Quinn's buddy Ryan served briefly and upon being honorably discharged entered the priesthood.

By the time the war ended almost three hundred and fifty Loyola men had performed some variety of military duty. This number exceeded the total enrollment (high school and college) for even the best year. Most were alumni but a significant number (one in five) were students at the time of their enlistment. One in four received commissions, twelve served as chaplains, and one went over as a recreation worker for the Knights of Columbus. Almost half went into the army and, although they were assigned to a variety of units, there was a noticeable contingent of Loyolans in the 115th and 313th Infantry Regiments, units recruited from Baltimore. Father Zeigler said Mass for them at Port Covington.

Another thirty or forty joined the navy, some in the air service. Among the naval fliers was Lieutenant Edward McDonnell (1911), who had already been awarded the Medal of Honor for "extraordinary heroism" during the brief encounter between the United States and Mexico in 1914. In the World War, his were the first American bombs dropped on Austrian installations in the Adriatic sector. A brother, John Chilton McDonnell (1907), became an aviator in the army. Navy and army air service duty beckoned almost one of ten Loyola servicemen—evidence of a venturesomeness that some may be surprised to find among Baltimoreans.

The first casualty occurred among the aviators. John Ganster (1916) enlisted in the navy a month before the declaration of war and was in the first American contingent to reach France. Shortly after his arrival, Ganster served in a squad giving full military honors to the first American who was killed "over there." The ritual, he thought, was "an empty honor, but the French made much of it." He would be wounded and recover but die in a seaplane accident. Because of Ganster's view of military honors, it might be well to note distinctions he cherished more. In 1912 he was a member of the water polo team representing the United States at the Stockholm Olympic Games. He was also a member of the Baltimore Athletic Club's swimming team that established a record for the 160-yard relay. Other Loyola men who died while on military duty included Joseph Hanlon (1912), Cyril Emory (1915), William Keating (1916), John McCarthy (1918), and Frank Weatherly (1920). Their sacrifice along with that of John Ganster was commemorated in simple stained-glass windows installed shortly after the war in the new student chapel.

Departures from Loyola during the war years were not limited to students; several lay instructors also left. Cyril Keller (1910), who taught college German, departed in February of 1918 to take a position with a federal agency. Increasing demands on American manpower opened the way to "a more lucrative post" for another instructor who left Loyola shortly before the end of the school year. Some of these departures were not entirely voluntary. Congress in May of 1917 passed the Selective Service Act, and under its terms an instructor of high-school arithmetic was drafted.

There was a stigma attached to being conscripted. A Loyola spokesman noted with pride that less than 4 percent of the men associated with the college entered the military service through the draft. The overwhelming majority were volunteers. As vacancies occurred on the

Loyola faculty, classes were reorganized and instructors reassigned to cover the gaps and to keep the school going.

• •

War brought material shortages and governmental orders to deal with them. During the winter of 1918 elementary schools and factories involved in nonessential production were closed for a time to conserve coal. Colleges were required to close only for ten Mondays. Briefly the weekly holiday at Loyola was again shifted from Thursday to Saturday to support further the fuel-conservation program.

Hardly had the necessary adjustments been made when the federal government (presumably finding more coal above ground than had been estimated) rescinded its orders for school and factory closings. Congress then instituted a more general method for saving fuel. On March 1 (Easter Sunday) clocks all over America were to be advanced to save an hour of daylight. Farmers and railroaders, in particular, objected to this tampering with the natural order, but daylight-saving time survived even a postwar return to normality. In July 1918 the minister applied for certificates to cover the three pounds of sugar that was the monthly allotment for the Jesuit community of over twenty members. [21]

There were opportunities for more direct aid to America's war effort. Students could purchase savings stamps at the school. When they had accumulated a certain amount they converted the stamps into an interest-bearing Liberty Bond. The alumni association began buying these bonds almost as soon as they became available to the public.

The war and the effort to win it lent a patriotic tone to the commencement of 1917. Indeed, the newspaper reports took special note of the colorful mingling of Loyola's blue and gold with the darker blue and gold of the naval uniforms worn by some of the participants, the army khaki of others, the purple robes of monsignori, the black cassocks of the Jesuits, and the black gowns of the graduates.

The commencement address was delivered by Doctor Charles Wellman Mitchell of Baltimore and Princeton University. He received an honorary doctorate of laws for his humanitarian services, but in his speech he attacked two enemies: Germany and modern education. Germany had started on the road to war, Doctor Mitchell asserted, when that nation expelled the Jesuits and shifted its educational emphasis from the classical liberal arts curriculum to one aimed merely at training for material betterment. He smote American educators who urged a similar course. Mitchell remained content to follow in the footsteps of such defenders of traditional values as Woodrow Wilson, Theodore Roosevelt, William Howard Taft, and Elihu Root.

A no less patriotic but more positive note was sounded in regard to the other honorary doctorate. Admiral William Shepherd Benson was the first incumbent of the newly created post of chief of naval operations. His wife of many years hailed from Baltimore County and he had long since become a convert to Catholicism. When he stood in full uniform to accept the award the band struck up "The Star Spangled Banner" (not yet the national anthem). After the war and his retirement from active duty, Admiral Benson was honored by a number of other Catholic institutions.[22] The nation then was in the midst of yet another wave of nativism (marked by the revitalization of the Ku Klux Klan). These colleges and universities were apparently attempting to declare again that devotion to both America and Catholicism was not only compatible but ideal.

President Ennis's concluding remarks at the 1917 exercises continued the patriotic theme, but he combined that with a warning to the undergraduates: "All honor to the boys who have enlisted . . . but . . . when the country calls for our best men, it ought to be given the best service that is in them and that can best be given after their education has been completed."

Despite Ennis's plea the total at the next September registration was significantly smaller. Fewer than 190 enrolled, down from the preceding three years, when the number had been well above 300. However, heeding President Ennis's plea, and ignoring both the draft and other attractions, 40 students registered for college classes. Although this ratio of college students to total enrollment had been common since the start of the college, college varsity sports were now eliminated, and the traditional "prize night" was not held. Instead, the diplomas and awards were given individually.

But what did all these changes and abbreviations portend? Was thought being given to eliminating college classes entirely? Or were the changes occurring merely for convenience and then being ascribed to the supposedly small college enrollment? The start of the next academic year (1918–19) seemed to provide an unwelcome answer.

. .

As might be expected, the *Annual* for 1918 was replete with references to the war. Father Fleming and the rest of the Jesuits made a conscientious effort to secure the name and address of every Loyolan in the military services; and Fleming corresponded regularly with them all, asking for letters and pictures that could be printed in the *Annual*.

The 1918 issue was dedicated to Cardinal Gibbons on the fiftieth anniversary of his consecration as bishop. Between this dedication and an editorial entitled "Loyola at the Front" there were nearly one hundred and twenty pages of correspondence and photographs from Loyola's servicemen. There were pictures of officers and privates, of sailors and aviators, of doctors and chaplains, in dress uniforms and fatigues, in camp and on leave—in the usual circumstances of Americans doing their military duty.

The letters had many things in common. Almost uniformly they refer to a continuation of religious observances even under the trying conditions in which the authors found themselves. Meetings with other alumni or men from Baltimore were recounted. Reference (mostly humorous) was made to the discomforts and ironies of military life. All testified to their happy memories of the college and of association with the Jesuits. Few expressed detailed views on the war, except to deprecate its waste, even its stupidity, and to insist that the "Boche" could never win.

One exception was a letter from Ray Furlong (1921), who had joined the army at the end of his sophomore year. He took a broader view of the war than did his schoolmates. From somewhere in France he objected to a peace proposal that he feared might be gaining support among Americans. This "no annexations, no indemnities" approach would result, he thought, in a "comic opera affair." First victory and then peace negotiations was what he urged.[23]

Furlong's expression of this view was noteworthy not so much because of its militant spirit as because it differed so directly with Pope Benedict XV's appeal of August of 1917. The pontiff had urged both sides to stop the battlefield slaughter immediately and to begin negotiating on the basis of "peace without victory." Furlong's interest in the subject makes it unlikely that he was unaware of how his program differed from that of the pope. Even more interesting was the willingness of his Jesuit mentors to reprint the letter without deletions. This may have been only because Furlong made no direct reference to the pope's appeal, but even that bespeaks a sophistication not usually ascribed to American Catholics of the era.

The remaining sixty pages in the 1918 *Annual* were given to the traditional components. One sad note was an obituary for William Lapsley (1879), who had served at Loyola as porter since 1888. In addition to minding the entrance, he sold tickets for all the plays, movies, lectures, and games from a cubicle near the front door, and he always had an ample supply of chances for one raffle or another. Even Father Ryan's *Historical Sketch of Loyola College* was on sale at Lapsley's "lodge."

First panel of the centennial plaque located on the Holliday Street side of the War Memorial Plaza near the site where Loyola College started in 1852. The plaque was designed by Albert Sehlstedt (1919) and executed by Henry Berge.

Engraving of "the College," 1856. This engraving was a regular feature of Loyola's catalogues until the 1890s. The spires were never built.

Detail from 1869 Sachse View of Baltimore showing Saint Ignatius Church and Loyola College near the right edge (MHS)

Father John Abell Morgan, S.J., president from 1891 to 1900

Father William Ennis, S.J., president from 1911 to 1918

The College Theatre, now home of Center Stage, was erected in 1899.

Ground breaking for science building (now Beatty Hall), June 12, 1922. Father Joseph McEneany, S.J., president of Loyola College from 1918 to 1927, observes Archbishop Michael J. Curley turn the first shovel. The students are attired for commencement exercises, held the same day.

Father Edward Bunn, S.J.,
president from 1938 to 1947

Father Justin Ooghe, S.J.,
professor of philosophy
from 1918 to 1931

George Carrell Jenkins (1837–1930), a generous benefactor during the 1920s

"Madonna of the Stars," a photograph taken by Father John Delaney, S.J., professor of physics, on the night of December 10–11, 1939. The camera shutter was left open on a moonless night, and the rotation of the earth created the star tracks.

Father Vincent Beatty, S.J., president from 1955 to 1964, greeting then-Senator John Kennedy, who was the speaker for the alumni banquet on February 18, 1958. Jim Lacy (1949) is to the left of the senator, and John Fetting (1949) appears between Kennedy and Father Beatty.

Father Joseph Sellinger, S.J., president since 1964

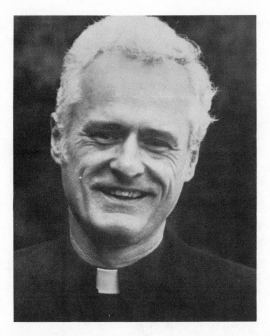

Father Eugene Ahern, S.J., coordinator of campus ministries and assistant professor of theology, for whom the Ahern Apartments are named

Loyola–Notre Dame Library, dedicated in March of 1973

Donnelly Science Center, dedicated in December 1978

Part Three

1918–1947

Evergreen

11

Evergreen Instead

C hanges of various magnitude and kind were evident in the post-war world, including at Loyola. In the general swirl it was possible to sense a pervasive release—although from what or to what was unclear. Parents and social critics worried over the "problem" of the younger generation, but the objects of that concern hailed their era as one of "wonderful nonsense." The summer and fall of 1918, however, were still punctuated by climactic battles in Europe. A German offensive was stalled by the French, British, and Belgian armies reinforced by the Americans. An Allied counteroffensive followed and finally forced Germany to sue for an armistice—and then for a peace based on President Wilson's Fourteen Points.

．．

The contemporaneous events at Calvert Street could not match European developments for high drama, but here too change was taking place, albeit more orderly and purposefully. On July 27, 1918, Father Joseph McEneany assumed the responsibilities that he would bear for more than eight years. The most visible event of his term was the transfer of college classes to Evergreen and the separation of the college from the high school. In this act President McEneany could be considered the second founder of Loyola College because it became a different kind of institution from what it had been. The paucity of records makes it impossible to claim for McEneany the title of savior of Loyola, but there is reason to believe that the institution came very close to having its college-level programs suppressed in 1918.

The most pertinent element of Father McEneany's preparation was eight years as minister at Woodstock. As the training ground for Jesuits, Woodstock was always staffed with exemplary teachers and administrators, and Father McEneany as minister was responsible to the rector for daily order and operations of the resident community. Except for the date of his birth (April 12, 1868), that he attended school in New York City, and that he entered the Society at the age of 25, nothing of his early background is recorded. He taught for several years at Boston College, when Read Mullan (1879) was its president, and continued his studies at Woodstock. He suffered from asthma, a condition that must have been aggravated by the humidity and industrial smoke of Baltimore. He was a short man who struck a Napoleonic pose when photographed. There is little from which to construct a biography—not even an obituary in the *Woodstock Letters.* He was 50 years old when he came to Loyola.

• •

His immediate concern was the reopening of classes in the face of the demand for soliders and workers. One resource for Loyola was to secure a unit of the Student Army Training Corps (SATC). This was a hastily organized program to prevent the collapse of American higher education and to provide at least lightly seasoned recruits. A school with an SATC unit was paid full tuition and a dollar a day subsistence for each enlistee. The Jesuits thought they would be more successful in applying for these units by limiting their participation to Georgetown, Fordham, and Boston College, with qualified teachers from the others reassigned to these schools. The result for Loyola was the suspension of college-level classes in September of 1918 and the transfer of its college teachers to Georgetown.

The Loyola students who had not enlisted in SATC were horrified by the discontinuance of college classes and protested to Father Fleming. Those who anticipated becoming college freshmen were especially aroused. They pressed for a reopening of college classes, if only for them. Fleming offered some encouragement, if enough recruits could be found. Emmet Bradley (1922), for one, scoured his neighborhood and acquaintances for likely prospects. In his mind, and probably that of others, the issue was nothing less than saving Loyola College from extinction. The discontinuance of collegiate classes at Mount Saint Agnes earlier that year—though unconnected to Loyola—fed the fear that a similar fate was about to befall the college program at Calvert Street.[1]

The situation of the high school was notably less precarious. On September 16, 1918, when classes resumed with the traditional *schola brevis,* almost two hundred students registered. There was an additional contingent of unknown number who had heeded the government's call in the spring for farmhands and would return after the harvest in late October.

Despite an auspicious start, Loyola, with all other schools in Baltimore, closed at the beginning of October because of the raging influenza epidemic. Unlike earlier contagions, this one was a national disaster. The death rate in the major eastern seaboard cities rose by 700 percent and people were ill and dying in virtually every state of the Union. Fear spawned rumors and bizarre theories as to the source and cause of the epidemic. Viral infection was not a familiar idea, and doctors did not know how to treat their patients beyond prescribing aspirin and bed rest.

In Baltimore the health authorities took what action they could to limit the spread of the disease. A few days after the closing of schools all theaters and churches were shut. Despite these precautions fatalities continued to mount in the city, with 240 people dying in one twenty-four-hour period. By the end of October, the epidemic had run its course; restrictions were gradually lifted, and on November 4 even schools were permitted to reopen. On that day Father Fleming recorded the toll among Loyola students as 1 dead, 15 with deaths in their immediate family. But 230, including 9 new registrants, were on the school rolls.

Among them was the nucleus of a college freshman class that had in fact been organized on the eve of the flu outbreak. Then a squad of eight young men (Emmet Bradley among them) presented themselves to Fleming, who promptly got Father Philip Finnegan to instruct them in Latin and Greek, a scholastic to teach them mechanics, and a layman to explain trigonometry.

Hardly had the normal schedule been resumed in November when it was joyously disrupted. Three days after a false report, authentic headlines declared: THE WAR IS OVER. On the morning of November 11 a few eager students arrived at the usual time, but Father Fleming shooed them home. His diary continues: "Great spontaneous demonstrations in the city. All business & schools suspended."[2] After a delirious celebration, most Baltimoreans—including the students—were found the next day at their normal pursuits.

The rest of the semester proceeded uneventfully, except for a midday recess on December 13 so that Loyola students could join the crowds watching Baltmore's victory parade. This year, as in others since the start of hostilities, the post office asked Loyola for helpers to sort and deliver the mail during the Christmas season. How many responded is not known, but Christmas post-office work became a firmly established feature that would be familiar to teachers and students for the next forty years.

• •

Toward the end of this *annus mirabilis,* President McEneany tried to revive a full college course. He wrote the provincial to ask for a return of the Jesuits who had been reassigned to Georgetown. The SATC program was being disbanded, he noted; the teachers could be freed and the enlistees would be returning. His arguments may have been prompted by the understandable desire to lead the institution to which he was first assigned rather than a truncated version of it. In the cautious rhythm associated with that office, the provincial did not act immediately but sent the Jesuits back to Loyola by the end of the Christmas vacation. On January 6, 1919 (the feast of the Epiphany), the full schedule of college classes was resumed—but for how long?

The question was being asked in regard to the whole Jesuit educational enterprise in America. If its polemicists were publicly defending the quality of the order's schools, other members of the Society in private were asking for serious evaluation of the future of Jesuit colleges. Too many were seen as "inadequately staffed, underfinanced, and unevenly administered." Continuing to maintain such lackluster institutions was not in accord with the genius of the Society, and in this postwar period a study and consultative process was begun to reform and revitalize American Jesuit education. This reform would proceed at what seemed a glacially slow pace and would not be embodied in a formal structure until the founding of the Jesuit Educational Association in 1934.[3] This association was controlled by the provincials, advised by an annual conference of institutional president-rectors on educational developments and issues. Except for the stress it placed on securing accreditation, this general movement had little direct impact on Loyola.

For various reasons including an old-fashioned disdain for statistics, Father Fleming did not bother in January of 1919 to note in his office diary how many students were enrolled in Loyola's newly reopened college classes. The catalogue at the end of the year, however, listed twenty-one freshmen, ten sophomores, six juniors, and five seniors. If few they still represented the usual balance between college and high-school students. Their number was sufficient to persuade the provincial after his March visit to Calvert Street to continue the college program, but it was several months before he informed Father McEneany of this decision.[4] The delay heightened the belief of McEneany and others that serious consideration had been given to suppression and that it had been averted by the narrowest of margins.

Continuation of the college program was not the only matter that absorbed President McEneany at that time. He was working steadily on the transfer to Guilford—whatever the school's educational level was to be. Early in August of 1918, he traveled to Atlantic City in the company of Father Ennis to meet Thomas O'Neill. Because international hostilities had not yet ended, they agreed that construction could not begin. Even the end of the war brought no immediate lowering of costs. And then, on April 6, 1919, Thomas O'Neill suddenly died, activating the trust arrangement he had made for his wife and relatives. As a result there might be at the least an indefinite delay in the plan to move Loyola and Saint Ignatius Church. With the rest of Baltimore, the Jesuits joined in mourning this generous and public-spirited man.

In due course O'Neill's will was submitted for probate and (as is common) questions were raised about how his intentions were to be understood and fulfilled. About his bequest to Loyola, did O'Neill's gifts and several codicils, taken together, indicate that he had intended that the full amount of the bequest be delivered to the Associated Professors despite the provisions made for the family trust? Was a late gift of almost $82,000 in securities, not accounted for in a codicil as other donations had been, part of the whole sum or an addition to the original bequest? What might seem simple to a layman has often been found quite complex by practitioners of the law. One of O'Neill's trustees (an experienced banker and trust manager) favored Loyola's position and would have handed over the bequest augmented by the $82,000. Another trustee, however, who happened to be an alumnus, staunchly defended the opposite view and persuaded the others that the way to settle the issue was to join the college in a friendly suit.

It took almost two years to secure a definitive judgment. On January 21, 1921, the Maryland Court of Appeals ruled for the O'Neill trustees. This meant that the part of the bequest not yet paid to Loyola would not be delivered until after the death of Mrs. O'Neill, and the amount that Loyola would receive then would be only $218,000. Meanwhile the $282,000 that O'Neill had transferred to Loyola during his lifetime, and the Guilford land, had to be retained until the whole bequest could be used for its intended purpose—the building of a church. However, the relocation northward of Saints Philip and James Church about this time made it even less likely that the Jesuits could open one on nearby

University Parkway.[5] Soon the new archbishop, Michael J. Curley, made clear that he wished Saint Ignatius Church to remain at Calvert Street, but he promised to cover any loss to the Jesuits as a result of his decision.

• •

After nine years as prefect (an unusually long term), Father Richard Fleming was transferred in June of 1919 to Brooklyn, where he continued his decanal service at a new Jesuit school. His hapless successor at Loyola, William Stinson, whose title was changed from prefect of studies to dean, became the central figure in the great strike of 1919. This event was compounded from customary extracurricular concerns of students: securing holidays and vexing authority. (Changing the title of the office of perfect should be seen as a step in the continued adaptation of Jesuit education to prevailing American practices.)

As the first anniversary of the armistice approached, a quickly circulating rumor had it that the day was going to be celebrated at the college, as at other Baltimore schools, with a full holiday. Dean Stinson thought otherwise, and President McEneany was out of town in connection with the dispute over the O'Neill will. A college junior (a returned veteran) insisted that Father McEneany had promised that Armistice Day would be a school holiday. Stinson, who had served a number of years as dean at Saint Joseph's in Philadelphia and who should have known better, responded with a temporizing accommodation that seemed to sanction a holiday only for the college juniors and seniors. This struck the underclassmen and high-school students as grossly unfair.

On the morning of November 11 they gathered in the college yard before the bell sounded for classes. A deputation was sent to the dean and he came out on the balcony and conceded dismissal at noon for all. If the bell had rung at that moment, probably nothing would have happened (or so one participant later thought), but there was a ten-minute interval for students to consider the prospect of a morning of recitations and study. One of the bolder spirits in the pack shouted "Let's strike!" and seventy-five young rebels rushed through the archway to Calvert Street and then downtown, where in front of the Sunpapers building they held a rally. They shouted general defiance and a variety of Loyola cheers to the applause of amused onlookers.

Of course, such behavior could not be condoned. The remedy was a familiar one in Roman administrative tradition. From ancient times the traditional assumption has been that no group moves spontaneously;

there must be leadership and this has to be punished. All absentees were closely interviewed on their return to classes. A few had to bring their parents for a conference with the dean, and two high-school seniors already known as troublemakers were suspended. They chose not to appeal the action and departed from Loyola. Their peers accepted this denouement indifferently and were especially impressed by the fact that having a brother in the Society of Jesus did not shield one of the culprits.[6] On President McEneany's return the measures already adopted were ratified, but a program of half-holidays and other concessions followed to regain the students' good will. Father Stinson was quietly transferred at the end of the academic year; Loyola was not the brightest moment in an otherwise substantial record of service.

An intensive effort to reform American society was then being launched. The Eighteenth Amendment, which prohibited the manufacture, transportation, and sale of alcoholic beverages, was ratified early in 1919. The roots of this Prohibition movement were deep and varied, but its most persistent support came from people inspired by American nativism, and this made it obnoxious to Catholics.

When national prohibition was enacted it was seen by many Marylanders (especially important political leaders) as impinging on states' rights. As a result, police in Maryland generally avoided enforcing the ban on alcohol unless a riot or some other serious crime was immediately involved. This policy prompted some wags to create a new motto for Maryland—the Free State—apparently by analogy with the Irish Free State and other enclaves around the world that were declaring their independence from surrounding authority.[7]

What the Jesuits generally thought of this "noble experiment" is unknown, but there are a few indicative touches in the house diary. Independence Day in 1920, the first national anniversary after Prohibition went into effect, was celebrated on Calvert Street in the traditional manner by displaying the flag and toasting the occasion with a glass of wine for dinner. Whether the latter part of the ritual was continued in subsequent years was discreetly left unrecorded.

Three years later, some event must have touched off the accumulated exasperation of the diarist, for on October 23 he exclaimed: "Prohibition—foolish and unjust law." He feared that enforcement might become so restrictive that it would be impossible to obtain the wine needed for the sacrifice of the Mass. He also feared for "Liberty, freedom and independence, America!! may the Lord keep us from benighted citizens whether Christian or otherwise."[8] No similar outburst appears later in the house diary, but this writer was doubtless not alone in holding such sentiments—or stronger.

· ·

In this postwar era the Jesuits of the Maryland–New York province joined their fellow citizens in discharging one of their civic responsibilities. Late in 1918 the provincial recommended that all qualified members of the Society register to vote. Except for occasional reminders against identification with any political group, there had probably been no rule against Jesuits voting, but the constant shifting from one location to another militated against it. What prompted the provincial's recommendation at this moment is uncertain, but the emergence of democratic governments around the world must have been taken into account. The traditional Jesuit reliance on influence with the elite and an apparent disdain for the electoral process now appeared to be anachronistic. Furthermore, the effort to enfranchise women in America nationally had come very close to success earlier that year. It may have seemed only a matter of time till they too would be voting; then, why not the Jesuits?

Loyola's Jesuits obeyed the provincial and registered to vote. Their first opportunity to exercise the franchise came during the fall of 1919, when Albert Ritchie was elected governor in a very close election. There is no way to establish whether voting by the Jesuits had any effect on his victory. Accounted an able executive and political leader, Ritchie repeatedly won election during the next decade or so and was considered a serious candidate for the presidency in 1932. Some of his early popularity with the Maryland voters arose from his opposition to federal Prohibition laws and to women's suffrage—at least until the Nineteenth Amendment was ratified.[9]

The change in Maryland's governmental leadership was paralleled by a major change in the church. On March 24, 1921, James Cardinal Gibbons died. Loyola's faculty and students joined the rest of Baltimore and the nation in mourning the death of "everybody's Cardinal." Forty-four years—half his lifetime—had passed since he became the archbishop of his native city. This able, tactful, but frail man had exercised his authority so skillfully that an editorial writer for the *Sun* declared, "Humanity is better and purer and nobler because of the life that has come to its earthly close."[10]

It was eight months before his successor, Michael Curley, arrived. Among the dignitaries who escorted the new archbishop into Baltimore was Father McEneany, and at Mount Royal Station a waiting throng cheered as Curley stepped from the train. They continued the din as he entered an automobile for the drive to his new residence. Initially, Archbishop Curley seemed unable to decide what to make of this demonstration. As the motorcade passed an assemblage of Loyola students who rhythmically chanted "Arch-bishop Cur-ley—Arch-bishop Curley," however, his face finally broke into a broad smile.

He differed from his predecessor in a number of ways. Physically, he was tall and imposing. In temperament he tended to command where Gibbons might have moved by indirection. He was quietly generous to those in need, but harsh and even sarcastic with those whom he judged incompetent or at fault. Archbishop Curley believed in the punctilious observance of all rituals of deference due his office. He was an able, zealous churchman who stressed the importance of a Catholic education, the requirements of social justice, and the need to oppose anti-Catholic forces in Mexico and Spain. He was an effective orator— judged by some to have been among the most eloquent archbishops of Baltimore.[11] On November 30, 1921, he was formally installed as archbishop of Baltimore at the age of 42.

. .

There was an addition to the leadership cohort of Maryland at this time who had a Loyola connection. The president of the Baltimore Federation of Labor since 1920 was Henry Broening, an alumnus (class of 1901). Broening's father operated a horseshoeing shop near Camden Station; he hedged his bets by apprenticing his son to the trade and sending him to Loyola College. A cousin, William Broening (later memorialized with a highway to Annapolis), was then the mayor of Baltimore.

Henry Broening effectively capitalized on being both a laborer and a college man. He became the head of the Horseshoer's Union and embellished his speeches with classical allusions and references to ancient history. In 1922 he got Archbishop Curley to address the Maryland Federation, and His Grace took the occasion to denounce the effort of some owners to promote the open shop. He, like Gibbons and other American churchmen, supported labor's right to organize. Elected to the state legislature, Broening became labor's leading and most effective advocate; he enjoyed the confidence of Governor Ritchie. He used his expertise in workmen's compensation to help inmates of the state penitentiary file claims. It was there that he resumed his friendship with a schoolmate, Father Joseph Ayd (1903), who in addition to his teaching duties at Loyola served as the prison chaplain. Thereafter, whenever a union occasion required the presence of a clergyman, Broening saw that Father Ayd was invited.

On his election to the presidency of the Maryland and District of Columbia Federation of Labor, Broening's dedication, talent, and influence gained a larger field of operations at a crucial time. The labor movement in America was then suffering from the opposition of organized capital, from political demagogues who used the fear of communist revolution to smear union organizing, and from its own tactical failures. Union membership was declining nationally so that by 1923 it was only a little over 3.6 million. Morale was low and rival unions were squabbling over who was to organize various groups of workers.

The situation might have discouraged a lesser man, but Broening worked to turn it in a more hopeful direction. While promoting the interests of workers, he strove to maintain the harmony of management and labor that has always been characteristic of Baltimore unionism and contributed significantly to the booming economic development of the region. He led a drive to organize more unions with little success at first—but his efforts finally resulted in the founding of over thirty more organizations after the Great Depression hit. In fact, the organizing drive and his work to mitigate the effects of the economic crisis brought about Broening's sudden and untimely death in 1933.[12]

• •

The plan to move Loyola had been muted by O'Neill's death and the adverse court decision, but it had not been entirely forgotten. Two communications forced renewed action early in 1921. One was a letter from the Middle States Association, and the other was the provincial's decision on the Guilford project.

The letter from the Middle States Association was a reminder of its new program for accrediting colleges. This was part of a general movement involving state agencies as well as such private bodies as the Catholic Education Association. No immediate reply was given the letter from the Middle States (which seems to have perplexed the MSA staff), but Father McEneany and his colleagues knew they could not postpone the matter for very long. The 1921 report of an inter-province committee urged all Jesuit schools to seek accreditation—but all accrediting agencies reserved their approbation to colleges that had no direct connection with a secondary school. This qualification was obviously intended to raise the standard of instruction at both levels and to make the high school serve a variety of objectives, not merely college preparation. Loyola had been moving toward such a division for many years, but since income from the high-school level financed the college, not much progress had been made. Emergence of the accreditation movement made decisive action necessary—otherwise, Loyola graduates would eventually be denied admission to the best professional and graduate schools.[13] The determination and energy that became evident in McEneany's activity from 1921 onward arose from a variety of causes, but one of the most urgent (even if not openly acknowledged) must have been the realization that Loyola would soon have to try for accreditation and that it could not afford to fail.

About the same time, the provincial and his consultors came to the conclusion that there was no future for either the college or a church in Guilford. A magnificent Protestant Episcopal cathedral was being erected on a site diagonally opposite the Loyola property, and this would overshadow the church. The college, on the other hand, would be only a few blocks from the Johns Hopkins University after it moved to its Homewood campus, and the provincial and his consultors thought Loyola might suffer by comparison.[14] Another site therefore had to be found for a Loyola College that would not be connected to either a high school or a parish church.

The local reasons for this separation were reinforced by another general change in the attitude of Americans toward higher education. Various arguments had been urged for completing a full collegiate program before the war, but these had not been effective. College, most continued to believe, was only for those who planned to become doctors, lawyers, or clergymen. The war changed all that when a significant number of people suddenly and simultaneously learned that those with any college training got preferential treatment in the military, in industry, and in government service. What one knew, as certified by a college transcript or diploma, made a big difference when commissions or jobs were distributed. As a result, the demand for admission to institutions that could provide such advantageous credentials rose quickly.

Among Catholics there were additional factors promoting college attendance. According to a notable historian, American Catholics had come to believe that they were the inheritors of an integral culture based on Thomistic philosophy that could be transmitted most effectively through church-affiliated schools. This Catholic culture, in the frenzied and disorderly society that emerged after the World War, could serve as a vehicle for redeeming the period. Even some Catholics were worried by the tone of smugness they detected among their co-religionists.[15] Others considered the attitude of Catholics as naive or a perverse refusal to face current realities except as formulated by church authority. This increased the disjunction between Catholic and other American institutions.

• •

Within two months after the provincial's decision against Guilford, President McEneany found a suitable alternative. Though it is nowhere recorded, circumstances suggest that he learned of the site from George Jenkins, who had been peripherally connected to the Guilford project and who was personally acquainted with the prospective sellers. An attractive parcel of land about three miles due north of the Calvert Street location and with almost twenty acres stretching northward on Charles Street Avenue[16] and eastward on Cold Spring Lane had just become available.

Most recently the handsome half-timbered Tudor-style mansion and its grounds had served as a rehabilitation center for men blinded during the war. Although the area was not under direct control of the Roland Park Company, it faced the upper limits of Guilford across Cold Spring Lane and was within the environs of the Homeland section of the District. The tract, known as Evergreen Junior, was an appanage created just before the turn of the century by the Garrett family for one of its scions. The mansion had originally been an 1895 wedding gift but the unfortunate recipient died while on a trip to England before it was completed. The building is sometimes erroneously attributed to Stanford White but was actually the work of Renwick, Aspinwall, and Renwick, a firm that had around that time designed the spires of Saint Patrick's Cathedral in New York City.

Until 1918, when the boundaries of Baltimore were expanded to their present dimensions, the area had been mostly rural in character. Sometime in the early 1850s, the Broadbents, a prominent Catholic merchant family, built a country seat on what they chose to call "Glenmary." Their nearest neighbor was an orphan asylum conducted by Father James Dolan, who in the early 1850s had welcomed Loyola's founder, John Early, to the city. During the Civil War the Broadbents sold the property, and even the land of the orphan asylum passed into other hands.

In 1871 part of the tract was acquired by the School Sisters of Notre Dame, a community of nuns from Bavaria who had been working in Baltimore for over twenty years. They were seeking a location where they could open a suitable boarding academy for young ladies. It was opened in 1873 and twenty years later was augmented by the first Catholic college for women in the United States, the College of Notre Dame of Maryland. Meanwhile John Garrett, builder of the Baltimore and Ohio Railroad, acquired the Broadbent seat in 1878 and expanded it to fit the needs of one of Maryland's leading families. In the interim it was renamed "Evergreen."[17]

That McEneany or the Jesuits were aware of these associations is doubtful. They knew a good piece of real estate when they saw it, and they had to move quickly. And move quickly they did. It took only a month for President McEneany and his colleagues to inspect the site and to secure the permission of the provincial. The archdiocesan authorities agreed without delay, but they carefully stipulated (this was during the interval between Gibbons's death and Curley's arrival) that the new site was not to "be used for a church or public chapel without the special permission of the Archbishop of Baltimore."[18]

Then difficulties arose from the Garrett side. They had mixed feelings about selling to the Jesuits. They appreciated, on the one hand, the reputation of the Jesuits for tenacity in holding land but, on the other hand, they were worried about various nuisances. They were most directly worried about bells, and even George Jenkins's assurances that Jesuits did not covet such noisy appurtenances did not convince them. Into the deed went a stipulation that the college could not install any bells or chimes without the written consent of the Garretts. Loyola's neighbors were protected against a belching smokestack from a power plant or laundry by a requirement of prior notice and time to negotiate the location of such a facility. The deed permitted the erection of a chapel and of several other facilities but stated that the land was to be used for a private educational institution for "white persons." More than sixty years later this may seem an awkward requirement for both parties, but it and the remainder of the deed, prohibiting odoriferous enterprises and livestock, were standard provisions for deeds in the area. They were not so much aimed directly at Loyola College as at protecting the neighborhood against what might be erected on the site if the Jesuits were forced to sell the tract.

What notice, if any, Father McEneany took of the stipulations in the deed is unknown, but he agreed to the price—$240,000—and signed the contract. The price in today's dollars (ignoring any change in real estate values) would be $874,000. Fortunately, more than half the amount needed became available just before the agreement was signed. Mary Ann Farmer, a parishioner of Saint Ignatius Church, completed the transfer of over $155,000 to the Associated Professors, mostly in liberty bonds, and agreed that these funds could be used to buy the Evergreen parcel.

· ·

This money had come to Mary Ann Farmer by a tortuous route, involving among other things a lawsuit by her nephew and nieces. Mary Farmer and her sister had to appear in court to defend themselves against the charge that they had acquired the fortune—in the hyperbolic and comprehensive language of the courts—through "improper influence and dominion" over their aunt. In September of 1920, a Maryland court ruled against the nephew and nieces.[19]

To thwart their kin the Farmer sisters decided to give the money to Loyola College on condition of receiving an annuity during their lifetime. This has been a common, if not generally publicized, practice among a variety of institutions, but it entails some risk. Georgetown in 1834 accepted a gift subject to a life annuity, and the donor survived to receive more than twice the amount of the original gift. Mary Farmer was then only about 50 years old. The death of her sister shortly after the court decision in their favor prompted Mary Farmer to complete the transaction. She endowed two professorships as memorials for the Quinn-Farmer families and deposited over $155,000 with Loyola's treasurer. On this account she was to receive about $6,500 a year, the same as the interest on the bonds she gave to Loyola.

The arrangement was formalized in a legal document emerging from a transaction that stretched over eight months. When Father McEneany proffered a copy of the deed Miss Farmer refused to accept it because she did not want to keep anything around that might inform her nephew and nieces of what had happened to her money. "When my eyes are closed," she told a friend, "theirs will be opened."[20] For the same reason, she later rejected a suggestion that the mansion on the Evergreen campus be named the Quinn-Farmer Memorial Building. Mary Farmer's reticence about her finances was shared by other Baltimoreans of that period.

For the next nine years, she maintained close relations with Loyola. Soon she moved away from the neighborhood, which held painful memories for her, to a small house a few blocks south of Cold Spring Lane. At Hadley Square West she lived with a servant and several cats. She was a regular visitor on the new campus that her generosity had made possible; as the result of a nearly fatal accident, she would later become a source of legal difficulties for the college.

· ·

The formalities of the purchase of Evergreen stretched from July to November of 1921. Even before the formal transfer of title, President McEneany spent the late summer preparing for the opening of classes in September. There was neither time enough nor suitable space to shift the laboratories immediately and so for a few years chemistry, physics, and biology students had to commute between Cold Spring Lane and Calvert Street. Futhermore, there were no plans yet for the Jesuits to move into the mansion, so they too would have to commute.

The distance involved made it clear that a separate dean was necessary for the college classes, and Father Philip Finnegan, who was scheduled to teach the junior class, accepted this additional responsibility. He was, however, freed from supervising high-school classes, which now became the responsibility of another officer called "the principal." However, the formal division of the Jesuit community, which still served both the college and the high school, took several years.

July and August were busy with necessary modifications and additions to the mansion. On the fifteenth of September, volunteer scholastics drove a truck from Woodstock to haul the books, desks, tables, chairs, and other paraphernalia up Charles Street.[21] However many trips it took, the task was completed in one day. All the essentials were in place for the start of classes four days later, on September 19, 1921— sixty-nine years after Loyola College first opened its doors on Holliday Street. Evergreen afforded a broader vista both physically and in terms of possibilities. "Education *de luxe* is what the Loyola College students will enjoy in their new home at Evergreen," declared the *Catholic Review* on the weekend before the start of classes in 1921.[22] In such bucolic surroundings students and teachers sensed a release from the grim-walled concrete school yard at Calvert Street.

· ·

Those who arrived early on September 19 shared a cheerful expectation of the future. Most had come on the trolley up Saint Paul Street to Bedford Square (a few may have come by the alternate line on York Road). From Bedford Square to the campus the direct route was across a field, and students would soon wear a path on this land. Eventually dwellings and fences forced them to walk up Charles Street.

The Charles–Cold Spring intersection was then guarded by a sound-actuated traffic light installed to accommodate the sparse traffic on Cold Spring, still a narrow two-lane roadway. Students, familiar with the system, could shout into the sound receptor and suddenly change a green light to red, forcing motorists to halt. The widening of

Cold Spring Lane, an increase in traffic, and the advance of technology soon brought an automatic time-switch to the intersection, and the students lost this means of annoying the citizenry.

Among the early arrivals on that first Monday was Father Henry McLoughlin. Surrounded by a crowd of students, he hoisted the flag on the pole left by the federal hospital that had occupied the site. To instruct them in measuring by triangulation, he calculated the height of the pole by pacing its shadow and that of a bystander.[23] In working out the proportion, he found the pole about sixty feet tall from the concrete base to the ball finial.

By half past nine, the sixty students, some alumni, and the faculty formally opened the school year. Dean Finnegan started "with a prayer to the Holy Ghost." Then Father McEneany delivered a brief address. In his characteristically precise enunciation and slightly pompous manner, he announced, "This is a day of days; it is a day the Lord hath made." He reminded the audience of the dangerous past, when during the war "Loyola's doors were so nearly closed forever." He briefly rehearsed the difficulties that had to be overcome before the college could move to its new site.

Finally he offered a few thoughts about the future. President McEneany predicted that the small band of students before him would in a short time increase to a thousand and that Loyola would become a university in fact, as well as in the words of its charter. This vision thrilled his listeners and induced "a resolution to study and accomplish things."[24]

• •

The shift to Evergreen was accompanied by less welcome changes. Tuition, which had hovered around $60 a year until World War I, when it had risen to $80, now became $125 for the college students and would three years later rise to $150. The catalogue for 1921–22 carried no information about the high-school program or tuition. The issuance of separate catalogues signalled the approach of a formal division, which would be achieved a few years hence.

A change in the demography of Loyola's clientele—a change that may have begun a few years earlier—became evident after the move to Evergreen. At least during the decades that bracketed the turn of the century, the college had attracted the sons of some of Baltimore's social and civic elite. Furthermore, Loyola's graduates were well accepted in the management of a variety of local establishments and enterprises. The general experience during World War I made many Americans aware of how valuable a college education could be. This, the restlessness of the younger generation, and the general prosperity of the 1920s combined to make it possible for many whose fathers and uncles had attended Loyola to go away to college.

This choice meant a relative decline in but not the disappearance of that stratum among the new Loyola's student body. If the college at Holliday Street and then later at Calvert did not focus its efforts mainly on the sons of recent immigrants, now not by preference but because of general developments, the proportion of students who had parents of modest economic means and social background increased at the new Loyola. The college as a result lost some of its former social cachet. It now served a student body more nearly like that at many other Catholic colleges. By this time Baltimore was completing the change from a center of commerce and finance to an industrialized economy.[25] For American Catholics World War I marked the end of their immigrant era and the start of a general advance into the middle class with a concomitant emphasis on a college education.

Loyola's new focus on the college level prompted its offering of more options. The Jesuit provincial in 1919 had suggested a number of amendments to the curricula offered by the schools under his jurisdiction. At Evergreen this meant that Greek became merely an alternative to an equivalent number of mathematics courses. A bachelor of science degree was made available to regular undergraduates; it had been listed around the turn of the century among the university extension offerings. The bachelor of science program carried the same course requirements as the bachelor of arts, except that additional science classes and laboratory sessions were substituted for Latin.

A bachelor of philosophy, also formerly only an extension listing, became available in 1927 to regular undergraduates. It was a lineal descendant of the old English (commercial) course but had acquired a greater dignity than that accorded its barely tolerated ancestor. Upon completion of the bachelor of philosophy program, a student received a regular college diploma and not merely a certificate of attendance. Loyola's "philosophers," like their confreres in the arts and science curricula, took all the generally required courses but substituted the study of ancient civilization, political science, economics, and the history of philosophy for Latin and Greek. The provincial's suggestion had warranted the establishment of a premedical program that took only two years but included a substantial amount of philosophy and religion. It was even more heavily weighted with biology and chemistry courses, but not quite heavily enough for the Johns Hopkins Medical School, which for a while admitted Loyola students only conditionally.

Table 11.1 offers a comparison of the four curricula offered by the college at Evergreen in the mid-1920s. A comparison of the major subjects and their relative weights in the A.B. curriculum between 1895 and 1928 reveals the steady substitution of philosophy and religion for ancient literature as the main vehicle by which the Jesuits sought to impart a liberal education (Table 11.2).

The aspiration to aesthetic and humanistic development was still clearly embedded in the required core of studies, but it yielded primacy to instruction in a rigorously reasoned philosophy of life. As much as anything, the carnage of World War I and the subsequent revolutions

TABLE 11.1   Curricula Offered, 1927–1928

	A.B. (N hrs.)	(%)	B.S. (N hrs.)	(%)	Ph.B. (N hrs.)	(%)	Premed. (N hrs.)	(%)
Latin	18	11.5	0		0		0	
Mathematics	16[a]	10.3	16	10.5	16	10.3	0	
Greek			0		0		0	
English	14	8.9	16	10.5	16	10.3	8	9.5
History	6	3.8	6	3.9	6 ⎫ 16[b] ⎬	14.1	0	
Political Science	0		0		6 ⎫	11.5	0	
Economics	0		0		12 ⎭		0	
Philosophy	36	23.1	36	23.6	36 ⎫ 4[c] ⎬	25.6	24	28.6
Sciences	16	10.3	30	19.7	8	5.1	36	42.9
Languages	8	5.1	8	5.3	8	5.1	8	9.5
Religion	(16)	10.3	(16)	10.5	(16)	10.3	(8)	9.5
Elocution	(2)	1.2	0		(4)	2.6	0	
Electives	24	15.4	24	15.8	24	14.4	0	
Total	156	99.9	152	99.8	156	100.0	84	100.0

NOTE: No credit was given for the religion or elocution courses. They are included to provide a full summary of the requirements. Only Catholics were required to take the religion course.

[a]Students enrolled in the A.B. program could choose either Greek or mathematics.

[b]These 16 semester hours were for the ancient civilization course.

[c]This was the history of philosophy course.

TABLE 11.2 Subject as a Percentage of A.B. Curriculum, 1895–1928

	1895	1912	1928
Latin	22	16	12
Mathematics	21	4	0
Greek	15	10	(10)
English	13	7	9
History	0	7	4
Philosophy	12	23	23
Science	10	14	10
Languages	3	2	5
Religion	2	9	(10)
Elocution	2	2	(1)
Electives	0	6	15
Total	100	100	99

NOTE: In 1928 Greek was no longer required but could be chosen as an alternative to an equal amount of mathematics. Religion and elocution were required for Catholics but no credit was given for these courses.

were seen by many as convincing proof that a heightened appreciation of beauty or style was no longer an antidote for barbarism. The civilizing effect of the study of literature, thought the Jesuits and other Catholic educators, had to be reinforced with larger doses of scholastic logic, metaphysics, ethics, and religion. At other American colleges for men, culture courses were retained as electives—ornamental survivors of a bygone era—but the demand was for the natural sciences and engineering.

• •

During the 1920s a number of refinements were introduced into Loyola's catalogues that anticipated the standards of various accrediting agencies. Course work, for instance, was now defined in terms of semester hours, and this meant a standard lecture period per week or twice that amount of time in the laboratory; the standard lecture period was fifty minutes.[26] Classes started at nine o'clock and ended by two in the afternoon.

The term *major* appeared briefly in the catalogue, but it was mainly a device to organize the choice of electives. A similar usage appeared in the catalogues of Saint Joseph's and of some other Jesuit schools.[27] After a year or two the term was dropped from Loyola's catalogue, but it left one important residue: the requirement of a 3,500-word thesis on a philosophical topic. *Philosophical* was construed broadly by deans and faculty, so that virtually any reasonably coherent subject was accepted. The exercise came in the senior year, and Father Ooghe was the favorite mentor. The finished product was meant to demonstrate the student's diligence and ingenuity in research as well as his ability to organize data in a coherent and even in an interesting fashion. The senior thesis did not survive the Second World War as a general requirement, and the move to a new library in 1973 was probably the occasion for the disappearance of the manuscripts of the early theses.

In 1928 tuition and generally required fees for labs, student activities, and graduation during four years at Loyola amounted to $720 for a bachelor of arts; $745 (or $770, if an extra biology course was chosen) for a bachelor of science; $700 for a bachelor of philosophy; and $450 for the two-year premedical course. It is difficult to translate these figures into today's terms. The style and standard of living has changed drastically during the intervening half-century and general histories of higher education as well as chronicles of institutions delicately tend to pass over information about increases in tuition.

Nevertheless, several points for comparison are available. The average four-year cost at Loyola ($720) was in 1928 equivalent to the annual per capita income of Americans. This figure provides an arbitrary reference point for fifty years later, when the per capita income was ten times as high while Loyola's four-year tuition was more than twelve times as high. Except for farmers, times were pretty good in 1928. Wages were higher than they would be after the depression struck, and work was available. Of the fifty dollars a week he got as a floorman at Hutzler's department store, one alumnus recalls paying half for room and board in Baltimore near the end of the 1920s.[28] This suggests that a frugal fellow working during the summer could reasonably expect to save the $150 that he needed to pay next year's tuition.

How did the cost of an education at Loyola compare with the cost elsewhere? The Johns Hopkins University charged the same tuition that Loyola did—$150 a year—and this was lower than the tuition at many other schools in the nation. The cost of living in Baltimore then and until after World War II had a reputation of being lower than that in Philadelphia and other cities. As for the cost of education, Saint Joseph's in Philadelphia, with a tuition of $200, was nearer the national average. Dartmouth, Amherst, and Cornell charged between $230 and $240, according to a report published in the *Sun* on December 8, 1924. At an extreme, Williams was listed as asking $1,600 a year (but the reporter may have included residence expenses in the figure.)

What is clear from thte the *Sun* article is that nowhere did tuition fees cover the colleges' total cost. Institutional expenses exceeded tuition by more than 100 percent, with income from endowments and donations making up the deficit. Loyola and Saint Joseph's did not have such financial resources; nor could they expect opulent gifts. Instead, they relied on balancing their books through the continuing generosity of their nonsalaried Jesuit faculty.

At all American schools the general subsidy was increased by scholarships. In 1928 Loyola listed forty scholarships with which it sought to recruit students. These, plus the continuing demand for a college education, swelled enrollments from fifty-nine in 1921 to almost three times as many seven years later. This rate of increase was the same as for Catholic colleges in general during the 1920s.[29]

In addition to the regular offerings, Loyola instituted a special extension program at the request of Archbishop Curley. Like Cardinal O'Connell in Boston, he wanted teaching nuns to continue their education, and in 1927 he asked Loyola to provide degree programs and courses acceptable for certification by the state authorities. Scheduling was difficult, because almost all the nuns taught during the day, and they were still subject to restrictions on travel and use of time. Nevertheless, courses in English, history, chemistry, Latin, and various modern languages were offered that first year. The classes were scheduled for late afternoons on weekdays and on Saturday morning. More than twenty women from the Mercy, Saint Francis, Charity, and Saint Joseph sisterhoods enrolled in 1927, as did several women not affiliated with any teaching order. A few years later the names of some men appeared on the register. If only in a very restricted form, coeducation made its appearance at Evergreen in much the same fashion as it had first appeared earlier at Marquette. Though coeducation went counter to papal directives and was opposed by some Jesuits, it caused no difficulty or controversy at Loyola. It was very limited; it was a community service; and it brought in revenue.

During the next years, this program at Loyola expanded both in courses offered and in numbers enrolled. Courses in sociology, philosophy, and education were added. Over the first five years enrollments increased nearly to three hundred and at the high point, in 1932, the tuition paid by the various sisterhoods amounted to $8,000. During the next four years, under the financial stringency imposed by the Great Depression, enrollments fell and so did revenues, to less than a quarter of the 1932 level. When no one from one sisterhood registered in 1934,

Dean Thomas O'Malley visited the mother superior, who frankly indicated the reason as lack of funds. To his offer of a full remission of tuition, she said "they could not take advantage of this offer."[30] For the other communities he arranged to relieve them of the cost of traveling to the campus by sending teachers to them. Eventually this program was absorbed administratively into the evening division when that structure was formed in 1945.

• •

Even as negotiations for the new site were underway, it was evident that additional buildings had to be erected at Evergreen. A combination classroom-laboratory-office structure was to be the first order of business. Until such a facility was constructed, classes would continue in the mansion, and therefore it could not be used as a Jesuit residence. Their daily trek from Calvert Street to Cold Spring Lane was eased by a generous parishioner who gave them a Packard (then a name even more awe-inspiring than Cadillac later became).[31]

Determined to ensure an orderly development of the new campus, President McEneany engaged the architectural firm of Otto Simonson and Sons to prepare a site plan. The Simonson plan, with several modifications, was followed for nearly forty years. On the Simonson plan, erection of six buildings arranged around a large quadrangle was projected. Off to one side a gymnasium was positioned between the mansion and Cold Spring Lane, about in the middle of the long axis of the athletic field. Near the boundary with the Garrett estate, an engineering building was drawn approximately where Maryland Hall now stands. Farther eastward and in the dell, almost even with the front of the mansion, was to be a cruciform chapel, its transept pointing across the narrow side of the quadrangle to a rather small building. This appears to have been merely a formal reservation of space rather than a firm commitment. A few years later what is now Jenkins Hall was built on this site. Westward, with its back likewise to Cold Spring Lane, was the proposed chemistry building—the first structure to be started. The public face of Loyola, the main entrance, was supposed to be a large, multipurpose building tentatively called "Recitation Hall," sited along the Charles Street axis of the quadrangle.

This plan was accompanied by a sketch that provided a three-dimensional interpretation. The buildings were in the Gothic style, with brick as the major material. They looked serviceable enough, but heavy and generally without grace. Someone with good taste, possibly George

Jenkins, suggested substituting stone for brick. In fact, McEneany suggested to this benefactor the possibility of adopting a new name for the college. What did he have in mind, Jenkins University? Jenkins contributed generously, and the first building would bear his name, but three-quarters of the building's financing ($150,000) came from a donor who preferred to remain anonymous. That name appears only in the history of the house written by Father Peter O'Carroll, who supervised the whole project. For January of 1922, O'Carroll noted that Joseph Kelly (not otherwise identified, but in fact a political leader in the Tenth Ward who invested in real estate and kept a saloon) gave Loyola $15,000 to level and mark the athletic field for football and baseball. He promised another gift ten times this amount, and Father O'Carroll soon became worried when it was not delivered on time.

The delay was occasioned in part by a noisy diversion in May of 1922. A squad of federal Prohibition agents suddenly swooped down on Kelly's saloon. Instead of hauling the owner and his forbidden stock away, the agents found themselves besieged in the middle of a massive gridlock created by Kelly's loyal friends and neighbors. Just who pulled the fire alarms or reported a riot to the police or called the gas and the trolley companies for repair crews or called for an assortment of taxicabs no one reported. Distraction of the federal agents permitted some adept urban guerrillas to get close enough to puncture the tires on their trucks, thus preventing any quick resolution of the tangle. From a distance, young toughs lobbed bricks and bottles on this scene of utter confusion. It took six hours to disentangle the mess, but eventually Kelly and his illegal stores were taken into custody.

In such circumstances, a public announcement of Kelly's donation to Loyola College was inopportune, and for several reasons Kelly was himself against it. He was by temperament a diplomat more than a brazen boss and, like others of his generation and background, he had a passion for keeping his affairs—especially financial—very private. His sensitivity permitted attention to be focused on George Jenkins, who committed himself to give $150,000 at the same time. This coincidence allowed the Jesuits to publicize Jenkins's generosity and to entertain the hope that he might increase his commitment to Loyola.

As for Joseph Kelly, the denouement in court made any publicity for his gift to Loyola even more unlikely. He was acquitted of the original charge of illegal possession and sale of alcohol (the Free State of Maryland was a name well deserved). Later he was tried again, this time for interfering with federal officers. He was finally convicted and sentenced to nine months in jail. The warden, an old friend, saw to it that Kelly was not seriously discommoded by his confinement. Rumors of his anonymous generosity—none of them connected to Loyola—persisted until his death a decade later.[32]

12

The New Loyola

The first commencement exercises at Evergreen, held on June 12, 1922, were supplemented with a ceremony to bless the site and to break ground for the Jenkins Science Building (recently renamed Beatty Hall). President McEneany beamed noticeably when he handed the new silver spade to Archbishop Curley, who did the honors. This implement has served on most such occasions since.

On election day of 1922 His Grace came back to lay the cornerstone. In his brief remarks he elaborated on his persistent theme that Catholics had to support high-school and college education. They must urge their children to continue through college, or else Catholics as a group would remain little more than "hewers of wood and drawers of water." The featured orator, James Flaherty, national leader of the Knights of Columbus, pointed to the new building as proof that church institutions had never been the enemies of science. The invitation to Flaherty was probably suggested by Father O'Carroll, who then served as chaplain to the Maryland branch of the Knights.

The speed with which the science building was constructed is evident from a photograph taken hardly more than a year later, which shows a nearly completed structure, with the small cupola in place and surmounted by a flag. In two more weeks the shell was weatherproof. Because of the usual delays, especially when installation of complicated interior fittings is involved, classes in the building were postponed till the start of the spring semester. Father McLoughlin, however, saw no reason for waiting, and moved his operations into the new building just before the start of the Christmas vacation. Because he had designed its scientific facilities and had constantly badgered the builders, his act of appropriation was approved by the student body.

. .

By the time classes opened in February 1924, commuting for both students and Jesuits was ended. Fathers Finnegan, Ooghe, McLoughlin, and Weisel and several scholastics took up residence in the Tudor-style mansion. A few months later the Jesuit community at Loyola College was formally separated from the brethren left at Calvert Street. At that time, McEneany, still president of Loyola College, but rector now of a smaller band of Jesuits and no longer pastor of Saint Ignatius Church, also moved to Evergreen.

The new science building of locally quarried stone, measuring 147 by 64 feet, provided much-needed facilities. Near the entrance was the dean's office, from which he could espy most late-comers or early-goers, and here too was the master clock that regulated all the bells. An assembly hall and chemistry labs occupied the rest of the first floor. Above it were a physics amphitheater and a laboratory as well as a chemistry lecture room. The third floor held a smaller amphitheater initially assigned to philosophy. Next were a small classroom, a dissecting room, and a biology lab.

The basement was the domain of the students. Here were their lockers and a well-furnished recreation room where seniors were permitted to smoke. Nearby were the student library and a lunchroom. In unspecified nooks around the building there were lodged a student counselor, the alumni association, and a bookstore. The students and their teachers were favorably impressed.

The third-floor amphitheater in the new building became Father Ooghe's realm, where another set of anecdotes about him was spawned. A student with a minor talent for imitating animal noises practiced his art during the philosophy class. Whenever Père Ooghe illustrated a point with a reference to an animal, an appropriate sound effect was provided by this fellow—to the amusement of the class and apparently of the instructor. However, during one lecture Ooghe deliberately made a reference to a rabbit and, in the ensuing silence, beamed triumphantly at the class.

He was visibly confounded on another occasion when, as he was passing out notes, one student bounded out of his seat, ostentatiously ripped a sheaf of papers in half, declared that this stuff was all rot, and threw the remains out the window. Ooghe did not know what to do, but, his face turned livid, he managed to continue the lecture. The interval gave the culprit time to ponder the consequences of his performance. After class was dismissed he explained to Father Ooghe how he had substituted another set of papers and showed that he indeed had kept the duplicated notes. The student-protagonist graduated with his fellows. A few years later he completed his medical training and settled down to a respectable practice.

Some alumni recall an exchange between Father Ooghe and Dean Finnegan that displayed the personality of each. On a warm spring day when the windows of the new building were open, Dean Finnegan was startled as he was walking around the third-floor hallway to hear raucous laughter emanating from the philosophy class. Uninvited he entered the room and warned the students to behave like proper gentlemen. The workmen on the scaffolding across the street would be scandalized, he said, and might spread stories about the unseemly goings-on at the college. When the dean left, Father Ooghe turned to the class and quietly but firmly said, "Gentlemen, continue as before." This evoked another subdued but nonetheless hearty round of laughter. It was not surprising that the students supplemented the official school cheers with one that went:

Big 0, little o,
g. h. e.
Ooghe! Ooghe!
Oui! Oui! Oui!

His indulgence of students was evident in that he never corrected their pronunciation of his name, which is approximated as *Ocher.*

There was a less charming side to this faculty idol that was remembered by his former students. Although Cardinal Gibbons had taken an irenic, even ecumenical, view of what were then called "mixed" marriages, Father Ooghe ended his final discourse each year with an adamant condemnation of them and issued a dire warning against marrying anyone who was not a Catholic. He never explained his stand, and one might speculate that it rose from some misfortune in his own family; such sentimental theorizing may, however, be wide of the mark, because he was if anything a relentlessly logical man. A mixed marriage in his mind was a strong solvent of Catholic fervor. As on all such matters, though, the auditors merely noted his seriousness and later did what they thought appropriate for themselves.[1]

• •

The science building was not the only project underway. Even before ground was broken for that building, an informal campaign had begun to raise funds for a gymnasium. At the alumni banquet in February 1922, the principal speaker, Archbishop Curley, pledged $1,000 for this new building. Little else was heard of the matter until the following

January, when a surprisingly modest goal of $50,000 was announced. The unstated plan may have been to rely for the remainder on Jenkins's earlier commitment.

Despite careful planning and evident enthusiasm, the scope of the building had to be reduced. By the end of the fund-raising campaign only a bit more than half the goal had been pledged. A second round was out of the question, because there were competing appeals already underway. Another fund-raising effort would have delayed the completion date, and so the plans for the gymnasium were merely scaled down to essentials, with completion of the swimming pool and of the alumni wing postponed.

Ground was turned ceremonially on a rainy June afternoon in 1924, but the steam shovel for full excavation was not brought in until the following February. Construction was completed with borrowed funds. On January 20, 1926, a revitalized Loyola College Athletic Association held a dance in the new gymnasium, and a week later the varsity basketball squad drubbed an alumni team in the inaugural game. Loyola's gymnasium was for many years considered one of the finest in the state of Maryland. For a time it served as the home court of the Loyola High School squad, and for many years it was the site of the Maryland scholastic basketball championships.

What disappointment arose from the need to modify the gymnasium plans was offset by two welcome additions to the campus. The first was a small chapel brought from Mount Washington. Dean Finnegan may have mentioned to his friend, the pastor at the Shrine of the Sacred Heart, that since the move to Evergreen, Mass for the students was being said in a room of the Jesuit residence, and the pastor generously donated the chapel.

Systematically disassembled, it was trucked to the Evergreen campus in the fall of 1924. Its reconstruction took the remainder of the year. Fittings from the temporary chapel in the residence were transferred, along with the plaque commemorating the generosity of the pioneer band of students who had raised over one thousand dollars during their first year on the new campus to furnish it. Candlemas (February 2) of 1925 was marked by the formal opening of Saint Francis Xavier Chapel.

The other addition—a marble statue of Mary under her title of the Immaculate Conception came later in 1925. A statue of Jesus with the emblem of the Sacred Heart arrived on campus, during the first year, but nothing about its origins is recorded. The new statue was a gift from

Loyola's benefactress, Mary Ann Farmer. She had intended that it be placed inside the Jesuit residence, but the Carrara marble proved too heavy for the flooring. It had to be moved to a pedestal outside, where it faced the entrance of the student chapel and, past that, the heart of Baltimore.

Its most memorable use and representation appear in a photograph taken by Father John Delaney in December of 1939. On a clear but moonless night he positioned a camera so that it would take a picture not only of the statue but of the North Star directly over its head. Leaving the lens open for twelve hours, he captured the circular tracks made by the stars as a result of the rotation of the earth. The picture was widely distributed and was acclaimed in an out-of-state paper as "one of the most amazing photographs ever made." It has been imitated many times since and has illustrated Christmas cards used by the college community.

• •

Shortly before his departure, President McEneany took measures that left a curious and ambiguous legacy. Ostensibly it was a building project that was supposed to be completed for the college's diamond jubilee in 1927, but its grandeur suggests a less tangible aim. He instructed Lucius White to plan a greatly expanded and elegantly elaborated version of Recitation Hall—the centerpiece of the original site plan. The Arts Building, as it was now tentatively called, would have been three stories high with twelve window bays across a 320-foot front and a tall square tower in the center. Its English collegiate Gothic style was meant to impress the students and passersby with a "sense of Oxford."

This embodied McEneany's vision of what the new Loyola should become. He wanted to centralize most campus needs and functions in this one building, so that a close contact would unavoidably be maintained among all the elements and processes that went into Loyola's corporate life. Even living quarters and a domestic chapel for the Jesuits were included. Within the walls of the Arts Building were to be an auditorium for a student body grown to a thousand, a commodious hall in the form of a senate chamber for debating, offices for student publications, lecture halls, libraries, a cafeteria, administrative offices, and assorted recreation rooms. The proposal still envisioned completion of an engineering building and of a permanent chapel, but left the site for the unnamed companion to the science building on Cold Spring Lane to future contingencies.

McEneany's dream has not been realized, and one element of it raises doubt that it was meant to be physically completed. White's sketch included a large clock in the tower, and the description made clear that its mechanism was to be connected to a full set of chimes, which would toll the hours. Such an installation was a notable feature of the new Boston College, but that school was not encumbered by the restrictions in Loyola's deed. In view of this and of the earlier opposition to ringing bells around the college, there was no likelihood that the Arts Building as planned could be completed in time for the diamond jubilee. It might serve, however, as Father McEneany's summary guide for Loyola's future development.

• •

During all this close-packed planning of Loyola's new physical fabric, persistent attention was given to its intimate life. Both the students and the Jesuits had thought about the kind of community they hoped to create on the new campus. They agreed that Loyola was to become collegiate like other American schools and that the involvement of the student body should be expanded, but how was a question on which there were different views.

Rather early, some students sought to introduce the practice of hazing. However, a sprained wrist sustained during a melee between the lowly frosh and the lordly sophomores evoked a prohibition from Dean Finnegan. Upon his departure in 1925, a renewed effort succeeded in establishing a formal rite of initiation. A committee of sophomores became responsible for enforcing the rules drawn up by them and approved by the school authorities. These required freshmen to wear coats and ties and what was then called a jockey cap (later a pup cap), to attend all varsity games played in Baltimore, to memorize all school songs, yells, and athletic schedules, to address the upperclassmen only as "Mister" and "Sir," to use only the concrete walks, to stay out of the poplar grove unless accompanied by an upperclassman, and to carry matches at all times for the instant relief of an upperclassman in the throes of a nicotine fit. These rules are reminiscent of cadet life at Annapolis and West Point as portrayed in films, and seemed a small enough price to pay for an eventual welcome into the corps. The initiation could in fact be justified on the grounds of promoting school spirit, polite behavior, and a kempt appearance.

There were, however, two provisions that gave these rules a less commendable twist. By one, the vigilance committee had plenary authority to exact any punishment it deemed appropriate for a violation of the rules. By the other, interpretation of the rules was left to the will of the same group of sophomores. Similar practices had by then become part of the American collegiate ethos, and Loyola's students wanted to share in this national rite of passage. Significantly, those who instituted the system were themselves never subjected to it.

For almost a quarter of a century hazing was a minor but integral part of student life. Periodic efforts were made to break the cycle, but these never proved effective. Occasionally encounters between classes resulted in physical injuries—none particularly serious, but public enough to gain the attention of a dean. A damper would then be put on such activities until a new group of enthusiasts reimposed the system in full rigor.

Somewhere along the way it developed that release from caps and rules could be gained before the end of the first semester if the freshmen were victorious in a late autumn football game. Later this was changed to rugby. Because few knew the rules of rugby and because referees (when there were any) were tolerant of violations, freshmen under the cover of the game could retaliate against their tormentors on the sophomore team. Eventually it became almost traditional for the freshmen to win. The arrival on campus of World War II veterans who would not submit to such treatment brought an end to hazing.[2] Even its last remnant—the rugby game—was discontinued during the 1960s for lack of willing participants Thus, for a time, these initiation rituals disappeared from the Loyola campus, only to be revived in a different form after dormitories were erected in the 1960s.

. .

The students at Loyola's new campus sought to develop a community and collegiate spirit. Shortly after classes were inaugurated at Evergreen, members of the debating society suggested to Dean Finnegan that "certain details of discipline be looked after by a committee of students." He was amenable to the proposal, at least to the extent of putting a senior in charge of the lunchroom.

Early in 1926 students raised the question in much the same terms. A council was urged as a useful means to direct student activities and to act as an intermediary with the faculty. The main aim was to protect the good reputation of the student body as a whole against the misdeeds of a few. The proponents were most concerned about unsavory language, disaffected carping, and "grave misconduct." A council, they thought, could quickly detect and effectively deal with any miscreant. No immediate action was taken on this proposal, but the disciplinary emphasis of the students is interesting as a clue to their ethos.

It was not till March of 1928 that Loyola's first student council was formally inducted. Nevertheless, this was five years prior to the establishment of a student council at Canisius College. Thomas "Nat" Ferciot (1928) and some friends wrote the constitution and secured approval from the school authorities. What was included in the text must be surmised, because no copy of it has been uncovered; more than likely it conformed to the aims stated earlier. The council consisted of the four senior class officers (with the senior class president the presiding officer of the student council), three junior class officers, the president and vice-president of the sophomore class, and the freshman president. It was a simple and notably hierarchical arrangement with no trace of the principle of "one man, one vote."

In fact, just the opposite principle was applied. The senior class, normally the smallest, had the largest representation, but no one then seemed to think this inequitable. On the contrary, their disproportionate weight was justified by the seniors on the ground of their maturity and as a means for maintaining school spirit and tradition.

An additional guarantor of order and continuity was the student counselor—a Jesuit—who acted as faculty moderator for the council. From 1928 onward this institution was reasonably successful in achieving its main objectives: student life at Loyola appeared similar to that at other American schools, the council provided liaison with the faculty and various national organizations of students, and, finally, the council afforded prizes (if only honorific titles) for the ambitious.

• •

The students, feeling the need for an additional channel to express their views, started a newspaper. William McWilliams and "Charlie" Max Ways, both of the class of 1926, were its founding spirits. For different reasons, they were viewed by other students as outsiders. The first commuted from "Crabtown" (Annapolis) and the second, though a Baltimorean, was considered a nonconformist. Also, they shared a fascination for the writing and exploits of H. L. Mencken that separated them from their peers. Later, McWilliams became a distinguished justice on the Maryland Court of Appeals, and Ways served as an editor of *Fortune.* Both have been generous benefactors of the college.

When they first broached the subject to Father McEneany, he promptly and firmly said no—a common enough response from authority. Not daunted, they waited for a favorable opportunity to raise the matter again. This appeared in the person of Stan Coffall, the new football coach, who recognized the value of a newspaper in promoting student and alumni enthusiasm. When approached by McWilliams and Ways, he gave them his support, and this seems to have persuaded the school authorities.

The editors and staff of the *Evergreen Chatter*, as the paper was named, meant it to be more than a vehicle for boosting sports. In their November 16, 1925, manifesto, they declared it to be "the official mouthpiece of the students." To this end, they solicited comments on campus life; even more significantly, they set aside time during their staff meetings for their fellows to discuss campus issues. In an early edition of the paper the question of establishing a student council was raised on the front page. In another the editors indicated their preference that enrollments at Loyola be limited to about five hundred (half the goal that President McEneany had envisioned) and their aversion to Loyola's becoming "a real boarding school."[3] They liked what they had and did not want any admixture from beyond the environs of Baltimore.

After the graduation of its founders, the *Chatter* appeared only once during the next fall. No definitive explanation has been offered for its demise, but the most likely cause was a lack of funds. The founding staff seems to have relied mainly on advertising. For a time funds were sufficient to persuade an indulgent printer to publish the paper, but bills mounted and finally he called for payment. Thus came the end of Loyola's first student newspaper.

• •

In the autumn of 1927 a new group of leaders emerged, and they planned action on several matters. Baltimore sportswriters were using a variety of nicknames to designate Loyola's varsity teams, including "the Jesuits" and "the Irish." These students thought something more distinctive was needed. To deal with this, Edward Tribbe (1928) and Hugh Meade (1929), with the assistance of the class presidents, called a meeting of the student body. They wanted to revive the newspaper with a new name that would serve as mascot for the football team. In addition, the totem somehow had to embody the new school colors: green and gray. This complicated set of requirements inspired one wag to nominate the parrot; a peer more partial to gray proposed the squirrel. Although these conformed to the guidelines and might have been appropriate on the masthead of the paper, they hardly could serve as an inspirational symbol for a football team.

Some sounder mind (probably Tribbe's) suggested the greyhound. It was then thought to be the fleetest animal in the world (the speed of the cheetah had not yet been established). Furthermore, the greyhound, it could be argued, had been bred by the Irish and was associated with the ancient Romans, who imported the dogs for racing. All thought the suggestion appropriate and immediately agreed.[4] The varsity teams got a proper mascot and the student paper had a new name.

Originally only four pages, the *Greyhound* appeared semi-monthly —more or less—until the 1960s, when it became four times as large and a weekly. Its continuing existence was assured when, shortly after its revival, the whole student body became subscribers by assignment of some of their general activity fee to the newspaper. Its stories and notices have chronicled the doings of the students, faculty, and alumni. Book and theater reviews, features, and editorials provide an interesting record of student sensibilities and opinion and of how these changed over the years. Editorials are particularly valuable as evidence of stands taken on various public issues—some quite different from what might be expected. Changes in prevailing styles and mores are evident in the advertising.

The quality of the paper has varied with the cycle of additions to and departures from the staff. In 1948, however, when several issues were evaluated by national college press associations, they received high scores. For a few, membership on the staff was an apprenticeship to careers in writing or journalism. For most others it became a pleasantly remembered episode of their days at Evergreen.

. .

As already mentioned, the school colors changed when Loyola moved. Some time during the first year Dean Finnegan asked the students for suggestions on a new combination. There was, as Monsignor William Sweeney (1922) explained at the dedication of the new student center in 1960, no question that one of the colors had to be gray. Many Baltimoreans still cherished a sentimental attachment to "The Lost Cause." Then, there was the example of Jesuit institutions to the immediate north and south. Georgetown's colors were blue and gray, Saint Joseph's crimson and gray.

The mystery of the source of the companion color—green—was finally solved when Monsignor Sweeney publicly admitted authorship. He was vice-president of the first class to graduate at Evergreen, and his devotion to all things Irish was duly noted in the yearbook, now renamed the *Green and Gray*. His confession should finally dissipate the suspicion of many of his schoolmates that no student had suggested the combination. The shades of green and gray were not specified, and over the years some awkward combinations have been used (it is after all a difficult pair of colors to balance). The official hues now are forest green (the darkest) and pearl gray (the lightest). If somewhat cool in feeling, this arrangement is not without a certain harmony.

Loyola's new livery was soon seen on the playing fields and courts of the region. The 1920s were the golden age of athletics in America, so it was not surprising to find a strong interest in sports at Loyola. One Jesuit, somewhat bemused by this devotion, described the office of faculty moderator for athletics as "a very important position hereabouts."[5]

Basketball had survived the move to Evergreen. Until the new gymnasium was built, however, the old court at Calvert Street was used for practice and games. Bill Schuerholz was still the coach and he was fortunate to have the championship team from Loyola High School— John Cummings (1926), "Big Jim" Lacy (1926), Ray "Shorty" Helfrich (1927), Robert "Doc" Lyons (1926), and John Menton (1926)— continue to play for the college. This team amassed a respectable record. During their final year they won eleven of their fourteen games and were acclaimed the Maryland collegiate champions. Local sportswriters named Cummings, Menton, and others to their all-star teams. As soon as the athletic field and the tennis courts were in playing condition, baseball, track, and tennis were inaugurated with modest but generally favorable results.

The most eager effort, however, was put into football. A beginning of sorts was made during the 1923 and 1924 seasons, but the coaching and results left much to be desired. The team's mentor for the second season could think of no more urgent way to motivate the players than with an exhortation to "fight for the good Jesuit fathers and for my job." When the Johns Hopkins University walloped the green and gray by 87 to 0, all recognized that some changes were needed.

The mediocre showing of the Loyola football squad allowed a group of alumni to propose a plan that they had been discussing for some time. A new coach—someone with the Knute Rockne touch—and experienced players would obviously have to be brought in. All this would cost money. Led by August Bourbon (1914) and Isaac "Ike" George (1901), the group submitted a remedial proposal to President McEneany. They wanted the alumni association freed from Jesuit tutelage, at least to the extent that its faculty moderator would no longer have to approve every action. Secondly, a group of alumni was to be incorporated as the

Loyola College Athletic Association and to assume responsibility for the cost of building up the football team.

As Bourbon, George, and company analyzed the situation, it would take about twenty thousand dollars to finance this development over the next five years; the sum was needed at the very beginning of the process. They raised the funds by selling small-denomination bonds that matured in five years and paid 5 percent interest. They expected that three good years on the gridiron would increase the revenue from admissions to such a level that the football program would become self-sustaining and the bonds would be retired on schedule. The plan combined two of the most attractive growth industries of that era— football and investing. Early in 1925, McEneany gave his approval.

By March the athletic association had signed a new coach, Stan Coffall. He had been an all-American at Notre Dame—and a Rockne protégé. After graduation he moved to Los Angeles, where he coached and also managed a new motion-picture company. This did not last long, and he moved to Philadelphia, where his football teams brought him a measure of local fame. As Loyola's new coach, Coffall used his contacts around Philadelphia and New Jersey to recruit players. (The addresses listed in the catalogues give no support to the often repeated canard that he brought these men in from the Pennsylvania coalfields).

Housing had to be provided for the players, and most of them lived at Kernewood, another Garrett property a block east of the campus but facing away from Cold Spring Lane. The cost of the lease was borne by the athletic association. Sometime after the football players had taken up residence at Kernewood, the owners offered to sell the mansion and its surrounding land to the college. Unfortunately this offer came at a time when funds were critically needed for additional buildings on the main campus. Loyola's inaction on the offer annoyed the Garretts, who then sold the land to a developer. In the 1926 deed, building a school, apartment house, or charitable institution on Kernewood land was prohibited.[6] Although this stipulation was vague, it was probably meant to discourage future dealings with the nearest school and eleemosynary institution. The estrangement between Loyola and the Garretts was still an active memory thirty years later when the college became interested in acquiring more land.

With the start of practice in the fall of 1925, many felt that gridiron glory was about to descend on the college. Not all were persuaded that such a result was worth the price. Some of the players who had suffered the heat of the previous two seasons were angered at being displaced by newcomers favored by Coffall. Father Joseph Ayd, serving briefly as dean, saw some of the new athletes as unpromising academic material, and his judgment was shared by more than one member of the faculty. Coach Coffall worked to contain these adverse opinions by helping the athletic association and the student body. He and his wife assisted with various fund-raising projects, and his support for a student newspaper has already been noted. After a decisive victory over Johns Hopkins, Loyola students threw a party for their team, indicating general satisfaction with the progress to date.

During his three years at the college, Coffall scheduled games with a variety of opponents. Some, like games with the Army Tank School and Juniata, resulted in easy victories. Other opponents, like Villanova, Navy, Catholic University, Loyola of New Orleans, and Western Maryland, severely tested the endurance and determination of the green and gray. Among the players who were wreathed with athletic laurels were James "Hap" Enright (1928), George "Lank" Tanton (1928), Paul Byrne (1928), and James "Desprit" Desmond (1929). (The last played in the first postseason game sponsored by the Shriners.) The general playing style and record of Loyola's new team had been noteworthy but lacked the drama that was to come with later squads. The anecdotes of their behavior around the campus, especially "Pauly" Byrne's, mark them as raffish and insouciant characters. The overall record for these three years was ten wins and sixteen losses, somewhat disappointing to the alumni. Seeing no future for himself in Baltimore, Coffall accepted an offer from Wake Forest in 1928, and some of the players also departed— a few before graduating.[7]

The new campus enhanced the social activities of the student body. There had been an annual "Parents' Night" and dance at Calvert Street since World War I. In 1926—now that the gymnasium was completed—the leaders of the junior class decided, like counterparts on other campuses, to hold a prom. Three hundred couples, students and alumni, attended the affair on May 7, with Bob Iula's "syncopating artists" providing the music.

In the 1920s, people attending such a dance still joined in the Grand Promenade that gave the affair its name. At half past eleven John Spellissy (1927), who was the organizer, and his partner started the march while the orchestra played the "Washington and Lee Swing." After several circuits and a final chord, congratulations and cheery good nights were exchanged. Spellissy later treated his co-workers to a banquet at the Hotel Rennert, then acclaimed by Mencken for serving the finest Maryland cuisine. Thereafter each junior class tried to outdo its predecessors in holding the most "unforgettable" prom.

• •

The most significant change in the life and operations of Loyola was the formal separation of the college from the high school. The process initiated during the 1890s was completed on July 31, 1924 (the feast of Saint Ignatius Loyola). At approximately the same hour, McEneany was "read in" as rector of the Jesuit community at Evergreen and Father John Duston (until then principal of the high school) was installed as rector of the Jesuits left at Calvert Street. This placed both houses on an equal footing within the Society of Jesus in relation to important questions of how to deal with the assets and liabilities of the original corporation.

By the time of the separation, an informal agreement had been reached on financial arrangements. This took definitive form in a memorandum prepared by the provincial at the beginning of September 1924. Based on the records for the previous few years, it was believed that the high school and Saint Ignatius Church would continue to enjoy an annual surplus of $24,000. The college, on the other hand, was expected for a time to suffer a substantial deficit. The high school had subsidized the college during the 1924–25 year to a total of $15,000, and Father Duston agreed to continue the support for two more years. The agreement provided for diminishing the subsidy if the income at the college was increased either by raising tuition or by adding of more students—both of which occurred. Should any of several other contingencies arise, the high school's subsidy was to be decreased proportionately.

Attached to the agreement were a number of appendices. Generally, where assets could be divided, half was assigned to each house. This was the arrangement for disposition of the bequest of $500,000 for the O'Neill memorial church. Archbishop Curley pledged to indemnify the college and the high school for any losses that might result from his prohibition against building a church on the Guilford tract. Other corporate assets that could not be divided were assigned to one or the other institution, with the totals for each meant to come out about equal—thus avoiding the Solomon-like decision at another Jesuit institution upon separation of the high school and the college, where odd-numbered volumes in the encyclopedias were assigned to the one and the even-numbered to the other. The Guilford tract was a special case. Title to the land was divided, with the college assigned one third (for the section where the O'Neill church was to have been built) and the high school given the right to dispose of the remaining two thirds of the tract. Bequests dated before July 31, 1924, were to be divided equally, but those made afterwards went to the institution named in each will.[8]

The care in preparing the agreement did not prevent all differences. Father Peter O'Carroll, who cast his lot with the high school, submitted a number of objections and observations to the provincial. In general he believed that the assets of the high school were overstated and its liabilities understated and that a reverse measure had been applied to the assets and liabilities of the college. He had other complaints and doubts about the operation at Evergreen and about President McEneany. In summary, O'Carroll thought "H[igh] S[chool] is not getting a square deal."[9] This impression was shared by others and lingered for several years.

Division of the Calvert Street property was a more complex matter. Even though finding a buyer for the whole tract and buildings seemed unlikely, selling them was intended and provision had to be made for distributing the proceeds. Upon sale, the college was to get half the price of the land. Money from the sale of the school building was meant for the high school. In regard to Saint Ignatius Church, the proceeds of the sale were to be divided equally between the college and the high school; to deal with any claims by the archdiocese on Saint Ignatius Church, canon lawyers at Woodstock prepared cogent arguments against any such right. "What if" discussions began, and the Jesuits considered which lawyer to engage if the dispute was taken to court. Fortunately this contingency did not arise then or since, and the Jesuits continue to hold Saint Ignatius Church.

• •

The appointment of Father McEneany as rector of the Jesuits at Evergreen amply demonstrated the order's extraordinary confidence in him. The separation of college and high school in 1924 made it possible to reappoint him rector after he had completed two canonical terms in that office, because he was to be rector of what was in effect a new community. He would thus have served for twelve years if he had completed his fourth term—but that was not to be.

In fact, serious difficulty with his health appeared shortly after his installation at Evergreen. He and Father O'Carroll went to Florida in October of 1924 to inspect a parcel of land given to Loyola almost a quarter of a century earlier. Since then it had meant nothing but semiannual tax bills, albeit small; but in the 1920s a land boom in Florida suggested that the tract might now be disposed of at a good price. It took considerable effort for McEneany and O'Carroll to locate the woodsy 240-acre tract near the center of the peninsula. There were no good roads near it, nor was there a settlement that might help attract a buyer. For the time being, selling was out of the question. (The matter would be settled in 1945 and the land sold for one thousand dollars.) Shortly after deciding the land could not be sold, Father McEneany suffered a severe attack of asthma, and his recuperation took almost two months in a Jacksonville hospital.

No attack of similar severity can be deduced from the notations for 1925, but several times during the next year McEneany was forced to enter the hospital. After a stay in December of 1926, doctors ordered him to convalesce somewhere away from wintry Baltimore, and they recommended El Paso, Texas. Shortly before Christmas he boarded a train for that warm, dry area, where neither fog nor industrial smoke would irritate his lungs. His return was not precluded, but a temporary replacement was named. A week of getting acquainted with the situation at Evergreen proved enough for the first appointee, and upon his departure the dean, Henri Wiesel, was named vice-rector and elected president pro tem of the college.

Father Wiesel thus found himself in delicate circumstances. On the one hand Father McEneany was still formally in charge, even though he was recuperating many hundreds of miles away. On the other hand there was continuing need for prompt decisions. For the next year and a half Wiesel discharged his responsibilities effectively without impinging on the prerogatives of his nominal superior. There was no evidence of a debilitating interregnum.

By May of 1927, Wiesel was acting as though Father McEneany would not be resuming his offices. On Wiesel's initiative a new heraldic seal was struck on the medals awarded at commencement. That year President McEneany returned to Baltimore for the graduation exercises—in effect, his farewell appearance. Archbishop Curley delivered an eloquent encomium on the work of the Jesuits and an imperative appeal for support of their efforts. Father McEneany as subject of his praise was obvious to the few who were aware of the situation.

After such an acknowledgement it would be reasonable to expect a prompt transfer of authority, but for some reason (probably the slow grind of administrative machinery) the appointment of Wiesel as rector and his election as president of Loyola College took another year and a half. Eventually Joseph McEneany would serve for a time at George-town and participate in the defense of Loyola College in a court case that arose from his agreement with Mary Ann Farmer. He spent his last years on the staff of the new Jesuit novitiate in Wernersville, Pennsyl-vania. As a result of his efforts Loyola College was well rooted at its new site and well equipped with the accouterments of a small liberal-arts college.

13

Accreditation and the Depression

The energy evident during McEneany's term flowed for several more years that were punctuated by a number of favorable signs: the conditions for accreditation were gradually realized; another building —containing the library—was erected; registration became more formal and admission procedures stricter; new student organizations and sports were instituted; most significantly, enrollments continued to rise. All these developments suggested that the basic hopes roused by the move to Evergreen were becoming realities.

•   •

These achievements were in the main the work of Father Henri Wiesel, who became head of Loyola College in 1927. Although some time elapsed before he was fully installed as rector and president, he did not allow the ambiguity of his position to slacken the pace. He joined Father Duston in a modest celebration of Loyola's diamond jubilee. The extension program for nuns and other teachers was inaugurated during this transitional period—as also was the student council.

A small act, but one indicating a sense of authority, was Father Wiesel's design of a new seal. He replaced the busy device created in 1915, when Loyola was supposed to move to Guilford, with simpler insignia. Like its predecessor, the shield on the new device alluded in part to geographical location but used two other segments to emphasize Jesuit origins. The lowest and horizontal third of the shield carried the Loyola wolves and kettle found on the emblems of many Jesuit institutions. The other two divided the upper part of the shield vertically. On the left was the flag of Baltimore, including the Battle Monument, and on the right appeared the seven maroon and gold bars from Saint Ignatius's coat of arms. (For some reason they were drawn incorrectly, but more decoratively, from lower left rising to upper right. The correct arrangement would slant these bars downward.) The Wiesel seal was a clearer and more attractive emblem than the one that preceded it, and Loyola's publications and displays carried it for about a dozen years. Diplomas and other official documents, however, continued to be imprinted with the corporate seal adopted in 1853.

Henri Wiesel was the second alumnus to become president of Loyola. In 1903 he joined his older brother, Boiseau Wiesel (1907), in attending the Calvert Street school. In due course the latter graduated and went to the Johns Hopkins University for a doctorate in chemistry. His later life was marked by exemplary devotion to his Catholic faith and a substantial career as a paint chemist. Shortly after his brother was graduated, Henri left Loyola to enter the Society of Jesus. After the usual alternating stints of study and teaching, he was ordained in 1922. Two years later he was assigned to the college and, as Father McEneany's health declined, Wiesel was moved into the post of dean and eventually that of president. Although photographs of Father Wiesel convey a certain reserve—possibly the effect of round eyeglasses and hair neatly parted in the center—he was highly esteemed by students for his warm but judicious character and because he was a supporter of Loyola's new athletic program.[1]

• •

At Wiesel's accession to the presidency, there were several important and connected items on Loyola's agenda. Progress toward accreditation required revising the catalogue and programs to make them comparable to those of other American colleges and understandable to those unfamiliar with Jesuit educational tradition. There were also physical standards to be met, especially for classroom space and a library. Both were included in the grandiose plan for the Arts Building, but Father Wiesel had no hope of raising the enormous sum required for that project.

Nevertheless, hope for progress was offered by George Jenkins. The death of his wife, Kate Key Jenkins (granddaughter of Francis Scott Key), and a sense of his own mortality impelled him to volunteer another $250,000. Generous as this was, it was not nearly enough for the Arts Building. The need to proceed quickly, however, dictated that plans for a new building be adapted from sketches for the Arts Building.

The result was a useful if architecturally undistinguished structure. From his earlier plan the designer, Lucius White, took one wing—tall, simple, and boxlike, with a facade of five window bays extending from the ground to the topmost floor. He placed the main entrance in the middle bay facing the campus and embellished it with a Gothic arch. One added feature was Loyola's new heraldic emblem, carved as a decorative escutcheon above the doorway. The pressing need for a library and full financial support from Jenkins made a fund-raising campaign unnecessary, and so President Wiesel omitted any formal announcement of plans for the new building.

For many years the large, high assembly hall on the top floor had to serve two not always compatible purposes. As the main college library it required book stacks and tables. This furniture, however, restricted the use of the room as an auditorium (even though the big tables could be moved into the alcoves between the stacks). For the debaters, lecturers, singers, instrumental soloists, choirs, and dance bands who appeared there, a small platform backed with dark wood panelling was placed at one end. Thus the claims of individual scholarship or study occasionally had to yield to social demands.

At least the architect designed the library space with more attention to aesthetics than was paid in other parts of the building. The tables, the wooden panels to mask the ends of stacks, and the panelling around the rest of the hall were neatly coordinated and carved in Gothic style. The high ceiling was gently pitched and supported by heavy wooden beams ornamented in the same fashion. White gave the room the feel of an old college library. Unfortunately, its location on the third floor (with no elevator until 1974) was ideal for neither a library nor an assembly hall. Construction of the building took more than a year. Groundbreaking passed with less notice than usual, but the cornerstone was laid with due ceremony after graduation exercises in June of 1928. Jenkins Hall opened just before Thanksgiving in 1929.

• •

With more than enough classroom space for the college's 160 students and an operative library, President Wiesel thought Loyola had a plant adequate for accreditation. To oversee the less tangible details of the process, a new dean, Father Thomas O'Malley, a native of Scranton and son of a steelworker, was appointed. Soon he and Father Wiesel began attending the annual meetings of the Middle States Association and of other educational organizations. They were forming impressions of the officers, becoming acquainted with the jargon, and gathering other information about these bodies.

The repeated references to regular procedures and high academic standards at association meetings fortified Dean O'Malley's resolve to enforce the college's stated policies vigorously. The old ad hoc and paternal style of administration did not disappear, but it was amended during Father O'Malley's tenure to more orderly procedures. Until then, enrollment occurred when a student first applied to the college— only once. Thereafter it was the dean's responsibility to ensure passage to graduation. Although a date was specified for registration each year, no likely lad was turned away or made to wait until the start of the second semester just because he was a few days or even a month or so tardy. Such accommodations had become fewer even before O'Malley's appointment, but he ended them entirely and exacted a small financial penalty for lateness. Furthermore, each student now registered every year.

The admission procedure became more formal and more formidable under Father O'Malley. During some earlier catalogue revision, graduation from high school was announced as a prerequisite for admission to Loyola College. After the move to Evergreen a precise definition of the necessary units of secondary-school work appeared. These prerequisites Dean O'Malley strictly enforced. If an applicant had taken a required course during his last two years of high school but failed to achieve a grade of seventy-five, he would have to take an examination in that subject. Students from other colleges or universities were rejected if they had failed any course in their major. On the other hand, applicants from the "A" course at Baltimore's Polytechnic Institute or its equivalent were now given advanced standing, as had been the practice at other institutions familiar with these schools' high standards.

Dean O'Malley announced these policies, and his office diary records decisions that reflect their enforcement. Applicants with inadequate credentials were rejected. A number of these had attended out-of-state schools (football players?), but he found even the records of several applicants from Loyola High School and from City College seriously wanting. Some potential transfers from the University of Maryland and Johns Hopkins got no welcome.

This stringency was applied by O'Malley not only to those at the threshold of Loyola College but to those already matriculated there. Loyola students were periodically warned not to expect recommendations to graduate, law, or medical school unless their average was above seventy-five. To secure regular attendance at class, unscheduled holidays disappeared from the life of the college, and an unexcused absence resulted in a loss of two points from the semester's grade. Double that penalty was exacted from any who chose to work for the post office at Christmas time. If the grade fell below sixty-five the student was not permitted to take the regular final examination, but was allowed to take the conditional examination, which normally was for those who had done satisfactory work during the semester but failed the regular final. The highest grade for a conditional examination, however, was a minimum pass.

• •

The quality of the faculty was an important factor in accreditation, and this was registered on forms they filled out for the Maryland Department of Education in 1929. Father Ooghe, now in his twenty-fourth year of college teaching, was the doyen of the faculty. His nearest competitor for this distinction (from among those with a close and continuing connection with the college) was Father Joseph Ayd (1903). Father Ayd had ten years of classroom experience—mainly in sociology, psychology, and ethics. His service as chaplain at the Maryland penitentiary was almost equally long, and he took particular note of this experience on his application form. In addition, he listed his contributions to such magazines as *America, Catholic Charities Review,* and *Thought,* as well as to the newspapers of Baltimore. Several years hence he would produce two widely respected books: *Introductory Manual to Psychology* and *Summary of Sociology.*

Father Ayd's association with Henry Broening (1901) has already been noted; he was by this time also acquainted with H. L. Mencken. Their friendship arose from a common concern for, though they held differing views on, capital punishment, crime, and other issues. Of Father Ayd, Mencken later wrote, "No more useful man ever lived in Baltimore."[2] He was warmly loved and vastly admired by generations of Loyola students—even though his sharp wit and readiness to use it discouraged them from the byplay they enjoyed with others.

Mencken was acquainted also with Father John Hacker, with whom he shared a love of music and of their common German cultural heritage. At first meeting, Father Hacker's appearance was rather startling, because he was a diminutive hunchback (four feet ten inches, according to the form he submitted to the Maryland Department of Education); but his physical deformity did not seriously impede him or linger for long in the consciousness of his companions. He was remembered as a kindly teacher of German—if also as something of a "character," a term of affection not defined more precisely.

Beyond the classroom, Father Hacker's love was music. He published a hymnal and organ score for which there was a steady demand until the fashion in ecclesiastical music changed. There were also shorter compositions by him. One of these was a musical setting for Tennyson's *Ode to Virgil,* which he conducted at Loyola in 1930 for the celebration of the bimillenium of the ancient Roman poet's birth. An audience of Baltimore classicists—still a formidable force at Johns Hopkins, Goucher, and City College—gave his work hearty rounds of applause and praise. For this occasion, Father Hacker organized a student orchestra and chorus, which he maintained and directed until his death fifteen years later. His musicianship and skill in directing the students brought the college a solid local reputation.[3]

A similar ethnic linkage made Father Richard Schmitt another Loyola-associated acquaintance of Mencken's. Almost six feet in height and weighing over 190 pounds, he was the physical antithesis of John Hacker. His temperament had the same sharp edge as Henry McLoughlin's, whom he had replaced a few years earlier. Schmitt brought to Loyola a new technique, which he learned at New York University from a student of the Nobel laureate who discovered it. Microanalysis requires only a minute drop of liquid or a grain or two of a solid to support the identification of the substances present. The *Sun* reported that during this period there were only twenty other American institutions equipped to teach microanalysis.

In fact, Father Schmitt acted as a kind of local promoter by arranging to bring his old instructor and other associates to Baltimore to lecture and to demonstrate the method. Among the people interested in the process was J. Edgar Hoover, who in 1924 was appointed director of the Federal Bureau of Investigation. In publicizing his fight against Prohibition- and depression-related crime, Hoover emphasized detection and conviction through scientific methods. On several occasions he sent agents from the bureau's crime lab to study Loyola's equipment. Father Schmitt's professional interests made him generally impatient with student callowness. Nevertheless, he could invite a tired laboratory assistant to join him in a cocktail from the departmental refrigerator at the end of a trying day[4]—by then Prohibition had been repealed.

Other teachers also completed the forms for the Maryland Department of Education. It might seem from the selection above that the faculty had acquired a strong Teutonic cast. At this time, however, there were ten of German ancestry—only one more than the total of Celts on the faculty. The remaining four teachers had Belgian, Spanish, or vaguely American origins.

In 1929 two laymen taught part time at Loyola: George Renehan (1918) and John Egerton. They were not expected to stay long because laymen at most Catholic schools were still considered disposable auxiliaries. Renehan would in fact leave at the end of 1929 after teaching at Loyola for only three years. Egerton, already in his sixties, would remain for another ten years. Renehan taught eight hours of inorganic chemistry a week, and his peer was responsible for a similar load in algebra and calculus. Each was paid eight hundred dollars a year. If they had been carrying what then was considered a full load (as measured by the hours assigned to the senior Jesuits), they would presumably have been paid twelve hundred dollars. At that rate, in an irony often cited by academics, they would have earned half as much as that other layman at the college—the football coach.

George Renehan is interesting for another reason. Some years before joining the faculty he had organized "the Philomaths," a group of alumni who continued the study and discussion of philosophy under the tutelage of Father Ooghe. The membership included Bert Hoen (1918), Clarence Caulfield (1922), Harry Casey (1921), Leo Johnson (1919), John O'Connor (1918), Joseph Kirby (1918), Albert Sehlstedt (1919), and Joseph Garland (1918). Renehan was a lawyer and O'Connor became a doctor; the others included an editor of the Sunpapers, a chemist, and several businessmen. Gradually their attention shifted from abstract philosophical questions to the papal encyclicals on labor and other social concerns. They became in effect a cell for spreading Catholic ideas on issues raised during the depression. The group survived Father Ooghe's death in 1931 by acquiring a congenial moderator from Woodstock but was dissolved in the late 1930s because the lives and interests of the members finally diverged.

. .

As part of the accrediting process, the credentials of the instructors at Loyola were submitted in April of 1929, along with other documents, to state authorities. These materials were augmented with data gathered by an official visitor who soon came to the campus. He was favorably impressed with the Loyola College library—listing its holdings as thirty thousand volumes. He thought the best word to describe its condition was *growing* rather than the alternatives listed on the form: *static* or *decadent.* He characterized the equipment and furniture in the science laboratories as "magnificent." Such a favorable impression pointed to formal approval, and that was voted by the state board on June 21, 1929.

It may not have been entirely coincidental that two days after the visit of this officer a formal invitation was sent to Governor Ritchie. He was in recent years regularly asked to attend Loyola commencements, and he usually took the seat reserved for him on the platform. At this appearance in 1929, the college gave Albert Ritchie an honorary degree—a practice that has been continued with many of his successors. To that June 10 audience, Dean O'Malley read the citation, which acclaimed Ritchie an "unselfish statesman . . . guardian and promoter of education, foe of bigotry, champion of toleration . . . and above all fearless defender of the Constitution of the United States." This tribute gave voice to the general approval Marylanders afforded Ritchie, who was then enjoying his third term and would be reelected in 1930. Ritchie and many voters thought that 1932 might be the year when a Marylander would win the Democratic nomination for president, but this was not to be. The victor was Franklin Delano Roosevelt, governor of New York. Two years later Ritchie lost his gubernatorial office to the Republican he had defeated in 1919.

Anticipating approval by the state department of education, Fathers Wiesel and O'Malley had already applied to the Middle States Association, but its review proved to be unexpectedly difficult. In October of 1929, the regional organization sent a visitor to the college and, had all gone well, Loyola College would have been voted to full membership at the association's next meeting. Unfortunately, doubts arose in the visitor's mind about two important matters. For unknown reasons, Wiesel chose not to show the inspector either the temporary library facilities in use since the move to Evergreen or the recently erected but not yet formally opened Jenkins library building. The other matter was whether the college's admission standards actually conformed to requirements of the state of Maryland. As a result of these notations in the inspector's report, the Middle States Association postponed action on Loyola's application.[5]

Early in March of 1930, Loyola's president and dean submitted a formal justification for reviewing its original application. They offered logical evidence to demonstrate the adequacy of Loyola's library. Also, Father Wiesel insisted that the college maintained the same admission standards as other Maryland institutions, and Dean O'Malley's more detailed presentation on this point supported that assertion. The association, however, continued its postponement and asked for additional evidence that the college was complying with state standards on admissions. The library, at least, had passed muster. Father Wiesel was annoyed by this question because among the documents submitted to the association was a letter from the Maryland Department of Education testifying to Loyola's full compliance. The association's director, in reply, confessed a lapse of memory. And well that might have been true, although some on the faculty may reasonably have suspected that the delays served first to increase anxiety and, later—if Loyola was finally admitted to membership—pride of accomplishment. Among Jesuit schools generally this was a moment of discouragement not so much because of the Great Depression as because of the failure to achieve distinction.[6] Average is too low a rating to be acceptable among Jesuits.

Though action was promised at the fall 1930 meeting, nothing happened for another year. Meanwhile the responsibility for decisions on admissions, which in practice had been assigned to the dean, was formally shifted to a committee consisting of the president, dean, dean of discipline, and school physician (who happened to be an alumnus). This might have seemed to assure more consistent application of admissions policy, but in fact the other members of the committee generally deferred to the dean. In any case, Loyola's procedures took on a form familiar to those who came to scrutinize it.

On a mid-November morning in 1931, Ryland Dempster, registrar at Johns Hopkins, arrived at Evergreen as the representative of the Middle States Association. He thoroughly examined the admission records, science facilities, and library. At the end of the day he told the dean "that he was highly pleased with the inspection" and expressed confidence that Loyola would finally be voted membership and thus, in present terminology, to full accreditation. This occurred on November 27, 1931. By that time 40 percent of the Catholic colleges in America were accredited; in eight years this figure rose to 76 percent. However willingly, they were adjusting to the general pattern of American higher education—but, as previously, only after a chronological lag.[7] Then the association did not have a program of periodic reviews, and once on its approved list an institution held a reasonably secure status. This policy would be changed in the mid-1950s and would result in an even more trying experience for Loyola College.

There was one brief corollary to the first episode. When the school sought to have its bachelor of science and bachelor of philosophy degrees recognized by the New York State Department of Education (its A.B. awards having been accepted in 1909), that agency questioned the Middle States decision because none of the department heads at Loyola held doctoral degrees. The association's director noted in reply that all were Jesuits and their traditional training was accepted as "sufficiently equivalent" to the work required for a Ph.D.[8] This explanation proved effective, and the catalogues thereafter carried approval by New

York's authorities. In time a similar warrant was obtained from the National Catholic Educational Association.

One added note. The letters sent by Father Wiesel to the Middle States Association were dictated to and typed by Catherine McDonald —her initials appear on the identification line. There may have been volunteer or temporary secretarial help earlier, but "Miss McDonald," as she was usually called, became the first woman engaged in a regular position. Her employment, unremarkable as it might seem now, came after earnest but unrecorded discussions among the Jesuits. In the end it was justified by making her responsible not only for the president's correspondence but for that of the treasurer's office; she also assisted the librarian. This last responsibility was soon yielded to another woman who came in 1931, and Kitty McDonald became the registrar. In that capacity she was a charming and resourceful presence who for over thirty years provided an important strand of administrative continuity. More than one student and teacher, and perhaps a dean or two, were saved from misfortune by her generous concern, knowledge, and experience. Her retirement in 1966 evoked many affectionate testimonials.

• •

News of Loyola's accreditation prompted the dean to press the advantage, with the premedical program as the first object of his attention. By first requiring a third and finally a fourth year, he phased out the earlier short program. Father O'Malley arranged an exchange of visits with the dean of admissions at the Johns Hopkins Medical School. These get-acquainted sessions produced an agreement that Loyola's recommendation would ensure admission to the medical school, but only "A" students were to be nominated. In this cordial glow, the medical school's earlier practice of conditionally admitting Loyola students slid quietly into oblivion.

Success prompted another initiative by Father O'Malley. He discussed the two scholarships awarded each year by the Johns Hopkins Engineering School with its dean. No formal arrangement on this matter was possible, but O'Malley obtained a schedule of mathematics courses that, if followed, would permit students to transfer and complete the Johns Hopkins program in only two years. Exactly how many took advantage of this connection is not known, but more than half a dozen of the very small number of alumni from this period went to Hopkins and pursued careers in engineering.

At this time Fathers Wiesel and O'Malley interested themselves in a public issue that affected Loyola as well as a number of other institutions in Maryland. For some time the state legislature had appropriated money for scholarships, but the students assisted were required to attend certain schools. The League of Women Voters thought the arrangement too restrictive and campaigned for a program of scholarships that allowed the students to pick their own schools. Father Wiesel seconded this motion with a statement to the *Sun,* and Dean O'Malley got the alumni to register their support with the league. After several years the state legislature enacted a more liberal policy. Criticism of various aspects of the state scholarship program has continued, but the principle of student choice has not been seriously questioned.

The dean's activism altered several intramural practices. He streamlined the programs for student assemblies and for commencement. During the assemblies, Father O'Malley discontinued the practice of reading every student's grade; only those with grades of eighty or higher were now publicly recognized. By this, the less gifted or lazier students were spared embarrassment (a loss some still decry), but the able and diligent now gained a greater visibility. Later, when such convocations themselves were abandoned, these honors were maintained by posting the dean's list.

O'Malley's attention to academic distinction led to the inscription of honors on the diploma. The first to graduate with such a notation— cum laude, as it happened—was Robert Peddicord (1935); this was followed in the next year with a magna cum laude attached to the degree of John Higinbothom (1936). It would be two more years before the highest distinction, summa cum laude, was awarded, to William Mahoney (1938). Many years later the distinctive Greek letters identifying members of various honor societies with which Loyola had become affiliated were also added to their letters patent.

The move to Evergreen had no noticeable effect on the perennial concern about students' gambling. At the start of each year the dean of discipline warned against games that involved betting. This was not from any general aversion to gambling, but from a desire to prevent student sharpies from winning the pocket money of their fellows. Periodically reports of gaming reached the ears of the school authorities, and appropriate warnings were repeated.

Rules on proper attire have existed since the founding of Loyola. The earliest catalogue required "clean and becoming apparel" without defining the terms or indicating a means of enforcement. This declaration apparently secured adequate compliance. After the mid-1920s, freshmen were indoctrinated during the hazing period to wear coats and ties, and the sophomores ensured their conformity—at least for one semester. Thereafter the matter was left to the faculty, with the dean periodically reminding students of their responsibility. The main problem was sweaters. These could be worn under a coat, but if the coat was removed students were not permitted to enter or to stay in a classroom.

．．

More significant and poignant concerns arose. A week before commencement in 1930, the college community and Baltimore were saddened by an event that could not have been unexpected. On June 5, George Carrell Jenkins died, at the age of 94. The students registered their grief in the *Greyhound* with a declaration: "Loyola will not soon find another such friend."[9] Similar sentiments were included in the minutes of the trustees and in other college records. In his will Jenkins left another one hundred thousand dollars to the college—a half million in all. With similar but more public notice, Baltimore also mourned the passing of one of its leading citizens.

The day of Jenkins's death brought even more distressing news. Loyola's other major benefactor, Mary Farmer, was found semiconscious in her house. She had fallen down the stairs and broken her hip and an arm, and had lain there for two days until discovered by her cleaning woman. Her rescuer called Miss Farmer's close friend, who had her rushed to the hospital; then she called Father O'Carroll. The doctors doubted that a woman of her age and infirmities could survive the ordeal, but after the initial crisis she began to recover. First one niece and then another, and finally her nephew, visited her in the hospital—and they became reconciled.

One of the nieces moved in to nurse Miss Farmer, now a semi-invalid and often confused. During one of her more lucid periods she was persuaded to give her nephew a power of attorney, and he used it in September of 1931 to institute legal proceedings against Father Peter O'Carroll and Loyola College to recover the $155,000 she had given to the college a decade earlier. The accusation of the nephew and nieces cast a sinister light on what supposedly happened in 1921. The bonds and currency had been given, the complaint now said, not as an outright gift conditioned on a life annuity, but only as a loan. Father O'Carroll was accused of using his "controlling and dominant influence" to get Mary Farmer to sign an agreement that she had not read and did not understand. Her nephew and his sisters, acting in the name of their helpless aunt, asked for full restitution and a like amount in damages.

For a number of incidental reasons the legal process stretched across two and a half years, to March of 1934. The initial complaint and an amended version were summarily dismissed by the judge who first heard them. Three times the dispute was brought to the court of appeals, and there was another trial at a lower level. All these actions were brought by the Farmers, and all failed to secure any judicial support. This route, however slow and tortuous, ensured the close scrutiny of both the facts and the applicable legal doctrines.

Part of the delay arose from the death of Father O'Carroll in August 1932 and, about ten months later, of Miss Farmer. This meant that her relatives could now press the suit in their own right. Mary Farmer was the last family member buried in the Quinn-Farmer plot near the center of the small cemetery maintained by Saint Mary's Church in Govans near the campus. A month after Miss Farmer's death, on May 20, 1933, Loyola's president celebrated a solemn requiem for the repose of her soul. In this way the Jesuits honored Mary Farmer's generosity and indicated their recognition that her surviving relatives were the source of the legal challenge they continued to face.

Less than a year later the state's highest court rendered its final judgment, which like all previous decrees completely vindicated Father Peter O'Carroll and Loyola College. In such cases the burden of proof falls on the defendants, and the college had presented convincing evidence that Mary Farmer clearly understood the nature of the original agreement and acted afterwards in ways that conformed to that understanding. By an irony common in the legal profession, the law firm headed by William Galvin (1908), which defended the Jesuits in the Farmer case, would appear in a similar dispute seven years later—but as counsel for another group of complainants against Loyola and another president.[10]

• •

The anxiety-inducing episodes associated with Loyola's accreditation occurred simultaneously with the onset of the Great Depression. With the crash of Wall Street in late October of 1929, the market economy that Europe and the United States had developed during the nineteenth century almost collapsed. In America, thirty billion dollars in stock and bond values—more than the national debt—vanished over a few weeks. President Herbert Hoover tried with little success to convince the nation that panic itself was the main enemy. He acted to stimulate American industry and trade in various ways, some adopted and expanded by his successor, Franklin Roosevelt. What he could not bring himself to do was use federal power for direct relief of individual Americans, because he thought such action was unconstitutional and corruptive of basic national values.

Hoover's actions were not enough to stop the continuing downward curve of all economic indicators. By 1932 American industry was producing half as much as it did in 1929, and wages were 60 percent lower. One of four workers was unemployed, and men with jobs were paid only twenty or thirty cents an hour; women's wages were even lower. The cherished notion that hard work drew opportunity to itself was shaken by a disaster that engulfed indifferently both the diligent and the feckless.

For a time some Baltimore leaders thought their city situated somehow above this ruinous economic tide. By December of 1932, however, even the association of commerce admitted that the city was no longer secure, because more than half of the Marylanders out of work and in need of assistance lived in Baltimore. The mayor established a free employment service, which was quickly swamped by five times as many applicants as there were jobs.

Private agencies tried to relieve the needy. In 1931 civic activists organized a self-denial campaign in which affluent Baltimoreans abstained from some luxury during Lent and contributed the saving to relief. This collection yielded ninety thousand dollars, and a parallel appeal to business and industry brought more than seven times as much. But private generosity was not enough. Maryland authorities, who at first disdained federal assistance, finally applied for the state's share of federal relief appropriations.[11] Distasteful as this was, Marylanders like other Americans accommodated themselves to the situation by recalling that governmental intervention in the economy during World War I had proven effective. They considered this economic disaster an "analogue of war," and they were willing to accept controls and leadership.

When Franklin Delano Roosevelt accepted the Democratic nomination in 1932 he responded to this climate of opinion by issuing "a call to arms" and promising a "new deal." The most quoted phrase from his inaugural address—"The only thing we have to fear is fear itself"— reiterated his hapless predecessor's sentiments, but people believed President Roosevelt. He capitalized on their trust with a "tornado of action": measures to stabilize banking, to stimulate business and public works, to provide federal relief for the nation's needy, and to reform the institutions and policies that had brought America to its sorry economic state. Though neither as revolutionary (he had after all only promised a "new deal," not a new deck) nor as successful as his partisans insist, President Roosevelt, through his actions, saved the country from the monstrous remedy that about the same time was being prescribed by Adolf Hitler for Germany . . . nazism. The general effect of the federal government's intervention in the national economy was a 40 percent rise in prices. For school administrators this meant rising costs, and some, Jesuits among them, were not long enamored of Roosevelt's new deal.

* *

Like other institutions Loyola College was hurt by the depression, but its effect on the college was mild. The provincial in 1932 urged Jesuits to keep expenses down and to increase revenues. At Evergreen this meant keeping outlays below $60,000 (the 1931 total), which was done; in 1934 and 1936 expenditures fell to $50,000. Income during the same period rose from $53,400 in 1931 to more than $61,000 in 1936. Part of the increment came from stipends for priestly ministrations of the Jesuits, for their direction of retreats, and for their teaching at other institutions. Some of this income by special exemption from the Jesuit general was not shared with the province, and stipends for services performed at Saint Ignatius Church were charged against the college's indebtedness to the Calvert Street Jesuit community. Favorable as the overall balance between income and outgo appears, there were year-by-year deficits ranging between $8,000 and $22,000, with small surpluses only in 1935 and 1936. The mystery of continual deficits and continuing operations is as fascinating and apparently as unfathomable as the smile on the Chesire cat.

Major contributors to Loyola's financial health were an increase in enrollments and a rise in tuition. A student body that numbered only 167 in 1928 doubled in the ensuing ten years. This occurred for reasons including retrenchments by more than one Baltimore family who decided against sending a son away to college and chose Loyola instead. With work not readily available and a college education recognized as essential, more fellows and their families were willing to invest four years and almost $1,000 to be better prepared when the depression ended. The rising demand for admission to Loyola, while enrollments elsewhere were generally falling, convinced its officers that they could safely raise tuition to $200. To ease the increased burden, the alumni association established a revolving loan fund with repayment deferred until after graduation. Other students merely chose to delay paying tuition. Loyola permitted this arrangement, although the dean regularly reminded such students of both current charges and arrears. In one year, these deferred tuitions amounted to more than $7,000. The only sanction was the threat to withhold diplomas and transcripts till all debts were paid.

Individual students found various other means to cover their costs. A few from affluent families had chosen to come to a local college and so were freed of costs of room and board that they would otherwise have paid. Many students at Loyola had fathers who were policemen, firemen, magistrates, or other civil servants. Their family income may not have been high, but it was steady. Others delayed enrolling for a few years, working full time until they earned enough to pay their tuition. Some chose to work only during the summer months, as lifeguards, salesmen, or truck drivers, or by swinging a pick and shovel. For laboring nine hours a day six days a week they received an average of two hundred dollars for the season's labor—enough to cover tuition. A historian of the University of Detroit recently noted a financial paradox: "The depression was a mixed blessing since, if money was harder to come by, [the students] did not need quite as much as formerly."[12]

Another source of support came from an assistance program instituted in 1934 by the federal government. The National Youth Administration (NYA) paid students fifty cents an hour up to twenty dollars a month for work they did around a school. By 1937 NYA had almost six hundred thousand on its rolls, but only sixteen Loyola students—7 percent of Loyola's total enrollment—were receiving such assistance. Why the proportion of Loyola students in the NYA program was so much lower than that at nearby institutions is unclear. Because so few Loyolans were involved in the NYA program, the treasurer suggested that a unit of the Reserve Officers Training Corps (ROTC) be brought to the campus, but provincial authorities, fearing federal control and interference, withheld approval. This noteworthy attitude would change in the 1950s.

A few Loyola students favored a more enterprising method for dealing with the effects of the depression. Thirty of them organized an escort service. They offered to take ladies from out of town (with no age limit) on a tour of Baltimore, to dinner, or to the theater for expenses and an hourly fee. Often members of this service merely served as a stag line at nearby women's colleges; on such occasions their remuneration barely covered the cost of renting a tuxedo, but they could enjoy a pleasant date without net cost to themselves. Several of the Jesuits were amused and favorably impressed by the enterprise—as were the *Sun* and its cartoonist Richard "Moko" Yardley.[13] For one social season the escort service established by Loyola's students provided a cheerful topic of conversation and recreation for its members.

In the main, Loyola's financial needs were met during the depression by borrowing—particularly from the province. Obligations to a total of $250,000 were carried on the college's ledgers by July 1934. A part of the debt had been refinanced that year, when Loyola College was brought to the verge of bankruptcy because it could not pay the interest on $87,000 that remained from the loan to complete the gymnasium. Catastrophe was averted when the province advanced the sum and charged it against the still unrealized remainder in the bequest from Thomas O'Neill. In such circumstances it is not surprising to find a provincial procurator (treasurer) threatening President Wiesel jocularly that he would "have to bring bailiff, or sheriff . . . to institute foreclosure proceedings" if the interest on Loyola's borrowings "from the Province were not paid."[14] Instead of carrying out the threat, the procurator merely added the charge to the principal—as he would do several more times.

Similarly, the procurator would write off ten thousand dollars that the Jesuits at Evergreen had failed to pay over the years. This was for the annual per capita assessment levied by the province on every house under its jurisdiction to support the scholasticates and the central administration of the province. It was not until 1939 that the Jesuit community at Loyola would resume payment of this intramural tax. The province gradually got the college and other institutions to turn over management of their investment portfolios to the procurator, and at the least this stabilized their income.

• •

These years, although shadowed by threat and worry, had a productive side. The economic disaster, coming as it did on top of the trauma of World War I, forced people to address basic questions about society and civilization. Some thought they found the answer in a Marxist-Leninist utopia; others sought salvation in the competing totalitarianisms of Mussolini, Japanese militarism, and Hitler. In America the media, expanded by the development of radio, publicized a variety of movements, personalities, and solutions for the nation's ills. The air was thick with competing schemes, but it had become possible to gain a hearing for any strongly held view.

This was the atmosphere in which Loyola students managed their affairs in the early 1930s. The relatively light tone of the *Greyhound* and yearbooks of the first ten years at Evergreen was subdued (though not eliminated) by more serious interests. The sodality, which till then had emphasized personal piety, expanded its horizons to include activities subsumed under the phrase "the lay apostolate." What this or its cognate—Catholic Action—meant was subject to endless discussion and many distinctions. To rehearse these exercises in logic is less enlightening than to identify the underlying aim of the general movement: to rouse Catholics to full and effective participation in society. In Europe this resulted in an obscure but protracted competition between Catholic activists and the Fascist-Nazi authorities. (This drew no contemporary journalistic interest but has begun attracting attention among historians.)

In America the situation was quite different: there was no such palpable antagonist. The force against which American Catholics had to struggle was identified by Father Daniel Lord as their own sloth. In one appearance at Evergreen he charged that "the most characteristic quality of the Catholic college man is apathy." On another occasion he asked, "Where are the Catholic leaders?"[15] His was not the only voice urging consideration of these themes.

Special targets of Father Lord were American politics and the diplomatic service. In politics he found the influence of Catholics "bewilderingly slight," even though they made up 16 percent of the population. In the foreign service he discerned an infinitesimal percentage of Catholics. Father Lord urged his listeners to commit themselves wholeheartedly to the study of their religion and to preparation for leadership in these vital fields, and his call came at an opportune juncture. President Roosevelt cultivated the Catholic vote with respectful references to the papal encyclicals on labor and by appointing Catholics to the federal judiciary and to other prominent posts.[16]

Writers referring to this movement among Catholics have been tempted—and have too rarely resisted the temptation—to reduce its motive force to anti-communism. Admittedly, the menace of a Red revolution was a major concern for Catholic churchmen, Jesuits included, but it was a fear they shared with many others. Loyola students, reflecting this climate of opinion, argued during many a lunchtime whether or not the New Deal was a Trojan horse for communism. A few independent spirits among the students were suspected of favoring the Reds, but this was about as serious as labelling a fellow with a crew cut a "stormtrooper."

Such name-calling was taken lightly in those years. A tour of Russia was not deleted from the advertising for student travel offered in the *Greyhound* for the summer of 1930. Whether anyone inquired further is unknown, but seven years later a group of students from Loyola drove down to Mexico City, then thought by many Americans to be a hotbed of Marxists and revolutionaries. They went to participate in a rally of students from North and South America sponsored by the Jesuits, but they also sought an interview with Leon Trotsky, the Russian arch-revolutionist in exile. His fear of Stalinist assassins (a fear soon justified) closed his doors against casual contacts. Nevertheless, these student-adventurers published a full report on their return to Baltimore, indicating they harbored no apprehensions of being considered subversive.[17]

The studied views of Loyolans were aired in a series of brief commentaries for Baltimore radio station WCBM in 1937 and in their own newspaper. The threat of communism was the subject of only four of the twelve radio talks; the rest covered a variety of subjects including a plea for the return of the *Constellation* to Baltimore. The enemy, in the view of Loyola's students, was not communism alone but all forms of totalitarianism. In this category they lumped fascism and nazism together with communism. The antidote to these alien ideologies, according to the *Greyhound*, was to eradicate popular grievances—an attitude some might well characterize as liberal.

Around the college, fundamental problems of social justice drew more attention than the Red menace. One WCBM talk urged profit sharing. The development of an alumni group, the Philomaths, has already been mentioned. They carried the message of the papal encyclicals on labor to many groups around Baltimore, including the local American Federation of Labor. The college itself offered extension courses in social work and evening lectures on Christian social justice at Calvert Street.

There were other traces of this liberal approach. The *Greyhound* in 1931 reported Father John A. Ryan's call for a five-billion-dollar national public works program. Four years later the newspaper editorialized against a loyalty oath for Maryland's teachers on the grounds that it was unnecessary and would deprive the state of the services of able foreign scholars. Despite lobbying by the American Legion, the governor refused to sign the loyalty oath bill. (A similar bill in Massachusetts drew the same response from student journalists at Holy Cross.) The *Catholic Worker*, published by Peter Maurin and Dorothy Day, drew notice and praise in Loyola's student newspaper.

Even clearer signs of this attitude appeared in regard to Father Coughlin, "the radio priest." The sophomore class in 1935 listened to a debate on the proposition that it "formally approve and endorse the activities, the social and economic principles and objectives of Father Charles E. Coughlin." Despite this radio orator's charisma the class voted against the resolution, among other reasons because Father Coughlin was perceived as a radical even before he had begun delivering anti-Semitic diatribes. Futhermore, Coughlin's influence among American Catholics—a firmly held dogma among liberal intellectuals even today—has been exaggerated. A Gallup poll of the period puts his approval rating at only 42 percent, with 25 percent of Catholics disapproving and 33 percent expressing no opinion. (Something of the same phenomenon and misjudgment of Catholic support appeared again in the early 1950s when Senator Joseph McCarthy essayed the demagogue's role.)[18] Loyolans were wary of Adolf Hitler. When he became chancellor in Germany many people were ill-informed about his aims. Even at that early stage, however, a *Greyhound* editorial called the Führer's solutions to Germany's problems simplistic and expressed fear of the fanaticism of the Nazi movement.

• •

Other Baltimore Catholics—notably Archbishop Curley—held similar opinions. At Loyola's commencement in 1925 he denounced Nordic claims to racial superiority. In June of 1934, after Hitler came to power, Curley launched a noisy crusade against the *Sun.* One of its foreign correspondents had ended a dispatch from Germany by comparing the leadership and strength of will displayed by Adolf Hitler with the same qualities in Ignatius Loyola. A number of people, including Fathers Wiesel and O'Malley, objected in letters to the editor to a comparison they considered odious and prejudiced.

After this reaction appeared Archbishop Curley sought to rally public opinion against the *Sun.* (He thought the paper had been less cordial to him and his endeavors than to his predecessor, Cardinal Gibbons.) Just before leaving for his annual vacation in Ireland the archbishop urged subscribers and advertisers to boycott the paper until it printed a full retraction and apology. He left it to others to settle this brouhaha—if they could.

The effect of the boycott was real but the management of the paper refused to surrender to such tactics. Meetings between representatives of the archdiocese and of the Sunpapers produced little progress until the most ardent partisans on both sides left town for vacation or turned to other matters. Then agreement was reached (with the help of H. L. Mencken) on a statement that allowed each side to claim success in principle. When the archbishop returned at the end of the summer, he accepted the accommodation. This disappointed Mencken, partly because he expected the *Sun* to win, an outcome that would encourage other American newspapers to resist such pressure.[19]

This contretemps did not unfavorably affect the attitude of the *Sun* toward Loyola College. In March of 1935 it publicized a poll that summarized the thinking of Loyola students on questions of war and peace. The poll was an extension of another poll conducted earlier that year by the *Literary Digest* in 150 other colleges and universities. Virtually the entire Loyola student body answered the same seven questions, and their attitudes can be compared with those of students elsewhere. This material is presented in Table 13.1.

The most striking thing about these responses is that with one exception (question 4) these American students generally agreed on what was likely to happen and what ought to be done. Loyola and Boston College students differed from their peers at other schools in that they favored a large military establishment. Given the pessimism of those at Loyola, their preference for a large army and navy seems logical.

Lest unwarranted conclusions be drawn from the agreement of Loyola and Boston College students, it is well to note that the responses of the students at the Jesuit schools were not identical. For instance, the fellows at Boston College, like those at Johns Hopkins, were much more willing to support American aggression (question 3) than those at Loyola or than the national average. Why this was so cannot be simply explained.

Evergreen was more pessimistic about the prospects of peace (question 1) than the rest. It was the seniors at Loyola who were most convinced that there would be another war and that America would be involved. The sophomores displayed the most negative attitude on all questions except joining the League of Nations: the freshmen most staunchly opposed membership, by 95 percent.[20] (As polling became more sophisticated, analysts came to believe that young adults favor conservative responses.) Furthermore, it is not unreasonable to assume that these young men, particularly the freshmen, reflected the thinking of their parents.

Shortly after publication of the poll the threat of war in Europe became quite real. In the Spanish civil war of 1936 Germany and Italy

TABLE 13.1   Literary Digest War-Peace Poll, 1935
(In Percentages)

	1		2		3		4		5		6		7	
	Yes	*No*	*Yes*	*No*	*Yes*	*No*	*Yes*	*No*	*Yes*	*No*	*Yes*	*No*	*Yes*	*No*
Nationally	69	31	84	16	18	82	37	63	91	9	82	18	49	51
Loyola College	56	44	98	2	18	82	66	34	95	5	76	24	17	83
Johns Hopkins University	68	32	88	12	32	68	42	58	88	12	86	14	36	64
Boston College	66	35	94	6	35	65	79	21	86	14	72	28	18	82
George Washington University	73	27	88	12	20	80	48	52	90	10	87	13	45	55
University of Pennsylvania	68	32	82	28	17	83	39	61	83	17	77	23	48	52

1. Can the United States stay out of war?
2. Will you fight if the United States is invaded?
3. Will you fight if the United States is the invader?
4. Should the United States have the largest army, navy, and air force?
5. Should the government control production of munitions?
6. In wartime, should capital and labor be conscripted like men for the military service?
7. Should the United States join the League of Nations?

NOTE: Results were not available for all participating schools. Those chosen provide geographical comparison or, in the case of Boston College, comparison with another Jesuit institution.

supported the nationalists led by General Francisco Franco. The equipment and tactics tested in his campaigns across the Iberian Peninsula would a few years later be seen again in the blitzkrieg against Poland, Greece, Holland, Belgium, France, Britain, Norway, and Russia. The Soviet Union was involved in the Spanish civil war, but on the side of the republican forces. It supplied arms for international brigades recruited under the aegis of the Spanish republican government. Americans were among the partisans on both sides. Ernest Hemingway commemorated the Spaniards and idealists who fought against Franco in *For Whom The Bell Tolls*. Though Catholics were assumed by many other Americans to favor Franco's nationalists overwhelmingly, opinion among them was divided. Fifty-eight percent, aware of the antagonism and persecution that the church had endured under the republican government, sided with Franco's nationalists, but 42 percent favored the republican loyalists.[21]

Articulate students at Loyola expressed their opinions on the Spanish civil war in the *Greyhound* and in their talks for radio station WCBM. The theme of their comments was "Let's get the story straight."[22] In this endeavor, quixotic midst rising passions and preparations for war, a *Greyhound* editorial supported Mencken for his courage and "intellectual honesty" in expressing doubts about the republican charge that the nationalists had senselessly bombed the unprotected village of Guernica—still a cause célèbre. Students admitted that Franco's forces were supported by Fascists but insisted that other political factions were active among the nationalists. They were appealing for reason, not issuing full-throated calls to arms against communism. Their stance, tenuous and delicately balanced as it was, resembled that of *America*, the Jesuit national journal of opinion, and the *Catholic Review*, the archdiocesan weekly.

• •

The serious tone at Loyola during the 1930s spread to student activities. The chemists' club organized by Father Schmitt in 1929 alternated presentations of student papers (on such topics as "Hydrogen Ion Concentration" and "Bakelite, Phenol-Formaldehyde Resins") with lectures by recognized scientists from Johns Hopkins, Princeton, and New York University. Lecturers were employed by the National Bureau of Standards and other governmental agencies, or by local industries. The aim was to bridge the gap between classroom chemistry and the science as it was rapidly developing in research and industrial centers.

A few years earlier the biology and premedical students organized the Mendel Club—named for the Austrian scientist and monk who confirmed the laws of genetic inheritance—but little publicity was given its operations for some years. Unlike the chemists, the biologists relied almost exclusively on student presentations. When Father Joseph Didusch (1898) returned to the college in 1935, the preparation of papers for the Mendel Club became even more thorough and detailed.

Not to be outdone by their science-minded peers, Loyolans with an interest in history organized in 1927. They named their association in honor of John Gilmary Shea, "the father of American Catholic history." At the first meeting of each year the students chose a subject such as the French Revolution or the Middle Ages or nationalism, and then volunteered to deliver papers on various subdivisions of the year's topic.

Membership generally averaged about twenty—a number large enough to share the labor and small enough to ensure cohesion.

About this time the history academy inaugurated "a more pretentious program" (so described in its minutes book) by supplementing the student papers with those of mature scholars. Father Joseph Thorning, a leader in the Catholic Association for International Peace—an organization formed to promote support of the League of Nations—discussed "Sea Power and World Power." He ended his discourse with a plea for limiting naval armaments. The other featured speaker in 1929 was Father Gerald Walsh, professor of history at Woodstock College. More than 125 students and others attended his evening lecture on the norms for scientific history.

This modest experiment proved so successful that throughout the rest of the 1930s a series of such lectures was offered each year. Among the better-known speakers were Carlton Hayes and Parker Moon of Columbia University, Lee Bowen of Johns Hopkins, and Father John LaFarge. These lecturers recurrently appealed for more American support for internationalism.

• •

The yearly programs of the history, chemistry, Mendel, and other clubs were printed in leaflet form and widely distributed. What notice was taken of them cannot be discovered, but they provide information about what was going on at the college. The public was welcome, especially at the presentations by academic celebrities.

The best-known local scholar was Doctor Elizabeth Morrissey, who. taught economics at the College of Notre Dame of Maryland for many years. She also served on various commissions of the federal and state governments. After hearing her talk on "Nationalism in the Nineteenth Century," Dean O'Malley confided to his diary: "Possibly largest audience of the year attended—It was a superb lecture—Definite propositions lucid and authoritative development."[23] Not surprisingly, he asked her to teach a history course for the extension program. She thus became the first woman to join the Loyola faculty, if only on a part-time basis, and also the first woman to receive an honorary degree from Loyola. The citation in 1957 acclaimed Elizabeth Morrissey's "zeal for social improvement," her "efforts to remove racial prejudice," and her work "to insure industrial peace and economic well-being."

Other organizations were formed at the college. Repeated efforts had been made to reestablish a dramatics club, but early attempts foundered on lack of a place to rehearse. In 1937 the Mask and Rapier

Society, as Loyola's resident company was now named, staged *Everyman* at the old Calvert Street auditorium. The following year it essayed *The Amazing Dr. Clitterhouse* at Notre Dame's LeClerc Hall. Under such circumstances it took determination and ingenuity to continue, but as enrollments increased it became easier to find the necessary actors and to entice enough of them into the latest production. The ambitions of the Mask and Rapier Society grew accordingly.

Interest in the theater was promoted by "Loyola Night," inaugurated in April of 1936. Neill Miller (1937) suggested it, and Fathers Hacker and August Fremgen (back at the college after a lapse of twenty-five years) arranged a program featuring the glee club and several one-act plays. With no place on campus to stage the show, they rented the hall at the Alcazar (now the Baltimore School of the Arts). An appreciative crowd of four hundred attended, and their reaction encouraged students and faculty to do it again.

The same general format was employed for the second and most memorable "Loyola Night." It was scheduled for December 11, 1936, again at the Alcazar. Neill Miller, now a senior, thought his spot on the program, a performance of his own compositions, ought to be embellished with a vocalist—a girl. He was putting himself through college by playing piano around the city and he was well acquainted with local show business people. Father Fremgen immediately objected to this request, but his diminutive colleague interjected, "Why not girls? We all had mothers—and sisters." Fremgen relented, but only on condition that the singer stand immobile during her performance.

There was a large audience for this second "Loyola Night." The glee club's part in the program, standard light-classic pieces, went so well that Father Fremgen relaxed at the rear of the hall and lit a cigar. Then it was Neill Miller's turn. He followed onto the stage a gorgeous girl in a fire-engine red satin gown. Fremgen bit harder on his cigar and puffed nervously. As instructed, the vocalist (who had a fine voice) began her performance standing quite still, but the students in the front row clapped and tapped so provocatively that she warmed to her audience and began to move.

The coup de grâce fell during the last number, an updated version of the Adam and Eve story. The first chorus went:

Adam never treasured fame
For Eve had always acted sane
Until one day

When she raised Cain.
Oh! Adam!

The vocalist emphasized the words with apt and ample movement, to the delight of the front row and the fury of Father Fremgen. And there were still three more verses and a finale to go. At intermission Fremgen stormed at Miller for the "disgraceful" performance. "Not at all," rejoined Father Hacker, "—the best thing in the show."[24]

Fortunately, this episode did not doom a good idea. Thereafter "Loyola Night" was put on every year to generally favorable reviews. The death first of Father Fremgen, and then a few years later of John Hacker, removed the main supports for its musical portions, but this was balanced by the addition of skits satirizing campus life and personalities.

For a number of years the moderators and directors of the Mask and Rapier Society, especially Father John Scanlan throughout the 1950s, took responsibility for recruiting and rehearsing the performers. By the 1960s, however, this assistance, never obtrusive and mostly to ensure aesthetic quality, came to be viewed by some student activists as an interference with their spontaneous creative impulses. They objected to rehearsals and used various ploys to evade faculty involvement. Instead of an artistic flowering, the overall result was an obvious decline in quality. When several rescue efforts failed, all except the few who wanted to perpetuate "Loyola Night" regardless of its style regretfully welcomed its demise.

The 1930s were the beginning of the big-band era, and groups traveled around the country playing one-night stands. They became quite fashionable as the main attraction at school dances. Not to be outdone by their peers on other campuses, the managers of the junior proms at Loyola sought bands that would be near Baltimore in the spring. Included were some that became famous: Ozzie Nelson and Harriet Hilliard (1934), the Dorsey Brothers with Bob Crosby as featured vocalist (1935), Russ Morgan (1937), Jimmy Dorsey (1938), and Harry James (1939). Teddy Black (1932), Glenn Garret (1933), and Ted Fio Rito (1936) are less well remembered today, but in those days they had many fans.

June Week, the pause between final exams and commencement, made its appearance at Loyola now—possibly in imitation of the nearby United States Naval Academy. To secure approval in 1931, a philosophical disputation was included in the schedule for the first June Week.

This distinctive (and incongruous) element was immediately discarded, a course probably made easier by the death later that year of Loyola's premier philosopher, Justin Ooghe. In the typical program, a student could choose among freshman and sophomore beach parties, junior and senior dinner dances, the senior stag party, and the senior ball. Although each event was the responsibility of a specific class, the small number of potential ticket-buyers forced promoters to open them to all. As the number of students increased, especially after World War II, the fear of deficits faded and this end-of-the-year series of dances and parties was retitled Senior Week—with an obvious narrowing of its focus to the revels of those who had made it.

• •

Despite small enrollments during the early 1930s, Loyola's football team achieved a brief moment of distinction, although the scheme to finance the team by the sale of bonds failed. The moment of glory came largely through the efforts of a new coach, Walter "Tony" Comerford, who had been an outstanding player at Boston College in the years before World War I. He joined the staff of Frank Cavanaugh, his mentor, and when the "Iron Major" left Boston for Fordham, Comerford in 1928 accepted Loyola's offer. His first year in Baltimore had only one bright spot—a solid win over Washington College. This was not much when balanced against seven losses, including a 69 to 0 rout by the "Green Terrors" of Western Maryland. Comerford knew that another such disastrous season would be his last.

He spent the next semester and summer recruiting players. From his days at Fordham he remembered a light but imperturbable passing quarterback named Laurie Dallaire (1932). No longer at Fordham, Dallaire accepted an invitation to come to Loyola. In Vincent Carlin (1933), Comerford got a hard-running halfback who also had left Fordham. Loyola's new coach persuaded Michael Plotczyk (1933), a big, tough center, and John "Punk" Ryan (1932), another fast back (both from Worcester, the home of Holy Cross College), to register at Loyola. To this nucleus from New England, Comerford added local talent, including Ken Curtis (1932), Maurice Egan (1933), and George Waidner (1934).

The beneficial effect of these reinforcements was immediate. The 1929 football season was marked by five wins and four losses. More could be expected from this new team because it had scored on Western Maryland when few others had succeeded. Ike George (1901), a leader in promoting football at Loyola, yelled so loud after the green and gray scored on Western Maryland that sixteen people around him were deafened. Or so he later claimed. It was, to be sure, not a win, but the "Green Terrors" had finally been scored upon and little Loyola had done it.

This drama provided a welcome distraction for the ten thousand spectators in Homewood Stadium, because it was played on Armistice Day only two weeks after the stock market crash. The sports headlines for several years thereafter seemed bigger and blacker than those in the news section. Editors may have avoided assaulting their readers with bad economic or international news by drawing attention instead to athletic contests, which offered symbolic evidence that conscientious effort, and a bit of luck, still produced something like a victory.

It would be satisfying to report that in the next season's game between Loyola and Western Maryland the green and gray toppled the giant, but it would not be true. Loyola's team scored again but could not deny Western Maryland a tally of forty points. The final record for 1930 was an acceptable but indecisive four and four. Though the sum for the next season was not much better statistically, the gridiron campaign of 1931 struck a note of victory or something like it. What happened during the first four games can be passed over, but it was in the fifth game, with Western Maryland, that the green and gray team demonstrated the prowess that moved Baltimore's sportswriters to acclaim them the "Eleven Iron Men."

Loyola's students sought to evoke winning spirits for the game with Western Maryland through a unique Halloween rally. Freshmen gathered around the Washington Monument after dusk and waited, clad in pajamas and nightshirts and wearing the required green-and-gray pup caps. At the appointed hour a group of local hucksters drove their wagons and horses into Mount Vernon Place. Quickly the freshmen mounted these unlikely chariots and with shouts, blaring horns, and flashy signs, the procession started down Charles Street to the center of Baltimore. Upperclassmen followed the wagons in a variety of tin lizzies and flivvers bedecked with appropriate banners. The cortege emptied at Sun Square for round after round of cheers and shouts of defiance against the Green Terrors. When the rally ended the students formed a snake dance and with undiminished din wended their way back up Charles Street. If some citizens objected to this raucous display, the energy at least had been concentrated and expended less annoyingly than in traditional Halloween pranks.

The next day, in cold and threatening rain, four thousand spectators at Baltimore Stadium watched a game that exceeded the expectations of all but a few of Loyola's most ardent partisans. The first quarter ended with neither team scoring—an unusual start for Western Maryland, especially against so light a team as Loyola and a squad with so few substitutes. Furthermore, Dallaire was not passing, as expected, but sending the green and gray into and around the line. When the Green Terrors finally scored in the second quarter their rooters must have been relieved—and sure now that the customary march to victory had begun. Instead, the Loyola eleven charged back so hard and so often that Western Maryland remained on the defensive throughout the next two quarters. Long runs, and even a touchdown, by Loyola were nullified when the officials called some infraction of the rules.

With only minutes left to play, Western Maryland punted. Vin Carlin caught the ball at Loyola's forty-five-yard line and charged toward the goal line. Running for the left side, he eluded the first rush of tacklers. Reversing his field, he evaded another pack of harriers. By now Carlin had picked up blockers, and it looked as though there was no way to stop him from scoring—but the last opponent tripped him and Carlin fell four yards short.

After a Western Maryland time out, Dallaire sent Carlin through a gap he spotted earlier on the left side, and Loyola's hard-charging halfback was stopped only a foot short of the goal line. Dallaire then sent Maurice Egan into the line for no gain. An indirect pass to Egan on the third down failed. On the final down, the opponents slammed Loyola's linemen upward so Egan could not dive over the heap of bodies, but it did not matter. Laurie Dallaire ducked behind the charge and carried the ball in himself. Pandemonium! Dallaire held the ball for Joe Morisi (1934), who made the extra point. The kickoff gave the ball to Western Maryland, but before it could line up for another play time ran out. Not only had the green and gray tied Maryland's football powerhouse, but the eleven starters for Loyola College had played the whole game without relief.[25] "Eleven Iron Men," indeed.

In 1932 Loyola's students and team prepared for an even better year. The rally before the Western Maryland game was bigger and noisier than a year earlier. The campus was the starting point for the procession downtown, and a cheerleader at the game was attired in a greyhound costume. But these rites proved unavailing. Dallaire and company had graduated and no comparable group had been recruited. Loyola lost to Western Maryland 28 to 6. The season's tally was a dismal lone victory against seven losses. The results next season were no better.

. .

Despite this record, plans were made for the 1934 season, but several events combined to bring an end to varsity football at the college. Two years earlier the general of the Jesuit order had issued regulations severely restricting scholarships and other forms of financial assistance for athletes. American Jesuit schools reacted in various ways and with varying alacrity. Loyola became parsimonious with its athletic scholarships. Father Wiesel was aware that his term as rector would end shortly after commencement in 1934; he could therefore afford to take an unpopular action and spare his successor from having to start his term under a cloud. Finally, that spring the Johns Hopkins University announced that it was considering abolition of football, reorganization of varsity athletic programs, and greater emphasis on intramural sports. These developments made similar action by Loyola seem timely and prudent to President Wiesel and his colleagues.

When the announcement appeared on May 1, alumni and students were stunned by the decision and by its suddenness. An alumnus-sportswriter for the *Sun* counseled patience, predicting that a football team in green and gray would be seen again in a few years. Plans were laid to raise the question after a new president was installed. But another obstacle arose. Tony Comerford found an attractive football coaching position elsewhere. His departure did not entirely discourage those seeking to revive football, but now they had to plan without him as a natural rallying point.[26] Whether or not this contributed to declining enrollment cannot be determined, but during the next two years the student body dropped by a fourth when the economy was no worse than it had been.

As athletic director the college engaged a young man who had been an outstanding Loyola basketball player, William Liston (1931). As a guard he averaged twenty points per game in his senior year. His employment indicated a continuing interest by Loyola in basketball and baseball. He and his immediate superior in the administration, Father John Jacobs (dean of discipline), faced the crucial task of involving the disaffected students in an expanded intramural program. With students avoiding the gymnasium, and giving facetious answers to polls designed to discover what sports they were willing to play, this was no easy process.

Gradually Liston and Father Jacobs made headway. Under Liston's coaching, the varsity basketball team tied Mount Saint Mary's for the Maryland championship several years in a row. In 1935 a postseason game was played to break the tie, with Loyola's opponents winning on a final basket. On the next occasion Coach Liston insisted on a three-game series, which unfortunately ended the same way. Income derived from admissions, however, was used to equip the team, and the remainder supported the general athletic program.

As graduation dispersed students who remembered football at Loyola, the antipathy toward intramurals dissolved. Father Jacobs suggested indoor baseball, scheduled around the lunch hour. It was a fast game: one strike, batter out; two balls, a walk. In time almost half the student body was enrolled in a league of ten teams. Kelly's All-Stars and Ferrarini's Hounds played for the championship, with the latter team winning. A similarly vigorous basketball league was instituted, and plans were made for touch football. These developments were encouraged in 1936 by a new dean of studies, Father Lawrence Gorman, who made participation in an extracurricular activity and in athletics (varsity or intramurals) a requirement for graduation. When Bill Liston (1931) took a position with the federal government in the fall of 1937, the transition to a brighter and more stable era of athletics was well along.[27] It would not be stretching matters too far to apply this judgment to the college as a whole.

14

Hopes and Fears

The president and rector who held office as the grip of the depression began to ease was Father Joseph Canning. He was an amiable man whose main extramural interests (it seemed to his associates and to the students) were baseball and the Buick that the college provided for his use. He relied on the dean to keep the school operating smoothly. Arriving at Evergreen just in time for the fall semester in 1934, he had as his only stated objective to raise registrations over 300—a modest though not an insignificant goal. The rolls of the college had been reduced by 15 percent since the spring and stood then at 217. The loss for the next year was smaller (only 13 percent), but that loss brought the total enrollment to only 188. Such a decline meant a severe loss of revenue and obviously had to be reversed.

• •

Despite this unfortunate turn (one that in the early days of the college resulted in a short tenure for the incumbent president) no thought was given to replacing Father Canning, but after the graduation ceremonies in 1936, Father Thomas O'Malley was transferred to Saint Peter's College, where he continued as dean. This was part of a general process of reassignment within the province and not, as was later rumored, because a smile from O'Malley during commencement exercises was deemed insufficiently respectful by Archbishop Curley. There is no evidence for this story—the archbishop was not even present at the 1936 graduation—but the rumor illustrates the passions that were aroused after 1940 when relations between Loyola and the archbishop became severely strained.

The June 1936 ceremonies at Evergreen were otherwise distinguished. Four women were among the recipients of degrees: Cleta O'Hara, Christolinda O'Neill, Ignatia Tyrell, and Estelle Watson. They were all Franciscan nuns enrolled in the extension program.[1] By the rules and customs of that day they were not permitted to accept their diplomas in person, and for some sisterhoods that would still be true as late as the 1960s.

Shortly after Dean Lawrence Gorman replaced O'Malley, he discussed his educational philosophy with a *Sun* reporter. "Truth for truth's sake" was the whole purpose of Loyola College and of the Jesuit system of education, he said. He contrasted this aim with persistent attempts throughout the world to make education subservient to "exaggerated nationalism."

From this interview and other sources Baltimoreans learned that Father Gorman was 37 years old and that he was from New York City, where he was graduated from Fordham and entered the Society of Jesus in 1920. He was a teacher of chemistry and acting dean at Georgetown before coming to Loyola. Gorman's mission was to heal the disaffection that had arisen among the students because of the elimination of varsity football and to provide administrative leadership. Although some of his Jesuit brethren doubted that Father Gorman was made of rectorial timber, his assignment to Evergreen did provide seasoning for an eventual return to Georgetown with larger responsibilities.

Soon after he took office Dean Gorman introduced a number of changes. His aim was to bring curricular practice and terminology into closer alignment with that generally used at other American institutions. The faculty was now organized into departments with a Jesuit as the chairman. This general form of organization had appeared at a few American insitutions of higher learning in the 1890s but was not adopted at Jesuit colleges until the early 1920s and appeared at Evergreen in tentative form by the early 1930s. However it functioned at other schools, at Catholic institutions departmental organization was more a matter of administrative convenience than of decentralization of authority.[2]

Academic titles had been in use for decades, but they were now refined. The catalogue restricted use of the title *professor* to a full-time teacher who was a Jesuit priest or a layman who held a doctoral degree. An assistant professor was a Jesuit scholastic or a layman who taught a full class load but had only a master's degree. An instructor was a regular faculty member without higher degrees or who taught only part time. The term *lecturer* was reserved for experienced part-time teachers with advanced degrees. The term *associate professor* would not appear in a Loyola catalogue for some years.

In 1937 there were twenty faculty members. Seven were laymen, four of whom had the Ph.D.; another was the school doctor, who was listed also as a lecturer. There were fourteen professors (four layman), three assistant professors (two Jesuit scholastics and a layman), and one instructor (a scholastic). William Thornton, Jr., a Ph.D. who taught at Johns Hopkins, apparently fitted none of the categories, so he was listed as "research chemist."

The only lay faculty member with a long-term commitment to the college was Edward Doehler (1930), a professor. Upon graduation from Loyola he enrolled in the history program at Georgetown and took his doctoral degree in 1935. Meanwhile he joined the Loyola faculty, and in addition to his class work moderated the Shea History Academy and advised the students who broadcast over WCBM. Students found him an excellent teacher, an able scholar, and an exemplary Catholic layman. His Jesuit colleagues were less vocal, but their esteem was shown by his continuous employment at a time when such things as faculty contracts and tenure were unknown at Evergreen.

Dean Gorman instituted changes that directly affected students. As already noted, he had made participation in extracurricular activities and athletics a condition for graduation. To ease any lingering disaffection he periodically convened round-table discussions with the students. These were informal but taken seriously enough to assuage feelings. This, along with Father Gorman's active recruiting at the Catholic and (more notably) the public schools, reversed the downward trend of enrollments. In September of 1936 there were almost a third more students than in the previous June. Two years later the number reached 332 and it continued to climb until late in World War II.

• •

One factor in this increase was the introduction of a new program, in business administration. The impetus came from Archbishop Curley, who was probably concerned that young Catholic men in Baltimore had no choice but to attend a non-religiously affiliated institution if they were interested in business or accounting. The archbishop suggested a business program at his first meeting with Dean Gorman.

This would not entail a complete surrender to Mammon. In addition to the required core of liberal studies, students elected eighteen semester hours from courses in accounting, finance, money and banking, marketing, and business law. Completion of the program qualified the graduate to take the state examination for certified public accountants. The faculty mainstay of the new program was a lawyer-accountant,

tant, Granville Triplett, who also taught at the University of Maryland. To publicize the program and to recruit able applicants, four scholarships were offered; to preclude any religious test, the nominations were made by a committee of the Junior Association of Commerce. This arrangement signalled the desire of the college for more direct and broader contacts with its surrounding community. In its first year the new curriculum accounted for a quarter of the incoming freshman class.[3] The students eventually acquitted themselves well academically, receiving graduation honors and admissions to Alpha Sigma Nu, the Jesuit honor society, in numbers comparable to other majors.

Father Gorman made other efforts to bring the college to the favorable attention of a larger public. In 1937 he invited Sumner Welles, undersecretary of state, to give the commencement address. Faced with challenging Nazi and Communist totalitarianisms, the United States and other democratic nations, Welles said, must strive for "the establishment of the foundations of international peace . . . and the foundations of social justice." Pope Leo XIII's encyclical *Rerum Novarum*, he declared, had contributed significantly to the growth of a new conception of social responsibility. "When the day comes that there are no underprivileged," he continued, "our democracy will be safer than it has been in these past generations."[4]

Gorman must have been pleased with the coverage by the *Sun*, which carried ample quotations from the undersecretary's speech. The *Sun*, however, delayed its report on Loyola's commencement one day so that it appeared in the same issue as the accounts of similar exercises at Goucher and Johns Hopkins. That readers paid much attention is doubtful. They were probably more interested in the accompanying stories about the sudden death of Jean Harlow and about Amelia Earhart's arrival on the west coast of Africa in her flight around the world, or in the rumor that the Duke of Windsor and his new wife planned to settle in her native Maryland.

In the latter part of 1936, some measure of fiscal relief suddenly arrived at the college. William Galvin, legal counsel to the archbishop, delivered a check for $207,000 to President Canning in December, apparently without a detailed explanation. This was certainly a welcome remittance, but it perplexed the Jesuits. They knew that Roberta O'Neill, Thomas's widow, had died recently, but the amount of the check differed from the sum held in trust since O'Neill's death seventeen years earlier.

Was it the O'Neill inheritance? Were they still bound to use it and the rest of the O'Neill bequest for building a church? Or could it be used for "educational purposes," as Archbishop Curley had agreed some years before? Intramural discussions proved inconclusive, so the questions were put directly to the archbishop, the residual legatee. Cavalierly refusing to discuss any arrangements made in the late 1920s, the archbishop said that the money discharged his obligation to do justice to the Jesuits and that the money could indeed be used for educational purposes in Baltimore.

The division of these assets took several years and cannot be traced in detail because of the paucity of records. Apparently an equal apportionment of the O'Neill bequest was made to the high school and the college, less unspecified amounts loaned to the college at various times. The O'Neill, Jenkins, and other bequests were gradually used by Wiesel and Canning to free the college of indebtedness. By the end of President Canning's term no funds had to be applied to payment of interest—and there was even a small reserve for capital improvements.[5]

• •

By the time the provincial status—the list of appointments—was published in late July of 1938, the situation of Loyola College looked much brighter than it had for a long time. The country too was recovering, if unsteadily, from the effects of the depression. To capitalize on this general upturn and in response to complaints that the provincial authorities in New York had not been sufficiently attentive to the needs of the Maryland region, a new and more dynamic president and rector was posted to Evergreen. He was Father Edward Bunn, 42 years old and an alumnus from the nonpareil class of 1917.

Improbable as it might seem now, Baltimoreans then detected a resemblance between Billy Rose, the famous New York World's Fair impressario, and Loyola's new president. There were superficial similarities in their slight build, obvious energy, and enjoyment of public attention. Father Bunn's clerical status precluded his adoption of the flashy dress of his supposed counterpart, but students and others thought the spats on Bunn were a sign of a spirit kindred to Billy Rose's. On several occasions he had produced theatrical pageants, duly noted in his vita.

It was his formal installation at Evergreen that fixed Bunn's image as a showman. No ceremony like it had been seen at Loyola College, although formally displaying a new college president was a well-established American academic ritual. (The indefinite tenure of presidents at other institutions made such installations more appropriate than at Jesuit schools, where the chief officer usually served only a short and canonically prescribed term.) In 1930 a new president of Fordham who had acquired a taste for academic ceremony during his years at Cambridge had himself inducted with appropriate pomp. It is unlikely that Bunn attended this event, because in 1930 he was completing his theological studies at Woodstock, but no doubt he heard inter nos comments about that affair.

At his appointment to Loyola, Father Bunn was directed by the provincial to give the college dynamic leadership and to make it "assume the position in the consciousness of Baltimoreans that its years of service and type of education warranted." There was something more involved in this directive than mere attention to a particular school. It was an application of the general determination of the recently formed Jesuit Educational Association that the order's colleges should assume a more active and "responsible role on the American scene."[6] How better initiate such a program in Baltimore than with a dramatic entrance?

• •

Nothing was stinted in the announcements or in the performance. Edward Bunn's installation was resplendent with pomp and color. About eight o'clock on the evening of October 29, 1938, the academic procession entered the gymnasium, whose bare walls were hidden behind satin hangings, flowers, and palms. A grand marshal, Father Schmitt, led the alumni and faculty. Next came a group of fifty or more representatives from various colleges, universities, and learned societies—arranged according to the foundation date of each. A few held degrees from European schools and wore caps and gowns of brighter hues and more imaginative form than the somber black of American academic robes. The notables following them included presidents of three other Maryland institutions: Harry Byrd of the University of Maryland, Isaiah Bowman of Johns Hopkins, and David Allan Robertson of Goucher. Next came recipients of honorary degrees: John Fenlon, president of Saint Mary's Seminary; John Hubbard, a Johns Hopkins professor; Judge Samuel Dennis of the Baltimore City Supreme Bench; and Francis Kirby, a surgeon and alumnus (class of 1903). At the end of the entourage was Father Bunn, accompanied by Robert Gannon, president of Fordham, who was to deliver the installation address.

The only notable absentee was Archbishop Michael Curley. He was confined to the hospital with an attack of shingles, a virus infection of the nerve endings that results in blisters on the skin. This is a painful affliction associated with forceful, irritable personalities subject to stress. The characteristic rash that gives the disease its name usually appears on the chest, but it can break out on the face and eventually cause blindness. It was the latter form of shingles that afflicted Curley. Since there was no effective treatment the archbishop was given bromides, which in that period did duty as tranquilizers.[7] (Such clinical detail is necessary to explain later developments in the relationship between Curley and Loyola.)

When all were seated Dean Lawrence Gorman rose to deliver a few introductory remarks and presented the college charter to its new president. After this the four recipients of degrees were invested as doctors of laws and doctors of letters, *honoris causa.* Then the dean of Fordham's graduate school read the Latin text of the honorary doctorate of laws that was conferred on Edward Bernard Bunn—a rare occurrence, because in Jesuit tradition such honors were not then awarded to members of the Society. Commenting later, a student wag thought this violated the constitutional rights of Loyola's new president, because the "accusation" had been read in a foreign language.

The final scene was a brace of addresses. In his, President Gannon stressed the vital need for small liberal arts colleges in the educational scheme of the nation. Father Bunn, after paying tribute to his predecessors, several of his teachers at Loyola, and Loyola's major benefactors, sounded a timely theme: "Ideologies which consider the individual only as a unit in the vast mechanism of an artificial state will destroy natural society." He portrayed educators not as disciplinarians but as artists who are driven by a lofty conception of human nature to "fashion and perfect this character in others." Their model for this work was "God, the Supreme Artist."[8]

Few in the audience could fault what was a familiar doctrine— although the emphasis on artistry may have seemed novel. The style of Bunn's performance impressed the audience, and yet in hindsight, something might have been added to heighten the drama of this inauguration. Presidential installations at other American institutions have sometimes been the occasion for important declarations on educational philosophy. Either Bunn or Gannon might have taken the opportunity to reply to Robert Hutchins, the young president of the University of Chicago who only a year before—more in a tone of fraternal correction than of anger—criticized American Catholic colleges for imitating the least desirable features of their secular counterparts (athleticism, vocationalism, and anti-intellectualism) and ignoring high standards and scholarship.

Hutchins's comments were not prompted by the Olympian attitude that inspired the strictures of President Eliot of Harvard a generation earlier. Hutchins was urging his Catholic colleagues to follow the best in their educational heritage—"to show that the intellectual tradition can again be made the heart of higher education." Some Catholic educators responded defensively and saw Hutchins only as a latter-day Eliot. Others insisted that pushing forward the boundaries of knowledge was a profitless enterprise for Catholic institutions. Truth was already in their grasp; scholarship and professionalism could only distract teachers from full, loving service to their students.

More notable spokesmen took the occasion of Robert Hutchins's remarks to revive the continuing discussion about the need to pay more attention to libraries, faculty workload, and other factors essential to promoting scholarship at Catholic institutions. The imminence of war made bold departures seem imprudent to those responsible for guiding church-related colleges and universities.[9] At this inaugural, Gannon and Bunn avoided the matter—probably because the criticism had been leveled at Catholic schools in general, or possibly because a record of action seemed a more substantive reply. Nevertheless, the questions raised by Hutchins and Catholic educational thinkers toward the end of the 1930s were given renewed attention twenty years later.

On that October evening in 1938, President Bunn's well-phrased but not startling sentiments and his confident performance drew approving applause from the more than twelve hundred people present. It had been a good show and was well covered in the *Catholic Review,* the *Sun,* and the *News-American.* Even the *New York Times* carried the news, with ample quotes from Father Bunn's address. Whether it was worth the effort and money was soon asked by some sobersides— students and alumni; but only time, experience, and the actions that followed could answer their query.

⋅ ⋅

Loyola's nineteenth president was a native of Baltimore and an alumnus of the college. His family originated in Hungary but sometime during the turmoil between the Reformation and the Thirty Years' War migrated to the Rhineland, where they were eventually assimilated into the German community. The Bunns were staunchly Catholic, and each generation produced at least one priestly vocation.

Edward Bunn was a third-generation American. His grandfather Philip Bunn arrived in Baltimore in 1852, probably during the summer before the opening of Loyola College. He supported his family as a laborer or well digger, and his sons became glassblowers. Philip's son Sebastian married Philomena Fortmann and established a household near his brothers and the factory in which they worked. Joy at the birth of a son, named Edward, on March 25, 1896, was shattered a short while later by the sudden death of Sebastian Bunn. The widow's difficulties were increased by the birth of a daughter soon after Sebastian's death. She supported her family by working in a neighborhood tailor shop and with the assistance of relatives who lived close by.

As Eddie Bunn (the name the cousins with whom he grew up still remember him by) was completing the eighth grade, a young priest who was a Loyola alumnus encouraged him to apply for a scholarship. A neighborhood chum already attending the school, Ferdinand Schoberg, put in a good word for the bright and studious but needy young fellow. In September of 1910 President Brady welcomed Bunn to the college.

Twenty-eight years later, Father Bunn paid tribute to the Calvert Street Jesuits, who made a lasting impression on him. In his inaugural address he mentioned Presidents Brady and Ennis as models of active and imaginative leadership. Which of his teachers startled him repeatedly with a shout of "Bunn, stop dreaming!" was not made clear, but among his mentors at Loyola were Fathers McLoughlin, Ooghe, and Charles Kleinmeyer—any one of whom was likely to have employed that goad.

Bunn maintained his friendship with Schoberg, and together they walked to school, about a mile and a half from home. They were friendly with classmate Herbert O'Conor (1917), who was instrumental in getting them jobs as floorboys at the Belvedere Hotel during the Democratic National Convention of 1912. The party hopefuls and notables were so generous that these diligent lads realized over ten dollars a day in tips. Bunn and O'Conor maintained friendly relations throughout their lives, but the son of Holy Cross parish thought the fellow from Saint Paul's was a bit "prim"—a view shared by O'Conor's biographer.[10]

As chance or providence would have it, O'Conor was elected governor of Maryland a few weeks after the inauguration of his classmate as president of Loyola. Catholic authorities in Maryland were generally eager to avoid embarrassing the new governor, so Bunn's contact with O'Conor was infrequent. Father Joseph Ayd, however, was not so reticent. As prison chaplain he repeatedly appealed to Governor O'Conor to grant a parole or commutation of sentence for "one of his boys" and was occasionally successful. The college in the late 1930s could not honor the governor, its most distinguished alumnus, with an honorary degree, because it had awarded him one when he became state's attorney for Baltimore City. Instead, O'Conor became the first recipient of the John Carroll Medal, instituted by Father Bunn in 1939 to honor alumni "for noteworthy and meritorious service on behalf of the College and its values."

While young Bunn and Schoberg hiked to classes they occasionally discussed their plans for the future. At one point Bunn seriously considered becoming a physician and was offered a scholarship to the Johns Hopkins Medical School. This early interest explains his lifelong nickname of "Doc." Dean Fleming, on the other hand, was sure that Bunn and Schoberg were interested in the law and had arranged their employment by a downtown firm while they attended law school. When just before graduation he met them in the corridor and gave them the good news, he was startled by their reply: "Too late! We have decided to become Jesuits."[11]

They did not arrive at Saint Andrew-on-Hudson on the traditional date, August 15, but informed their soon-to-be superior to expect them after Labor Day. For three carefree weeks they fished and crabbed around Queenstown, where Bunn's grandfather had owned a small cottage. When they arrived at the novitiate they began the usual course of training, study, and teaching. For Bunn, this meant a term at Fordham as assistant dean and director of dramatics. Then followed four years at Woodstock, where his former teacher, Father Kleinmeyer, was on the staff. He was ordained in 1930 by Archbishop Curley. (The identity of the ordaining bishop is often taken note of in the life of a Catholic priest.)

The next few years Bunn spent at Canisius College in Buffalo, where he taught philosophy in a manner that impressed his students. He was, they recalled, more apt to quote Shaw's *Candida* than the approved text, and he "assigned Eddington's *Nature of the Physical World* within a few months of publication." His grand manner and refined tastes were noted also by his Jesuit confreres, possibly in hopes that something would dampen his style—but this never happened. What leisure he had was spent on a centennial pageant that he produced for the city of Buffalo.[12] He could obviously manage complex and diverse enterprises with appropriate éclat.

In 1935 he was transferred to Fordham, where he became an assistant to Father Walter Summers, a psychologist who directed a guidance clinic for adolescents. Summers was famous as the inventor of the polygraph lie detector, which he demonstrated at Loyola in 1937 with Mayor Howard Jackson as his subject. Prudently, Summers avoided asking His Honor any of the questions suggested by members of the audience, but elicited the indicative reactions with more politic questions. Father Bunn, planning to become a psychologist, began to study Jean Piaget's work on child development—then not widely known. Before that program was far advanced he was appointed president and rector of Loyola College.

On several points, all who met Father Bunn agreed. He was direct, witty, and charming. To him, courtesy was a virtue because it brought people together. The greatest sin, he thought, was stupidity—"the failure to apply oneself to the obvious." He considered administrative activity not particularly praiseworthy in itself; rather, he thought "an innate respect and reverence for human beings . . . the important thing." This side of his character and attitudes gradually became evident to the students, his colleagues, and other Baltimoreans.

• •

President Bunn's activities to promote and develop the college had many interconnected threads to which he gave persistent attention. Of crucial importance was raising the visibility of the institution, and in this he was a most effective instrument. Bunn addressed a variety of groups, such as the Advertising Club of Baltimore, the council of social agencies, and the recreation workers. He appeared at academic events such as a commemorative banquet for the University of Maryland and a student assembly at the Polytechnic Institute. Among religious gatherings was a luncheon in the undercroft of the Protestant Episcopal Cathedral and a banquet in honor of Har Sinai's rabbi.

That was just the start. He invented occasions to bring various groups to the campus. In mid-May of 1939, for instance, he got the director of Fordham's placement bureau to address the student body on career opportunities, and he capped the day with a dinner for the speaker and a select group of business leaders. Some, like William Casey, vice-president of the Maryland Trust Company, and Charles Cohn (1897), vice-president of the Baltimore Gas and Electric Company, were already well acquainted with the college; but this reception at the Jesuit residence was an occasion for opening conversations with officers from Glenn L. Martin, the telephone company, McCormick, Southern Packing, and Crown Cork and Seal. Wisely, Bunn never marred these genial get-togethers with any pitch for financial or other assistance. Some subject, issue, or personality that interested his guests was chosen and invitations were limited. President Bunn knew Baltimore well enough to treat the powers that be in the customary style.

An offshoot of Bunn's cultivation of prominent community leaders was the establishment of an advisory council. It provided valuable support and consultation that at other private institutions was available from the board of trustees. Fordham a few years earlier had established such an auxiliary body. Loyola's initial group of eight included prominent men in banking, business, and the law, several of them not Catholic. It also included three alumni: Charles Cohn, Edward Burke (1906), and Clarke Fitzpatrick (1907). The eight met periodically with Father Bunn, but what they discussed and recommended remained off the record.

Educators and psychologists were attracted to the campus by a series of demonstrations on child development and testing. Familiar enough nowadays, the subject was then beginning to draw attention beyond the ivied walls. This growing interest was fed by refugee-scholars from Europe. At Loyola in 1939 a Viennese woman psychologist demonstrated a new process for ascertaining the intelligence of young children. A year later another psychologist, a woman from the Netherlands, put on a similar demonstration of measuring the motor ability of children.

In November of 1940, Joseph Donceel, a Belgian Jesuit recently added to the faculty, began presenting a well-attended series of afternoon lectures on the psychology of character. After completing his doctorate at the University of Louvain he came to America just before the World War II. He held the attention of his audience by analyzing the character of such people as Mussolini, Hitler, and Stalin. Father Donceel's lectures proved so engaging that a number of his auditors asked if they could be continued.

Happy at what may not have been an unexpected turn, Father Bunn encouraged Father Donceel to continue the series if at least ten people registered. His initial band drew more recruits, and these offerings served as nucleus for a revival of Loyola's continuing education program. It was at first handled quite informally. Prospective students indicated what subjects interested them, and the college administrators found likely faculty members to direct the courses. This would blend with later developments and lead in a few years to the establishment of a formally organized evening division.

The emphasis on psychology and testing that came with Father Bunn was applied in other ways. Placement tests were administered to freshmen during the first week of classes to determine the sections to which they would be assigned in modern languages, religion, and English. The college joined a nationwide testing program, and Dean Gorman was pleased to record that "Loyola freshmen ranked in the first third of 300 colleges."[13] This achievement should not pass unnoticed: it offers the first such comparative data on the academic quality of Loyola. The freshmen were also offered a personality test designed to help the student counselor advise them.

The heightening pace and broadening range of activity under the new president-rector touched the faculty and the Jesuit community. Both lay and religious members of the faculty were encouraged to join scholarly organizations and to attend professional conventions. Dean Gorman took note of these contacts in his diary. For intellectual stimulation of Jesuits in particular, a few notable guests were invited to dinner and an evening's conversation. The Loyola community had a reputation for hospitality among the members of the Society and it now employed that trait to obtain stimulus from a wider world.

Within a few months after Bunn's arrival, Fathers Hacker, Ayd, and Schmitt took the initiative and asked their friend Henry Mencken to join them for a convivial evening at Evergreen. Unfortunately, no Boswell recorded the banter and talk, but in his thank-you note Mencken warmly expressed his pleasure. Jovially he continued:

> Your way of life seems to me almost perfect. I begin to regret I didn't enter the Church in my youth, though I realize that my heresies might have caused difficulties. It is conceivable, though naturally certainly not probable, that I might have been a bishop by now, eating five meals a day and weighing 300 pounds.[14]

He was a bachelor at heart, with a decided preference for the elite, and this may have led him to perceive values in Jesuit life that he appreciated. Various contacts occurred between Loyola and Mencken, through occasional correspondence and meetings around Baltimore, but there is no record that he came again to the Evergreen campus.

• •

Not all Father Bunn's attention and energy was directed to building the college's public reputation. From the start of his term he was closely involved with the student body. He personally conducted the retreat before Thanksgiving in 1938. As from the foundation of the college, students who were not Catholics remained exempt from these exercises, but two years later they were invited to attend a series of six lectures on "A Philosophy of Life" delivered by Father Bunn. Student reaction, as recorded by Dean Gorman, was entirely favorable, so Father Bunn repeated the program—but it was no longer voluntary; absence was treated like absence from class. Whether this was being done at other Jesuit institutions is unknown.

Loyola's young president employed various means to maintain his visibility among the students. Jesuits, like other Catholic priests, are required to read their breviary every day. This is a book of prayers that follow the liturgical cycle, with origins in the early days of the church. It is a form of the daily office, whose common chanting is a chief responsibility of monastic orders. On clear afternoons, Bunn made it a point to fulfill his obligation while striding along the walk from the Jesuit residence past the library and science buildings. No student would have thought to interrupt him during this exercise, but he felt it important that he be a noticeable presence on campus. The reading of the breviary, like much else in the church's piety, has since been modified, and fewer priests are now seen walking, open prayer book in hand, reciting the ancient prayers.

Father Bunn sought more direct channels for communicating with the student body. He suggested broadening representation in the student council by adding the elected heads of extracurricular groups and limiting class representation to presidents. This doubled the membership and included representatives from a wider variety of constituencies. All student elections were shifted from September to May to provide greater continuity at the cost of eliminating seniors from being elected to office but not from voting. Some seniors offered a clever—not to say jesuitical—defense of this practice. Allowing the seniors to vote just before they were graduated obtained this final measure of their wisdom and devotion and was justified as a proxy for the yet-to-be-admitted freshmen. Continuity thus was more highly prized than political responsiblity—and anyway it was only a matter of student offices. Father Bunn took the responsibility as Jesuit moderator of the student council and suggested than it choose a layman as faculty adviser. Initially, and for many years to come, the students selected Edward Doehler, professor of history.

With minor amendments, which President Bunn accepted, the revised council structure was ratified by the students. Thereafter their representatives met with Father Bunn every Thursday at noon in his office. The exchange of views (in the words of an interested and neutral observer) was "very forceful"—not least because Bunn encouraged open dialogue. Students enjoyed these weekly sessions, which were marked by "diplomatic bickering and intra-mural logrolling," according to the yearbook. No one was so crass as to keep score on these exchanges, but there is evidence that not all the points went to Loyola's president.[15]

. .

Reorganization of student government and the prevailing administrative attitude raised the attention of students to the world beyond the Evergreen campus. Some Loyola students joined their peers at Goucher and Johns Hopkins in founding the Baltimore Youth Conference, which quickly succumbed to the strains and pressures of wartime. Others, with Doctor Doehler's assistance, organized the International Relations Club (IRC) and affiliated with both the Carnegie Endowment for International Peace and the Catholic Students Peace Federation. These organizations held regional and national conferences to which the Loyola IRC regularly sent delegates. In 1940 Jere Santry, a senior, was elected treasurer of the Maryland-Washington group of the Catholic Students Peace Federation.

In another national student association Loyolans played a more prominent role. When various radical groups during the 1930s sought support from college students, a balancing movement was launched in 1937 among students on Catholic campuses. Its aim was to publicize the papal encyclicals and to promote solidarity among the students, especially by developing student government. In 1940 this movement culminated in a constitutional convention held in the District of Columbia. Among the sixty delegates from Catholic schools were Eugene Bracken (1941) and Frank Horka (1943) representing Loyola.

After the draft constitution of the National Federation of Catholic College Students (NFCCS) was adopted, Frank Horka was elected delegate for the Baltimore-Washington region. The following year Horka was unanimously elected national president and, more significantly, was elected for a second term in 1942. In the aftermath of the bombing at Pearl Harbor, he organized a conference to plan student contributions to the war effort and development of student leadership for the future. A third presidential term was foreclosed by Horka's graduation and departure for military service. On his return to civilian life Frank Horka earned a degree from the Yale Law School and served as counsel to one of Baltimore's leading banks until his early death.

Not all Loyolans were enlisting in such noble causes. Some, preferring the whimsical opportunities of campus life, organized a society to honor Robert Benchley. Charles Barrett (1942) and Ed Kaltenbach (1942) found the gently sardonic and humorous spirit of this drama critic and author of *My Ten Years in a Quandary* more to their taste. Finding kindred spirits equally devoted to "the master," they supposedly met at improbable locations, where one or another of the members discoursed on a subject such as "Pre-Hittite Madrigals" or "Peruvian Influences on Albanian Wallpaper Designs." Authority among the Benchleyians was apportioned among such dignitaries as Custodian of the Privy Seal, Keeper of the Royal Lizards, Poet Laureate, Lord High Werewolf, and Lector of Forbidden Books. Although some Jesuits were amused by this spoof, the shenanigans of the Benchley Society were not appreciated by Father Bunn; prudently he let time, graduation, and the call to military service work an inevitable remedy for such a minor annoyance.[16]

The president's preference in student activities was conservative. In 1940 nine Loyolans were named to *Who's Who Among Students in American Universities and Colleges.* Although this publication had been started in 1934, these were the first nominations from the college. This group of campus leaders was chosen by Father Bunn, Dean Gorman, and the student council. Bunn's object was to promote a sense of general competence in those honored, to strengthen a belief that they could hold their own in the company of the nation's student elite, and to inspire emulation among the underclassmen.

Similar motives resulted a couple of years later in the establishment of a chapter of Alpha Sigma Nu, the Jesuit honor fraternity. Outstanding qualities of scholarship, loyalty, and service to the college are norms for admission. In 1942 the initial cohort of Loyola's *aristoi* (Thomas Thaler, Casimir Zacharski, Robert Bachman, John Helfrich, and Donald Schmidt, all seniors) was selected by Fathers Bunn and Gorman. Thereafter, the incumbent members have nominated their successors—subject to approval of the dean and the president. Care is taken to impress the new initiates with the distinction they have achieved and with their obligation to apply the high standards for admission to their successors.

For all the glamor that inheres in this fraternity, the inauguration of Loyola's chapter combined humor and true grit. To do the honors, a delegation from Saint Joseph's in Philadelphia was commissioned by the fraternity's national office, and Palm Sunday was chosen as the date. Unfortunately, that March 1942 holy day found Baltimore blanketed with an unexpected snowfall that ultimately measured twenty-three inches. The car of the hapless brothers from Philadelphia got stuck twenty blocks from Evergreen and was abandoned. Undaunted, the men slogged their way to the campus. The ceremony was completed with due solemnity, except that the presiding celebrants (though properly robed) invoked blessings and administered the oaths in their bare feet because their shoes and socks were wet. Appropriate folk remedies against pneumonia were applied as soon as the ritual was completed.[17] None of the later inductions to Alpha Sigmu Nu were touched with such drama.

The efforts of Loyola's faculty and officers toward student academic achievement were given statistical form in the first quarterly grade report for the 1941–42 school year. The overall average was just a shade below B (78.92), with the senior A.B. students averaging 84.82 and the sophomore Ph.B.s at 74.10. When this information is combined with the fact that Loyola students scored in the top third on a nationwide test, there is reason to conclude that Loyola was a least as demanding as most other American schools of this period.

Another measure of a college is what its students accomplish after graduation. Members of the class of 1940, according to Father Gorman's note, garnered four scholarships: two from the Johns Hopkins engineering program, one from the Georgetown graduate school in history, and one from Georgetown Law. Six other members of the class were enrolled in various law schools; four entered medical school; two were in the air corps; two joined the Jesuits; and one entered Saint Mary's Seminary. After the next year's commencement exercises the dean proudly noted without much detail that one-third of the class of 1941 was enrolled in graduate or professional schools; among these, one was at Yale Law, another in the foreign service; the military claimed four more; one entered a Benedictine monastery; another went to Saint Mary's. Loyola's was obviously a solid record.

• •

These efforts and several of greater significance were diligently pursued despite the rising specter of war. During the late summer of 1939 Hitler's armies marched into Poland, and Britain and France honored their commitments by declaring war on Germany. What policy the United States should follow became a subject of continuing debate for the next two years. Many in both business and labor argued for strict neutrality.[18] "America First!" was their slogan. Others urged support for the European democracies, to protect this endangered species of society and as a bulwark against totalitarian expansion to the American hemisphere.

At this critical juncture the attitudes of Loyola students and their peers at other Catholic institutions were recorded in a poll conducted by the editors of the Jesuit public affairs magazine *America*. The responses of Loyola's 362 students, obtained only a month after the outbreak of hostilities in Europe, were filed in the dean's diary, permitting a comparison of opinion here with the opinion of Catholic college students nationally, with the opinion of male Catholic college students nationally, and with the opinion of Catholic college students in the mid-Atlantic region (Table 14.1).

The results of the poll give a sharp summary of what the views of Loyola students and their peers in October of 1939. The young men at Evergreen differed with students at other Catholic schools on a number of points. Only a miniscule percentage of all these students favored entering the war, and Loyolans were a shade firmer in opposition. Such an "isolationist" sentiment, according to Samuel Lubell, a respected political analyst, appeared in areas where a significant proportion of the people came from either a German or an Irish background. Both the Germans and the Irish had historic grounds for holding an anti-British attitude, and both groups were prominent in Baltimore. The names of Loyola students in this period indicate that at least half were of Irish or German ancestry.

The four years since the *Literary Digest* poll had only intensified the pessimism of the men at Loyola. Of the 1935 group, 56 percent believed America could remain neutral. This was a much smaller percentage than the national average and than that obtaining at the Johns Hopkins University. Four years later belief among Loyola students that the United States would escape being drawn into war declined by 5 percent. A slightly higher proportion of students at Loyola than elsewhere believed that American involvement would prove beneficial to the cause of peace (question 3). Their relatively low support for a national referendum before a declaration of war probably arose from the traditional repugnance Baltimoreans feel for altering constitutional procedures. The group that answered the 1935 poll was similarly less willing than their peers to support government control of business and labor in wartime. The Loyola results in the 1935 and 1939 polls are statistically significant because virtually the whole student body responded.

The responses to the fifth 1939 question may seem surprising today. Not only did these young men register a general unwillingness to serve

TABLE 14.1   National Poll of Catholic College Students, 1939
(In Percentages)

	Yes	No	Doubtful
1. Do you favor United States entry into the war?			
Nationally	2.5	96.5	1.0
Loyola College	1.4	97.2	1.4
Males nationally	2.6	96.4	1.0
Regionally	1.7	96.6	1.7
2. Do you expect the United States to be drawn into the war?			
Nationally	45.0	29.0	26.0
Loyola College	49.0	29.0	22.0
Males nationally	46.2	29.1	24.7
Regionally	45.9	30.8	23.3
3. Do you think that United States intervention with military force would help create a stable peace?			
Nationally	6.7	79.3	14.0
Loyola College	8.6	81.5	9.9
Males nationally	6.9	80.8	12.3
Regionally	6.0	80.0	14.0
4. Should there be a national referendum before war can be declared?			
Nationally	74.8	19.8	5.4
Loyola College	70.0	26.0	4.0
Males nationally	74.4	20.9	4.7
Regionally	74.7	20.3	5.0

5.   If war were declared today, would you:

	Volunteer	Await Conscription	Seek Conscientious Objector Status
Nationally	22.9	41.4	35.7
Loyola College*	18.0	38.6	43.4
Males nationally	20.3	44.0	35.7
Regionally	21.8	40.0	38.2

*Seven Loyola students did not respond to this question.

in the military, but those on Loyola's campus were the least prone to volunteer and the most willing to consider claiming conscientious objector status. Their predecessors at Evergreen had responded in 1935 with a similar reluctance, but only to a theoretical question about supporting American aggression. In October of 1939 the aggressor and his probable targets were known. In their attitudes on volunteering and on conscientious objector status, Loyolans differed from their peers at Catholic schools in the mid-Atlantic region.[19] These attitudes undoubtedly reflected the sentiments of their parents, but such sentiments were not taken into account by—if known to—strategists in Tokyo. The Japanese decision to attack Pearl Harbor two years later aroused an underlying patriotism as nothing else could.

• •

The specter of war in 1939 did not seriously inhibit preparations for a major celebration. The following year was the four hundredth anniversary of the formal establishment of the Society of Jesus. Jesuit institutions around the world scheduled special commemorations.

To the extent that wartime conditions permitted, the occasion provided a rationale for a general tidying up at Evergreen. President Bunn added a wing to the Cold Spring end of the Jesuit residence to house twelve additional teachers who would be needed because of rising enrollments. The architect, Lucien Gaudreau, designed the addition so carefully and matched the materials so well that the original structure and the new wing are indistinguishable. Father Bunn, not one to miss an opportunity, asked Gaudreau to offer elective courses in art and architecture, and for several semesters these attracted a number of students. The appearance of the Evergreen campus was further enhanced by the planting of more than sixty conifers.

Father Gorman had two unconnected projects on his agenda for 1939–40. The more impressive was completion of the swimming pool, which for fourteen years had been a noisome hole in the basement of the gymnasium. It was finished by May of 1940 and provided a small (twenty-five yards by five) practice facility for the new varsity swimming team, large enough for dual meets. Funds for the pool and the addition to the Jesuit residence came from the O'Neill and Jenkins bequests.

Dean Gorman's other project was a revision of the heraldic emblem of the college. He retained the general arrangement of the 1929 shield but recast it in the form of a round seal. The celebration of the Society's quadricentennial seemed an appropriate moment for correcting the slant of the seven maroon and gold bars downwards—visually a less pleasing arrangement, but true to the way they appear on the coat of arms of Saint Ignatius.

Although some may consider this change merely aesthetic, it indicated an enlargement of Loyola's constituency. The Battle Monument, which appeared on the center of the upper left section of the 1929 shield, was deleted. The emblem of the city of Baltimore was eliminated and what remained was the Calvert arms associated with the state. The college was not denying its association with Baltimore so much as quietly expanding its horizon to identify with the state. Gorman, during his tenure as dean, led the way in making Loyola better acquainted with the educational leaders and officials of Maryland.

Father Gorman's projects were probably intended as farewell gestures. His superlative work at Loyola convinced the provincial authorities that he was ready for greater responsibilities. He was slated to be named president of Georgetown—probably in July of 1940.

• •

His putative successor was already on campus. Father Richard Grady, after serving briefly as dean at Canisius College, had been transferred to Evergreen in 1939. He conceived, directed, and produced the centerpiece of Loyola's celebration of the Society's four hundredth anniversary. This was an imaginative revival of *Cenodoxus,* a seventeenth-century morality play written by a Swabian Jesuit, Jacob Bidermann. Grady's attention was drawn to the play by its successful Viennese revival in 1933 and its banning a year later by the Nazi regime of Germany. He found an old copy at Georgetown and translated it from Latin into English.

From its early years the Society of Jesus used the theater to extend its educational mission. Schools were established for young men, but the theater served as a net to catch adults, as a means to pose basic life issues dramatically to people who might not attend church. The popular theater allowed the Jesuits to present their argument in much freer forms than were allowable within the confines of a church. The Jesuits operated a number of theaters throughout Europe during the sixteenth and seventeenth centuries, and even after these declined they retained the drama in the education they offered.

At its Munich opening in 1609, Father Bidermann's play was an instant hit, and productions were mounted in other parts of Germany and in Austria, Bohemia, the Netherlands, and France. Bidermann based his play on a medieval legend about the fate of a proud but hypocritical Parisian doctor of laws whom he named Cenodoxus (derived from the Greek words for *empty show, vainglory*). The Jesuit dramatist challenged his audience to examine their conscience and to imagine what the judgment of Jesus Christ might be on each of them. The trial scene, even in translation and more than three centuries after its first performance, could still elicit a descriptive "towering" from a blasé *Time* magazine drama critic.

Father Grady worked hard to produce something worthy of the occasion. For the lead he engaged a professional actor, Philip Huston, already familiar to Baltimore audiences. Major roles were given to actors from local theater groups including the Vagabonds, the Hopkins University Playshop, and the Hilltop Players. Members of Loyola's Mask and Rapier Society provided the rest of the cast. Four years before the dream-ballet in *Oklahoma* made such interludes virtually de rigueur on Broadway, Grady incorporated local ballet dancers in a dream sequence and bacchanal. Musical themes to vary and intensify the drama were selected by a member of the Baltimore Symphony Orchestra from among the works of Bach, Stravinsky, and Respighi. Students from the Maryland Institute and others contributed much time and talent in stage design, scenery construction, costumes, makeup, and the myriad chores attendant on a serious theatrical production.[20] With his energy and charm Father Grady got so many people involved that this question might have arisen: How many were left to watch from the other side of the footlights?

This question was answered decisively on opening night (Thursday, February 29, 1940) and at the three performances that followed. Newspapers, magazines, and radio in Baltimore generously gave notice of Loyola's dramatic offering. That first night the Auditorium Theater (at Howard and Franklin) was packed, with the mayor's party filling one box, representatives of the city's consular corps filling another, and the rest holding a sparkling array of Baltimore society. President Bunn enjoyed the evening in the company of his peers from Fordham, Georgetown, and the Catholic University, and of his former teacher, Father Charles Kleinmeyer, now the provincial treasurer. With the tolling of the final bell the audience thrice raised the curtain with enthusiastic applause. For the Saturday matinee police were posted to manage the crowd of ticket-seekers. Three hundred had to be turned away.

Reviews in the *Sun* and the *News-American* were rave. Although the visiting critic from *Time* magazine praised Loyola's production, he faulted the old Jesuit playwright for having burdened his main character with so abstract a flaw as pride—however universal a trait it might be. He would have preferred "a few of the more scarlet sins . . . [to make a] Faust and Don Juan, a really immortal sinner."[21]

Discounting this small "carp," Father Grady thought of reviving and adapting more old Jesuit dramas for modern audiences, but his program was stopped by a variety of circumstances. Of major significance was a real trial. On Saturday, while the character Cenodoxus was arraigned on stage, Archbishop Curley (through an intermediary) informed Loyola's lawyer that Father Bunn would be brought to judgment.

• •

Overtly, the cause for this startling turn was a dispute about the testament of an elderly lady, Frances Stuart. There were, however, other tensions among the principals, including conflict between the secular clergy (Archbishop Curley) and the regulars (Bunn, a Jesuit) that may have been heightened by the archbishop's failing health and the obvious energy and dynamism of Loyola's president. The suit was initiated not by the archbishop but by the executor named in Miss Stuart's first will after he had been replaced in her second will by Loyola's corporate counsel, R. Contee Rose. Rose had been chosen as the college's legal adviser in place of William Galvin (1908), who had served the college for many years but who also was counsel to Archbishop Curley and to a number of Catholic institutions. Of necessity such a combination of responsibilities was fraught with the possibility of conflicting interests, and Bunn transferred the management of Loyola's legal affairs to Contee Rose, a well-established counselor with a sterling reputation.

The dispute was over the validity of the will Frances Stuart made just a few days before she died. This involved several changes in the terms of an earlier will: besides the change of executors already noted, she consolidated a number of smaller bequests previously assigned to the archbishop and to several Catholic institutions, including Loyola, and named only Loyola and Woodstock College as institutional beneficiaries. Under Miss Stuart's first will the archbishop, Loyola, and other institutions would each have received about $9,000; in the second will Loyola and Woodstock would each receive $60,000.[22]

But money was not the main objective on either side. Archbishop Curley eventually made clear that he sought the subjection of the Jesuits, while they were mainly concerned with defending the honor of their order and the honesty of Edward Bunn. They offered to give Curley and the other Catholic institutions all that they would have received under Frances Stuart's original will.

How did such an extraordinary proceeding—an archbishop accusing a Jesuit college president in a civil court—come about? The account herein is derived essentially from the trial testimony and conforms to the rulings and decision of the court. It is not possible or appropriate to rehearse all aspects of the Curley-Bunn dispute here, but since it affected the development of Loyola College it must to that degree be explained.

Miss Stuart's first will, made in 1937, had been drafted under duress. Shortly before his death her brother, whom she was nursing in her apartment, refused to make her his sole beneficiary unless she made a will that conformed to his specifications. Frances Stuart was described by all as a strong-willed woman and was quite knowledgeable in business affairs because she worked for many years as the personal secretary to Captain Isaac Emerson, producer of Baltimore's gift to the overindulgent—Bromo Seltzer. When her brother died a few months after Miss Stuart made her will, the estate became entirely her property. She likely had assets of her own and was under no legal obligation to abide by the will her brother forced her to make.

Father Bunn became acquainted with Frances Stuart in the course of the courtesy calls to benefactors of the college that are customary for a new president. Although Miss Stuart was still able to get about, her health was declining (from arthritis and a heart condition) and she no longer had any close family. Father Bunn became a regular, although at first not a frequent, visitor.

Quite early she confided to him her dissatisfaction with the will her brother had forced her to make and asked him to recommend a lawyer. After President Bunn had decided on Contee Rose for the college he mentioned Rose's name to Miss Stuart and probably added that Rose came from an old Maryland family and was married to a daughter of Eugene Didier (1859), the Poe scholar. Rose was a convert to Catholicism who became active at the Manresa retreat house and associated with the Jesuits at Woodstock.

As Miss Stuart's health declined and she became virtually confined to bed, Father Bunn became a more frequent visitor, and the lonely old lady found the priest very cheering company. (There would be much testimony about these developments at the trial.) On January 9, 1940, Miss Stuart sent for Rose and handed him a memorandum in her own hand defining how she wanted to dispose of her estate. All the bequests to relatives and friends of her brother remained the same or were increased, but the institutional bequests were consolidated and assigned to Loyola College and Woodstock College. Four days later, Contee Rose returned to Miss Stuart's apartment with the new will, which he read to her. Finding it satisfactory, she asked her practical nurse and a neighbor who handled small financial chores for the household to witness her signature. Frances Stuart signed her name to each of twelve pages firmly and in her distinctive script.[23]

Three days later her condition became so critical that she was taken to a hospital, where in a few days she died. Even before she was buried her brother's business agent, who had been named executor in the earlier will, made known that he intended to challenge the new one. Not only had a bequest to her brother's business agent been diminished, but he had been deprived of the office and perquisites of executor. He appears to have persuaded some of Miss Stuart's relatives to join in his complaint, even though bequests to them had been increased in her second will.

The last to file challenges to Miss Stuart's will were Archbishop Curley and the two religious corporations. Their complaint repeated doubts that the legal requirements for a valid will had been fulfilled and asserted that Miss Stuart was not mentally competent to understand what she signed. Contee Rose, Loyola College, and Woodstock College were formally accused in the archbishop's complaint of perpetrating a fraud and of exercising "undue influence" on Frances Stuart.

. .

Why did the archbishop choose a civil court in which to try this case when he and the other Catholic corporations might have sought justice (as they saw it) in a church court? Probably because trying a case in a church court is often a slow process and, furthermore, would not have been binding on the heirs who were not Catholic. Two trials—one under canon law and the other under the civil code—raised the unwelcome prospect of dividing the complainants and complicating the situation beyond practical remedy. Joining the suit already instituted by the executor of Miss Stuart's first will was simpler and raised the pressure on the Jesuits to settle on Curley's terms. The archbishop proceeded quite deliberately. Before having his caveat filed he personally interviewed some of the witnesses—certainly to secure a comprehensive account and possibly to judge the ability of the witnesses to withstand courtroom interrogation. His lawyer, William Galvin, filed the caveats against his better judgment and only on direct written order from the archbishop—or so he told Contee Rose. Some among the archdiocesan staff later claimed that Galvin had urged Curley to take action and assured the archbishop that the plaintiffs would win the case.

This was the culmination of a major struggle between the church heirarchy and religious orders over their papal exemption from the jurisdiction of local ordinaries that was waged during the 1930s. The exemption of religious orders had been a cause of persistent difficulties with bishops for centuries, no doubt made more acute by the world wide economic depression. The Maryland Jesuits were convinced that Archbishop Curley was particularly urgent in expanding his control over them despite their papal exemption because he had secured the transfer of five Jesuits beyond the bounds of the archdiocese.

The Jesuits responded by seeking some way to accommodate Curley. Father Bunn, on learning of the archbishop's intentions, asked for an audience, but his request was curtly spurned. He and the provincial authorities offered the archbishop and the other two Catholic orders all that they would have realized under the 1937 will. This was not an admission of fault, but reciprocated in principle what Archbishop Curley had done earlier in regard to the O'Neill bequest. This offer was rejected.

It took a while to discover what Curley and his counsel wanted as the basis for a quiet settlement. Stripped to essentials, the second Stuart will was to be invalidated, and Father Bunn would be removed as president and rector of Loyola College. Some Jesuits appeared willing to agree to these humiliating terms. Father Charles Kleinmeyer, however, strenuously objected because the settlement was contrary to the evidence. Furthermore, it could not certainly forestall court action by other parties to the dispute. Kleinmeyer persuaded the provincial to refer the matter to the Jesuit general in Rome. Probably anticipating similar tactics from other churchmen, the general cabled back laconically: RECTOR NOT TO BE REMOVED.[24] This left the initiative to the complainants, and the archbishop was seen as the crucial factor among the Catholics for proceeding to trial.

• •

The decision was reached during the winter of 1941 when Archbishop Curley was in Florida, recuperating from the combined effects of overwork, high blood pressure, and the flu. There his medical problems were compounded by overdosage with bromides to relieve the discomfort he suffered from shingles. This medication, his chancellor noted, had the effect of confusing and dulling his mind.[25] (Later, Kleinmeyer, not aware of these medical circumstances but relying only on what he could see of the archbishop's behavior, raised the question of whether Curley had been fully responsible during this period.) By the time Archbishop Curley returned to Baltimore on March 16, 1941, the die had been cast: it was to be a public fight with no quarter given.

The reactions around Baltimore were what one might expect. In these latitudes such brawls, especially among people who should know better, have usually elicited expressions of contempt and discomfort. The question most Baltimoreans asked was whether the dispute could not be settled more quietly. Apparently those who were not members of the Catholic church took little satisfaction in the embroilment of the archbishop and the Jesuits. Catholics were embarrassed and avoided discussing the affair. No notice of the trial appeared in the *Catholic Review* or the *Greyhound*, although it was fully and properly covered by the *Sun* and the *News-American*. Main points of testimony from both sides were reported without sensationalism during the trial, which lasted ten days—from May 12 to May 22, 1941.

The various caveators presented their arguments and witnesses first. There was much testimony about Father Bunn's ingratiating manner, the growing dependence of Miss Stuart, and the circumstances surrounding preparation of the second will. At the end of this presentation Judge Emory Niles ruled that the charges of technical inadequacies in the preparation and attesting of the will, fraud, and undue influence had not been proven. He instructed the jury to find for the defendants on these points. That left only two questions to be decided: whether Miss Stuart was mentally competent during the six weeks prior to making her second will and whether she knew exactly what was in the document she signed.

On these points, Loyola, Father Bunn, and codefendants were fortunate in being represented by a thorough and slow-talking but keen-witted attorney, Edward Burke. In his deliberate manner Loyola's lawyer produced the original memorandum in which Miss Stuart had instructed Rose; a comparison between it and the final will failed to uncover any significant differences. Burke then called to the stand Doctor Manfred Guttmacher, one of Baltimore's leading psychiatrists and chief medical officer for the city courts. He was regularly called upon to assess the mental competence of people involved in judicial proceedings. Doctor Guttmacher said "I heard no facts presented which would lead me to believe that Miss Stuart was incapable of making valid deed or contract on January 13."[26] The jury was impressed by his testimony.

Burke's final problem was the assertions of the two witnesses to the signing of the will. They said that Frances Stuart was confused and so drowsy from illness and medication that she did not know what she was doing. They claimed that they witnessed her signature against their better judgment to avoid angering her and bringing on a fatal attack. Burke produced records of checks and other documents signed by Miss Stuart or by the witnesses at her request. Several of the checks had in fact been signed by Miss Stuart on the very day she made her last will. These were made out to the witnesses, who later cashed the checks, demonstrating that they had considered her competent when it was to their advantage. It took the jury about three hours to persuade a lone dissenter that the only reasonable course was to uphold Frances Stuart's second will.[27] This finding completely exonerated Father Bunn and Contee Rose. It came on May 22—Ascension Thursday.

Understandably, this result disappointed the archbishop, who, although he took an inconspicuous role in the subsequent proceedings, supported an appeal. Meanwhile his attorneys worked for a more expeditious settlement, but unfortunately they sought to have Loyola pay part of the court costs. This might have tied up the loose ends more quickly, but it would also imply an admission of fault. Ned Burke would have none of it. He recommended against losing in camera what had been won in open court. On the other hand, he advised the college to join in procedures to minimize costs and to speed delivery of bequests to Miss Stuart's relatives.[28]

Father Bunn and the Maryland Jesuits benefited from this affair in other ways. The fortitude of Loyola's president, and his ability to withstand a searching public inquiry into his conduct and character, aroused much sympathy. The vague unease—if not disdain—that people felt at his flamboyant entrance onto the Baltimore scene was replaced by admiration and confidence. Among Jesuits, he was a hero not only for how well he had conducted himself during the ordeal but because they never again suffered another assault from Archbishop Curley.[29]

During the years after the trial Bunn sought to heal the breach—if not with Curley, at least with the archdiocesan clergy. Slowly but with increasing frequency, important and representative monsignori and priests were invited to college functions and to participate in some official capacity. Even after 1947, when both principals had left the scene, Loyola's Jesuits tended to rely on the healing qualities of time. Eventually the cordial relationship between the college and the archdiocese was fully reestablished.

．．

That the trauma of the Stuart trial did not dampen spirits on campus is evident from several contemporaneous events. Starting well before the opening of court proceedings, Father Grady and the students were in rehearsal for a musical revue entitled *Your Town or Baltimore— By and Large.* It was presented in the college gym on June 6, 1941, before an audience of over five hundred.

The play was modelled on *Pins and Needles,* a popular Broadway revue, but was muted to the sensibilities of the Chesapeake meridian.

Opening suddenly with a loud crash and assorted noises characteristic of Baltimore, it treated the audience to a witty lampoon of familiar targets: the *Sun*, Curley Byrd (energetic and ambitious president of the University of Maryland), Governor Herbert O'Conor, the Junior League, Mrs. Roosevelt ("Four More for Eleanor"), the horsy set in Green Spring Valley, Fort Meade, and Druid Hill Park.

To set the mood, Richard "Moko" Yardley, cartoonist for the *Sun*, contributed a familiar tableau that served as the curtain. On it, his tubby little alter ego and companion cat were fiercely pursued by his demon-editor, resplendent in the habiliments of a Wall Street tycoon and flailing at the underlings with a whip. Periodically, Yardley incorporated such episodes in his cartoon comments on local politics and life.

The verve of the eighteen sketches and many songs became evident with the opening number, a piece in the fashion of the popular "Ballad for Americans." One verse read:

So stand! raise your glasses for a toast
To Baltimore, Your Town,
To the town we call home and we love the most!
To her beauties of world-wide renown!
To her wisdom and her folly,
To her Mencken and her Wally [Duchess of Windsor],
To the sails on her waters,
To the eyes of her daughters,
A toast, drink it down!

To Baltimore, your town. Skits and songs of similar felicity drew rounds of laughter and applause. These sovereign remedies dispersed whatever gloom lingered from the drama played out recently in the courtroom.

The most durable piece in this revue was the finale. It was a song composed by John Ozazewski (1940, then attending medical school) with lyrics by Father Grady. "Alma Mater, Dear Loyola" proved so appealing that the college asked if Ozazewski would relinquish his musical rights so it could be adopted as the school anthem. He readily agreed.

15

Adjustments: War and Postwar

Loyola's president did not slacken his pace during the early months of 1941. Even as he prepared for his ordeal in court, Bunn hosted a dinner and symposium on "Functions of Private Colleges in an Industrial Democracy" at the Jesuit residence. The featured speaker that April evening was the president of Tamblyn and Brown, a leading firm of business and industrial consultants. Father Bunn's guests were officers from a number of Baltimore's most important manufacturing firms. More significant than the meeting was an agreement under which the New York consultants were to conduct a survey for the college.

The year 1942 was the ninetieth anniversary of Loyola's founding, and President Bunn thought it an appropriate time to launch a major development campaign. What should be done, how it was to be financed, and what was feasible were the questions that the consulting firm was hired to answer, and its report provided a framework for Loyola's development. The firm had probably been recommended by Fordham's president, who two years earlier had Tamblyn and Brown do a similar job in preparation for the university's centenary.

. .

In August of 1941 the report was submitted to Father Bunn. It provided a comprehensive summary of the opportunities and problems facing the college. Baltimore and its environs, the report noted, had a bright economic, scientific, cultural, and educational future. Although Catholics composed less than a quarter of the city's population, at 210,000 they continued to provide Loyola with a large pool from which to select qualified applicants. Baltimoreans from other religious traditions sent sons to Loyola—they made up about 12 percent of the 1941 enrollment—so the associations with non-Catholics established at Holliday Street had been maintained.

Young men gave the interviewers various reasons for attending Loy-ola. The most often repeated were the recommendation of high-school counselors, the fine reputation of the science departments, the choice of a business career, the historic reputation of Jesuits as teachers, the preference for religion in the curriculum (cited by Catholics and oth-ers), the low tuition (still only $200), and the proximity of the school to their home. The Tamblyn-Brown interviewers reported that Loyola was described as "the best college in Baltimore or in the State."[1] Such praise was less impressive to Father Bunn because the report also said that the college was not well known and that people were confused about its nature. Some thought it was a secondary school, a mistake easy to make in Baltimore because City College was only a high school and there was a Loyola High School; others believed it was a prepara-tory school for those who were considering entrance into the Jesuit order, even though this vocation was actually chosen by very few stu-dents. Although Bunn was making progress on getting the college bet-ter known around Baltimore, obviously there was still a lot more to do.

Viewed in the simplest terms, the balance sheet was discouraging. An endowment of only $88,000 shrank in value during the depression to less than half that sum—a difficulty experienced by most other in-stitutions. Eighty percent of the college's income came from tuitions and fees; its students now came from families who relied on salaries for income and whose resources would not be increasing rapidly. For this reason the consultants recommended against raising any charges. Fur-thermore, this dependence on student payments meant that any decline in enrollments—as a result of the newly instituted Selective Service System, for instance—would severely curtail income. Despite these pinched circumstances, over one-third of Loyola's students were attend-ing on scholarships or receiving some other form of aid, mostly Na-tional Youth Administration assistance.

Applying a variety of accounting techniques that were standard in business but were only then being applied in education, the consultants demonstrated that Loyola's financial picture was not as bleak as it ap-peared. If appropriate salary values were assigned for the services of the twenty-six Jesuit teachers and administrators (something not previously done) and if the expenses for their maintenance were subtracted from this total, a surplus of $45,000 would result. This sum could be consid-ered "free services" (or in later parlance "contributed services"), and when it was factored into the balance sheet a much brighter picture emerged. The Tamblyn-Brown report recommended that "contributed services" be considered income on a "living" endowment, and at a conservative 3 percent return, Loyola's capital funds could properly be recalculated to total nearly $1.6 million. Such accounting procedures were normal in business and among educational institutions in other parts of the country where they served to qualify Catholic schools for accreditation. Adopting these procedures would make Loyola's balance sheet more intelligible to a broad public.

Under the new procedures recommended by Tamblyn-Brown, administration (including salaries for the president and deans) now represented only 15 percent of the outgo; faculty salaries (lay and Jesuit) would account for 54 percent of total expenditure; and there would be no line on the balance sheet for maintenance of the Jesuits. With this adjustment for "contributed services" and "living" endowment, Loyola's capital structure and operating accounts resembled those of such institutions as Hobart, Kenyon, Western Maryland, and Davidson.

Inclusion of regular salaries for religious teachers and administrators on the balance sheets of Catholic institutions gives a realistic picture of economic costs but has another, more subtle, effect. When regular salaries are assigned to members of the religious community, the financial cost of lay instructors no longer seems disparately high, and addition of faculty appears less threatening to institutional solvency. Comparable salaries blurred the difference between the employment of religious and lay faculty. An aversion to lay teachers remained strongly entrenched, but the change in accounting concepts made it possible for administrators at Catholic colleges to consider in practical terms what previously had been unthinkable and after the war would become quite necessary.

While the survey was being conducted for Loyola, Father Kleinmeyer independently suggested changes in the financial practices of the institutions in the province. He urged shifting to double-entry bookkeeping and the adoption of formal budgeting procedures for each year. To guide the financial officers at each of the province's institutions, Kleinmeyer circulated simple explanations of what was to be done and of why and how to do it. His calm persistence gradually got the Jesuits throughout the New York–Maryland province to adopt the discipline of annual budgets, but these were not formally introduced at Loyola until after Father Bunn's departure in 1947—even though Kleinmeyer's recommendations had been seconded in the Tamblyn-Brown report.

• •

That report made suggestions for Loyola's future development. Although President Bunn was encouraged to seek support from individual donors, the consultants judged a general fund-raising campaign inopportune. Loyola, they thought, needed time to promote a better understanding of its nature and objectives before it embarked on a public appeal. The report recommended that the membership of the advisory council of local civic and business leaders that President Bunn had established be expanded from eight to fifteen. The council then could provide the publicity and support offered by a lay board of trustees without being directly involved in the decision-making process.

Once the college achieved wider recognition it could embark on a campaign to increase its enrollments and to add new facilities. A more direct and persistent recruitment effort involving the faculty and alumni was suggested. This was to be aided by large brochures made attractive "with a wealth of action pictures which depict the college at work and play"—but emphasis was to be on "quality not quantity." To accommodate a student body of six hundred, a new multipurpose building, a better-designed chapel, and a larger library had to be added. The estimated cost of these additions was $850,000.

There were other recommendations in the Tamblyn-Brown report. An additional $150,000 was included to support professors in business, sociology, and education. An unspecified amount was to be raised for scholarship grants and for loans to students. Among these miscellaneous suggestions were ones to expand the existing public relations office and to establish an office for alumni affairs.[2] Very few obvious possibilities had been omitted.

This report and its appended shopping list of needs today provides a useful picture of Loyola in 1941 and at the time sketched a practical agenda for its future development. Not all of its many recommendations could be realized. The most significant contribution was its emphasis on explaining Loyola College to its constituency before making any attempt to seek general support. The advice came on the eve of America's entrance into World War II; this circumstance made it easy advice to follow.

The survey had taken special note of Loyola's athletic programs. At an average annual cost of less than five dollars per student there obviously was "no 'overemphasis' of athletics at Loyola." Nevertheless, the college offered a large, varied, and active schedule of intramural sports. In addition, it had varsity teams in ten sports: basketball, baseball, lacrosse, track, swimming, fencing, wrestling, soccer, tennis, and golf.

This achievement was almost entirely the work of Emil "Lefty" Reitz, who became director of athletics in 1937. Except for a brief stint in the navy, he devotedly served the college and its students for over thirty years. Namesake and son of an alumnus (class of 1908), Lefty was running the program on a budget of approximately two thousand dollars. This covered his salary as athletic director and coach of the basketball and baseball teams as well as honoraria for the lacrosse, track, swimming, and fencing coaches (the last of whom also served as mentor to the nearby Naval Academy team). Wrestling, soccer, tennis, and golf were temporarily coached by students. How traveling and equipment needs were met on such slender finances is one of many mysteries of Evergreen and Loyola.

The rising threat of war and the recently enacted draft produced new apprehensions; in typically Jesuit fashion these resulted not in paralysis but in practical action. Lefty Reitz set up a physical-conditioning program that included calisthenics, an obstacle course, sports, and informal exercise. The obstacle course, located in the dell (now covered by the College Center), was built to specifications of the navy so that Loyola students could qualify for its various reserve programs. All students declared fit after a physical examination were required to run and exercise at least three hours a week.[3]

For those who saw their future in the skies, a more elaborate "defense" program had been established even earlier, in October of 1939. A federally subsidized pilot-training program was established at the college, with twenty students enrolled in the first group. The head of Curtiss-Wright Airport and of the Baltimore Flying Service was the instructor. In three months the first class completed its ground training and solo flights. To maintain their new proficiency they organized a flying club. Officers of the Army Air Corps made campus appearances to attract recruits for cadet training. The increasingly tense international atmosphere noticeably allayed the fear of outside control among Jesuit authorities that only a few years earlier had blocked introduction of ROTC to the campus.

• •

Nineteen forty was a year of disasters for Britain and France. Norway fell to the German onslaught in a campaign that lasted only a month. The conquest of the Netherlands, Belgium, Luxembourg, and France took only a few days longer than that. By the end of June the British were under siege in their home islands. President Roosevelt, claiming authority as commander in chief, gave the British fifty overage destroyers in exchange for strategic bases. Just as classes resumed in September, Congress enacted what was technically a peacetime draft. All men aged 20 to 36 had to register; this left 18 and 19 year olds the option of starting college. Students received no general exemption, but they could postpone induction until the end of the academic year in which they were called. The first year of the draft brought over a million into the army.

Until the age was lowered to 18, the draft had no statistical effect on enrollments at Loyola. From September 1940 to June 1943 registrations continued rising, to peak at over 410. (At least 20 percent of the student body was then not Catholic.) Father Bunn, like his counterparts at other Jesuit institutions, supported the nation's draft policy but used every opportunity to emphasize President Roosevelt's declaration that it was the "patriotic duty" of youth to persevere in their education. Without minimizing the gravity of the current situation, Bunn urged students to look beyond the war: "Democracy is not defended solely by militarism." It needed educated leaders prepared to cope with the problems of the postwar era. In word and deed, he emphasized this long-term view throughout the war years.

Dean Gorman, whose appointment to Georgetown had been delayed by the Stuart trial and a change of plans at the university, included more martial notes in his office diary. A few months after the pilot-training program started, he wrote that a graduating participant received an Air Corps commission and his wings. Loyolans continued to volunteer for flight instruction. With evident pride, he recorded that Loyola alumni among the naval reserves constituted the largest single group selected for the December 1940 training cruise on the battleship *New York.*

These and other portents came into a sudden sharp focus on Sunday, December 7, 1941. The bombing of Pearl Harbor resulted in the shelving of plans not directly connected to the war effort. Priorities for the next several years were measured on a very different scale; Loyola, like many other American institutions, adjusted to this new circumstance.

Democratic societies have historically appeared unsuited for warfare. When involved in hostilities they often suffer initial periods of confusion and defeat. So it proved for the United States during the months after Pearl Harbor, when Japanese forces captured one strategic position after another in the South Pacific. The Philippine Islands, where a number of Jesuits from Baltimore were serving as missionaries and teachers, fell to the invaders, and it seemed only a matter of time before the enemy landed on the beaches of Australia.

The reaction to these early disasters was a mixture of fear and determination. Newspapers reported the defeats but sought to hearten their readers with stories of individual acts of heroism or defiant bravado from beleaguered outposts. The national mood could be gauged, however, from the nightly blackout of West Coast cities and the yielding of public authorities to prejudice and hysteria in rounding up all persons of Japanese ancestry. This frenzied atmosphere gradually dissipated under the press of an increasingly coherent drive to win the war. The battle cry was "Remember Pearl Harbor!" and complaints were squelched with "Don't you know there's a war on?"

Patriotic persons and groups pledged their loyalty and support to the war effort. The enemy was perceived as evil incarnate; this now made assistance to the Soviet Union acceptable even to Catholics. The struggle was seen as something more than an episode in a game of international chess. It was viewed as an apocalyptic battle in which the stakes appeared to be nothing less than the survival of civilized values and institutions. This aroused a national solidarity such as was not evident in any other American war—before or since. Among many pledges of support sent to President Roosevelt was one from American Jesuits. In addition, they offered their colleges and universities for "the defense of the country or the promotion of the common welfare."[4] Graciously alluding to Saint Ignatius Loyola, the soldier-founder of their order, Roosevelt accepted this pledge.

It would be seven months before the string of military defeats was interrupted. In June of 1942 an American fleet repelled an attack on Midway Island and crippled Japanese naval air power. Few could be sure, however, that the tide had turned; occasional setbacks still occurred and everyone anticipated a long, hard effort before final victory was achieved.

A few months after the battle of Midway, Charles Broderick (1939), home on recuperative leave, gave Baltimore papers an eyewitness account of the action. He had been an officer in charge of the torpedo shop on the aircraft carrier *Yorktown* when he was wounded. During the battle his ship was heavily damaged and had to be taken in tow; *Yorktown* listed so badly that the crew was evacuated. Later, when Lieutenant Broderick learned that the ship was sunk by a submarine, he admitted going "into a tailspin."

Broderick lightened his graphic description of the battle of Midway with an anecdote from an earlier engagement. During a lull in the fighting the *Yorktown*'s commander discovered that there was only one large piece of steak left in the larder. Instead of enjoying it himself he offered the precious slab of beef as a prize to a small group of shipmates chosen by lot. While the drawing was being held the trophy was ceremoniously paraded around the deck, guarded by a squad of marines and accompanied by a band. With an even grander flourish the steak was cooked and set before the winners of the lottery while the rest of the crew enviously watched.[5]

The obvious (though unstated) point of Lieutenant Broderick's story was the solidarity and high spirits of America's sons even in the midst of a battle. Gallantly, Broderick acknowledged that the Japanese pilots were "good fighting men . . . just like ours." He ended the interview on a morale-boosting note: "At Midway the Japs meant business [and] the business was what they got."[6] Similar stories were repeated in hometown papers across the land for three more years. Grimmer reports of casualties were recorded in the same papers and by the gold stars on service flags that churches, schools, and neighborhood associations prominently displayed.

. .

War and the mobilization to win it were insistent realities for all Americans. Gasoline, rubber, coffee, sugar, meat, silk, and other commodities were rationed, though less stringently than in Allied or enemy countries; the effects of rationing were mitigated here as elsewhere by the black market. Synthetic substitutes—nylon among them—were diligently sought and quickly put into production by all nations. A presidential order increased the ordinary workweek to forty-eight hours, and special efforts were made to resolve labor disputes and to prevent disruption of war production. Rents and prices were controlled. Daylight-saving time became the year-round norm, with the clock set forward a second hour during the summer. A federal commission was appointed to manage the manpower resources of the nation.

This commission and the draft posed the greatest threat to the operation and even the existence of the country's colleges and universities. Enrollments dropped sharply—at some schools by as much as 50 percent. In contrast, Loyola's registrations (probably because of travel restrictions and family anxieties that kept Baltimore students at home) continued to increase until 1943, when they peaked. The following year showed a 25 percent loss, and for 1944–45 registrations at Evergreen fell below 120. Estimates varied on how many institutions would close if the war continued long; some thought it would be at least five hundred smaller institutions—almost a third of the nation's colleges. By the fall of 1944, President Gannon of Fordham was certain his university would be among the casualties if the war lasted two more years, and pessimistically he doubted that many of these institutions could later be revived. [7]

To survive, American colleges and universities adopted a variety of strategies. Those with women in their classes increased the proportion of coeds. The University of Detroit followed this policy but Canisius chose instead to join a co-operative program in nursing education. Neither alternative appeared feasible for Loyola. Schools with well-established engineering and management courses got support from the federal government to retrain people needed for the direction and expansion of war production. This involved on-the-job training, with men and women attending classes after their regular shift in the factories. Boston College and the University of Detroit volunteered for this service. Fordham chose a variant of this option by augmenting its adult education offerings and becoming involved in other programs supported by the government. [8]

Because Loyola's circumstances resembled those of Fordham, Loyola followed a similar plan. In February of 1942 the small adult-education program began under Father Donceel's aegis was supplemented by a civilian-morale course. The United States Office of Education urged the establishment of such programs to explain the rise of totalitarianism and the fundamental values for which Americans were fighting.

In 1944, as enrollments in the day sessions declined, courses with regular college credit were added to the evening schedule—although they were not yet a part of any degree program. President Bunn's rationale for this was that many young people had gone directly from high school to factory assembly lines. He thought some might have planned to go to college, and this seed could be cultivated. Enrollments in all the evening courses rose from 13 in the fall of 1943 to a peak of 146 a year later and were still over 120 by February 1945.

In the next year several black people applied and were accepted in the evening courses without note or comment. Although ugly race riots occurred in various parts of the country during the war, the need for national solidarity mitigated—though not nearly enough—the application of discriminatory practices, and the racism of Hitler made Jim Crow less respectable. Loyola College did not openly challenge the prevailing mores of its region, but it never adopted a rule or practice denying entrance to blacks. The war-induced prosperity and the paucity of other opportunities encouraged some Baltimore black people to register in Loyola's evening courses. [9]

The situation of Jewish students in America remained unchanged, but Loyola did not need Hitler to embarrass it out of anti-Semitism. During Loyola's earliest years Jews applied to the college and were accepted. Their continuing presence is sufficient testimony to the favorable reputation of the college in Baltimore's Jewish community. In 1945 a mother gave concrete expression to that feeling. Her son had been offered scholarships to Loyola and to another Maryland institution. He accepted Loyola's offer and found there were other Jewish students receiving assistance. One of his co-religionists was named to *Who's Who Among Students in American Universities and Colleges*. "This is a true example of democracy in action, where all have equal opportunity, regardless of religious convictions."[10] She contrasted her son's reception at Loyola with the treatment of Jewish students at Maryland institutions where anti-Semitism was still in vogue.

To hold students attending the day sessions, Dean Gorman counseled them about the various army, navy, and marine programs that would allow them to continue. About 115 Loyolans joined the naval reserve. The military services made special arrangements for premedical and predental students, and several continued their studies at the college under this formula.

Partly at the suggestion of the federal government, but also in response to the threat of the draft, Loyola like its sister institutions shortened its four-year program to three years, and later cut it to two and a half years. This was accomplished mainly by eliminating holidays and vacations, conducting classes during the summer, and increasing the weekly load. It is not necessary to trace each amendment of the schedule. Suffice it to note that the dean periodically announced yet another adjustment to ensure that as many as possible could get their diplomas before they were called to active duty; as already noted, these changes helped maintain Loyola's major source of revenue: tuition.

Wartime acceleration had other effects. Because high-school students were being graduated in February, it became necessary for colleges to hold registration more often. There were, as a result, two or more groups of freshmen in every year, and this required adjustments, with promotion and graduation ceremonies scheduled for January, July, and October. The last traditional ceremony, held in June of 1942, was marked by the unexpected appearance of Frank McDonough, who wangled a very short leave from pilot training and caught a flight to Baltimore. As he stepped forward to accept his diploma, McDonough —a popular athlete—got the heartiest cheers. Twenty months later his bomber crashed in Italy. At the first winter graduation, in January of 1943, Governor Herbert O'Conor was invited to hand the diploma to his son and namesake, who reported to the army on the following day.

If wartime reduced the customary pomp, attention was still given to the selection of commencement speakers. Walter Lippmann, Raymond Gram Swing, and Robert Baukhage had for their commentaries a wide audience in the press and on radio. As a relief from the journalists, Father Gannon returned to the campus for the January 1944 commencement, and a year later Felix Morley, president of Haverford, sustained the academic tone.

An incidental effect of this wartime acceleration is still evident: the ordinal number for graduations is anomalously greater than the number of years since the first ceremony. For instance, the year in which Loyola celebrated its one hundred and twenty-fifth anniversary was ended with its one hundred and twenty-ninth commencement.

. .

Experimentation and adaptation convinced some educators that the time was ripe for more drastic changes. Robert Hutchins called for a program that would graduate people from college by the age of 18. He thought only six years were needed for primary schooling, three for secondary, and three for college. Few among Maryland's educational leaders supported Hutchins's plan, but Stringfellow Barr, president of Saint John's College, believed there was "a raft of stuff" that could be dropped from the "educational system and never be missed." Father Bunn was willing to concede that the plan might be acceptable at some future date, but he thought "the best immediate results [could] be obtained by changing the curriculum to meet wartime needs."[11]

This did not mean that he was joining those who called for a suspension of the humanities for the duration. They were urging instruction in only mathematics, chemistry, physics, and geography—subjects that had an immediate application in the military service. One prominent figure at another Maryland institution denounced liberal education as an elitist luxury, useless in wartime and fundamentally dangerous to a democratic society.

As during World War I, voices were raised in defense of traditional education. Wendell Willkie declared "preservation of our cultural heritage" the very essence of that for which Americans fought. Father Bunn thought the nation's winning edge was its "elasticity and ingenuity," and that these qualities came from "a highly developed imagination—one of the products of liberal arts training."[12]

Nevertheless, some adaptation had to be made in Loyola's offerings. As elsewhere, the focus of several courses shifted from abstract theory to military applications. Problems of navigation and trajectory were included among the demonstrations of mathematical principle, and Vincent Beatty, then a Jesuit scholastic, organized a sequence in military chemistry. After January 1943 the science curriculum was emphasized. Despite such measures, Loyola's devotion to the humanities remained intact, because even its science degree contained a substantial proportion of philosophy, religion, history, and literature. Had the war lasted longer than it did, what further measures might Father Bunn have been forced to take?

On all campuses, unease prevailed. In 1943 a columnist for the *Sunday Sun* characterized the situation of America's colleges and universities "as a cross between confused organization and regimented chaos."[13] The situation was compounded that year when the War Department announced its Army Specialized Training Program (ASTP). Institutions of higher learning were invited to negotiate contracts under which they were to provide instruction in engineering and languages for a select group of enlisted men.

What were the objectives of the Army Specialized Training Program? Concretely, it infused a large number of students—over four hundred thousand—and federal funds into many schools at a critical time. The year Fordham housed a unit brought the university over half a million dollars, and though the amount was not clear profit, it provided a sorely needed flow of cash.[14] The army derived specific benefits. The program secured billets for a rapidly expanding force without erection of additional facilities and kept a healthy, intelligent reserve distracted for about a year. (However querulous this interpretation may seem, it arises from my memories of participating in an even more dubious enterprise —the Army Specialized Training Program Reserve, a junior offshoot for those who had not yet turned 18.) In any case, it was light duty in pleasant surroundings.

Georgetown was among the first to apply for an ASTP unit. For the university, the detailed and tedious negotiations with the army were conducted by Father Lawrence Gorman. His outstanding record at Loyola prompted his Jesuit superiors to name him president of Georgetown in December of 1942. He left Baltimore after a testimonial banquet attended by state and local educational, religious, and civic leaders.

The army negotiators at Georgetown found the problem of compensation for Jesuit instructors difficult to comprehend. Their experience did not include the special accounting procedures that Loyola and other Jesuit institutions had recently adopted to make their financial statements conform to accepted business standards. Army guidelines allowed only for "actual costs," which meant salaries for lay instructors. Although there was now a salary listed in the ledgers for each Georgetown Jesuit, this consisted of both actual living expenses and "contributed services." The government's negotiators, arguing to keep costs down, agreed to compensate for expenses, but not for "contributed services." On their side the Jesuits noted that this would give the army highly trained instructors at a scab rate. Eventually the differences were resolved and the solution accommodated the Jesuit view. At least Georgetown, Fordham, Boston College, and the University of Detroit participated in the ASTP program. Father Bunn made a serious effort to secure inclusion of Loyola. Although the army inspectors were laudatory of what they saw at Evergreen, they doubted that Loyola could properly feed the number that might be assigned to the college. There were, as a result, no soldier-students or federal funds to tide the school over 1943–44.

After the invasion of Europe in June of 1944, the army closed its marginal instructional programs. All the men in the Army Specialized Training Program, anti-aircraft officers' candidate school, and the like were transferred to the infantry. There they became replacements for the casualties suffered during the final drives into the heartland of Hitler's Europe and into the Japanese Empire.

• •

While these climactic campaigns were being planned, life on campus had a hectic, anxious quality. Two statistics were ever-present reminders of the war. The first was the number of Loyola alumni in uniform, which only a few weeks after Pearl Harbor already stood at a hundred, including several career officers but mostly recent volunteers. By the time the Japanese surrendered four years later this number exceeded a thousand, about a third of them commissioned as officers.

Like the ubiquitous Kilroy, Loyolans served everywhere—in every branch, theater, and circumstance. Among the daredevils was Bernard O'Neill (1939), who commanded a PT boat in the Pacific. Severn Lanier (1943) preferred an even more fragile mode of transportation; he joined an underwater demolition team—the frogmen. Among the more methodical tasks of war was the Atlantic anti-submarine patrol, and William Sanford (1942) drew this duty.

Even wartime, however, is not all shot and shell. William O'Donnell (1937) served as counsel for navy men subject to court-martial. At the very end of the war he was recalled from a discharge furlough to defend a captain who suffered the misfortune of having his cruiser sunk. To keep home-front morale high, motion pictures were produced with stories about heroism in the branches of the service. One such wartime feature, entitled *Bombardier* and starring Randolph Scott, was a fictionalized account of John "Paddy" Ryan's career (class of 1927). Between the wars he had worked on perfecting the technique of high-level bombing.

There were stories of narrow escapes. Robert Overbeck (1937) was captured at the fall of Corregidor and became a prisoner of war. Late in 1944 his captors marched Lieutenant Overbeck and almost two thousand other prisoners into the small hold of a transport headed for the home islands of Japan. En route the ship was torpedoed. Despite great danger and hardship, Overbeck and a few others survived. On D-day off the Normandy beachhead, Ensign Fran Mueller (1943) dove off his ship and rescued two seriously injured men. These and innumerable other reports about servicemen-alumni were clipped and pasted into thick scrapbooks. Periodically the *Greyhound* printed an honor roll of Loyolans in the military service.

The second statistic that could not be ignored by the students still on campus was the number of casualties—missing, wounded, and dead. The first to be killed after Pearl Harbor was Frank Brown (1940), a navy flier. He had been a member of the lacrosse team and of the first class to receive pilot training at the college—"a splendid type of Catholic gentleman," the dean noted in his diary. He was the grandson of another Frank Brown, a politically independent governor of Maryland who held office from 1892 to 1896. Wartime restrictions permitted only the most meager details. The *Greyhound* and the Baltimore papers merely reported that Brown crashed at sea—only that and a brief biography. By the end of the war almost thirty more such notices for Loyola men appeared.

The students and faculty expressed their feelings in various symbolic ways. The bombing of Pearl Harbor was remembered a year later with two distinctive events. The senior class, led by James McManus (1943), donated a ship's lamp, which was fastened to the base of the statue of Mary. This lamp was the first gift to the campus from a graduating class. At the same time the staff of the *Greyhound* (attending more directly to the business of war) organized a bond-and-blood drive. In a week, Dean Joseph d'Invilliers proudly noted in his diary, students purchased $6,500 in bonds, and a third of the seniors had each given a pint of blood. This achievement was given publicity by radio station WITH, and campus biologists thought the time was ripe for a series of lectures on blood and blood plasma in the treatment of wounds. When the Red Cross became the agency for promoting these drives, the sodality became responsible for recruiting volunteers on campus. Subsequent bond drives brought in as much as $20,000 at a time.

There were other expressions of student and faculty sentiment. The annual Parents' Day ceremonies were continued throughout the war with an added feature—the raising of the college's service flag, each time with more stars, both blue and gold. At the beginning of the war, farewell parties were notable events. In February of 1942, when Father Arthur North became an army chaplain, students and alumni flocked to a reception in his honor and contributed a small purse. As such events became more frequent and there were fewer people available for gatherings, less notice was given to them. Wishes for a safe return were converted into rosaries, novenas, and masses added to the normal cycle of religious observance at Evergreen.

. .

As best they could, faculty and students tried to maintain a full program of extracurricular activities. Not enough time and talent were available for the *Evergreen Quarterly,* and publication had to be suspended "for the duration." Yearbooks—when they appeared—contained little more than pictures of the dwindling number of graduates. The *Greyhound* was issued regularly, filled as much with news of servicemen-alumni as of campus doings. The tradition of oratorical skill was maintained by entrants in national contests sponsored by the Hearst papers; Ray Chartrand (1944) was a finalist in 1943, followed two years later by Thomas Lalley (1947). Each year one or two dramatic presentations were offered, but these were mostly one-act plays or short comedies with a limited number of characters.

Despite restricted numbers, "Loyola Night" was regularly staged and each presentation managed to include a show-stopper. In 1943, for instance, Dan Silverstein (1945) started his piano recital with a technically difficult piece by Rachmaninoff. Having demonstrated his mastery, he responded to the applause with a fiery Spanish dance. When the audience demanded still more he "struck out a jerky rhythm on the lower end of the keyboard, and was off on the boogiewoogie special."[15] The glee club's more sedate selections made the audience receptive to an original one-act play.

To maintain all these activities even as enrollments dropped, it became necessary for students to participate in several organizations. This could not be done easily, because most students now had part-time jobs and the accelerated program meant heavier course loads. Early on the faculty discussed the problem but could not agree on specific remedies. One Jesuit thought everything would work out as the students adjusted to wartime circumstances. Prosaic and complaisant as it may sound, his laissez-faire approach worked, and a remarkably full schedule of student activities was maintained.

A similarly persevering spirit was evident among Loyola's athletes. The sports program under Lefty Reitz became more than merely a matter of competition. With large responsibilities and limited resources for management, he established an apprenticeship system for developing student assistants. These kept the varsity squads and intramural games on schedule and produced the statistics and information beloved of sports writers and broadcasters. Every year Lefty recruited a likely group of freshmen, which was winnowed, and those who remained were rewarded with the responsibilities and experience they sought. Among the best-known products of Lefty's system were James McManus (the American Broadcasting System's "Jim McKay") and Vince Bagli (1949), who for many years has provided sports news for local viewers over WBAL-TV.

Reitz worked to break down the cliquish spirit of the varsity teams. He fostered the Block L Club, which included all athletes in green and gray. Each year's athletic wars ended with a feast at which sweaters and letters were awarded to those who qualified under an elaborate point system designed to reward ability and commitment. Under Lefty Reitz's direction athletics at Loyola—varsity and intramural—was not so much a mechanism for generating favorable publicity (although it did) as part of the school's extra- or even co-curriculum.

Just before America's involvement in the war the old Maryland collegiate league disintegrated and was replaced by the Mason-Dixon Conference. Loyola College was among the charter members of the new organization and took pride that the first commissioner was Paul Menton (1922), sports editor of the *Evening Sun*. Reitz welcomed the new organization because it made possible a regular schedule of games in a reasonable number of sports and with nearby schools similar in student and financial resources.

Before all the benefits of the Mason-Dixon conference could be realized the outbreak of war put a damper on its activities. Fewer players were available at every school. The accelerated study program discouraged participation in sports—and government limitations on gasoline and tires affected players and spectators. Nevertheless, Loyola maintained a full card of varsity sports. During these years the green and gray won more than their share of games and titles.

In July of 1943 Reitz started to work with James Lacy, Jr. (1949), the scoringest basketball player in the history of the college. Lacy's father, who had played at Loyola High School under Coach Schuerholz (as had Lefty Reitz), established a record—thirty-seven field goals in one game—that withstood even his son's determined assault. Although the elder Lacy had registered at the college and played basketball for a year, his father's death forced him to abandon formal education to manage the family's iron foundry. Later the younger Lacy's record at Loyola High School attracted attention from several collegiate institutions. Family ties and a favorable account of life and play at Evergreen from former teammate Aloysius "Wish" Galvin (1948) tipped the balance, and Jim Lacy, Jr., stayed in Baltimore. He started playing on the varsity and scored over four hundred points during his first season.

About the time that Lacy first registered at the college, the navy ordered Galvin and about fifty other young Baltimoreans to report to Mount Saint Mary's in Emmitsburg to continue their preparations for service. Galvin's desire to play basketball was so strong that he even donned a Mountaineer's uniform.

As luck would have it, the finalists in the 1944 Mason-Dixon tournament were Loyola and Mount Saint Mary's. The game was hard fought—a classic nip-and-tuck struggle—with the lead shifting fifteen times. In the final minutes the score was Loyola 39 and Mount Saint Mary's 38. Galvin caught a rebound and from near mid-court gracefully arched the ball through the hoop—his specialty. Seven Loyola attempts—three by Lacy—all bounced off the rim of the basket, and the final score stood Loyola 39, Mount Saint Mary's 40.[16]

Before the next season Lacy joined the navy, and shortly after the 1944 tournament so did Reitz. With another athletic director the college continued to field varsity teams throughout the war.

• •

Like other institutions, Loyola watched the start of the veterans-on-campus phenomenon, but President Bunn was aware that his canonical term as rector had been completed in 1944. Each general review of Jesuit personnel thereafter had to raise the possibility of his transfer. At most, Father Bunn might remain at the head of the college till 1947, unless the offices of president and rector were separated. Such an arrangement was then being tested at Fordham, but this example was not repeated in Baltimore immediately, partly to wait for the results of the Fordham experiment and partly because the Maryland Jesuits were no longer directly connected with their New York brethren. In 1943 the Jesuits beyond the Delaware River had been reconstituted into a separate province. The union established in 1880 was abrogated and a Jesuit provincial was again in residence at Calvert Street. One effect of the reorganization was the naming of Father Bunn as prefect of schools for the Maryland province.

Even though his days at Loyola had a limit, his determination to provide for the future was evidently not slackened. A matter to which he gave attention was dormitories for resident students. At the 1944 alumni banquet, President Bunn announced that housing for at least a hundred students would be constructed as soon as the war was over, and the policy of the college thereafter would be to house at least one-fourth of the student body at Evergreen. This was not welcomed by all. Some among the alumni, students, and faculty feared that residents would loosen Loyola's ties to Baltimore. Probably neither Bunn nor they could recall that Father McEneany had envisioned a school with resident students after he moved Loyola to Evergreen.

Bunn was interested in maintaining the accelerated schedule because the three-year program had amply proven itself. Shorter and fewer vacations meant fewer distractions and better grades for the students, even though for the faculty it meant an unremitting cycle of labor. Father Bunn favored the shorter program because it allowed graduates to start their careers and families sooner. At a February 1945 meeting of the Maryland province's educational leaders, he worked to secure agreement on maintaining the accelerated schedule. He even proposed that the high-school course be cut to three years, with additional provision made for early admission to college—something close to the educational change Robert Hutchins had suggested early in the war.

Bunn's proposal was referred to a committee, which a month later came back with a watered-down recommendation. The institutions of higher education in the Maryland province would continue on the accelerated schedule, but no firmer commitment was made, and nothing at all was said about shortening the high-school program.[17] Each Jesuit community has always guarded its independence, and none was ready to yield its ability to respond to special circumstances. Such tenuous conformity has always been characteristic of American Jesuit education, but notice of it has not been taken until recently.[18] At Loyola, the last accelerated class was graduated in July of 1950, three years after Father Bunn's departure.

Well before victory, America began planning its transition to the postwar era. All were agreed that there was to be no repetition of the political, economic, and social disasters that followed World War I. What was needed was clear to all: a peace-keeping organization stronger than the League of Nations, avoidance of the customary postwar depression, and quick reintegration of former servicemen into society and the economy.

This last objective was particularly worrisome because by mid-1944, when over a million soldiers and sailors had been discharged, the press carried stories of nasty, even violent, incidents involving veterans. The fears aroused by such reports were given a larger and more ominous frame by an American Legion spokesman testifying before a congressional committee. He noted that after World War I idle and dissatisfied veterans were a leading element in the revolutions that wracked Germany, Italy, Russia, and other nations. Obviously, delay on any of the three major postwar objectives could be ruinous.

At all levels Americans were concerned about what international structures would replace the League of Nations. As the tide shifted against Germany and Japan, more attention was given this subject, and a variety of groups were formed so that people could participate in the discussion. Among educators, one of the most prestigious was the Universities Committee headed by Harvard's Ralph Barton Perry. Started in 1944, this committee provided guidance and liaison among campus groups around the country. Father Bunn went to Princeton for an orientation session sponsored by Perry's committee. On his return to Evergreen he constituted the senior members of Loyola's faculty a committee and assumed its chairmanship. Through this body Loyola participated in this nationwide endeavor. Loyola's committee attempted to engage student attention by reprinting discussion guides in the *Greyhound*.

The substance of these deliberations at Loyola cannot be reconstructed accurately, but their probable tenor can be inferred from two later acts. In April of 1945 the students assembled in the chapel to offer their prayers for the success of the conference then opening in San Francisco to draft a charter for the United Nations (UN). When in July the Senate quickly ratified the United Nations Charter, Father Bunn joined several other Baltimore religious leaders in urging people to express their gratitude for both the ratification and the expedition with which the senators had acted.[19] Hopes were high that the UN would be an effective instrument of international order, but fears engendered by the explosion of two atomic bombs were even higher.

Contemporaneous with the emergence of the United Nations was the elaboration of domestic policies to avoid depression and to absorb the veterans quickly. Government leaders at all levels were agreed that both objectives could be served by diverting the veterans from the job market into school. This would immediately lessen the problem of unemployment and, they hoped, would still any postwar agitation for a bonus.

Not all educators were equally enthusiastic. Robert Hutchins, for one, opposed using the nation's colleges and universities for such a purpose because he feared the program would dilute the intellectual content of higher education and lower admission standards. These high-minded complaints fell on insensitive ears, because many college presidents, treasurers, and trustees eagerly awaited increased enrollments and federal funds. Nevertheless, many educators were afraid that an educational program for veterans would increase centralization.

• •

These trends and concerns prompted Thomas Pullen, state superintendent of education and one of John Dewey's leading students, to prepare a broad postwar program for reforming and reconstructing Maryland's educational system. Governor Herbert O'Conor, who did not want to see bread lines or veterans selling apples, gave vigorous support to Pullen's ideas. To mobilize public support and to share the onus for any unpopular decisions, the superintendent early in 1944 organized the Maryland Educational Conference.

With finesse and attention to protocol, Pullen easily secured the selection of Father Bunn as chairman of this new body. This choice was readily accepted because of the high standing Loyola's president enjoyed among the state's educational leaders after six years. Evergreen, where the conference was launched, was readily accessible to all and a neutral meeting ground for public, private, and religiously affiliated schools. It could not have escaped notice (even if it was not mentioned) that Bunn was a classmate of Governor O'Conor's. The date for the conference—March 25—was not only a state holiday (the 310th anniversary of Maryland's first settlement), but also Edward Bunn's forty-eighth birthday. The luncheon before the meeting, all agreed, conformed to Loyola's well-deserved reputation for hospitality.

Details of the structure of this Maryland Educational Conference are not necessary. Its plenary sessions afforded a common meeting ground for two hundred representatives from every kind of educational institution or interest in the state except (understandably enough) church-related elementary schools. The active agencies of the conference were an executive committee headed by Bunn with Thomas Pullen as vice-chairman, and a legislative committee composed of only three members: Bunn, Pullen, and the superintendent of the Baltimore City schools. The Maryland educational conference was served in effect by an interlocking directorate in which Loyola's president played a major role.

Just as this Maryland agency was forming, the national program for returning veterans started through the congressional mill. Federal support in buying a home, starting a business, and going to school was to be made available to veterans according to how long they had served. As this program, popularly called the GI bill of rights, took shape, many educators became alarmed at a provision that gave the director of the Veterans Administration exclusive authority to determine which schools were eligible to participate.

It was easy to mobilize pressure to amend this provision. Father Bunn and Thomas Pullen joined spokesmen from other states to stop this centralization of power. All argued that state agencies had already reviewed and certified schools within their jurisdiction and that these determinations should be accepted by the VA. It took only a note to enlist Governor O'Conor in this effort. By the end of May 1944 the nationwide campaign forced Congress to amend the law, which a month later was enthusiastically passed.

There remained, however, one unresolved matter of special concern to Father Bunn. His earlier work and continuing interest in psychology made him press for an amendment to remedy an omission from the GI bill of rights. Although vocational counseling was provided for disabled veterans, no such service was offered the other veterans. The need for such counseling had been recognized at the earliest meetings of the Maryland Educational Conference. Initially, Bunn and Pullen urged the Baltimore office of the Veterans Administration to support such a service. When several rounds of correspondence prompted them to think they were encountering a bureaucratic stall, they began to develop a state-supported system. This need was obvious to others, and before the Bunn-Pullen alternative was ready, a national program for counseling all veterans was authorized, with Loyola listed among the centers in Maryland.[20]

From August of 1945 to May of 1949 a veterans guidance center occupied two classrooms in the basement of what is now Beatty Hall. It provided a broad range of vocational testing and advice from counselors, some of whom were Loyola faculty members. The college received a small rental fee for the space and twenty dollars for each person who completed the process. From this income Loyola paid the salaries of two counselors and the cost of utilities. No record of the number who came to Evergreen has survived, but the financial records indicate that at least two thousand returning servicemen, both disabled and not, were advised at this center. Most, obviously, went to schools other than Loyola; counselors were not permitted to use their position to promote attendance at any particular institution.[21]

• •

Even before the war ended, the first veteran arrived at Evergreen. The name Howard Strott (1945) appears on the dean's list for November 1943, seven months before Congress passed the GI bill. It was mid-August of 1944 when the VA finally transmitted the check for his tuition and books. By then Gerard Connolly (1945), a returning veteran, was attending the college. By October they were joined by two more ex-servicemen. At the time, the number of students at the college was less than 120. These few veterans were, however, harbingers of a much larger flock that would arrive soon enough.

The main wave came two years later. In February of 1946 there were 425 students attending Loyola, 75 percent of them veterans. A year later registrations increased to 860, with only a hundred of that number entering directly from high school. To accommodate the enlarged student body, recreation and locker rooms and other unused space were converted into classrooms. The faculty was nearly doubled—mostly with laymen (there was even one in the philosophy department); some of the new teachers were veterans themselves. By the summer of 1947 the college had to admit that there was no place on campus "to study or even to sit between classes."[22] The peak was not reached until September of that year, when almost 1,100 were accepted for the day division and another 450 registered for evening courses. Thereafter the flow of veterans ebbed, with the last full-time day students of the World War II brigade graduating in 1952.

Almost two years after the arrival of the first veteran at Evergreen the war in Europe ended. As in the finale of World War I, there were rumors and false alarms for days before the German forces finally surrendered, on May 8, 1945. That day victory celebrations preempted the centers of most major cities around the free world. The people of Baltimore blocked downtown streets and carried on with an enthusiasm remarkable in view of the heavy morning rain. By midafternoon, however, the city was back to its normal business. To those who participated in the carryings-on elsewhere in the nation (which continued well into the night) this behavior may seem odd, but it may be taken as an example of one of the things that distinguishes Baltimoreans from other Americans: a preference for a quiet and matter-of-fact approach to life.

The observance at Loyola was even more sedate than the citywide celebration. Students collected in the library to listen to the formal announcement over radio. The voice they heard was not that of Franklin Delano Roosevelt, because he had died almost a month before; Harry Truman was now president. Regular Tuesday morning classes were held, and at noon the faculty and students assembled in the chapel for prayers of thanksgiving.

Three months later—after American planes dropped atomic bombs on Hiroshima and Nagasaki and the Soviets finally declared war on Japan—the fighting in the Pacific theater ceased. The announcement came almost as an anticlimax. Below the triumphant headlines on August 15 appeared reports that the navy had cancelled contracts worth over six billion dollars and that the Glenn L. Martin Company had immediately instituted a regular five-day, forty-hour workweek. The postwar transition had begun.[23]

During the interval, enrollments at Loyola were rising spectacularly, and these required immediate accommodation. Like other institutions facing the same problem, the college began buying surplus government materials. Rather than hoard the things built or bought for the prosecution of the war, the federal government, after victory, made virtually everything available to schools and other nonprofit institutions at nominal prices. One of Loyola's earliest requisitions included platinum electrodes and crucibles, analytical balances, and other equipment for the chemistry laboratory.

The biggest item acquired from the government was the dell building, a structure compounded from bachelor officers' quarters and an administration building left standing on a nearby abandoned navy base. The need for additional classroom and office space was quite evident by July of 1946, when a newly arrived dean of students, Father Robert Arthur, took the initiative. He received only mild support from his colleague, Dean Joseph d'Invilliers, and a negative reaction but no outright disapproval from President Bunn—slight encouragement but enough for a brave Jesuit to proceed on.

Originally the buildings were to be erected at a different site, fitted into the empty space (now occupied by the Andrew White Student Center) between the gymnasium and Millbrook Road, enclosing a small quadrangle. Either the starkly utilitarian architecture of the new building or the distance of the site from other campus buildings prompted a shift to the dell, which had previously been reserved for a permanent chapel. This site shielded the structure from the view of all but those with business on campus.

The government's official description of the building said it contained approximately nine thousand square feet divided among "five classrooms, seven offices, three toilets, two storage rooms, three entrance vestibules, and one boiler room." Teachers and students who had classes there will wryly recall three major distractions: the Y-shaped supports that occupied the center aisles, the excessive heat, and the buzzing fluorescent lamps that cast a glaring light from the ceiling. Contrary to the widely held belief that the government required such buildings to be torn down after a certain number of years, their life span was determined by nothing but institutional need. This building was opened just in time for the eleven hundred students who came to Loyola in September 1947. (These details have been included because they are the only ones left of this once-familiar campus feature. In 1982 the dell building was dismantled in a couple of hours to make way for the college center.)

. .

By the start of classes in 1947 a number of familiar figures had reappeared on campus. Lefty Reitz was by far the best known and most welcome. Discharged from the navy in December of 1945, he came back in time to rebuild the athletic program—varsity and intramurals—before the flood tide of students arrived. A year later brought Jim Lacy back into green and grey togs for the start of the brightest episode in Loyola basketball (a story recounted in the next chapter).

Graduation in 1947 was accompanied by the reappearance of two campus publications: the quarterly and the yearbook. The first postwar issue of the former—now self-consciously literary and ignoring the broad scope of the prewar editions—arrived early in July. Except for an article by a faculty member who had lived in Hungary during and after the war, short stories and poems filled the pages. The editorial board of the quarterly, like those of its predecessors, solicited comments and got good reviews and suggestions from H. L. Mencken and from Robin Harriss, then editor of *Gardens, Houses and People.*

In hard silver-and-green cover, the yearbook for 1947 was an equally creditable production. Its editors were more deferential to the past than were their peers at the quarterly. They reprinted photographs from the 1922 edition, the first produced at Evergreen. There was a picture of Archbishop Curley stooping to lift a shovelful of earth, with Father McEneany benignly looking on.

The contrast in the pictures of the classes of 1922 and 1947 measured the distance in time and custom that twenty-five years had wrought. The sixteen earlier graduates were attired in academic caps, gowns, and formal white bow ties, and, though not wearing pompous expressions, they all looked at the viewer with solemn dignity. There were almost six times as many in the class of 1947, and they were photographed in their ordinary jackets and ties—all but one of them four-in-hands—and most were smiling.

The catalogue for 1946–47 carried details of a co-operative arrangement with the Peabody Conservatory of Music: a Loyola student could substitute fifty credits in music for major courses and electives and receive a bachelor's degree. Less visible was the institution of contracts for lay faculty members. Although these specified general conditions of employment (including a workload of fifteen semester-hours), much was left to the discretion of the dean. At least these contracts provided the faculty with a legal claim on their salaries—and automatic renewal unless written notice was given prior to the expiration of the agreement. The issuance of contracts was connected with the gradual implementation of the budgeting procedures recommended earlier, in the Tamblyn-Brown report, and in memoranda of the provincial procurator, Father Kleinmeyer. Presumably contracts for lay teachers were instituted at other Jesuit schools in the same period, and were an informal acknowledgment that laymen were no longer merely temporary auxiliaries.

• •

The most significant feature in President Bunn's postwar plans was a building program, well publicized in handsome brochures and in student publications. The endpapers of the 1947 yearbook had a new site plan—much less coherent than the one drawn in 1921. In fact, the Bunn plan seems only a sketch that displayed his major concerns rather than a fully developed program for Loyola's future growth.

The alumni memorial chapel and auditorium was the only structure to be erected approximately where President Bunn planned. He did not choose to locate the chapel at the site reserved for it in the 1921 plan of the campus—the dell building had preempted that location. Bunn wanted the chapel built near the corner of Cold Spring Lane and Charles Street, balancing a proposed administration and classroom building. The choice of this site for the chapel obviously meant at least postponement of the dormitory, a project President Bunn had mentioned to the alumni only a year or so earlier. Why the change? Why was priority now given to a chapel rather than to a student residence? If someone asked these obvious questions at the time no one thought to record the answers, but this change and the size and style of the chapel suggest an extramural priority.

The fund-raising campaign for the chapel began in March of 1946 with $400,000 as its goal. Nine months later about half that amount had been collected or pledged—a disappointing result. One reason was a restriction of the appeal to Loyola's alumni and friends, probably to forestall any dispute with the archdiocese over the title to the chapel— a possibility if the appeal had been more general. A bequest of $100,000 from Charles Cohn (1897), president of the Baltimore Gas and Electric Company and chairman of the college's lay advisory council, brought the sum closer to the goal, but by then postwar inflation had added 50 percent to the original estimate. Under these circumstances construction was delayed.

The length of President Bunn's term (nine years) and the shortfall of the funds needed for the chapel suggested the time had come for a new hand at Evergreen. Although the decision to transfer Father Bunn had been made much earlier, it was not announced publicly till after the death of Archbishop Michael Curley in May of 1947. This sequence prompted some archdiocesan clergy to speculate that the Jesuits had kept Bunn in Baltimore beyond expiration of his canonical term to remind everyone of his vindication in the face of charges brought by Curley. The chancellor, Monsignor Joseph Nelligan (1922), was pleased when he later learned that no such intention had been at work. The decision to transfer Bunn had been taken earlier and his successor had privately received his commission dated March 25—months before the archbishop's final illness. [24]

There was will and time enough for educators and religious and civic leaders from Baltimore and around the state to attend a testimonial banquet in Father Bunn's honor. Thomas Pullen presided as toastmaster. President Byrd of the University of Maryland avowed that he would miss the "practical guidance" he had from Father Bunn. An assistant superintendent of Baltimore schools said that Loyola's president had "brought about mutual confidence between the administrations in the public schools and in the parochial schools." William Casey, chairman of the Commission on Governmental Efficiency and Economy, declared that Father Bunn "left an inheritance to the city—an inheritance and a future for an institution which fills a large part of the city's educational pattern. What he built here is enduring." There were similar tributes repeating and elaborating these sentiments.

After Baltimore, Father Bunn was briefly director of the labor school at the University of Scranton. In 1952 (the hundredth anniversary of Loyola's founding), he was named president of Georgetown University where, like the founder of Loyola, Father John Early, he filled his last office—another twenty years—and came to be numbered among its most distinguished leaders.

Part Four

1947–1964

Renewal

16

Centenary Preparations

The postwar years, if fraught with tensions, were generally marked by "an unprecedented material and social well-being." The grim, teeth-clenching mood of the 1930s was replaced for about twenty years by a euphoria based on long delayed but desperately needed social reforms and an evident prosperity in which Marylanders gained more than the national average.[1] The postwar mood did not ride one continuous wave but was affected by various currents. Like the community it served, Loyola College rode this rising tide with a characteristic Baltimore caution.

In the summer of 1947, Loyola's prospects continued to glow with the achievements of Father Bunn and were heightened by hopes engendered by the appointment of Father Francis Xavier Talbot. More than a thousand students were enrolled, and over the previous nine years the college had caught the favorable attention of Baltimore's leading citizens. With the new president and rector a nationally known figure, it was reasonable to expect that the institution would become even more sophisticated and broaden its horizons. Planning for the centenary of Loyola's founding (1952) focused on how best to capitalize on that event. The aura attached to Father Talbot's name gave hope that Loyola would emerge from his term with an even brighter glow—but, for reasons beyond his control, that did not happen.

. .

Father John LaFarge, a close associate during Talbot's years in New York, recorded perceptive impressions. This elder brother-in-religion thought Talbot "blessed with an inimitably gracious, encouraging manner" tempered by a certain restlessness that seemed to increase with age. This was coupled with a readiness to initiate—to get things moving—sometimes without full appreciation of the complexity of the issues. Father Talbot himself located the source of his administrative difficulties at Loyola in an inability to say no.[2]

His appointment, somewhat anomalous because of his lack of experience in academic administration, seems to have been intended to provide Loyola with a literary and intellectual celebrity at its helm, with the mundane aspects of the operation covered in other ways. Provisions were made to alleviate the problems President Talbot might face by having Father Bunn prepare an organizational chart (probably the first in Loyola's history) and define the duties of the major school officers. Bunn remained a member of the board of trustees so that his experience would be readily available to his successor.

The treasurer, deans, and some other officers were constituted a committee to meet with the president twice a month to plan and to review the development of the college. Each officer was required to prepare a budget for his division; these estimates were reviewed by the committee and incorporated into an annual budget for the college. Among Jesuits such changes are only gradually applied, and although the budgeting policy was announced early in Talbot's term it was not fully operative for another eight years.

Oversight of daily operations and routine matters was assigned to a young and energetic dean, Matthew Sullivan. These arrangements and the old Jesuit can-do tradition left little room for doubt; in addition, they seemed to ensure that Father Talbot would have the time to add a history of Loyola College to his already substantial list of publications. At 58, he was the oldest man ever appointed president of the college.

Loyola's twentieth president arrived in Baltimore by a circuitous route. The youngest of seven children, he was born in Philadelphia on June 25, 1889. An elementary-school nun suggested that he take the scholarship examination for nearby Saint Joseph's—which he did, successfully. Talbot's four years at that institution ended with his entrance into the Society of Jesus at age 17. His training included a teaching stint at Boston College, and after ordination he was named in 1923 to the editorial staff of *America*; its editor in chief, Father Richard Tierney, recruited Talbot for this important apostolate.

During the next twenty-two years Francis X. Talbot tried to refine and broaden the literary interests of his co-religionists. His aim was to bring Catholic readers and authors into the literary mainstream without sacrificing either their aesthetic sensibilities or their theological heritage. Such quests, quixotic as they may seem, have been persistent among Jesuits, who have sought salvation in the world as it is rather than in some utopia.

In January 1930 Talbot delivered a series of lectures in Baltimore under the auspices of Saint Ignatius Church, in which he explained his literary ideas. He opposed censorship and deplored the production of "pandering books," and the remedy he offered for these twin evils was a refinement of taste among readers. If there were no general market for objectionable literature, there would be no plausible argument for prior censorship. One concrete example of Talbot's approach is his defense of the sexually explicit novels of Sigrid Undset against the moralistic criticism of American Catholic reviewers. When films were still a suspect medium, Father Talbot worked to adapt the canons of literary taste and criticism to this branch of popular entertainment. He was, in a word, a skillful and dynamic doer in things literary.

Early at Campion House (the New York City headquarters of *America's* staff) he wrote a number of books that were favorably received. The first, in 1927, was a diamond-jubilee history of his alma mater, Saint Joseph's College. The next, a biography of Richard Tierney, was a tribute to his mentor, the Jesuit who more than anyone set the tone, breadth of interest, and standards of quality that raised *America* to national attention. There were also books of literary criticism and several anthologies.

By the early 1930s his organizational efforts and increasing editorial responsibilities made Talbot discontinue such time-consuming productions. He turned his attention to public affairs. In 1936 he was appointed editor in chief of *America* and assumed editorial responsibility for the *Catholic Mind*, a pocket-sized documentary and reprint magazine. A few years later he became the religious superior of the Jesuit community at Campion House.

Shortly after Father Talbot became editor of *America*, the Spanish civil war erupted, in 1936. He saw the division in that tragic event—to put his views in the simplest terms—as between a defense of "Christian and traditional Spain" and a determined assault by atheistic revolutionaries. Some of his fellow editors at other American journals of opinion did not agree; they characterized the forces supporting the Spanish republican government (in latter-day terminology) as freedom fighters, and they attacked the forces led by General Francisco Franco as agents of Fascist reaction.

In Father Talbot's mind this was misleading because it described "not two deadly enemies to world peace and human freedom [fascism and communism] but only one [fascism]." His aim was to redress the balance by emphasizing Communist activities among the republicans when the editors of other American journals concentrated only on the Fascist menace. It is a position hard to view objectively today because of the terrible aftermath in Europe. For the next three years, while Spaniards killed one another with assistance from Italy, Germany, Russia, and brigades of international volunteers, *America* emphasized the double threat and countered what it considered pro-republican propaganda as a matter of editorial policy.

Talbot's position at the time led him naturally into a major fundraising effort, with a sequel that occurred after he came to Loyola. In 1936–37 Americans responded with typical generosity to appeals for aid to war victims and orphans in the areas controlled by the Spanish republican forces. To help sufferers on the other side, Father Talbot organized the *America* Spanish Relief Fund in May of 1937. Over the next few years he raised almost $100,000, which was distributed not by rebel authorities but by the Cardinal-Archbishop of Toledo.[3] This succor would be remembered, and a decade later, while president of Loyola, Father Talbot was honored for his service to the Spanish people.

Because some of his ideas reportedly irritated church authorities outside the Society, he relinquished the editor's chair to John LaFarge in 1944. Talbot filled the days of his rustication with work on the saga of Jesuit missions and missionaries in North America; he projected at least five volumes to complete the story. Of these, he finished *Saint among Savages,* a biography of Saint Isaac Jogues, and *Saint among the Hurons,* an account of the life and martyrdom of Saint Jean de Brebeuf (published while Father Talbot was at Loyola). He was engaged in research at Georgetown when in 1947 he received news of his transfer to Evergreen.

His commitment to the historical project drew him away from Baltimore shortly after he arrived; for several weeks during the fall of 1947 he worked at archaeological sites in northern New York. By the end of November Talbot was confiding to a friend: "I have found Baltimore most cordial and charming. The life of a president is far more bearable than that of an editor."[4] He thought public relations his main responsibility at the college.

• •

Father Talbot set December 3, the feast of his patron saint, for the inaugural ceremonies, and the delay provided time for the necessary arrangements. The customary forms were observed—with two notable additions. The proceedings were broadcast over WMAR, Baltimore's first television station, which had begun regular operations only a few months earlier. James McManus (1943) provided the commentary. President Talbot credited the presence of the television cameras with getting the procession started almost on time and with imposing a welcome limit on the speeches.

To his predecessors and the faculty he pledged, "I shall expend whatever strength and talent God may endow me with, in a stubborn struggle to raise Loyola College to even higher peaks." He promised that the school would continue striving to make better men and citizens of its students. This could be done, he said, only if "we can make them aware that the human being does not stand alone," only if "we can show them the glint of the blinding splendor of God."[5] It was judged a satisfactory performance.

The other note of distinction was the recipients of honorary degrees. The award to Thomas Pullen, Maryland's superintendent of education and close associate of Father Bunn, provided an apt local connection. An ecclesiastical dimension was an honorary degree for one of Cardinal Spellman's auxiliary bishops. The third and most significant award was granted in absentia to "Evelyn Arthur St. John Waugh, A.B., Author" (as he was listed in the program). Even though British travel restrictions prevented Waugh's personal appearance, his name lent an international and literary color to the ceremony.

The award to Waugh was made for better reasons than merely the cachet that his renown brought. Between the two world wars Evelyn Waugh brightly limned the confusion and pretensions of Britain's upper classes with a pen dipped in acid. His novels had a loyal audience, and few paid attention to his becoming a Catholic until his publication of *Brideshead Revisited* in 1946. Although most reviews were favorable, some Catholic critics objected to Waugh's portrayal of a none-too-edifying family of English Catholic aristocrats. This reaction annoyed Waugh and bothered Talbot, who decided that an honorary degree from a Jesuit institution would stop the moralistic carping—and it did, to a remarkable extent. Grateful for this gesture, Waugh donated his much-emended proofs of *Brideshead Revisited*, bound in leather, to Loyola College.

The year after President Talbot's inauguration he got Waugh to agree to come to the United States for a lecture tour. *Life* magazine, in addition, engaged Waugh to do a lengthy piece on American Catholicism, which brought him to Baltimore in November of 1948. Father Talbot arranged for Waugh to meet the directors of important archdiocesan offices at a dinner in the Jesuit residence. Waugh asked to meet H. L. Mencken, and a luncheon date was set for November 24. What the meeting between these two conservative lambasters of sham and social pretensions might have produced must be left to conjecture, because it had to be cancelled. The evening before, Mencken suffered an incapacitating stroke. He would live eight more years but was never able to continue the literary activity that had brought him and his native city such fame. Saddened, Waugh left for New Orleans to continue his research on the article for *Life.*

After returning to Britain for the Christmas holidays, Evelyn Waugh came back to America in February of 1949 for his lecture tour. In Baltimore during the first week of February 1949 Waugh lectured at the Maryland Casualty Auditorium under the auspices of Loyola College. His subject was the spiritual odyssey of three other English converts: Ronald Knox, Gilbert Keith Chesterton, and Graham Greene. Some in the audience of more than twelve hundred were disappointed that Waugh did not include his own story, but the chapel fund was enriched by a small but welcome sum.

Waugh's essay on American Catholicism for *Life* magazine documented that America's colleges were successfully raising a proletarian group to the bourgeois level. This was a perceptive observation at the time, one that would eventually be supported by statistics on per capita income and become commonplace. Under Talbot's urgent tutoring, Waugh was impressed that even business administration majors in Jesuit schools had to take solid courses in philosophy and theology (Loyola's catalogue provided the concrete evidence).

Much later, when a selection of Waugh's letters was published posthumously, the author's comments on Baltimore and Loyola were of a piece with so much else he wrote his friends: witty, entertaining—and vicious only if taken seriously. He was, if these letters were to be believed, bored, unimpressed, and embarrassed.[6] Private correspondence is a genre for indulgence and posturing, even more for writers than for ordinary people, and Evelyn Waugh used this license with gay abandon.

• •

During the first year of President Talbot's brief term, Loyola's name was wreathed in athletic laurels. The campaigns of 1947 ended with Mason-Dixon Conference championships in golf, baseball, tennis, and basketball. A major contributor to the tennis and basketball victories was Jim Lacy (1949), back from the navy. In thirteen tennis matches he was undefeated. For his even more spectacular performance on basketball courts, Lacy was hailed by sportswriters and opposing coaches as "the greatest collegiate . . . shot" who was "excellent on defense and . . . an outstanding playmaker."[7] During his final three seasons the green and gray won seventy games and lost only twenty-seven. In 1948 and 1949 Loyola's team was invited to national tournaments after the regular schedule had been completed.

Because these games were played in Kansas City and Denver, many local fans could not afford to attend, but they wanted at least to hear how Lacy and Loyola were doing while the ball was actually in play. Bill McElroy, track coach and bookstore factotum, arranged for a telegraph and telephone relay—a setup used in those days for broadcasts of major league baseball games. An on-site telegraph operator transmitted the essential data to the studio, and over the clickety-clack of the telegraph key an imaginative announcer converted the sketchy information into a continuous and exciting commentary—as if he were actually watching the action. Vince Bagli successfully "re-created" the games for the nearly two hundred fans who came to the gymnasium on each occasion.[8] Although no national championships resulted, the team and its rooters knew that the Greyhounds were included among the country's best. Jim Lacy amassed one less than twenty-two hundred points as his career total—a national record that swelled the pride of students and alumni.

These events gave a notable lift to campus spirit. Student-veterans using their military training abducted a 500-pound bronze terrapin—totem of the University of Maryland—on the eve of an important basketball game. This, along with Lacy's dominance on the court, so demoralized the opponents that Loyola won—by two points. When Strom Thurmond, the Dixiecrat presidential candidate, came to Baltimore in 1948, a *Greyhound* reporter, David Maguire (1952)—arrayed in the uniform of a Confederate brigadier—interviewed Thurmond. Even *Time* thought that stunt worthy of notice. More staid students organized a veterans' club, another for married students, and also a baldness anti-defamation league. Although the last secured a properly qualified moderator, Father Edward Hauber, it was denied recognition by the student council because of its genetically determined requirements for eligibility.

Loyolans, with their peers on other campuses, shared larger concerns. The movement to form a national students' organization received major impetus from the spectacle of Communist domination of the International Students Union meeting in Prague in the summer of 1946. It took more than a year for America's student leaders to convene their own founding convention, and Loyola was represented at that meeting. In the judgment of Loyola's delegate, Dudley Shoemaker (1948), the work of the convention went smoothly and special issues pressed by Communist-oriented delegates lost to the will of the majority.

Without weakening its general support for the new National Students Association, Loyola's spokesmen demurred to certain provisions in the draft of an academic bill of rights. Loyolans objected to a claim that a college education was everyone's due and preferred a clause asserting the right only for those who were qualified. Some might sense an elitist or even racist overtone in this amendment, but for its authors it was merely a truism. They wanted to halt the dilution of the intellectual content of higher education (a concern similar to that propounded again at this time by Robert Hutchins).

Loyola's delegates wanted to limit an assertion that the right to free speech and a free press was absolute. They were not objecting to the freedoms of the First Amendment, but they thought the immaturity of students and circumstances of some educational institutions, especially private, religiously affiliated ones, justified modification of these rights. How many and what other schools registered similar amendments? Too few to change the draft. But their failure to get their way did not inhibit the co-operation of Loyola's students with the National Students Association. They had made their point. The student council acted as campus liaison for this organization and also for the National Federation of Catholic College Students.

One prewar institution—hazing—was significantly curtailed in September 1947. The sophomore class by an overwhelming vote refused to inflict the old rules and penalties on freshmen. When the freshmen arrived on campus a year before, their numbers and the high proportion of veterans among them had intimidated their would-be tormentors into suspending the twenty-year-old custom. Generously, the sophomores were unwilling to inflict what they had not suffered; anyway, veterans were exempted (a prudent rule), which meant that only the few freshmen directly from high school could be subjected to hazing.[9] Hereafter, initiation into the Loyola community consisted merely in wearing pup caps, ostensibly till after victory in the rugby game; but after a week or two even the callowest newcomer knew that he could be doff this symbol of servitude without fear of reprisal.

• •

Some campus spirits reacted against this press of numbers and sought to form exclusive associations. One group started operations around the middle of 1945 under the title the Foamy Twelve. As its membership increased and improved, it chose the classier name of the Esquire Club—derived, no doubt, from the men's magazine of that name. Near the end of 1947 another group that eventually numbered about thirty formed the Evergreen Club and rented quarters in downtown Baltimore. The attraction of these groups, beyond conviviality, was the availability of beer at a time when school rules forbade the beverage at campus affairs and state law prohibited possession by anyone under 21. Whether or not it was a good law, it was the law, and the college believed it could not act as a shield for violations.

The Esquire and Evergreen clubs made no effort to secure recognition from the student council. A *Greyhound* editor pointedly reminded Evergreen members of Loyola's aversion to such organizations. The only perceptible result was an article a month later detailing the clubs' aims, membership, and location. This and a few incidental notices in the paper and the yearbook suggest that an informal modus vivendi had been achieved. When the original members of these clubs graduated they retained control and failed to recruit any new members. As a result they ceased to be a factor in campus life, although they continued their activities for a few more years.[10]

These examples inspired imitation in a form that became a longtime annoyance for the college and an amusement for some students. John Corcoran (1950), before the war as a student at Baltimore Polytechnic Institute, had joined a fraternity named Zeta Eta Theta and become a chapter leader. On returning to Loyola from military service, Corcoran and some friends decided to organize a fraternity. Sometime during the process they inquired about affiliation with Alpha Delta Gamma, a national fraternity active at several Jesuit institutions, but nothing came of this because every chapter in Alpha Delta Gamma had to secure recognition from its school. That was no more forthcoming from the authorities at Loyola in 1946 than six years earlier. The deans no longer claimed that social fraternities were unknown on Jesuit campuses; nor did they urge that these fraternities existed mainly in schools in the Midwest, an area noted in the order for other deviations from tradition. There was simply no practical way for Loyola to provide a faculty moderator for an off-campus chapter house—and the college would not recognize any student organization without a moderator.

Unwilling to accept this refusal as final, Corcoran and company formed an autonomous fraternity using the name Zeta Eta Theta, although it had no connection with the existing organization. The members, mostly veterans, saw themselves as exercising their natural right of association. Beyond refusing recognition, the college authorities took no action against the organization or its members. Unlike the Esquire and Evergreen clubs, the fraternity restricted membership to enrolled undergraduates, and this gave it a continuing life. Upon graduation its members could join an alumni association, but the chapter and its house remained under the direction of those who still were students.

The fraternity worked persistently, though quietly, to resolve its relationship with the college. They invited faculty members, Jesuit and lay, to the chapter house in hopes that the experience would alter opinion. The founding brethren were identified in the 1950 yearbook, apparently to convince the college community that they were a responsible group. Their successors again sought recognition and again failed. An even stronger and more explicit policy against social fraternities was written into the Loyola catalogue, but did not inhibit this and a few shorter-lived brotherhoods.

As a result Zeta Eta Theta took on all the glamor and attraction—especially to adolescent males—of a clandestine association. Like other such bodies, it claimed a much earlier origin—not 1946 but before the war—and hinted at membership and support from distinguished alumni. The members' claims of power in student affairs and elections made fellow travelers of some campus politicians, but few who sought the most prestigious offices risked formal initiation into the brotherhood.

Zeta Eta Theta offered prospective recruits the customary mumbo-jumbo rituals, swank parties, and a file of term papers and helpful information on courses, teachers, and tests. Periodically, neighbors of the chapter house complained to Loyola after a particularly noisy affair, and college authorities answered by disavowing any responsibility. When circumstances forced the fraternity to move, it merely involved a new set of neighbors in the trials of living next to an active and occasionally boisterous group of young men.

Over the years Loyola authorities tried various strategies to undermine Zeta Eta Theta. Some meetings of the history academy were held off campus in the homes of members, and this permitted serving beer without institutional responsibility. School dances were scheduled to conflict with the major affairs of the fraternity, and the most popular local bands were engaged. These maneuvers severely limited the fraternity's income—for a time.

In 1959 the arrival of a much younger group of Jesuit administrators occasioned a thorough review of Loyola's policy and experience with social fraternities by a faculty committee. The complete membership list, constitution, and house rules of Zeta Eta Theta were carefully studied, along with the academic and disciplinary records of the brethren. The faculty committee found ample grounds for recommending against recognition of Zeta Eta Theta, but suggested procedures and norms for establishing a social fraternity if other students wished to organize one.[11] That proved not to be the case.

When, like other states, Maryland lowered the drinking age to 18 in 1974 and Loyola erected dormitories and expanded its on-campus activities, the main attractions of fraternity life disappeared. Whether the undergraduate chapter of Zeta Eta Theta survived could not be determined even by inquiries among its alumni, who continue to cherish their fraternal memories and associations.

· ·

There was plenty of activity on campus in the late 1940s. The limited income of most students and a shift of fashion made name bands for proms passé. Attention went instead to tuxedos, corsages, and boldly striped taffeta strapless evening gowns. Christian Dior's "new look," which lengthened skirts for streetwear, evoked only a brief satirical piece in the *Greyhound* on the shortening of men's trousers—replete with picture.

In May of 1947 the junior sodality, led by Joseph A. Sellinger (then a Jesuit scholastic, but who seventeen years later would become president of Loyola College), sponsored a new feature in the campus social whirl: the Queen's Ball. Even though it was quite successful, at least one older Jesuit grumbled against diversion of the sodalists to worldly activities. Over the years sponsorship changed several times, until the college's 125th anniversary celebration, when it became the President's Ball. As it started, so it still is the most elegant evening of the campus year.

Dramatics, always a major campus activity, was especially lively and imaginative in the postwar years. For a while the Mask and Rapier Society offered a monthly fare of old film classics (*The Count of Monte*

Cristo, The Prisoner of Zenda) and dances. Its revival of the play *Every-man* was staged among the columns of the Baltimore Museum of Art, and it was televised. George Herman (1949) sparked and produced a variety of shows. In collaboration with Don Swartz (1950) he created several memorable revues. One, *Marelyn* (not a damsel but the name of the state in local patois), sang the praises of:

> Beautiful skies of velvet blue,
> The smell of lilacs
> Fresh with dew.
> That's Marelyn! Mah Marelyn!

"Moko" Yardley, cartoonist for the *Sun,* again obliged with drawings to enhance the program and patiently bore another stage incarnation of himself. After graduation, Herman and Swartz pursued productive careers in show business.

The *Greyhound,* no less than dramatics, had its stars. Even as his father presided over Baltimore City's affairs as mayor, Thomas D'Alesandro III (1949) worked on the campus newspaper. After graduation he became president of the city council and later mayor. The editor in 1948–49 was Frank Gallagher (1949), who later served in the state legislature and became a leading figure at the Maryland constitutional convention of 1968. Only his early death, some thought, prevented his winning the highest public offices at the disposal of the voters.

During Gallagher's term as editor he commented vigorously on a variety of subjects. When the state legislature failed to dismantle the system of discriminatory racial laws, he denounced the inaction as "idiotic political suicide." Frank Gallagher was sure that President Truman's reputation was enhanced by his defense of civil rights and would outshine the memory of his Dixiecrat opponents. An "Old Grad" objected to such comments from a mere student and urged the *Greyhound* to restrict itself to campus doings and problems.

Joined to young Gallagher's liberalism was his even more vehement opposition to the Communist menace. In December of 1948 he urged his fellows to demand that President Truman take effective action to prevent the fall of China to the forces led by Mao Tse-tung (now written *Mao Zedong*). Two months later he worked to rouse support for the Ober Act, which had been submitted to the voters of Maryland in a referendum. This law, like others passed in neighboring states and by Congress, required all public employees and candidates for office to affirm their loyalty to the United States and to deny any connection with or support of subversive organizations. Even as President Truman proclaimed his Fair Deal for America's needy and poor, he instituted a loyalty-security program in the executive branch of the federal government. Whether or not internal security warranted such a dragnet, it protected Truman's flank from political attack and helped justify his appeals for vastly increased foreign aid, ostensibly to stop the spread of communism.

However incongruous some of these actions and positions may seem today, then many Americans were alarmed at the advances of what seemed a unified and threatening force. In 1948 Czechoslovakia lost the last semblance of democracy when its Communist leaders suppressed all other political parties. At the same time the forces of Mao Tse-tung were steadily advancing southward in China. West Berlin was blockaded and supplies reached that beleaguered city only through a British-American airlift. Americans wanted to avoid the mistakes of the Munich period and to stop aggression before it developed irresistible momentum. The voters of Maryland approved the Ober Act, and thereafter every public employee and candidate had to sign a long, complicated oath affirming loyalty and denying subversive intent or activities.

Only a public sense of a massive external threat with internal ramifications can explain the shift of opinion from the 1930s. Then, the *Greyhound* and newspapers at other Jesuit schools had resolutely opposed the imposition of loyalty oaths; now, at least at Evergreen, the editorials supported such requirements. Who even thought to recall what had been written only ten years earlier? The anti-communism crusade of the late 1940s and early 1950s was not solely a concern of Catholics. Maryland Masons and members of Kiwanis and other Baltimore civic clubs and trade associations were equally vigilant and active against the menace they perceived.[12]

On March 31, 1949, President Talbot lent himself to an event that was meant to help secure the inclusion of Spain in the North Atlantic Treaty Organization (NATO). Communist successes in Europe and China had shocked the leaders of the United States and western Europe into form this alliance against the Soviet Union. As the negotiations were getting under way Talbot accepted the Spanish government's offer of the Order of Isabella—a nineteenth-century decoration awarded to those outside Spain who resisted revolutionary influences. Sponsors of the ceremony, held at the Sheraton-Belvedere Hotel, included George Radcliffe, a historian and United States senator from Maryland; Thomas Pullen; Gerald Johnson, an author and journalist with solid liberal credentials; the Reverend Arthur Kinsolving, a well-known

Protestant Episcopal minister; and Isaiah Bowman, president of the Johns Hopkins University.

While Talbot expressed his gratitude for the honor, he confined the rest of his acceptance speech to general historical observations. William Casey, a prominent member of the Baltimore establishment, struck a more urgent, contemporaneous note. On the authority of Winston Churchill and James Farley, he insisted, "Spain is an essential link in the North Atlantic Security Pact" and inclusion of Spain was equally vital to "our planning for world peace."[13] The only public objections to this whole affair were made by the Young Progressives of Maryland, who picketed the hotel entrance, and the editors of the Johns Hopkins *Hullabaloo.* This Baltimore event had no effect on the course of diplomatic negotiations, probably because it was so isolated. Spain was not accepted into NATO, but instead signed a bilateral defense arrangement with the United States.

· ·

The growing and active student body at Loyola required enlargement of the faculty, and this meant more laymen. A few years before Talbot's accession to the presidency several noteworthy additions to the lay teaching staff occurred. In August of 1945 John Sweitzer (1928) was brought back from New York to revitalize the business administration and accounting programs in day and evening divisions. For several years the business law courses were taught by Francis Burch, an alumnus (1941) and a graduate of Yale Law School. As his legal practice became more demanding, Burch stopped teaching in the 1950s; eventually he was repeatedly reelected attorney general of Maryland. Edward Kaltenbach (1942), while he attended the graduate school at the Johns Hopkins University, joined the faculty in 1946 to reinforce the program in classics.

On the eve of Father Talbot's arrival a change was made in the history department. Edward Doehler (1930), after nearly two decades at Evergreen, transferred to Mount Saint Agnes, which in 1947 revived its four-year collegiate program. In his stead came Harry Kirwin, who soon secured a doctorate from Fordham and became a leading force in promoting the scholarly and professional elements of faculty life. For the students, he was one of the most popular teachers ever in the employ of the college.

A preeminent force at Evergreen, from his arrival in 1939 till his retirement over thirty years later, was Father Thomas Higgins. Philosophy was his field, ethics his specialty. Because of what he taught and how he counseled the students, and what he wrote in his textbook *Man as Man,* a generation of Loyola students had to face the ultimate questions of life's meaning and of how to live. His influence extended far beyond the campus, because his ethics text was adopted at many other institutions. Father Higgins, a serious man, never developed the personal rapport with his students of an Ooghe, but his immense influence is attested by all.

Heading the faculty was a genial new dean, Father Matthew Sullivan. As already noted, President Talbot relied entirely on him to manage the daily workings of the college. Sullivan had a large and difficult responsibility for which there was no precedent or experience among the Jesuits. Thirty-two of the nearly fifty regular teachers were laymen. A similar or greater imbalance was developing at most Jesuit institutions. Its cause, in the judgment of Father Albert Poetker, formerly president of the University of Detroit, was not so much the tide of veterans as the earlier decision to separate Jesuit colleges from their secondary schools. This committed the order to serve a much larger number of students at the collegiate level with no prospect of any significant increase in the number of Jesuit teachers. By 1946 the figures made it clear that Jesuit schools would have to rely more heavily on lay instructors than ever before.

This realization met an adverse reaction within the Society. Some feared the schools would lose their distinctive Jesuit identity; others feared loss of control to the lay faculty. Even Father Poetker, who urged his brethren to accept laymen as an "*essential* and *permanent*" part of their institutions, including in the departments of philosophy and theology, nevertheless considered it congruous to have Jesuits as department chairmen and as deans of the college of arts and sciences.[14] Any other arrangement raised the specter of secularization—the path already traced by many leading institutions founded by Protestant denominations. Such concerns may well have prompted one of Loyola's trustees to secure amendment of the graduation ceremonies. Degrees were no longer awarded in the name of "the President and Faculty," but by the "President and Associated Professors," that is, the president and trustees—all Jesuits.

Although membership in scholarly organizations had been encouraged at least since Father Bunn's term, this encouragement did not extend to the American Association of University Professors, because of that organization's promotion of academic freedom and collegial governance.[15] Membership in AAUP was considered incompatible with the distinctive spirit of Jesuit education. One teacher, queried at his hiring interview about membership in the AAUP, thought an organization that inspired such concern was worth investigating, and after he investigated he joined. It was a movement toward professionalism that other faculty members also found natural, but no serious effort was made to organize a chapter on campus for fifteen years.

. .

The main objective of Father Poetker's 1946 address to the Jesuit Educational Association was to focus attention on what was needed as a result of accepting laymen as a permanent presence on Jesuit campuses. Since it was necessary to recruit lay teachers and they could no longer be considered temporary, he urged the institution of formal rank and tenure policies and provision for decent retirement. In this he was merely publicizing what had already been mandated by Jesuit authorities in Rome.[16] As always, these directives were left to local circumstances and judgment.

Dean Matthew Sullivan's activities reflected these ideas in many ways. He engaged the whole faculty in the process of drawing up a statement of objectives. Various facets of the grading system and attendance requirements were discussed, voted on, and implemented in accordance with the faculty's expressed will. Father Sullivan drafted a short statement defining Loyola's rank and tenure policy, distributed via department chairmen for review before it was provisionally put into operation in 1948. This original statement has remained the basis of Loyola's policy and although it has been much amended and elaborated, there has been no need to change any provision substantially.

Nevertheless, there was a limit to Dean Sullivan's progressivism in regard to both faculty and students. He was responsible for the good order of the school and he zealously promoted what he saw as Loyola's best interests. He had to contend with a large student body and a faculty that had grown too quickly for the normal process of socialization to have its inevitable effect. As a result, Sullivan tended to assume functions previously performed by others.

The limitation in Dean Sullivan's thinking became evident during the discussions of a faculty retirement program. He appointed a small committee with two lay faculty members and a Jesuit, the college treasurer. After careful study the committee unanimously preferred the individual contracts offered by Teachers Insurance and Annuity Association (TIAA), an agency started years before with Carnegie seed money specifically to provide an economical retirement for American academics. For some time after its establishment the Carnegie foundation would not deal with any religiously associated institution, and Catholics suspected that its objective was to secularize American higher education.[17]

By the time the question of the Carnegie-sponsored TIAA retirement program arose at Loyola, the earlier restriction to non-church schools had been abandoned and Dean Sullivan was probably not aware of the original basis for wariness about Carnegie projects. Such attitudes, however, have a way of lingering even when the factual basis is no longer known or applicable. Dean Sullivan's objections to TIAA were entirely pragmatic. It permitted a young instructor to begin his career at Loyola, gain experience, and then leave, taking not only his own contributions to the retirement program but those of the college.

To professors everywhere portability is one of the main virtues of the TIAA retirement program, but Father Sullivan thought it would reward those least loyal to Loyola and create a constant drain on the college's funds.[18] He apparently could not envision the other side of the coin—that well-qualified teachers might be attracted to Evergreen precisely because they could retain membership in a nationwide retirement program.

In addition to whatever apprehensions he had about the academic mainstream, there must also have been at work the deeply imbedded Jesuit preference for institutional autonomy within the order and freedom from all agencies outside the order. The dean's attitude was not unique. TIAA had recently been rejected by the authorities at Saint Louis University for many of the same reasons adduced by Sullivan, and only four of the other twenty-five Jesuit colleges in the United States had signed up with TIAA.[19] Even many publicly supported colleges and universities preferred locally established retirement programs.

The dean and the committee each submitted their recommendations to President Talbot, who passed the matter to the board of trustees. After considering a presentation by the treasurer (speaking for the committee) and by Dean Sullivan, the board chose the latter's proposal. Thus, a locally structured retirement program, rather than TIAA, was established for the faculty at Loyola College.[20] The teachers —at least laymen—were not pleased with this outcome or impressed with the procedure by which the decision had been made, but they saw no alternative but to accept it. There were, furthermore, no obvious signs that Father Sullivan's cordial relations with the faculty had been disturbed by this affair. He was still personally popular with them.

• •

As the management of Loyola's affairs became more routine, Father Talbot began preliminary work on a history of the college. He collected what few documents remained in the office files, numbered the minutes of the board of trustees, and had significant portions transcribed. He discovered a cache of old registers, deans' diaries, and other records that had been brought from Calvert Street to Blakefield when Loyola High School moved to that location.

Father Talbot wrote to his predecessors and other former administrators asking them for brief accounts of the events and issues with which they had dealt. The return was meager—often merely a reference to someone who could supply a more detailed narrative. Talbot prepared an outline of what was to be a rather small book, like his earlier history of Saint Joseph's College in Philadelphia. These preparations suggested that Loyola College and its alumni would have a well-written commemorative volume about the time of the centennial in 1952, but events made this an unrealized hope.

Meanwhile Father Talbot presided over the expansion of the evening division and the inauguration of graduate programs. His associate in this was Father John Wise, who came to Evergreen at the end of World War II. Wise was a new breed of Jesuit. In addition to the traditional education and a doctoral degree from the Gregorian University, he had taken graduate courses in education to qualify for a second doctoral degree. Accrediting agencies were less willing now to accept a Jesuit's long education as the functional equivalent of a doctorate, and the additional work required for a doctoral degree from the Gregorian University did not seem satisfactory anymore. Wise supplemented his education with four years as dean of freshmen at his alma mater, Georgetown. Early in 1946 he was named dean of the evening school— as it was called then.

The breadth, drive, and style of the man may be deduced from two unrelated incidents. Instead of dribbling the library budget out on various individual works, Father Wise as director of the library assigned the money one year to the purchase of Migne's *Patrologia,* more than three hundred untranslated volumes of writings by early Greek and Latin fathers of the church. A Catholic and liberal arts college library, he thought, should have this treasure for use by faculty and students, even if at first only a few might dip into it. In another episode, he sought to have the general rule against alcoholic beverages at student affairs suspended for his much older clientele. His colleagues on the committee of executives, however, would not agree to any modification, probably because they feared it might rouse the veterans and older students in the day division to ask for similar privileges.

Wise was quite successful in expanding the scope of the division for which he was responsible. The loosely organized evening courses were formally organized into undergraduate degree programs: one in business administration and the other a catch-all bachelor of science in social science with concentration in economics, education, history, political science, or sociology. To increase the cohesion and visibility of these programs, Dean Wise began issuing a regular catalogue in January of 1946. He started an undergraduate summer-school program in 1949, at a time when the day division was unable to make such offerings because its students were still on a three-year cycle and took regular courses during the summer.

The main and enduring objective of Dean Wise was the establishment of a high-quality graduate program. He carefully prepared his proposal for a master of arts degree in education, counseling, or school administration. The requirements were the usual ones, and Father Wise placed particular emphasis on the preparation of a research thesis. This, he thought, would save the program from ever becoming a vehicle for those educators mainly interested in accumulating credits to qualify for salary increments. There were already ample opportunities for that in the region. What Dean Wise wanted was something more distinguished.

Not everyone on campus supported Wise and his plans. Although in these years Harry Kirwin regularly taught evening classes, he thought that "the Evening School should be moved downtown to Calvert Street," where if the old building were air conditioned it "would make money hand over fist." At Evergreen, he said, "the night school and day school climb over each other's back."[21]

How many others agreed with Doctor Kirwin is unknown, but in 1949 Father Wise was unexpectedly transferred to the University of Scranton. He was appointed dean—indicating no loss of esteem for his abilities on the part of his Jesuit superiors. His office at Loyola was briefly filled by Father Arthur North, who had left Baltimore as an army chaplain in the midst of World War II and had most recently served as dean at Scranton. After a couple of years and the departure of Talbot and Sullivan, Wise returned to the college. This circumstance suggests that some unresolved difference among them had played a role, however slight, in the exchange with Scranton. Upon his return in 1952 Father John Wise resumed work to broaden and deepen the graduate program for eighteen more years, until his retirement in 1970.

• •

Signs of a growing estrangement between President Talbot and a significant group of Jesuits showed in connection with the building of the chapel. As it had been to his predecessor, the alumni memorial chapel was for Talbot the center of his building program, and he was diligent in raising the necessary funds. Early in 1949 the two-acre remnant from the old Guilford project was sold to a developer. This brought in $25,000, which some (Father Bunn among them) thought too low a price. Talbot's willingness to sell may be explained by the need for capital, the absence of other offers, and the continuing drain of property taxes. With this sale the last physical tie to the pre–World War I plan to move Loyola and Saint Ignatius Church to University Parkway was severed.

By the end of September 1949 President Talbot was ready to start the chapel. Even before the contracts were signed he arranged for a ground-breaking ceremony, with the new archbishop, Francis Keough, doing the honors. A few days later the college trustees met to decide how to handle the bidding. This resulted in an unusually detailed series of motions, the full import of which cannot be deduced from the text. The vote on the final motion found eight trustees opposed and only one, presumably President Talbot, in favor. The cause for this decision was not recorded and it is not otherwise apparent (nor could any memories be plumbed for its recovery). The important point is the division evident between President Talbot and the rest of the trustees.

The next meeting of the board was held three weeks later. After the reading of the minutes of the previous session, a member who had not been present moved to expunge the final vote. This motion failed, with only three votes in favor (presumably the mover, Father Talbot, and one other trustee who had changed his mind) and seven opposed. Talbot then "made a statement to the effect he regretted any misunderstanding . . . and that, if it were in his power, he would repudiate the action of the trustees."[22]

Though such differences had undoubtedly occurred before (given the effects of original sin), it was extraordinary to record the matter so explicitly in the minutes of the board. A longtime friend and confidant learned later from Talbot that a source of difficulty was his reluctance to "attend wakes . . . [and] alumni clubs . . . and to make appeals for more funds."[23] Some on the other side, however, perceived a man who had imbibed the ways and attitudes of New Yorkers and who could not accept any suggestion based on Maryland or Baltimore experience—a familiar and widespread local plaint. It had become an unhappy situation for all involved.

Naturally enough, notice of these differences did not spread outside the circle of those directly concerned. The bulldozers set to work on November 10, 1949, and, depending on the weather, construction was to be finished in a year. Shortly before its completion the chapel was described by Paul Gaudreau, son of the architect (quoting Ruskin), as a "prayer in stone." Gothic styling had been chosen to harmonize with the existing campus buildings. The chapel's long, narrow nave is sited along an east-west axis, with a shorter crossing transept at the foot of the sanctuary. Inside and out the architects stressed soaring lines and verticality to inspire the lifting of minds in prayer. Instruction in the Catholic faith and its history is provided in large stained-glass windows at the four terminals of the nave and transept. Along both sides of the nave, at a higher level, there are sixteen windows depicting major Jesuit saints. At eye level, seven small windows represent historic shrines from around the world dedicated to Mary. It is as impressive as a church built for an upper-class neighborhood parish.

The signature-statue, above the front facade, is Our Lady of Evergreen, Queen of Peace—donated by Fulton Oursler. He was a friend of Father Talbot's, a Baltimorean, and senior editor of the *Reader's Digest*. Royalties from his most famous book, *The Greatest Story Ever Told*, were the source of his gift to Loyola. The chapel's builder, John McShain, voiced the judgment of virtually all observers: "Up until the present time, including the Jefferson Memorial [another of his projects], the Loyola Chapel is the most beautiful building we have ever built."[24] Formal dedication was reserved for the start of Loyola's centenary, September 15, 1952—over which Father Talbot did not, as expected, preside. He was transferred two years earlier.

• •

The climax of Talbot's brief term at Evergreen was not the centenary celebration but an even more significant event. Blacks with the required academic credentials—including students from nearby Morgan State College (now University)—had been enrolled in evening courses during the war and in graduate programs since their inception. This made it possible for the college to claim a tad more virtue than all but four of the twenty-six institutions of higher learning conducted by

American Jesuits. In the figures on black enrollments published annually in *Social Order,* only Saint Louis University, Loyola University (Chicago), the University of Detroit, and Fordham (all much larger institutions) had more black students than Loyola. Even so, the number for all Jesuit schools was small—amounting to no more than one percent in 1946–47. It would be pointless to offer any comparison with other American schools, since few had much to note with pride on this subject.

In 1946–47 the issue was raised directly at Evergreen. Two Josephite priests sought President Bunn's assistance for several young black men who wanted to attend a regular Catholic college. His reply saddened them. He feared "that his faculty and alumni would be violently opposed to black students" attending regular undergraduate classes. After the installation of President Talbot the Josephites returned, and the new president's response was, "I was waiting for you to come." He would personally take the job of dealing with faculty and alumni.

A year later the theoretical discussion had to be applied in a concrete case that presented certain technical difficulties. Charles Dorsey, formerly a student in a Josephite seminary, applied for admission to Loyola. Dean Sullivan would not approve him because his qualifying courses had been taken at schools not accredited by a regional agency such as the Middle States Association. Dorsey, whose Catholic roots went back for generations, was not deterred; he was determined to get a Catholic education. Another exchange between Josephites and Jesuits ensued; Dorsey renewed his application and finally was accepted.[25]

Father Talbot announced this fact (without naming the student) at an alumni banquet in April of 1950. As one might expect, the reaction was mixed. Some accepted it with more or less grace. Others were anxious and confused. A few parents thought to ask their sons if they wished to transfer to another school. None of the students wanted to leave Loyola, but for some this decision probably reflected little more than a determination that "if anybody's going to go, it'll be Dorsey." As it was, he stayed and participated freely in all the school's social activities. When he accumulated sufficient credits he transferred to the University of Maryland Law School. After being admitted to the bar Charles Dorsey joined Maryland's Legal Aid Bureau (of which John O'Shea [1924] was co-founder) and eventually rose to become its executive director. He has remained an outstanding and exemplary member of the Catholic church and in 1983 was awarded an Andrew White Medal by Loyola College.

The announcement of Dorsey's admission to Loyola attracted wide attention. In 1947 the Sidney Hollander Foundation began giving an annual award for outstanding contributions "toward the achievement of equal rights and opportunities for Negroes in Maryland." The award jury for 1951 cited Loyola's action, not merely for admitting blacks (others had claims on priority) but for fully integrating minority students into both its curricular and its extracurricular activities. The presentation was made by the president-emeritus of Morgan State on television. [26] However, one righteous blast does not quell a social evil—even at Loyola. Five years later a decisive sequel involved Charles Dorsey's brother-in-law.

The difficulties between President Talbot and the trustees were resolved during the summer of 1950 when three veteran members resigned and Dean Sullivan was transferred. He was replaced at Evergreen by Father Joseph Drane, an able troubleshooter for the Maryland province. What he found was a lack of systematic attention to the predictable decline in enrollments. The wave of veterans had crested and there was no replacement for them on Loyola's immediate horizon. Fewer students meant lower income, and this would necessitate cutting faculty, staff, and other budget items. No contingency plans had been prepared— even before the eruption of the Korean police action near the end of June, which made such planning even more imperative.

At Evergreen there was a sense of drift. Father Talbot seemed unable to rise to the occasion even in his capacity as rector of the Jesuit community. In these circumstances he tendered his resignation and was replaced before the start of the new school year. He returned to Georgetown, where he resumed work on his history of the early Jesuits in North America, but no additional volumes were published. Father Talbot reappeared at Evergreen on September 15, 1952, to deliver the sermon at the solemn dedication of the chapel. A year later, on December 3, feast day of his patron saint and the sixth anniversary of his installation as president of Loyola, Francis Xavier Talbot died of pneumonia. [27]

17

An Interim

Loyola's new president and rector, Father Thomas Murray, was almost the same age as his predecessor and also from Philadelphia, but he had lengthy and varied experience in academic administration. He taught at Loyola in the late 1920s, when students dedicated a yearbook to him. Father Murray was then sent to the Philippines, where among other accomplishments he established a school at Zamboanga. On his return to the United States in 1936 he served for five years as dean of the school of business at Fordham, and almost ten years as regent of Georgetown's foreign service school. It was from that post that he was transferred to Evergreen, where his term lasted from 1950 to 1955.

· ·

Few doubted Murray's administrative abilities, but some thought he was less at ease in dealing with people. Apparently he was not a relaxed, gregarious man. Even his Jesuit colleagues, it was said, had to submit formal requests for interviews. In temperament, and even in appearance, he resembled Joseph Canning, Loyola's president during the mid-1930s—another period of retrenchment. There was no formal installation ceremony.

Only an abbreviated celebration of Loyola's centenary now seemed appropriate. Yet there was more than enough activity to mark the hundred years of the college's association with Baltimore and Maryland. The year opened with the formal dedication of the chapel (as already noted), on September 15, 1952. Father Murray used the occasion to indicate that he planned no additional building but would continue to concentrate on scholastic matters—the dean's domain. Three weeks later a plaque, designed by Albert Sehlstedt (1919) and executed by

Henry Berge, was unveiled at the City Hall Plaza near the spot where Loyola College first opened its doors.

This anniversary was commemorated with a long, loud parade. Among the marchers were units from the various armed services, drum and bugle corps from neighboring schools and associations, a full contingent of Shriners, Jewish War Veterans, Mercy Hospital nurses, Knights of Columbus, and many other well-wishers. It was a community celebration reviewed at the city hall by church and civic notables.

An editorial in the *Sun* succinctly summarized the paper's view of the significance of Loyola's hundred years of service to the region.

> The point is that Loyola College has always taught
> essentially as and what it taught a century ago. In a
> sense, it has outlived some educational extremisms. No
> single system or philosophy can serve our various people
> in this complex age. But Loyola maintains in 1952, as
> in 1852, one of the perennial wealths of Western
> education and Western civilization.[1]

Because there was neither the time nor the will to produce a formal history, Father Joseph Drane, the dean, published a brochure that covered the ground tersely and with many pictures. It projected the image of an up-to-date, vital, patriotic, and devout institution with deep roots in Baltimore and Maryland.

Much the same impression could be derived from a tabulation of the careers pursued by Loyola's alumni in 1952 (Table 17.1). There were significant differences between this group the smaller group that existed at the fiftieth anniversary. Four times as many alumni were now on the rolls, and the proportions in the learned professions of law, medicine, and sacred ministry had declined. At the golden jubilee these learned professions had accounted for almost half the alumni, but fifty years later they represented less than a quarter of the total. What had not changed was the large proportion who were involved in business or industry—not surprising in a city like Baltimore.

• •

Table 17.1 was derived from the alumni directory prepared for Loyola's centenary. The main impetus for this project came from Frank Boland (1894), a native Marylander who successfully combined his knowledge of law, hotel management, and public relations into a solid career. After World War II he and his wife because owners of the Hotel

TABLE 17.1   Careers of Selected Loyola Alumni, c. 1902 and 1952

| | Numbers | | Percentages | |
	1902	1952	1902	1952
Doctors	105	182	19	8
Lawyers	74	160	13	7
Clergymen	80	139	14	6
Businessmen	164	886	30	39
Government officers	10	210	2	9
Teachers	7	132	1	6
Accountants	11	114	2	5
Graduate students	17	104	3	4
Engineers	8	82	1	4
Writers	11	35	2	2
Military officers	0	210	0	9
Retired	0	27	0	1
Miscellaneous	68	0	12	0
Total	555	2,281	99	100

Commander in Cambridge, Massachusetts. Their hostelry opened onto the green where George Washington took command of the Continental army, and this circumstance inspired Boland to collect Washington memorabilia.

Now in retirement and without children, Boland undertook a number of good works and among these was the development of his alma mater. From 1950 till his death seventeen years later Frank Boland made substantial donations to the college, but this was only a token of his broad concern. From Father Talbot's time onward, he and Loyola's presidents were constant correspondents. In many of his letters he included newspaper clippings of worthwhile ideas to rouse the alumni into becoming a major source of support for the college and to broaden the planning horizons at Evergreen.

His first concrete suggestion was an alumni directory. He saw this as a basic tool for all later developments. He would not finance the project alone (though he could have) but insisted on establishing a partnership with like-minded graduates. Boland's constant theme was the superiority of co-operative activity and persistent involvement over solitary, unconnected grand gestures.

The finished typescript of the directory went to the printer in the fall of 1952. It provides a compendium of what Loyola's alumni were doing and who they were. Almost half pursued further study, and most of these earned graduate and professional degrees. About 30 percent of the alumni who were awarded advanced degrees between 1903 and 1952 got them in law. This proportion is quite a bit lower than that cited in a contemporaneous study attributed to Catholic colleges in general. It found the "production of lawyers from Catholic institutions" to be "phenomenally high."[2] Twenty-four percent of Loyola's alumni with advanced degrees got them in the health professions, and 12 percent got an unspecified Ph.D. or M.A. More than 80 percent lived around metropolitan Baltimore, although one or more could be found in each of the other states but five and in eight foreign countries.

The year 1948 was used to refine family statistics to take into account that graduates after 1948 had not time enough to establish their families, and indeed more than half of them were still unmarried. Twenty-three percent of the pre-1948 alumni were single, even though much fewer than half of these were clergy or religious. Another 13 percent was married but childless, and the remaining 64 percent averaged only 2.7 children per family—not much different from the national norm, and hardly in line with the usual assumptions about fertility among a substantially Catholic population. Unfortunately similar data were not collected for the next or later editions of the directory, so no comparison is possible.

This record, in some measure, may reflect instruction during the final semester of senior year when the required course in religion centered on the sacrament of marriage. Only Catholic seniors were required to take it. Earlier it had been the special domain of Father Ooghe, but from 1948 to 1965 the guide through this vital territory was Father John Scanlan. He was a cheering Irish presence on campus—in the classroom, directing a dramatic production, and at Loyola Night. His students described him as a "veteran performer . . . [and] a conscientious teacher and a dedicated priest" in the the 1961 yearbook.

If the family statistics for one class (1956) are typical of others, then the profile in the 1952 alumni directory was later repeated. The married members of the class of '56 and their wives averaged 2.4 children at their tenth class reunion but 3.3 offspring by their silver anniversary. In collecting the data the class secretary (something of a wag) asked graduates to list the names of their children; to the third blank space he attached an asterisk, noting: "If you've passed this point you should have stayed awake during Father Scanlan's lectures." Father Scanlon probably had explained what Father Higgins wrote in his ethics text: "The intention of avoiding conception is not itself wrong," although the only canonically licit methods for controlling conception were either total abstinence or confining "intercourse to a sterile period."[3]

• •

During the early 1950s institutional indices at Evergreen presented a mixed picture. Enrollments in the day sessions fell more severely at Loyola than at Johns Hopkins or the University of Maryland. The bulge of veterans had passed and there were barely six hundred students attending undergraduate day classes. The drop in students was accompanied by a 20 percent reduction in the full-time faculty, but the student-teacher ratio improved from 20:1 in 1949 to 17:1 in 1955. Solvency was managed by raising tuition from $350 in 1950 to $500 five years later and by the more than $140,000 in donations and legacies received during President Murray's term. These increments permitted an increase in financial assistance to the students from 5 to 10 percent.

About twenty students a year were aided through a new on-campus work program. Unlike the now-defunct National Youth Administration assistance, this involved work not for the college but for the federal government. In 1952 Loyola signed a contract to calculate the trajectories of various kinds of projectiles tested at the nearby Aberdeen Proving Grounds. The work was explained in general terms when the Aberdeen Project (as it was called) was first announced. The memory of these explanations quickly faded and later students and faculty supervisors, unsure what comments were permitted, became reluctant to talk about what they were doing. In effect, their work became secret—and subject to the glamor and suspicion that accompany secrecy.

Some of the projectiles on which they worked were models with unusual configurations. When news and pictures about the nation's space program and the various space capsules, including the moon lander, were published, the capsules proved to be very much like some that Loyola students had worked on earlier. The habit of secrecy, however, did not permit them to claim any credit. When the project was started Frank McGuire (1954) was the student supervisor; he later returned to Loyola to become its first lay dean.

During the early years faculty responsibility in the Aberdeen Project was shifted several times because of departures from the campus. Finally supervision was assumed by Charles Jordan (M.A. 1954), a reliable and congenial teacher of Spanish who had been a bomber pilot during World War II. The income for the students and faculty was not much. The students got $1.50 an hour at the beginning, and their income depended on how many photographs were delivered for processing. Nevertheless, the Aberdeen Project provided a source of money for twenty years, till the nation's expenditures on space exploration were curtailed.[4]

A major factor in maintaining Loyola's financial stability was the evening and graduate programs, with Father William Davish as dean from 1952 to 1957. Enrollments in the evening classes remained constant at about six hundred, with occasional increments due to special offerings such as the multifaceted description and analysis of the Baltimore community presented in 1953. City leaders were recruited to share their knowledge of the social, economic, and political character of Baltimore. Among the subjects covered was the rich and varied ethnic character of the city—an exotic subject for that period.

Graduate registrations increased, but rather slowly, from 66 in 1949 to almost 110 six years later. One factor in this development was the introduction in 1951, while Father North was dean, of a new master's degree in education. North, unlike his predecessor Father Wise, was more concerned with adding to enrollments and income. This did not require a research thesis but only completion of thirty credits in graduate work and was meant to attract those who wanted to qualify for a salary increase. The announcement of this new program was reported to the Middle States Association by the president of a neighboring institution, who thought this was "something to watch."[5] No immediate inquiries were made, because Loyola was to come up "for reevaluation in the next two or three years" and that would provide better opportunity for reviewing the graduate offerings at the college. Tuition for the evening and graduate courses accounted for almost one-third of the school's total income.

• •

Another way the college sought to become more attractive to potential applicants, especially for the day sessions, was to establish a Reserve Officers Training Corps (ROTC) unit. At whatever high school he visited during these years, Father Vincent Beatty (now back at Evergreen) was asked several predictable questions—among them whether Loyola offered ROTC. This interest among young Marylanders was due not to any latent militarism but to avoid a peacetime draft instituted in 1948. Anticipating the drastic effect this might have on Loyola, the Jesuit provincial recommended that it apply for an ROTC unit—a reversal of the position taken in the 1930s, when a similar suggestion was rejected by provincial authorities. Times had changed and wartime experiences mitigated fears of outside interference.

No action was taken until after Fathers Murray and Drane took office. By then the situation had become even more urgent with the outbreak of the Korean War. As soon as they could manage, Loyola's new president and dean sought the support of Lansdale Sasscer, an influential Maryland congressman. The initial cost of setting up the unit was not small and included a deposit of $25,000 for uniforms and a grant of $2,500 for relocating the first group of instructors. At the normal pace of the army bureaucracy it took two years—until September of 1952—to process Loyola's bid.

As the centennial year began at Evergreen, a unit of the Reserve Officers Training Corps began operating on campus.[6] Thereafter and until the late 1960s all freshmen and sophomores were required to take ninety hours of instruction and drill each year. The military staff identified likely prospects for advanced training and encouraged them to continue through the remaining two years. These advanced cadets got a heavier schedule of instruction, and for this they were paid twenty-seven dollars a month (during summer camp their compensation nearly tripled). This was not much, but it provided pocket money at a cost that many students found acceptable.

The presence of ROTC brought noticeable changes in campus life. Haircuts were obtained more frequently and hair was uniformly short; shoes were diligently shined, especially for Wednesday afternoons when in good weather the playing field resounded with the commands of would-be officers drilling their platoons. In bad weather the new auditorium under the chapel echoed with equivalent duty.

Most students bore this burden only as long as required. Their general attitude was evident in their reference to the Reserve Officers Training Corps as "rot-see"—and in comparative statistics. At the height of the Korean War 210, or 9 percent, of the college's living alumni were in the armed services. Ten years later, before the escalation of the Vietnam War, that figure dropped to 66 or 2 percent. Alumni were obviously willing to do their duty, but few saw the military service as their life's work.

· ·

Loyolans, like all Americans, were made anxious by the invasion of South Korea. President Truman, determined not to repeat the mistakes of the generation that faced Nazi aggression, dispatched American forces to that peninsula and obtained a United Nations' sanction for what he disingenuously called a police action rather than a war.[7] Students were asking again whether it was wiser to enlist now or to get their degrees first. Other voices raised the question of recompressing the college curriculum to three years. Several Loyola instructors and students were recalled to duty. Stories of casualties again began to appear in the *Greyhound.* Was this the beginning of World War III? Would the atom bomb be used again?

Fathers Murray and Drane repeated the advice of their predecessors: continue your studies as long as you are permitted; the country needs well-trained leaders not only to fight the war but for the more complicated tasks that will inevitably come afterwards. Dean Drane waited for the draft requirements to be defined before he committed Loyola to an accelerated program, but he was ready to revive what had been phased out only a year before. The way the draft was administered made that unnecessary.

The Korean War, pitting as it did the United States against Communist forces, fueled the nationwide argument about subversion, security, and the need to mobilize against the threat of communism. A number of public figures vied to lead that crusade, but Joseph McCarthy, United States senator from Wisconsin, emerged as the symbol and spokesman of those demanding extirpation of every trace of communism and any other unwelcome idea that might taint American life and thought. In their attitudes toward McCarthy, Catholics like other American were divided. Their support exceeded that of Protestants by only 7 to 9 percent but a few leading Catholic figures, wary of the demagogue, avoided challenging him, and this reticence was taken by liberal intellectuals as indicating a basic sympathy for McCarthyism.[8]

The emergence of McCarthy as a national figure was facilitated by attention focused on two Marylanders: Alger Hiss and Owen Lattimore. The former, a rising figure in the State Department, was convicted of perjury in 1949, and the latter, a professor at the Johns Hopkins School of International Relations, became the central figure in McCarthy's proof of subversion in the State Department. A Senate investigation into McCarthy's charges against Lattimore was chaired by Millard Tydings of Maryland, who got a majority of the committee to agree that McCarthy's proof amounted to nothing more than "a fraud and a hoax." This curt dismissal led to the notorious "back alley campaign" in the senatorial election of 1950.[9]

How did the members of the Loyola community view the anti-

Communist crusade? They responded with the same diversity and in the same low key in which they had responded to earlier fevers that wracked the American body politic. There were McCarthy partisans. Edward Fenlon, a lay professor of philosophy, denounced Tydings on television for the "indignities" heaped upon Joseph McCarthy.[10] The students also responded variously. The *Greyhound* staff was inclined to accept court testimony that Harvard was "a leading proving ground for Communist leaders," but it continued to be skeptical about Senator McCarthy. A clue to campus opinion appeared in a September 1954 poll when, by two to one, incoming freshmen were inclined to favor McCarthy—much to the dismay of the campus newspaper. The views of the other students were not sought. No one, however, registered anything but laughter in response to Loyola Night skits lampooning the anti-Communist hysteria and an investigation conducted by "Senator Joe Blowhardy."

The result in November of 1950 was the election of a Republican to replace Senator Tydings, of a Republican governor, Theodore McKeldin, who however avoided hysterical rhetoric about the Communist threat, and of three Republican congressmen. In the next national election none of the candidates in Maryland devoted attention to the Communist issue, although it took several more years before this fever died down nationally. A perceptive historian of this episode concluded that the anti-Communist movement in Maryland "was more intense . . . than in most states, but it also faded rapidly and actually did less damage to liberty and liberalism than might have been expected."[11]

A revival of the generally temperate way of looking at things was evident in how Loyolans regarded the various issues and incidents of the Korean War. A congressional attempt to hold up grain shipments to the starving people of India until India's neutralist government converted to anti-communism was denounced as inhumane. Arguments for and against diplomatic recognition of Red China were outlined in one editorial printed in the *Greyhound.* Another denounced a nationally prominent monsignor who had missed the whole point of intercollegiate debating. The national topic was the diplomatic recognition of Red China, and the monsignor insisted that it would be unconscionable for any Catholic to present an affirmative case. Formal diplomatic ties with the new Chinese government were not unthinkable—at least not for some Loyola students. A random sample of student opinion found no support either for trying to end the war with atomic weapons or for

General Douglas MacArthur after he was dismissed by President Truman.

One student defended the proposition that a preventive war in Asia was unnecessary and not likely to be effective. Communism was an ideology and thus could only be defeated "by better ideas more widely known."[12] Furthermore, the combined land and population mass of China and Russia offered no prospect of victory—only endless war and internal disintegration for the United States. Few on campus were willing to rush to Armageddon. Like many of their fellows, they "liked Ike" (Dwight Eisenhower) and saw in his election to the nation's presidency in 1952 what appeared to be a welcome surcease, if not a solution, to the problems and issues that bedevilled the country and the world.

• •

There was a more immediate threat to Loyola and other private institutions in the region during these years. The University of Maryland, located near the District of Columbia, for a variety of reasons wanted to establish a branch to which Baltimoreans—about one-third of its regular clientele—could commute daily. A branch in or near Baltimore would slow the growth of the main campus, which university demographers predicted would exceed thirty-five thousand in twenty years if no action was taken. Such a branch would expand the university's sphere of operations, and that would mean a formidable, tax-supported competitor for the schools already established in the city. Even the alumni and partisans of the state teachers' college at Towson objected.

Loyola served as the center for coordinating the brief for Baltimore's private institutions. At the 1953 alumni banquet, President Murray questioned the need for a branch of the University of Maryland near the city. Loyola and other private schools could easily absorb the potential applicants from the area at less cost than would be needed to open a new campus. Other states, like New York, were coping with similar problems by including both private and public institutions in their educational planning. (Maryland in 1971 would follow this example.)

A few months later this message was reinforced during commencement exercises at Evergreen. The speaker, Stewart Macaulay, provost of the Johns Hopkins University, avoided too direct an allusion to the issue but offered a cogent argument couched in theoretical terms: "There have been a few cases in recent history which point up the danger of total government control of higher education. One of these was Nazi Germany; the other is Soviet Russia."[13] In addition to vigilance

against such a development, Provost Macaulay called for increased support for private institutions from a variety of sources including the public treasuries. A similar message was smoothly incorporated into the
citation for a doctorate of humane letters, *honoris causa,* awarded to
Governor Theodore McKeldin on the same platform.

This effort succeeded—at least for a while. The report, prepared
under the direction of Thomas Pullen (no stranger at Evergreen), recommended expanding two-year community colleges and the existing
state teachers' colleges as the preferable means of alleviating pressure on
the University of Maryland. Ten years later, the University of Maryland
Baltimore Campus was finally established and located about as far from
Towson as is geographically possible.[14] There, by formidable and persistent efforts, it has become a recognized asset to the community, and
university spokesmen claim it has not yet realized its full potential.

. .

Under Father Drane's direction, a number of changes were made in
academic practice at Loyola. Terminology was amended but not sim-
plified by dropping the degree of bachelor of philosophy and replacing it
with a bachelor of science in social science—already available to evening students. This alteration was prompted by a desire to adopt generally accepted forms without dimming the aura historically associated
with the bachelor of arts degree from a Jesuit school. Grading was
changed to conform to the practice at most Jesuit and leading American
institutions. Since the Civil War, numbers had been used to signify the
quality of a student's work in a course, but these were replaced now by
letter grades: A, B, C, D, and F. The letters in turn were convertible
into numbers (4, 3, 2, 1, and 0) so the course grades could be averaged
in a form accepted by graduate schools. One familiar component in
evaluating a student was dropped. After twenty years, a senior thesis
was no longer a general requirement for graduation—much to the relief
of students and of many faculty members.

Alumni and students continued to gather laurels during Father
Murray's term. In 1951 William Rogers, Jr. (1948), was elected national
president of Alpha Sigma Nu, the Jesuit honor fraternity. Thomas Lalley
(1947) was among the first to benefit from the new Fulbright program
for using United States assets in foreign countries to support advanced
studies. He was followed by George Sills (1952) and by Hal Sanks
(1955), who was also offered a prestigious law scholarship by New York
University but joined the Society of Jesus instead. A decade before the
establishment of the Peace Corps and similar programs of assistance,

John Connor (1948), already a lawyer, became a co-missionary of the Jesuits and went to Jamshedpur in India, where he taught labor relations.[15]

More pertinent to Loyola's development was the addition of new faculty members in the natural sciences and the humanities. Father Frederick Koehler (1941) became head of the mathematics department and, together with Georges Farre, an ebullient Frenchman with wide-ranging interests, revised the course offerings and standards in mathematics and physics. To the English department were added Frank Voci, a medievalist, and John Toland, who for a time directed dramatics. Shortly after theater-in-the-round was embraced by some Baltimore amateur companies, Loyola's Mask and Rapier Society produced *The Hasty Heart* in this innovative format.

More pertinent to Loyola's development was the addition of new faculty members in the natural sciences and the humanities. Father Frederick Koehler (1941) became head of the mathematics department in the evening division) appeared in the regular cast, ushering in the dawn of a new era. For the next twenty years female roles were filled by students from the College of Notre Dame and from Mount Saint Agnes College. Only Baltimore's Paint and Powder Club retains an allegiance to all-male casting, but even it has admitted women to roles in a few of its productions.

• •

Loyola College broke new ground in its efforts to educate the Baltimore public on the nature and uses of atomic energy. Father Vincent Beatty of the chemistry department organized a course on the use of radioisotopes in the teaching of science. News accounts identify it as the first such course offered anywhere in the country. The instructors were physicists and chemists with the Atomic Energy Commission or on the faculties of the Johns Hopkins University and the University of Maryland; another of the lecturers was the redoubtable Admiral Hyman Rickover. To reach an even larger audience, a summary presentation was televised by WBAL. A year later Loyola, in cooperation with the University of Maryland, the Sunpapers, and the city board of education, sponsored an atomic energy exhibit in the Fifth Regiment Armory.[16] The following year (1954) Father Beatty effectively suggested to the Baltimore Association of Commerce that it sponsor a conference on industrial applications of atomic power.

As a student counselor, Father Beatty was attending the "college nights" held at various high schools to acquaint the students there with the programs offered at Loyola and with the college's general character. He was often asked three questions: Did Loyola have ROTC? Did it have an engineering program? Was there on-campus housing for students? His report of the first query had already strengthened the decision to establish an ROTC unit at Evergreen.

Beatty's interest in an engineering program was encouraged by Father Edward Hauber, his local mentor, and Edward Donnelly, an engineer and a member of Loyola's lay advisory board. In conversations with Father Beatty, Donnelly deplored the narrowness of his own education, which slighted the humanities. Beatty initially thought to combine training in business administration with training in engineering, but such a program—though offering something unique—would have been complicated to achieve and might not prove attractive to the many students whose primary interest was technical. So Father Beatty revised his plans to emphasize engineering. What he finally outlined was a curriculum of mathematics, physics, and allied subjects within the traditional Jesuit frame. Although it did not qualify a student as a particular kind of engineer, it provided a broad and solid foundation on which any of the major engineering specialties could be erected with additional study.

How much would such a new program cost and where was the money to come from? President Murray approved the program but suggested that extramural support be found for it. With Father Bunn's assistance and encouragement, Beatty explained his plan to the executive director of the Jesuit Educational Association, who helped prepare a budget and supporting exposition. One fact that Beatty used to gain financial assistance was that only 10 percent of the members of the local engineers' club ordered fish on Friday. There was, Father Beatty deduced, a dearth of Catholic engineers in Baltimore, and this became part of his presentation to the Raskob Foundation, which had been organized to support Catholic activities. Beatty estimated the total cost of his program as $100,000—mainly for additional faculty members. The college was responsible for one-fifth of this sum, and the foundation was asked for a remaining $80,000. Father Beatty's presentation was successful and the new physics-engineering option was inaugurated in September of 1955.[17]

His attention was drawn to smaller projects. His contribution to Loyola's centennial celebration was a directory of those graduates who had majored in chemistry or whose later careers brought them into this field. Father Beatty produced a consciousness-raiser for the alumni and the college community, but he included data in the directory that made it useful also to dispel the stereotype of Jesuit education as antipathetic to the natural sciences. Three hundred of Loyola's twenty-two hundred alumni were listed, and a significant number had completed or were pursuing doctoral studies—and even more were involved in master of science programs. Their advanced degrees were earned at Columbia, Johns Hopkins, Ohio State, Michigan, Yale, Fordham, Georgetown, and Notre Dame. When a few years later *Sputnik* roused fears that America was neglecting education in the sciences, Father Beatty was proud to publicize a federal study that listed Loyola College among the top 10 percent of American colleges and universities whose graduates earned science (not including medical) doctorates. Indeed, Catholic colleges in the 1950s did better in encouraging advanced study in the sciences than in any other field of scholarship, although the overall ratio of Catholics in graduate schools was low.[18]

Father Beatty chafed at the restrictions imposed on Loyola's development by its twenty-acre campus, and his interest in enlarging the campus showed the direction of his thought. Earlier, when planning directly concerned itself with only a few hundred students, the campus seemed large enough. But a growing and more diverse student body required more and more varied facilities. Father Talbot, early in his term, had inquired tentatively about the unoccupied tract on the northwest corner of Cold Spring Lane just across Charles Street from Loyola, but he did not actively pursue the matter. In 1953 Beatty attempted to revive this project with an appeal to Father Bunn. Nothing immediately resulted from their correspondence, and the proposal seemed doomed when shortly thereafter a group of two-story apartment houses called Charleston Hall was built on the tract. These would be acquired by Loyola in 1979 and converted into student residence facilities.

The association of Fathers Beatty and Bunn led to a consequential meeting early in 1954. The older Jesuit invited his confrere to a dinner where he could chat with a small group of Baltimore's civic leaders who were friends of Bunn's and who were also on Loyola's lay advisory board. They were William Casey, Henry Irr, and Felix Goldsborough.[19] No record survives of their conversation or of the impression Vincent Beatty made on the others, but it must have been very favorable, because these three men would significantly aid the college's development during the next nine years, when Father Beatty served as Loyola's president.

At most the change of leadership had been advanced by only a year.

Father Murray was near the end of his canonical term as rector, and some of his closest associates detected signs of lassitude or exhaustion. With Loyola College facing the Middle States Association's new accreditation process in a year or two—a matter fraught with considerable anxiety in view of the unfavorable report on the University of Maryland recently made public—a firm and consistent administration was essential.

On June 24, 1955, the Jesuit residence was severely damaged by fire. Had a decision not already been made (likely it had been), it was certainly reached within a day or two after the fire. On July 10 Father Vincent Beatty officially became president of Loyola College with a full agenda demanding his immediate attention. At the age of 42, he had the competence, energy, and stamina for the responsibilities he assumed. The students had presciently registered their approval earlier by dedicating their 1955 yearbook to Father Beatty. They saw him as "a typical small college teacher, a man who believes in close student-instructor relations."[20]

18

New Leadership

The cause of the fire in the Jesuit residence was never determined; even where it started was not pinpointed. Suspicion settled on the old furnace. A fireman told a reporter that it was "an old house, tinder dry"; the fire spread quickly inside the walls and burst through the roof on the north side of the building. Flames and smoke shot more than twenty-five feet into the air, creating an updraft and intensifying the blaze. As eight alarms were sounded, almost a score of fire trucks and other equipment rushed to the campus, as did a crowd of spectators. It took two hours to bring the fire under control. By then the roof had collapsed, injuring twelve firemen (none was disabled). The timing of the fire—at noon on a Friday after the regular school year had ended—could not have been more fortunate. Summer classes continued without interruption.

There was great damage to the building and its contents. Flames, smoke, and water had splintered and streaked the plaster, buckled the walls and flooring, and ruined the bedding, books, and clothing of the Jesuits—and knocked out all the water and electrical systems. Except for the south wing, constructed during Father Bunn's term, the residence was uninhabitable. Books and periodicals from the library, stored in the basement, were soaked with water. The most regrettable loss was a considerable collection of items on Baltimore assembled by Henry Watts, a spry factotum long associated with the college. Those beyond salvage were tossed onto a pile of rubble; the others were carried to the gymnasium and spread to dry. Records of scholarship endowments stored in the president's room were lost to the flames and eventually had to be reconstructed. One thing that survived in Father Murray's room was the original charter of Loyola College. Although flames reached within a few feet of it, there was no scorching or other damage.

• •

In addition to the usual preparation for the start of classes in September and planning his formal installation, Father Vincent Beatty had to oversee the restoration of the Jesuit residence. Temporary quarters were immediately found among the Jesuits at Loyola High School, and by the end of the summer one section of Charleston Hall across Charles Street from the college was rented for most of the community. The south wing of the residence, as soon as it had been thoroughly aired, quartered seven of the company and an office for the new president and rector.[1] The fire, devastating as it was, had not entirely evicted the Jesuit community from Evergreen.

Many people offered help immediately and in several forms. The most touching offer was a mite collected by three young neighborhood girls, which they delivered a day after the disaster. Pending final settlement, the insurance company (Lloyd's) advanced $50,000 to begin the recovery. The cost of restoring the structure and replacing the losses in furniture, clothing, personal effects, and books had to be documented, and this began even while rubble was being carted away. The settlement totalled almost $460,000, and final payment was received only four months after the fire.[2]

Historians, although not without compassion, view disasters a bit differently than other people. The burial of Pompeii under volcanic ash and lava left a historical record similar to a candid photograph. Such catastrophes freeze action at an unexpected moment and offer an uncensored record of how people actually lived. So it was with the fire at Evergreen. The insurance claims provide a description of the domestic life of the Jesuit community. This was not opulent. Individual claims for all categories of loss—furniture, clothing, typewriters, and the like—averaged only $700. The few higher ones were mainly for books or, in the case of the community minister, for photographic equipment. This picture of modest living is corroborated by a more general figure. The annual living expense for each Jesuit in 1955 as recorded in the house accounts was $3,500, and with allowance for postwar inflation, that figure had not risen during the previous ten years.

Loyola's new president and rector saw the fire not as an obstacle to be overcome but as an opportunity to be used. In addition to plans to make the residence habitable again, he had blueprints drawn for a new wing at the damaged end. This would hold a community chapel, small parlors for interviews, a more accessible presidential office, and living quarters for the additional Jesuits who would be needed for a much

larger student body. Father Beatty never formally announced an enrollment goal, but the working figure in his earliest official correspondence
was a day registration of one thousand. That was a nice, round number
which seemed ultimately possible if not immediately realizable. He
probably was unaware that a student body of that size had been President McEneany's dream when the college first moved to Evergreen.

Beatty was fully aware, however, that the executive director of the
Jesuit Educational Association had given the green light for expansion
of Jesuit schools.[3] Father Beatty wanted to use the occasion of the fire to
enable college representatives to answer affirmatively the third of the
common questions asked by applicants—whether or not Loyola had on-
campus living facilities. He asked Paul Gaudreau to prepare sketches for
a building to include a dormitory, offices for student activities, a cafeteria, and a dining room for the lay faculty. This three-story structure
was to be erected on what then was called the northern parking lot,
now the site of Maryland Hall.

It was impossible to fit so large a facility on the campus as it was
then measured, so Father Beatty applied to the owners of the neighboring tract—the Johns Hopkins University—to purchase the needed
land. For several months correspondence was exchanged with the university on this proposition. At the same time Father Beatty was writing
to the president of the College of Notre Dame about a complicated arrangement involving all three institutions. This project did not succeed
immediately but these discussions when they were resumed several years
later had important consequences, which are described in the next
chapter.

Beatty planned to finance building at Loyola with a mortgage from a
federal agency. In 1950 it had become national policy to offer long-
term, low-interest loans to certain institutions as a means to provide
needed shelter and employment. The negotiations with the government proved quite difficult and were ultimately unsuccessful. Playing
neither Santa nor Scrooge, the agency informed President Beatty three
days after Christmas of 1956 that it had disapproved Loyola's application
because the proposed facility was "ineligible" under law as recently
amended.

Loyola's plans were snagged by the Eisenhower administration's policy to limit federal government activity in areas where it believed private resources adequate—a familiar Republican preference. Because
the apparent snag was the amount requested by the college and not the
request itself, Loyola submitted a new application two weeks later for

less money to rebuild the Jesuit residence. This also proved unsuccessful. Loyola therefore relied on local resources and benefactors to complete this essential project about a year later.

The exercise was not as futile as it might seem. What he learned during this encounter with the federal government President Beatty put to productive use when the college applied in 1958 for a loan to erect a student union building. In this brief episode, Father Beatty demonstrated his energy and adaptability—and his reticence in giving early public notice of his plans or ideas, a familiar trait of Jesuits of that period and earlier.

• •

Much of what Vincent Beatty eventually accomplished depended on his personality and character. At first encounter, he was impressive not so much for an aura of power as for his warmth, honest concern, and relaxed manner. His refinement and sense of proportion kept him from moving too far ahead of the group with which he was dealing. At least one senior lay faculty member groused about his soft handshake. He would have preferred a sterner and more aggressive approach than was Beatty's habit. Although a native New Yorker, Beatty had come to appreciate the softer tone and slower rhythm of life on the shores of the Chesapeake.

Everybody found him easy to talk with, and he listened. Father Beatty was chagrined if he could not remember someone's name—which happened rarely. As a religious superior, his brethren (even the most senior) judged him a rock of common sense with courage to act in difficult situations. He was, in the words of one who knew him long and well, "a happy man; involved in the human situation and acutely aware of other people."[4]

Beatty's family and nurturing contributed to the development of his attractive personality. He was born in Brooklyn a few months before the outbreak of World War I, the youngest of a vigorous group of brothers and sisters. In 1932, he entered Georgetown University in the midst of the Great Depression. At graduation he was honored as the best company commander in the Reserve Officers Training Corps.[5]

A few months later he went to Wernersville to join the Society of Jesus, but he was so sure of a brief stay that he did not bother to pack a suitcase. The rector of the novitiate suggested that he stick it out at least until he got his cassock—and later, at least until after the long retreat. The completion of Saint Ignatius's Spiritual Exercises resolved Beatty's doubts about his vocation. His quiet presence made Vincent Beatty stand out in a crowd so much that when he was assigned to Evergreen, a community prophet confidently predicted he would eventually be appointed rector.

His Jesuit training followed the usual pattern—making allowances for wartime conditions. He studied at Innisfada near Manhasset, Long Island. From there he was sent to Spring Hill in Alabama to continue his studies in philosophy and the natural sciences. From 1942 to 1944 he taught chemistry to a dwindling student body at Loyola, and three years later he was ordained at Woodstock. He returned to Evergreen in 1949, again to teach chemistry and to serve as a student counselor.[6] His lay colleagues found him one of the most approachable and sympathetic members of the Jesuit community; the similar judgment of the students was cited in the previous chapter.

Even before his formal installation, occasions were found by the publicity staff and Henry Irr, chairman of the lay advisory board, to introduce Loyola's new president and rector to the Baltimore community. Beatty and Loyola College were the subjects of extensive coverage in the *News-American*. He was interviewed on a local radio station, WFBR, and presented on WMAR-TV with presidents of five other Maryland colleges and universities on the panel. This publicity may not have made Beatty's name a household word, but it promoted early recognition among a large audience.

It is not clear why November 3 was chosen for the inaugural ceremonies, since it marked no event in Father Beatty's life and is a blank in the church calendar. If there was a rationale, it seems to have been merely general convenience. About eleven o'clock the program began. Fifteen college and university presidents were among almost two hundred academic delegates. Civic dignitaries included Governor Theodore McKeldin, Baltimore's Mayor Thomas D'Alesandro, Jr., and former Senator Herbert O'Conor (1917). Honorary degrees were awarded to Archbishop Francis Keough, Charles Ghequiere Fenwick (1908), a leading scholar in the field of international law, Admiral Hyman Rickover, and Edward Flanigan, a Baltimore contractor and philanthropist. Georgetown University conferred an honorary doctorate on Father Beatty, and its president, Edward Bunn, gave the main address.

In his own remarks, President Beatty quickly went through the traditionally appropriate references. He proposed "to adhere to the century-old principles and traditions of Loyola College . . . [and] make them more operative in the life of our nation and especially in the free state of Maryland." For his keynote he chose a quotation from an eminently respectable source. Abraham Flexner, an outstanding American educator, had praised the practical value of what others derided as useless knowledge. Flexner was convinced that "the ceaseless quest for theoretical and speculative learning" was paradoxically often "productive of the greatest good." After illustrating this point with several instances from the sciences, President Beatty stated his conviction "that this type of 'useless' knowledge, intrinsic to liberal education, is the most effective for a happy and useful life."[7] Indeed, this pursuit of learning beyond mundane concerns always had been the core of the education offered by Loyola.

The newspaper coverage of Father Beatty's installation was full; radio station WFBR recorded his inaugural address for replay that evening.[8] It was an excellent beginning and displayed Loyola's new president to advantage. The style was contemporary, the rhetoric spare. The allusions were understandable and attractive to a wide audience. The deft but clear emphasis was on Loyola's roots and long service in the Baltimore and Maryland community.

• •

Throughout his nine years, President Beatty administered with an apt blend of direction and flexibility. The lines of authority were defined, and he was the center of Loyola's operations. However, he expected other officers to perform effectively and avoided intervening in their areas of responsibility. He anticipated the best from everyone and worked quietly but effectively to elicit it. He relied on his colleagues to deal sensibly with items on the agenda, even in his absence. Studies have produced evidence of two general predispositions among leaders. Some are results oriented; others are people related. Beatty's style was more the latter. He certainly produced notable and desirable results but Vincent Beatty was also concerned with "achieving good interpersonal relations."

The success of his relaxed approach was facilitated by the indoctrination administrators had undergone during the preceding ten or more years. They had been practiced in the budgeting process so thoroughly that President Beatty could now vigorously apply the rules. He normally, though not invariably, attended the budget committee meetings—where he participated as a colleague. Another officer, not the treasurer, served as chairman. Reports and preliminary drafts were discussed in detail. The natural tendency to defer to the person responsible for a section of the budget was subordinated to a determination to question not only budget items but general policy. The fact that final drafts represented practical plans collegially created made it easier to secure formal approval from the board of trustees. After the operating budget had been adopted, there still remained traditional, informal procedures for securing funds for worthwhile projects that arose unexpectedly. This fiscal discipline was further strengthened in 1957 and thereafter with annual audits by an independent firm of both college and Jesuit accounts. There are no earlier records of such a procedure.

A previously established but not fully applied management aid was the college statutes drafted in the early 1950s by a small committee of senior Jesuits in response to a general suggestion from the order's authorities in Rome. The statutes codified and elaborated existing practices and principles and were in effect a written constitution, stating generally who was supposed to do what. However, their status remained vague until Father Beatty responded to a question during a faculty meeting preparatory to accreditation. The college statutes were in force, he said, and should be used to describe the organization of the college. Recommendations for amendment were equally in order, as far as he was concerned.

The statutes attended little to committees. Although the committee of executives, or administrative board, established earlier had been clearly defined, no other agencies received such treatment. There were references in the text to a committee on rank, tenure, and salary and an academic council, but nothing beyond their names appeared. These brief notations, however, laid the foundation for later developments.

Father Beatty was directly responsible for initiating an active committee on rank, tenure, and salary. The original rank and tenure policy statement drafted in 1948 referred to a five-member group, but no one had been appointed during the intervening eight years. Decisions continued to be made through informal consultations among the president, the deans of the day and evening divisions, and the treasurer—all full-time administrators and Jesuits. In the late summer of 1956, however, President Beatty appointed Father Robert Hoggson, dean of the day division, chairman of this committee. The other members were Father William Davish, dean of the evening and graduate divisions, Father John Scanlan, professor of psychology, Doctor Harry Kirwin, professor of history, and Doctor Edward Kaltenbach, professor of classics. They were by any standard among the most able and judicious people available.

Some might consider the composition of the committee less than ideal because it still contained administrators, all the members were appointed, and there was a Jesuit majority (but not seriously dispropor-tionate to their numbers among the faculty). The composition of the committee had in part been dictated by the need that members not per-sonally benefit from their appointment. The noteworthy advance over previous practice was that most members were experienced teachers still in the classroom. Hereafter, the process of promotion and the granting of tenure included judgment by peers, not merely administrators, even though the final decision remained with the president.

The need and propriety of peer review is not well understood—in or out of academia. It is very different from the performance appraisal process employed in business and industry. There managers evaluate their subordinates and their decisions are reviewed only by higher man-agement. The business-industry model is inappropriate to college teaching because the process of education is not properly analogous to an assembly line or a sales campaign. In such endeavors quantitative norms may be readily applied because soon enough effectiveness may be judged by whether or not profit is produced.

The development of understanding and maturity in students, how-ever, is not so readily judged or measured. The less easily quantified norms applied in judging the performance and potential of teachers in quite disparate disciplines require a substantial involvement of experi-enced peers. A closer though admittedly weak analogy would be peer evaluation in other professions. (The more complicated and much mis-understood matter of academic tenure will be discussed later, in the context of when the policy came up for its next major revision.) The establishment of a formal rank-and-tenure policy and peer review at Loyola, more or less contemporaneous with those of the University of Maryland, antedates their appearance at many other Catholic, even Jesuit, schools, though such a policy and peer review had been recom-mended by the order around 1948.[9]

In addition to dealing with specific cases of promotion and general salary patterns, Loyola's new committee undertook a revision of the pol-icy statement. Doctor Kirwin, a lawyer by earlier training, sought to delete verbiage, to clarify the vague, and to secure adoption of signifi-cant amendments. He raised the issue of applying the policy to Jesuits and laymen alike, and all agreed. He was, however, alone in seeking review of ranks assigned to Jesuits during the previous seven years. (That is, since the policy was nominally in force.) His colleagues were unwilling to reconsider decisions already made by others, but Kirwin's initiative and independence did not diminish their respect for him. Later he would raise questions about the composition of the committee, but he did not hurry action on these matters. This first revision of the rank-and-tenure policy took more than a year. The committee actively solicited and got suggestions from the rest of the faculty and submitted the revised policy directly to the board of trustees, which promptly approved it.

• •

President Beatty lost no time in beginning to plan for Loyola's longer-term development. Relying on the advice of Henry Irr, chairman of the lay advisory board, Beatty decided to engage the American City Bureau, which enjoyed a high reputation in planning and fund raising. It had recently aided the campaigns of several Jesuit institutions in the Midwest. In Baltimore, it had effectively served Johns Hopkins, the Community Fund (predecessor to the United Way), and others.

Basic to the process was identifying Loyola's main objectives. The immediate goals were to be enlargement of the campus, augmentation of faculty salaries from increased endowments, and erection of a student union building and an engineering and general classroom facility. Neither at this point nor later in President Beatty's term did on-campus housing for students again figure prominently in his planning. This was not because he had entirely abandoned the idea, but only because he and his Jesuit colleagues considered it less than essential in his limited term and a potential source of difficulty in the college's relations with alumni and Baltimore.

No firm dollar goals were mentioned during the initial discussions or in the presentation to the advisory board in February of 1956. Nevertheless, round sums of three or more millions were offered as estimates. Even more would be needed later for a new library, an addition to the gymnasium (which had been mentioned during President Talbot's term), and more endowments. After a probing discussion, the advisory board unanimously recommended employment of the American City Bureau, and a few weeks later the board of trustees registered its assent. Unlike his predecessors, who had used the lay advisory board merely to gather ideas and suggestions, Beatty quietly made it part of the decision-making process.

By April the firm submitted a brief but complete statement of aims, plan of organization, and schedule of operations. The goal was set at $6,550,000: $2,550,000 for the immediate goals, the remainder for the library, the gymnasium addition, and increased endowment. A contract was signed, and Frank O'Hern came to the campus as Loyola's first director of development. His function was not to collect a dollar but to act as a "diplomatic irritant . . . to keep the College group working, and working effectively, to advance" the agreed-upon plan.[10] This was Loyola's first major fund-raising effort since the mid-1920s and the first ever employing professional assistance.

Various phases of the campaign were started on schedule during the ensuing year. By November of 1957, when the contract with the fund-raising firm ended, almost $600,000 had been pledged, with a fee of between 10 and 12 percent, depending on how certain contributions were counted, going to American City Bureau. It was by far Loyola's most successful effort to date. At his departure, O'Hern outlined plans for continuing the development program. Its main objectives—in money and in buildings—were achieved over the next five years.

In both their initial presentation and its formal summary, the consultants had suggested that the college reorganize its relations with the alumni. Frank Boland (1894) had been urging such a course for several years, and on being asked by President Beatty he contributed the salary for a new secretary. It was expected that in a year or two this operation would become self-supporting.

· ·

It was at this point that Beatty offered the post of alumni secretary to William Lefevre, night news editor for radio station WFBR. They had met casually during the early publicity surrounding Beatty's appointment and his inauguration. Lefevre was so impressed by what he saw in Father Beatty that although he had never considered any position other than the one he held, he was ready after only a two-hour conversation to join the staff of the college. Because Loyola could not offer him much financially he continued his night work at the radio station, but the college had first call on his time. His radio work reinforced Lefevre's recognition among the alumni and throughout the city. A few words and a handshake with the president was the only agreement between Lefevre and the college. In preparation for his new responsibilities, he took a quick, private course in alumni relations under the tutelage of Frank Boland and the alumni secretary at Boston College.

Boland thought a physical facility essential to revitalize the alumni association. With his personal and financial assistance the college acquired Millbrook House in 1957. It was a three-story mansion built around the time Loyola College moved to Evergreen and is on two acres of land just across the road that traced the eastern edge of the campus. (A few years later the college took an option to buy the property north of Millbrook but let the option lapse because of the price; that property was acquired in 1981. The handsome mansion south of Millbrook, whose last owner was the publisher of the *Sun,* was acquired by the college in the 1970s and has since served as the president's house.) Although the whole first floor of Millbrook House was reserved for alumni offices and meeting rooms, the upper floors were used as faculty offices. This was not what Boland had in mind; he wanted the whole building as an alumni center. Boland's ideas, however, ran counter to a deeply ingrained Jesuit preference for multiple, rather than exclusive, use of all college buildings. After registering his point, Boland accepted the multiple use of Millbrook House in light of the limited space then available on campus.

The crucial task assigned to Bill Lefevre was to convert the alumni association from a small social club with only a nominal connection to Loyola into a strong financial resource for the college. Before 1956, membership waxed and waned but averaged less than a quarter of the living alumni. Dues and special events—oyster roasts, dances, communion breakfasts, and banquets raised less than five thousand dollars annually. That was used in the main to cover the expenses of the association and contributions to the scholarship fund.

The need for change had been recognized by some of the association's officers even before the appointment of Lefevre. In 1949 Lingard Whiteford (1917) proposed adoption of what he called the Fordham plan. The Fordham Alumni Association had resolved itself into a department of the university and abolished dues and substituted an annual campaign for contributions from all who had ever attended the school. Whiteford's suggestion got no immediate attention, but Frank Boland took up essentially the same theme in the notices he kept sending to Loyola's presidents about what alumni at Harvard, Radcliffe, Bucknell, and other schools were giving annually to their alma mater. The reluctance to follow these examples arose from ambivalence; there was desire for stronger support but also a fear of lay influence.

It took a while for Bill Lefevre to reform the alumni association. Membership dues were eliminated in 1959 and an annual campaign, called the Evergreen Fund, was instituted. Even the fund's first year brought more than $12,000 from over eight hundred alumni, and both these figures have risen steadily ever since. By 1962 the alumni had contributed a total of $350,000—a tangible expression of their generosity and their continuing affection for Loyola College.

• •

This prevailing climate of initiative and change evoked significant efforts from the student body and its faculty advisers. The broadest was a revision of the student council's constitution—an exercise that too often becomes merely a futile diversion. This time, however, basic changes in procedure and principle were effected. The new draft, unlike preceding drafts, which had been internal transactions between the members of the council and the college president, was submitted to the student body in the first referendum in Loyola's history. The students overwhelmingly approved the new constitution and, by a vote of two to one, chose the more democratic council structure.

There were other notable achievements by students during this period. Jerome Langan (1958) organized a student congress on Soviet-American relations with the assistance of Doctor Kirwin and the members of the International Relations Club. Early in November 1957 more than a hundred delegates from as far away as Connecticut spent an enlightening weekend on campus. They talked about issues raised by the cold war and listened to experts from neighboring campuses and the government. At the close of the congress they adopted resolutions that ignored the anti-Communist crusade and called for general disarmament under United Nations inspection. That might appear utopian but at least did not echo the xenophobia that had wracked the early 1950s.

The Eisenhower years are generally considered quiet times, particularly compared with what preceded and what followed them. Comments (whether approving or disappointed) on student inattention to public issues were common. One popular tract-for-the-times, *The Organization Man* by William H. Whyte, characterized their mood as "obtrusive in no particular, excessive in no zeal." Even the most important issue that seared education during these years, public school desegregation, was watched by most Americans from the sidelines. The *Greyhound* editorial writers found little to comment on. They deplored the rioting in neighboring Delaware that followed the Supreme Court's 1954 decision, and student shenanigans at several Baltimore schools. One piece, and that was all. Baltimore authorities and civic leaders, however, responded by quickly eliminating the Jim Crow rules declared unconstitutional by the Supreme Court. There was no "massive resistance" in Maryland and no dramatic confrontation such as occurred in Little Rock, Arkansas.

Opinion in Maryland was generally united on obeying the law—however distasteful it might seem. Some, although willing to yield in regard to the public schools, were determined to protect their private social milieu from contact with blacks. That left the decision on serving food or renting facilities to owners who refused to deal with blacks and who enforced this determination by invoking the law against trespassing.[11] This situation created a problem for Loyola with which President Beatty dealt personally and decisively.

• •

Shortly after Charles Dorsey (1953) left campus, Paul Smith applied for admission to the college. There had been several other black students on the campus during these years, but Smith played a role in putting the college in clear opposition to racial segregation. At the time of his application there was no evident connection between him and Dorsey; later Dorsey would marry Paul Smith's sister.

Smith applied to Loyola at the suggestion of Father William Driscoll, who had met him at a mountain resort where Smith was working during the summer. Father Driscoll was deeply impressed with Smith and his desire to become a priest. Driscoll found a benefactor who provided Smith's first year's tuition. Because he had graduated from Frederick Douglass High School, his application did not raise the technical problems that initially stalled Dorsey.

Throughout his four years at Evergreen Paul Smith was a diligent student, a participant in student activities, and generally accepted by his peers. For several years he managed the lacrosse team and was a member of the sodality. He served on the *Evergreen Quarterly* staff during all his years at Loyola, although Smith's name appears on only one published piece—an editorial dealing with the effects of the Supreme Court's decision to desegregate the public schools. After outlining the historical origins of "Southern sentiment" (as he termed it), he called for understanding and warned that "unless carefully treated," the disease of Southern sentiment would "contaminate those who would effect the cure."[12]

Despite his moderation and friendliness, Smith created a dilemma for the officers of his class that arose dramatically when they began to plan their junior prom. Since the 1940s these affairs had been held off campus, but virtually none of the fashionable ballrooms or country clubs around Baltimore then would rent facilities to groups that included blacks. Acting mainly by their own lights, the junior-class officers, Wayne White and Thomas Ferciot, engaged the only acceptable ballroom available under these conditions. It was at the Friendship (now Baltimore-Washington International) Airport terminal, subject to federal regulations against discrimination in public accommodations.

The distance to the airport and the drab facilities prompted a number of students to insist that nicer arrangements be made next year for senior week. A new set of officers scheduled a full round of dances and parties—all at the best country clubs and facilities. Senior week that year was going to be—in the customary language advertising such events—memorable for everyone. On the eve of the first event four members of the class, George Brown, Thomas Coyle, Morton Barnett, and John McLaughlin, noticed that all events had been booked into facilities that never before had accepted black patronage. They and some of the senior-class officers were members of an American constitutional law course in which they had recently reviewed the Supreme Court's decisions in the public school desegregation cases. These students asked the lay instructor—a first-year tyro (me)—for time to discuss the problem. Three positions were espoused. Some raised the practical question whether anything could be done at such a late date. Others appealed to majority rule for going ahead as planned. Brown, his cohort, and a few others thought Catholic college students should act by a more generous standard.

An indecisive result (the instructor gave them only half the period) prompted the four students to consult Father Beatty. He accepted the practical impossibility of amending arrangements for the very first event, but he directed that remaining senior week events be open to *all* members of the class. By diligent effort the program managers willingly got all their contractors—except one country club in Anne Arundel county—to agree to this condition.

This county was then noted for its strong opposition to racial integration. The owner would accept the whole class for an afternoon party so long as the black did not take a dip in the pool. Should Brown et al. return to Beatty or should they settle for this much progress? On consulting some of the senior Jesuits, they were persuaded to accept what they had already achieved in opening these facilities. Their young lay instructor could offer no better advice than to defer to the judgment of people versed in the distinctive mores of Maryland.

Looking back, it would have been more pleasant if the episode had ended with a flourish, but human life and effort are not so simply organized. At least this episode established that Loyola students could and would contract only for outside facilities where no one was excluded by reason of race. When the state of Maryland finally passed a public accommodations law about ten years later, the need for such a rule was obviated. Paul Smith was eventually ordained a Roman Catholic priest and later became principal of Holy Angels School in Chicago, the largest black school in the nation.[13]

• •

One of the most important and pressing concerns of the first half of President Beatty's tenure was the reaccreditation of Loyola College by the Middle States Association. The postwar expansion of American colleges and universities had convinced many educators that the old system of permanent accreditation was inappropriate. Periodic review, it was thought, would ensure the maintenance of proper standards and encourage needed development. There were three major stages in this new procedure: self-evaluation, during which the institution examines itself and prepares answers to a series of probing questions posed by the association; a campus visitation by a team drawn from other member institutions; and a report by the team to the association.

Among the first institutions in the region to undergo this new process was the University of Maryland, which was visited by a Middle States team during the early 1950s. Because that university's evaluation report became an issue in the gubernatorial election of 1954, the board of regents felt obliged to publish a "painfully honest" summary. The regents denied a widely circulated rumor that the school of medicine had been placed on "probation" but explained that the association had voted to "reconsider" the whole university in two years.

The regents also listed the "most critical areas" for the second review: a highly centralized administration, lack of faculty participation in educational policy making, the condition of library, the status of the school of medicine, and intercollegiate athletics. After the second visitation the university's new president, Wilson Elkins, proudly announced the institution's reaccreditation in 1958.[14] Despite the differences in size and status of the institutions, there were, as it turned out, many similarities in the experiences of the university and of Loyola College that in some measure may have been the result of the newness of the process and the zeal of some of the evaluators.

Originally evaluation of the college had been scheduled for the spring of 1955. Unforeseen circumstances—the change of presidents and the Jesuit residence fire—prompted the association to postpone the process for two years. Meanwhile Beatty, following his own inclinations and the suggestions in the Middle States guide, established a notably open procedure for preparing Loyola's self-evaluation report. Eleven small faculty committees were assigned groups of questions from the association's guide and prepared preliminary answers, with the faculty as a whole to review them for amendment. Presiding over these plenary sessions was Father Thomas Higgins, a judicious senior member of the faculty. On first assuming the chair early in May of 1956, Father Higgins made clear that this phase was "to be approached in a spirit of complete candor"[15]—and he was taken at his word.

The faculty's interest and dedication may be measured by an average 80 percent attendance rate at eighteen two-hour meetings during May and part of June. Furthermore, Xavier Hall, the site of the meetings, had no air conditioning, and the windows were kept closed to ensure privacy. Anybody familiar with the climate of Baltimore will recognize what this meant.

The candor of the faculty particularly in the recommendations appended to the committee reports disturbed some of the older Jesuits. The Roman tradition in its emphasis on unity and obedience is wary of explanations to outsiders or proposals for change. The faculty committee recommendations smacked of "washing dirty linen in public" and were taken as carping criticism of established practice and standards. These expressions of dismay were temporarilly allayed by assurances that the recommendations were merely intended to lay a foundation for orderly development after the accreditation process was completed. They did not have to be included in the final report to the visiting team.

The anxieties of the older Jesuits flared up again in a little while. To speed the plenary sessions a new rule was announced; on the model of congressional proceedings, it restricted each member to two interventions per report. A few, Jesuit and lay, vigorously objected to this restriction and walked out of the meeting—eliminating the "left" in parliamentary terminology. When objections to the new rule continued, one senior Jesuit (an alumnus) was recognized and stated the fear that aroused basic anxiety. He declared that Jesuits would never submit to laymen taking over the college. Father Beatty firmly but calmly assured his brother-in-religion that he discerned no such revolutionary intention but only a sincere, cooperative effort to improve the institution— and the objector fell silent, effectively disposing of the "right." The "moderates," Jesuit and lay, practically nullified the new rule by gaining recognition more than twice on the same report, which kept the discussions uninhibited (if also prolonged) during the remainder of the meetings.

Noteworthy it was that many of the most active participants were young and not tenured. Their apparent vulnerability did not deter them from discharging their responsibilities to Loyola as they understood them. Their sincerity, if not their finesse or wisdom, was generally accepted—and experience has ever been considered the most effective teacher of prudence.

• •

The "moderates" focused their attention on promoting the establishment of an academic council. Such an agency would ensure that committee recommendations would be given serious consideration after the accreditation process was completed and would continue to deal with the development of Loyola systematically. Few participants evidenced awareness (and certainly none of the laymen knew) that the Jesuit Educational Association had been recommending establishment of such a body on each campus for a number of years. On one campus for sure, and probably on a number of others as well, this recommendation was not acted upon because a faculty senate, it was thought, "would waste time, encourage crack pots, and slow down administration." Good decisions (it was traditional to believe) came from an able and conscientious officer—not from a group of subordinates. Fordham would not overcome this attitude until 1964, with the University of Detroit following a year later and Canisius College in 1968. In the Maryland province, no school preceded Loyola College in establishing a faculty senate but others took action later, in the 1960s. In the ambit of American higher education, there was no greater willingness to involve the faculty directly in governance. The University of Maryland got a faculty senate only shortly before Loyola. Columbia University, for one, continued to rely on traditional, administrative, procedures until the end of the 1960s.[16]

The handle used to push acceptance of an academic council was the reference to one in the college statutes. What was needed, however, was some definition of its structure and a rationale for its operation. These were supplied by Father John Wise, professor of education, who thought:

> there should be a continued departmental sharing in administration such as in employment of personnel, regulation of curriculum and approval of majors. None of these functions should be [carried out] in isolation. *Departments,* as well as department heads should know what is going on. I think the department heads should act continuously as an executive *academic council.* A sense of proportion in judging indi-

vidual departmental needs would then be more readily assured. *Standing academic committees* should perhaps work in conjunction with this council. All functions of department heads, singly and collectively, would be advisory, but this can be . . . consistent, with normal administrative operation[;] such practice and *spirit,* in my opinion, are indispensable for *effective,* not to say *creative,* academic achievement [emphasis added].[17]

His views (without attribution) were circulated by one of the "moderates," encouraging the faculty to express similar sentiments during the plenary sessions. The cumulative effect of these suggestions convinced Loyola's leaders that it was time to move. On the agenda for the trustees' meeting of January 18, 1957, appeared an item: "Examination of the proposal on the Academic Council." However, no action was taken until after the Middle States Association team had been to the campus.

• •

The seven-member team headed by Robert McEwen, president of Hamilton College, arrived at Evergreen during the last week in February 1957. McEwen was a forceful, dynamic man who had taught or served as president at several small, private, liberal arts colleges with religious associations. Upon being appointed president of Hamilton College in 1949, McEwen transformed a school immobilized by internal divisions into a solidly developing institution. His success was not without its cost in the antipathy of some faculty members toward him, but he was proud of what he had accomplished in a short time.[18] By reason of his experience, McEwen seemed an appropriate choice to head the team to evaluate Loyola—even as a last-minute replacement.

In the main the evaluation went smoothly. Only during the departure meeting, when McEwen outlined the team's report in very general terms but allowed no questions to be asked or observations offered, was there a ruffle. He terminated the meeting abruptly on a claim of having to catch a train. This strange treatment roused the concern of President Beatty and some others who were at the final meeting with McEwen. Faculty members who had been interviewed by various members of the team reported that they had been treated courteously except by Chairman McEwen. He chose to talk only to faculty members who had not completed their doctoral studies and he seemed blunt, even rude, during these conversations. This unusual behavior coupled with his abrupt ending of the departure meeting roused the suspicion that he had come to Evergreen with some definite ideas about what he was going to find. (Whether or not he had been influenced by the general deprecation of

Catholic and other church-related colleges among American educators
—e.g., Eliot of Harvard—cannot be ascertained).

Once the possiblity of prejudice was recognized, President Beatty
wrote McEwen and sought to invoke provisions in the Middle States
guide that permitted communication between them on the preliminary
draft of the team's report. President McEwen answered that this was
"quite impossible." Since the avenue to correction of factual errors had
been foreclosed by this reply, Beatty appealed to the Middle States Association on the grounds of possible prejudice on the team. This effected no change in the status of McEwen's final report, which raised
serious doubts about Loyola's accreditation. The report was practically a
"show cause order," but the association offered its assistance in preparation for another visit in two years.[19] This cast Loyola then into the same
academic limbo as the University of Maryland, which would not
emerge shriven and with its accreditation reaffirmed for another year.

• •

On reading the evaluation report, a staff member at the association
(probably its executive secretary, F. Taylor Jones) made notations on the
cover, and these may be taken as the main points of approval and difficulty. Among Loyola's apparent assets were its basically sound financial
position, the coherence of its degree requirements in the evening division, the quality of its student activities, and the proper role it assigned
to athletics.

There were, on the other hand, many problems listed in the report.
Faculty salaries (to no one's surprise) were too low. The evaluators also
thought not enough teachers had their doctoral degrees—less than 25
percent. By this time, the general training of Jesuits was no longer considered the equivalent of a Ph.D. and only those who personally acquired that degree were included among the doctorates. The evaluators,
possibly unaware of the progress achieved during the preparatory meetings of the faculty and the plans to establish an academic council, found
too little participation by the teachers in the governance of the college.
Several of these points, especially the last, appeared also in the critique
of the University of Maryland and reflect the concerns of the 1950s
among American educators.

Certain mechanical features and rhetorical flourishes in Loyola's
self-evaluation report, even shorn of the recommendations for improvement, may have contributed to the team's unfavorable judgment. Faculty data were listed not for a single group but for two distinct categories: Jesuit and lay. Such a dichotomy could easily have played into the

suspicion that lay teachers were still considered only temporary auxiliaries and not integral members of the faculty. The editing committee had thought to enlighten the visitors about the character of Jesuit institutions with a prefatory note on organization. This reduced the internal policy-making process to what was termed "directed initiative," which was described as the president giving direction, with the faculty merely supplying "initiative" in following these commands. The authors were innocent of how such a description might be read by educators who considered such a decision-making process obsolete and unacceptable in an American context. The preface ended with a triumphal assertion: "The soundness of this organization is proven by more than four hundred years of recognized academic success."[20]

What impact such bravura may have had on McEwen and other visitors cannot be determined directly. Nevertheless, the Jesuit who edited the report submitted to another team two years later avoided these notes. In the 1959 report, data on the faculty were tabulated without distinction between Jesuit and lay teachers, and any mention of the virtues of "directed initiative" was noticeably absent.

The main complaint in the evaluation report was that Loyola College, while professing to offer a liberal arts program, was in reality providing instruction in certain professions. The basis for this astounding judgment was the heavier than normal requirements for graduation and for concentration in a major. Loyola's students had to complete 140 semester-hours of credit for a bachelor's degree, while the usual requirement in a liberal arts program was only 120. To people unfamiliar with academia, a heavier workload for a modest tuition might seem praiseworthy. However, it was the combination of heavy credit requirements and strict specification of required courses that drew the evaluators' adverse judgment. They shared a belief that fewer courses (especially in philosophy and theology) and more electives were a better foundation for a liberal education. This would permit students to explore disciplines outside their majors and the required core of subjects.[21] On its face the report required the college to conform to a general pattern, to give up what it considered distinctive in its curriculum. American educators have in principle decried a tendency to homogenization, but here in practice homogenization appeared to be at work.

Beatty and the deans, reviewing the report, considered it deeply flawed because "it lacked constructive spirit, factual accuracy, unity and balance"[22]—the characteristics of a good report as specified in the association's guide. The Middle States officers and commissions would not publicly concur in that description, but their later actions come as close to confirmation as academic politesse permits. At a workshop for evaluation teams held in November 1957, authoritative comments included suggestions that could have forestalled most of Loyola's difficulties. In the future chairmen would have less control over the members of their teams and there would be a continuing dialogue between the president of the institution and the team—not merely a brief departure interview. The contribution of Loyola's difficulties to these sensible changes in procedure should not go unnoticed.

Loyola College and Beatty clearly needed help, and this was provided by the Maryland province in the person of Father Joseph Drane, already familiar with Evergreen. Since his departure from Loyola in 1953 he had acted as overseer of all the colleges and universities in the province. Drane retained that responsibility and was named academic vice-president of the college. His leadership style—more results oriented than people related—complemented that of Father Beatty. His main function was to direct the continuing reform of Loyola and to coordinate preparations for the visit of another team of evaluators in 1959.

19

Breakthroughs

In September of 1957 President Beatty and Father Drane initiated the process that would prepare for the return visit of a Middle States Association team and for the orderly development of Loyola for the next seven years. Their first step was the establishment of an academic council that consisted of academic administrators, the chairmen of five standing committees, and department chairmen—twenty-two members in all, or almost half the full-time faculty and academic administrators. There was almost an even balance between Jesuits and laymen and this approximated the proportion of each group on campus. Any member of the college community could propose business for this new body, and the council, not its chairman (Father Drane), decided whether or not a proposal merited further study. If a majority of the council agreed, the proposal was assigned to one of the new standing committees, to which all regular faculty members were appointed. Over the next seven years there were incremental changes, making the structure more responsive to constituent views. But more than adjustment of institutional structures is needed to make such a process work, and a general spirit of openness and cooperation was fully operative during these years.

• •

Major credit for introducing this collegial style of governance is due Fathers Beatty and Drane, but the prior agitation of the faculty should not be slighted. This development at Evergreen appeared earlier than at most Jesuit schools—indeed, more than 70 percent of the faculty senates at Jesuit insitutions were founded after 1964—and was comparable to that at Notre Dame, Boston College, and Saint Louis University. The smaller size of Loyola and the lack of publicity may partly explain the failure to include Vincent Beatty's name among the progressive

Catholic college and university presidents cited in the most recent history of this period.[1] It may be that, like the banyan tree, which permits nothing to grow in its copious shade, attention to the most visible leaders in Catholic higher education obscures similar achievements at smaller institutions. In our justified anxiety to avoid claiming too much we may have fallen into the congruent error of claiming too little.

Within five months of its establishment the academic council approved a revised statement of objectives (what is now called a mission statement) and a revision of the basic curriculum. Loyola College would continue to be what it had been all along—a liberal arts institution—but now phrased its objectives in a more generally understood vocabulary. The overall requirement for a bachelor's degree in the day sessions was reduced to 120 semester-hours, but Catholics were required to take 16 additional credits of theology. A core of humanities, including philosophy, accounted for 66 credits. All major fields were restricted to eight courses at the junior and senior levels, with the credits varying between the science courses (with their requirement of laboratory work) and the other subjects. The remaining 30 credits were to be assigned by individual departments to prerequisites for majors and to electives. This meant that all departments had to review the effects of the new policy on their offerings and to submit a progress report at the May of 1958 meeting of the academic council—which they did. These were only the first installments of what was a continuing process.

There were significant differences of opinion among members of the council but they were resolved by accommodation, not fiat. For instance, the education department submitted a program for teacher training in the day sessions (there was already such an offering in the evening division). Father Drane and Dean Hoggson were both opposed to the proposal and they urged against it the strictures of the Middle States Association on professional training. The rest of the council, however, thought the proposal worthy of study and referred it to a committee. The opposition of the academic vice-president and the dean was still active when the committee returned a favorable report; nevertheless, over the ensuing years the day sessions' teacher-training program was slowly but incrementally developed and then reinforced by Loyola's merger in 1971 with Mount Saint Agnes College.

Although no major difficulties appeared in the operation of these new structures and procedures, complaints soon arose about the number of council and faculty meetings. Collegial governance requires more attention from more participants than the traditional style of administration. Nevertheless, it brings to the process a larger pool of experience and information, makes prudent decisions more likely, and normally assures a greater commitment to a decision than one framed through old-fashioned methods. It may bemuse current faculty members to know that the complainants were objecting to attending four meetings during 1957–58—albeit some that extended over a whole day.

As the new report for the Middle States Association was being compiled, there appeared an indicative difference on how it was to be reviewed. Some, operating on the familiar premise that the report was supposed to be a faculty product, wanted the draft reviewed in plenary sessions just as the 1957 report had been. Father Drane, more partial to efficiency through subordination, thought that unnecessary because of the faculty's "proper representation" in the academic council. He thought the council's approval sufficed and wanted to avoid the earlier tedium. An experienced layman, Vincent Colimore, suggested a preliminary review by departments, with comments and approval registered by the chairmen in the council. Although the faculty had no practical way to enforce its desires, Vice President Drane willingly acceded to this suggestion. That was the style of this Jesuit.

The 1959 evaluation visit came in February, almost on the anniversary of the earlier one. Fortunately, that was the only point of similarity. The association's executive secretary, F. Taylor Jones, had been extremely helpful in advising the college on preparations for this visit. Because of another last-minute withdrawal, he had to serve as the team's chairman. This time there were no later reports from the faculty of rudeness, and Father Beatty met with the team at the end of each day. One team member thought this practice "completely satisfactory," largely because of Beatty's knowledge and charm.

To the three fundamental questions of whether or not Loyola College had clearly defined its objectives, had established practical conditions to realize them, and had made substantial progress in that direction, the team replied with a confident yes.[2] The evaluators found (as such functionaries usually do) a little dust on their white gloves. They wondered about a graduate program narrowly focused on educational methods and theory in a professedly liberal arts institution. The association team believed some provision should be made to acquaint teachers with subject matter along with educational methods.

Whatever the evaluators intended, this notation justified a request by the association for a progress report in another two years (fortunately without another campus visitation) and also impelled an obscure, tangled conflict between the education department and much of the rest of the faculty that lasted into the 1970s and need not be recounted here. The association's letter confirming Loyola's accreditation congratulated President Beatty on his "personal leadership and the diligence and devotion" of his faculty. The final sentence was: "We are confident of Loyola's future."[3]

· ·

During the years when accreditation was the center of attention, President Beatty was taking action on other matters. One of the most basic was faculty salaries. They were too low for the faculty members already in the employ of the college, and they hindered recruiting new teachers, especially those who had or soon would earn doctoral degrees. At Father Beatty's accession to office in 1955, lay faculty salaries ranged from $3,400 to $5,700, with the higher figure allotted only to the athletic director, who had been at the college longer than anyone else. Making allowance for the difference of eight years and inflation, these figures are comparable to those in a study of faculty salaries at eastern Catholic colleges in 1947.[4]

In May of 1958 the board of trustees approved a new and more comprehensive policy that was aimed at raising the general level of compensation, providing a longer-term and more predictable schedule of increases, and augmenting rewards to those who acquired doctorates. The increase was derived in part from a Ford Foundation grant. The foundation sought to raise the generally depressed salaries in American higher education. The first year the new policy was applied, faculty salaries spread between $4,000 and $8,000, with the latter amount allotted to the senior classroom teacher. The main aim of the new policy was to encourage greater effort in securing a Ph.D. The minimum salaries assigned to each rank were higher for doctorates than for those without a doctoral degree. Furthermore, annual increments, which were not granted automatically but required favorable recommendation from the committee on rank and tenure, were defined as 5 percent of the base salary on the doctorate and non-doctorate scales, and this meant a noticeable difference between the two sets of merit increments.

The new salary policy was accepted by most of the lay faculty. The salary ceiling on non-doctorates was worrisome to those whose personal circumstances did not permit continuation of their work toward that degree, but most would not be reaching the limit for several years. Those working to complete their doctoral studies saw a shift in the not too distant future to the higher schedule. Mainly for professional reasons (although not ignoring the new financial incentives), those who had nearly completed the degree requirement redoubled their efforts. This and the active recruiting of new faculty members raised the percentage of doctors on the faculty from less than 25 percent (Jesuit and lay) in 1957 to over 30 percent two years later, and that figure rose steadily thereafter.

However, the new salary policy could not be applied in all its particulars over the period for which it had been established. Questions of justice arose when some teachers without doctorates reached the upper limit. They had ably and faithfully served the college and their students for many years, and it seemed unfair to apply the ceiling in its full rigor. Ad hoc accommodations above the limit were made. Similar adjustments became necessary because of a general rise in teachers' salaries during these years. The demand for teachers rose because of the increasing number of college-aged people produced by the postwar baby boom. The federal government, responding to an outcry raised after the launching of *Sputnik* by the Soviets in 1957, began to lend money for tuition and to award grants for faculty research.

This combination induced competition among institutions and an unprecedented mobility among the professoriate. As a result faculty salaries rose faster than anyone had predicted, and for Loyola to recruit qualified teachers it had to offer more than the salaries listed in the 1958 schedule. As the salaries for newcomers rose, equity demanded occasional adjustments for those already in service at Evergreen. Loyola could not and did not attempt to outbid all other schools, but its financial offerings and working conditions had to be made acceptable to prospective faculty members who in those days savored the luxury of several job offers. The 1958 salary schedule was not formally replaced; administrators merely made individual adjustments as required.

• •

The need to increase the proportion of faculty with doctorates prompted an active campaign of recruiting. Among the Jesuits who came to Loyola in these years, the most notable were Father Gerard Campbell, a medieval historian, and Father Henry Lavin in English literature. Some years later Father Campbell would be transferred to Georgetown and be appointed president of the university. Father Lavin, at Loyola a few years longer than his colleague, served briefly as dean and then became headmaster of Georgetown Preparatory School.

For various practical and theoretical reasons, President Beatty instituted a policy of recruiting qualified alumni to teach in the sciences.

Among educators such a practice is not favored because of a fear of intellectual "inbreeding." This is pertinent in graduate schools, but in Loyola's case the new faculty members had been off campus and studying at Princeton, Johns Hopkins, Notre Dame, Purdue, Carnegie-Mellon, and institutions of similar quality for three or more years. Many, in addition, had experience in various phases of industry or research.

Candidates with similar qualifications would have been sought and hired even if they had not been alumni. The experience of these alumni with the college and their connections with Baltimore made them even more attractive prospects for the faculty. During Father Beatty's term of office this effort brought James Gumnick (1953) in physics, Bernard Weigman (1954) in physics, Frank McGuire (1954) in chemistry, F. Xavier Spiegel (1961) in engineering, Mel Miller (1957) in chemistry, and Norbert Zaczek (1958) in chemistry, back to alma mater. They proved vital additions to the faculty and all but one are still with the college.

There were other noteworthy additions to the faculty. Offerings in the English department were strengthened and broadened after the arrival of Charles Hands, who soon got his doctorate from the University of Notre Dame. Hans Mair in political science and Morgan Pritchett in modern languages completed degree requirements at the Johns Hopkins University. In the same cohort was Doctor Doris Duffy Boyle, the first woman employed by Loyola College as a regular faculty member. She had attended the neighboring College of Notre Dame, where Doctor Elizabeth Morrissey (the first woman among Loyola's adjunct faculty) impressed her with the need for well-prepared Catholic scholars in the social sciences and with the opportunity such a background afforded for introducing Catholic thought on social justice into America's life and economy. Doris Duffy (she would later marry the talented editor and author George Boyle) studied labor economics at the Catholic University of America, which awarded her Ph.D.

Before she came to Evergreen in 1958 Doctor Boyle alternated between teaching, government service, and involvement with labor unions. After World War II she and her new husband left the United States to join the Antigonish movement in Nova Scotia. This was a self-help effort promoted in Canada by Saint Francis Xavier University and the Catholic church. The objective was to ease the numbing poverty of the local farmers, fishermen, and coal miners and their families so they could pay attention to something more than the drudging effort to avoid starvation. Doctor Boyle taught at the university, helped the provincial government mediate labor disputes, and contributed think pieces to the newspaper her husband was publishing.

Unfortunately George Boyle's health gave out, and after his death Doris Boyle returned to her native Baltimore to continue her career and apostolate at Evergreen. Her qualifications and ideals made her admirably suited to fill Loyola's needs, and she was appointed to the faculty at the rank of full professor.[5] For about ten years she remained at Evergreen, but eventually the call to return to Canadian life and politics proved irresistible.

In 1959, after the notice of accreditation had been received, important changes were made in administration. Additions to the faculty, it was thought, required new faces in decanal offices. Father Aloysius Galvin (1948) was appointed dean of the day division. His opposite number as dean of the evening and graduate divisions was Father John Burns, and Father Frank Bourbon was named dean of students. Although the last was not an alumnus, he was the son of August Bourbon (1914), who maintained close ties with the college.[6]

They were a young, active group of Jesuits who had been ordained only shortly before their posting to Evergreen. They seemed so young that they were affectionately, if also jocularly, referred to as the "boy-deans." Some of the alumni, at least, facetiously suggested that Father Galvin's appointment was a penance imposed by his provincial superiors for his having thrown the basket that won the Mason-Dixon championship in 1944 for Mount Saint Mary's—Loyola's arch-rival in athletics. Under Vice President Drane's guidance they effectively assumed their new duties, and by the time of his departure in 1961 they had demonstrated commitment and judicious behavior in their work at Evergreen. Upon Drane's departure, the office of academic vice-president was assigned to Father Galvin, who carried the responsibility effectively and unobtrusively for five years.

• •

The problems of facilities and land were not overlooked during these developments. The need for a larger and more attractive dining room and a center for student activities had been recognized by Beatty at the start of his presidency. In 1958 the college again applied to the federal government for $550,000, and in contrast to the experience of two years earlier, this loan was quickly approved. An additional $200,000 was assigned to the project from the development fund. This ended the "debt-free" status that Loyola College had enjoyed for many years, but the new debt never proved the grinding burden that earlier loans had been. The program of engaging alumni and a wide range of benefactors to support Loyola freed the administration from the worst anxieties suffered by their nineteenth- and early twentieth-century predecessors. The college debt, like that of a business concern, was managed prudently rather than liquidated before further commitments were made.

The location of the proposed student center changed several times before the center was built. Beatty's early plan to combine it with a dormitory and to erect it on land to be acquired from Johns Hopkins has already been described. That was not the only possibility he was working on in 1956. Father Beatty was also considering a location near the present site of the Loyola–Notre Dame Library. While he was corresponding with Hopkins's administrators, he wrote to Sister Mary Matrona, president of the College of Notre Dame, located on the other side of the tract owned by Hopkins. He raised the possibility that the two Catholic colleges might co-operatively build a new student center to serve both campuses. Hopkins at the time seemed interested in acquiring a buffer strip along its northern boundary with Notre Dame. Beatty was suggesting a three-sided arrangement and laid several proposals on the table. Success depended on the willingness of both Johns Hopkins and Notre Dame, but the ruling powers at each did not assent, partly because of a reluctance to engage in joint ventures then and partly because of a need to plan their own development more carefully. Although these discussions were not immediately productive, Beatty had broached the subjects of land transfer with the university and a joint venture with the College of Notre Dame, and both would be brought to the brink of realization before the end of his term.

Failure of these initial efforts meant that Loyola's new student center had to be erected entirely on the campus as it then existed, and for various reasons it was finally positioned on the east side of the gymnasium, abutting Millbrook Road. Ground was broken in the autumn of 1958, and the finished structure was dedicated with appropriate ceremonies at the end of January 1960.[7]

The Gothic lines and ornamentation of the older building were not directly imitated. That style of construction had become prohibitively expensive, and Father Beatty wanted to give the campus a modern look that did not clash architecturally with the buildings already in place.

The stone on the gymnasium was sandblasted so that the two buildings could age together. Inside was much needed space. The first floor was occupied by a student cafeteria, dining facilities for the lay faculty, and the bookstore. On the second floor were offices for student activities and a well-furnished lounge. Some had argued for furniture that would withstand the most determined abuse, but Father Bourbon insisted that approach would only encourage the very behavior that was anticipated. He thought Loyola's students, given the chance, would act like mature gentlemen, and he was not disappointed—generally. Air conditioning made the building useful for the whole year, including during oppressive Baltimore summers.

The name of the building—the Father Andrew White Student Center—was chosen because of important historical associations. Father Andrew White was the leader of a small Jesuit band that joined the first expedition to Maryland in 1634. By naming its student center for this Jesuit pioneer, Loyola College sought to keep his memory alive and to emphasize the long and fruitful association between the Jesuit order and Maryland. The point would be given greater emphasis a few years later when a medal in Father White's honor was established on President Beatty's initiative.

• •

The desire to promote academic excellence and to get more students interested in continuing to graduate school prompted President Beatty to inaugurate a series of events and a persistent campaign of publicity. A fall honors convocation was instituted in 1958. After the Mass of the Holy Spirit, which traditionally begins the Jesuit school year, the faculty in their academic robes and the student body assembled to honor an outstanding scholar and those students who had garnered academic distinctions during the preceding year. The speaker at the first convocation was William Foxwell Albright of the Johns Hopkins University, whose lifelong study of Semitic languages and archaeology had revolutionized the translation and understanding of the Bible.

In September of 1960 Monsignor John Tracy Ellis was offered as the exemplar of fruitful scholarship and public concern. It was five years since Ellis's famous address in which he reopened the discussion of the intellectual caliber of American Catholic colleges and universities. After duly congratulating the students who had won various distinctions, he challenged them, their fellows, and all his audience to more, more ambitious, and higher quality intellectual endeavors. Ellis gracefully but firmly rejected the argument that Catholic institutions could not be expected to produce scholars because they had only recently been established and had during their short existences dealt mostly with the children of recent immigrants.

Ellis did not attack this excuse directly but cited instead the example of Reed College in Portland, Oregon. Within less than a half-century it had gained "a reputation for extraordinary achievement among its alumni"—a reputation that had brought to Reed "the admiration of discerning educators in every section of the land."[8] The fundamental source of this admiration was the emphasis that Reed's faculty had placed on "hard work" from the college's very beginning. In Reed's first prospectus, in 1911, the priorities of the new school were clearly proclaimed. The diversions of "college life" were eschewed, and only those who wanted "to gain the greatest possible benefits from their studies" were welcome at Reed College. Such determination had in fifty years produced a small, private, liberal arts college with an outstanding reputation for academic excellence.

Ellis's style and subject were not intended to inspire the sort of fervor that Urban II's address aroused in the crusaders, but it engendered a renewed determination to excel in the academic and intellectual tasks at hand. Near the end of the school year the *Greyhound* printed notices of scholarship awards for graduate study garnered by Loyola's seniors. In one of these years (and the others were comparable) a third of all the graduates would continue their education—most in law or medicine. Awards from the National Science Foundation were much fewer, as might be expected, but still sufficient on a per capita basis to rank Loyola first among all the Jesuit colleges and universities in America, even though Loyola had one of the smallest enrollments.

This notable record was being promoted by a new faculty committee. For a number of years there were individual advisers who assisted students in seeking prestigious awards for graduate study, but these were now organized as the fellowship committee. Its tasks were to identify promising candidates early (preferably by the sophmore year), encourage them to begin thinking about graduate school, guide them in securing the necessary credentials, and later help them to prepare their applications. The committee, taking the word *fellowship* in a broad sense, invited recent graduates who were already in advanced programs back to the campus before Christmas vacation to meet students with a potential for graduate study. This general affair supplemented the continuing

exhortations of the faculty with practical information and encouragement from successful alumni not much older—perhaps even former
course mates.

The effectiveness of this effort was evidenced by the many items in
the student newspaper about the award of a graduate scholarship to yet
another Loyola student. After each semester, the *Greyhound* printed
the names of all paragons on the dean's list according to their majors.
On other occasions its front page featured those elected to Alpha Sigma
Nu, the Jesuit honor fraternity, or *Who's Who in American Colleges.*
Such persistence and saturation made it virtually impossible for a student to escape the question of whether or not he too should continue to
graduate school.

A more formal addition to this general campaign appeared in Loyola's course offerings by 1960 in the form of honors projects. These were
intense seminars offered in lieu of basic required courses. The opportunities and difficulties inherent in the honors courses were explained
to selected freshmen and sophomores. After listening to the prospectus
a few chose to remain in their regular classes, but more (probably heartened by this show of confidence in their abilities) volunteered to transfer to one or another of the honors projects.

Directors of these alternative courses were volunteers, and all came
from among the ablest scholar-teachers on the faculty. For them to
teach an honors course was a mark of distinction and an opportunity to
work with students more homogeneous and higher in ability. These
honors courses permitted teachers to experiment with subject matter, to
include interdisciplinary connections, and to try new instructional materials and formats. They were directed to pitch the level of the courses
high enough so that a successful student would deserve an A, and except for a failure no other grade was to be given.

The first honors projects were offered by the English, history, modern languages, and philosophy departments. The initial experience
made both the students and the faculty so enthusiastic that these
courses were continued throughout the 1960s and inspired imitation by
other departments that shared responsibility for courses required of all
students. Periodically faculty members engaged in these honors projects
suggested combining them into a comprehensive honors program like
those established at Fordham, Georgetown, and other Jesuit schools.
The smaller number of students at Loyola, and a wariness among some
of the faculty (Jesuit and lay) about elitism, discouraged formal consideration of the idea. No claim to originality is made for these efforts at

Loyola. The need to encourage superior students was a general concern of American higher education during these years; the college was merely applying that concern to its own circumstances. These honors projects prospered for about ten years and then fell into desuetude when a more imaginative and more thorough revision of the curriculum was adopted.

• •

This emphasis on academic excellence and scholarship was not restricted to the students. Beatty included notices of scholarly activity and publication by faculty members, Jesuit and lay, in his annual reports to the college community, and these notices were quite substantial. Even greater publicity to faculty scholarship was afforded through the *Greyhound.* For a two-year period student reporters compiled a list of six books and fifteen articles produced by the faculty, which is quite a respectable record in a group of fewer than fifty members. Nevertheless, this attention to faculty research did not mean adoption of the "publish or perish" dictum that afflicted other institutions of higher learning in America. Teaching then and since remains the first concern of the college, but sholarship was recognized as an activity essential to making instruction at Loyola comparable to that at other liberal arts colleges.

What kind of things was the faculty studying and writing about? One of the most interesting was the effects of lysergic acid (LSD) on basic developmental and physiological processes. The head of this government-funded study, which included several student-researchers, was Father Joseph A. Burke. Because of limited facilities and for the sake of simplicity, he chose to study the effects of LSD only on earthworms, starfish, and albino mice. This research continued for several years.

A solid contribution to scholarship was made by Harry Kirwin, whose biography of Herbert O'Conor was published in 1962. Doctor Kirwin spent several years gathering data for the book he entitled *The Inevitable Success.* It described the life and political career of one of Loyola's most distinguished alumni. For more than twenty years since the early 1930s, Herbert O'Conor had served Marylanders as state's attorney for Baltimore, attorney general, twice as governor, and finally as United States senator. A genuinely shy and cautious man, O'Conor nevertheless was shrewd in his judgment of public affairs. He was described by political observers as a conscientious, crisply efficient public servant. Kirwin recounted O'Conor's eventful life in detail, and his documentation, though thorough, was not excessive. Bradford Jacobs, a knowledgeable political reporter, reviewed the book for the *Sun* and described Kirwin's narration as "friendly, even warm, but in no way worshipful of O'Conor."[9]

Tragically, publication of this work was followed shortly by Doctor Kirwin's death after a year or so of illness. The college community deeply mourned his loss and the history academy and student council joined in seeking a suitable remembrance of his devoted service. This finally took the form of the Harry Kirwin Memorial Lounge in Maryland Hall where a bronze bust of "Doc"—as he was affectionately known by all—benignly surveys the comings and goings of his erstwhile colleagues with the trace of a knowing smile. The editor of the *Greyhound* wrote a heartfelt tribute to him as "an outstanding teacher . . . a scholar . . . a man of great wit and personal charm."[10] The most vital monument to him, however, must be sought in the lives and memories of his students and fellow teachers.

Much less public but occurring at the same time as these academic developments was a prescient modification in the bylaws of the college corporation adopted April 30, 1959. Under the new bylaws a distinction was made between the "members of the corporation" and the trustees. Only the former are successors of the original six Jesuit incorporators of Loyola College, and they retain title to all corporate assets. Ordinarily this body meets once a year, and its regular business is to elect members to the board of trustees, who are responsible for the management of the college's property and business.

This may seem like lawyerly busywork and it had no noticeable effect during the remaining years of President Beatty's term. However, it assured a continuing Jesuit presence in the ultimate control of Loyola but at the same time opened the door for diversifying the membership of the board of trustees. That was not undertaken until a decade later— after Vatican II and after serious legal problems arose in regard to government aid for church-related schools. Where did this useful innovation, as it proved, come from? Directly from Loyola's legal adviser, but he may have been alerted to this device by discussion at a 1953 national conference of financial administrators at Jesuit institutions.[11] What was of little moment in the late 1950s became a major developmental resource for Beatty's successor.

· ·

For some time, President Beatty had been concerned with finding a suitable means to emphasize Loyola's connection with the community in which it had been operating for over a hundred years. The device he selected was to celebrate March 25—the date of the landing of the first settlers in 1634—with appropriate ceremonies. Although it is a state holiday and a few private organizations still commemorate the event, Maryland Day draws little attention around the state in general.

Loyola's Maryland Day program in 1961 included an address by Father Robert Gannon, formerly president of Fordham, and the award of medals named in honor of Father Andrew White to distinguished citizens of the state. The first recipients of this award were Bishop James Walsh, a Maryknoll missionary then imprisoned in China; Brother Gabriel Cecilian, principal of Calvert Hall; Samuel Hecht and Patrick Roche, both respected business and civic leaders; and Judge Morris Soper of the federal bench. The occasion was made more festive by a fife-and-drum corps, uniformed in the style of soldiers in the American Revolution. The high point of the celebration was ground breaking for Maryland Hall. (An account of how that long-desired project was realized appears below.)

Since that first Maryland Day, the Andrew White Medal has been awarded to more than seventy recipients including Marylanders in a number of fields. Among the churchmen were Lawrence Cardinal Shehan; Noble Powell, the Protestant Episcopal bishop of Maryland; Monsignor Joseph Nelligan; and Father Edward Bunn. The educators have included Milton Eisenhower of the Johns Hopkins University, Martin Jenkins of Morgan State, Sister Mary Cleophas Costello of Mount Saint Agnes, Otto Kraushaar of Goucher, Richard Weigle of Saint John's, Sister Kathleen Feeley of the College of Notre Dame of Maryland, and Richard Franko Goldman of the Peabody Conservatory. The arts have been represented by Ogden Nash (comic poet), John Dos Passos (novelist), Richard Quincy Yardley (editorial cartoonist), R. McGill Mackall (historical muralist), and Clarisse Mechanic (theater builder and owner). Other Andrew White recipients were Governor Millard Tawes; United States Senator Charles Mathias; Vernon Eney, who presided over the abortive effort to revise Maryland's antiquated constitution in the 1960s; Juanita Jackson Mitchell, a civil rights activist; Brooks Robinson, for many wonderful years third baseman for the Baltimore Orioles; and James Rouse, widely respected for establishment of Columbia, Maryland, and for contributions to the revitalization of Baltimore's inner harbor. The other Andrew White laureates were as distinguished. Loyola, acting as proxy for the general community, has honored these Marylanders for their outstanding service to the common weal or for notable personal achievements.

Less publicly, Father Beatty pursued his objective of broadening

Loyola's connection with the community by reviving President Bunn's practice of inviting small, select groups of Baltimore's business and civic leaders to dinner at Evergreen. The chief executives of well-established firms received invitations, not merely for a social evening but for an opportunity to meet outstanding national figures. The first such attraction was Admiral Hyman Rickover, whose acquaintance Beatty had made some years earlier. Among the others were John J. McCloy, considered by many observers to be "chairman" of the American "establishment"; General Lyman Lemnitzer of the joint chiefs of staff; and Neil McElroy, secretary of defense. The yeast for this heavy fare was such Jesuit luminaries as John Courtney Murray and Gustave Weigel, who then were active participants in the exciting and widely publicized developments at the Second Vatican Council.

As in Bunn's term, no direct pitch for aid to the college was made; participants just shared a quiet, informative evening together. Some guests were so favorably impressed that they suggested the names of others who might find such presentations of interest, and soon invitations were actively sought by still other Baltimore executives.[12] Similar efforts at cultivation gradually spread President Beatty's circle of acquaintances, and he was able to recruit other prominent leaders to assist Loyola in its development programs. These efforts were coincidentally followed by a steadily increasing flow of grants from a variety of corporations.

• •

The early 1960s was a buoyant, exciting time, for none so much as younger members of American society. The election of John Kennedy as president of the United States was viewed by many—young and old—as a watershed marking a new era of activity and development in many fields. Kennedy's poise, sophistication, and success lessened the psychological defensiveness of Catholics. Their sense of acceptance was further enhanced by the favorable reaction to Pope Johns XXIII's initiatives, especially the convening of the Second Vatican Council. The president and the pope attracted widespread media attention and made "good copy." The result was a ferment of rising hopes and expectations especially among the 42 million American Catholics who had grown to compose 23 percent of the population. They were also becoming aware that Catholics as a group were beginning to outrank Protestants in economic terms.[13]

This buoyant mood expressed itself in the willingness of a surprising number of Americans—old and young—to volunteer for the Peace

Corps. Although the program had been suggested by others, it was popularly identified with Kennedy and became a symbol of his invigorating effect on the nation. Among the earliest Peace Corps volunteers were three from Loyola: Bernard Zubrowski (1962) worked in East Pakistan (now Bangladesh), Helen Rupp (1962, evening) taught in Nigeria, and Victor Corbin (1962) served in Costa Rica. In later years a steady, if small, number continued to volunteer for the Peace Corps, and later still for its domestic counterpart. Others offered their services to similar efforts sponsored by the Catholic church for Latin America (PAVLA) or to a more diversified program associated with the Jesuit order. Although the number of Loyolans involved in all these efforts was never very large, their disposition to offer two years of their lives to serve others is ample testimony to the generosity of their spirit.

The spiritual ferment that resulted from the Second Vatican Council came later and more slowly, because the council was not convened until October of 1962 and then took a while to formulate its decrees. One of the subjects to which the council fathers gave attention was the need for more active participation by the laity in liturgical services. This subject had in fact engaged the attention of a number of people for at least a generation before the opening of the council, but the prescriptions then in force allowed nothing better than a "dialogue" Mass. While the celebrant and server performed the ritual according to the rubrics, the faithful in the pews recited the server's prayers—sometimes in the vernacular, but more often in Latin. The congregation, however, repeated the priestly prayers only in summary, to avoid any blurring of the distinction between the priest and the laity. Many found this "dialogue" Mass instructive and some wondered if more could be done: congregational singing, for instance.

Interest in a more vital liturgy was then more apt to be found on Catholic college campuses, where it was easier for priests and lay faculty members interested in the subject to recruit the devout. Early in 1960, long after similar developments had appeared at other Catholic schools, Loyola's student sodality introduced the "dialogue" Mass and hoped to add congregational singing eventually. This transitional stage—so easily forgotten during the noise and furor roused by the later, more dramatic, and more extensive changes in the liturgy—needs to be recalled to place that later trauma in perspective.

• •

An aspect of liturgical practice that engaged the attention of many more Loyola students at this time was the requirement that Catholics attend Mass on campus on the first Friday of each month. This is a traditional devotion associated with the Society of Jesus and the rule antedated transfer of the college to Evergreen. Enforcement was had by collecting attendance slips at the end of the service. The sanction for absence was a double cut from religion class, which might make a student liable for a failure in that course. With a certain callow shrewdness, Loyola's students did not attack the requirement itself but only the method of enforcing it. They thought collecting attendance slips was demeaning to college men and was too reminiscent of high-school practices. The student council persuaded the dean to institute a three-semester experiment during which no individual attendance records were kept, only a count of the total number present. If attendance regularly fell below 65 percent of Loyola's Catholic registration, individual attendance slips could be reinstituted.

Attendance during the first semester of the experiment remained above the danger point—often enough. As time wore on and memories dimmed, however, fewer students attended first Friday Mass despite the efforts of the student council to promote attendance. The dean supplied the council with attendance statistics after the last Mass in this series. One of the seniors introduced the motion necessitated by the evidence—to restore individual attendance slips. Half the members of the council voted for his motion and half were still convinced that such disciplinary procedures were not consistent with the dignity of college men (to put the best face on their objection). The tie left the decision to the president of the student council, Thomas Dwyer (1960). There was a long silence, broken first by the parliamentarian, who noted that postponement of his vote was permissible. Dwyer, however, ended the matter with four words: "The motion is passed."[14]

That was not the end of the matter. Four years later, after the Vatican Council fathers issued their decrees on liberty of conscience, the question was raised again, but this time the point of attack was not enforcement procedures but the obligation to attend first Friday Mass. The premise for the renewed attack was supplied by an editorial in the *Catholic Review,* the archdiocesan newspaper, disapproving of compulsory chapel attendance at the nation's military academies: "It is always wrong to force a grown person to perform an act of worship. . . . [Religion] must always be basically a matter of personal decision and free choice. When it is not, shallow religion or hatred of religion is the likely result."[15] If such reasoning applied to the midshipmen at Annapolis, Loyola's students saw no reason why it did not apply to them as well.

The college officers, however, did not respond and the issue was left dormant until the late 1960s. Whether or not they shared the views of their confreres on other campuses is not clear but elsewehere some Jesuits were sure that elimnation of required attendance at Mass or the annual retreat meant losing the distinctive character of their schools. As the 1960s wore on, an even more anxiety-producing question arose: at what number or proportion of Jesuits does a college cease to be recognizably a Jesuit institution?[16] At Evergreen the first Friday Mass requirement and annual retreat quietly disappeared in the late 1960s when the class attendance rules were significantly modified and when the decrees of the Second Vatican Council began to have a noticeable effect.

Up to 1963 the involvement of Maryland Catholics in the civil rights movement was primarily a matter of individual conscience. Early in that year and to mark the centennial of Lincoln's Emancipation Proclamation, Archbishop Lawrence Shehan issued a pastoral letter in which he noted the failure of Catholic legislators representing heavily Catholic districts to vote for the repeal of racially discriminatory city ordinances. "Such a failure is all the more regrettable since our Christian faith imposes upon us all a special duty of both justice and charity toward all men, no matter what may be their racial and social origin." On this principle he enjoined that there remain no "racial segregation" and no distinction "based on racial difference" in Catholic churches, schools, charitable institutions, and hospitals, or in personal relations.[17] Shehan's 1963 pastoral lent the weight of the organized church to the efforts of other religious leaders in the community.

This appeal to conscience emboldened Loyola's students and Jesuits along with other Catholics to participate in the civil rights movement. William Scholtes (1965) wrote a commentary on Archbishop Shehan's pastoral letter for the *Evergreen Quarterly*. When the interdenominational ministers' alliance called for a march on Easter Monday in 1964, thirty Loyola students and four Jesuits joined the more than twenty-five hundred Baltimoreans who publicly demonstrated their support for ending racial discrimination in America. One would like to report something more substantial or dramatic, but at least a claim to honor and decency was saved by the few.

By this time a durable fad had established itself at Evergreen and throughout the country. Rock-and-roll music first appeared at a freshman mixer in 1962—to mixed reviews. Some liked the simple, strong beat and simple repetitive themes, but no one even tried to make sense of the lyrics. A few lay faculty members could not believe that rock-and-roll would be more than a passing phenomenon and wondered what was next. They were of course mistaken and would eventually learn the twist, the hully-gully, and the mashed potato. As more and larger amplifiers were added to the bands, faculty chaperones took what refuge they could in small acoustical deadspots or in the vestibule and wondered what all this noise and frenetic activity (it did not seem like dancing) portended.

• •

Much more serious matters were at hand at Evergreen at the same time; President Beatty was directing the process that resulted in the erection of Maryland Hall. He had the assistance of several notable people in this project. Father Beatty acknowledged the vital role of Patrick Roche, vice-president of the National Brewing Company, in various ways including awarding him one of the first Andrew White medals. Everyone associated with Loyola was aware of the need for more classroom and laboratory space, but Roche suggested a practical way to obtain the million dollars that would be needed to establish it. Pat Roche was an alumnus of Loyola High School, having entered before World War I. During his business career, he made a point of getting acquainted with people in leading positions around Baltimore and cultivated their friendship with a genuine concern for them as individuals. He had met President Beatty at various functions and they became acquainted. When Roche learned of Loyola's need for a new physics-engineering building he suggested seeking the funds from the state government, but Father Beatty was reluctant to enter that tangled thicket.

Roche, however, persisted; he noted that before World War I the state had provided the money for an engineering building at another private institution, Johns Hopkins. Further reflection convinced Beatty of the justice of such an appeal, but he was not willing to connect Loyola's request to the precedent. The grounds for Loyola's approach were Maryland's evident need for professionals trained in the sciences and the solid record of the college. Furthermore, all but 5 percent of Loyola's alumni had come from Maryland, and 80 percent of them still lived and worked around metropolitan Baltimore. State aid to Loyola could be viewed in this light as an appropriate and fair use of the taxpayers' money.

The next question was how to get the public funds. Pat Roche arranged for Father Beatty to meet Theodore McKeldin, who had recently completed his term as governor. Although McKeldin was a Republican in a state where most voters register as Democrats, he was a widely respected public figure and repeatedly won elections as mayor of Baltimore and governor with Democratic support. McKeldin provided the know-how for enlisting legislative leaders. In April of 1959, at the very end of the general assembly session, a measure was passed that granted $750,000 to Loyola College on condition that Loyola raised a matching amount. [18]

To this end, President Beatty organized several committees. One, consisting of friends and associates of William Hilgenberg, appealed for a memorial. Hilgenberg, a member of Loyola's development advisory board, had died recently. He was a distinguished civic leader who had served as state banking commissioner and as the potentate of the Shriners' Boumi Temple on Charles Street just north of Evergreen. Governor Millard Tawes and Mayor Harold Grady (1942) vigorously endorsed the Hilgenberg Memorial. [19] A group of Baltimore's business leaders was formed to solicit funds more generally, and alumni and friends of Loyola provided the remainder. These appeals raised the $750,000 to match the grant from the state of Maryland, and the ceremonial shovelfuls of earth were turned on March 25, 1961.

It took only fourteen months to complete the five-story building located near the northwest corner of the campus. This height was necessary to accommodate the small space available, but because of the building's low site Maryland Hall does not tower over the chapel or the older structures on campus. The height of the new building required a zoning variance, which was given without difficulty.

This new building added seventeen classrooms and nine laboratories to Loyola's facilities. The transfer of the physics and mathematics departments to the new building enlarged the space available in the old science building (now Beatty Hall) for biology and chemistry. By far the most welcome—though not always reliable—feature of the new building is air conditioning. Glazed green bricks constitute the main outside wall, but to harmonize the new building with the existing structures a facing of stone in the form of tall Gothic arches was applied. The stone for this feature and for the connected lecture hall came from the old Calvert Hall building at Mulberry and Cathedral streets that was replaced about this time by the Catholic Center. [20]

A notable appendage to the new building is a 200-seat lecture hall donated by Doctor Frederick Ruzicka. Doctor Ruzicka's father was an immigrant from Bohemia who came to Baltimore in the early 1880s and worked as a clothing cutter. In that period the local garment industry, if not as large as that of New York City, was nevertheless a major element in Baltimore's economy. Bohemian immigrants, men and women, made up a large part of the work force. The fifth son in a family of eight, Doctor Ruzicka had his elementary education at Saint Wenceslaus School, part of a Bohemian parish, and he continued his education at Loyola College, from which he was graduated in 1912. His medical training was completed at the University of Maryland; then he interned at Hebrew (now Sinai) Hospital. For twenty years Doctor Ruzicka maintained a general practice before specializing in internal medicine and cardiology.[21] He donated $100,000 for the new lecture amphitheater, and in his honor it is named Ruzicka Hall.

The new facility was dedicated on September 20, 1962, as part of the ceremonies for the start of a school year. Archbishop Lawrence Shehan blessed the new building, the name of which was changed at the last minute from a description of its main function—physics-engineering—to Maryland Hall as an acknowledgment of the grant from the state government.

• •

New things have a way of lifting the human spirit, and so it seemed at Evergreen after the opening of Maryland Hall and other innovations contributed to a buoyancy on campus. On September 25, 1962, the board of trustees voted to name Joseph May (1935) treasurer of the college. He had served as assistant to many Jesuits who for longer or shorter terms held that office since his return to the campus in 1943. A discreet, genial, and conscientious man whose ability and devotion to Loyola were now recognized, Joe May became the first layman given an important administrative responsibility, and a significant threshold for the college was crossed. About half the Jesuit schools by then had appointed laymen to such technical positions but not to positions such as dean of the college of arts and sciences.[22] Unfortunately May's service as treasurer proved short. Only five years later he died of a heart attack. A plaque donated by the students was placed on the wall of the treasurer's office and there perpetuates the memory of Joe May—"a man who never thought of himself while serving the College."

During the latter half of President Beatty's term there were two obituaries that carried special significance. Father Herman Storck (1897), after an active life as a Jesuit missionary in southern Maryland and northern New Jersey, had settled at Evergreen to serve as spiritual father to the Jesuit community and as a counselor to the evening students. He was a generous man who once confided to a younger member of the faculty that among the souls for whom he regularly prayed was that of Joseph Stalin. Father Storck died in February of 1962. His brother-in-religion, Father Joseph Didusch (1898), long a mainstay of the premedical program at Loyola, died in October of 1963 only a few months after celebrating the golden anniversary of his ordination. The death of these two Jesuits and alumni severed a living connection with the highpoint of Loyola's development at Calvert Street. Both men had entered the college in the late 1890s when Father John Abell Morgan was president and rector.

The world beyond the bounds of Evergreen or even of the United States could not be safely ignored. The use of atomic energy for peaceful purposes—the generation of electricity, for instance—and the radiation hazards from nuclear explosions were described by various speakers invited to the campus. For the most part they made the problems seem amenable to rational control. The international situation in the early 1960s, however, grew so grim that President Kennedy addressed the nation and urged the building of bomb shelters. Some took his advice—to the delight and profit of contractors ready to supply this demand—but gradually this seemed an unlikely solution for people living near or downwind from probable targets like Pittsburgh or Washington, D.C.

This public discussion of nuclear warfare was confusing, and so Leo O'Donovan, then a Jesuit scholastic, organized a program in which a physicist, a political scientist, and an ethicist from the faculty addressed the basic issues. The greatest impact on the audience came from the physicist's graphic description of what would happen if an H-bomb was dropped on Baltimore. Little, he said, would be left standing or alive within the ring of the recently constructed beltway around the city, and he gave the dimensions of the radioactive crater that would be left.

A short interval later, the United States and the Soviet Union, as an aftermath of the Cuban missile crisis, negotiated a treaty banning all tests of nuclear weapons in the atmosphere. This would stop the pollution of the earth with deadly and persistent radioactive isotopes and might slow the development of even dirtier bombs. Many Americans were then dubious about ratifying the test-ban treaty for fear the Soviets might gain an advantage. Important as this subject was, only one student thought to address it in the *Greyhound*. He acknowledged that there were risks in the agreement with the Soviets but thought them "worth taking."[23]

What seemed a much smaller cloud on the horizon was the involve-ment of the United States in Vietnam. In the early 1960s this seemed a remote concern. Nevertheless, even then Vietnam cast its shadow across the land. A new biologist had come to Loyola after serving there as a parasitologist for the Pasteur Institute; he thought of writing an account of his experiences in Vietnam, but circumstances restricted his exposition only to vivid conversation—generally favorable to the French. Among the students was the son of a Vietnamese province chief assassinated by the guerrillas. Speakers on this current topic were invited to the campus, and soon some of the ROTC cadre included sol-diers and officers returned from Vietnam. Each was asked about the sit-uation, and campus discussion more and more included references to that far-off battleground.

As attention turned to such global subjects that would later grow in importance, so also was attention given to more pleasant local topics. In these years Loyola began an active program of cooperation with Mount Saint Agnes College and the College of Notre Dame of Mary-land. Women from these schools enrolled in various courses, especially in mathematics and chemistry, and in exchange Loyola students regis-tered at the other campuses for foreign languages and fine arts. All agreed that the arrangement made better use of facilities at these three Catholic colleges than would occur if each tried to provide all courses desired by its own students. However, the distance between the cam-puses made scheduling difficult, and few students were persistent enough to surmount the various obstacles. The nearness of Notre Dame prompted students on both campuses to try to coordinate their extra-curricular and social activities—with modest success.

• •

Nevertheless, these efforts were harbingers of later developments. The most striking product was a joint library, eventually built by Loyola and Notre Dame, but crucial to that development was acquisition of a tract of land that gave the two institutions a common boundary. Presi-dent Beatty's final achievement was the purchase of ten acres from the Johns Hopkins University.

Father Beatty had broached the subject of purchasing land from Johns Hopkins shortly after his accession to the presidency, but it took nine years to complete negotiations. Several factors contributed to this delay. During the first year the impending change in the presidency of the university hindered communications. When it became known in 1956 that Doctor Milton Eisenhower was to be the new president of

Johns Hopkins, a new problem for Loyola arose. A suitable residence was needed for Doctor Eisenhower, and one possibility for its location was on the back acreage of Evergreen. During an early discussion at the university, Albert Hutzler, chairman of the buildings and grounds committee and a prominent Baltimorean, looked at the map and noted that any construction there would effectively block Loyola's development. Father Beatty became aware of these discussions but waited before appealing directly to Eisenhower. It took him two weeks to draft a suitable exposition of the problem. [24] Beatty's letter proved successful and an alternative living arrangement was made for the university's new president. At least the door to future consideration of the property issue remained open.

The ensuing lull gave ample opportunity for a chimera to stalk the process. Whenever the subject of securing Evergreen land is raised in a conversation involving people associated with Loyola, someone is bound to repeat the old (and therefore undoubtedly true) story that there is something in the Garrett will that prohibits Johns Hopkins from transferring any Evergreen land to the college. Quietly but firmly Beatty tried to scotch this many-lived rumor by announcing to the faculty that a careful review by legal counsel for both institutions had uncovered no obstacle to a well-prepared transaction. Even after the transfer this bit of local lore has proven resistant to the obvious fact. There are still people in Baltimore who are sure there is a testamentary obstacle to any transfer of Evergreen land to Loyola. No silver bullet or wooden stake has been found to kill this story, and mere words and deeds have no magic against it.

When in the early 1940s John Work Garrett and his wife informed the trustees of the university that they intended to bequeath Evergreen to the Johns Hopkins, a thorough review of their intentions and wishes was made. Evergreen mansion and its parklike surroundings—one of the last such magnificent tracts left within the bounds of Baltimore— were to become the property of the university upon the demise of the Garretts. Anticipating contingencies, the Garretts made it abundantly clear that the university's trustees were free to dispose of the property to meet future necessities. [25] The formal transfer of ownership to Johns Hopkins did not occur until 1952.

Seven years later, after President Beatty had broached a transfer, a new complication arose. The university asked the city for an adjustment of its boundaries at Homewood that would encompass over seventy acres of Wyman Park. Some of Loyola's friends in the municipal government and around Baltimore wanted to use this request as a lever to pressure the university into making an equivalent accommodation at Evergreen. Father Beatty repeatedly asked these partisans to desist because the university was very sensitive about any process that smacked of a three-way deal.[26]

In mid-February of 1960, Father Beatty conferred with Doctor Eisenhower and they agreed that the time was ripe to begin formal negotiations. A month later, Loyola College submitted a request for land to the trustees of Johns Hopkins. This merely stated Loyola's need, affirmed Loyola's esteem for the achievements of the university, and joined in expressing "the gratitude of the community for the public benefactions of the late Mr. Garrett."[27]

. .

Doctor Eisenhower finally invited both Loyola and Notre Dame to a meeting in mid-May of 1961. He wanted them to know that, although Johns Hopkins planned to move some of its special collections to the Evergreen mansion, it had decided to build a new library on the Homewood campus. This meant that some Evergreen land could be made available to its neighbors. The president of Notre Dame saw no urgent need for additional space for her school but was ready to assist Loyola in its quest.[28] Father Beatty, of course, was overjoyed, but it was another eight months before detailed negotiations began.

Loyola's interests were ably represented by Henry Knott, a well-known Baltimore business leader and an alumnus (class of 1929). The main issues were defined in a memorandum dated January 12, 1962, which limited the tract under discussion to ten acres, and this practically meant the section east of a line drawn from the intersection of Millbrook Road and Westway. The last point was the price to be paid. Two appraisers for the university suggested a basic rate of $15,000 per acre, which made Knott quite angry because he thought it too high. There was, however, no practical alternative, and President Beatty was anxious to start a fund-raising campaign to cover the costs of this additional land and of a new library. In October of 1963 a formal agreement was signed that transferred ten acres of Evergreen to the ownership of Loyola for almost $166,000, with some additional cost for the construction of new homes for the groundskeepers of Evergreen.[29] One of the participants in the process expressed the sentiments of many when he told Father Beatty: "I don't believe anybody else but you would have been successful in acquiring the land . . . for the College, at any price and on any terms."[30]

While negotiations with Johns Hopkins were in progress, President Beatty gave impulse to an even more impressive project. He had begun discussions with the president of Notre Dame, to which Henry Knott was privy, that the two institutions establish a joint library. The additional land from Hopkins made Loyola and Notre Dame neighbors divided only by a chain-link fence. Beatty was reviving a subject that had engaged his interest in 1955 and 1956 when he suggested several facilities that could be erected through the combined efforts of Loyola and Notre Dame. (Since the realization of this joint library would not occur during his term as president, the description of how it was finally accomplished is left for later.)

Father Beatty's direction of Loyola College ended quietly in July of 1964. Few were aware of any impending change during his last semester at Evergreen, although he had held the office of rector for three years longer than usual. It was pleasant but strange when, near the end of that semester, small groups of lay faculty were in turn invited to meet informally with Father Beatty in the lounge of the Andrew White Center. Over drinks there was easy, friendly conversation, but no apparent theme or concern. Nobody offered a good answer to the question: What is this all about? It was evident only later that these small get-togethers were Father Beatty's quiet way of saying goodbye.

After his departure, he served for a time as director of the retreat house at Manresa-on-Severn and later as president of Georgetown Preparatory School. Father Vincent Beatty would, after a full and graceful life, breathe his last in November of 1979.

Part Five

1964–

The Sellinger Years

20

Dormitories and Other Changes

On July 13, 1964, Father Beatty sat down to dinner at the place designated with a napkin in a ring and his successor, Father Joseph A. Sellinger, took the seat opposite him. At the appropriate moment, the minister read the announcement that Father Sellinger had been appointed the new rector of the Jesuit community at Evergreen. Beatty then stood and relinquished to Sellinger the place at table marked by the napkin ring. This was probably the last occasion when a napkin ring played a role in this little ritual. At the next such occasion in 1970, there was no special place reserved for the rector because such things had come to be viewed as remnants of a style of life not compatible with the renewal of the Society of Jesus.

• •

There had been many changes at Loyola College since its founding but in no previous sequence were there so many, such basic, and such pervasive developments as during the Sellinger years. To describe only selected highlights of this conversion will take the next four chapters, but to get some sense of the scale of change several indices may be helpful. In 1964 the annual operating budget for the college amounted to only $1.4 million; by 1984 that had risen to $24 million with an endowment that grew similarly but at a slightly lower rate—impressive achievements even when discounted for inflation. At the end of President Beatty's term, the Evergreen campus included eleven buildings on thirty-three acres. Twenty years later, the area had doubled and there were twenty-seven buildings, including six dormitories and student residences. A jointly supported library now serves both Loyola and Notre Dame. Though the Evergreen campus remains the center, there are several satellite operations.

Enrollments during these twenty years grew from 1,300 students to

6,000, with all divisions coeducational including the undergraduate day sessions, while the number of full-time faculty rose from 50 to 160. In 1964 graduate offerings were restricted to education; in the ensuing twenty years graduate degree programs in business, engineering science, modern studies, psychology, pastoral counseling, and speech pathology were added. Management of the property and business of the college was transferred from an all-Jesuit board of trustees to one on which a majority of members are lay people. It is not too much to say that under the leadership of President Sellinger the institution has become a really new Loyola College that nevertheless retains its basic original character. These increments and changes were not the result of a specific plan relentlessly pursued, but rather the product of a basic vision of excellence and timely response to circumstance—a typically Jesuit approach.

The year 1964 marked a significant turning point in Jesuit education generally. Where previously provincials had closely monitored changes and developments at the schools within their jurisdiction, they now tacitly permitted the institutional presidents to expand with little reference to "higher superiors." It would take another six years to work out the implications of this mandate and to reformulate the relationship between provincials and presidents. The result, as one close observer described it, was that "these Jesuit institutions glided smoothly into the mainstream of American academic life and discovered that their vessels were seaworthy."[1] Significantly, this process was begun among Jesuit colleges and universities before the *Horace Mann* case of 1966 impelled an even broader review of how church-related institutions were affected by their religious sponsorship.

• •

In 1964 Father Sellinger was no stranger to the Evergreen campus. As a Jesuit scholastic he taught freshman chemistry and German, served as the registrar for the evening division, and was moderator of the junior sodality for three years immediately following World War II. His initiative in promoting the Queen's Ball—as well as the grumpy judgment of an older Jesuit on such nonspiritual innovations—has already been noted.

That earlier tour of duty produced an anecdote that provides an enlightening sketch of the young Mister Sellinger. After brief acquaintance, his students began calling him "Antimony Joe." Considering the essential use of that element as a hardening agent, he accepted the nickname, believing that it referred to his emphasis on discipline in the chemistry laboratories and high standards in the classroom. One day while writing the formula for a chemical reaction involving antimony on the blackboard, Mister Sellinger suddenly realized that his nickname was a double-entendre: the chemical symbol of antimony is Sb. This flash of recognition instantly propelled the eraser in his hand toward the semicircle of students and evoked the sort of laughter heard when the point of an in-joke is grasped.

Joseph Sellinger is a second-generation American. His parents, although ethnically German, were born in Rumania in villages less than a hundred miles apart. His mother and father emigrated separately to America before World War I. They met, married, and settled in the Germantown section of Philadelphia, where the elder Sellinger found employment hauling supplies for a knitting mill. The marriage produced two ambitious sons, Frank and Joseph. Joseph was impressed with his older brother because Frank sought a solid education at Saint Joseph's Preparatory School and there displayed his formidable prowess in football. About the time that Father Sellinger became president of Loyola College, his brother was rising in the business world to become president of the Jos. Schlitz Brewing Company.

When Joseph Sellinger completed his elementary education, he followed his brother to Saint Joseph's. His disposition to follow his brother's example was reinforced by the partiality for Jesuits expressed by a favorite elementary-school nun. Whenever he was asked about his future, the younger Sellinger usually answered with a vague reference to medicine. It was a laudable ambition for a lad in his modest circumstances, and it saved him from having to mention his forming interest in the Society of Jesus.

He finally disclosed his desire to become a Jesuit to his mother when she was seriously ill and about to enter the hospital. On being informed of these plans, his father was not impressed, because he believed they arose from his son's diffidence about having the means to complete a medical education. To prove that was not so, Joseph Sellinger garnered scholarships to LaSalle and Saint Joseph's, which, he thought, demonstrated that he could go on if he wished. That point having been made, he applied instead for admission to the Society of Jesus and entered on July 30, 1938. After the long retreat prescribed for all entering the order, Joseph Sellinger was visited at Wernersville by his parents, and his father was reconciled to Joseph's decision.

• •

After seven years in the Society, Sellinger was at Spring Hill College in Mobile, Alabama, completing his course in philosophy. This and his earlier encounter with classical literature convinced him that his basic interests lay elsewhere. The provincial prefect of studies, Father Edward Bunn (then also president of Loyola College), arrived at Spring Hill on one of his periodic visits. Anticipating increased enrollments at Evergreen, he mentioned the need for a chemistry instructor, and Mister Sellinger volunteered for the post.

When his three-year stint at Loyola was completed in 1948, he was attracted to the study of theology and even hoped to pursue it at the graduate level. To complete his basic course of studies Sellinger was sent to Louvain and was ordained there in 1951. He completed his tertianship at Münster and returned to the United States in 1953. The swelling enrollments at the schools of the Maryland province made heavy demands on the available Jesuit manpower, and Father Sellinger had to postpone the start of his graduate work. Instead, he was sent to Georgetown to teach theology and to act as prefect in one of the dormitories until arrangements could be made to release him for doctoral studies.

But that release never came. He was co-opted into administration as a student counselor and master of the dormitories. In 1955 a Middle States Association accrediting team suggested the need to reorganize the university's administrative structure under an academic vice-president. This new responsibility was given to the incumbent dean of the college of arts and sciences. To lighten the dean's load, Father Sellinger was named his associate, and two years later Sellinger became dean.[2]

Over the next seven years, Dean Sellinger was one of the most visible and active members of the Georgetown administration. He became involved with various national educational organizations and took to heart John Tracy Ellis's speech on the need for emphasizing academic excellence in Catholic schools. In his new post Father Sellinger set about recruiting faculty members whose personal scholarship and high standards would encourage excellence. As these teacher-scholars were added to the Georgetown faculty, he organized an honors program with emphasis on the classics and modern literature. He was, according to an alumnus from this period, "constantly pushing and challenging" all the undergraduates to do better, but especially the students enrolled in the honors program.

Little of importance escaped his attention, and nothing roused his ire so quickly as any critical allusion in the school newspaper. After any uncomplimentary reference a hapless editor was immediately called to

Sellinger's office. His theme, asserted loud enough to be heard throughout the building, was: "If you don't like Georgetown as it is, go elsewhere."[3] In this he was acting like other Catholic educators of that period. Father Theodore Hesburgh was delivering the same message to student-critics at the University of Notre Dame. These administrators were anxious to maintain the accustomed order while they worked diligently to improve their institutions, and their experience to date had not accustomed them to such behavior.

Slowly at first but inexorably, the apathy that had characterized the campuses in the 1950s was giving way to the frenetic activism of the 1960s, and Catholic institutions were no more successful than others in erecting bulwarks against the rising tide. In what proved to be Father Sellinger's last year at Georgetown, a few students and faculty members came to believe they had a moral obligation to join sit-ins and other demonstrations in support of the civil rights movement. They were convinced that they were putting into practice the principles they were being taught or were teaching.[4] Many of their peers, however, viewed such departures from generally accepted norms of decorum with disdain if not outright hostility.

• •

By the early 1960s Father Sellinger's energy and dedication made him appear a likely candidate to succeed Father Bunn as president of Georgetown University, even though he would have been only 44 years old when the transfer was due. His relative youth appeared to be no obstacle because of a new attitude in the order. To revitalize the Society and to keep pace with general developments, authorities in the Society let it be known that younger members had to be given greater responsibility. In addition, Father Bunn became Sellinger's mentor. The hoped-for succession, however, was not realized. Father Sellinger's identification with efforts by some rank-and-file members of the Georgetown Alumni Association to reform the association's operations aroused opposition. His mentor quietly suggested that this activity could be damaging to his hopes for the presidency, but Sellinger persisted in what he thought to be a proper and timely course.

In the spring of 1964 he was perplexed to learn that he was slated to become president of Loyola College. Father Beatty, after nine productive but exhausting years, had asked to be relieved. The provincial, partly on Beatty's advice, designated Sellinger as his replacement. Father Sellinger conferred with his superior and explained why he preferred to remain as dean at Georgetown. His efforts to promote academic excellence were just beginning to produce noticeable results—admission of Georgetown to Phi Beta Kappa was one—and he thought the university's development had been hampered in recent years by the lack of stability in the decanal office. The provincial listened attentively, but his next letter to Father Sellinger informed him that he was to report to Evergreen in July. Almost ten years later, Sellinger explained to a federal court how transfers had been managed in the 1960s: "A Jesuit was assigned to a college, or whatever occupation . . . the superior wanted him to go, and he went. . . . In [those] days, when you did not do something [you were told to do], heads did roll."[5]

In preparation for assuming his new responsibilities, Father Sellinger was given a thorough briefing by his predecessor. Beatty stressed the plan to establish a library jointly with the College of Notre Dame of Maryland but suggested that no fund-raising campaign be started until full agreement with Notre Dame had been achieved. Since Sellinger at that time found raising money distasteful, Beatty's caution gave him an excuse for delaying action on this project. Administrative changes at Notre Dame that took several years made full negotiations impractical. Later, reflecting on the delay, he came to believe that considerable momentum had been lost and that earlier attention to the joint library project would have been better.

The only other major project Father Sellinger had in mind initially was the erection of a dormitory. From his days as a scholastic at Loyola, he thought the campus suffered from a provincial tone. His later experience at Georgetown convinced him that resident students had a beneficial effect on the educational process and on general campus life. While he was dean, the number of dormitories at Georgetown had grown from four to nine.

Attracting students from beyond Baltimore and even Maryland had been considered by two of his predecessors. Father Bunn had included a residence among his postwar projects, and Beatty had proposed a dormitory in his first plan for developing the college. In 1964, however, Father Beatty offered Father Sellinger no encouragement for this idea. During the intervening years Beatty apparently became convinced that a dormitory might alienate alumni who thought that a residence would weaken Loyola's commitment to its traditional Baltimore constituency.[6]

• •

Sellinger's inauguration was scheduled for November 12, 1964, when the occasion was brightened by the presence of Father Bunn, who in the name of Georgetown University bestowed an honorary degree on its former dean. Loyola awarded honorary degrees to Austin Murphy, auxiliary bishop of Baltimore; Max Ways (1926), co-founder of Loyola's first student newspaper and then the managing editor of *Fortune* magazine; and Theodore Distler, president of the Association of American Colleges, the organized voice of liberal arts colleges in the United States.

When President Sellinger stepped to the microphone, the audience saw a man of medium height who looked to have the physical energy and power of a halfback. His crew-cut hair and steady eyes gave him the appearance of a Marine Corps officer, and this impression was strengthened by his forceful, resonant voice. Over the years since, presidential peers have described Joseph Sellinger as "a wonderful warm person with a good sense of humor," "very earnest, very determined, if sometimes impatient," and "a fine priest and an exemplary Jesuit."[7]

He tried to lighten the occasion with incidental pleasantries scattered throughout his inaugural address, but its dominant tone was quite serious. After the formal acknowledgments, Father Sellinger briefly alluded to his dreams of erecting "a library . . . and also, I hope, a dormitory for boarding scholars."[8] His use of the word *scholars,* rather than the more common *students,* indicates the practical advantage he anticipated from the introduction of a resident population to the campus. Dormitories meant that Loyola could become even more selective in the students it admitted.

His main theme was that "education is . . . for the essential good of man." For Sellinger, the chief organon in this endeavor remained "the great literatures of Greece and Rome." He illustrated this point with references to Homer, to Cicero, and to Alexander Pope's *Essay on Man.* Approvingly he quoted Russell Kirk's trenchant criticism of American higher education for abandoning its classical, humanistic heritage and replacing it with "mere congeries of vocational and specialized courses with no central core."[9] In effect, President Sellinger was promising, as had all his predecessors, that Loyola College would remain true to its essential tradition. What was different was his renewed emphasis on the humanities at a time when natural sciences generally held a certain pride of place at American colleges.

At about the same time but in a different place Loyola's new president commented on the problems and opportunities he discerned in Jesuit education. To the scholastics at Woodstock he suggested that Jesuit administrators should no longer be satisfied with "regular screw-tightening here and there, with an occasional new paint and polish job."[10] Such complacency had relegated them to be "mere followers" of the Ivy League and "secular education." What Jesuit schools needed was vigorous experimentation, and that required freedom from regulations that had "cabined, cribbed, and confined" them in the past. How aware the scholastics were that provincials had decided to provide just such a bracing atmosphere is not clear.

He also offered some observations on students and their relations with the faculty. Progress at Jesuit schools depended on recruiting an "excellent student body" and this objective should not be subordinated to financial need through increased enrollments. Institutional budgets could be balanced, he thought, by seeking additional support from other sources. About the students Father Sellinger expressed considerable optimism.

> The great majority . . . are ready as never before; they are eagerly ready to have us capitalize on their interest by a challenge which will require the best of the college and the best of them. This generation of students . . . is, by and large, aware of its growing pains and often eager for something better.[11]

His hopeful message could not do other than engage the commitment and dedication of the young Jesuits he was addressing.

• •

Sellinger immediately made changes in several administrative positions closely associated with his office. Others occurred in the normal rhythm of the province's development. In 1965, the academic vice-president and dean, Father Aloysius Galvin, was appointed president of the University of Scranton and was replaced as Loyola's dean by Father Henry Lavin, formerly chairman of the English department. In a few years, the order's emphasis on extending responsibilities to younger members was applied to the lay faculty with the replacement of several department chairmen by experienced but recently employed members. Symbolically, the office of marshal in formal academic processions was transferred from a longtime incumbent to a junior member of the faculty. Not all these changes were universally welcome or handled with equal finesse. Together they manifested President Sellinger's style of leadership, which, while exhibiting a concern for good human relations, places greater emphasis on producing defined results.

President Sellinger delegated broad authority and did not interfere so long as the job was being done but was quick to change administrators when he judged their performance inadequate.[12] In addition, he pursued several projects simultaneously rather than concentrating neatly on one at a time. This makes a simple, sequential narrative of his term difficult, because many things were going on at the same time. Energy, activity, and substantial achievement were keynotes of his tenure.

Administrative matters did not engross Father Sellinger's attention as he tried to give direct impetus to a renewed emphasis on the humanities. As a pilot project, planning was begun for a preceptorial system in the historical survey of Western civilization. There would be greater emphasis on student initiative (a traditional aim of Jesuit pedagogy), a wide range of ideas, and close contact with the faculty. Appropriate memoranda were drafted and preliminary discussions with Father Sellinger were held, but despite general enthusiasm for introducing a preceptorial system nothing practical resulted, apparently because there was not enough experience on campus to prepare an effective presentation for seeking a grant to fund this innovation. It took a while but eventually the necessary expertise was developed and aided in supporting many changes in Loyola College.

A less formal but more successful intellectual enterprise was launched early in 1965. A small group of Jesuit and lay faculty members sponsored a wide-ranging discussion series entitled "Problems in Belief." The coordinator and guiding spirit was Stephen McNierney, a recent addition to the philosophy department. This series provided an opportunity for students and faculty to discuss issues raised by the Second Vatican Council, the civil rights movement, the war in Vietnam, and the unrest on America's college campuses. "Problems in Belief" was a species of teach-in, but it offered little opportunity for the assertive rhetoric and emotionalism that characterized such events on other campuses.

The discussions at Loyola had almost a tutorial air. Volunteers—faculty members, students, guests from other institutions and from the general community—chose a timely subject and either prepared an exposition or made a collection of pertinent readings. These texts were reproduced and distributed before the session, and the discussion leader started with a twenty-minute summary of the main points. What followed was a dialogue, with everyone present licensed to make whatever point he thought could contribute to the process. Titles for a few of the earliest sessions were "Phenomenology of Belief," "The Unbelief of the Believer," "Black Power: Background and Analysis," "The College Student and the Draft," and "The Rebellious Student." For many it was a heady experience merely to hear the variety of opinions expressed, to see faculty members openly—if decorously—disagree with one another and to find themselves daring to question generally accepted views.

The presentations varied in quality, and attendance during the three years of operation was not consistent, but it was always large enough to ensure a lively discussion. "Problems in Belief" provided a forum in which questions that were bothering students and faculty members could be raised. It provided a safety valve for some, and for many others it was an experience that assured them that such free-ranging discussion was not necessarily a harbinger of anarchy and discord. This example was not lost on leaders in student government, who began holding periodic "town meetings" during which campus concerns were aired directly in dialogue among the students, faculty, and administrators.

. .

The renewed emphasis on academic excellence had an unexpected and unwelcome effect on enrollment in 1966–67. Although over 200 freshmen had been admitted in September, only 160 of them were permitted by the new dean to register for the spring semester. The grades for the other 40 were below the level required by the college. Such effects have multiple causes, and a review of admissions and counseling procedures was quickly instituted. The practical result of this loss, however, was to raise the specter of budget deficits. Loyola has always had to rely on tuition as the main source of its income because it has not been able to increase its endowment faster than the rise in costs. The loss of 40 freshmen left a gap in enrollment that would remain for at least the next three and a half years. During this period enrollments hovered around 830 and then fell in 1970 to 801.

The composition of the student body was changing during these same years in accord with the other major point Father Sellinger made in his inaugural. In December of 1966, the *Greyhound* excitedly reported that ground for Loyola's first student residence would be broken in two months and that the dormitory was expected to be in operation by the start of classes in September 1967. Habits of discretion dictated that the full scope of the plan remain obscure, but the unstated intent was to erect at least three dormitories over the next five years. These were meant to accommodate about four hundred students, or almost half the undergraduate day enrollment. To fill these facilities with qualified students, Loyola's recruiting area was enlarged to spread north and west from the metropolitan area around New York City to Chicago and everything in between. The total cost of the dormitories was estimated at over $2 million. It was no small scheme and would in the main be realized.

Construction usually involves delays, but virtually on schedule Loyola's first dormitory was ready in the early fall of 1967. It was named in memory of I. H. Hammerman, a leader in Baltimore's business community and a longtime friend of Fathers Bunn and Sellinger. Located well away from the main buildings (which are covered with light grey stone), the three storys and simple rectangular form of Hammerman House are faced with red brick and a mortar tinted to the same hue, accented only by the bronze window frames and ventilators. The interior was designed to avoid the familiar banes and complaints associated with college dormitories. Rooms do not open directly on a long, echoing corridor but are clustered in groups of four around a lavatory and other service facilities. Except for the hot-water heaters, there is no central plant; each room has its own heating and air-conditioning unit, which can be adjusted to the preference of its inhabitants.

While the dormitory was under construction, some discussion occurred about regulations to govern activities of the residents. Loyola's administrators and faculty were aware of the travail on other campuses. With the rest of the nation, they read in their newspapers or saw on television the vehement demand of students that they be freed of curfews and be permitted to invite friends of either sex to their rooms. To avoid any similar agitation in Loyola's new residence facility, some faculty members recommended a minimum of rules—only those absolutely essential to communal living: no firearms in the rooms, for instance.

This approach did not prevail because the college still considered its responsibility in loco parentis, and so the curfew and other restrictions in force at Georgetown were applied with only minor amendments. This code would soon enough provide the text for objections and demands from the students, but meanwhile Hammerman House had almost eighty residents (about 60 percent of its capacity) during the first year of operation.

Careful planning had kept difficulties to a minimum, and even complaints about the cafeteria food—the most persistent annoyance among college students—were few. The success of the new dormitory prompted a decision to proceed immediately with erecting another. Built essentially on the same design but with an added story, this twin residence was named for Thomas Butler, one of Baltimore's leading bankers and a moving spirit in the Greater Baltimore Committee, which planned and coordinated what has become known as the Baltimore renaissance. Sellinger found a "good chemistry" in his relations with Butler and was deeply impressed with Butler's desire to promote co-operation with Mount Saint Agnes and Notre Dame. Butler saw cooperation among Catholic institutions as an earnest of the talk about ecumenism.[13] Butler Hall was completed in 1969—also on schedule—and this meant that over 160 students, or almost one-fifth of Loyola's total day enrollment, would now be residents. It was another two years before a third living facility was added to the campus, and that was organized differently.

These first dormitories had been carefully sited, but their location alienated Loyola's nearest neighbors. Doctor Jacob Fisher (1949), formerly a member of the biology department but now in charge of college planning and development, oriented these new buildings in such a way as to avoid removal of large old trees. Unfortunately, the buildings' location on a small rise placed them in a position overlooking the backyards of four substantial private homes.

The owners had understood when the college acquired the tract from the Johns Hopkins University that it was to be used for an athletic field, and there was a period during Father Beatty's term when that was the intention. Originally, he could think of no better place to build the new library that Loyola needed than on the old athletic field at the corner of Millbrook Road and Cold Spring Lane. In that case, it would have been necessary to relocate the field on the newly acquired tract. But matters changed significantly when the creation of a library jointly with Notre Dame became a real possibility. The library would likely be erected on land then in the possession of Notre Dame. That eventuality made the land acquired from Johns Hopkins the only practical location for the dormitories. Cogent as this explanation might seem to others, it was not acceptable to the neighboring homeowners. Shortly after Loyola's first dormitory was erected, one of them complained to Father Sellinger that he could not drink his morning cup of coffee without seeing "that building."

A later effort to explain Loyola's future plans and to allay the fears of these neighbors only contributed to the estrangement. One woman gasped when she looked at the map on which Loyola's future development was outlined and saw that new tennis courts were projected on her property.[14] Such faux pas are produced by the best-intentioned organizations and usually are eventually surmounted, but in this case the apprehensions aroused in the late 1960s made leaders of the Kernewood

Association distrustful of the college. When new conditions later necessitated other changes in Loyola's development they would object and attempt to obstruct.

. .

In the midst of all this, Father Sellinger gave impetus to an important development involving the faculty. At a Christmas party in 1965, he asked two laymen (Doctor Charles Hands and myself) "Why doesn't Loyola have an American Association of University Professors chapter?" The two faculty members looked at each other and told him that they had been unable to muster seven interested members (seven being the minimum required for organizing a chapter). Also, they said, there was a feeling that the college administrators had seemed averse to the idea. Sellinger's question appeared to provide enough warrant, however, and the two instructors started the process.

This was a remarkable initiative because Catholic schools and teachers generally have been wary of involvement with the AAUP. Since it was organized in 1915, the AAUP has been identified with the protection of professional standards of academic freedom, tenure, and faculty participation in governance. It is the largest single organization of the American professoriate and numbers over sixty thousand members. The concepts of academic freedom, tenure, and faculty participation in governance were until recently considered an unacceptable interference with the proper functioning of authority at Catholic institutions. Furthermore, the organization of a campus chapter ran against the deeply ingrained Roman attitude that cohesion among subordinates is tantamount to conspiring against authority. Even at the end of the 1960s, the general secretary of the AAUP took note of the continuing reluctance of Catholic professors to join as individuals or to organize campus chapters.[15]

Father Sellinger's question, however, came in the midst of the ferment among Catholics roused by the Second Vatican Council. The council's general call for openness to the world encouraged among other things a greater willingness on the part of Catholics to cooperate with those who were not members of the church and in organizations that had not originally been sponsored by it. The council's specific declaration on Christian education was authoritatively interpreted as being against isolation from the rest of the world and in favor of working in and, "in a sense, *for* the world."[16]

This general attitude was given concrete application to higher education in the 1967 Land O'Lakes Statement. Father Theodore Hesburgh of Notre Date impelled and guided the process that produced this remarkable declaration of principles, and three outstanding Jesuits— Fathers Michael Walsh of Fordham, Paul Reinert of Saint Louis, and Robert Henle, later to become president of Georgetown—were among the leading draftsmen. These Catholic educators ringingly affirmed the fundamental necessity of academic freedom in all subjects taught at Catholic universities, including theology. The necessary though un-stated consequence of this affirmation was that tenure would have to be respected by Catholic authorities. Two years later at a national work-shop in Denver the Jesuits extended the principles enunciated at Land O'Lakes to their colleges as well as to their universities.[17] These devel-opments made academic freedom, tenure, and faculty participation in governance the general rule, with implementation according to institu-tional circumstance.

President Sellinger's encouraging question was evidently part of a large movement, and the local sequel was a careful process of recruit-ment and organization. One or two of the older lay instructors at Loyola joined the AAUP but expressed a preference for limiting recruitment to laymen; they were apprehensive about Jesuit influence in the chap-ter. Most, however, were convinced that the chapter would be more effective if it avoided any us-them dichotomy. Father Fred Homann was elected vice-president of the new chapter, with Doctor Hands as secretary-treasurer and myself as president. By its third year, in Loyola's AAUP chapter had risen to thirty-eight members including six Jesuits, in a regular faculty of only sixty members. By this means, Loyola's fac-ulty developed an even more effective voice in the decision-making process. Two factors had attracted membership: the chapter was active, and it was generally successful on important issues in its early years.

• •

The first issue pursued by Loyola's new chapter was the transfer of the lay faculty's retirement program from the insurance carrier chosen in 1949 to Teachers Insurance and Annuity Association. This did not involve much exertion—merely care and persistence. A proposal was submitted to President Sellinger who, as he had done on most such matters, referred it to the board of trustees. The board in turn advised that because the proposal involved the whole faculty it ought to be con-sidered by the academic council. This formality was easily managed and TIAA soon became the agency for Loyola's retirement program. This provided an attractive feature in efforts to recruit new faculty members.

The next issue raised by the chapter was the establishment of a more rational method for reviewing the salary policy for faculty. Before Father Sellinger's arrival, general policy was drafted by the committee on rank and tenure and individual salaries was determined by informal consultation among the dean, treasurer, and president. In line with his desire to expand participation in the decision-making process, Sellinger chose to consult a board of administrators, which included several who had no experience in academic matters, and which had no faculty members. The absence of the latter and the presence of the former seemed anomalous to the faculty, especially because this board awarded merit increments.

To remedy this situation, the AAUP chapter proposed the election of a small group of faculty representatives to confer with the new academic vice-president. This office was reestablished in 1967 to oversee Loyola's general academic affairs and the incumbent, Father William Kelly, accepted this proposal; all four of the chapter's nominees were elected. These included Stephen McNierney of the philosophy department and Father William Byron, then in economics but a few years later successively president of the University of Scranton and of the Catholic University of America.

These salary discussions, completed early in January of 1968, were brief but efficient and need not be detailed. The overall program would increase the faculty salary cost to the college by 23 percent during three years. The pay of a typical full professor was to increase from just under $12,000 to over $14,700, and a typical assistant professor's salary would rise from $8,500 to $10,200. It was noteworthy that the rate of increase at both levels was almost the same, whereas the common practice among Catholic schools was then to favor the lower ranks.[18] The task of awarding merit increments was now assigned to the committee on rank and tenure, of which a majority were teachers.

The faculty generally approved the program as a good start in making Loyola's salary structure competitive with those at similar institutions. By the second year of the program, however, the Vietnam War–induced inflation rate rose much higher than the one assumed as the basis for the new salary policy. This wiped out the merit increment and eroded the purchasing power of the salaries paid to the faculty. Inflation would be a continuing problem during the 1970s.

The year 1967 was brightened by an innovation in American Jesuit education. Until then the deanship of undergraduate arts and sciences continued to be occupied by Jesuits even though laymen had been appointed to various other administrative positions. Marquette in 1964 had even named a layman to serve as academic vice-president.[19] The first break on the decanal front came at Loyola with the appointment of Frank McGuire (1954), age 31, as dean of the undergraduate day division. A native Baltimorean, he had been student supervisor of the Aberdeen Project on campus and was graduated from Loyola with honors. McGuire took his doctorate in chemistry at the Johns Hopkins University and worked for several years as a research chemist in Wilmington before returning to Loyola in 1963. Among his peers he was judged a quiet and thoughtful man of independent views and of integrity. Although the announcement noted that Doctor McGuire was the first layman named as dean at Loyola, the appointment's larger significance was not mentioned, and comment on this advance subsided rather quickly.

• •

During these same early years, the foundation was figuratively laid for the establishment of a new library jointly with the College of Notre Dame of Maryland. A month before he left Loyola, Father Beatty secured an agreement in principle to move forward on the project and Father Sellinger outlined the concept at the first faculty meeting after he took office. There were then only a few cooperative libraries in America, and these merely integrated the holdings and services of nearby institutions without otherwise modifying the existing corporate structure.

What was envisioned in regard to Loyola and Notre Dame was unique. The two institutions were going to create a third body, a library to serve both of them. This arrangement finessed the problems inherent in formal cooperation between two distinct religious orders, and it promised each a larger and better library than either could individually afford. It also provided a nexus that might later impel more extensive forms of cooperation.

Moving firmly but cautiously in such unfamiliar territory, Father Sellinger arranged for discussions to proceed at several levels. The faculties of both schools were engaged through the establishment of a small committee from each to confer jointly on the characteristics of the proposed library. These discussions were frank and detailed, with the questions raised and answers proposed periodically communicated to each constituency. A few continued to wonder whether the advantages could outweigh the disadvantages. Of the former, the most important was the prospect that Notre Dame would contribute the necessary land. Among the latter was concern that a separate institution might not be as responsive to the faculty and students as a library subject to the same authority as the faculty.

Methodically these concerns were resolved in a detailed agreement between Loyola and Notre Dame. The third party, the Loyola–Notre Dame Library Incorporated, was not created until all the provisions had been settled. The agreement covered all the main issues involved in building and operating the library. It was closely scrutinized by the joint conference committee and the two boards of trustees. The agreement was accepted in September of 1967, and the library was formally incorporated early in the next year.[20] By their diligence and good will, William Kirwan, then Loyola's librarian, and Sister Ian Stewart, librarian at Notre Dame, contributed significantly to this fortunate resolution. It would take several years before building began, and that phase is described later.

• •

In the judgment of an insightful religious historian the 1960s were marked by a disconcerting shift in the "substructures of the American mind." There was evident a lessening attraction from the supernatural and sacral, with a greater inclination toward the natural and the secular. Some avant-garde writers were discussing "the death of God" while others sought a secular interpretation of the gospel and still others were working to demythologize the biblical message. Proponents, opponents, and commentators on the various concepts got much time and space in the mass media. There was a spreading perception of the disparity between what Americans professed and how they acted, and consequently a growing "revolt against the hypocrisies and superficialities of conventional moral codes." Finally, Americans were becoming less assured that the customary ecclesiatical, political, social, and educational institutions could remedy the nation's malaise.[21]

At least at the beginning of the 1960s many American Catholics still tended to believe that these regrettable phenomena were extrinsic to their communal life. During the 1940s and 1950s pressure for reforms in the church came from below and was contained, but in the 1960s reform was mandated by the Second Vatican Council and the pope. In a little more than a decade Catholics had to cope with "the riddle of religion and modernity" that had puzzled Western civilization for over two hundred years.[22] It was an exhilarating and perplexing time marked by more than the usual number of difficulties.

After the Second Vatican Council, the Society of Jesus began a careful effort to discern how the teachings of the council applied to its life and activities, and how to reorganize or reorient its operations for greater effectiveness. It was a wrenching experience in a number of Jesuit communities and during the process of discernment, a number of members of the order sought permission to leave the priesthood. This along with increasing enrollments at Jesuit schools prompted a Jesuit sociologist to predict that by 1978 Jesuits would represent only 5 percent of the full-time faculty and only 15 percent of administrators at Jesuit schools.[23] No general figures are available to test this prediction but in 1978 at Loyola Jesuits represented 6 percent of the faculty and over 20 percent of the administration, even though the overall enrollment in Jesuit schools continued to increase. The departures from the Society and the decline in applications for admission were forcing the order to think seriously about whether or not it would be able to honor all its commitments. Questions were being raised about whether the traditional ministries of the Society were still valuable in the life of the church. These doubts focused especially on higher education. There might come a time when some of the priests and scholastics committed to the operation of Jesuit colleges might be more effectively deployed to other apostolates.

Given such a prospect and the decline in membership, serious thought had to be given to the possibility of transferring control of at least some Jesuit colleges and universities to boards of trustees consisting largely of lay people. This issue had come under intramural discussion even before the Second Vatican Council was convened. Father Robert Harvanek, prefect of studies for the Chicago province, predicted in 1961 that Jesuit colleges and universities would eventually come under lay control, and he argued that this transfer should be sanctioned by the provincials.[24]

This was not a welcome prospect. Even as late as June of 1966 a majority of Jesuit presidents rejected a resolution permitting one or more of their institutions to add lay trustees to their boards. A statistical study of the laicization process after it was virtually completed demonstrates that among Catholic schools generally it began between 1960 and 1965, that is, before the full impact of Vatican II was felt and before the *Horace Mann* case. The process of laicization was not undertaken because of external forces but from an internal desire for more effective development of these Catholic insitutions. Some (even laymen) feared that diluting religious authority would result in the secularization of Catholic schools just as it had in Protestant institutions during the past century. A well-known Jesuit theologian, Father John Ford, raised the specter that addition of lay trustees would violate canon law against the alienation of ecclesiastical property; furthermore, these additions offered no means for assuring the Catholic character of the colleges.[25]

These tides and cross-currents impinged on life at Evergreen. While the question of adding laymen to boards of trustees remained unresolved, a step was taken in the mid-1960s that would facilitate further development—whatever it proved to be. Jesuit institutions were advised to reform their governing boards so that they could play a more effective role in governance. Up to then Jesuit boards tended to consist of the deans, the treasurer, and a few reliable senior Jesuits. If this arrangement had the virtue of expediting business, it provided also a parochial perspective and the possibility of domination by the president-rector. The mid-1960s advisory meant the replacement of campus officers and those subject to the policy directives of a board with Jesuits from other communities and institutions. When the deans of the day and evening divisions yielded their seats in the spring of 1967, the members of the corporation chose Father Charles Costello, president of Loyola High School, and Father Joseph Drane, quondam dean and academic vice-president of the college and now the provincial prefect of studies. Near the end of 1967 the members of the corporation added Edward Donnelly, a prominent Baltimore business executive and an outstanding Catholic who had served on Loyola's lay advisory board. His observation to Father Beatty about the limited character of an engineering education has already been noted. Donnelly was soon joined by Don Zeman (1959) an officer in one of Baltimore's leading accountant firms.

How had this threshold been crossed? The remote preparation for this innovation was the 1959 change in Loyola's corporate bylaws, but there were two more immediate factors. In the *Horace Mann* case, Maryland's highest court had ruled in 1966 that state aid for building facilities at the College of Notre Dame, Saint Joseph's College, and Western Maryland College was unconstitutional because the ethos that permeated these institutions made it impossible to differentiate between the religious and secular aspects of their operations. The refusal of the United States Supreme Court to review the *Horace Mann* decision left in doubt whether any church-related college or university could qualify for federal or state aid. Frank Gallagher (1949), who defended the Catholic colleges involved in the *Horace Mann* case, advised the Jesuits to open their boards and administrative positions to laymen.[26]

The other and possibly more effective factor was the powerful example of Saint Louis University and the University of Notre Dame. About the same time that changes were taking place in Loyola's board, President Reinert and President Hesburgh announced in June of 1967 that their respective institutions would thereafter be fully governed by boards on which members of the religious communities that founded their institutions would be in the minority. Reinert's announcement was particularly significant because while he remained president of Saint Louis he would also serve as president of the Jesuit Educational Association. His presence eased the transition to full rule by the presidents of Jesuit institutions rather than by the provincials. These precedents were reinforced in the plan for renewal adopted by the Maryland province in 1969.[27]

• •

Without knowing much about the structural changes that were occurring at Loyola or their long-term significance, a faculty member (me) proposed that its corporate emblem be amended and stabilized to prevent the proliferation of the casual changes that had been introduced over the years. This suggestion arose from a review of the way the college had managed its corporate insignia. The official seal adopted in 1853 was rarely displayed in the twentieth century except on diplomas, and was never otherwise referred to or explained. It was treated like a remnant from a fading past. As noted at several points in this narrative, various heraldic seals had been used by Loyola and replaced—the last version appearing in 1940. Over the ensuing years, this seal had been reproduced with a number of anomalies and it lacked a motto or any reference to the school colors.

The absence of these elements and such offhand treatment of the college symbol bespoke a tenuous sense of identity and continuity. With the aid of the American College of Arms, a Baltimore institution, a new seal was designed; its dominant theme is an acknowledgment that Loyola College has benefited from two vital traditions, that of the Society of Jesus and that of the state of Maryland. Its main feature is a quartered shield. The lower half reproduces elements from the coat of arms of Saint Ignatius Loyola—the two wolves and a kettle and the seven alternating maroon and gold diagonals that are emblazoned on the seals of many Jesuit schools. The upper half of the shield refers to the location of the college. One quarter contains the Baltimore coat of arms, and the other, composed of a dark evergreen on a light gray field, identifies the site of the campus in the school colors. Unfurled beneath the shield is the college motto: STRONG TRUTHS WELL LIVED. This was taken from President John Quirk's toast on the occasion of Loyola's fiftieth anniversary. In an elegant and heraldically proper form, this seal summarizes what the college has stood for in the past and what it continues to consider most important and most dear.

To protect it from casual alteration, the new emblem was submitted by Father Sellinger to the augmented board of trustees. Arriving as the new seal did just after the addition of a lay trustee (Edward Donnelly, chairman of the lay advisory board, was elected to the board of trustees in September of 1967), its adoption offered a way to symbolize the new context in which Loyola College would be operating. On January 30, 1968, the board of trustees unanimously adopted the new design for a corporate seal. The new insignia, although well publicized through the *Greyhound,* was at best a short-lived curiosity among the students. Like their peers in this traditionally irreverent cohort, they quickly parodied the motto as strong booze well swilled. Such a commonplace reaction was in a way reassuring: even in the late 1960s students did not seem to have changed much.

. .

There were, however, more perplexing freshets in the flow of student opinion then—even at Loyola. Its students were hearing and seeing the same words and images that elsewhere were rousing others to dramatic displays of bad manners, disordered thinking, and callow violence. Nothing spectacular occurred at Evergreen, but campus life could not but be affected by what was happening elsewhere. One accounting merely from January to mid-June of 1968 lists 221 major demonstrations involving 39,000 students at over a hundred colleges and universities.

What was the source of all this turmoil? Who can say with certainty even now? There was, as there should have been, much talk of Vietnam. By June of 1968 it would become America's longest war. It had already claimed twenty-three thousand American lives and involved more than half a million troops—with the commanders asking for more. Predictably this meant that more young men could anticipate a draft call, and that raised for each of them the question of how he should respond. The situation was so complicated that no simple summary of responses is possible. Things were very different from World War II or even the Korean "police action." Many still went dutifully; some sought status as conscientious objectors; a few broke the law in various ways and some of these were prosecuted. Loyola's students responded like their fellows and could be found in all the major categories of this spectrum.[28]

When questioned about the cause of their behavior, America's youth referred to Vietnam, racism, and poverty. But how these issues could be resolved by dynamiting, burning, trashing buildings, or roughing up college presidents and deans was never explained. This violence seemed to be an expression of impotent rage. Some analysts point to a demographic push. During the 1960s the median age of the American population fell from 30 to 25. This meant many more young people in proportion to the rest of the population, and for these their earliest recollections were of postwar affluence rather than of the stringencies of the depression and World War II. To growing numbers may be added the evidence of increasing economic power. Business and advertisers had become aware of young consumers who together had twenty-five billion dollars a year to spend. Products and enticements were tailored to this younger taste.[29]

Contributing to the atmosphere that produced the student turmoil were a series of national traumas beginning with the assassination of President John Kennedy in 1963 and reaching a bewildering climax in 1968 with the killing of the Reverend Martin Luther King and Robert Kennedy. Incongruously, the death of Doctor King, "an apostle of nonviolence," set off "the worst outburst of arson, looting, and criminal activity in the nation's history."[30] Almost 170 cities and towns suffered from a week-long orgy of rioting. The nation's capital was the most severely ravaged. In downtown Baltimore, people attended Palm Sunday services under the protection of the National Guard. The editor of the *Catholic Review* described a nightmare with troops near the old Basilica and "fires flaring against the crisp night sky."[31] To channel the grief and perplexity Loyola College with Mount Saint Agnes and Notre Dame sponsored a well-attended memorial service for Doctor King, but it took more than fifty-thousand troops to contain and finally extinguish the nationwide conflagration. Two months later, after Robert Kennedy's death, some openly wondered whether the United States had degenerated into a banana republic.

If the causes were hard to identify, the results were clear enough. Responsible national leaders, black and white, redoubled their efforts "to remove, as far as possible, the roots of such bitter racial antipathy."[32] Meanwhile there was still abroad in the land a lambent and ill-defined discontent with things as they were. Liberalism, conservatism, and other "accepted modalities of social thought" were indiscriminately lumped together as "The Establishment"—and protestors under age 30 were against it. It should be noted, however, that almost three-quarters of the students never took part in any demonstration during their four college years. For all the dramatic incidents graphically displayed in the media, American students in the late 1960s were afflicted more with a quibbling and contentious mood than with a steely determination to overthrow "The Establishment."[33]

Some of this miasma seeped into activities at Evergreen, but here it did not result in the confrontations that bothered other institutions— including a few Jesuit schools. A majority of Loyola's students were still commuters who left the campus each day. The small corps of activists lacked a critical mass or a ready support, and they pursued their goals, more often than not, in good temper. As they saw the situation, the college was overdue for a drastic reformation, and "what [Loyola] will be, we must decide."[34]

ROTC was their most opportune target, but no serious effort was mounted to abolish it. To dramatize their disgust with the Vietnam War, some students organized the Martin Luther King Peace Society that in May of 1969 held a demonstration, which was rather decorous, to say the least. An antiwar Jesuit from Georgetown gave a talk; there were films and a Mass in the center of the campus. The climax was a silent vigil, which coincided with the annual president's review of ROTC cadets. After the march-by a number of ROTC cadets joined this peace demonstration. There was respectable attendance at these events by faculty and students, but before "Peace Week" had even begun, the practical issue had been eliminated. Bowing to nationwide pressure, the army dropped the compulsory requirement and relied instead on scholarships and other inducements to attract volunteers for ROTC. This timely action limited but did not entirely eliminate opposition to ROTC even at Loyola.

• •

Others among the student body aimed their protest against the course requirements in philosophy and theology, and here too a timely adjustment avoided greater conflict. The door to modifying philosophy and theology requirements was left ajar after a 1962 national workshop for Jesuits, and change came to each campus according to local initiative.[35] Under the leadership of Stephen McNierney among the philosophers and Father James Connor among the theologians, the departments agreed on a sequence of two required courses and two electives in each discipline, with a required course in ethics to be taken at the student's discretion under the aegis of either department. This meant a substantial diminution of the time assigned to these subjects. Philosophy and theology still accounted for an important segment of the curriculum, but not for nearly as much as they had since just before World War I. When this proposal was submitted to the academic council, it made some of the faculty, both Jesuit and lay, uneasy because the centrality of philosphy and theology to Jesuit education had been virtually an article of faith for so long.

After two long, searching discussions, the proposal was approved after the philosophers affirmed their commitment to "the existence of God, the immortality of the soul, and the freedom of the will," although they were "not wedded to any particular philosophical expression of these commitments."[36] In practice this meant an end to the Thomist monopoly. Even with these assurances, at least one Jesuit member of the council—not by any means the oldest—registered his opposition. This did not matter in practical terms, because eighteen of his colleagues voted in favor of the revision. Similar adjustments were being made in these years at most other Jesuit institutions, but at Loyola this change in the philosophy-theology requirements was the beginning of an even broader revision. A faculty committee was appointed to review the whole curriculum and the academic calendar. In the nature of such efforts, it took several years before the new curriculum and calendar were submitted to general scrutiny and discussion.

The hottest campus issue was the rule requiring students to wear coats and ties when not engaged in athletics, and this too was managed with an appropriate modification. Until the late 1960s this regulation had by and large been observed, and little attention was paid to it. Two factors weakened it, and another made it an issue. The dormitory students were no longer under the watchful eye of their parents, and the cut system was modified so that ejection from class for improper dress carried no other penalty. And the college officers now diligently tried to enforce the rule. At a February of 1968 "town meeting" President Sellinger declared: "I want to make this real clear, this is my rule. . . . I want it and we shall keep it."[37] To this the student reaction was mixed. One student noted that Father Sellinger had brought about many changes in the life of the college and it seemed only right to defer to him on this point. Some regretted the impasse but accepted the situation.

Others, however, were not so willing to let the issue rest. In April of

1968 about two hundred students attended a "town meeting." After rehearsing their grievances, they decided to march—*orderly* was their watchword—to the president's office. One leader sternly warned any of faint heart to drop out now and then more than half the assembly strode the short distance from the student center to the Jesuit residence. While the main body blocked the roadway, their spokesmen went in to confront Father Sellinger. His secretary expressed regrets that he could not meet with them because he was in Annapolis, but, she added, they could have an appointment for early Monday morning—an offer they accepted.

Still determined to demonstrate about something, the students now sat on the traffic bump in the roadway just outside the door to the residence. These bumps were one of the lesser but nevertheless strongly felt grievances—not merely among the student body. The bumps had been unexpectedly installed during a Thanksgiving vacation and were so constructed as to jar and rattle the heaviest vehicles. While the students blocked the roadway, a bell sounded to announce the end of a class period. In ten minutes another ring would mark the start of class. First one, then another, and then a third student arose and half-apologetically walked off. Marylanders, even young ones, are nothing if not practical, and few wanted to throw away a fraction of tuition already paid. The game of confrontation was not nearly as important to the students as their work.

This student fiasco was not the end of the matter. Afterwards, Father Sellinger appointed a small committee of students, faculty, and alumni to review the subject of a dress code. Its report was a model of circumspection, listing the arguments for and against relaxation but leaving a decision to the president. Read closely, however, it contained a clear indication that some modification would not be unacceptable, even to the alumni. The final straw was a chance conversation between Father Sellinger and an alumnus who groused about his son's long hair and casual dress, but who anticipated that Loyola would soon remedy these because his son had been accepted as a freshman. Father Sellinger did not believe that was the most important function of a college. Although he would not concede complete autonomy to students, he agreed that "we should divest ourselves of many responsibilities we have clung to in the area of student affairs."[38]

Furthermore, a former Marine Corps officer, Morgan Lavin, had become the new dean of men. (Another Jesuit bastion in the structure of the college had been yielded to a layman.) Lavin thought young men had "the right to be responsible." To him this meant working with the students and faculty to enlist social pressure for compliance rather than merely attempting to enforce rules. In September of 1968 the coat-and-tie rule was modified, although it was not entirely abrogated. Time and lessened attention gradually ended the problem—to everyone's relief. Coincidentally and with a minimum of fuss, representatives of student government were accepted as members of the academic council—another national phenomenon.

The question whether or not the student furor of the late 1960s was worthwhile elicits—as one might expect—a variety of answers. There were no doubt a number of minuses and pluses, and temperament, point of vantage, or experience is likely to determine which of these a respondent emphasizes. On balance, however, the attitude among Loyola's activists from this period was probably best summarized later by Dave Townsend (1969), president of the student body during the climactic year, who said after graduate work at Harvard:

> I had a good education and a handful of the best teachers I have encountered. I was able to think seriously about serious theological and philosophical questions and to be taken seriously—if not always with affection. And I believe, perhaps arrogantly, that the College was much better when I left than when I came . . . and I think I had something to do with the improvement.[39]

There is a reminder in these words that along with the sound and fury —such as it was—the process of education continued during these years. The bubble of agitation burst in May of 1970 when four students at Kent State and two at Jackson State were shot. Activists continued to harangue but they could no longer mobilize significant support.[40]

• •

There was a more attractive side to campus acitivities in the mid-1960s. In January of 1965 Father Frank Bourbon sparked the establishment of Loyola Students for Social Action (LSSA) after reading about a similar development at Georgetown. The aim of the new organization was to help the Baltimore community and to familiarize Loyola's students with what it means to live in the inner city. The student leaders of LSSA were Francis and John Knott (1969), scions of that energetic tribe.

LSSA was an ambitious operation. It created a network of volunteers from Notre Dame, Mount Saint Agnes, and other nearby colleges and high schools—both church-related and public. These served as instructors in remedial reading and as paramedics, or supervised study halls for students who did not need any tutoring, just a quiet place to do their homework; some worked as trainers for "unteachables" at a facility for the mentally retarded. The report of LSSA activities of the end of its first year of operations was painfully honest. The volunteers quickly found that enthusiasm and good intentions were not enough and they willingly undertook the required training.

One of the most spectacular and most enduring projects started by LSSA was a marathon flag-football game. All the proceeds were dedicated to Santa Claus Anonymous, a Christmastide charity created by the local Junior Chamber of Commerce (Jaycees). Learning that a Jesuit school on the West Coast claimed a world record for playing the game continuously for seventy hours, Loyola students led by John Knott were determined to set a new record. But organizing the marathon game was easier said than done. The opponents would have to provide the field, and insurance liability had to be covered. These were satisfactorily worked out, and students from Towson State College (now University) accepted the challenge.

From noon on Friday, December 9, 1968, until noon of the following Monday, Loyola students in squads of nine chased similar groupings of Towson students up and down the field. In flag-football there is no tackling, and blockers have to remain on their feet. A runner is downed if an opponent snatches one of the brightly colored flags worn on each side of the waist. About fifteen teams for each side ran, passed, and punted in two-hour stints. More than fifteen thousand Baltimoreans came to view this spectacle. At the end, the score was Loyola 580 and Towson 904. One of Loyola's tired and mud-spattered players explained the disparate result: "Towson State's got a bunch of physical education majors playing. All we have is philosophy majors."[41] Anyway, Santa Claus Anonymous was richer by about seven thousand dollars.

Institutional authorities may have been complaisant that this first game would exhaust a lot of youthful energy and would probably not be repeated, but the game was held the following year with a larger donation to the charity. Eventually the affair was incorporated, and teams from practically all the colleges around Baltimore (including "powderpuff" squads of competing women) were attracted to join the melee. Two decades later, a weekend early in December will be rent by the signals, shouts, sweat, and cheers of young men and women playing flag-football. The time devoted to this pastime has varied according to the number of teams and on occasion has exceeded a hundred hours. LSSA has long since disappeared from the roster of student organizations, but its functions have been absorbed into the campus ministries' volunteer services and outreach programs.

21

Take-Off

For Baltimore the years between 1967 and 1971 were alarming. The riots after Doctor King's death only added to a soaring crime rate. Exodus to the suburbs peaked in this period and narrowed the city's tax base, just as bonds for previous renewal projects matured. Throughout the country people were saying that America's major cities were dying and were becoming ungovernable.[1] It was the unfortunate lot of Thomas D'Alesandro III (1949) to serve as mayor during this troubled period in Baltimore's history. He has eloquently expressed the anguish he experienced as mayor, walking the streets of his city while troops and tanks occupied strategic positions in an attempt to restore order.

For Loyola the years between 1966 and 1973 had a very different character. It was during these years that the master's program in business administration was inaugurated; that the lay presence on the board of trustees became effective; that the college became fully coeducational as a result of the merger with Mount Saint Agnes; and that enrollments began to increase. These developments have been identified by Rhoda Dorsey, president of Goucher College, and Steven Muller, president of the Johns Hopkins University, as marking the emergence of a new Loyola College. Muller noted that if things had gone badly, Father Sellinger would have been blamed; thus, credit must go to him for things having gone so well. Father Theodore Hesburgh, former president of the University of Notre Dame, agreed but cautioned that such a complex process was not the work of one person—no matter how talented or determined.[2]

. .

Father William Kelly was a leading figure during the first three years of this period. He had a reputation in the Maryland province as a troubleshooter, and his abilities would be particularly useful in preparation for Middle States evaluation in 1969. He was effective in the executive aspects of his labors because he was a careful, indefatigable worker; a softspoken man, Father Kelly was of medium height and portly, and, like Sellinger, he wore a crewcut.

Upon arriving on campus in 1966, Father Kelly was given operative responsibility over the graduate program and one of his projects was the addition of a master of business administration (M.B.A.) degree. Changing what had become the customary procedure for dealing with such matters, President Sellinger appointed a small task force, including Father Kelly, Bill Carton, chairman of the business department, and Ron Biglin, an assistant professor, to prepare a feasibility study. By then, an M.B.A. had become a desirable credential nationally, and quite a few schools were offering it. Among these was the University of Scranton, the school from which Father Kelly came to Loyola. No institution in or near Baltimore then offered such a program, even though a Junior Chamber of Commerce survey documented the existence of over one thousand potential applicants. Here was an opportunity that some school was bound to notice soon—why should it not be Loyola?

The task force completed its report by the end of November, and Sellinger asked the academic council to consider the proposal at the next meeting. The usual difference of opinion appeared with some members favoring it, some opposed, and others wanting more time to analyze its implications for the future development of Loyola. The need and carefully estimated cost and revenues having been demonstrated in the report, the proposal for establishing an M.B.A. program was adopted by a substantial majority without further study. Nonetheless, this summary procedure disturbed several members of the faculty and administration.

Deliberation did not end there, since correspondence aimed at dissuading Father Sellinger continued. An opponent among the experienced Jesuits on the board of trustees feared that the expansion of the professional focus of the graduate division would dilute Loyola's commitment to the liberal arts at the undergraduate level. The proponents of the M.B.A. argued that the college had long since accepted a dual commitment to both the liberal arts and professional training. That threshold had been crossed seventeen years earlier when the graduate program in education was established.

By February of 1967, Father Sellinger accepted the reasoning of the proponents. He perceived an opportunity in the new program for dealing with "the ethical implications of management and decision-making" without diluting the program's professional quality. The M.B.A. program would also serve as a hedge against the economic crisis, anticipated during the next five years, for small liberal arts colleges. Furthermore, Sellinger saw the M.B.A. program as "an opportunity for Loyola to tie itself into the business community and thus derive substantial financial support for the overall operation."[3] His initial appeal to Baltimore business leaders might, he thought, be in the half-million dollar range, with only a part to be earmarked for the new program and the rest for general support.

The M.B.A. program was inaugurated in September of 1967 with over seventy students and a departmental faculty augmented by Father William Byron and Doctor Paul Ergler. Any new program brings a few problems, and in this one it was the rustiness of the mathematical skills of the students. It was more than a few years since many of them had wrestled with the intricacies of algebra or calculus, and knowledge of these is basic to the new techniques of management. Within a few cycles, this deficiency was remedied. By 1970 over four hundred students were registered in the M.B.A. program, and from then until the end of the decade yearly enrollments, while fluctuating within a wide range, grew at an average rate of 13 percent. This singular and high-quality program brought Loyola to the attention of more and more business and civic leaders. This ended the relative obscurity under which the college had labored since its founding.

. .

By the time the M.B.A. program was in operation, Father Kelly had been appointed academic vice-president—an office vacant since Father Galvin's departure. In the summer after his promotion in 1967 Kelly appointed a task force, composed of several leading faculty members and the deans, to revise Loyola's rank-and-tenure policy. This was a timely exercise, but in addition the AAUP chapter shortly after its formation had requested the college formally acknowledge its reliance on the 1940 Statement of Principles on Academic Freedom drafted jointly by the AAUP and the Association of American Colleges (AAC). The former represents the views of the American professoriate; the latter is an organization composed of those responsible for the operation of America's liberal arts colleges. Such joint sponsorship probably accounts for the acceptance of the 1940 statement by so many of America's finest colleges and universities. In the years since its promulgation more than eighty professional organizations, including the Catholic historical and philosophical associations, have formally adopted it as the norm for their memberships.

To focus the committee's discussions, Father Kelly distributed a preliminary draft that incorporated the basic principles of the 1940 AAUP/AAC Statement on Academic Freedom. This meant that Loyola College formally affirmed what had in fact been its practice: that all its teachers were entitled to undertake any research and to publish whatever flowed from their scholarship; that in the classroom all teachers were free to discuss the subject matter as required by that discipline; and that they were not subject to any institutional censorship or discipline merely for exercising their rights as American citizens—with the proviso that they take care that their personal views not be imputed to the college.

Though most often associated in the popular mind with the protection of a controversial professor against arbitrary dismissal, academic freedom has a broader, social, justification. Russell Kirk identifies it as a "high moral value ultimately derived from a religious conception" of human nature. Other proponents see it as "an intrinsic part of an open, democratic society." For still others, such as Robert Hutchins and Sidney Hook, academic freedom has an "instrumental value in the improvement of life in our society."[4] These last in particular have drawn from historical experience the lesson that repressive societies have not been as broadly productive as those that have institutionalized the defense of freedom. Which has been more generally admired for the quality of its life, ancient Athens or Sparta? Current examples are obvious.

Tenure, the other side of the same coin, was dealt with almost as expeditiously by Father Kelly and the 1967 task force. As defined in Kelly's draft, tenure was "an expectation of continuing employment given to a teacher by Loyola College," and the college pledged "that the service of a teacher shall not be terminated except for adequate cause."[5] This is the general understanding of academic tenure and had been established at Loyola by the early 1950s. In a few particulars the process for granting tenure at Loyola differed from that promoted by the AAUP, but these were eliminated by Father Kelly.

His most statesmanlike act was the resolution of an anomaly. Loyola's tenure policy required teachers to acquire a doctorate by the end of the seven-year probationary period or they would be denied promotion to the rank of associate professor and their employment terminated. Up or out is the general principle, but during the years since Loyola first established its policy it had engaged several able teachers who from various circumstances—some entirely beyond their control—could not complete their doctoral work. Instead of dismissing them at the end of the probationary period, the college waived its up-or-out requirement. As far as the college was concerned these teachers were not tenured, but the AAUP treats any full-time teacher retained after the probationary period as tenured de facto and judges dismissals on that basis.

Father Kelly cut the Gordian knot by announcing that the few faculty members in this anomalous position—mostly laymen—were now recognized as tenured by Loyola College. This took care of the past and avoided a possible conflict when the revised policy was submitted to the faculty. For the future, tenure was not specifically tied to the rank of associate professor, although the possession of a doctorate remained a normal condition for employment at Loyola.

The grant of tenure is considered by many outside academia as most unusual because they believe it means lifetime employment. This is a common but careless use of the word *lifetime.* Crowned sovereigns hold office on such tenure and this is why revolutionaries execute kings and emperors. Death is the only release from a *true* lifetime position. A tenured professor, on the other hand, has a conditional right to employment only until retirement age is reached, or unless the professor's behavior is provably improper or the institution faces grave financial difficulties.

What tenure means practically is that a professor can be dismissed before retirement only for a serious cause. The procedure requires an institutional officer to file charges of incompetence or misconduct and to prove the accusation to a small body of professionals—senior faculty members. Even if this group judges the institution's case to be inadequate, the faculty member may be fired by action of the president or trustees. Academic tenure has never been an invulnerable shield; it merely raises the threshold at which the discussion of dismissal takes place.

Although attention is generally focused on dramatic instances, this is not the most important facet of the tenuring process. Its most common and most pervasive effects impinge on the planning and hiring process and on the supervision of teachers. Tenuring forces an institution to plan its development carefully, with emphasis on long-range objectives. Once a teacher has completed the probationary period and acquired tenure, it becomes much harder to fire him or her than to fire an office worker, and so care must be taken in the recruitment of a teacher. The certainty of having eventually to make a decision about tenure implies close attention to and supervision of a teacher during the probationary period. Laxness on the part of those responsible for administering the multistage tenure process has, on occasion, led to institutional embarrassment, but occasional abuse is grounds for reform—possibly only of personnel—not for the elimination of a policy that contributes to institutional stability and excellence.

Finally, tenured faculty are a resource for the steady, balanced development of a school. Administrative officers do not enjoy tenure but serve only at the "good will and pleasure" of whoever appointed them. As a result, they are more easily disciplined. High-quality educational institutions, however, are not likely to be produced in a situation where every whim or fad is immediately put into operation. That has been tried within the last two decades in America without notable success (e.g., at Parsons College). Although education like almost everything else must be subjected to financial restraints, it is too complex and cooperative a process to adopt a marketplace ethos wholesale. The decisiveness of administrators needs to be balanced by careful thought, and that ideally comes from a school's tenured faculty.

. .

The only tenure issue that caused any discussion at Loyola in 1967 was how the process applied to Jesuits. Father Kelly proposed that if a Jesuit acquired tenure it was to be contingent on his remaining a member of the order. Departure from the Society—a phenomenon frequent in the late 1960s—abrogated the college's pledge of tenure. This was an attempt to secure the authority and practices traditional in religious orders but was not acceptable to the AAUP. The system of tenure had grown in American institutions without significant involvement of religious communities, and the professoriate viewed contingent tenure as no tenure.

The question had been discussed in March 1967 at a national conference of Jesuit educators, who were unable to reach a specific conclusion. They chose instead to leave the matter to the experience and determination of the faculties at Jesuit schools.[6] One university did adopt the general principle proposed by Father Kelly and in 1976 found itself censured by the AAUP for the way it handled a tenured Jesuit who left the order.

When the draft containing contingent tenure for Jesuits was circulated among Loyola's faculty, laymen and Jesuits objected—the latter more vigorously. They argued that Loyola College had only one faculty, subject to one set of rules for promotion and tenure, even though the faculty were in different states of life. This had been the formal rule since 1956 when the committee on rank and tenure began its operations. Prudently, Father Kelly deleted this principle from his draft.

In the revision process, the last point that drew attention was the composition of the body that formally recommended promotion and the granting of tenure. Since 1956 these recommendations had been the responsibility of an appointed committee chaired by the dean or the academic vice-president. By 1967 the other four members were all teachers and a majority were laymen. No one suggested changing the number of members, and everyone agreed that the faculty members should no longer be appointed but should be elected by their peers. Father Kelly went one step further by proposing that the new board on rank and tenure have only faculty members. He acceded to the argument that in a process with several stages involving administrators, it was valuable to have a clear statement of the faculty's judgment. To some a board composed entirely of faculty may not seem much, but it made Loyola College one of a very few Catholic colleges that vested responsibility for these matters in an elective board made up entirely of active professionals. [7]

The final product from the task force was not considered ideal by anyone. Such documents rarely achieve perfection in principles or language, but this one's major provisions marked a definite improvement. The faculty, which had been consulted periodically during the drafting process, reviewed the final text under the aegis of the AAUP chapter and registered its strong assent. The academic council made a few additional changes and recommended approval by the board of trustees, which acted favorably shortly thereafter.

. .

The operation of the new board on rank and tenure ran into an unexpected crisis during the first year. Its five members consisted of all four members from the old committee, including Father John Wise, with Doctor Charles Hands added. The board elected me as its chairman. Near the end of the fall semester in 1968, the new board had to deal with an unusually heavy load because applications for promotion and tenure were then processed together and there were thirteen applicants for promotion and ten for tenure (seven were to be reviewed for both). A sense of responsibility and a desire to do well on this first round caused the board to work even more systematically and more slowly than the old committee.

After recommendations had been agreed upon, not all unanimously, the board met once more to review its recommendations as a whole. In three instances, it finally recommended against promotion for reasons such as the applicant's having been a member of the faculty for so short a time that no clear impression of the person's teaching ability was available. Recommending tenure is a more significant decision, and the board in three instances supported such a grant even though there was one or another technical credential missing. The overall competence of these teachers justified exceptions. These and the other recommendations were transmitted in February of 1969 to Father Kelly in the customary form but instead of undergoing the customary executive review, the recommendations were submitted to the board of trustees as provided in the new policy. This change had been introduced by Father Kelly and aroused no discussion.

Faced with having to approve twenty recommendations, a few trustees asked for additional information on all the recommendations. Not having anticipated this unprecedented request, the board on rank and tenure thought it would not be helpful or informative to attempt to reconstruct the reasoning of more than a month earlier. The faculty members believed that they had explained the exceptional instances and would now be forced to justify all their other recommendations. This seemed a futile exercise. They thought it was obvious that the absence of an additional note on a recommendation meant that the applicant had in their judgment fulfilled all the requirements of the college's policy. What the board suggested was that the trustees accept or reject the recommendations and, as provided in the policy, return those it rejected to the board on rank and tenure for reconsideration.

While this exchange was in progress, Father Kelly suggested significant changes in the structure and procedures of the new board on rank and tenure. His basic premise was that the board was "attempting to set itself up in an adversary position to the Administration of [the] College."[8] His remedy was reintroduction of the academic vice-president as a member of the board and addition of the deans. Furthermore, he drafted a set of guidelines, the main objective of which was to slow promotions. Although the policy stipulated a three-year requirement in the rank of assistant professor for promotion to associate professor, he thought this a bare minimum and that the average time in rank should be at least five years. The board acknowledged that this might be a legitimate concern for an academic vice-president, but it was constrained to act according to the explicit terms of the policy.

In form at least, Kelly's suggestions would have marked a return to the structure established in 1956 when administrators deliberated directly with the faculty on promotion and tenure. In spirit, however, it would have been a reversion to an even older mode of operation. This was a tense and difficult time for the board members. Because of the confidential nature of their responsibilities, they felt unable to explain the situation to the rest of the faculty or appeal to them for support.

The problem was resolved in mid-March when President Sellinger arranged a meeting of the trustees and the chairman of the board on rank and tenure. The trustees were interested in how the board had gone about its work, and after satisfying themselves on this they approved all the recommendations except one in which the board had advised *against* a promotion. The review of promotion and tenure recommendations by the trustees continued, though with much less difficulty, until the early 1970s, when the board augmented by an experienced lay academic administrator delegated this function again to the president.

• •

Father Kelly was more at ease in larger, more specifically administrative, ventures. He worked hard to increase cooperation with Mount Saint Agnes and was aided in this endeavor by the strong commitment of Sister Cleophas Costello, president of Mount Saint Agnes College. Throughout the country there was a notable increase in academic consortia and cooperative programs of various kinds after 1965, when federal assistance became available for such ventures. There was also more thought being given to mergers, especially between previously all-male and all-female institutions.

The approaching evaluation of both schools by the Middle States Association was viewed by Father Kelly as an opportunity for achieving several goals simultaneously. Loyola and Mount Saint Agnes arranged with the Middle States to be visited in 1969 by the same team, so that not only each school, but also the degree and quality of their inter-institutional cooperation, would be evaluated. To promote the general process, Sister Cleophas was elected a member of Loyola's board of trustees in October 1968, after she had resigned the presidency of Mount Saint Agnes.

About nine days later, with Sister Cleophas in attendance, Father

Kelly submitted a proposal to the Loyola trustees for the establishment of "the Federated Colleges of Maryland," of which Loyola and Mount Saint Agnes were to be the first members. Such an arrangement left both institutions intact but coordinated their operations so that "mine" and "yours" were converted into "ours."[9] The trustees of both schools were to retain full title of all property, buildings, and endowment funds and the right to review plans for future development. However, the operational responsibility for both institutions and their future development was to be vested in a board of regents. The anticipated savings in personnel and other operating costs was estimated at seventy-five to eighty thousand dollars a year.

Despite this cautious avoidance of a merger, discussion of the proposal was postponed in December 1968. The new president of Mount Saint Agnes, a layman, asked for the delay, and this seriously disappointed Father Kelly. He thought a "critical period" had been reached in the process and, unless forward movement was maintained, apprehensions on both campuses about a loss of identity might become too formidable to overcome.

This postponement of the federation proposal did not interfere with other cooperative efforts. Loyola College singly, and in combination with Mount Saint Agnes on the one hand and with Notre Dame on the other, applied to the federal government for grants in varying amounts during the last few years of the 1960s under the guidance of Father Kelly. His diligence and grantsmanship provided a capability that had earlier been lacking at Evergreen.

The most significant application, in cooperation with Mount Saint Agnes, was a program for joint deliberations by the faculties of both schools in preparation for the Middle States visitation. There were also projects to rationalize plant operations on both campuses and to coordinate record-keeping procedures. They were to be assisted by consultants from the Johns Hopkins University and from Lybrand, Ross Brothers, and Montgomery, one of Baltimore's leading accounting firms. Loyola, in addition, was seeking funds to computerize its operations; the J. E. Greiner Company, an engineering firm, served as consultant on this project. The opportunity was provided mainly under Title III of the Higher Education Act of 1965, which had been passed after Lyndon Johnson became president. The law was intended to support developing institutions and cooperative programs.

Another element of these applications involved Loyola and Notre Dame. They were seeking federal support for the early phases of the establishment of a joint library. This meant planning the facilities and recataloging both collections so that they could eventually be combined. Although the federal agencies approved these applications, they did not grant all the money sought—a common practice that provides evidence of care in the disbursement of public funds and is anticipated by knowledgeable applicants. In May of 1968, a press release announced a federal grant of $100,000, and a year later a similar announcement took note of an additional $86,000. All the most important projects were funded either from federal funds or from other sources. To continue and expand this successful fund-raising effort a development office was reestablished with Father Daniel McGuire as its head.

• •

Part of the federal grant was put to immediate use in preparation for the Middle States visitation. The faculties of Loyola and Mount Saint Agnes participated in a three-day working seminar before classes began in September of 1968. Separately the Loyola and Mount Saint Agnes faculties reviewed the reports they had prepared for the Middle States evaluation and together by departments they proposed ways to increase interaction. Other events were arranged to encourage people to become better acquainted.

Such exercises produce many reports, and the Woodstock seminar was no exception. Father Kelly and Sister Judith Schmelz, dean of Mount Saint Agnes, were quite satisfied with the results. When interviewed by a reporter, Father Kelly explained the reason for seeking closer ties: "With the competition we're facing, we must ask ourselves, can we as a small institution produce an excellent product?" Such a result seemed more likely through greater cooperation but not, he carefully noted, in the form of a merger. Maintaining the two colleges as separate institutions would capitalize on the main advantages of smallness—"A more personal approach to education and a chance for getting better acquainted with students."[10]

During the ensuing year, the usual process of preparing for the accreditation inspection was completed. The faculty and students at Loyola reviewed the various reports—not as exhaustively as in 1957 but still in a manner that made everyone feel involved. These reports and comments were edited and combined by a steering committee that included faculty, students, and administrators. In over two hundred pages, with copious tables and statistics, Loyola College described its aims, operations, and outcomes to the Middle States Association. The evaluation team visited both campuses in mid-November of 1969, and in a few months produced searching, helpful, well-balanced, and favorable reports on both schools. There was no repetition of Loyola's earlier experience with this process. Its accreditation was reaffirmed, as was that of Mount Saint Agnes.

About the cooperative efforts of the two colleges, the Middle States team delicately tried to convey a sense of urgency. It commended the schools for their efforts but noted that "the central question they must resolve is not whether and how they can improve their programs, but whether they can survive another decade."[11] This comment prompted thoughts among the officers of Mount Saint Agnes "of the necessity for the inclusion of Notre Dame in a cooperative program."[12] Much the same idea appeared in the report of the Middle States team that visited Notre Dame in mid-February of 1970. These promptings from the Middle States Association gave renewed impetus to the search for a mutually acceptable formula for greater cooperation among Baltimore's Catholic colleges.

• •

That process, however, would not be directed by Father William Kelly, because in May 1969 President Sellinger reorganized the administrative structure of the college. He named Kelly to the new post of administrative vice-president with responsibility for budgeting, grant proposals, and general oversight. The office of academic vice-president was now filled by Stephen McNierney, a young layman who had served as chairman of the philosophy department. A number of factors impelled this change, but the most significant was that Father Kelly had proven more adept at planning and getting things done than in dealing with some of the harder problems or in relating to the peculiar mentality of academics. There had been no dramatic incidents to prompt the change, just the gradual development of a sense of unease. The Middle States team took note of this atmosphere and expected that the appointment of McNierney, which had occurred before the visitation, could "be of great value."[13]

The change produced a mixed reaction. A few of the Jesuits—not necessarily the oldest—were less than elated at the prospect of having a young layman as Loyola's leading academic administrator. They were made anxious as were some of their confreres on other Jesuit campuses by similar developments and the transformation of governing boards. Generally, however, McNierney's appointment was approved by the faculty and students because many saw him as a charming, even charismatic, fellow. He was 32 years old and had received his bachelor's degree from Baltimore's Saint Mary's. After studying at the Gregorian University in Rome and the University of Paris, and receiving a master's degree from the Catholic University of America, he joined Loyola's philosophy department in 1963.[14] As already noted, he originated the "Problems of Belief" series and was instrumental in securing a reduction in the philosophy and theology requirements. He was of medium height with a pudgy face, thinning hair, and a deserved reputation as a raconteur. Much was expected of his leadership and much he achieved between 1969 and 1977.

The minutes of the day-long meeting of the board of trustees held on January 17, 1970, are more than usually full, but only two subjects would attract attention today. One was the registrar's recommendation that Loyola's diplomas be translated from Latin into English, presumably in keeping with the substitution of the vernacular for Latin in the liturgy. From the minutes, it would seem that this subject, in view of more important business, occupied the attention of the board for hardly more time than it took to look around the table. The English text remained faithful to the Latin inscribed on the college's diplomas 117 years earlier. The 1970 graduates were probably unaware that there had been any change, but if it had been brought to their attention they would most likely have approved this sign of modernization.

Another subject was raised in an unusual procedural context. After lunch, Edward Donnelly assumed the chair while President Sellinger absented himself briefly from the meeting. The board had to decide what course to take in view of the provincial's recent notice to Father Sellinger that his term as rector would end in June and that "the continuance of a President, or the appointment of a new President rests solely with the Board of Trustees."[15] It voted unanimously to retain Joseph Sellinger as Loyola's president and expressed its "profound gratitude . . . and . . . appreciation of his handling of complex problems, his contributions to the academic and administrative improvement of Loyola College, and his leadership in Catholic higher education."[16] Father Jerry McAndrews was already acting as superior of the Jesuit community and in June was formally installed as rector. Sellinger could now concentrate his attention and efforts on the development of the college, with results that have been remarkable. Studies by Father Andrew Greeley and others demonstrate that the distinction or mediocrity of a college or university depends more on the talent of the president than on any other single factor.[17]

After Father Sellinger resumed the chair at the January 17 meeting, the board asked the Members of the Corporation (the six Jesuits in whom legal title to the college is vested) to review the charter and by-laws with a view to "clarifying the separate identities of the educational institutional and the Jesuit community."[18] The board was eager to have the question of separate incorporation of the Jesuit community resolved so that it could begin functioning as the effective governing body at Evergreen.

• •

These changes and questions at Evergreen reflected a general process through which American Jesuit education was passing. The transition from control by the provincials organized as the Jesuit Educational Association to the leadership of institutional presidents in the form of the Association of Jesuit Colleges and Universities was completed early in 1970. This was a necessary step in the transfer of governance to lay boards of trustees.

To clarify the situation, the newly elected Jesuit general, Father Pedro Arrupe, propounded a series of questions to his American brethren. One question raised a basic issue: "Why should the Society of Jesus permit its name to be identified with an institution in which the responsible superiors of the Society can exercise no authority?"[19] The reply was that a firm commitment to "a style of education that emphasizes traditionally Jesuit values" was more important to the identity of an institution than juridical authority. On how to maintain an institution's Jesuit character without a provincial's oversight a practical consideration was urged. Any college that too closely resembled its state-supported or non-church-affiliated competitors would lose the reason that made it attractive to its clientele.[20] Although the question of what number or proportion of Jesuits was necessary to maintain an institution's Jesuitness was raised repeatedly, no entirely satisfactory reply was formulated. There was general agreement on the need for a Jesuit president, some trustees, and some teachers, but otherwise reliance had to be on quality rather than quantity—the very genius of the Society of Jesus.

There were a number of good reasons for undertaking this difficult process. The Second Vatican Council noted the emergence of the laity and gave further impetus to this development in the life of the church. The main limitation on the development of Jesuit colleges and universities as defined in 1966 by Father Paul Reinert, president of Saint Louis University, was underfinancing.[21] There was little hope of attracting the necessary level of support from private, corporate, or governmental sources except through the presence and commitment of lay trustees. Furthermore, the increase of lay people engaged as teachers and as administrators required a more professional style of governance. These lay people were familiar with generally accepted standards, and they could not be expected to participate for long or wholeheartedly in a system where essential control remained a Jesuit monopoly—especially when extramural authority was exercised. What was needed was the combination of generally accepted standards of academic practice with traditional Jesuit values.

. .

The one really difficult point was the provision in canon law prohibiting the alienation of church property, which seemed to preclude the transfer of governance at Catholic institutions to lay trustees. This difficulty was overcome in 1968 by Father John McGrath, a diocesan priest and canonist who was then lecturing on comparative law at the Catholic University of America. He contended that institutions that had not been incorporated under church law (and this was the condition of virtually all American Catholic colleges and universities), but that had been chartered under civil law, were governed under civil law. According to this doctrine, Catholic institutions in America, including the Jesuit schools, had never legally been the property of the founding religious communities, even though most members of those communities believed otherwise. Title to the land and fiduciary responsibility had always been vested in the incorporating body—no matter what had been the common understanding of the founding religious communities in the past.[22] This meant that the transfer of governance to a lay board of trustees did not violate canon law.

The transfer of governance to new boards of trustees and the incorporation of Jesuit communities separate from the particular institutions they served alarmed some members of the Society. They warned about the loss of ownership and sensed the prospect of a loosening of ties with the institutions that had been their bailiwicks. What once had been "family business" pursued informally among confreres would now be discussed in another—and, to some, less congenial—forum. The rector of Georgetown (which had completed the incorporation process) reported in 1971 a momentary "diminishing of confidence and partisan enthusiasm for the University."[23]

Some Jesuits feared that the change opened the door to secularization—a fate that had already befallen many colleges established under Protestant auspices. The announcement by faculty activists on one

Jesuit campus that the proper objective for that school was to become a "Catholic Amherst" increased these apprehensions and made some Jesuits more wary of participating in open dialogue with those who were not members of the order. More terrifying examples could be cited. Only a few years earlier, Webster College in Saint Louis had renounced its connection with the community of nuns that had founded it, and its president successfully applied for laicization.[24]

Nor were all the participants in this process convinced that it could be legally effective. In 1971, Ruth Cessna, attorney for the Jesuit community at the University of San Francisco, argued that, despite the reconstitution of governing boards and the separate incorporation of Jesuit communities, the Society itself remained, as it had always been, the ultimate, legal owner of all the institutions it had established. Her challenging brief was scrutinized carefully at all levels in the Society and by legal counsel for each of the Jesuit colleges and universities, who answered her contentions, relying in the main on the cogent reasoning of Father McGrath.[25]

While these matters were being pursued elsewhere the Jesuit community at Evergreen carefully and prayerfully considered the question of incorporating itself separately from the college. These deliberations continued off and on from 1969 through 1974. Some favored the change, but they were unable to convince the community as a whole that the change would benefit Loyola College or the Jesuits associated with it. This result was not unique. Although most Jesuit communities were incorporated, those associated with about half a dozen of the smaller colleges had arrived at the same consensus as their brethren at Evergreen.[26] The Jesuit community remained fully committed to the development of Loyola College but had found no compelling reason for formalizing its commitment through another charter of incorporation. Existence of "Associated Professors" seemed a sufficient guarantee for the Jesuit character of the college. To complete the sorting out of the relationship between Loyola College and the Maryland province, Father Sellinger resigned as a Member of the Corporation and Edward Donnelly was elected chairman of the board of trustees in 1971, and all his successors since then have been laymen.

• •

Although such developments were widely discussed on some other Jesuit campuses, little of it was the subject of conversations at Evergreen because things were managed quietly and slowly. Revision of the academic calendar and of the curriculum were the most common topics of faculty and student discussion in 1969 and 1970. As noted earlier, some attention had been given to curriculum revision, with a significant reduction of the time allotted to philosophy and theology. This left an inviting slackness in the schedule. Such an opportunity could not be ignored by various campus groups with favored projects for changing the curriculum still further. Dealing piecemeal with what inevitably would have been competitive and contradictory proposals promised more sweat and residual dissatisfaction than a comprehensive approach.

In September of 1968, Father Fred Homann had been named head of a committee to prepare a comprehensive revision of the calendar and of the undergraduate curriculum. Its members were selected because they enjoyed the confidence of their peers and had evidenced receptivity to innovation. They went through the standard drill: searching the literature, employing several consultants, visiting a variety of campuses, and discussing ideas with members of the faculty.

After a year of diligent effort, the committee proposed an attractive resolution of various calendar and curricular issues. The new calendar kept the usual four months for the fall semester, but classes started a few weeks earlier and final examinations were completed before the Christmas vacation. In the old calendar, classes started later in September and the two weeks of classes and examinations in January had always been an annoyance to many teachers and students. This post–Christmas-holiday appendix had a very limited pedagogical usefulness, but it had been too deeply lodged to be removed easily; now the scrutiny to which higher education was being subjected permitted questions about the calendar. Furthermore, the installation of air conditioning made it possible to ignore the heat and humidity that blankets much of the country in early September.

The second semester also would last four months starting early in February. The month of January was devoted to a variety of innovative academic courses or programs among which a student could choose to concentrate on one. Understandably, such an academic calendar is simply described as 4-1-4. Small liberal arts colleges of such stature as Colby, Clark, Macalester, Saint Olaf, Smith, and Williams were then operating under it. Loyola added a component of its own to this pattern. The phrase *4-1-4* at Evergreen referred not only to the number of months but also to the number of courses a student normally took. This meant a reduction from the customary forty courses for graduation to thirty-five, with sixteen courses allotted to subjects included in the traditional liberal arts core. What was yielded in breadth was to be gained in the opportunity to study fewer subjects in greater depth.[27] Similarly, the time spent in the classroom by faculty members was reduced from four to three courses per semester, with an obligation to teach two out of three January terms. This reduction of the faculty workload allowed more time for class preparation, scholarly research, or travel.

By the time the Homann committee's report was finished Steve McNierney was the academic vice-president and his first big project was to secure assent to the new calendar and curriculum. He discussed and settled certain details with each department and by October of 1969 the final text was distributed to the faculty and students for their judgment. Although there was general assent, some of the faculty—mostly in the natural sciences—feared that Loyola students would not be well enough prepared for graduate school, but over the life of this curriculum their fears proved unfounded. Some students expressed concern that the emphasis on greater depth would mean more work for them—a too common fear among American students. The expression of these views did not alarm a strong majority of the faculty and students, and on November 4, 1969, the academic council approved the new 4-1-4 calendar and curriculum.[28]

The transition from the existing calendar and curriculum entailed much effort in each department, but a detailed description is not necessary. Once the 4-1-4 program was fully operative it gained the approval of all but a few diehards. Periodically during the 1970s and early 1980s someone would mount a new assault on the 4-1-4 program on one pretext or another, but each was turned back by students, faculty, and administrators who saw the program as preferable to anything suggested.[29] No curriculum is without flaws—there are good arguments for adding this or changing that—but the proponents of change never successfully identified the problems they had with 4-1-4 or persuaded others that the scheme required more than minor adjustments until 1985.

Curriculum revision is an exercise indulged in periodically and the late 1960s and early 1970s was a period when academia generally went at it with a will and with mixed results. The history of the University of Detroit and that of John Carroll University describe what happened there; the product of these efforts, though retaining the humanities emphasis, differed in other particulars from what was produced at Loyola.[30] Unfortunately, the histories of some other Jesuit institutions disdain dealing with the subject.

．．

At the same time that the 4-1-4 program was being discussed, McNierney initiated two developments in student relations of contrasting character. The first was a stern policy statement to discourage disruptive activities on campus, adopted by administrative action rather than being considered by the college council. Demonstrators who ignored an order from the dean of men to desist were liable to suspension or arrest, and there would be no amnesty or retraction of a legal complaint. This was strictly precautionary and some faculty members suggested that the issuance of such a statement in the otherwise calm atmosphere on campus might incite what it was meant to prevent, but this did not dissuade Vice President McNierney. However, he quickly balanced the statement with the establishment of a student-life commission to deal with all nonacademic aspects of campus life, subject only to a veto by the dean of men with an appeal to the trustees.[31] This commission composed of faculty and student representatives played an active and effective role in the early 1970s and did much to save Evergreen from the drama and tension that afflicted other campuses. Its was a characteristically deft and politic performance.

Not all developments of this period were initiatives of the new academic vice-president. Over the years, the academic council had grown, and Father Kelly's effort to streamline its operations by the formation of a steering committee had not proven satisfactory. Absenteeism, never so pronounced as to threaten the presence of a quorum, was becoming noticeable, and those who were regular in attendance occasionally expressed annoyance with their more casual colleagues. A remedy was suggested by a veteran faculty member (myself): a smaller number of elected representatives—all of whom would have volunteered for the position—could be substituted for the more than a dozen department chairmen who represented the faculty and who had other responsibilities.

A broad consultation produced a new structure in which six faculty representatives were elected by constituencies to serve with four academic administrators and a representative of the student body. This system, adopted on April 7, 1970, has endured with minor adjustments to the present. To assimilate this into the general climate of innovation, the name was changed from the academic to the college council. Its effectiveness has varied, but it continues to be an acceptable forum for the discussion of general community concerns.

Some developments at Evergreen followed a different trajectory. The movement toward reliance on administrative decision-making and the use of *ad hoc* bodies that had begun during Father Kelly's brief incumbency continued under McNierney. The academic council's steering committee, created at Kelly's suggestion, was easily dispensed with by his successor, and this left the preparation of the college council's agenda to its chairman, the academic vice-president. In the general euphoria engendered by Steve McNierney's appointment, this and similar developments passed with little immediate notice. The process of consultation seemed unchanged and faculty members were loath to question his actions that early.

In December of 1969 the Evergreen campus was the site of a small event of wide import. The Second Vatican Council had in general terms decreed a more sympathetic and more theologically valid attitude toward Judaism and the Jewish people. After the council adjourned, the secretariat for Christian unity, of which Cardinal Shehan was a member, drafted guidelines for implementing the council's decree in all dioceses of the church. On the occasion of a "duologue" between Catholic and Jewish people sponsored by Loyola, Mount Saint Agnes, and Notre Dame, the text of the secretariat's guidelines was given to the press by Cardinal Shehan and reprinted throughout the world before it had been officially released.

Such publicity forestalled any curial tendency to make the guidelines ambiguous or for bishops to delay their implementation. The episode passed so quickly and quietly that few were aware of its importance, and no reference to this subject appears in Cardinal Shehan's memoirs. Although one close associate later reported that Cardinal Shehan suggested that the release was inadvertent, there is better evidence for considering it a deliberate leak.[32]

• •

Just as governance was being transferred to lay boards there was a renewed emphasis on interinstitutional cooperation—even thoughts of mergers—among American Catholic colleges and universities. It is convenient to refer to Catholic schools as if they were an entity with common characteristics, but diligent and perceptive observers realize that except for sharing the faith, American Catholic colleges and universities have always operated in a context of "pluralism verging on anarchy" because they were founded by autonomous teaching communities. This is true not only between schools conducted by different orders but even between schools within the same community such as the Society of Jesus. Some of its schools by the late 1960s had more in common with other Catholic schools than with some institutions conducted by Jesuits.[33]

The difficulty of getting religious communities to cooperate has already been noted, but the financial and demographic pressures of the 1960s were forcing Catholic institutions to consider ways to moderate their competition and to apply their limited resources more effectively. Jesuit participation in such ventures was viewed by others as little more than an expression of academic imperialism. The concern of certain Jesuit administrators was the protection of their own institutions, although there were Jesuits who were demonstrably well intentioned toward their peers at other institutions.[34] Such reactions are understandable; joining a religious community is an act of unreserved commitment to that community. Furthermore, those communities which are smaller and less dynamic tend to be sensitive, and this tendency is heightened when there is a gender difference.

Cooperation among Baltimore's Catholic colleges reached a climactic stage during 1969 and 1970. Ill health forced the resignation of Mount Saint Agnes's new lay president in June of 1969, and Doctor Elizabeth Geen, formerly dean at Goucher College and more recently assistant to the president of Mount Saint Agnes, was appointed in his place. Doctor Geen accepted the office for one year on condition that the college negotiate with the other two institutions for a merger based on the principle of collegiality. The deadline implicit in her acceptance was dictated by the precarious financial situation of Mount Saint Agnes— and by demographics. Mount Saint Agnes had a debt of over $300,000; enrollments had stabilized at about five hundred; and by this time all educators were aware that the postwar baby boom had ended.[35] For the next twenty years there would be fewer people graduating from high school. During the ensuing year, the representatives of Mount Saint Agnes pressed for a federation based on equality and the representatives from Notre Dame made clear that they remained eager to cooperate, especially in regard to the library project with Loyola, but that they preferred to wait until they could evaluate the federation experience of the other two colleges.[36]

The summer of 1970 was marked by progress on federation with Mount Saint Agnes and on the joint library with Notre Dame. Bilateral negotiations on an instrument to establish the federation were begun in earnest and continued into late August. The representatives of Mount Saint Agnes preferred a joint board that embodied the principles of collegiality and equality and Father Sellinger was prepared to go a long way toward accommodation. Loyola's trustees, however, pointed out that the resources that Mount Saint Agnes would contribute to the federation were much less than Loyola's. Moreover, the continuing decline of undergraduate enrollments at Loyola, especially noticeable in freshmen that year, gave added urgency to these negotiations.[37]

Notre Dame came to realize that the joint library might prove more of a drain on its resources than it had originally envisioned. Initially both schools were to make equal contributions to the establishment and operation of the library, but this did not take into account the difference in enrollments or in the diversity of programs at Loyola and Notre Dame. When these points were at last raised, a distinction between "joint" costs and "use" costs was offered by Loyola. The former were to be borne equally, and included such things as construction, debt financing, and insurance. The remainder, or "use" costs, were to be apportioned according to the number of students attending each school.

In the summer of 1970, Notre Dame's representatives indicated that even this arrangement was too burdensome and asked that all costs be allocated in proportion to student enrollments. Some among Loyola's leaders were willing to ensure this enterprise by accepting the terms suggested. Most, however, preferred to make a counteroffer in which several items previously assigned to "joint" costs were transferred to the "use" category and subject to apportionment according to enrollments. This position was defined on July 24 and was accepted a few weeks later.[38] With this breakthrough, the attention of those responsible for the joint library shifted to the practical details of fund-raising and construction.

• •

In late August the moment of decision arrived in Loyola's relations with Mount Saint Agnes. On August 21, 1970, Loyola's trustees offered what amounted to an absorption of Mount Saint Agnes students and those faculty members and administrators who were willing and qualified to take positions at Evergreen. This proposal was a shock to the Mount Saint Agnes negotiators; if it were accepted, there would be no federation and the word *merger* could be used only loosely. When questioned years later, no one seemed able to recall how this sudden change came about beyond recognition that there was no sensible alternative. The expiration of the deadline set by Doctor Geen when she accepted the presidency of Mount Saint Agnes appears to have determined the timing.

Mount Saint Agnes could accept this offer or close at the end of the next school year. President Geen was determined to ensure fair treatment for the faculty and students and, failing that, to close the college. The Sisters of Mercy were no less committed to just treatment for their college's loyal faculty and students, but they wished to follow a course that would best contribute to the continuing development of Catholic education in Baltimore.[39]

The announcement that Mount Saint Agnes might merge with Loyola next year was greeted with general approval. For a short while consideration was given to housing the young women at Mount Saint Agnes with a shuttle bus to bring them to and from classes, but the Mount Saint Agnes students adamantly rejected such an arrangement. They had no intention of becoming commuters, so Hammerman, Loyola's new dormitory, was reserved for women. President Geen and her staff raised a scholarship fund so that all the transfers could afford the higher tuition at Loyola.

At the level of faculty and administrators, the process of integration proved almost as easy. A few from Mount Saint Agnes chose to seek employment elsewhere or to retire. The credentials of the rest were reviewed by the appropriate departments or officers at Loyola. Those who held the rank of associate or full professor were, as required by Loyola's internal policies, reviewed by its board on rank and tenure. By Christmas, twenty teachers and five administrators signed contracts for the next school year; more than half the total were Sisters of Mercy. The dean of Mount Saint Agnes, Sister Judith Schmelz, and representatives from the faculty and students, were invited to meetings of the Loyola College council, and room was made on all faculty committees at Evergreen for the soon-to-be colleagues from Mount Saint Agnes. During the spring term, balloting in faculty elections covered both campuses.[40]

Loyola gained a great deal in this merger. Its undergraduate student body suddenly increased from about eight hundred to twelve hundred, a level that conventional academic wisdom identifies as optimal for the use of faculty and physical resources. Instantly, Loyola became coeducational across the four years of college, and thereby was avoided the sense of strangeness that a pioneer group of women would have felt and engendered if women had been admitted only in the freshman year. Tuition from the students who transferred covered the cost of salaries for the faculty members who were added. Where there had been only six women on Loyola's faculty, there were now almost a score.

Loyola College benefited in many other ways. It could now offer well-developed programs in speech pathology, elementary education, and medical technology.[41] Doctor Edward Doehler (1930) returned to the daytime classrooms at Evergreen and brought with him a conscientious, demanding Russian linguist and historian, Doctor Andrew McCormick (also a Loyola alumnus, class of 1951). Doctor Hanna Geldrich and Malke Morris strengthened the teaching of German, French, and Spanish. The speech pathology program had a steady center in Elaine Saltysiak. Sister Judith integrated the formerly solidly male preserve of academic administration, while Sister Monica Yeager brought her skill with numbers and accounts to the treasurer's office. Loyola's board of trustees was enlarged by four: Sister Mary Michelle Carroll, chairwoman of Mount Saint Agnes's board, President Geen, and two young but knowledgeable laymen, Ross Jones, from the administration at the Johns Hopkins University, and Thomas Wolff, a rising business figure. Sister Cleophas Costello, former president of Mount Saint Agnes, was already a Loyola trustee.

The transition was completed by 1973 and managed with notable smoothness. Much of the credit for this result is due Loyola's academic vice-president, Steve McNierney. His finesse and diligence rounded several awkward corners and capitalized on the evident good will of all participants in the process. The Sisters of Mercy, for their part, were determined to carry off the closing of Mount Saint Agnes in good spirits and with class—and they did. Reflecting fifteen years later, Sister Judith observed that the federative equality sought in 1969 did become effective in practice at all levels.[42]

Public approval of the merger was broad and strong. News reports and editorials were invariably favorable. A year after the merger, Father Sellinger, who had made clear his preference for an all-male school, reported: "The environment is, let's say, exhilarating."[43] In an address to the Association of American Colleges, he summarized the experience by avowing: "Loyola is an appreciably better college than it was this time last year." A few years later, Father Sellinger concluded that the change from an all-male to a coeducational institution made Loyola a "happier place," and no one disagreed.[44] From 1972 enrollments have continued to rise even as the demographic pool of prospective applicants declined. Catching the spirit, Father Sellinger allowed his now much grayer hair to grow a little longer—gone was the crewcut that he had worn since his arrival at Evergreen.

• •

One might well expect that all this activity engrossed Father Sellinger's attention to the exclusion of any other commitments, but such was not the case. In July of 1970, the media reported thirty-six deaths, and many times this number of seriously ill elderly patients, at an "above average" local nursing home. The cause was salmonella poisoning—which occurs usually through the careless handling of food. Various efforts were made to assure the public that the state government had discovered the cause of the outbreak and was taking steps to prevent a recurrence, not only in that facility but throughout the state.

The public, however, was not easily convinced. Skepticism and the continuing pressure from groups of concerned citizens prompted Governor Marvin Mandel to establish a "blue-ribbon" commission in June of 1971. He asked Father Sellinger to head it, because by this time Loyola's president had become a familiar and welcome presence among influential people around the city and state, and Sellinger had no connection with any of the interests involved. He had served on a number of corporate boards and on a variety of Baltimore and Maryland committees. This exposure brought him a widening reputation for reliability, balance, and thoroughness—and for getting things done.[45]

The nursing-home commission was indeed thorough, and it took about a year and a half to complete its work. Most hearings were held in the State Office Building in Baltimore, but some crucial hearings were conducted in the large first-floor parlor of the Jesuit residence. The commission's staff director, for one, believed this occasional change of venue elicited more honest answers on critical issues. There are no detailed reports of how Father Sellinger conducted these hearings, but others who have observed him in action note that he contributes insightful questions and observations without attempting to dominate a group. The commission's staff director, relying on Sellinger's talent for "brokering" points at issue, questioned witnesses quite aggressively. Whenever the atmosphere in the hearings became "edgy," the staff director noted that Father Sellinger would fill and light his pipe, and this pause eased the tension.[46]

Father Sellinger was deeply shocked by the callous attitudes expressed by physicians and attendants involved in caring for the aged. This, he was convinced, resulted from the profit motivation that prompted establishment of many nursing homes, and from the lack of clear and adequate governmental supervision. The commission's final report was presented to Governor Mandel in September of 1973. By then a number of the derelictions uncovered had been dealt with by executive or legislative action, and many of the recommendations for administrative improvement had been put in operation. The long-range solution, recommended by the commission, was a reworking of federal, state, and local methods of payment to include community-based services for the elderly who remained at home.[47] Under such an arrangement, fewer would seek admittance to nursing homes and more would be tended by personal physicians and relatives. Due notice was taken of the commission's work and Father Sellinger was thanked for his public service.

. .

The most tangible development in these years was the Loyola–Notre Dame Library. Its unique corporate structure (previously described) was matched by the distinction of its architecture. In January 1971, the colleges joined in a two-and-a-half-year campaign to raise $5 million, but to avoid delaying the start of construction the library corporation borrowed $3 million from the state retirement system and secured an interest subsidy from the federal government.[48]

The four-level building is sited on the bank of a small stream, which was dammed to create a reflecting pool. The land was donated to the library corporation by Notre Dame in lieu of part of its matching contribution of money and is at a point where the two campuses meet. The functional brick-and-glass structure provides three times the space of the libraries that Loyola and Notre Dame had available before its construction. It has a basic shelf capacity of over 300,000 volumes, or about double the number of volumes already on the shelves of its two predecessors.

As usual with such construction, it was completed a few months later than promised—in February of 1973. Its dedication with appropriate ceremonies was held on May 12. On this occasion, honorary degrees were awarded by the two colleges to the new institution's progenitors, Father Vincent Beatty from Loyola and Sister Margaret Mary O'Connell from Notre Dame, and to its most generous benefactors, Henry Knott (1929) and his wife, Marion Burk Knott.

A few months later the American Institute of Architects and two library associations recognized Richard Ayers and his building for its distinguished design. The judges described it as a "bold, well-sited" structure. They also commended it for "the exciting masonry, clarity of materials used, integration of building systems, strong functional plan, and quality of library equipment."[49] In the years since the library's opening, two-thirds of its original capacity has been filled, and it now houses a collection of first editions of the works of Henry James, a collection of works by Gerard Manley Hopkins, and an outstanding collection of volumes with fore-edge paintings donated by Mr. and Mrs. Knott. There is also the bound revised page proofs of Evelyn Waugh's *Brideshead Revisited.* The Loyola–Notre Dame library has continued to grow and to serve effectively the two colleges that created it, but no similar success has attended their other efforts at cooperation.

• •

In the afterglow of the decision to build the joint library, student journalists at the two colleges decided early in 1971 to publish one newspaper for both constituencies. Imaginatively enough, they titled their new publication *Twain*, but imprudently the editor accepted an advertisement for the first issue from a clinic that offered abortion counseling and services. The authorities at Notre Dame acted first and *Twain's* second issue was its last.[50] A similar misjudgment later by a Loyola editor prompted the promulgation of a policy against accepting advertisements from abortion clinics or referral services.

The *Greyhound* too gave attention to the abortion issue—with predictable results. Some students, including several coeds, thought this was a matter better left to the decision of an individual woman and her doctor. Others and a Jesuit ethicist insisted that such a position was incompatible with church teaching.[51] Neither side succeeded in convincing the other, and periodically the argument has reemerged with other protagonists. For a time, the vehemence of the students and faculty (more often lay than Jesuit) opposed to abortion made it difficult to discuss the problem in any but the narrowest terms. The tiresome repetition of arguments and the 1984 presidential campaign, however, broadened and calmed the discourse—though there was no alteration of positions.

The presence of female students on a formerly all-male campus brought minor and transitory problems. The only overt charges of "sexism" arose with regard to athletics. The green and gray livery was worn by women's varsity teams in basketball and field hockey, and sports reporters took to calling them the "Lady Greyhounds." The team members and their partisans believed that they did not get even-handed treatment in regard to the use of facilities, publicity, and scholarships. After these complaints were publicized in the *Greyhound,* the athletic staff and college authorities rectified the situation.[52]

The difficulty arose in part because the staff responsible for athletics was new. After over thirty years of service, "Lefty" Reitz, Loyola's athletic director, retired when, as he reported, "my doctor told me the job was getting on my nerves and told me to get out."[53] Over six hundred alumni and friends attended the October 1973 banquet tendered in Lefty's honor. The testimonial speeches acknowledged his positive attitude and that Lefty Reitz was "a person determined to bring out the best [in a] person or . . . a player." He had achieved one of the best overall records as a basketball coach in a small college—349 wins against 228 losses (207-48 in Mason-Dixon Conference play)—and a 290-245-2 record for the baseball teams he coached. On such occasions, people commonly say that it is the end of an era and it was. That the memory of his service to Loyola suffer no dimming the main court in the new college center has been named the Reitz Arena.

22

"Not Pervasively Sectarian"

With the benefit of hindsight it is easy to identify the upturn in Baltimore's fortunes with the inauguration of William Donald Schaefer as mayor in 1971. During the course of his four terms Schaefer would come to be acclaimed as "the hardest working mayor" in Baltimore's history and the "best mayor in America."[1] Schaefer, a bachelor and married to his job, demanded hard work and loyalty from his staff. His success in raising the morale of Baltimore's citizens and boosting the city into the rank of American municipalities enjoying a "renaissance" was due to his positive attitude toward every endeavor, to his engagement of competent personnel, and to his ability to increase spending through state and federal assistance. Mayor Schaefer's ability to get things done was an important factor in attracting new investment to the city.

Although a college is not a municipality, there are significant analogies between the accomplishments of President Sellinger and those of Mayor Schaefer in approach, methods, and success. Indeed the two men were personally acquainted and for ten years Father Sellinger served as a member of Baltimore's board of ethics. The years between 1972 and 1977 for Sellinger and Schaefer read like an account of comparable achievements although in the service of two very different institutions. Some years later, Schaefer described Sellinger as "a leader of tremendous integrity" who is impressive for his "energy, diligence, and keen knowledge of the business world." Even after becoming governor of Maryland, he welcomed Father Sellinger's input and considered himself fortunate to have Sellinger as "a colleague and friend."[2]

. .

As already noted, the student body continued to grow after Loyola became coeducational, and this growth encouraged planning for additional residences. The college had completed two of the four dormitories it originally planned, but by the early 1970s there was an evident aversion among students throughout America to dormitory life and regulations. Few institutions succeeded in modifying their rules quickly or basically enough to satisfy the students. Administrators were finding that dealing with dormitory residents posed baffling problems. Dormitories brought students together and this concentration made it easier for protests to develop and to be sustained. Some other living arrangements had to be devised if the hectic cycle of demands and protests was to be ended.

At Loyola, an avenue for a new accommodation appeared in the offer of some neighboring real estate. The owners of a small and still rather new garden-style apartment complex that bordered on Loyola and the new library indicated a willingness to discuss either leasing or selling it to the college. The Underwood Apartments, as they were then called, were acquired in 1972 for about $250,000 by means of a mortgage and with the aid of a federal subsidy. This added thirty-two apartments that could accommodate almost one hundred more students.

The complex had, of course, been built to commercial rather than institutional specifications. It was not a dormitory with a limited number of entrances but a series of individual housing units; curfews and other restrictions could not be enforced as readily as in a dormitory. The college accepted this reality by emphasizing its role as landlord without entirely yielding what it considered its regulatory responsibilities. It reserved this new housing for juniors and seniors, who were presumably more mature, and assigned separate areas to men and women. Each furnished apartment was leased for the school year to a group of three or four students who accepted liability for any damages and responsibility for observance of the visitation rules. Peer pressure was to be relied on to enforce the rules more than the customary systems of having the students sign in and out and of monitoring by residence counselors.

This development was noted with interest by the sophomores and freshmen living in the dormitories, and predictably these students concluded that a similar modification of the curfew and visiting rules was in order for them. The more adventuresome men in Butler Hall treated the regulations as a dead letter, and this prompted the housing authorities to various actions aimed at disabusing them of this belief. The women in Hammerman House took a different course. Early in November of 1972, they drew up a petition that convinced Loyola's housing officer that some amendments were in order—at least in regard to that dormitory.

What the housing officer accepted was sensible enough, and the modified regulations are less notable than the reaction of the student life commission. This august body did not really object to the new rules for Hammerman; it was rather the summary procedure by which they had been adopted that roused the ire of the commission members. They appealed to the commission's mandate to be "the primary agent, under the board of trustees," for making or altering policy in regard to the nonacademic aspects of student life. To this the housing officer responded with the claim that such an arrangement interfered with his responsibility to such a degree that it made his position superfluous. That their positions could be reconciled does not seem to have been understood by either party to this exchange. Having expressed itself, the commission merely resolved to take action (otherwise unspecified) if such administrative fiat were repeated.

As much as anything, this deferential attitude of the students indicated a change. What only a few years earlier might have agitated the campus for several weeks with editorials and "town meetings" was quickly ended with only a notation of positions in the commission's minutes, which had a limited distribution. In 1964 all but 4 percent of the student body voted in campus elections, but in 1973 hardly 30 percent of the students cast their ballots, and editorials on student apathy again appeared in the *Greyhound*.

This change was not lost on other administrative officers, who became aware that they could discharge their responsibilities with less concern for dialogue and prior consultation than in the 1960s. An increase in the ratio of administrators to faculty contributed to this shift in attitude. The number of faculty members and administrators increased between 1971 and 1976, but the growth rate was 10 percent higher for administrative officers. Although there seemed to be generally no overt intention to revive the old fashion of exercising authority, a growing sense of confidence and of professionalism among administrators made the new style increasingly hard to distinguish from the old one. The style was more genial, but natural tendencies found among managers were also discernible.

This evolution was promoted in some measure by Father Sellinger's confidence in the team of administrators he had finally assembled and by his reliance on their judgment. In the years since Father Kelly became academic vice-president, Sellinger had become less visible to students and faculty and comments could be heard similar to those made on the absences from campus of Father Theodore Hesburgh, Notre Dame's president. For both, public relations and fund raising could be pursued more diligently because of the competence of their administrative officers, and they gave credit as it was due.

• •

Since the early 1970s, all additions to the residence facilities at Evergreen have been apartment units. In 1974 a tract of land beyond the Underwood Apartments was purchased and stretched the campus northeastward to Notre Dame Lane. The original building on this property was replaced in 1977 by a quadrangle with apartments for almost one hundred and fifty more students. The new residence facility was named McAuley Hall to commemorate Catherine McAuley, a young Dublin woman who in 1831 founded the Religious Sisters of Mercy. With this addition, Loyola could accommodate over six hundred residents.[3]

These extensions of the campus brought Loyola property into contact with a well-established section of small, generally working-class residences. Occasional difficulties over parking and noise arose but the college authorities and the neighborhood associations worked out a system of communication and consultation that has, in the main, proven tolerable to both sides. Loyola's relations with neighbors along the other sides of the campus, however, have been less amicable. These are regions with larger residences inhabited by articulate and well-connected professionals.

The Underwood Apartments, named for the street on which they stand, were renamed in 1974 for Father Eugene Ahern. He was a Jesuit who came to Evergreen in 1971 to head the new office of campus ministries. Most American colleges have traditionally been served by chaplains who viewed their responsibility largely in terms of providing religious services—whatever the denomination. The Danforth Foundation in 1969 suggested broadening this concept to include "prophetic inquiry" into campus community issues, and counseling.[4] In response to this call, Father Ahern was engaged by Loyola to supervise such a development on campus.

A little more than a year after he arrived at Evergreen, Ahern suffered a kidney failure and for a while was treated on a dialysis machine. Three times a week he had to go to the hospital, where it took many hours each time to complete the process. Although the procedure sustained his life, he found that it depleted his energy. Rather than continue to exist at this restricted level, Father Ahern chose to undergo a transplant, which was made near the end of May in 1973. This resulted in a recovery of energy—indeed, a new lease on life—but it also meant having to live with the ever-present danger that his body would reject the transplant.

When he returned to the campus, Father Ahern added a new project to his agenda of good works. He publicized the opportunities for organ donation to the Kidney Foundation and the Maryland Eye Bank. On a day early in April of 1974, campus ministries with his assistance got almost eighty students, Jesuits, and lay faculty members to sign kidney and eye donation pledge cards. Carried in one's wallet, these cards notify medical personnel in case of a fatal accident that the eyes or kidneys can be taken for transplantation. A few months later, unfortunately, Father Ahern had a rejection that could not be controlled and he died.[5] That his generous example not be forgotten, Loyola's first apartment residence for students was renamed Ahern Apartments.

Too often less attention is given the achievements of locally familiar personages than those of distant celebrities. To avoid this common failing, notice must be given the role of Doctor Charles Graham (1962) in the development of corneal transplantation and eye banks, not only in America but also internationally. After returning to teach at Loyola in 1966, he was a key agent in bringing to Baltimore a new medium for storing corneas, about which he learned during postdoctoral research at Marquette University. There a graduate student had developed the medium that made it possible to prolong the useful life of corneas for more than six hours. In 1971 Doctor Graham was engaged to teach the new technique to the staff and technicians of the Maryland Eye Bank, established in 1962 through a grant from the American Legion. The Maryland Eye Bank is unusual because it is not associated with either a hospital or the practice of a particular eye surgeon. Such independence made innovation easier.

After becoming the bank's laboratory director in 1974, Graham expanded the pool of technicians by carefully training John Requard (1974) and several other premedical students at Loyola. The eye bank was averaging six hundred corneal donations a year in 1971 when Graham joined the agency; by 1974, donations had risen to one thousand, and they doubled over the next four years. This was due in part to the extension of the viability of the corneas to two days. The director of the eye bank reported these advances to a national conference, along with the 10 percent greater success rate achieved by his agency than elsewhere; this persuaded other eye banks to follow the lead of Maryland. After the Maryland agency decided to establish branches in Florida, California, Delaware, and West Virginia, Graham decided that he could not adequately discharge his teaching responsibilities at Evergreen, so he yielded the position at the eye bank to John Requard but maintained his connection with an expanding network of eye and tissue banks. This American group has provided support for the development of similar facilities in Great Britain, France, Italy, Greece, and Israel, with Charles Graham one of the leading consultants in the process.[6]

• •

Concern over the fiscal health of Loyola was not peculiar to the 1970s, but steeply rising costs and a nationwide decline in the college-age bracket made that concern more urgent than it had been for some time. From 1970 to 1981, excluding the year when President Nixon imposed a price freeze, the annual inflation rate in the Baltimore area averaged almost 9 percent. This meant that the college, like all educational institutions, had to find more money to cover rising costs. Tuition remained its main source of revenue, but the population boom that had started in 1946 ended around 1964, and no general demographic upturn was likely to appear before the early 1990s. That Loyola did not merely survive the 1970s but indeed began to thrive is evident, and this noteworthy achievement was due in large measure to the fortitude of President Sellinger, the new administrative staff, the new board of trustees, and a cooperative faculty.

The two most urgent fiscal problems at Loyola in the early 1970s were the budget deficits incurred during the preceding years, and the expenditure in some budget categories of more than had been authorized. Such problems were not unique to Loyola; they appear to be endemic among charitable and educational enterprises in America. Inflation and the spectacle of campus disorders made the general public less willing to contribute what colleges and universities said was needed to sustain their operations. Fiscal reform was no longer merely desirable; it had become essential. Deficits at the Johns Hopkins University between 1969 and 1971 had become so critical that Milton Eisenhower was recalled from retirement. By cutting expenses and raising money Doctor Eisenhower reduced the deficit in the budget for fiscal 1973 to acceptable proportions and yielded the university's presidency again, this time to Steven Muller.[7]

Efforts to deal with Loyola's fiscal problems had begun under Father

William Kelly, but the catalysts for solving the problems were two additions to the college community. Thomas Wolff, vice-president for industrial development at the Rouse Company, was a new trustee brought over from the Mount Saint Agnes board in the early fall of 1970. The other was Paul Melanson, Loyola's vice-president for finance and administration, who replaced Father Kelly about the same time.

At the first meeting of Loyola's trustees that he attended, Thomas Wolff coupled a motion to accept a revised budget for the current year with a suggestion that a *pro forma* budget for the next fiscal year be submitted when the board met again, and Father Sellinger agreed. A month later when the draft budget was presented, several of the trustees (not otherwise identified) suggested that no deficit would be accepted, even if this necessitated a salary freeze. Others raised the possibility of phasing out programs deemed not essential to the "aims and objectives of Loyola as a private Jesuit college." Wolff introduced the idea of long-range planning, and repeated his urging in September of 1971. Father Sellinger agreed to have a five-year plan of goals and objectives ready at the earliest possible date. These developments indicate how seriously the trustees took the situation and how effective the revised structure made the board. Father Sellinger delegated the budget problems to Melanson and the five-year plan to Vice President McNierney. Both responded effectively and in a timely fashion.

The process for achieving a balanced budget and fiscal discipline did not trace a simple trajectory but the goals were reached rather quickly, if not easily. By June 30, 1971, income exceeded expenditures by over $87,000 and in the following year this figure almost doubled. This excess was not plowed back into operations but was used to liquidate the $440,000 in deficits accumulated during the late 1960s—some in short-term notes and other forms of forward financing.

Loyola's development during the late 1960s was not matched by increases in revenue, and payment of some bills was delayed until the cash flow covered the most urgent demands. How long such practices could have been continued is conjectural, and there were probably other ways of handling this problem, but the one chosen by Father Sellinger and Paul Melanson was to liquidate the entire accumulated deficit in a short period of time. Within four years, this item was eliminated from the college budget notations—an achievement recognized by the Association of Independent Colleges of Maryland with its highest rating in management and by a handsome bonus from the funds raised cooperatively by the association. A single comparison may make this feat clearer: in 1979, Columbia University succeeded for the first time in twelve years in balancing its budget.

How was this remarkable result achieved? Vice President Melanson employed the familiar practice of underestimating revenues when he drafted budgets. These lowered revenue estimates created pressure against increasing expenditures and, at the end of the year, yielded a larger than projected excess. He also used a chart of accounts, with Sister Monica Yaeger policing expenditures, so that everyone stayed within the totals authorized in the budget. Cash outflow was checked monthly, and the balance between revenues and expenditures was reported quarterly in general terms to the trustees.[8] It all seems rather obvious, and all the elements in the process had probably been announced earlier at one time or another, but what made the 1970s different was the determination to live strictly within the terms set down in the budget.

A number of other factors contributed to the improvement of Loyola's fiscal health. The alumni and development offices were becoming more effective in dealing with their constituencies. The alumni responded to the annual giving program, and the value of annual gifts from businesses, foundations, benefactors, and friends generally followed an upward curve. The total for 1970 in what was now called the Evergreen Fund was nearly $320,000, and this figure almost doubled by 1980 and by 1986 was just over $1,042,000. Tuition increases were modest, as they were generally in America; if inflation was discounted Loyola's tuition during the 1970s did not rise. In October of 1976 an education at Loyola was rated a bargain by the Kiplinger magazine *Changing Times*—along with educations at fewer than seventy other American colleges.

· ·

Loyola's largest operating expense, as in most small colleges, has been faculty salaries, and the budget could not continue in balance without close attention to this line. The projected faculty cost in the original 1971–72 budget had included provision for nine new positions; this was cut to three as a temporary expedient, with all the positions filled and more added in subsequent years. Salaries were not frozen, but an overall ceiling to match the rise in the cost of living was imposed. The funds for salary increases were then divided into two parts: an increment up to half the inflation rate was apportioned to virtually all the continuing faculty; the other portion was assigned by "merit."

Merit increments are a hardy perennial in American education, but they have rarely achieved the goals urged by proponents. References to merit as the basis for salary increments appear in Loyola pronouncements back at least to the 1950s. The success of the AAUP chapter in shifting the apportionment from an administrative committee to the board on rank and tenure in the late 1960s has already been recounted. McNierney's innovation in the early 1970s was the transfer of the decision on merit to the academic vice-president, the dean, and each department chairman. These negotiated, however, under an overall ceiling and an average per department. The system was flexibly applied and generally kept the cost of salaries within the limits set by the budget.

The faculty adopted a wait-and-see attitude; some were pleased to receive notice that they had merited one of the higher awards. Not initially connected to the scheme of merit pay, a process of student evaluation of teachers was instituted in the early 1970s. This, it was eventually argued, gave some evidence on classroom performance—the most important element in judging merit—but at first little credence was given the data derived from the student responses on the questionnaires.

After several rounds of the merit process, even those honored with the higher awards recognized that their salaries were hardly keeping pace with the rate of inflation. The trustees also were concerned; savings on faculty salaries might result in the loss of the more able or more mobile teachers. During the budget review early in 1973, Thomas Wolff asked whether faculty salaries at Loyola were still competitive. Father Sellinger could truthfully reassure the board on this point, partly because the erosion of academic salaries and purchasing power was nationwide.

The growing unease about this situation prompted Father James Salmon, an associate professor of chemistry and member of the college council, to propose a way to deal with faculty salary policy more openly and rationally. What was needed, he thought, was some procedure whereby the faculty and administration could review Loyola's compensation policy as a whole—and consistently, rather than piecemeal just before contracts were issued. This could be done by an elected faculty committee that met regularly with the academic vice-president. McNierney did not openly oppose this proposal; instead he gave timely notice of it to the board of trustees and assured them it would be closely monitored for "possible union implications."[9]

The college council in May of 1973 adopted Father Salmon's proposal, and the committee continues to function. It has served to focus the discussion of salary policy and has proven most effective when the members mustered the attention and support of the faculty, but as might be anticipated with such a body, that has not invariably been the case. The merit program went through one more minor revision and was soon allowed to lapse while Steve McNierney served as academic vice-president. The inflation rate kept rising, and the rewards for merit proved meager.

• •

The most significant contribution to Loyola's fiscal health came from a new program of general aid adopted by the legislature in 1971. Faced with a serious financial crunch, private institutions in the state organized the Maryland Independent College and University Association (MICUA). One of its first endeavors was to explain the desperate situation threatening Maryland's private colleges and universities to Governor Marvin Mandel. MICUA's delegation included Father Sellinger and the presidents of Goucher College and of the Johns Hopkins University. They convinced the governor that it would cost the state less to help private institutions now than to wait for disaster and then be forced to pay either to absorb private schools into the state system or to expand public institutions to accommodate students from closed private schools. The governor was aware that contributions from private sources could not be increased enough or in time to prevent a serious crisis. New York and Illinois had already dealt with a similar situation by providing general-purpose grants based on the number of students graduated.[10]

The Maryland law that Governor Mandel got through the legislature in 1971 was merely a stop-gap measure which apportioned $2 million a year among twenty-four private colleges and universities. An immediate effect of this interim law, however, was to give Loyola only a claim to the funds because, as everyone anticipated, a suit was instituted in March of 1972 to block payment of any state monies to church-affiliated colleges. This affected Western Maryland, College of Notre Dame, Mount Saint Mary's College, Saint Joseph College, and Loyola. Until this suit (*Roemer v. Board of Public Works*) was resolved, the state grants to them were held in escrow. An amendment was added to the law, prohibiting explicitly what was otherwise taken for granted —that none of the public funds could be used for sectarian purposes.

To prepare the permanent program of aid, a small commission was appointed by the governor in the summer of 1972 and it recommended several changes; among them: the basis for making grants was shifted from the number graduated to the full-time enrollment, and the commission pegged the annual cost of the program at 15 percent of the amount appropriated for students in public institutions. The first change recognized the service being performed by private colleges in regard to adult education, while the latter insured the program against future erosion by inflation. The new formula for state aid almost doubled the amount the private colleges were to receive.[11] (Loyola between 1972 and 1976 was involved in the *Roemer* suit; an account of this episode is narrated near the end of this chapter.)

Some of the data later used by the plaintiffs in the *Roemer* suit were derived from the five-year plan drafted by Vice President McNierney. This was a startling and unanticipated use of that document, but not its most pervasive application. The plan consisted of nine major goals and more than seventy objectives distributed under those headings. All were stated as simple declarations of purpose without exposition, argumentation, or data, and a detailed summary of the plan's contents seems unnecessary.

The draft was distributed to the faculty and students before it was considered by the college council, and only a few and relatively minor amendments bubbled up during this consultative process. The final version was approved by the council on March 20, 1972, and was transmitted to the board of trustees, which a few weeks later expressed its appreciation to Father Sellinger and all those who had participated in its preparation. Formal adoption was delayed to allow detailed study, especially of the plan's financial feasibility. What had drawn the attention of several trustees was the expansive tone of the plan. The statement of goals and objectives bespoke a variety of new programs promoted with such adjectives as *vigorous, distinctive, superior,* and *first rate.* The board, which is responsible for the fiscal soundness of the institution, wanted time to discover what all this enthusiasm might cost.

• •

Goal four dealt with curriculum, and the tenth objective under it proposed a historic change. It read: "Establish courses and a requirement for all students that they explore the religious dimension of human existence"—theology was to be required of *all* students, not only Catholics.

From the time it first opened its doors, Loyola had never required students of other faiths to attend religion classes. This practice had been adopted generally by Jesuit schools in America to forestall any accusation of proselytizing. But Father Sellinger had always considered this an anomalous arrangement. Historically, Catholic educators have denominated theology "the queen of sciences," and he, like Cardinal Newman, thought liberal arts without theology to be truncated and deformed. Such a curriculum was simply not the best that a Jesuit school should offer its students.[12]

His thinking on this point came as the culmination of a general and gradual development. The controversies inspired by the Reformation had made Catholic educators and authorities wary of including theological studies in the curriculum for laymen. It was not until the 1890s (as already noted in this narrative) that specific courses in religion made their appearance in Loyola's schedule. Their nature and the training of the teachers made requiring them of all students impossible. The courses as then taught were essentially a prolongation of the catechetical process begun in parochial school and thus were inappropriate for students who were not Catholics. Any Jesuit who had completed his general training that included advanced study in philosophy followed by a four-year concentration in theology could be assigned to teach them.

By the 1940s, some Jesuits decried this situation and began their efforts for reform modestly by arguing that the title of the courses and the department teaching them should be changed from *religion* to *theology*. This was not mere repackaging. The change was meant to reorient the subject matter to scriptural and solid theological sources and to demand that the teachers be qualified by doctoral studies in theology.

At Loyola, the title of the department did not change from *religion* to *theology* until 1956. Information about when it took place at other Jesuit schools is not readily available, but the historian of John Carroll University notes that the change was made there in 1956, and that John Carroll was the last institution in the Chicago province to do so.[13] It took longer to deal with qualifications of teachers, but by 1969 at Loyola a Jesuit teaching in the theology department could not expect to be granted tenure unless he had completed his doctoral studies and was engaged in normal scholarly activities. Furthermore, Abraham Shusterman, an eminent Baltimore rabbi, had been teaching courses on Judaism for several years, and efforts were made to employ lay theologians whose scholarly interests were in fields other than Catholic theology, but without immediate success.

The most significant addition to the theology department was Father Felix Malmberg, a Dutch Jesuit who after a long and distinguished career of teaching and publication in his native land was recruited in 1970 by Father William Davish, chairman of the department. Upon retirement, Malmberg accepted invitations to lecture at various institutions, and after teaching at Loyola for a semester he was persuaded to settle at Evergreen. When questioned later, during the *Roemer* trial, Malmberg explained his decision in terms of the opportunity Loyola presented. "It is . . . a very open college; a very understanding college. They understand the importance of Theology."[14]

One factor in Father Malmberg's decision was undoubtedly a requirement that all students, not merely those who were Catholic, take two semesters of theology. After adoption by the college council in December of 1972, the requirement was implemented at the earliest opportunity—September of 1973—and this meant that thereafter all students took the introductory semester in "Theological Anthropology," which was an "inquiry into the nature of human belief [and] the concepts of religious dialogue." Catholic students were required to take the second semester; others could elect any other theology course. Malmberg was well satisfied with this arrangement and served as chairman of the theology department from 1971 to 1979. His was a jaunty, cheerful presence on campus.

Even before the trustees formally adopted the five-year plan, it was used by college authorities as a general but flexible guide. Various provisions served as rationales for new projects; others, less favored, were left in limbo. And new ideas, not included in the plan, were entertained as opportunity suggested. As the term of the first plan was nearing, Vice President McNierney cranked up the machinery to produce a new, improved version early in 1977—on the eve of his departure from Evergreen. All the salient points of the first plan were repeated and supplemented with new objectives and goals. The faculty and students used it as grounds to propose representation on the board of trustees, but that idea did not survive final review because it was deemed inappropriate to include those subject to policy decisions in their final approval. Nevertheless, most of the trustees declared themselves in favor of the principle: "all those who are affected by a decision should have some voice in . . . [its] formation."[15]

• •

Although the college had intermittently offered instruction at off-campus locations after the late 1920s, these never rose to the formality of satellite operations. They were merely conveniences for groups such as communities of nuns who needed courses to qualify for teaching certificates. In the summer of 1971, however, Loyola began to offer graduate courses in education and business administration in Columbia.

Columbia, sited in formerly rural Howard County between Baltimore and Washington, has been described as "one of the most successful new towns built in America in this century." It was opened in July 1967 by James Rouse, a Marylander, a successful mortgage banker, and builder of shopping malls. Rouse's experience prompted him to diagnose the problems inherent in America's postwar urban sprawl as those "of scale, absence of place, [and] absence of physical form of community." His solutions were embodied in Columbia, and among the goals set for this new town was "education as a life-long process." This and its other characteristics attracted a young, affluent population whose careers in business or government could be furthered through additional education. Such a clientele soon drew the attention of Antioch College, the Johns Hopkins University, and Loyola.[16]

With enrollments growing at Columbia, Loyola sought additional ways to serve its new clientele. In the fall of 1972, graduate courses in psychology were added. A year later, a new master's in modern studies was inaugurated. This is an interdisciplinary liberal arts degree organized around three central themes: ways to be, ways to see, and ways to say. In 1976, with assistance from a Rouse company officer, Loyola's Columbia operation occupied several floors in the American City Building, then the tallest structure in the center of the new town. Here a master's degree in pastoral counseling and a selection of non-credit professional development programs were offered. The college preferred to lease facilities in Columbia and moved several times, but the advantages of ownership finally prompted building a center there in 1987.

In 1976, Loyola extended its executive master of business administration (X.M.B.A.) curriculum to Columbia. The success and growing reputation of Loyola's M.B.A. stimulated the members of the department to search for ways to expand their offerings. The X.M.B.A. program had been started three years earlier on the Evergreen campus by Ron Biglin, director of the M.B.A. program and then an associate professor. Doctor Biglin's entrepreneurial spirit was roused at a professional conference where Biglin learned of such a program recently established at Wake Forest. At that time few other institutions in America were offering an X.M.B.A. degree, but five years later fifteen schools listed the offering, with Loyola alone among the Jesuit colleges and universities. Securing the support of his departmental colleagues and of Vice President McNierney, Biglin guided the development of Loyola's newest and most glamorous outreach to the business community.[17]

The curriculum was fashioned to appeal to vice-presidents, division heads, and managers of business firms and of governmental and non-profit agencies. Their careers were too advanced for them to commit the time required by the regular M.B.A. program, but such people felt the need for "retooling." They were offered a broad range of courses in such subjects as management, quantitative methods, industrial relations, ac-counting, and marketing, with classes meeting only one day a week, alternately on Fridays and Saturdays, over a two-year period. Tuition started at $2,500 but rose over four years to $4,000, with the sponsoring firms generally paying.

From its inception, the X.M.B.A. program attracted a substantial number of applicants. In 1973 it enrolled 105 participants, one of whom was Steve McNierney, and over the next five years it averaged an annual increase of 24 percent. The leading sources of participants were Bendix, Westinghouse, Black and Decker, and the United States Department of Health, Education and Welfare. The X.M.B.A. program, targeted for leaders in the local business community, yielded a strategically posi-tioned and growing constituency for the college.

. .

Sensing a favorable tide, President Sellinger early in 1975 engaged an experienced firm of consultants—Brakeley, John Prince Jones, Inc.—to verify this impression and to suggest the best means to capital-ize on it. There were, as might be expected, many similarities between the Brakeley and the earlier Tamblyn-Brown report, but the differences were striking. In the 1941 report, Loyola was acknowledged as "the best college in Baltimore or in the state," but known to very few; its educa-tional mission was even less well understood. Thirty-four years later, these conditions had in some degree been transcended. One respon-dent averred: "One could not conceive of Baltimore without Loyola College."[18] It had acquired a reputation, especially under Father Sel-linger's leadership, for being quickly responsive to needs perceived in Baltimore. Indeed, Loyola's president was held in such high regard by all categories of people interviewed that the report stated: "A wholly accurate statement of his standing . . . defies description."[19] This and the "excellent morale" found among administrators, faculty, and stu-dents in regard to Loyola's general development and educational mis-sion put the college in an extremely favorable position for a major fund-raising campaign. For the past twenty years Loyola had engaged, the report noted, in short-term efforts focused on single major projects. Its most recent exertion in behalf of the joint library had fallen a bit short of its goal so that the project had to be completed with loans. Loyola could choose "more of the same" or summon the courage to "take fullest advantage of its potential."[20]

What was needed was a more aggressive and coherent "advancement" team (development, alumni, and public relations) with a substantially larger budget and stable professional fund-raising assistance. A new vice-president for development was appointed. To ensure a smooth start for the new campaign and as a reward for his achievements to date, Steve McNierney was given a new title, executive vice-president, and general oversight of the effort and greater involvement in the "advancement" side of the college's operations. The other stipulations on the budget and on professional assistance were managed in due course.

The tentative financial goal startled some alumni and business leaders who were interviewed. Ten million dollars seemed much too ambitious. Few alumni had risen higher than middle management, and the branch-office character of Baltimore was cited. Others noted the depressed state of the national economy and similar cautions. When, however, Loyola's tentative goal was compared to the $100 million the Johns Hopkins University had recently announced for its extended fund-raising campaign, and the needs at Evergreen were defined more concretely, the reaction became "Then, that's what the campaign should seek."[21]

Of critical importance to the success of this endeavor were the trustees, and they also were initially hesitant about the tentative goal. The Brakeley report noted that trustees on average contribute 15 to 20 percent of a fund-raising goal, but this seemed more than could be reasonably expected from so small a number with so few lay members as then sat on Loyola's board. This was not a new problem; virtually the same point had been made in 1941, but the recent re-formation of the board made the remedy easier to apply. In September of 1975, seven new lay members were added, members who contributed effectively in various ways to Loyola's campaign. Among the pros and cons of the Brakeley report was one indisputably encouraging note: a former trustee made a commitment of $500,000.[22]

There is no need to go further in describing what became known as the Decade of Decision campaign. Suffice it to note that the goal for the initial phase was set at $8 million, with another $5 million to be raised during a second stage. These sums were committed to a new science building, outdoor athletic facilities, renovation of certain buildings, an athletic and recreation center, and endowment for student aid and faculty development. By November of 1979, almost all of the initial goal of $8 million had been pledged and the new science building at the corner of Charles Street and Cold Spring Lane had been dedicated. In the judgment of a former trustee this campaign transformed the climate of opinion, planning, and effort at Evergreen.[23]

• •

Loyola's successful development during the 1970s brought unanticipated costs. On October 31, 1975, Steve McNierney applied to the federal government for a grant under the advanced institutional development program. This was a follow-up on the earlier federal grants that had assisted in the merger with Mount Saint Agnes, but a much larger sum was sought—$4 million.

The aim of this 1975 application was to match the development of Loyola's physical plant with the maturing of various processes and programs. About a quarter of the total sought was to be used to establish a more effective management information system. The college had, during the preceding five years, demonstrated its ability to set goals and to achieve them, but this process had suffered from a lack of timely and accurate data. Over an eighth of the grant was to support a comprehensive career-planning program for the students. Most of the money sought was assigned to academic developments proposed in the main by the faculty, such as an honors program, an increase in fine arts, recruitment of minority students, a center for quantitative techniques of research in various disciplines, a political research center, and a fast-track program in business administration for women and minority students.

The need for the grant and the ability of the college to use the grant effectively were amply documented in a volume two inches thick. All to no avail; the federal bureaucracy responded three months later with a declaration that Loyola could no longer be considered a "developing" institution under the guidelines set in the law.[24] Thus Loyola's success had foreclosed one avenue of support; aid for the plans and programs enumerated in the grant proposal had to be sought from other sources. Bit by bit, the most urgent or important elements were installed over the years that followed through the normal procedures of the college.

• •

A localized problem arose in the mid-1970s over the use of the house at the corner of Millbrook Road and Cold Spring Lane purchased in the fall of 1970 from the estate of the publisher of the Sunpapers. Father Sellinger in September of 1975 moved from the Jesuit residence when he realized that the new fund-raising campaign necessitated the holding of receptions and meetings and that this would infringe on the privacy of his confreres. To emphasize that he was now only the president of the college and no longer rector of the Jesuit community, he moved to the house across from the athletic field.

For a number of years, the socially and financially comfortable homeowners in the area, organized as the Kernewood Association, had been sparring with the college over the liquor license for a rathskeller that operated on weekends in Millbrook House next to what became the president's house. The association's real animus was directed against the dormitories erected on the land behind their homes, but there was no legal procedure available to stymie the erection of these buildings. President Sellinger's change in residence, however, roused the association to challenge what it viewed as violation of the residential character of the area. To heighten the challenge, the use of Millbrook House for alumni, public relations, and development offices, which had continued for almost twenty years, was included in the association's zoning complaint.

There were several stages in this legal process. Initially the zoning appeals board split the difference by discovering no violation in the uses associated with the president's house, while finding that the administrative offices in Millbrook House were incompatible with residential zoning. Such a decision satisfied neither party, and it was appealed. In August of 1977, a Baltimore judge upheld the zoning board's ruling on the president's house and overturned its finding on the building next door. "College does not consist," said the judge, "only of classrooms. Administrative offices and parking areas are as essential to the functioning of the college as purely academic structures."[25] The court of special appeals later affirmed this ruling.

Another real estate matter was settled in this period. As a matter of public record, ownership of the old Calvert Street buildings was still vested in the Loyola College Corporation, although effective management of them had long been transferred to the Maryland province. By 1970 the cost of rehabilitating the property was estimated at $500,000, and such a sum was beyond the means of either Saint Ignatius Church or the province. Private efforts to sell proved unsuccessful, and so availability of the property was publicly announced.

No suitable buyer appeared until four years later. A fire destroyed the theater then used by Center Stage, a repertory company that had been operating in Baltimore at various sites since 1963. Needing a new home and aware of the availability of Loyola's large old auditorium, Peter Culman, managing director of Center Stage, initiated negotiations that by reason of their complexity have been described as "nothing short of Byzantine." In schematic outline what happened was this: the city bought three-quarters of the old Loyola site, leaving enough for a rectory to serve Saint Ignatius Church; the city then sold the structure to Center Stage for $5; and Loyola and the province donated the proceeds of their sale to Center Stage.[26]

This merely provided a physical location. The cost of converting the buildings to the demands of modern stage productions was estimated at nearly $2 million. This was financed through long-term bonds backed by the credit of Baltimore, a loan from the Ford Foundation, a loan from a local consortium of banks, a grant from the National Endowment for the Arts, and the financial reserves of Center Stage itself. What was produced by this effort was a remarkably innovative playhouse. It is set more or less diagonally in the old auditorium, with none of the five hundred seats more than thirty-five feet from a moderated thrust stage. Workshops, rehearsal halls, and a small second theater for experimental productions occupy the rest of the space. Complicated as the process had been, a full schedule of plays was presented in the new home of Center Stage hardly more than a year and a half after the fire that had forced it to move. The curtain rose in the late fall of 1975 on Moliere's *Tartuffe*. Four years later, Culman triumphantly dispatched the final repayment to the Ford Foundation.[27]

Not only had this endeavor contributed to preservation of the neighborhood but it ensured the vitality of a major cultural resource for Maryland. Elsewhere in the city landmarks such as Mount Royal Station, Fells Point, and Federal Hill were being recycled, and the old City Hall was thoroughly rehabilitated instead of being displaced by a modern glass-and-steel box. How much all this contributed to the "renaissance" of Baltimore is hard to estimate—but contribute it did.

· ·

Capital, buildings, and real estate were not the only categories within which developments occurred at Evergreen during the 1970s. Before federal regulations to aid the physically handicapped were promulgated in June of 1977, Loyola established a committee to survey the campus to determine what changes would be needed. Ramps had been installed to make the classrooms and offices in Jenkins Hall accessible, and several units for the physically handicapped had been included in the plans for the McAuley residence.

The federal edict merely extended this concern to cover the whole campus systematically. Parking spaces near buildings were reserved for the handicapped. Curbs were modified to increase mobility and other adjustments were made in and around the buildings on campus. It was such a simple and obvious thing that one wonders why we Americans had not done it before. Bringing the physically handicapped further into the mainstream of life and work has benefited all of society immeasurably.

In regard to black students, Loyola had made an effort to attract more of them during the 1960s and early 1970s, but with indifferent success. By 1976, minority students represented less than 4 percent of the undergraduate enrollment. Individually they participated in campus life as they chose, and together they organized the Black Students Association. This activity was not unique: a Jewish Students Association and a Christian Bible-study group were active. Something more was needed, especially in recruiting black students, because Loyola was such an unfamiliar entity in that community.

Review of the second five-year plan early in 1977 and other circumstances gave a decisive impetus to Loyola's efforts in regard to minorities. A recent general congregation of the Jesuit order had mandated a commitment to the theme of "faith and justice." The Society was not merely to teach general principles but to become involved in practical applications of them. When the text of the new five-year plan was submitted to the board of trustees, it was accompanied by several amendments proposed by the administration. One of these called for an effective program for recruiting and supporting minority students.

This generalization was soon made concrete in what became known as the LOY (Loyola Opportunity for Youth) program. Its specific goal was to double the proportion of minority students in five years. Even that meant only an increase from 62 to 124 in an undergraduate student body of 1,800. To this end, more than $400,000 was committed over the next five years. This money was to pay for an admissions counselor, an academic counselor, a coordinator of student services, and additional financial aid. To start the LOY program, the college needed some assistance and successfully sought it from the Morris Goldseker Foundation.[28]

Repeated throughout the discussions and memoranda was an insistence that Loyola could not provide remedial assistance and would not lower its admissions standards. What it was seeking was to alert minority students to the opportunity it offered and to support those who had a reasonable expectation of being able to complete the course. By the end of the first year, the recruitment goal had been exceeded. This surplus was a serendipitous effect of a larger and better coordinated publicity effort, because a number of new black students enrolled outside the LOY program. Since then the recruitment program has been broadened to include Asians and Hispanics. The total in 1985 was more than 210, with Asian students now the largest contingent among Loyola's minority enrollments.

• •

These events, important as they were to the development of Loyola College during the 1970s, served merely as an obbligato over the most persistent concern of the period. After the passage in 1971 of the Maryland program of assistance to private colleges, the law was challenged as a violation of the "no-establishment" clause of the First Amendment. *Roemer v. Board of Public Works,* as the legal controversy was entitled, was not resolved until June of 1976, when the Supreme Court upheld the state's program of assistance. The decision in the *Horace Mann* case (1966) has already been described, but because the Supreme Court had refused to allow an appeal in that case, the legality of government assistance to church-related colleges and universities remained in question.

On June 28, 1971, the court sought to resolve this ambiguity by its decision and opinion in *Tilton v. Richardson.* By a vote of five to four, it ruled that construction aid to church-connected colleges did not violate the "no-establishment" clause, under a threefold test: government aid had to be given for a secular purpose; the primary effect of such aid could neither advance nor hinder religion; and the program could not entail "excessive entanglement" of government with religious bodies. If these criteria were satisfied, the mere fact of a church relationship was not constitutionally disabling, and a concurring opinion reached the same conclusion without bothering about "excessive entanglement."[29] The four dissenting justices held that a church-related college was by its nature as sectarian as any parochial school.

Immediately after the *Tilton* decision, the American Civil Liberties Union (ACLU) and other like-minded organizations made clear that they were set on securing a reversal of *Tilton.* The earliest and most attractive opportunity arose in the form of the 1971 Maryland program of general state aid to private institutions. Here was no mere one-time grant, but a program that annually disbursed tax money to colleges, in-

cluding those with church connections. In late March of 1972, the lo-
cal chapters of the ACLU and of Americans United for Separation of
Church and State challenged what they viewed as a violation of the
First Amendment.

Because of a ruling by the federal district court, their original complaint had to be converted into one filed by John Roemer, then executive director of the Maryland ACLU, Edd Doerr, director of educational relations for Americans United, and two other taxpayers. Their
petition read:

> Each of the institutional defendants is a sectarian, educational in-
> stitution which is engaged in the teaching and practice of religion and
> a substantial purpose of which is the inculcation of religious values.
> Each . . . is controlled in whole or part by a particular church.
> Each . . . compels obedience to the doctrines and dogmas of a par-
> ticular religion, requires instruction in theology and doctrine, and
> does everything it can to propagate a particular religion.[30]

Because of this alleged sectarianism, the plaintiffs sought an injunction
against further payments to the defendant colleges—Western Maryland, Notre Dame, Mount Saint Mary's, Saint Joseph, and Loyola—
and demanded that all funds already authorized be returned to the state
with interest.

Fortunately, lawyers for both sides treated the dispute as a serious
matter of constitutional law rather than as an occasion for arousing passions and prejudices. During the pretrial proceedings, both sides made
extensive use of their opportunities to secure depositions and replies to
various interrogatories. These seem livelier and more searching than
the trial transcript, which is more like a formal exposition to highlight
cogent points rather than a record of dramatic cut and thrust. Although
the primary objective for each side was a favorable decision, equally
important was the tenor of the court's findings of fact. These would provide the basic data on which the Supreme Court would eventually deliberate, as no one seriously doubted that the lower court's decision
would be appealed by whichever side lost.

Court proceedings began near the end of May 1973 and continued
for a month. Presiding was Joseph Young, a federal district court judge,
who in the absence of a jury was joined by another district court judge
and one from the circuit court of appeals. Counsel for John Roemer *et
al.* was Lawrence Greenwald, a serious, careful young lawyer serving *pro
bono publico.* The board of public works, the state agency involved in
administering the aid program, was represented by its own counsel—

as were the defendant institutions. Loyola's cause, on Father Sellinger's decision, was represented by Paul Connolly, an alumnus (class of 1943) who was a member of a nationally renowned firm headed by Edward Bennett Williams (the lawyer who represented the Catholic colleges in *Tilton*) and Joseph Califano. Another member of the partnership represented Mount Saint Mary's. The defendants' table, as a result, was crowded by more than a dozen counselors and principals, while Greenwald sat alone. These very serious proceedings were not without their lighter moments. During a recess, the president of Mount Saint Mary's smilingly offered to provide some company for the plaintiffs' counsel, but the offer was not accepted.[31]

• •

Loyola's portion of the trial occupied only two days—June 18 and 19—near the end of the proceedings. By then, the same testimony with a few variations had been repeated several times. Paul Connolly's aim was to show that the Maryland program did not violate the First Amendment because it conformed to the criteria enunciated in *Tilton*. This in turn required him to demonstrate that Loyola College was not controlled in any way by the Catholic church, that it did not compel obedience to the doctrine and dogmas of the church, that theology was taught as an academic discipline, that contrary to the plaintiffs' complaint Loyola did not do "everything" to propagate a particular religion, and that religion did not seep into or permeate its secular educational function. In a word, Loyola was not the kind of institution described in the charging allegations of the plaintiffs' complaint but was indeed substantially like the Catholic colleges involved in the *Tilton* case.[32]

Loyola's autonomy was established through the testimony of many witnesses, but first and most important was President Sellinger. Connolly capitalized on the publicity about the Second Vatican Council and stressed the basic changes in thought and practice that had resulted from it. Sectarianism, especially as a means of proselytizing, had been positively prohibited by the Second Vatican Council. When asked to characterize the essence of the post–Second Vatican attitude in Catholicism, Father Sellinger replied that it was "the freedom of personal conscience" and applied to the way Jesuit provincials exercised their authority: where formerly they had demanded "blind obedience," their function now was "more as a guide and a counsellor."[33] In his turn on the stand, the elderly Jesuit Felix Malmberg reinforced this point. The teachings of Second Vatican could, he said, be rephrased: "Let [the provincials] form men who are free, responsible people who decide on their own judgment."[34] This attitude operated not merely in relations with religious superiors but within each Jesuit community. "There must be dialogue," Father Malmberg insisted.

Greenwald, in his cross-examination of Father Sellinger, tried to elicit an admission that the Maryland provincial could still exercise control over the president of Loyola College. Sellinger responded by distinguishing his responsibility as president from that as a member of the Jesuit order. Loyola's board of trustees was his only boss in regard to his performance as head of the college, but the provincial could guide and counsel him in regard to his progress in the religious life. When Greenwald averred that the provincial could resume the old mode of exercising authority and could use the vow of obedience to secure Sellinger's compliance, Connolly objected. Judge Young mused that this was "probably tilting at windmills to a degree." Significantly he added: "I think that, first, the Provincial would not issue such a directive."[35]

Recruiting for the theology department got a lot of attention in the testimony because the five-year plan included several goals expressing a desire to increase the "presence" of Jesuits and Sisters of Mercy on campus, but this according to testimony merely indicated the college's desire to maintain its historic character and did not mean preferential hiring practices except in the field of theology. Even there, however, all candidates for employment underwent the same process of review, involving the departmental faculty and the academic vice-president. What these people were concerned with was the quality of the candidates' academic credentials, not just whether or not the candidates were members of the Jesuit order or Sisters of Mercy. Among a regular faculty of more than ninety, there were only ten Jesuits and six Sisters of Mercy, and a substantial proportion of the total—41 percent of the faculty— had no affiliation with the Catholic church. The preference for academically qualified Jesuits and Sisters of Mercy in the theology department was explained by Father Sellinger and Vice President McNierney as resulting from the fact that most students were Catholic and there were only a certain number of teachers the college could employ in this field. Furthermore, Sellinger noted, "I think Jesuits are pretty darn good theologians."[36]

The testimony of Sharon Burns, a member of the Mercy community and of Loyola's theology department, corroborated what was already in the trial record. She had respectable academic credentials including a master's degree in theology from the University of Notre Dame and a doctorate from Catholic University. Her description of the courses she taught demonstrated their breadth and academic substance. On cross-examination, Lawrence Greenwald was unable to elicit any hint that she or any of the other theologians used the classroom to indoctrinate students in the Catholic faith.[37]

Sister Sharon's testimony included two other pertinent points. She, along with a number of other Catholic theologians, had signed a protest against Pope Paul VI's encyclical affirming Catholic teaching against contraception, but she had not been brought to task by either her provincial or Cardinal Shehan. The other point was a graphic contrast between the nun's habit she had worn before Second Vatican and her dress now. Ten years ago, Burns said, she wore an enveloping black gown with a "coif and guippe," spelling these unfamiliar words for the court stenographer and explaining the exotic garments to which they referred. When encouraged by Connolly to describe the ensemble she was wearing, Sister Sharon noted a pink dress ("that I made") of "contemporary" length, silver accessories (earrings, necklace, and bracelet), and white pumps.[38] (Mention of such trivia is necessitated by the emphasis placed on "religious garb" in the complaints of those who oppose government aid to church-related schools.) Burns's testimony reinforced the point that priests and nuns on campus wore what clothes suited their personal preference.

Later, when the court formulated its findings, it noted the special nature of recruiting for the theology department but chose not to state whether the courses were taught as an academic discipline or to deepen the students' religious faith. Rather, it relied on the evident atmosphere of academic freedom and respect for the individual teacher's concept of professional standards to conclude that "the primary effect of aid to these defendants is not to advance religion."[39] This was a crucial finding under the criteria enunciated in the *Tilton* case and avoided the issue of "excessive entanglement." A definite characterization of the theology courses as "academic" would have provided grounds for the plaintiffs to insist that this quality had to be ensured, and that could only be done by constant oversight, which is constitutionally disabling.

• •

The conviction of the court that academic freedom was operative at Loyola arose not merely from the testimony of Father Sellinger and Vice President McNierney but from that of various faculty members. A philosopher who had served as president of the AAUP chapter, Doctor Bernard Nachbahr, strongly denied that any Jesuit, nun, or college authority ever suggested what he should say or teach. The chairman of the

English department, Doctor Thomas Scheye, affirmed his Jewish faith and the atmosphere of freedom at Evergreen. Doctor Alan Plotkin, a psychologist who is also Jewish, recounted how his courses in adolescent psychology necessitated very frank discussions of sexual problems, and how these were conducted according to the intrinsic requirements of the discipline rather than in conformity with church prescription. A sociologist, Antonia Keane, corroborated this testimony in regard to social problems and the solutions some proposed for them. Professor Edward Doehler (1930), a historian soon to add "emeritus" to his title, made clear that controversial aspects of history, including the role and activities of the church, were taught in the required core courses according to the evidence and not with a view to vindicating positions espoused by churchmen.[40]

The last faculty witness was Father James Maier, an earnest, bearded young Jesuit who had just completed his first year at Loyola. He explained in detail how he had been recruited for the biology department and confirmed that "a Jesuit—as any other professor—has to submit his credentials and compete with other candidates for any particular position."[41] In regard to his teaching, Maier described how he handled such frontier bioethical problem areas as *in vitro* fertilization, cloning, and genetic screening in a class. Although as a Catholic he could not but bring his conscience to the discussions, his starting point was akin to that of Doctor Albert Schweitzer. The way to deal with such issues, Father Maier said, was to consider them in the light of broader questions: "Are we preserving what is best of the traditions of both sciences [biology and theology]—and I think of religion—as a reverence for human life and what it means?"[42]

With some brief additional testimony from Vice President Melanson on how the state funds had been handled, the Loyola phase of the trial ended. On June 26, with all three judges present, Judge Young commended all the counselors for the thoroughly professional manner in which the evidence had been presented and for their diligence in preparing the evidence.

· ·

It took eight months for Judge Young to formulate the findings of fact because of detailed review of earlier drafts by both sides. Even more than the court's decision these findings of fact would influence the Supreme Court. The tenor of the findings was favorable to the state and to the defendant institutions, which disappointed the plaintiffs and Lawrence Greenwald. They had hoped at least for some differentiation among the schools according to the degree of sectarianism, but Judge Young discovered no clear grounds for this. They were also disappointed that the court had not given greater weight to the testimony that some teachers began classes with a prayer.[43] Because this ritual was not required by any of the institutions, but permitted as an aspect of the teacher's academic freedom, the court found no constitutional significance in the practice.

The court's opinion, drafted by Judge Young, was not published until October of 1974. The plaintiffs' petition for an injunction against further state grants and for repayment of the sums already appropriated was denied. The grounds for this decision closely paralleled the reasoning of the Supreme Court in the *Tilton* case, and the verdict was rendered on the basis of the actual characteristics of the defendant institutions:

> An atmosphere of academic freedom prevailed on each campus. Each of the . . . schools admitted students and hired faculty who were not members of the affiliated church. None of the schools required attendance at religious services. Although all of the schools required students to study theology, the courses were taught according to the academic requirements of the subject matter.[44]

The court labored long over the question of "excessive entanglement" but resolved that in favor of the defendants on the grounds that they were "substantially autonomous" in regard to the churches with which they were associated. The other district court judge concurred in this opinion.

However, the third judge, Arthur Bryan, dissented. He conceded that the purpose of the Maryland grant program was clearly secular, but he insisted that the defendant institutions were undeniably church related and that the issue was not whether state funds had actually been used for sectarian purposes but what potential use might be made of the public funds. Nothing in the original law prevented the assignment of state funds as salaries for theologians, some of whom also served as chaplains. Furthermore, the secular and sectarian could not be disentangled in "menial or professional services, or building and ground maintenance."[45] Judge Bryan was not convinced that the presence of academic freedom necessarily obviated possible "overtones of indoctrination" in the theology courses; he quoted a passage from the majority opinion almost conceding as much. Finally, he noted that close scrutiny of the content and teaching in theology courses or the detailed supervision of how state funds were spent would inevitably involve "excessive en-tanglement" and generate controversy.

These differing opinions afforded the Supreme Court alternative readings on the constitutionality of the Maryland grant program. The majority had weighed all the sticking points and found on balance that they were not disabling. Judge Bryan, emphasizing the potential misuse of public funds and the necessity of close supervision, found the law invalid.

• •

Hardly a week later, John Roemer, Edd Doerr, and the other plain-tiffs filed their appeal with the Supreme Court, and on February 18, 1975, its clerk formally notified all parties that "probable jurisdiction is noted." Oral presentations for the appellants and appellees were sched-uled eventually for mid-February in 1976.

During the intervening year, several significant developments oc-curred. The most notable was an agreement reached between Western Maryland College, on the one hand, and John Roemer and the com-plainants, on the other. This agreement, made about a month after the notice that the Supreme Court had allowed the appeal, permitted West-ern Maryland to withdraw from the suit. A number of conditions were stipulated, and these included the removal of all "religious symbols and indicia of church-relatedness" from the campus. Various practices also were proscribed, and quotas were set for non-Methodist teachers of religion and philosophy and for trustees who were not Methodist ministers.[46]

Removal of crosses from the chapel upset some people who over the years had been closely associated with Western Maryland. However, twice in ten years its authorities had been forced to explain its relation-ship with the Methodist church—tenuous as it had become. How many more times would it be dragged into suits where all the other defendants were Catholic-sponsored institutions? This turn was not entirely to the liking of the complainants, because the withdrawal of Western Mary-land left an aura of "Catholic bashing."[47] A few weeks after receiving a copy of the agreement, the Supreme Court approved the withdrawal of Western Maryland.

As the time for oral presentations approached, the two parties agreed to permit the filing of a small number of *amicus curiae* briefs. In support of the appellants, Leo Pfeffer, winner in the *Horace Mann* case, submitted a lengthy exposition reiterating the contention that secular and sectarian functions were so inextricably mixed in church-related colleges that there was no way to assure that state funds would be used only for secular purposes. The state and the defendant institutions had the benefit of two *amicus* briefs. The one for the Association of American Colleges and allied organizations urged a full determination of the issues raised, in order to establish the standards that must be used in judging the "academic integrity" of religious studies departments in state colleges and universities. It was the contention of the association that "the academic study of religion [is] . . . an essential part of a liberal arts education."[48] The other brief supporting the defendants was filed for the United States government. Any ambiguity in the Court's decision or the overturning of the *Tilton* decision would result in widespread confusion and difficulty in administering federal aid programs that in 1975 alone disbursed over $215 million to a variety of colleges and universities, some of which were church-related.[49]

Oral arguments were heard on February 23, 1976, and the verdict and opinions were announced five months later. By a vote of five to four, the Court agreed that the Maryland program to aid private colleges did not violate the "no-establishment" clause of the First Amendment. In practical terms, this meant the addition of $750,000 annually to Loyola's revenues. Justice Harry Blackmun, in his opinion, applied the *Tilton* criteria and found Loyola and the other Catholic colleges were "not pervasively sectarian." Therefore, state aid for their secular educational functions was constitutionally permissible.[50]

The leading opinion among the dissenters was delivered by Justice William Brennan. He noted his consistent opposition to governmental support that promotes the "type of interdependence between religion and state which the First Amendment was designed to prevent." He not only would have reversed the decision of the lower court but would have required the defendant colleges to refund all payments they were entitled to under the Maryland law.[51] The dissenting justices seemed unable to discern changes in ethos and relationships developed at church-related schools since the mid-1960s. Church-related schools were controlled by church authorities and their publicity had stressed the permeation of all campus life and study with religious values. This is what a church-related school was meant to be and this is what it should remain. That is why government aid for church-related schools was unconstitutional according to the dissenters.

During the *Roemer* trial, Paul Connolly denied that this common definition of the character of church-related schools was justified in the 1970s. He conceded that plaintiffs' counsel could even then cite verbiage from catalogues, bulletins, and speeches that used allegorical language and rhetorical imagery to appeal to a certain audience. However, he characterized this as little more than "the familiar penchant of all Mankind to use or ascribe loftier and commendable attitudes and objectives to one's loyalty, be it Catholic, American, or Democratic."[52] Loyola, he admitted, is a value-oriented institution, but the values taught are those taught in any proper liberal arts college—despite Loyola's preference for religious terminology. The Supreme Court dissenters obviously did not subscribe to Connolly's argument and the institutions had no occasion to comment on it publicly.

. .

As soon as the Court announced its decision, telephone lines to Baltimore, Emmitsburg, and other pertinent locales buzzed with the news and congratulations. Father Sellinger immediately issued a short statement:

> I am happy that the decision which the United States Supreme Court has rendered today makes it clear that a college such as Loyola can be Catholic and can still be eligible for state support for its obviously public purposes. . . . The Court's decision acknowledges that a diversity in American higher education is both desirable and constitutional and that religious programs are clearly separable from secular ones.[53]

He sincerely thanked those who had staunchly supported Loyola during this four-year ordeal.

In addition to the hasty and diligent dispatch of this statement to the media, the public relations office organized a cheerful bash for all who had contributed to the victory. Father Sellinger again thanked everyone assembled on the lawn of the president's house and expressed particular satisfaction that he had not "given up any part of Loyola's Catholic tradition to achieve the victory."[54] The "literary" highlight of that evening was Steve McNierney's dramatic reading of *The Epic of Roemer*, a *jeu d'esprit* loosely derived from *Paul Revere's Ride* by Longfellow. The penultimate verse read:

Then, yesterday morning, the news comes, we've won!
Sellinger faces the cameras and says, "Son of a gun!"
Four didn't buy it—we all make mistakes
But five of them did—and that's all it takes.

Congratulatory telegrams and letters poured in from all over the country. The bishop of Mobile summarized the general sentiments:

"Congratulations on winning what I know has been a long and tiresome fight. We are all in your debt."[55] A confrere, the president of Loyola University in Chicago, thoughtfully enclosed a substantial check to defray part of the costs incurred during the long litigation. Ross Jones, a Loyola trustee, was heartened "that patience and righteousness still have their just rewards."[56] The president of the University of Baltimore warned Sellinger not to "rush to spend it all at one time."[57]

The *Roemer* decision attracted widespread newspaper comment. The resultant clippings and editorials fill forty-two large scrapbook pages. The *Cincinnati Enquirer* hailed what it called this "landmark decision" as putting the Court "clearly on the side of those who wish to preserve the strengths and diversity of church-affiliated colleges and universities." The *Washington Post* took a different tack. Its editorial writer saw "the wall of separation tumbling down, at least so far as education is concerned." The *Christian Science Monitor* recognized "the difficult legal terrain" traversed by the Court and regretted the "move closer to the church position." A Columbia, South Carolina, daily favored the outcome but worried about the possibility that state aid might eventuate in governmental regimentation of private institutions. The *Post* of Frederick, Maryland defined the issue as aid to education rather than to religion.[58]

Of what significant effect was the *Roemer* decision? Immediately it made secure programs operating in Illinois, Louisiana, and Pennsylvania. Reflecting nine years later, former Governor Marvin Mandel, who had initiated the Maryland aid program, was sure "it gave the green light to similar programs in other states."[59] Government aid, until *Roemer*, had been limited to capital construction, general student aid, and assistance for minority students. Such categorical aid was useful only for the expansion of facilities or services. What the *Roemer* decision did was allow block grants that could be utilized as the needs of individual institutions dictated rather than according to a governmentally predetermined general formula. It is probably no exaggeration to say that the *Roemer* decision made the difference between life and death for many church-related institutions. Over the ensuing ten years, state assistance to Loyola increased from $750,000 to almost $2.7 million a year for a total of nearly $19 million. In order to comply with the law's prohibitions against using the money for sectarian purposes, it has been generally apportioned to faculty salaries, excluding the salaries for members of the theology and philosophy departments, the pastoral counseling program, campus ministries, and for any priest or nun. This reliable resource has played a not insignificant role in the development of the college.

• •

Even as the *Roemer* affair was reaching its conclusion, the brisk pace of campus development that had become characteristic under President Sellinger continued. A number of initiatives were undertaken in the months immediately before and after the announcement of the Court's decision. The undergraduate programs in the both day and evening divisions became the responsibility of Dean Frank McGuire (1954) when his decanal colleague in the evening division was given a leave of absence. A young second-generation Loyolan, Marie Lewandowski, ran in March of 1977 against four young men and was elected head of student government by a majority of votes cast. The student center and Millbrook House were renovated and the campus grounds generally refurbished during the summer of 1976. The approach of the 125th anniversary of Loyola's founding (September 15, 1977) prompted a decision to celebrate it with appropriate events and ceremonies beginning on Maryland Day (March 25) and continuing for a year. The state granted $1.85 million for a new science building, with the start of construction scheduled for early April in 1977.

The most significant but not the most welcome initiative came early in 1977. In mid-February, Steve McNierney announced to the college council that he was resigning as executive vice-president to take a position with Black and Decker. Few could recall campus news of comparable impact. Those who had speculated on such things predicted a college presidency as McNierney's next step. And in the early 1970s he had been interviewed for such a position at a small southern Catholic institution but had been urged by Loyola's board of trustees to remain at Evergreen. Others, noting his participation in several political campaigns and his service on the Baltimore school board, anticipated he would eventually fill some public office. With the benefit of hindsight, the only clue to a shift in his orientation might have been his enrollment in the executive M.B.A. program when it was inaugurated. However McNierney came to his decision, everyone now knew that he would be leaving Loyola a month hence.

Anxious not to lose momentum during a long search process, President Sellinger pursued a summary procedure involving the college council, which, it should be noted, includes representatives of the faculty, students, and administration. It took only a few weeks for the name of Loyola's new academic vice-president to be announced. Daniel

Degnan was graduated from Georgetown in 1950 and then studied law at Seton Hall University. After several years of practicing his profession in Newark, Degnan entered the Society of Jesus. Ordination was followed by completion of a master's degree at Harvard Law School, and he was a visiting professor at the Georgetown Law Center when the vacancy at Loyola suddenly appeared. President Sellinger thought the appointment of Father Degnan would fit neatly into the policy of increasing the Jesuit presence on campus.

McNierney's departure was marked with suitable expressions of regret and felicitations for his future. The *Greyhound* gave a full page of pictures and text to a recital of his career at Evergreen and to expressions of campus opinion. Father Sellinger opined: "I am losing my strong right arm, but I can't help but be happy for him." The president noted Black and Decker's close ties with Loyola and expressed relief that McNierney was not leaving for any of Loyola's competitors. Sellinger had found him "extremely helpful . . . because of his creativity and imagination. . . . [He] was on call seven days a week . . . and his tremendous sense of humor kept me sane when things were tough."[60] After a few years in his new position, Steve McNierney and his family moved to Texas, where he served among the managers of a large land-development conglomerate. There in December of 1986 he succumbed to cancer at the age of 50.

23

School of Business

This account of the years between 1977 and 1986 has a dual character. It is a narrative and analysis of events derived from available sources and is itself a document that should be of some use to the historian who picks up the work on Loyola's subsequent development. It is unreasonable to require that historians avoid dealing with anything closer than a generation or even a decade ago—so long as the changing nature of the narrative is understood. In music there are symbols for increase and decrease, and on some dashboard thermostats in automobiles these symbols placed together let one recognize and regulate the mix of fresh air and heat. Something of the same process can be applied to a historical narrative as it comes closer to the present.

Among significant developments at Evergreen during these nine years were the emergence of a new style of planning, the shift to a predominantly resident student body, the building of new science and college centers, a rise in the socioeconomic status of the student body, and the emergence of the school of business and management as a distinct entity. This listing is not in chronological order but is meant to highlight what was important. In these years there appeared signs of local recognition, including a 1979 declaration by *Baltimore Magazine* that among the area's institutions of higher learning Loyola College had become the "in" school. If not definitive, this nevertheless was a straw in the wind.

· ·

The first few years of the period were affected by the Decade of Decision campaign to raise over $10 million. To generate a steady stream of favorable publicity during this effort and to celebrate a milestone in Loyola's development, 1977 and 1978 were devoted to the celebration of Loyola's 125th anniversary. On such occasions a committee is appointed to plan a tasteful and interesting series of events. The chairman was Doctor Stuart Rochester, a young historian and alumnus (class of 1966); other young faculty members headed various subdivisions of the committee. Between Maryland Day in 1977 and in 1978 the schedule was full of various programs, colloquia, and dramatic presentations. One other development related to this celebration was the establishment of the college archives to preserve Loyola's records and to have ample material on hand for the next such celebration.

Just before mid-September the *Sunday Sun* devoted more than a full page to Loyola's festivities and to describing the institution. Among the highlights in this description were the college's continuing record of balanced budgets, the new fund-raising campaign, and the new science center under construction. Loyola's academic quality was indicated by a faculty on which two-thirds held doctorates, by a student body of which a majority were recruited from the top fifth of their high-school classes, and by a ratio of one teacher for every sixteen students.

To the question whether or not the college "had lost ground spiritually, Father Sellinger responded: "Today's religiosity is manifested in a different way. . . . Our students . . . are just less inhibited and they don't think they are as hypocritical as their elders are . . . or were."[1] A few years later Father Andrew Greeley gave a more sociologically detailed answer to this question. He concluded that the decline in church attendance by Catholics in their twenties did not mean they were "inherently less religious than those who went before them but they [were] only passing through an inherently less religious phase of the life cycle."[2] Greeley had data to show that in their thirties and forties about half of these young Catholics would again be regular churchgoers and in their fifties and sixties almost two thirds.

The *Sun* writer took note of some other matters. A parking garage was included among the projects on which the new funds were to be expended. Residents to the south and west of the campus were upset by the preliminary sketch they saw of the new science center. Material was being collected to support Loyola's application to Phi Beta Kappa. The solid credentials of its faculty and students gave hope that it would eventually gain this widely recognized cachet of academic excellence. Admission of Georgetown University to Phi Beta Kappa was one of Father Sellinger's last accomplishments when he was dean there. Finally, a fine arts center with a 300-seat theater was on Loyola's developmental agenda.[3]

September 15, 1977—125 years after Loyola College first opened its doors on Holliday Street—was marked by an honors convocation. The marshal of the procession held aloft a glistening ceremonial mace. This handsome piece of silver craftsmanship was given to Mount Saint Agnes College only a few years before the merger with Loyola by an anonymous donor, and it had been transferred to Evergreen. It consists of a staff fashioned from white ash with a stylized silver spear-point at the lower end and a four-sided silver lantern on the other. Until a few decades ago American colleges and universities were loath to add this bit of pomp to their public rituals, but one after another has adopted such an ornament. To indicate the formal presence of the corporate entity, Loyola College, this ceremonial mace is carried at the head of academic processions and placed upright near the speaker's lectern.

February of 1978 was dedicated to a retrospective exhibition of the paintings of Jacques Maroger at the Loyola Gallery, then located in the old Calvert Street building. Maroger, after a noteworthy career as technical director of the Louvre's laboratory, had escaped to America ahead of the Nazi conquest of France, and taught painting at the Maryland Institute of Art from 1940 to 1959. While working in the Louvre laboratory he had rediscovered the method of processing oils and pigments used by the old masters to produce pure, luminous colors. The "Maroger medium," as it is called, is easily recognizable, and is used by thousands of artists around the world. His steadfast championing of representational rather than abstract work at a time when there was a vogue for the latter prompted his retirement from the Maryland Institute shortly before his death.[4]

The idea of a Maroger retrospective arose from several circumstances. His widow still had a large collection of his canvases, and lived in a studio located on campus between the Hammerman and Butler dormitories. This was not the first or only artistic fling for the college. Early each fall since 1966 it has sponsored an invitational show to display the work of Maryland's professional artists. Furthermore, during several summers in the early 1970s, the campus served as the home for the now-defunct Maryland Ballet Theater.

• •

Not as an encore to the anniversary year but merely as a continuation of the college's development, the Donnelly Science Center was opened in September of 1978, even though it was not quite finished. Construction workers and installers continued to bustle about for several months while the students and faculty managed as well as they could amid the clatter and debris.

The need for a new science facility was obvious. Increases in the number of natural-science majors and the introduction of a computer-science program in the late 1960s were taxing the limited capacity of Maryland Hall, in which most of the space was assigned to general classrooms and offices. The facilities in the original science building, now more than fifty years old, were seriously outmoded. (The old science building would soon be reconditioned with state assistance to serve as a center for career-planning and placement offices, for the education department, and for several of the social-science departments. After renovation, it was named Beatty Hall in honor of Father Vincent Beatty, Loyola's president from 1955 to 1964). Half the cost of the new science center was covered by a matching grant of $1.85 million from the state of Maryland, authorized in 1976.

The site selected for the building—the corner of Charles Street and Cold Spring Lane—was one of the last unoccupied spots on campus. This location inspired the architect to design the new building as a formal entrance to Evergreen. Above a wide, open stairway, a glass-enclosed diagonal section connecting two wings is held up by a series of exterior arches. To the right and left of this stairway are five-story wings placed parallel to the streets, with the first floor of each wing below ground, and windows on the street-side walls were kept to a minimum to deaden outside noise. The building's general style is contemporary; the architect sought to evoke "a feeling of Gothic" to make it compatible with the nearby chapel. Its location and form partially screen the chapel from a southern or western viewer.

In due course the college sought to inform the residents near the Charles Street–Cold Spring Lane intersection about its plans. Unfortunately, the artist's sketch used in this exposition was drawn for dramatic impact rather than literal accuracy. An exaggerated perspective made the structure appear a soaring behemoth, and its low placement suggested that the hill at the corner with its stand of old evergreens was to be flattened. A picture is said to be worth a thousand words but many more than that could not assuage apprehensions aroused by this sketch. Even people beyond the immediate neighborhood became concerned because Charles Street holds a mythic fascination for many Baltimoreans. Homeowners in particular feared that this "monstrosity" would so violate the tone of the neighborhood that people would become reluctant to buy property and that this would put the area on an economic and social down-spiral.

Because government grants are valid only for a specified time the college could not long delay construction, and no other site could accommodate the structure as planned. To avoid possible unpleasantness, President Sellinger decided to forgo a formal ground-breaking ceremony. He expected that when people saw the actual building take shape their apprehensions would be relieved—and so it proved. Once construction began, it became abundantly clear that the hill and its trees would not be bulldozed. The proportions of the steel skeleton showed that the building would not become a looming bulk of masonary brooding over the Charles Street intersection.

After a quarter of the structure had been completed, some residents of Guilford were interviewed. Their fears had indeed lessened. One or two affirmed their confidence that Loyola would never put up something unsuitable for the area. Others wistfully regretted loss of the "beautiful view" they had of the alumni chapel. Nevertheless, these interviews uncovered a lingering hurt expressed in complaints about poor communications with the college and concern over the parking congestion on the streets near Loyola.

This modification of opinion and the completion of construction permitted a formal dedication ceremony on December 3, 1978. Its climax was the unveiling of a plaque with cameo portraits of Edward and Anne Donnelly, generous benefactors of Loyola and of Baltimore. Ed Donnelly, it may be recalled, was the first layman elected to Loyola's board of trustees, and he was the board's first lay chairman. He was now retired as chairman of Easco Corporation, one of the region's leading industrial firms. This brief ceremony (on a very chilly day) formally made available five classrooms, twenty-five laboratories, three shops, a central computer, and a number of faculty offices.

• •

The opening of Donnelly Science Center coincided with a significant administrative change. Father Daniel Degnan left Loyola to become dean of the Seton Hall School of Law. The explanation of his sudden departure mentioned that such an alternative was offered at the time he came to Baltimore, and when the offer was renewed in the late summer of 1978 his acceptance disconcerted President Sellinger. To cover the academic year 1978–79 Father Sellinger named Doctor Thomas Scheye, then chairman of the largest department in the college — English, fine arts, and writing—as acting academic vice-president, and appointed the customary search committee.

The sudden change engendered mixed but generally favorable reactions, rather like those that some years earlier had greeted the appointment of Stephen McNierney. There are people who naively assume that a Jesuit administrator is bound to be more demanding and less responsive than a layman. Although there was little evidence of this expected pattern under Father Degnan, the appointment of Tom Scheye brought a flash of euphoria. He was 36 years old and had been a member of the Loyola faculty since 1970, when during a December class he glanced at his watch and announced, "I am now a doctor."[5] Scheye was casual about formalities, rarely wore a tie, and sported lush sideburns. Slight in physical stature, he acquired a reputation as a witty, incisive commentator on administrative doings.

After elementary school, Scheye enlisted for a full course of Jesuit education at Loyola High School and at Georgetown, where he was a member of the honors program initiated and attentively watched over by Dean Sellinger. Among Tom Scheye's activities was a brief stint as editor in chief of the student newspaper, and he vividly recalls this brought him on more than one occasion to Father Sellinger's office to explain, justify, or retract some less than favorable notice of the university that had appeared in the *Hoya*.

After receiving a master's degree from Yale and beginning doctoral work at the University of Pennsylvania, Scheye taught for five years at Towson State University. Upon transferring to Evergreen, he appeared as the host and writer of an engaging survey of English literature on Maryland's public television station for two years. Doctor Scheye's appearance about this same time as a witness for the college during the *Roemer* trial has already been noted. His testimony about the atmosphere of academic freedom on Loyola's campus probably gained weight from his Jewish ancestry.

Among his proudest accomplishments as a faculty member was the establishment of the faculty council in collaboration with a departmental colleague, Doctor Sue Abromaitis. Scheye saw the need for the faculty to respond to administrative initiatives and proposals with a unified voice; Mrs. Abromaitis was concerned with securing a more broadly based faculty agency than the AAUP chapter. Established in 1976 with strong faculty support and the sanction of the college council, the faculty council, like most such bodies, has varied in effectiveness over the years. Eleven years later it was reorganized as a faculty senate.

Upon his being named acting academic vice-president, something of Scheye's personal style became evident in his preference for being called Mister Scheye. His comments also were engagingly modest. To a student reporter, he expressed amazement at all the things people were now telling him. His main function, Scheye thought, was as a sort of dean of faculty—"the heart and soul of the school." His main theme, like Father Sellinger's, was "Loyola is a better school than people know," and his aim was to enhance both its distinctions and its recognition, because "people are buying quality."[6] Over time, campus observers noted the disappearance of his sideburns and the regular presence of coat and tie and other administrator's stigmata.

• •

The turnover in the academic vice-presidency, in process since early in 1977, did not noticeably slow significant academic developments. As an outgrowth of its computer-science major, the engineering-physics department proposed establishment of a master's program in digital systems. Loyola's undergraduate engineering program had, over twenty years, developed an enviable reputation among industrial employers and graduate schools for producing graduates who were creative problem-solvers rather than merely competent technicians. In seeking to upgrade the computer element of its offerings, the department under the leadership of Doctor Bernard Weigman (class of 1954) prepared what was ostensibly an undergraduate proposal, which was circulated among local engineering establishments for comments and suggestions. The responses not only were favorable but were accompanied by notices of interest if something similar could be offered at the graduate level. Such encouragement and an informal marketing survey indicated substantial interest in such a master's program.

What the physics department finally proposed was a non-research, non-thesis curriculum in digital systems. This practical orientation avoided duplicating the research-focused graduate offerings at the Johns Hopkins University and at the University of Maryland. The rapid development of microelectronics provided the general rationale. Though in the past a design problem had been assigned to a mechanical, civil, electrical, or chemical engineer, the inclusion of a computer engineer in the design process was becoming increasingly necessary. Futhermore, people who had become managers of engineers in one of the old specialties now had to cope with computer engineers. Having identified a need in its surrounding community, Loyola earnestly planned to meet that need.

Curricular, financial, and staffing details were carefully worked out. Essentially, the laboratory work was scheduled for the Evergreen campus, where equipment for the undergraduate programs was already housed; with the opening of the Donnelly Science Center this equipment would include a mainframe computer. General instruction was centered at Hunt Valley—Baltimore County's "most successful industrial park"—located north of the beltway near the Harrisburg expressway. In the vicinity are many technically oriented firms including Westinghouse, Western Electric, and BioQuest.[7] Starting with an enrollment of over forty (as predicted in the department's prospectus), the master's degree program in digital systems had by 1985 grown fivefold with no signs of levelling or decline.

Not all Loyola's academic ventures of the late 1970s were successful. The dean of the graduate division, Sister Magdala Thompson, discerned the need for a doctoral program focused on training middle- and high-level educational administrators. There were twenty-six hundred people in such positions in the Baltimore area alone. There was some question whether Loyola's program would duplicate one at the University of Maryland, but Loyola's administrators finally decided that any overlap was not sufficient to deter its proposal.

This program too was oriented to practical training in management skills rather than to abstract research. By reason of the broad powers granted by the state in Loyola's original charter, the college might have instituted this doctoral program forthwith but chose instead to submit the proposal to the State Board of Higher Education (SBHE). This was an agency recently established to straighten out what the *Sun* called "the mess in higher education."

SBHE was given power to require state-sponsored colleges and universities to submit their academic development plans for review in order to minimize duplication and wasteful competition. The board's powers in regard to private institutions were less clearly defined. Nevertheless, Maryland's program of general aid to private institutions offered a practical incentive for their cooperation. When Loyola submitted its doctoral proposal to SBHE, the board responded in June of 1977 with a rejection because it discerned an overlap between Loyola's proposed program and one already operating at the University of Maryland.[8] President Sellinger gave thought to relying on Loyola's charter powers to institute the program despite SBHE's rejection and had encouragement from other private institutions in the area, but the stakes seemed too high. The board was not entirely negative regarding Loyola's proposals: an application for a master's program in pastoral counseling was approved in 1977 and after a gradual development the program was expanded to the doctoral level with the approval of Maryland authorities in 1986.

The exchanges with SBHE were not without other positive results. The presidents of Loyola, Towson State, Morgan State, and the University of Baltimore (Loyola the only private institution) cooperated effectively in persuading the state board to reject the University of Maryland's plan to transfer its business administration programs from College Park to its underutilized Baltimore County campus near Catonsville. Sellinger and the other presidents contended that there was no need for such an "extremely costly [and] . . . clearly duplicative venture" in an area already served by the four institutions. Their case was so clear and so cogently presented that the planned transfer was aborted early in 1979.[9]

By this time the effectiveness of Father Sellenger in his representations to the state government on behalf of Loyola and of MICUA was readily evident. Close observers of his performance on such occasions note his acquaintance with many of the leaders in Annapolis; these in the 1970s included legislators, 60 percent of whom were Catholic. The observers refer to his personable, compelling presence with no political overtones, and a sincere style leavened by a sense of humor. All these characteristics have engendered trust in Father Sellinger as senior statesman in Maryland private higher education.[10]

. .

At Loyola, athletics no less than academics underwent a significant development in the late 1970s. The transition after "Lefty" Reitz retired was completed with the appointment of Tom O'Connor as athletic director and the resignation of Loyola from the Mason-Dixon Conference. By the late 1970s there was only one other small private college left in a conference now dominated by fourteen state-sponsored institutions. A better fit for the modest athletic budget of the college was found in the East Coast Atlantic Conference (ECAC) of the National College Athletic Association (NCAA). In this league, Loyola could schedule varsity sports with two hundred colleges and its athletes would be eligible to compete in various tournaments. Concretely, the shift allowed Loyola's soccer team to win the national championship in 1976.

The shift to ECAC and a desire to familiarize more students, especially residents, with "lifetime" sports (squash, racquetball, swimming, tennis, and the like) required more and better athletic facilities. During the Decade of Decision planning process, new athletic facilities were connected to additional parking. A field house with adjacent parking was to go on the land behind the dormitories, but it was blocked by zoning problems and the neighborhood's concern about heavy traffic on its narrow streets. The alternative—an underground parking garage roofed with an astroturf playing surface on the old athletic field—failed for much the same reason. After uncoupling the athletic and parking projects, Loyola sought to lease land for parking from Johns Hopkins. Although President Muller was very sympathetic to Father Sellinger's request, the trustees of the university and of the Evergreen Foundation strongly disapproved the proposal.[11]

In these circumstances, President Sellinger decided to delay action on a new gymnasium, swimming pool, and parking facility to concentrate on a better playing field. The surface had to take the tearing and pounding of cleated shoes for practice sessions and regular games in men's and women's lacrosse, field hockey, soccer, and a variety of intramural sports. During 1978–79 there were 250 varsity athletes and 1,100 intramural participants at Evergreen. No grass surface could recover from such hard use, and a decision was made to cover the field with astroturf. Specifically this meant an all-nylon rug spread over 15,500 square yards, or enough for two regulation lacrosse fields. A few years later the Johns Hopkins University erected a similarly covered playing field.

Bad weather delayed completion of the foundation, and the zoning board would not permit erection of permanent bleachers. Nevertheless, the new surface of the athletic field was ready for use in the fall of 1979. It was dedicated to John Curley, Jr., a local steel executive who had generously supported Loyola's development before his untimely death. The uniform green surface has become one of the features of Baltimore that can be easily spotted from a plane. Some questioned what they considered an increasing propensity to bigness, untypical of an earlier Baltimore. But the ethos of the city was changing, with more and taller and dramatic buildings going up around the inner harbor, and for Loyola there was no alternative.

• •

As winter approached in 1978, President Jimmy Carter sought to slow the pace of inflation by asking employers to hold price and wage increases to no more than 7 percent. Whether or not this guideline applied to nonprofit institutions was unclear, and a number of colleges and universities increased tuitions and salaries without reference to the guideline. The issue was raised at the November 7 meeting of the board of trustees, with some administrative opinion on the side of exemption. After reviewing President Carter's announcement, however, Loyola's trustees approved a rollback of the planned tuition increase to 7 percent; to keep the budget in balance, salary increases were held to the same level.

In announcing the tuition rollback, Father Sellinger noted that the guideline was clearly voluntary and that "Loyola College elects to volunteer."[12] The public reaction to this was strongly favorable and widely noted. Senator Charles Mathias, an independent Republican from Maryland, adverted to Loyola's dependency on tuition income and hailed its courageous action for the "common good."[13]

The faculty reaction, however, was different because action had been taken without notice or opportunity to consult. Since 1970, the AAUP salary surveys displayed the national erosion of faculty purchasing power due to increases that did not match the rate of inflation. The faculty compensation committee appealed to the trustees with a detailed exposition of how inadequate a 7 percent salary increase would be.[14] A committee of the board listened politely to the presentation but the decision to follow President Carter's guideline remained unchanged.

There were expressions of faculty displeasure and a strong demand for some kind of action. The officers of the faculty council and AAUP chapter combined to propose that the faculty inform itself on how to invoke the National Labor Relations Act to organize and bargain collectively. This was an option that college faculties during the 1970s were increasingly adopting. The example of organizing among federal civil service employees and among schoolteachers made similar activity more acceptable to the American professoriate.

In 1970 the National Labor Relations Board (NLRB) finally accepted jurisdiction over employees at private nonprofit institutions. When about the same time the faculty at Fordham sought NLRB assistance in its organizing drive, Fordham's governing board objected on the grounds that the faculty had a managerial role in the university and thus their status was not analogous to that of industrial workers. Although the Fordham faculty as a whole voted for "no agent" in the election conducted by the NLRB, its law school faculty opted for an independent organization to negotiate with the university and succeeded in being certified under federal law. By 1976 fifty private four-year colleges were operating under collective-bargaining agreements. Among these were eight Catholic institutions including three Jesuit schools: University of San Francisco, Regis College, and University of Scranton. One observer of this development noted that collective bargaining enhanced the power of a board of trustees because governance becomes more explicit, less ambiguous.[15]

Although there was a general willingness among the Loyola faculty to learn what was involved in the organizing process, several lay members made their adamant oppostion clear from the start. They were concerned about outside interference, the loss of a collegial atmosphere, and becoming involved with an institution identified with roughneck industrial workers and strikes. They did not see pertinence of the papal encyclicals on labor to the situation at Evergreen. Nevertheless, an educational program was systematically pursued for almost two years. In Feburary of 1979, representatives from the AAUP and the American Federation of Teachers addressed a meeting with 80 percent of the regular faculty in attendance.[16] Administrators took note of these developments but did not interfere in any way.

This episode ended indecisively for several reasons. There were apprehensions about dividing the faculty, and those opposed to organizing could not be converted. The wife of an AAUP officer asked him the common-sense question: "If collective bargaining is so great, why haven't more college faculties adopted it?" The college's salary proposal in the fall of 1979 included a 12 percent increase with a commitment for the future to maintain a certain level on the annual AAUP salary scale. Finally, in February of 1980, the Supreme Court in its *Yeshiva* decision ruled that college faculties are indeed managerial and so may not invoke the procedures of the National Labor Relations Act. This slowed the movement toward collective bargaining on college campuses.[17]

This episode was a jarring introduction to the world of academic administration for Tom Scheye. None of the faculty blamed him for the unfortunate situation. Early in April of 1979 the word *acting* was dropped from his title on recommendation of the search committee and by decision of Father Sellinger.

· ·

In American higher education the late 1970s were still marked by concern with enrollments and finances. Fears about the "baby bust" and a decline in the quality of applicants to private liberal arts colleges were again abroad. These signs could not be ignored by Loyola's administration, but the steady increase in enrollment of well-qualified students and in finances made them less worrisome. The Decade of Decision campaign was bringing in capital for a new college center, but zoning regulations made it difficult to fit on the campus.

A possible solution appeared when late in 1978 Sister Kathleen Feeley, president of College of Notre of Maryland, reopened the practical dialogue with Father Sellinger. He acknowledged that this offered a chance to "escape our history and start again."[18] These negotiations would continue from August of 1979 to May of 1982 but did not result in much. The one practical thing was provision of technical means by which Loyola could meet the zoning restrictions that were blocking erection of a new college center. The fivefold growth of Loyola during the 1970s and its development into a "comprehensive university" with a variety of graduate programs made the task of fitting its needs with those of Notre Dame into a package acceptable to both seem virtually unfeasible.[19] The lines of communication opened in this period remain intact and various proposals continue to be discussed. The actual experience with the predicted "baby bust" has been unaccountably less severe for Loyola, Notre Dame, and many others schools than had been feared. Neither enrollment nor the quality of applicants declined as predicted, and as a result the urgency felt at the beginning of the 1980s has lessened—for the time being.

While the discussions with College of Notre Dame were in progress, Loyola acquired a major prize in the fall semester of 1979. Campus housing had been packed beyond its orginally planned capacity. Space designed for three occupants now housed four, and where only two students were supposed to room there were three. Lounge areas had been converted to living accommodations. How long such overcrowding might be endured became moot when Loyola authorities learned that Charleston Hall, a large garden-style apartment complex directly across Charles Street from the campus, was about to be put on the market. The board of trustees immediately authorized negotiations for this two-million-dollar property, which it was estimated would accommodate four hundred students.

Unfortunately, rumors of the deal outraced formal announcement and made the Charleston Hall tenants apprehensive. Most were middle-aged, some retired, and some elderly. Many feared that they would be summarily evicted by their new landlord, although the college from the beginning had never intended anything of the kind. Apartments that were empty would be occupied by students in September of 1980. Tenants who chose to move before the expiration of their leases were not penalized for early departure. Those who were elderly, seriously infirm, or handicapped could renew their leases on a year-by-year basis. Others who encountered difficulty in finding suitable quarters had their leases extended for more than a year. Only the remainder not included in any of these categories and whose leases ended early in 1980 would not have them renewed. Under the best of circumstances moving a domicile is not a pleasant experience, especially for people who have reached a certain time and settlement in life, but when Loyola's full policy was sufficiently publicized and understood tenant apprehensions subsided.

Nevertheless, this short-lived confusion and emotionality added to the uneasiness of relations between the college and its neighbors. At this juncture, Loyola got a helping word from Baltimore's popular mayor, William Donald Schaefer. In October of 1979, Schaefer interrupted his election campaign schedule to tour Loyola's campus. After inspecting the Donnelly Science Center and the astroturf-covered field, he said: "This college is important to Baltimore. The community should not be unreasonable."[20] For those not attuned to Baltimore's civic discourse this might seem rather bland—but it helped.

After students began moving into Charleston Hall in late August of 1980, both the tenants and the college authorities were uncertain about results. There was an obvious generation gap. Most of the remaining tenants were middle-aged or older and had been conditioned by television and films to expect unmannerly behavior, noise, and wild parties. The first students assigned were carefully selected and instructed in the absolute necessity of being on their best behavior. It took a little while for experience to dissipate various apprehensions but by the end of the first year the tenants had found that living in Charleston Hall had not changed significantly since the advent of the students. When a few years later the college acquired Wynnewood Towers, a high-rise apartment complex bordering Charleston Hall, some of the remaining Charleston tenants volunteered to reassure their neighbors that living with Loyola students and with the college as landlord was not unpleasant.

. .

However, the winter of 1979–80 brought the most severe public relations crisis Loyola had ever experienced. For several years the college had been quite diligent in communicating with the surrounding neighborhood associations. From January of 1977 to July of 1979 there were forty-seven written communications or meetings with representatives of the Guilford, Kernewood, or Radnor-Winston associations. On several of these occasions, the Guilford Association did not respond. The associations appeared before the zoning board in July of 1979 to oppose the variance Loyola needed to build permanent bleachers on the renovated athletic field. On this point the board agreed with the associations but left intact the building permit that authorized erection of lightpoles around the field. Sometime—possibly at the end of this proceeding—a voluble city inspector was heard to say that if Loyola now installed the light fixtures its officials and those of the builder would be "thrown in jail."[21]

The college was loath to act in such an atmosphere but was advised in September to erect the lights or risk losing the legal right to do so. Anxious to proceed properly, Loyola made a formal inquiry to establish the validity of its building permit. That was confirmed early in December, but complaints from the neighbors had reached the mayor's ears and he ordered another hearing. This resulted on December 20 in yet another confirmation of Loyola's legal right to erect the lights. Unfortunately, most of this was known to only a few, and that made it possible for opponents to capitalize on Loyola's next step.

During the weekend before Christmas, eight lightpoles between eighty and ninety feet high were installed around the athletic field. Without knowing about the delays and the repeated validations of Loyola's building permit, a number of observers, even some on campus, supposed that the college had acted with cunning to create a *fait accompli* at an opportune time. This prompted a consortium of forty-seven Guilford and Kernewood homeowners to file a suit against Loyola, the mayor of Baltimore, and others. In addition these associations had two ordinances introduced into the city council, one aimed specifically at Loyola and the other including Johns Hopkins as a target. The first ordinance would have prohibited the erection of any light fixture higher than fifteen feet without the approval of the zoning board. The other would have prevented Loyola, Hopkins, and any other private school from building or expanding without specific permission of the zoning board. This was particularly discriminatory because state-supported schools could expand without the permission of the city zoning board and they were located in much more tightly compacted neighborhoods.[22] Supporters of Loyola and Hopkins testified so effectively that the council quietly killed the ordinances.

The court suit over the lightpoles languished until the late fall of 1982. During this delay Loyola authorities ascertained that the Guilford Association was reconciled to the existence of the lights and was interested only in how they were to be used. The judge hearing the suit repeatedly made clear that he wanted the parties to find a solution by direct negotiations. With some additional refinements, including the lowering of the lights by fifteen feet, the final agreement was framed in much the same terms as those Loyola drafted in March of 1980. The number of intercollegiate games played each year under an 11 P.M.

curfew was specified. There also were various restrictions on the use of a public-address system. [23]

The settlement eliminated an immediate cause of friction but it did not establish harmonious relations. That would take another crisis and another agreement. What this 1979–82 episode displayed was that Loyola College could hold its own even against "some of the city's wealthiest and most prominent business and professional leaders."[24] It had not sought a fight and had been willing to compromise from the beginning, but it had demonstrated that it could be quite formidable. That was not, however, the impression it wished to convey. Shortly after the trouble over the lights began, Father Sellinger sought professional advice from a public relations firm that provided a suitable plan for the instant situation and for the longer term.

• •

The eventfulness of 1979 was not exhausted by the start of the trouble over the lights. A less strenuous exercise was the decennial visitation of the Middle States Association. This time Loyola, viewing itself as a stable, thriving concern, chose an abbreviated form of review. Instead of the encompassing studies of 1957 and 1969, this accreditation process focused only on governance, the undergraduate curriculum, and the graduate programs. In its self-study prepared before the visitation from the Middle States Association, the college noted how its development over the past ten years had burdened its administrative structure and it proposed to group departments into four divisions, each under a director. This, it argued, would afford better communication and coordination among departments with similar disciplines. [25]

The bulk of the self-study report was devoted to the undergraduate curriculum and to graduate programs. This included a straightforward description of the 4-1-4 curriculum as it had developed since its introduction in 1971. Note was taken of the writing course added to the core and of the requirement of theology for all students, not merely Catholics. The expansion of graduate offerings to eighteen distinct master's programs—some off campus—and an enrollment of almost twenty-five hundred was thoroughly summarized. The question of specialized accreditation for some graduate programs was noted.

The two-day visitation took place early in November of 1979. The Middle States team noted the dramatic developments at Evergreen since the review ten years earlier and expressed appreciation for the "completeness," "straightforwardness," and "total candor" of Loyola's self-study. The team also remarked on the college's continuing dedication to liberal learning and religious values even as it expanded its professional programs. The evaluators suggested that Loyola might have to redefine its mission to account for its involvement in career-oriented programs.

The Middle States team was more direct concerning governance. The team doubted that the proposed restructuring into divisions would improve communication and coordination among departments. Anticipating continuing growth, especially in the graduate programs, it favored vertical integration among the undergraduate and graduate divisions through a school of arts and sciences and a separate school of business, but also noted that the development of a solid consensus among the administration and faculty required "comprehensive airing" of the issue. Furthermore, specialized accreditation of the business program by the American Assembly of Collegiate Schools of Business (AACSB) and of the speech pathology program by the appropriate body was seen as a logical next step. Monumentally demanding and costly as the procedures for such accreditation were, the team thought there were notable benefits to be derived. Specialized accreditation would enhance Loyola's general reputation for excellence.[26]

This development was not seen as displacing the fundamental basis for the high esteem of Loyola: its undergraduate curriculum. The Middle States team was quite enthusiastic about the "strong liberal-arts core and a committed, qualified faculty interested in teaching." More could be done with January courses, such as attaching credit for them to core or major requirements. The team noted the general paucity of electives, especially in the preprofessional majors. It emphasized the importance of faculty development through restrictions on workload, increased support for research, and sabbaticals. These would enhance the faculty's "reputation for good teaching and scholarship."[27]

The team reserved its most critical remarks for student services. The students, described as "attractive, above average in terms of statistical and test measures, and positive in their reaction to the quality of the educational experience they receive at the College," expressed concern about disparities between "institutional performance" and promises.[28] Services for the students were well staffed and well administered but the space and facilities available were inadequate. The student center had been built for a male population of eight hundred but now had to serve more than twenty-one hundred students, with a substantial portion of women. Few could object to this assessment or deny that Loyola's most traumatic problem was parking.

The team's report concluded that Loyola's "track record for meeting challenges in the past ten years has been good and this in itself is an optimistic sign. Add to this a clear unvarnished view of itself and one reaches the conclusion that Loyola is, on balance, ready to cope with its future."[29] Early in the report, this favorable development was ascribed in large measure to the energy, continuance in office, and public visibility of President Sellinger.

• •

An attempt to deal in a limited way with the provision of additional student facilities and parking resulted in an unexpected confrontation during the fall semester of 1980. At the opening of classes, a shuttle service was announced. Students, staff, and faculty could park their cars on the cathedral lot a mile away and be bused to and from the campus. Unfortunately, the shuttle service was used by only a few and a car-pooling program was treated with similar indifference.

A permanent solution was sought by using the field behind the Butler dormitory. The area would yield almost seventy parking spaces, four tennis courts, and a basketball court that could be flooded in winter for ice skating. The students were slow to respond to the announcement of this project. When objections and grumblings finally arose, George Andrews (1982), president of student government, mobilized the opposition. The student council passed a strong resolution condemning the plan. Then Andrews got Faith Finamore (1982) and Julie Taylor (1982) to coordinate a presentation to the student life commission.

Representatives of the student council, residents, commuters, the Rugby Club, and the freshman class emphasized two points: Butler field was a last bit of grass on campus, and it was the only plot that could be used without formal permission. Pickup games and practice for various intramural sports would become impossible. These students also thought that acceptable alternatives had not been fully considered. After hearing these representations, the commission chairman, Doctor Frank Cunningham, associate professor of philosophy, declared, "It was an extremely professional performance."[30]

It took the student life commission several meetings and many hours to arrive at a consensus against the plan to cover Butler field with asphalt. Administrators considered this response over the Christmas vacation and decided to abandon their original plan—much to the delight of the students. Over the summer of 1981, more parking spaces were laid out between the Jesuit residence and Cold Spring Lane, where the tennis courts had been. The courts were later transferred to the eastern edge of Butler field, which was elevated to the level of the patio behind the dormitory with dirt excavated from the new college center site—and resodded to accommodate a rugby field available for other sports as well. With a minimum of difficulty from the Radnor-Winston Association, the renovation of Butler field was completed in 1984. It was a felicitous accommodation for all.

Students were interested in more substantive matters. Having the right to vote gave them a sense of obligation about the presidential election in 1980. Ronald Reagan was not their favorite, as was evident in the Republican mock-convention held on campus. The ticket preferred by the participants was Gerald Ford with George Bush as his running mate. During the campaign, John Anderson's third-party candidacy roused more comment than the candidacies of Reagan or President Carter. The mood of the students, at least of those who wrote for the *Greyhound,* was evident in their preference for Anderson as a "noble gesture."[31] Ambivalence toward President Reagan and "Reaganomics" persisted throughout his first term. Cartoons reprinted in the *Greyhound* were generally critical of Reagan's fiscal and foreign policies except for the invasion of Grenada. Customarily, Americans support presidential military actions—at least in the beginning. But retrenchment of federal programs diminished the funds available to assist college students in paying their bills.

This change did not have a severe effect on Loyola's students because the college increased its financial aid even as it raised tuition. In 1980 more than 25 percent of the undergraduate student body had more than 25 percent of their costs covered by various kinds of assistance. Four years later the proportion receiving aid had risen to thirty-five percent while the proportion of aid to each student remained essentially unchanged. Nevertheless, the cost to Loyola increased because the number of students was greater and tuition rose from $2,775 in 1980 to $4,950 four years later.

Outside employment covered some of the remainder. More than 25 percent of the full-time undergraduates were employed part time, with a little over 3 percent managing a full schedule of classes and a full-time job.[32] In the past such statistics would have evoked unfavorable comment by some faculty members and administrators, but the practice was now so deeply rooted, and the unlikelihood of finding alternative sources of money was so apparent, that no one bothered to register any objection.

• •

In the aftermath of the 1979 Middle States vistation, several factors combined to promote the establishment of a separate school of business and a decision to seek specialized accreditation for its undergraduate and graduate programs. The business departments had submitted a formal and well-documented proposal to that effect in the spring. This proposal stressed the "baby bust" and the threat to Loyola's "dominant market position" posed by the plan to transfer the University of Maryland's business programs to its Baltimore County campus, as well as the decision of the University of Baltimore to seek accreditation by the American Assembly of Collegiate Schools of Business (AACSB).

This organization was created in 1916 by deans of the schools of business of Chicago, Columbia, Harvard, California, Pennsylvania, and other universities of note. Among its functions has been accrediting high-quality business programs. The first Jesuit schools to be accredited by the AACSB were Marquette (1928) and Fordham (1939). In 1971, the Association of Jesuit Colleges and Universities (AJCU) recommended to all its members that they seek membership and accreditation by the AACSB. By 1979, thirteen of the twenty-eight Jesuit institutions of higher learning had been accredited and three more were actively preparing for the process. [33]

Whether or not Loyola's business faculty was aware of the AJCU recommendation is not clear from the record, but interest in AACSB accreditation was noted sporadically in the department's minutes during the early and middle 1970s. The final campaign was organized under the leadership of Ray House, a tall, courtly southern gentleman who had become head of the business department in 1976 and acquired a number of connected titles and responsibilities. Doctor House made no secret of his desire for AACSB accreditation, which was contingent on the establishment of a separate school of business. He was no less forthright about his interest in becoming the first dean of such a school. [34]

Since this was not a matter of general discussion, the main obstacle to the development was Father Sellinger's concern about Loyola's losing its institutional identity as an excellent liberal arts college. House and the business department repeatedly avowed their commitment to Loyola's strong liberal arts core but emphasized the threat posed by their competition, the growth potential in the business programs, and their contribution to the cash flow of the college. Since 1973 the undergraduate business programs had grown at an average annual rate of almost 14 percent and by 1978 they accounted for almost a quarter of tuition income in the undergraduate division. The annual growth rate in the

M.B.A. programs was similar, but the annual average rate of increase in the X.M.B.A. was 24 percent, with all tuition amounting to three-quarters of the graduate division's income.[35] The department was cautious about implying that such a rate of growth could be sustained in the future but argued that no decline was likely. The persistence of the department and the threat posed by competing institutions finally convinced Sellinger of the need to establish a separate school of business and to seek AACSB accreditation. Loyola's business program needed this structure and stimulus to maintain its momentum and without this effort it might lose ground to its competitors.

To gain a realistic picture of the accreditation process, Loyola employed a consultant, Thomas Bausch, dean of Marquette's school of business and something of an "insider" in AACSB operations. In his report, Dean Bausch argued that Loyola's survival depended on a strong and accredited business program fully integrated with the operations of the college. The dean of a separate business school would be an active and visible advocate. Such accreditation would attract more and better students and faculty, whereas the absence of an AACSB cachet would require constant defense of the quality of Loyola's business programs. The estimated cost included $300,000 in salaries for a dean and twelve new full-time faculty members. Bausch cautioned againsts financing this development at the expense of other departments. The results in less than a decade, Dean Bausch confidently predicted, would be "one of the best schools of business . . . in the Jesuit network."[36]

Discussion of the Bausch report began in earnest after the Easter vacation. Some faculty members and students were concerned about the limited amount of time left in the semester to consider such an important matter. They were anxious about the cost and the possibility that this might be covered in part by phasing out other graduate programs. Their main concern, however, was an implicit devaluation of the undergraduate core into merely something to be gotten over before acquiring technical skills. After strong assurance from Vice President Scheye that the liberal arts core would "in no way" be affected by the proposal, the college council with only one dissenter endorsed the plan to establish a separate school of business, to study the impact of the AACSB accreditation process, and to appoint search committees for the two new deans.

In September of 1980, the new administrative structure was fully realized and was the subject of comment for hardly a week. Eventually

David Roswell, professor of chemistry and chairman of the department, was appointed dean of the college of arts and sciences. Choosing the new dean of the school of business and management, however, proved more difficult. Ray House left and the subsequent turnover in the deanship makes it unnecessary to follow the permutations. What is significant is that the difficulty in finding a suitable dean did not interfere with the process of hiring more full-time professors; nor were the other preparations for AACSB visitation slowed.

Indeed, neither was recruitment for the college of arts and sciences slighted. Between 1980 and 1986, the total number of Loyola College full-time faculty rose from over 125 to over 170, with three-quarters of them holding a doctoral or other terminal degree. This increase in the regular faculty held at bay administrative concerns over too high a proportion of tenured faculty members and affected revision of the undergraduate curriculum. In 1984 the school of business and management was retitled to include the name of President Sellinger because a publicly unidentified donor made that the *sine qua non* of a one-million-dollar gift. Preparations for AACSB accreditation continued unabated under the direction of Dean Charles Margenthaler, who in April of 1988 had the pleasure of informing President Sellinger that Loyola's school of business had been accredited on its first try—a rather rare accomplishment.

• •

By the time Loyola's second five-year plan ended in 1982, a number of dynamic and successful institutions were demonstrating the effectiveness of a new style of planning. The old style, "long-range," planning was exemplified in Loyola's five-year plans. They were framed in terms of discrete periods and assumed that certain factors would remain constant during the cycle. For the 1970s these represented the state of the art, but experience with a more competitive environment in a period when federal assistance and the number of college-age students were both declining required something more flexible and responsive.

"Strategic" planning was developed pragmatically. The administrators and faculties at certain institutions began planning differently. Their experience was eventually organized by George Keller, vice-president of Barton-Gillet, in *Academic Strategy: The Managerial Revolution in American Higher Education* (Baltimore, 1983). What makes "strategic" planning different is that the process is continuous, is closely tied to the budget, and focuses on an institution's "strengths, weaknesses, opportunities, and threats."[37] Instead of the long declarative list of goals and objectives characteristic of "long-range" planning, it relies on a clear, practical mission statement that embodies the main strategic goals of the institution.

To apply this new style of planning to Loyola's development, President Sellinger invited the trustees to meet with him and the vice-presidents at the Homestead in Hot Springs, Virginia, in the summer of 1982. This site is used for conferences because it provides comfortable facilities and seclusion. Here Vice President Scheye outlined the circumstances in which Loyola College had to operate and how the administration proposed to deal with the situation. Over the preceding decade the undergraduate population had grown by 71 percent, from about fifteen hundred to over twenty-five hundred, and the Scholastic Aptitude Test (SAT) mean score was now over 160 points higher than the national average. Graduate enrollments after a dip in the late 1970s had risen so that they were 24 percent higher than ten years earlier, and graduate admission test scores were also higher. In that same period the regular faculty increased from 102 to 138, or only by 35 percent. Scheye concluded, "Loyola was in fact doing more with less—and apparently doing it better."[38]

Turning to the current situation, he noted the strong competition Loyola faced. The quality of state colleges and universities was improving and they continued to attract applicants with low tuition. The private institutions with which the college had to compete already had well-established reputations for quality and could offer more in financial aid than Loyola. This obviously meant having to raise more money, but Loyola's administration did not propose to follow the very old practice of accepting more but less-qualified students. Instead both the number and the quality of the students would continue to be raised. Scheye noted later that when this objective was discussed with other very knowledgeable educators they shook their heads with incredulity but wished the college well.[39]

In his mind the cornerstone of the planning process was a new mission statement, which read:

> Loyola will be a medium-sized, very selective Catholic liberal-arts college, under the aegis of the Society of Jesus, in collaboration with the Sisters of Mercy, serving Maryland and the mid-Atlantic region, committed to education in traditional arts and sciences and tomorrow's business and technology.[40]

The core of this statement of purpose remained essentially unchanged from previous formulations, and the introduction of the terms *medium-sized* and the *mid-Atlantic region* merely recognized what was already fact. It was the stress on selectivity (in the face of rising costs) that was new and even courageous, and yet in essence it was prefigured in Father Sellinger's remarks to the Jesuit scholastics at Woodstock in 1964.

Complementary presentations were made by Paul Melanson on financial implications of the new plan and by Robert Sweeney on development prospects. During the working sessions that followed, the trustees demonstrated the special quality of their involvement. One former trustee has noted that members of Loyola's board have been more involved than is usual in business or in other institutions. At the Homestead they asked searching questions and offered pertinent advice, but the toughest questions were propounded by Father Sellinger.[41] Out of this searching review arose a consensus on Loyola's strategic plan for the 1980s.

. .

Loyola's development made it possible and its ambitious strategy made it necessary to adopt a policy that had been suggested much earlier. In 1968, Christopher Jencks and David Reisman wondered why Catholic colleges did not attempt to solve their problem of underfinancing by raising tuition and then providing financial aid to students who could not pay the higher cost. They suggested that such increases would limit the clientele to the upper middle class and that these might not be willing to pay an "Ivy League" price for a "streetcar" college.[42] The ability to increase tuition above a certain level depended on raising the quality of education and campus life. To some it may seem futile to raise tuition and to increase financial aid, but coupled with larger enrollments this process can result in a net surplus. At Loyola, and probably at most Jesuit schools, it was the members of the order who cautioned against tuition increases beyond what lower-middle-class families could afford, but the addition of lay trustees and a more dynamic approach to development tempered this advice at Evergreen, as elsewhere.

Looking only at the 1982 tuition increase at Loyola is misleading. It was 21 percent—from $3,250 to $3,950—but this obscures the relative stability of tuition from 1967 to 1981. Discounting each year's bill by the rate of inflation yields virtually the same figure ($1,100) at both terminals of this period. Like many other American colleges, Loyola had been holding the line on the cost to its students, but like other institutions, it could no longer continue this policy. The general shift in the academic marketplace took the danger out of tuition increases. Since 1982 annual increments in tuition have varied between 6 and 9 percent, with one spike up to 15.

One extramural resource eased the burden of these increases for some Catholic students from the archdiocese of Baltimore. In 1981 Henry Knott (1929) established a twenty-million-dollar scholarship fund named for his wife, Marion Burk Knott. The objective is to produce Catholic leaders and the awards are apportioned to elementary and high-school students but with 45 percent reserved for college scholarships. This category is further divided, with 45 percent to College of Notre Dame, 35 percent to Loyola, and 20 percent to Mount Saint Mary's. The scholarships are awarded competively: to qualify an applicant must achieve an SAT score of 1,200 and maintain a B average. By 1986, twenty-four young women and men had used their Marion Burk Knott scholarships at Evergreen.[43]

Henry Knott is usually described as strong-willed, fiery-tempered, and certainly generous. There are various estimates of what his philanthropies have amounted to over the past forty years but they have been enough to secure him a listing among "the most generous living Americans" in *Town and Country* magazine. Attempts to trace a connection with Leo Knott, an earlier benefactor of the college, have not been successful; the two Knotts' generosity appears to have been of a collateral nature. After his studies at Loyola High School, Henry Knott attended the college for a while but found academia too tame, so his father gave him the alternative of joining the family business as a bricklayer and he made his way eventually as a building contractor and real estate investor.[44] Knott was a major factor in the negotiations with the Johns Hopkins University for the acquisition of land in 1964 and for establishment of the joint library.

Rising tuition did change the socioeconomic profile of the Loyola undergraduate student body. Comparing them to students at other highly selective Catholic colleges indicates that at Loyola in 1983 less than half of the general average came from families with an income below $12,000 and 13 percent more than the average came from families with an income over $100,000. These statistics can be made more idiomatic by noting that a sailing club was now numbered among extracurricular activities, and a group of students pooled their funds to hire a boat for a cruise around the Bahama Islands.

Why were they choosing to come to Loyola? In a marketing survey done in this period the two reasons offered by more than 90 percent of the students was the availability of programs in mathematics, natural sciences, engineering, and business, and Loyola's general academic reputation. This was second only to the Johns Hopkins University's. The middling size of the student body and its behavior were other attractions. Even though only slightly more than half the respondents indicated any prior familiarity with Loyola, this represented an improvement. Nevertheless, the consultants urged more effort to gain "wider visibility" among potential applicants. [45]

• •

What followed the Homestead conference was a progressive application of decisions made there. The accreditation process for the school of business has already been described. Revision from the 4-1-4 curriculum adopted in 1971 to a 5-5 pattern became a subject of discussion during the early 1980s. To the question Why change? numerous answers were given but, except for the 5-5 plan's ability to offer more electives, they were nebulous at best. Student opposition, mobilized by Sue Godbehere (1982), student government vice-president for academics, noted that a five-course curriculum meant more tests and writing assignments with only minor gain for electives. Some of the faculty were skeptical; as one teacher put it, the shift "may be an excellent solution, but a solution to what?" [46] For the faculty the crux of the matter was the possibility of a heavier workload. Before 1971 a five-course student load meant a four-course faculty load per semester, and a return to such a faculty workload when publication had become an important requirement for promotion and tenure seemed cruel and excessive.

After the graduation of Godbehere, an agreement on maintaining a three-course faculty workload, and an increase in the number of faculty members whose only experience had been with a 5-5 curricular pattern, made it relatively easy to change. The general agreement was formalized by the college council in mid-December of 1985. Undergraduate courses would carry three credits and the normal student workload would be five courses each semester. This made eight additional courses available over four years and these were assigned as follows: two courses were added to every major, four elective courses had to be taken outside the student's major area, and the two remaining courses could be taken either within or outside the major area.

Although the change to a five-course student load was adopted with only one abstention, the course distribution was adopted by a single-vote margin. Some faculty members, mainly in the business departments, wanted more electives restricted to the major. Colleagues, however, argued that this would contradict the liberal tradition that was characterstic of Jesuit education, and would restrict the pool of students who could take humanities electives. The new 5-5 curriculum was instituted in September of 1986 with a minimum of *post factum* comment.

Around the periphery of these curricular concerns were several other important developments. Majors in music, arts, and communications were introduced seriatim on the initiative of interested faculty members. Courses in the ancient classics in translation and in the original were again offered and a classics department was reestablished. These had fallen into the shadows after Doctor Edward Kaltenbach (1942) was co-opted into the administration as dean of freshmen in 1973.

His failing health prompted the college to institute a more elaborate program for advising freshmen and sophomores near the end of this period. For ten years Dean Kaltenbach had interviewed every freshman and arranged a basic program to suit the desires and abilities of each newcomer. It was heroic service performed judiciously. In 1984, however, such diligence proved too taxing and Doctor Kaltenbach retired about two years before his death. Father Joseph Sobierajski (1965) proposed a new general advising system about the time of Kaltenbach's retirement. Almost thirty teachers of core courses were recruited to advise freshmen and sophomores, and were given a stipend for this service. The caseload of each adviser is limited so that the students receive close attention. In this manner, students continue to get the personal care that has ever been a characterstic of Jesuit education.

Similarly, the traditional Jesuit emphasis on writing skills was enhanced by grants from the National Endowment for the Humanities (NEH). In 1979 Phil McCaffrey and Frank Trainor (1951), teachers in the English–fine arts department, obtained $50,000 to introduce a new writing and logic program. As this fund was depleted, Jack Breihan of the history department and Barbara Mallonee of English–fine arts prepared another, more elaborate, writing program. This was not limited to a specific course but introduced writing exercises into all courses appropriate to the discipline and level. A 1981 grant of $140,000 funded the first three years of the writing-across-the-curriculum program, and the college financed its remaining three years. Students reacted initially with grumbling, but when they realized that this program had become a permanent feature of the curriculum they quieted and went about their work.

A related development was the establishment of an honors program in 1984. Since 1960, departments had been encouraged to offer intensive or advanced courses as honors projects, described earlier. These flourished for a while and generated considerable enthusiasm among student and faculty participants. The transition in the early 1970s to the 4-1-4 curriclum cast these projects into a limbo where they continued a shadowy existence until the early 1980s. A parallel but more ambitious development started in 1979, when two English instructors invited freshmen with high SAT scores to join an experimental course and got a very positive response. This experience laid the foundation for an honors program, which was developed methodically from 1981 to 1984. Loyola admissions counselors noted that interest in such a program "runs high among seniors at the high schools where Loyola traditionally recruits."[47]

Under the leadership of Doctor Jack Breihan and with the cooperation of students, a regular honors program was instituted in 1984. Admission was limited to twenty freshmen, for a total of eighty during the four-year program. They are offered an integrated set of courses in the liberal arts and social sciences; these substitute for their core requirements. Experiences at nearby museums, galleries, theaters, and symphony halls are incorporated into the schedule. There are Friday seminars, a foreign film series, and senior projects to provide a final polishing. Loyola's honors program has been structured to avoid the common bugbear of elitism but has been kept small enough to ensure the maintenance of its quality.

Funding of the honors program was derived in part from a 1983 NEH grant for a humanities center. Despite the title, the humanities center was not conceived as a brick-and-mortar affair by its author, Dean Roswell of the college of arts and sciences. Rather, it is a fund to promote interest in and experience of the humanities. In addition to the honors program, visiting professorships filled by senior and younger scholars and occasional lectures or performances are included. The grant was $500,000 conditioned on Loyola's supplementing it on a three-to-one ratio. This ensures that the humanities center will be a continuing feature of campus life. Vice President Scheye noted that Loyola's commitment to raising $1.5 million "says very loudly that Loyola remains a true liberal-arts institution."[48]

• •

In 1982, Loyola authorities revived consideration of a new college center—another product of the Homestead conference. The only suitable location was in the dell east of Maryland Hall and parallel to the nothern boundary of the campus. This meant the demolition of the dell building, but it also inspired the inclusion of a long, glass-enclosed passageway and a pedestrian mall from Maryland Hall—where most of the staff and many student and faculty are to be found—all the way to the cafeteria and bookstore in the student center. When the new college center was erected, it would no longer be necessary to dodge cars while walking on the steep roadway in the rain or against a cold winter wind. The swift disappearance of the dell building in mid-October of 1981 roused very little interest or comment. It was not a structure that inspired attachment or nostalgia, despite its more than three decades of service to Evergreen.

No other demolition was necessary. The student center and the old gymnasium were connected to the new structure. The interior configuration of the student center was modified and the bookstore was relocated in the lower level of the old gymnasium, which had been occupied by a swimming pool. The gymnasium itself was converted into a large hall now used for dances, meetings, and receptions. After it had been refurbished, an anonymous donor insisted that it be named McGuire Hall in honor of Father Daniel McGuire, who for many years has served an an assistant to President Sellinger in development projects.

The new athletic wing is attached to the west wall of the old gymnasium. On its lowest level is an Olympic-sized swimming pool. Above this is a gymnasium with space enough for three basketball courts. The center one is used for varsity games, and bleachers are unfolded over the remainder to accommodate three thousand spectators. This has been named Reitz Arena as a reminder of Loyola's long-time athletic director, Emil "Lefty" Reitz. In various corners of the athletic wing are squash and racquetball courts, athletic department offices, training facilities, and locker rooms.

Further west is the fine arts wing. Here are a fully equipped photography center and rehearsal-practice rooms for music, a small exhibition gallery and facilities for sculpture and visual arts. Classrooms and faculty offices are tucked in various corners and levels of this section. At the western end of the center, across a narrow roadway from Maryland Hall, is a 300-seat theater with dressing rooms, a construction shop, and rehearsal space. The sheer length and height of the college center makes it imposing, but the interior configuration gives a cozy feeling. The athletic and fine arts wings rise five stories and the whole building covers 148,000 square feet. The cost of almost $10 million was defrayed by funds raised through the Decade of Decision campaign and a small matching grant from the state.

At the ground breaking on October 23, 1982, Father Sellinger announced that the new building was named the DeChairo College Center for Ralph DeChiaro, a trustee and a builder prominent in the Baltimore region, and a notable contributor to Catholic causes.[49] Incorporated in the center and named for other donors are the Julio fine arts wing and the McManus theater. The start of construction came soon after the ground breaking. The mud and clutter of equipment necessitated transferring commencement exercises from Evergreen, where they had been held since 1922, to the downtown Civic Center. With regrets, the seniors accepted this arrangement. At least, no manager of this annual ceremony need worry about capricious rain—or the cicadas that every seventeenth spring fill the campus with the sound of their constant churring.

Inspired by the new campus milieu, Carolyn Davies (1987), editor in chief of the *Greyhound,* changed its format from tabloid to regular newspaper size. It was not to be compared any longer with scandal and gossip sheets but rather with regular journals of news and opinion. A year later, the name was changed as another indication that the campus newspaper was no longer merely an extracurricular activity but had become a practicum for communications and media majors. The point having been made, the original name was resumed a year later.

· ·

At the ground breaking for the college center in October of 1982, President Sellinger was introduced not cryptically as "out of the construction business and into acquisitions."[50] This referred to the announcement a month earlier of negotiations to purchase Wynnewood Towers, a twenty-year-old high-rise apartment complex west of the Charles–Cold Spring intersection and partly adjoining Charleston Hall. This time the announcement preceded the rumors; still it roused the anxiety of Wynnewood tenants and revived opposition of the Guilford and Kernewood neighborhood associations. The decision to buy Wynnewood came at a time when undergraduate applications had increased to eight thousand but the number from students who would be living at home had begun to decline. Now Loyola's recruiting policy was to keep the undergraduate number stable but to fill it with 60 percent residential students and 40 percent commuters.

At the end of October, Father Sellinger and five staff members met with Wynnewood tenants who were assured, as the Charleston Hall tenants had been assured earlier, that existing leases would be honored and that special consideration would be given the elderly and infirm. There were almost twenty apartments vacant but no students would be moving in for a year. Father Sellinger answered questions and assured the tenants that only "responsible students" would be assigned to Wynnewood. The exchange helped, but prudently the tenants organized an association to protect their rights.

A year later a hundred students moved into Wynnewood Towers and were greeted by a tenants' welcoming committee. For the moment this was probably little more than an "if you can't beat 'em, join 'em" strategy. Nevertheless, an elderly resident told a *Sun* reporter that she was pleased with the politeness of the students. "I haven't heard so many 'yes ma'ams' and 'thank you ma'ams' since I was in Dallas, Texas."[51] Even with strict regulations against late parties and loud television or stereo equipment, there were complaints about noise, and so the students and tenants formed a joint committee to deal with such problems —and with some success. By 1985 when the purchase was completed, there were still over forty original tenants in Wynnewood.

The opposition of the neighborhood associations was not so easily relaxed. They revived their efforts to secure city ordinances that would require all private colleges and universities to secure zoning board approval for any building or expansion plans. This was a nuisance; it had been unsuccessful earlier and got no better hearing this time. In addition, the associations got bills introduced into the city council and the state legislature to block any kind of public financing for Loyola's purchase of Wynnewood Towers. All this meant was that the college had to seek private investment, which proved easy because of the value of this real estate. To convert relations with its neighbors into something more positive, several attempts were made to establish bilateral committees, but none of these efforts brought lasting results. If anything, they probably contributed to the atmosphere of distrust because of their ineffectiveness.

Meanwhile, complaints from the neighborhoods were given attention by municipal authorities in 1983. A new vice-president for development and a trustee laid out Loyola's case to the city planning department, which proved sympathetic and ventured an opinion that using the back acreage at Wynnewood for parking would not require action by the zoning board. A similar presentation to a mayoral task force, in which the assistance and sympathy of Notre Dame and Johns Hopkins were duly noted, produced a similar reaction. Early in 1984, Father Sellinger was pleased to report to the trustees that complaints from the neighbors had diminished substantially.

• •

What finally brought matters to a head was an even more rapid decline than anticipated in applications from live-at-home students. This was the result of a number of factors, including the rising academic reputation of some of Maryland's publicly supported institutions. The decline in registrations from commuter students could be balanced only by recruiting more residents, and that required more living space. It was in responding quickly to this situation that the new style of planning at Evergreen proved effective.

In the latter part of 1985, Loyola announced plans to build more residential units behind Wynnewood Towers and to extend the Charles Street wing of the Donnelly Science Center. Frustrated and angered by this unexpected turn, opponents organized as the North Baltimore Neighborhood Coalition (NBNC). This included—in alphabetical order—the Blythewood, Evergreen, Guilford, Kernewood, Keswick, Radnor-Winston, and Roland Park associations, a formidable array that represented twenty-five hundred householders. About the same time the legislature made a two-million-dollar matching grant available for the extension of the Donnelly Science Center.

Clearly nothing could be done in regard to this project until a settlement was reached with the coalition. An opening to agreement was made when early in 1986 Mayor Schaefer appointed a mediator. He chose an experienced lawyer, David Cordish, who had recently secured a binding truce between the Johns Hopkins University and the Wyman Park Association. The basic situation in the Loyola dispute seemed more amenable to resolution because Loyola owned the land involved and its plans did not require the cooperation of the zoning board, whereas the Hopkins-Wyman problem involved the use of city land and the zoning board.

Still, Cordish knew that he was dealing with a very hot situation. Town-and-gown controversies, whatever the causes, have often inflamed passions; in the Middle Ages they resulted in deadly riots. Proceeding cautiously, Cordish conferred with President Sellinger and his

close advisers. Among them he sensed that Tom Scheye, whose responsibilities had recently been augmented (and a new title—provost—
added to that of academic vice-president), was open to dealing with the
problem. Cordish made a similar selection among the representatives of
the coalition.

The next step was to get each side to present its case in such a way
that the other side could understand it. Loyola's presentation was complete with financial statements and other documentation. Such forth-
rightness impressed the coalition's representatives, and showed that
Loyola had to recruit more residential students and that it could remain
financially healthy with an undergraduate student body limited to
2,750. In turn, the coalition spokesman noted a lack of meaningful
communication over the past seven years. Members were worried that a
constantly expanding Loyola would retard the appreciation of the value
of their property (which has not in fact proven true). They also complained about the increased pedestrian and vehicular traffic and the unseemly behavior of some students. Better communication, a limit to
Loyola's physical growth, and better supervision of the students were
what they wanted.

Nothing essentially new had been said by either side, but a turning
point came during an afternoon walk around the college environs in
which Father Sellinger participated. He was shown where students had
forced a fence for a short cut, where students after an impromptu party
in a wooded glen had left paper and beer cans, and similar signs of indifference. He was embarrassed and said so.[52] The fact that Father Sellinger personally had listened to their complaints and had replied sym-
pathetically seemed to create a rapport between the two groups that had
been lacking for the past seven years.

On this turn, there followed a difficult and prolonged set of negotiations, with Scheye representing Loyola's interests. After a preliminary
statement outlined a satisfactory agreement, a final text was carefully
drawn by lawyers. The result is a long, tightly constructed agreement
binding on both parties for ten years. By its terms, Loyola's undergraduate enrollment is limited to 2,750, with over 2,000 of these living in
dormitories and apartments. Allowances were included for the vagaries
of enrollment statistics or a further decline among commuters. The
coalition accepted the construction of four small apartment buildings
behind Wynnewood with almost 150 parking spaces, another dormitory
north of Hammerman, the extension of Donnelly Science, and another
academic building. The coalition agreed with the college that these

plans should not be hindered by the prescribed 40 percent ratio of buildings to land.

Relations for the future are to be overseen by a council in which the majority of the representatives come from the neighborhood associations and at least one of Loyola's delegates has to be a vice-president. The main concerns of this council were specified: the reduction of pedestrian and vehicular traffic in the neighborhoods around the college, stricter supervision of student behavior, resolution of disputes, and the sharing of enrollment statistics and development plans.

Should any dispute arise over terms of the agreement, the chief judge of the circuit court of Baltimore would serve as an arbitrator but the process would not be binding.[53] By this agreement, Loyola and its neighbors have secured the prospect of a decade of relative amity. Its provisions cover all Loyola's anticipated needs at the cost only of a somewhat more formal development, planning, and communications process. As a result, Loyola no longer has any immediate interest in land owned by College of Notre Dame of Maryland or the Johns Hopkins University. This should alleviate some apprehensions that have affected interinstitutional cooperation.[54] If not an easy or simple solution to Loyola's longstanding problem of inadequate space, the agreement with the North Baltimore Neighborhood Coalition is nevertheless most welcome. The air has been cleared for Loyola College to pursue its drive for excellence less circumscribed than it had been for many years.

Notes

Abbreviations

AAB	Archives, Archdiocese of Baltimore
AMSA	Archives of the Middle States Association, Philadelphia
GUA	Georgetown University Archives, Washington, D.C.
LCA	Loyola College Archives, Baltimore, Maryland
LHSA	Loyola High School Archives, Towson, Maryland
MPA	Maryland Province Archives, now at Georgetown University, Washington, D.C.
SICA	Saint Ignatius Church Archives, Baltimore, Maryland

Chapter 1

1. Thomas T. McAvoy, "The Formation of the Catholic Minority in the United States, 1820–1860," *Review of Politics*, 10 (1948); 22–23; John Peter Marschall, "Francis Patrick Kenrick, 1851–1863: The Baltimore Years" (Ph.D. diss., Catholic University of America, 1965), 1–2, 43; Christopher J. Kaufman, *Tradition and Transformation in Catholic Culture: The Priests of Saint Sulpice in the United States from 1791 to the Present* (New York, 1988), 136–37.

2. Francis X. Talbot, *Jesuit Education in Philadelphia: Saint Joseph's College, 1851–1926* (Philadelphia, 1927), 38; David R. Dunigan, *A History of Boston College* (Milwaukee, 1947), 17; Edward J. Power, *A History of Catholic Higher Education in the United States* (Milwaukee, 1958), 33–35.

3. John J. Ryan, *Chronicle and Sketch of the Church of Saint Ignatius Loyola Baltimore, 1856–1906* (Baltimore, 1907), 1; Mémoire de M. Deluol sur la vente projetée du College aux Jesuites, etc., eu 1837, Sulpician Archives, Baltimore.

4. L. Deluol to Samuel Eccleston, March 4, 1848, *LCA* (copy).

5. Ignatius Brocard to John McElroy, December 27, 1848, *MPA*; William F. Clarke to Joseph Aschwanden, April 15, 1852, *MPA*. For a biographical notice of Father Damphoux see Kaufman, *Tradition*, 116–21.

6. Marshall, *Kenrick*, 34.

7. Marschall, *Kenrick*, 31–34, 39, 65; Hugh I. Nolan, *The Most Reverend Francis Patrick Kenrick, Third Bishop of Philadelphia, 1830–1851* (Philadelphia, 1948), 29, 219.

8. James Dolan diary, 1850–1852, LCA (copy), April 29, 1851.

9. Marschall, *Kenrick*, 1–2.

10. Ibid., 61; Brocard to McElroy, January 25, 1852, MPA.

11. *Church News* (Washington, D.C.), October 26, 1890; Annals of the Oblate Sisters of Providence, Archives of the Motherhouse, Mount Providence Junior College, Baltimore, 2:59–60.

12. Clarke to Charles H. Stonestreet, November 27, 1853, MPA.

13. John J. Ryan, *Historical Sketch of Loyola College, Baltimore, 1852–1902* (n.p., 1903?), 75.

14. Clarke to Brocard, October 13, 1851, MPA.

15. Clarke to Brocard, October 17 and December 23, 1851, MPA.

16. Clarke to Brocard, March 26, 1852, MPA.

17. Clarke to Aschwanden, April 15, 21, 22, 1852, MPA. Aschwanden to Joannes Roothaan, April 23, 1852, in Marschall, *Kenrick*, 62.

18. Peter Guilday, *A History of the Councils of Baltimore (1791–1884)* (New York, 1932), 178–79; John Tracy Ellis, *American Catholicism* (Chicago, 1956), 79–80; Peter Guilday, *The National Pastorals of the American Hierarchy (1792–1919)* (Westminster, Md., 1954), 191; Leo J. McCormick, *Church-State Relationships in Education in Maryland* (Washington, D.C., 1942), 173–82; Vincent P. Lannie, *Public Money and Parochial Education* (Cleveland, 1968), 11–12, 255–58; Douglas Bowers, "Ideology and Political Parties in Maryland, 1851–1856," *Maryland Historical Magazine* 64 (1969): 201–5.

19. James Dolan diary, 1850–1852, LCA (copy), April 26, 1852.

20. *Metropolitan* (Baltimore) 1 (1853): 88. This publication lasted until the outbreak of the Civil War—a long run for a magazine in Baltimore.

21. Anon., "History of Loyola College, 1852–1892," LCA, 9, 44–45.

22. Marschall, *Kenrick*, 63–64.

23. "College Notes," *Journal of Saint Ignatius Church* 15 (December 1908): 9; Joseph T. Durkin, *Georgetown University: The Middle Years (1840–1900)* (Washington, D.C., 1963), 48; House diary, 1871–1884, SICA, May 23, 1873.

24. *College Journal* (Georgetown) 1 (June 1873): 82–83 and Supplement.

25. Durkin, *Georgetown*, 5, 26; J. Fairfax McLaughlin, *College Days at Georgetown* (Philadelphia, 1899), 102.

26. Walter J. Meagher and William J. Grattan, *The Spires of Fenwick* (New York, 1966), 38–39, 45, 49, 60–62, 70; Frederick Rudolph, *The American College and University: A History* (New York, 1962), 133–34; Diary, Valedictory of James A. Healy at Holy Cross College, Holy Cross College Archives, Worcester, Massachusetts, February 27, March 6, 1849.

27. Meagher and Grattan, *Spires*, 51–56; John Early to Felix Barbelin, November 27, 1848, MPA.

28. James Dolan diary, 1850–1852, LCA (copy), September 21, 1851.

29. Early to Aschwanden, August 8, 1852, MPA.

30. Historia Collegii Loyolani Baltimorensis ab ejus exordio Kal. September MDCCCLII ad VIII Kal. April MDCCCLIII, MPA; Sam Lilly Diary, GUA, September 10, 1852.

Chapter 2

1. Talbot, *Saint Joseph's*, 58; Ryan, *Historical Sketch*, 65; Joseph Henry to James Ward, November 2, 1853, LCA.

2. "Church Notes," *Journal of Saint Ignatius' Church* 14 (January 1907): 5; "Bona Mors," ibid. 21 (November 1914): 7–8. For a more detailed description of this society, see Thomas P. Clifford, "Ritual, Community, and Reform, the Catholic Experience in Baltimore: St. Ignatius' Parish, 1853–1880" (Master's thesis, University of Maryland, 1986), 73–80.

3. Rudolph, *American College*, 133–34; Durkin, *Georgetown*, 38; Power, *Catholic Higher Education* (1958), 72–73; Charles H. Stonestreet, "The Church, the Guardian of Letters," *Metropolitan* 1 (February 1853): 3–11.

4. John Early, "Commencement Remarks," *GUA*.

5. Bernard C. Steiner, *History of Education in Maryland* (Washington, D.C., 1894), 207–17, 260–67; George H. Callcott, *A History of the University of Maryland* (Baltimore, 1966), 55–66, 98–99; James Chancellor Leonhart, *One Hundred Years of the Baltimore City College* (Baltimore, 1939), 18, 27–31.

6. Donald G. Tewksbury, *The Founding of American Colleges and Universities before the Civil War* (1932; reprint ed., New York, 1965), 9, quoting M. B. Anderson, president of the University of Rochester.

7. Colin B. Burke, *American Collegiate Populations: A Test of the Traditional View* (New York, 1982), 49.

8. Sebastian Anthony Erbacher, *Catholic Higher Education for Men in the United States, 1850–1866* (Washington, D.C., 1932), 84; Rudolph, *American College*, 68–71; Tewksbury, *Founding*, 55.

9. Burke, *Collegiate Populations*, 104, 108, 132–33, 229.

10. Emily Emerson Lantz, "Maryland Heraldry . . . Jenkins Lineage and Arms," *Sun* (Baltimore), February 25, March 4, 11, 1906. See also Mary Eleanora Smith, "The Jenkins Family of Baltimore" (Master's thesis, Catholic University of America, 1941).

11. Hamilton Owens, *Baltimore on the Chesapeake* (Garden City, N.Y., 1941), 24–27, 30, 32; *The Biographical Cyclopedia of Representative Men of Maryland and District of Columbia* (Baltimore, 1879), 277.

12. Harry W. Kirwin, *The Inevitable Success* (Westminster, Md., 1962), 31–32.

13. Rudolph, *American College*, 196–99; Allan P. Farrell, *The Jesuit Code of Liberal Education* (Milwaukee, 1938), 436–40; Burke, *Collegiate Populations*, 48.

14. Charles G. Herbermann, *The Sculpicians in the United States* (New York, 1916), 239–40; William Cabell Bruce, *Seven Great Baltimore Lawyers* (Baltimore, 1931), 17.

15. Ryan, *Historical Sketch*, 38.

16. Robert I. Gannon, *Up to the Present: The Story of Fordham* (Garden City, N.Y., 1967), 31; Power, *Catholic Higher Education*, 68–69.

17. Ryan, *Historical Sketch*, 38–39.

18. Ibid., 11, 40.

19. Early to George Fenwick, February 17, 1853, MPA.

20. Ryan, *Saint Ignatius*, 73–74; idem, *Historical Sketch*, 169.

21. "Record of Proceedings, Superior Court of Baltimore City." October 9, 1856, GUA. This was a record of final action on Father Early's citizenship and contains information about the preliminary application.

22. "Copy of the Original Charter to 'The Associated Professors of Loyola College in the City of Baltimore, Maryland' by the General Assembly of Maryland, April 13, 1853," SICA.

23. *Journal of the Proceedings of the House of Delegates of the State of Maryland, January Session, 1853* (Annapolis, 1853), 358, 393–94, 409; *Journal of the Proceedings of the Senate of Maryland, January Session, 1853* (Annapolis, 1853), 203, 210, 238; *Jour-*

nal . . . of the House . . . 1853, 475, 509, 510, 525. The initial vote to insist on the House version was 23 pro and 22 against; the vote to yield to the Senate was 38 to 1.

24. McCormick, *Church-State Relationships*, 178–79, 186; *Journal of the Proceedings of the House of Delegates of Maryland, January Session, 1880* (Annapolis, 1880), 869, 989, 1061, 1093.

25. Charles Stonestreet, "Note," April 17, 1853, GUA, 424–1.

26. Ryan, *Historical Sketch*, 79; Unidentified newspaper clippings, c. 1853–1856, LCA, July 13, 1853.

27. Early to Fenwick, July 1, 1853, MPA.

28. *Sun*, July 13, 1853; Unidentified newspaper clippings, c. 1853–1856, LCA, July 13, 1853; House diary, 1885–1898, SICA, May 28, 1891.

29. Dunigan, *Boston College*, 139; Rudolph, *American College*, 336.

30. Ryan, *Historical Sketch*, 28–29.

31. Rudolph, *American College*, 137–44; Ryan, *Historical Sketch*, 28; Gannon, *Fordham*, 52–53.

Chapter 3

1. Owens, *Baltimore*, 257–67; Raphael Semmes, *Baltimore as Seen by Visitors, 1783–1860* (Baltimore, 1953), 141–63; John C. Gobright, *The Monumental City or Baltimore Guide Book* (Baltimore, 1858), 12; *The British American Guide-Book* (New York, 1859), 59.

2. Ryan, *Historical Sketch*, 73–74.

3. Wilbur H. Hunter, Jr., and Charles H. Elam, *A Century of Baltimore Architecture* (Baltimore, 1957), 45; Richard Howland Hubbard and Eleanor Patterson Spencer, *The Architecture of Baltimore* (Baltimore, 1953), 96–101; *Sun*, September 26, 1853.

4. "Michael Roche in a/c with Loyola College and Saint Ignatius Church, Baltimore, January 7th, 1857," SICA.

5. Early to Fenwick, March 12, 1854, MPA.

6. "Expenses," 1854–1855, SICA. This appears to be Father James A. Ward's ledger.

7. Early to Fenwick, September 27, 1854, MPA.

8. Charles F. Kelly to Fenwick, February 16, 1855, MPA. After the departure of Loyola College, the houses on Holliday Street were occupied by a school conducted by Friedrich Knapp. The most famous alumnus of Knapp's Institute was H. L. Mencken.

9. *Sun*, February 22, 23, 1855.

10. Early to Fenwick, May 4, 1855, MPA.

11. Ryan, *Historical Sketch*, 12.

12. Ibid., 75.

13. Early to Fenwick, September 17, 1855, MPA; Ryan, *Historical Sketch*, 19; Durkin, *Georgetown*, 140–41.

14. Record of Loyola College, October 1855 to February 1856, LHSA, 2.

15. Charles H. Stonestreet, Instructions for Teachers at Saint Joseph's College, c. 1851, MPA.

16. Unidentified newspaper clippings, c. 1853–1856, LCA.

17. Guilday, *Councils of Baltimore*, 90–91, 180, 267–68; John Bernard McGloin, *California's First Archbishop: The Life of Joseph Sadoc Alemany, O.P., 1814–1888* (New York, 1966), 192–226, 253–76.

18. John T. Gillard, *Colored Catholics in the United States* (Baltimore, 1941), 78–79,

120–21; Ryan, *Saint Ignatius*, 5; *Saint Francis Xavier Church/Centennial* (Baltimore, 1963).

19. Burke, *Collegiate Populations*, 106.

Chapter 4

1. William Tyson et al. to Early, October 23, 1858, GUA.

2. Edmund Granville Ryan, "An Academic History of Woodstock College (1868–1944): The First Jesuit Seminary in North America" (Ph.D. diss., Catholic University of America, 1964), 19, 24.

3. Semmes, *Baltimore as Seen by Visitors*, 142, 163.

4. Sherry H. Olson, *Baltimore: The Building of an American City* (Baltimore, 1980), 137–38, 161, 169.

5. House diary, 1871–1874, SICA, August 9, 1872.

6. House diary, 1852–1863, SICA, June 15, 1860.

7. Stonestreet to Clarke, January 19, 1859, GUA. This reply is at the bottom of Stonestreet's original agreement to pay the ground rent, which is dated April 17, 1853. For Father Villiger see John J. Ryan, *Memoir of the Life of Rev. Burchard Villiger of the Society of Jesus* (Philadelphia, 1906).

8. Talbot, *Saint Joseph's*, 35.

9. Durkin, *Georgetown*, 15–17; McLaughlin, *College Days at Georgetown*, 120–22; Ryan, *Historical Sketch*, 75.

10. John J. Ryan, "Sketch of Loyola College, N. Calvert St., Baltimore" (August 1890), SICA, 23–24.

11. Joseph O'Callaghan to John Lee Chapman, April 13, 1863, SICA.

12. Rudolph, *American College*, 113; Power, *Catholic Higher Education* (1958), 57, 86; Meagher and Grattan, *Spires*, 125.

13. George L. P. Radcliffe, *Governor Thomas H. Hicks and the Civil War* (Baltimore, 1901), 130; Charles B. Wagandt, *The Mighty Revolution* (Baltimore, 1964), 19.

14. John Tracy Ellis, *The Life of James Cardinal Gibbons* (Milwaukee, 1952), 1: 46–47.

15. James S. Ruby, ed., *Blue and Gray* (Washington, D.C., 1961), 29, 86, 89, 90, 94, 96, 99, 115, 116.

16. Peter Beckx to Stonestreet, January 10, 1855, SICA; Angelo Paresce to O'Callaghan, February 23, 1862, SICA.

17. Harold R. Manakee, *Maryland during the Civil War* (Baltimore, 1961), 30–38; George William Brown, *Baltimore and the 19th of April, 1861* (Baltimore, 1887).

18. "Most Reverend Francis Patrick Kenrick," the *Catholic Red Book: Baltimore-Washington*, 1908, 88.

19. Leopold Blumenberg to John Morgan, June 15, 1864, MPA, Curiously, a student by the name of Mark Anthony Blumenberg enrolled at Loyola in September of the same year. His father, Julius Blumenberg, may have been related to the provost marshal, Leopold.

20. Owens, *Baltimore*, 289.

21. [Richard Malcolm Johnston], *Autobiography of Col. Richard Malcolm Johnston*, 2d ed. (Washington, D.C., 1901), 65–67.

22. Owens, *Baltimore*, 303. For a description of how the Democratic party recovered power in post–Civil War Maryland, see Jean H. Baker, *The Politics of Con-*

tinuity: Maryland Political Parties from 1858 to 1970 (Baltimore, 1973), and Margaret Law Callcott, *The Negro in Maryland Politics, 1870–1912* (Baltimore, 1969).

23. Anthony Ciampi to Clara Thompson, December 17, 1864, February 12 (year unknown), Ciampi-Thompson correspondence, 1863–1869; Holy Cross College Archives.

24. Ryan, *Historical Sketch,* 76.

25. Ibid., 77–78.

26. Ciampi to Thompson, April 15, 1866, Ciampi-Thompson correspondence, 1863–1869, Holy Cross College Archives.

27. Record of Consultations, 1865–1930, SICA, September 26, 1866.

28. Guilday, *Councils of Baltimore,* 191–92; Theodore Maynard, *The Story of American Catholicism* (Garden City, N.Y., 1960), 2: 27.

29. James Hennesey, *American Catholics: A History of the Roman Catholic Community in the United States* (New York, 1981), 160–65; Thomas W. Spalding, *Martin John Spalding: American Churchman* (Washington, D.C., 1973), 204, 240–43.

30. Guilday, *Councils of Baltimore,* 213, 217; "Filling in the Background," *Josephite Newsletter* (Baltimore) November–December 1966, January 1967. A similar effort was made by the Protestant Episcopal church. In 1872 nuns from the Anglican All Saints Sisters of the Poor arrived and the first group of sisters became associated with the parish of Saint Mary the Virgin, a new black congregation in East Baltimore.

31. Ryan, *Historical Sketch,* 63–64; House diary, 1871, SICA, December 5, 9, 1871.

32. "The Brick Bat Journal," GUA; Gannon, *Fordham,* 56–57, 81; McLaughlin, *College Days at Georgetown,* 130–33.

33. Ryan, *Historical Sketch,* 53, 58; Ryan, "Sketch of Loyola," SICA, 26.

34. *College Journal* (Georgetown), 1 (June 1873): Supplement.

Chapter 5

1. Clarke to Stonestreet, February 13, 1854, MPA; Edward Henchy to Burchard Villiger, October 9, 1859, MPA.

2. House diary, 1863–1871, SICA, July 31, 1870, February 11, 1871; Ryan, *Historical Sketch,* 81. For details of the disputed inheritance, see House diary, 1871–1874, SICA, June 20, 1872.

3. Rudolph, *American College,* 234–35, 324–25.

4. Tom Kelly, *Murders* (Washington, D.C., 1926), 47–55; *Sun,* October 4, 1905; Edward F. X. Sweeney, *The Story of the Mountain* (Emmitsburg, Md., 1911), 2:155, 270.

5. "Collegium Baltimorense," 1868–1876, MPA.

6. William Patrick Leahy, "Jesuits, Catholics, and Higher Education in Twentieth-Century America" (Ph.D. diss., Stanford University, 1986), 161–64, 168.

7. House diary, 1871–1874, SICA, November 3, 10, 1872.

8. Steven Marcus, *The Other Victorians* (New York, 1967), 16; Christa R. Klein, "The Jesuits and Catholic Boyhood in Nineteenth-Century New York City: A Study of Saint John's College and the College of Saint Francis Xavier" (Ph.D. diss., University of Pennsylvania, 1976), 254–55, 319–21.

9. Power, *Catholic Higher Education (1958),* 126–29.

10. Ryan, *Historical Sketch,* 72.

11. Diary of Loyola College Classes, 1883–1891, LCA, September 7, 1885.

12. Ibid., September 3, 1884. See also House diary, 1874–1885, *SICA*, September 3, 1884.

13. Loyola College Class Matter and Examination, 1878–1897, *LCA*, 7, 11.

14. Ibid., 14.

15. Ibid., 3, 4, 12.

16. Ibid., 3, 18, 20, 21.

17. Ibid., 17–18.

18. Burke, *Collegiate Populations*, 38, 61, 97, 141–42.

19. Ryan, *Historical Sketch*, 103.

20. Durkin, *Georgetown*, 60.

21. Ryan, *Historical Sketch*, 89.

22. J. A. Dacus, *Annals of the Great Strikes* (New York, 1969), 21–30, 63, 77.

23. Charles Hirschfeld, *Baltimore, 1870–1900: Studies in Social History* (Baltimore, 1941), 23, 30, 61, 95; Ellis, *Gibbons*, 1:164; Edward A. Krug, *The Shaping of the American High School*, 2 vols. (New York, 1964), 1:123.

24. [Edward McGurk], "Autobiography of Edward A. McGurk, S. J.," c. 1891, *GUA*; Ryan, *Historical Sketch*, 89.

25. Ryan, *Historical Sketch*, 169.

26. Ibid., 94; Meredith Janvier, *Baltimore in the Eighties and Nineties* (Baltimore, 1933), 35, 185; *The Early Eighties: Sidelights on Baltimore of Forty Years Ago* (Baltimore, 1924), 30.

27. Klein, "Jesuits," 166–67.

28. Ryan, *Historical Sketch*, 100.

29. Ibid., 93.

30. *Morning Herald* (Baltimore), June 26, 1879, clipping in *SICA*; House Diary, 1874–1885, *SICA*, November 27, 28, December 10, 17, 18, 25, 29, 31, 1880, January 2, 1881; Sweeney, *Mountain*, 1:141. For Ryan's birthplace, see Richard J. Purcell, "Ryan, Abram Joseph," *DAB*, 16:260–61.

31. Ryan, *Historical Sketch*, 106; Alumni Association of Loyola College, *Echoes from the "Questionnaire"* (Baltimore, 1925), 51; Francis F. Beirne, *The Amiable Baltimoreans* (Baltimore, 1984), 113. Shriver is more familiarly associated with his donation of a hall and a mural of Baltimore beauties to the Johns Hopkins University, from which he was graduated in 1891. The Shriver bequest provided for a reversion to Loyola if Hopkins did not accept it.

32. Ryan, *Historical Sketch*, 96–97.

33. Diary of Loyola College Classes, 1883–1891, *LCA*, May 28, 29, 30, 1885.

34. House diary, 1874–1885, *SICA*, October 11, 12, 13, 14, 1880.

35. *Pilgrimage of the Maryland Pilgrims' Association to Saint Mary's City, St. Mary's County, Md., May 15th, 1884* (Baltimore, 1884), 7.

36. House diary, 1874–1885, *SICA*, June 24, 1885.

Chapter 6

1. House diary, 1885–1898, *SICA* February 2, 1886; "In Memoriam, Father Francis A. Smith, S.J.," *Fordham Monthly*, January 1898, 124–25; Klein, "Jesuits," 236; Record of Consultations, 1865–1930, *SICA*, May 4, 1886; Ellis, *Gibbons*, 1:301–2.

2. *Sun*, June 25, 1887. For the early career of Bonaparte, see Eric F. Goldman, *Charles J. Bonaparte: Patrician Reformer* (Baltimore, 1943).

3. House diary, 1885–1898, *SICA*, June 10, 1886, June 15, 1887; Record of Consultations, 1865–1930, *SICA*, September 29, 1886.

4. Record of Consultations, 1865–1930, SICA, September 29, 1886.

5. *Journal of the Proceedings of the House of Delegates of Maryland, January Session, 1888* (Annapolis, 1888), 254, 1147; *Journal of the Proceedings of the Senate of Maryland, January Session, 1888* (Annapolis, 1888), 312, 365, 785. In neither house was a vote cast against the Loyola College charter amendment.

6. S. Z. Ammen, "History of Baltimore, 1875–1895," in *Baltimore: Its History and Its People*, ed. Clayton Colman Hall (New York, 1912), 1:271; *Sun*, March 13–17, 1888.

7. Janvier, *Baltimore*, 47.

8. Ammen, "Baltimore," 270; James B. Crooks, *Politics and Progress* (Baton Rouge, 1968), 5.

9. Ellis, *Gibbons*, 1:413; *Official Report of the Proceedings of the Catholic Congress, Held at Baltimore, Md., November 11th and 12th, 1889* (n.p., n.d.), 4. The Loyola men were S. H. Caughy (1879), Charles Grindall (1873), George May (1875), Edward Milholland (1856), Michael Mullin (1859), William Mullin (1861), William O'Brien (1883), Charles O'Donovan (1877), Alfred Shriver (1889), Mark Shriver, Thomas Whelan.

10. Ryan, *Historical Sketch*, 115; *Sun*, November 12, 13, 1889; Ellis, *Gibbons*, 1:389–94, 2:535–36.

11. Gannon, *Fordham*, 101–2; Rudolph, *American College*, 381–82, 429–30.

12. Jay P. Dolan, *The American Catholic Experience: A History from Colonial Times to the Present* (Garden City, N.Y., 1985), 335.

13. House diary, 1885–1898, SICA, June 29, August 4, 1886.

14. Ryan, *Historical Sketch*, 116; Leonhart, *City College*, 43.

15. Laurence R. Veysey, *The Emergence of the American University* (Chicago, 1970), 65, 89, 93–94, 117; Hennesey, *American Catholics*, 186.

16. House diary, 1885–1898, SICA, November 1890; John C. French, *A History of the University Founded by Johns Hopkins* (Baltimore, 1946), 289–93. After graduation, Francis Homer studied law and eventually became a Wall Street banker. His confrere Mullin also became a lawyer but died young; he was the son of Michael A. Mullin (1859).

17. Record of Consultations, 1865–1930, SICA, May 22, September 31, 1890.

18. Ryan, "Sketch of Loyola," SICA, 10.

19. House diary, 1885–1898, SICA, November, 1890; Gannon, *Fordham*, 90.

20. Record of Consultations, 1865—1930, SICA, November 21, 1890.

21. House diary, 1885–1898, SICA, May 17, 1891.

Chapter 7

1. Ryan, *Historical Sketch*, 131.

2. House diary, 1885–1898, SICA, May 17, 1891.

3. Burke, *Collegiate Populations*, 217.

4. House diary, 1885–1898, SICA, February 1892; Record of Consultations, 1865–1930, SICA, January 28, 1892.

5. Prefect of Schools, Loyola College (1890–1901), LCA, 27.

6. Record of Consultations, 1865–1930, SICA, January 12, 1897.

7. For more information on honorary degrees, see Stephen Edward Epler, *Honorary Degrees: A Survey of Their Use and Abuse* (Washington, D.C., 1943).

8. Beirne, *Baltimoreans*, 224–25.

9. [John A. Morgan], "Schola Brevis, Address, Textbooks," c. 1896, GUA.

10. *Biographical Cyclopedia*, 176–77.

11. Conversation with Gower Lawrence (1898), October 28, 1967.

12. House diary, 1885–1898, *SICA*, June 4, 1894; House diary, 1898–1907, *SICA*, March 6, 1899; House diary, 1918–1926, *SICA*, July 4, 1920, August 22, 1924.

13. *Folks* (December 1946): 3. This was a commemorative issue of the Baltimore Gas and Electric Company's house organ dedicated to Charles Cohn. On the preference for Loyola graduates see Olson, *Baltimore*, 265.

14. Ryan, *Historical Sketch*, 135–37; "Richard McSherry," in Hall, ed., *Baltimore: Its History*, 3:544–46; Henry Elliott Shepherd, *Representative Authors of Maryland* (New York, 1911), 98–99. On Johnston, see Jay B. Hubbell, *The South in American Literature* (Durham, N.C., 1954), 777, and his *Autobiography*.

15. Record of Consultations, 1865–1930, *SICA*, September 19, 1892, January 30, April 24, 1893.

16. James H. Bready, *The Home Team* (n.p., 1958), 16–17; Power, *Catholic Higher Education*, 135; Durkin, *Georgetown*, 161, 195, 237; Gannon, *Fordham*, 83–85; Dunigan, *Boston College*, 136–37.

17. Edward I. Devitt, "Loyola College, Baltimore, Maryland: A Sketch of Our Labor in College and Church during the past Quarter of a Century, 1879–1904," GUA, 7.

18. George Blake was a native of Ireland who was brought by his parents to Baltimore in 1846. On reaching his majority, he took Greeley's advice to "go west" but remained there only a few years. His return to Baltimore coincided with the outbreak of the Civil War; after its end Blake became an independent builder and contractor. His first major project was thirty-two "first class dwellings" at Jackson Square, which so impressed Baltimoreans that thereafter he and his brothers rarely lacked employment. (*Biographical Cyclopedia*, 156–57.) Blake's legacy to his daughters provided the means by which Loyola High School in the 1930s moved from Calvert Street to its present location in Towson. In honor of their generosity, the tract is known is Blakefield.

19. "Rev. John Abell Morgan, S.J.," *Journal of Saint Ignatius' Church* 4 (January 1907): 8. This obituary appeared in the November 28, 1906, issue of the Baltimore *News*.

Chapter 8

1. Prefect of Schools, Loyola College (1890–1901), LCA, 320. After his term at Woodstock, Father Brett returned to Boston College, where he taught philosophy. He so impressed his students that they set up a bronze memorial in 1915 after his death. Dunigan, *Boston College*, 199, 212.

2. "Father John F. Quirk," *Woodstock Letters* 54 (1924): 385.

3. Coleman Nevils, *Miniatures of Georgetown, 1634–1934* (Washington, D.C., 1934), 367–68.

4. Ryan, *Historical Sketch*, 185–88.

5. The review is signed "X.X.X." and appeared in a November issue of the *News*.

6. Diary of Loyola College, 1901–1910, LCA, 41.

7. Durkin, *Georgetown*, 76–77; William B. Faherty, *Better the Dream: St. Louis University and Community* (St. Louis, 1968), 250.

8. Gerald W. Johnson et al., *The Sunpapers of Baltimore* (New York, 1937), 373, 383, 388, 393; Beirne, *Baltimoreans*, 320; Harold A. Williams, *The Baltimore Sun, 1837–1987* (Baltimore, 1987), 117, 169, 220, 228, 245.

9. Olson, *Baltimore*, 165.

10. Janvier, *Baltimore*, 44, 51, 52, 83.

11. *A Survey of the Teaching of International Law in Political Science Departments* (Washington, D.C., 1963), 51.

12. Milton M. Gordon, "Assimilation in America: Theory and Reality," *Daedalus*, Spring 1961, 269–74.

13. Donna Merwick, *Boston Priests, 1848–1910* (Cambridge, 1973), 123–31.

14. Gannon, *Fordham*, 105.

15. Dunigan, *Boston College*, 177.

16. French, *Hopkins*, 64–71.

17. Olson, *Baltimore*, 341.

18. Newspaper clippings, 1901–1907, LCA, 57–58, 61–63. Clarke Fitzpatrick (1888–1973) obtained his early education in Baltimore's public schools and the parish school of Corpus Christi Church. He entered Loyola in 1898 on a scholarship and was graduated in 1902.

19. Elliott Ross (1884–1946) was the son of Cecilia Elliott and John R. Ross. He was educated at Saint Joseph's School and Gonzaga College in the District of Columbia before he entered Loyola in 1898. After graduation from Loyola in 1902, Ross obtained an M.A. from George Washington University in 1908. He joined the Paulists, an American religious community founded by Isaac Hecker, in the following year and was sent by them to Catholic University, where he studied sociology. In 1912 he was ordained a priest and was awarded his Ph.D. by Catholic University. Father Ross then served as director of Newman clubs at the University of Texas, Columbia University, and Iowa State. Simultaneously, he was publishing books on social problems. Among his titles are *Right to Work, Consumers and Wage Earners, Sanctity and Social Work, Christian Ethics*. He translated works from French and German. During the early 1930s he became the Catholic member of minister-priest-rabbi teams that toured the country under the auspices of the National Conference of Christians and Jews. This phase ended when he suffered a paralytic stroke in 1936. In his obituary, Father Ross was described as "of scholarly bent, questioning things taken for granted, and a priest of constant apostolic occupation." Lawrence V. McDonnell to author, September 3, 1975, LCA.

20. Diary of Loyola College, 1901–1910, LCA, 87–88. For an extensive account of the fire, see Harold A. Williams, *Baltimore Afire* (Baltimore, 1954).

21. House diary, April 1898–January 1907, SICA, May 30, 1904.

22. Leahy, "Jesuits, Catholics, and Higher Education," 45–49.

23. Diary of Loyola College, 1901–1910, LCA, 182.

24. The house diary indicates that Father Quirk was scheduled originally to remain at Loyola for the 1907–8 academic year, but the change to Father Mullan was announced late in August. House diary, January 1907–November 1907, SICA, August 25, 1907.

Chapter 9

1. Hugh Hawkins, *Between Harvard and America* (New York, 1972), 187–88; Dunigan, *Boston College*, 168–74, 176; Bliss Perry, *And Gladly Teach* (Boston, 1935), 170–71; Durkin, *Georgetown*, 256–57.

2. Hennesey, *American Catholics*, 186.

3. Dunigan, *Boston College*, 174; Durkin, *Georgetown*, 256–58; Charles A. Brady, *Canisius College: The First Hundred Years* (Buffalo, 1969), 100.

4. Hawkins, *Harvard*, 189.

5. Edward K. Hanlon, "Some University Impressions," *Loyola Annual,* 1910, 80–82.

6. Dunigan, *Boston College,* 166–68, 179.

7. Diary of Loyola College, 1901–1910, LCA, 184–85.

8. *Woodstock Letters* 33 (1914), 245–47.

9. Kirwin, *Success,* 37–38.

10. "The Gold and Blue," *Loyola Annual,* 1908, 1.

11. Diary of Loyola College, 1901–1910, LCA, 209.

12. Ibid., 218.

13. Ibid., 249, 267, 279; Diary of the Prefect of Studies, 1910–1920, LCA, 2.

14. Diary of Loyola College, 1901–1910, LCA, 281; Gannon, *Fordham,* 109–12.

15. Ibid., 279.

16. Kirwin, *Success,* 41.

17. *Sun,* November 8, 1910, 10.

18. "In Memoriam Father Francis Xavier Brady, S.J.," *Journal of Saint Igantius' Church* 17 (April 1911): 6.

19. Ibid., 8.

20. *Sun,* March 14, 1911, 7.

21. "In Memoriam Father Brady," 11.

Chapter 10

1. *Sun,* May 17, 1911; Kathryn and Jim Sullivan to author, June 13, 1967, LCA.

2. John A. Conway and Owen A. Hill, *History of Gonzaga College* (Washington, D.C., 1921), 235–37; Leahy, "Jesuits, Catholics, and Higher Education," 1.

3. "Father William J. Ennis," *Woodstock Letters* 54 (1925): 266–68.

4. "New Rector for Loyola," *Sun,* May 17, 1911.

5. Matthew Brenan to William Ennis, December 4, 1915, LCA.

6. "Thomas O'Neill," in Matthew Page Andrews, *Tercentenary History of Maryland* (Baltimore, 1925), 2:248–49; J. Joseph Gallagher, *The Story of Baltimore's New Cathedral* (n.p., n.d.), 2–4; conversation with Mr. and Mrs. A. Berthold Hoen, September 29, 1977. Thomas O'Neill was Mrs. Hoen's godfather. For a brief summary of the Peabody, Hopkins, and Pratt endowments and what they have meant to Baltimore, see Theodore R. McKeldin, *No Mean City* (Baltimore, 1964). On Cardinal Gibbons's love for the old cathedral, see Ellis, *Gibbons,* 2:451. There is an oral tradition deriving from Cardinal Gibbons's secretary that plans to shift the O'Neill bequest to Catholic University narrowly failed of acomplishment. Conversation with Lawrence Cardinal Shehan, May 22, 1979.

7. The most readily available source for the main terms of the O'Neill bequests is *Maryland Reports* 137 (1921): 546–48. These terms appear in the Court's opinion in a friendly suit brought by the College Corporation and the O'Neill trustees to resolve certain difficulties that arose after O'Neill's death. The case was entitled *The Associated Professors of Loyola College v. Hammond J. Dugan et al. Sun,* February 12, 1914, 5; Baltimore *American,* February 12, 1914, 9; E. H. Bouton to Ennis, February 11, 1914, Roland Park Company Records, Cornell University Libraries.

8. *Sun,* January 17, 1914; *News,* January 19, 1914; Dunigan, *Boston College,* 189.

9. Record of Consultations, 1865–1930, SICA, December 1, 1913, January 5, 1914; Minutes of a Meeting of the Archdiocesan Consultors, September 12, 1913, SICA; William Ennis to James Cardinal Gibbons, January 5, 1914, Gibbons to Ennis,

January 18, 1914, *SICA;* A. J. Maas (Jesuit provincial) to Gibbons, September 17, 1914, *SICA;* Baltimore *American,* February 12, 1914, 24.

10. House diary, 1912–1918, *SICA,* April 20, November 28, 1915, November 17, 1916; John T. Harwood to Ennis, October 20, 1916, Roland Park Company Records, Cornell University Libraries; Record of Consultations, 1865–1930, *SICA,* September 6, 1917, January 28, 1918.

11. "Pioneer of the Press," *Founder* (Mount Manresa, Staten Island) 6 (February 1948); conversation with Charles C. Conlon, Jr. (1938), August 4, 1977. On parish missions see Jay P. Dolan, *Catholic Revivalism: The American Experience, 1830–1900* (Notre Dame, Ind., 1978).

12. *Catholic Review* (Baltimore), September 11, 1931; Mary David Cameron, *The College of Notre Dame, 1895–1945* (New York, 1947), 77–81, 126–27; Kirwin, *Success,* 35. Conversations with John Sweitzer (1928) and Frank Fairbank (1927), October 10, 1967; William Taymans (1925), July 31, 1975; Bridget Marie Englemeyer, July 7, 1977.

13. Gannon, *Fordham,* 174–75.

14. Leahy, "Jesuits, Catholics, and Higher Education," 19.

15. Kirwin, *Success,* 34. Conversations with William Taymans (1925), July 31, 1975; Thomas Ferciot (1928), August 4, 1975. Brindley Mills to author, August 4, 1975.

16. Robert F. Reynolds, "Rev. Henry W. McLoughlin, S.J., 1872–1937," *Bulletin of the American Association of Jesuit Scientists* (Eastern States Division) 15 (December 1937): 46–51. Conversations with John Cummings (1926), May 22, 1975; Wilfred McQuaid (1927), July 27, 1978. The pertinent section of Goldsmith's poem is between lines 195 and 216.

17. House diary, 1912–1918, *SICA,* April 8, 1917; *Sun,* April 7, 9, 1917.

18. Paul Menton, "Schuerholz Dominated Basketball in the '20s," *Evening Sun,* January 25, 1946, 27; Kirwin, *Success,* 36–38.

19. In 1915, the winner of the nationwide finals was a Boston College student; a Holy Cross man came in second. Students from Jesuit schools won the regional contests that they were permitted to enter. Herman J. Muller, *The University of Detroit, 1877–1977: A Centennial History* (Detroit, 1976), 95.

20. Herbert R. O'Conor, "The League to Enforce Peace," *Loyola Annual,* 1917, 34–38; Kirwin, *Success,* 40.

21. House diary, 1912–1918, *SICA,* March 31, July 15, 1918.

22. Charles O. Paullin, "Benson, William Shepherd," *DAB* 11: 70–71.

23. R. B. Furlong, "Somewhere in France," *Loyola Annual,* 1918, 59.

Chapter 11

1. Gannon, *Fordham,* 152–53; Dunigan, *Boston College,* 217–18; conversation with R. Emmet Bradley (1922), February 28, 1967; Mary Magdala Thompson, "A Brief History of Mount Saint Agnes College, 1890–1959" (Master's thesis, Loyola College, 1959), 43–45.

2. Diary of the Prefect of Studies, 1910–1920, *LCA,* 250.

3. Paul A. FitzGerald, *The Governance of Jesuit Colleges in the United States, 1920–1970* (Notre Dame, Ind., 1984), 2–4, 7, 39.

4. House diary, 1918–1926, *SICA,* January 6, 1919; Record of Consultations, 1865–1930, *SICA,* May 26, 1919.

5. Record of Consultations, 1865–1930, *SICA,* October 27, 1919, November

23, 1920, March 22, 1921; House diary, 1918–1926, SICA, October 14, 1919, November 16, 1920; *The Associated Professors of Loyola College v. Hammond Dugan et al.*, *Maryland Reports* 137 (1921): 546–54.

6. House diary, 1918–1926, SICA, November 11, 20, 24, 1919. Conversations with Bernard Kirby (1924), March 27–28, 1968; John Cummings (1926), June 2, 1975; and William McWilliams (1926), April 1, 1979.

7. Kirwin, *Success*, 47; Frank F. White, Jr., *The Governors of Maryland, 1777–1970* (Annapolis, 1970), 260–61; Williams, *The Sun*, 216.

8. House diary, 1918–1926, SICA, October 23, 1923.

9. White, *Governors*, 259.

10. Ellis, *Gibbons*, 2:629.

11. House diary, 1918–1926, SICA, November 29, 30, 1921; Vincent de Paul Fitzpatrick, *Life of Archbishop Curley: Champion of Catholic Education* (Baltimore, 1929), 37–40, 41, 48; Lawrence Shehan, *A Blessing of Years: The Memoirs of Lawrence Cardinal Shehan* (Notre Dame, Ind., 1982), 101–3. Conversations with Edward Doehler (1930), May 7, 1975; James O'Hara (1956), March 3, 1977; Wilfred McQuaid (1927), July 22, 1978.

12. Maryland Commissioner of Labor and Statistics, *Thirty-First Annual Report of the Maryland State Board of Labor and Statistics, 1922* (Baltimore, 1923), 156; *Baltimore Federationist*, December 15, 1933, 3–5. Conversations with Mrs. Mary Broening, January 31, 1979, and Mrs. Vincent Lawler, February 23, 1979; Mrs. Lawler is Henry Broening's daughter.

13. Leahy, "Jesuits, Catholics, and Higher Education," 49, 63–69; Dolan, *Catholic Experience*, 356.

14. Record of Consultations, 1865–1930, SICA, February 8, 1921; Chairman to Philip M. Finnegan, November 27, 1922, AMSA.

15. Gannon, *Fordham*, 156; Brady, *Canisius*, 158; Philip Gleason, "In Search of Unity: American Catholic Thought, 1920–1960," *Catholic Historical Review* 65 (April 1979), 190, 196–99; Hennesey, *American Catholics*, 221, 255–56.

16. Charles Street is the main north-south thoroughfare in Baltimore. It was reportedly named for Charles Ghequiere, a prominent figure in Baltimore's early development. It has been compared by some bemused people to New York's Fifth Avenue, and it has always had some of the city's finest shops. However, it has a deeper, more mythic, quality for native Baltimoreans. Henry Barnes, traffic commissioner from 1953 to 1961, discovered the depth of this feeling when he reversed the traffic on the lower end of Charles Street to make it one way going north. He was astonished by the indignant outcry of those who objected to this tampering with the customary order. (See Henry A. Barnes, *The Man with the Red and Green Eyes* [New York, 1965], 153–57). The word *avenue* was probably tacked on by Baltimore County to differentiate the house numbers on the section of Charles that extended beyond the city limits. In 1918, Baltimore's boundary was moved farther north and eventually the word *avenue* was dropped from the designation of the annexed segment. To this day, one can find a Charles Street Avenue along an extra-municipal section of the road. Still farther along the name becomes Charles Street Avenue Extended.

17. Record of Consultations, 1865–1930, SICA, May 1, 1921; "Evergreen House" (descriptive brochure, n.p., n.d.); *Maryland Journal* (Towson), February 1, 1896, 3; Harold A. Williams, *Robert Garrett & Sons Incorporated* (Baltimore, 1965), 63; Cameron, *Notre Dame*, 16–19, 25, 35–38.

18. Owen B. Corrigan to Joseph A. McEneany, July 1, 1921, LCA.

19. *James Q. Farmer v. Mary A. Farmer et al.*, *Maryland Reports* 137 (1921): 69–88.

20. "A Statement Made by Mrs. Kate Keelan," c. 1931, *LCA*, 1. Mrs. Keelan had been a close friend of Mary Farmer's since childhood.

21. House diary, 1918–1926, *SICA*, July 5, September 15, 1921.

22. *Catholic Review,* September 17, 1921, 8.

23. Conversation with Bernard Kirby (1924), March 27–28, 1968.

24. "Junior Class Notes," *Green and Gray,* 1922, 82.

25. Shehan, *Blessing,* 235.

26. Dietrich Gerhard, "The Emergence of the Credit System in American Education Considered as a Problem of Social and Intellectual History," *AAUP 41 Bulletin* (Winter 1965): 647–68.

27. Meagher and Grattan, *Spires,* 240–43.

28. Conversation with William McWilliams (1926), April 1, 1979.

29. Leahy, "Jesuits, Catholics, and Higher Education," 77, 122–32.

30. Diary of the Dean of Studies, 1932–1936, *LCA*, 38; Dunigan, *Boston College,* 242–50.

31. House diary, 1918–1926, *SICA*, October 2, November 5, 1921.

32. *Sun,* August 14, 1930, 22.

Chapter 12

1. Conversations with William McWilliams (1926), April 1, 1979; John Sweitzer (1928) and Frank Fairbank (1927), October 10, 1967; John Cummings (1926), May 22, 1975; Bernard Kirby (1924), March 27–28, 1968; William Taymans (1925), July 31, 1975.

2. Conversations with Emmet Bradley (1922), February 28, 1967; Michael Ventura (1942), September 20, 1976; John Reilly (1948), December 23, 1970; John Evelius (1949), October 5, 1977.

3. Conversations with William McWilliams (1926), April 1, 1979; John Cummings (1926), May 22, 1975.

4. B. J. Mills to author, August 4, 1975, *LCA;* conversation with Thomas Ferciot (1928), August 4, 1975. Tribbe later joined the Society of Jesus and Meade entered politics. He held a seat in the Eightieth Congress.

5. Diary of the Prefect of Studies, 1921–1932, *LCA*, 157.

6. Deed, July 19, 1926, Liber S.C.L. 4625 folio 469.

7. Conversations with William McWilliams (1926), April 1, 1979; Thomas Ferciot (1928), August 4, 1975; Stanley Yakel, September 14, 1975; and Buck Henry, September 23, 1975.

8. House diary, 1918–1926, *SICA*, July 31, 1924.

9. "Rough Draft of Consultor's Letter to Rev. Fr. Provincial," *SICA.* Internal evidence suggests that this draft predates the agreement, and the handwriting is Father O'Carroll's. See also M. A. Clark, "Comments," c. September 1, 1928, *LHSA.*

Chapter 13

1. Conversation with Charles Conlon, Jr. (1938), August 4, 1977.

2. John W. McGrain, Jr., "Ayd and Criminal Aid," *Menckeniana,* Spring 1973, 11–12; Thomas J. Higgins, "Father Joseph J. Ayd," *Woodstock Letters* 87 (April 1968): 165–70; conversation with Thomas Ferciot (1928), August 4, 1975.

3. R. L. Slingluff, "In Memoriam: Rev. John G. Hacker, S.J.," Society for the History of the Germans in Maryland, *Twenty-Seventh Report,* 1950, 74.

4. Stirling Graham, "The Little Things in Chemistry," *Sun*, June 30, 1931; conversation with Charles Conlon, Jr. (1938), August 4, 1977.

5. Henri Wiesel, "Information Blank" (n.d.), *AMSA*; Adam Leroy Jones to Henri Wiesel, November 27, 1929, *AMSA*; Leahy, "Jesuits, Catholics, and Higher Education," 77, 91.

6. Wiesel to Jones, March 5, 1930; Thomas O'Malley to Jones, March 7, 1930; Wiesel to Jones, April 9, 1930; R. N. Dempster to Jones, November 24, 1931; Jones to Wiesel, November 28, 1931, all in *AMSA*.

7. Leahy, "Jesuits, Catholics, and Higher Education," 77, 91; Philip Gleason, "American Catholic Higher Education: A Historical Perspective," in *The Shape of Catholic Higher Education*, ed. Robert Hassenger (Chicago, 1967), 17.

8. Jones to Horace Field, August 18, 1932, *AMSA*.

9. "Builder of Loyola's Science and Library Buildings Ends Long Career of Charity," *Greyhound*, June 9, 1930, 8.

10. *Record No. 56, Transcript of Record . . . in the Case of Mary A. Farmer v. Peter J. O'Carroll etc.* (Baltimore, 1932), 19, 21, 23, 45; *Mary A. Farmer v. Peter J. O'Carroll et al.*, *Daily Record* (Baltimore), May 6, 1932, 2–3; *Mary A. Farmer v. Associated Professors*, ibid., June 27, 1933, 3; *James F. Farmer v. Associated Professors*, ibid., March 21, 1934, 3.

11. Charles M. Kimberly, "The Depression in Maryland: The Failure of Maryland, The Failure of Voluntaryism," *Maryland Historical Magazine* 70 (Summer 1975): 189–202; David Lamoureaux with Gerson G. Eisenberg, "Baltimore Views the Great Depression," ibid., 71 (Fall 1976): 428–42.

12. Muller, *Detroit*, 173. Conversations with William O'Donnell (1937), June 19, 1975; and Michael Ventura (1942), September 20, 1976.

13. "Collegians Set Up as Ladies' Escorts," *Sun*, January 29, 1938; conversation with Edward Heghinian (1940), June 16, 1980.

14. Francis Breen to Wiesel, August 19, 1934, *LCA*.

15. "Father Lord Calls for Catholic Leadership," *Greyhound*, January 29, 1932, 1, 6; "Are We Apathetic?" ibid., April 3, 1935, 2.

16. Hennesey, *American Catholics*, 260; conversations with William O'Donnell (1937), June 19, 1975, and Neill Miller (1937), June 23, 1975.

17. Diary of the Dean of Studies, 1932–1936, *LCA*, 82, 84, 87.

18. Hennesey, *American Catholics*, 274–75, 292–93.

19. "Prelate Denies Superiority of Nordic Peoples," *Sun*, June 10, 1925; conversation with Joseph Nelligan (1922), September 4, 1974; Carl Bode, *Mencken* (Carbondale, Ill., 1969), 201–2; H. L. Mencken to H. W. Seaman, August 9, 1934, in *The New Mencken Letters*, ed. Carl Bode (New York, 1977), 318; Williams, *The Sun*, 237.

20. "Loyola Students Hit Aggression by U.S.," *Sun*, March 13, 1935; "Thirty Colleges Point Way to Wipe Out War," *Literary Digest*, January 26, 1935, 6. See also the *Digest* for February 16, 1935, 7.

21. Hennesey, *American Catholics*, 272–74.

22. William W. Mahoney, "Let's Get the Story Straight," Radio Talk, May 17, 1937, *LCA*, 2.

23. Diary of the Dean of Studies, 1932–1936, *LCA*, 25. Elizabeth Morrissey came to Baltimore to continue her graduate studies at Johns Hopkins; her main scholarly interest was economics. See Cameron, *Notre Dame*, 84, 140; Anne Scarborough Philbin, *The Past and the Promised* (Baltimore, 1959), 155.

24. Conversation with Neill Miller (1937), June 27, 1975.

25. "Nag Supplants Lizzie as Loyolans Stage Whoopee Parade," *Sun*, October 31,

1931, 22; Craig E. Taylor, "Loyola Ties Western Maryland," *Sun*, November 1, 1931 (sports section), 1, 4; Laurie Dallaire to author, September 23, 1975; conversations with Vincent Carlin (1933), December 9, 1975, July 12, 1977.

26. Paul Menton, "It's All in the Viewpoint," *Sun*, May 2, 1934.

27. Conversations with William Liston (1931), June 18, 1979, and Emil Reitz, June 7, 1980.

Chapter 14

1. "Four Nuns among Grads," *Sun*, June 7, 1936.

2. Rudolph, *American College*, 398; Leahy, "Jesuits, Catholics, and Higher Education," 71; Powers, *Catholic Higher Education* (1958), 157.

3. "Association of Commerce Four Scholarships to Loyola," *Sun*, May 7, 1937.

4. Notes, "Sumner Welles Loyola Commencement Address 6/7/37," LCA.

5. Joseph Murphy to Michael J. Curley, April 7, 1937, AAB; same to same, April 24, 1937, AAB; Curley to Murphy, May 18, 1937, AAB, all in Curley Papers.

6. Father Bunn Testimony, GUA. Conversations with Edward Bunn (1917), c. May 1968; William O'Donnell (1937), June 19, 1975; Edward Kaltenbach (1942) May 12, 1978. Fitzgerald, *Governance of Jesuit Colleges*, 53.

7. [Msgr. Joseph M. Nelligan], Archiepiscopal diary, March 29, 1936, to June 18, 1947, AAB, October 18–21, 1938.

8. "President Officially Installed," *Greyhound*, October 28, 1938, 6.

9. Edward J. Power, *Catholic Higher Education in America: A History* (New York, 1972), 371, 388, 395.

10. Arthur Ciervo, "Father Bunn: 'With love and Distinction' until the End," *Georgetown Today*, July 1972, 4–9; Donald A. Casper, *"Doc" Bunn: A Remembering* (Washington, D.C., 1975), 9–11, 18; Kirwin, *Success*, 25–26, 224–28, 319; Brady, *Canisius*, 296–97.

11. Ferdinand Schoberg to author, August 21, 1978.

12. Brady, *Canisius*, 297.

13. Dean's Diary, 1940–1945, LCA, September 16, 1940; conversation with Joseph Donceel, May 28, 1979.

14. H. L. Mencken to John Hacker, June 3, 1939, H. L. Mencken Papers, Letters of Father John Hacker, Enoch Pratt Free Library.

15. Conversations with Catherine McDonald, February 25, 1975; Joseph Donceel, May 28, 1979.

16. Conversations with Joseph Donceel, May 28, 1979; Edward Kaltenbach (1942), January 3, 1980.

17. Conversation with Edward Kaltenbach (1942), January 3, 1980.

18. George H. Callcott, *Maryland and America: 1940 to 1980* (Baltimore, 1985), 29–30.

19. "National Catholic College Poll," *America*, November 11, 1939, 116–19; "Readers of *America* Poll," ibid., November 18, 1939, 144; Gerard Donnelly and Albert Whelan, "National Catholic College Poll," ibid., 144–46; "Final Report on NC Poll," ibid., 147.

20. Richard F. Grady, "Cenodoxus Redivivus," *Woodstock Letters* 69 (1940): 133–39; J. M. Loughborough, "The Story of 'Cenodoxus,'" *News-American* (Baltimore), February 18, 1940, E5; conversation with Richard Grady, May 2, 1968. Father Grady donated the script to the Loyola College Archives. A similar production was staged at the University of Santa Clara a year later.

21. [Louis Kronenberger], "Parisian in Baltimore," *Time*, March 11, 1940, 32.

22. Will of Francis Stuart, September 8, 1937, *LCA* (copy); Will of Frances Stuart, January 13, 1940, *LCA* (copy).

23. "Memorandum of the Very Reverend Edward B. Bunn," c. October 29, 1940, *GUA*. Conversations with C. Bowie Rose, June 25, 1975; Mary W. Johnson (1965), July 17, 1975; Claudia Fielding, July 23, 1975; Daniel Leonard, September 4, 1975.

24. Edward Bunn to Curley, March 2, 1940, *LCA*; Bunn to Zacheus Maher, June 26, 1940, *GUA*; Robert S. Grogan, "Recollections of the Case," July 4, 1975, *LCA*; Charles Kleinmeyer to James Sweeney, February 22, 1941, *GUA*; Edward Burke to Associated Professors, October 29, 1940, *GUA*; Maher to Bunn, March 17, 1941, *GUA*. Conversations with John Daley, May 21, 1968; Naomi May, June 18, 1975.

25. [Nelligan], Archiepiscopal Diary, *AAB*, January 5—March 16, 1941.

26. "Doctor Testifies in Stuart Case," *Evening Sun*, May 20, 1941.

27. [Nelligan], Archiepiscopal Diary, *AAB*, January 5–March 16, 1941; Kleinmeyer to Bunn, March 24, 1941, *LCA*; "Stuart Will Case Testimony Today," *Sun*, May 13, 1941; "Says Miss Stuart Unable to Attend to Any Business," *News-American*, May 14, 1941; "Judge Niles Says Fraud Absent in Stuart Will," *News-American*, May 19, 1941; "Defendants Win Stuart Will Case," *Sun*, May 23, 1941. Conversations with Henry Reisenweber, May 6, 1975; Mary W. Johnson (1965), July 17, 1975.

28. Burke to Bunn, July 17, 1941, *GUA*; Burke to Edward L. Ward and George M. White, August 7, 1941, *GUA*; "Stuart Will Litigation Is Ended Finally," *Sun*, September 4, 1941.

29. Kleinmeyer to Sweeney, June 10, 1941 (added note June 28, 1967), *GUA*; Kleinmeyer to Bunn, June 22, 1941, *LCA*; conversation with Edward Kaltenbach (1942), May 12, 1975.

Chapter 15

1. John Crosby Brown et al., "Survey of Loyola College . . . Report and Recommendations" (mimeographed), August 1941, 10.

2. Ibid., 56, 66–67, 74.

3. Ibid., 41; conversation with Emil Reitz, June 7, 1980.

4. Muller, *Detroit*, 210–11.

5. "Baltimorean Tells of Yorktown's Last Days," *Sun*, September 23, 1942.

6. "Lieut. Broderick . . . Tells of Jap Fighting Ability," *News-American*, September 23, 1942.

7. Gannon, *Fordham*, 237–38.

8. Geoffrey Perrett, *Days of Sadness, Years of Triumph: The American People, 1939–1945* (Baltimore, 1973), 113–15, 371–72; Muller, *Detroit*, 212–14; Brady, *Canisius*, 161, 166; Dunigan, *Boston College*, 288–89; Gannon, *Fordham*, 240.

9. "Loyola Morale Course," *Sun*, January 25, 1942.

10. "Bar of Public Opinion," *Catholic Review*, December 28, 1945, 28.

11. "Loyola to Cut Study Time for B.S. Degrees," *News-American*, January 10, 1943.

12. "Loyola College Head Lauds Philosophy of Liberal Arts," *Sun*, February 15, 1943; Perrett, *Sadness, Triumph*, 374.

13. Katharine Scarborough, "Confusion in the Colleges," *Sunday Sun*, January 17, 1943.

14. Perrett, *Sadness, Triumph*, 372–74; Gannon, *Fordham*, 241; Dunigan, *Boston College*, 296–99; Muller, *Detroit*, 215.

15. "Loyola College Freshman Scotches Musical Belief," *Sun*, January 15, 1943.

16. "Loyola Forms All-Athletic Organization," *Sun*, October 18, 1942; conversation with Emil Reitz, June 7, 1980.

17. "Maryland Again Becomes Center of Jesuit Province," *Sun*, July 2, 1943; Gannon, *Fordham*, 229–30; "Dr. Bunn Urges Short Course," *Sun*, March 10, 1945; "Jesuit Educators Meet in Council at Evergreen," *Catholic Review*, September 28, 1945, 10; conversation with Joseph Sellinger, August 26, 1980.

18. Christopher Jencks and David Reismann, *The Academic Revolution* (Garden City, N.Y., 1968), 344.

19. Perrett, *Sadness, Triumph*, 340–42, 378; Gannon, *Fordham*, 242, 245; "Clerics Asked to Show Gratitude over Charter," *Sun*, July 29, 1945.

20. Kirwin, *Success*, 359–61, 390–91.

21. Conversation with Patrick Coughlin (1944), July 3, 1980.

22. "Existing or Impending Shortages in Veterans' Educational Facilities," c. July 30, 1946, LCA.

23. "Jubilation Here Intense But Short," *Sun*, May 8, 1945, 8; "THE WAR IS OVER," *Sun*, August 15, 1945, 1, 15, 18.

24. "Memorandum to the Very Rev. Father Provincial from Father Kleinmeyer, June 10, 1941," GUA, Note no. 2, post-June 18, 1947.

Chapter 16

1. Callcott, *Maryland and America*, 29.

2. John LaFarge, *The Manner Is Ordinary* (New York, 1954), 195; idem, "Father Francis Xavier Talbot, S.J., 1889–1953," *Woodstock Letters* 85 (1956): 342, 344; conversation with Emil Reitz, June 7, 1980.

3. LaFarge, *Ordinary*, 197–299, 305, 392–94.

4. Francis X. Talbot to Fulton Oursler, November 21, 1947, LCA.

5. "Father Talbot Outlines . . . Objectives of Loyola College," *Catholic Review*, December 12, 1947, 13.

6. William Manchester, *Disturber of the Peace: The Life of H. L. Mencken* (New York, 1950), 311–12. Sara Mayfield's account of the Waugh-Mencken luncheon omits reference to Father Talbot. See Sara Mayfield, *The Constant Circle: H. L. Mencken and His Friends* (New York, 1968), 273. For Waugh's correspondence, see Mark Amory, ed., *The Letters of Evelyn Waugh* (New York, 1980), 263, 279, 292, 293 (for the editor's caveat on how to understand the letters, see p. viii).

7. "National Local Writers and Coaches Nominate Jim Lacy for All American Rating," *Greyhound*, February 21, 1947, 3.

8. Conversation with Emil Reitz, June 7, 1980.

9. Conversations with John Reilly (1948), December 23, 1970; John Corcoran (1950), July 18, 1980.

10. Conversation with George Fallon (1950), November 5, 1980.

11. "Three Honor Societies Are Only Fraternities Backed by College," *Alumni Newsletter*, March 1953, 4. Conversations with John Corcoran (1950), July 18, 1980; Joseph Drane, July 23, 1980.

12. Callcott, *Maryland and American*, 117–19.

13. "Spain Honor Father Talbot," *Sun*, April 1, 1949; Joseph F. Thorning to author, May 8, 1981.

14. Albert H. Poetker, "The Place of the Layman in Jesuit Schools," *Jesuit Education Quarterly* 9 (June 1946): 12–14.

15. Leahy, "Jesuits, Catholics, and Higher Education," 168–69.

16. Poetker, "Layman in Jesuit Schools," 17; Leahy, "Jesuits, Catholics, and Higher Education," 181.

17. Leahy, "Jesuits, Catholics, and Higher Education," 52.

18. Report of the Committee on Retirement and Group Insurance, April 8, 1949, LCA.

19. Paul C. Reinert, "A Retirement and Insurance Plan," *Jesuit Educational Quarterly* 9 (June 1946): 44.

20. Talbot to Joseph May, June 27, 1949, LCA.

21. [Harry Kirwin], Report of the Department of History, April 5, 1950, LCA.

22. Proceedings of the Associated Professors of Loyola College, 1947–1961, LCA, October 10, November 3, 1949.

23. Thorning to author, June 12, 1981, LCA; conversation with Joseph Sellinger, August 26, 1980.

24. Albert Sehlstedt, Jr., "A Prayer in Stone," *Sun*, October 24, 1951.

25. Francis A. Dynan to author, March 19, 1979, LCA.

26. "Loyola College to Receive Hollander Foundation Award," *Sun*, May 24, 1951; "Loyola to Continue to Avoid Racial Lines, Says President," *Sun*, May 26, 1951; conversation with Charles Dorsey (1953), February 1, 1979.

27. LaFarge, "Talbot," 337. Conversations with Joseph Drane, July 23, 1980; Joseph Sellinger, August 26, 1980.

Chapter 17

1. "Loyola College First Hundred Years," *Sun*, September 15, 1952.

2. John Tracy Ellis, "The American Catholic and the Intellectual Life," in *The Catholic Church, U.S.A.*, ed. Louis Putz (Chicago, 1956), 352.

3. Thomas Higgins, *Man as Man* (Milwaukee, 1949), 407–9.

4. Conversation with Charles Jordan (M.A. 1954) May 3, 1981.

5. David A. Robertson to Ewald B. Nyquist, c. April 13, 1951, AMSA; Nyquist to Robertson, April 19, 1951, AMSA; "Loyola to Offer New Degree," *Evening Sun*, April 11, 1951.

6. Conversations with Vincent Beatty, May 31, 1968; Joseph Drane, April 17, 1979.

7. Townsend Hoopes, *The Devil and John Foster Dulles* (Boston, 1973), 97–104.

8. Hennesey, *American Catholics*, 292–93.

9. William Manchester, *The Glory and the Dream: A Narrative History of America, 1932–1972* (Boston, 1973), 515, 517–29; N. Bancroft Williams, Jr., "An Examination of the Factors Leading to the Defeat of Millard E. Tydings in the Maryland Senatorial Election of 1950" (Master's thesis, Loyola College, 1966), 14–17, 39, 43–46; Callcott, *Maryland and America*, 125.

10. "Dr. E. Fenlon Wrote against Communism," *Sun*, March 18, 1964.

11. Callcott, *Maryland and America*, 121.

12. "A Good Offense," *Greyhound*, December 8, 1950, 5.

13. Private Schools Seen Threatened," *Sun*, June 8, 1953; James A. Newell, "Polytopics: A Degree Is Conferred," *Sun*, June 12, 1953.

14. Callcott, *University of Maryland*, 398–400.

15. John J. Quinn, "John S. Connor, Co-missionary," *Jesuit* 10 (January 1952), 29–30.

16. "First Ever Course on Radio Isotopes," *Sun*, September 24, 1952.

17. Vincent Beatty to Bunn, August 5, 1953, *GUA;* Bunn to Beatty, September 18, 1953, *GUA;* Beatty to Bunn, April 29, 1954, *GUA;* Bunn to Beatty, June 2, 1954, *GUA.* Conversations with Vincent Beatty, May 31, 1968; Edward Donnelly, April 19, 1988

18. United States Department of Health, Education, and Welfare, "Public Health Monograph #66," (1962); Ellis, "Intellectual Life," 353.

19. Beatty to Bunn, August 5, 1953, *GUA;* Beatty to Bunn, March 3, 1954, *GUA.*

20. "Evergreen Annual Honors Fr. Beatty," *Greyhound,* February 23, 1955, 1.

Chapter 18

1. "Eight Alarm Fire at Loyola College," *Evening Sun,* June 24, 1955, 1; "Faculty's Home Burns at Loyola," *Sun,* June 25, 1955, 26; "Blaze Wrecks Faculty House at Evergreen," *Catholic Review,* July 1, 1955.

2. "Loyola Teacher's Fire Loss Heavy," *Sun,* June 26, 1955.

3. Leahy, "Jesuits, Catholics, and Higher Education," 263.

4. Thomas Higgins, "Vincent F. Beatty, S.J.—November 10, 1979," LCA.

5. "Georgetown R.O.T.C. Review," *Herald* (Washington, D.C.), May 5, 1936.

6. "Loyola As Educational Force—For Individualism," *News-American,* September 25, 1955, 6B.

7. "Speech Presented by Father Beatty at His Inauguration," LCA, 2, 3, 4.

8. William Pyne, "Father Beatty Installed as Loyola's President," *Evening Sun,* November 3, 1955, 72; "Loyola Will Give Degrees at Inaugural," *Catholic Review,* October 28, 1955, 1.

9. Callcott, *University of Maryland,* 377–79; Power, *Catholic Higher Education* (1972), 422–24.

10. Frank O'Hern, Report on Loyola College Development Program, November 3, 1957, LCA, 1.

11. Manchester, *Glory and the Dream,* 576–81; Franklin L. Burdette, "Modern Maryland Politics and Social Change," in *Maryland: A History, 1632–1974,* ed. Richard Walsh and William Lloyd Fox (Baltimore, 1974), 814, 821.

12. Paul Smith, "Southern Sentiment," *Evergreen Quarterly,* Winter 1954, 26.

13. "We Put It All Together," *Time,* October 30, 1972, 70.

14. Dorothy Heindel, "Commission on Higher Education of the Middle States Association of Colleges and Schools" (Philadelphia), October 21, 1978; Callcott, *University of Maryland,* 361–63.

15. General Meeting of Faculty, Friday, May 4, 1956, LCA, 2.

16. Gannon, *Fordham,* 218–19, 295; Muller, *Detroit,* 320; Brady, *Canisius,* 340–41; Callcott, *University of Maryland,* 377.

17. John Wise to author, May 16, 1956, LCA.

18. "Meet the McEwens," *Hamilton Alumni Review,* January 1949, 57–60; Robert H. Hevenor, "The Closing of an Era," ibid., Summer 1966, 4–15; "Mr. McEwen Dies at 60," ibid., Summer 1967, 15–16; Frank K. Lorenz to author, July 5, October 3, 1979, LCA.

19. Nyquist to L. J. McGinley, March 12, 1957, AMSA; Nyquist to Beatty, May 2, 1957, AMSA.

20. Thomas Higgins et al., Data Submitted for Consideration . . . [to] Middle States Association, . . . 1957, AMSA.

21. Robert W. McEwen et al., Loyola College, Evaluation Report Based on Visit of February 26–March 1, 1957, AMSA.

22. [Vincent F. Beatty], Outline: Recent Relations with Middle States Association, October 3, 1957, *LCA*, 4.

Chapter 19

1. Power, *Catholic Higher Education* (1972), 419, 453; Gerard Hinrichs, "Faculty Participation in the Governance of Catholic Colleges and Universities," *AAUP Bulletin* 50 (Winter 1964): 336–42.

2. Charles J. Edgette to F. Taylor Jones, February 16, 1959, AMSA.

3. Nyquist to Beatty, May 7, 1959, AMSA.

4. Leahy, "Jesuits, Catholics, and Higher Education," 166.

5. Jeanne B. Sargeant, "In a Man's Field," *Evening Sun,* July 4, 1962.

6. "Father Galvin Gets Post as Dean at Loyola," *Catholic Review,* June 19, 1959.

7. John D. Hackett, "Loyola Student Unit Being Dedicated Sunday," *Evening Sun,* January 27, 1960.

8. John Tracy Ellis, "Honors and Work," *Evergreen Quarterly* 15 (Autumn 1960), 10.

9. Bradford Jacobs, "Books in Review," *Evening Sun,* June 20, 1962.

10. Frank R. Walsh, "Requiescat in Pace," *Greyhound,* March 15, 1963, 1; "Prof. Harry W. Kirwin of Loyola College Dies at 51," *News-Post* (Baltimore), March 12, 1963; "Prof. Kirwin Rites Today," *Sun,* March 14, 1963.

11. W. J. Maring, "Separating the Jesuit Community from the University," *Conference of Finance Administrators of Jesuit Institutions,* 1953, 71–74.

12. Conversation with Vincent Beatty, May 31, 1968.

13. Hennesey, *American Catholics,* 308–10; Leahy, "Jesuits, Catholics, and Higher Education," 1, 212.

14. "First Friday Mass Obligation Returns," *Greyhound,* March 4, 1960, 1.

15. "Against Compulsory Mass," *Greyhound,* March 20, 1964, 2.

16. Andrew M. Greeley, *The Changing Catholic College* (Chicago, 1967), 130, 178; Leahy "Jesuits, Catholics, and Higher Education," 168, 175.

17. Shehan, *Blessing,* 236–37.

18. Conversation with Vincent Beatty, May 31, 1968; "Loyola Maryland Hall Opens," *Sun,* September 23, 1962; French, *Johns Hopkins,* 167–68.

19. "Hilgenberg Tribute Set," *Sun,* January 10, 1960; "Loyola Gets $50,000 Memorial Gift," *Evening Sun,* December 6, 1960.

20. "Loyola Opens New Building," *Sun,* September 21, 1962.

21. "Francis Frederick Ruzicka, M.D.," in Andrews, *Tercentenary History,* 2: 864–65.

22. "Treasurer Named at Loyola," *Catholic Review,* October 5, 1962; Leahy, "Jesuits, Catholics, and Higher Education," 186.

23. Manchester, *Glory and the Dream,* 911–13, 985–86; Rudy Zea, "Test Ban Treaty," *Greyhound,* October 18, 1963, 2.

24. Beatty to Milton Eisenhower, October 9, 1956, *LCA*; conversation with Vincent Beatty, May 31, 1968.

25. D. Luke Hopkins, confidential memorandum, March 2, 1942, Ferdinand Hamburger, Jr., Archives of the Johns Hopkins University, Baltimore, Office of the President, 1903–1963, 936.4 (hereafter cited as Hopkins University Archives).

26. "Hopkins Seeks Park Land to Provide for Expansion," *Sun,* January 8, 1960, 38; "Foes Claim Park Sale OK'd before Disclosure," *Evening Sun,* February 1, 1960, 36;

Charles Garland, memorandum, March 8, 1962, Hopkins University Archives; conversation with Vincent Beatty, May 31, 1968.

27. Beatty to Trustees of the Johns Hopkins University, March 14, 1960, *LCA*.

28. Minutes of a Meeting Held at Evergreen House, Wednesday, May 17, 1961, Hopkins University Archives.

29. Beatty to Eisenhower, June 13, 1963, *LCA*; Beatty to Henry Knott, October 4, 1963, *LCA*.

30. Daniel B. Leonard to Beatty, October 21, 1963, *LCA*.

Chapter 20

1. FitzGerald, *Governance of Jesuit Colleges*, 188.

2. Priscilla Cummings, "No Matter What We Do, It's Misinterpreted," *Baltimore Magazine*, July 1983, 72; conversations with Joseph Sellinger, June 22, 29, 1982.

3. Conversations with Joseph Sellinger, June 22, 1982; Tom Scheye, July 8, 1982.

4. Francis E. Kearns, "Social Consciousness and Academic Freedom in Catholic Higher Education," in *The Shape of Catholic Higher Education*, ed. Robert Hassenger (Chicago, 1967), 226–27.

5. ACLU Lawsuit, Transcript of Trial, 1:1148, 1256; conversation with Joseph Sellinger, June 22, 1982.

6. Conversations with Joseph Sellinger, June 22, 29, 1982.

7. Theodore Hesburgh to author, May 4, 1988; conversations with Rhoda Dorsey, June 16, 1984; Steven Muller, June 15, 1988.

8. "Inauguration Speech of Very Reverend Joseph A. Sellinger, S.J.," November 12, 1964, *LCA*, 1.

9. Ibid., 8.

10. "Comments of Joseph A. Sellinger, S.J.," in *Proceedings of the Woodstock Institute on the Society of Jesus and Higher Education in America*, ed. G. Michael Crossin and Leo J. O'Donovan (Woodstock, Md., 1964), 15.

11. Ibid., 14.

12. Conversation with Edward Donnelly, April 19, 1988.

13. Conversation with Joseph Sellinger, June 22, 1982.

14. Conversations with Joseph Sellinger, June 22, 29, 1982.

15. Power, *Catholic Higher Education*, 424–25.

16. FitzGerald, *Governance of Jesuit Colleges*, 189.

17. "Land O'Lakes Statement: The Idea of the Catholic University," in *Guidelines for Jesuit Higher Education*, ed. Eugene E. Grollmes (Denver, 1969), 13; "Statement on the Distinctive Characteristics of Jesuit Higher Education," *ibid.*, 1; Power, *Catholic Higher Education*, 420–21.

18. Leahy, "Jesuits, Catholics, and Higher Education," 182.

19. *Ibid.*, 187.

20. "Trustees Chairman Appointed to Head Loyola–Notre Dame Library Corporation," *Alumni Greyhound*, March 1968, 1. The officers of the new library corporation were Truman Seamans, long associated with Loyola College and then vice-chairman of the board of Robert Garrett & Sons, was the president; Sister Ian Stewart of Notre Dame's library served as vice-president; Adrian McCardell, president of the First National Bank, was the treasurer. In addition to these, the board of trustees consisted of Austin Murphy, auxiliary bishop of Baltimore, as chairman; Thomas Butler, chairman of the board of the Mercantile Safe Deposit and Trust Company; Father James Connor of Loyola's theology department; George Constable, a well-respected lawyer; Henry Knott, a prominent Baltimore builder, Loyola alumnus (class of 1929), and member of

Notre Dame's board of directors; and Doctor Mildred Otenasek of Notre Dame's political science department.

21. Sidney E. Ahlstrom, *A Religious History of the American People* (New Haven, 1972), 1082–87.

22. Dolan, *American Catholic Experience*, 428–29.

23. Paul J. Reiss, "Faculty and Administration: The Jesuit-Lay Character," *Jesuit Educational Quarterly* 31 (October 1969): 107–10.

24. Robert F. Harvanek, "The Objectives of the American Jesuit University: A Dilemma," *Jesuit Educational Quarterly* 24 (October 1961): 87; Martin J. Stamm, "The Laicization of Corporate Governance of Twentieth-Century American Catholic Higher Education," *Records of the American Catholic Historical Society of Philadelphia* 84 (March–December, 1983), 83.

25. Leahy, "Jesuits, Catholics, and Higher Education," 175–76.

26. FitzGerald, *Governance of Jesuit Colleges*, 211, 294; Leahy, "Jesuits, Catholics, and Higher Education," 202.

27. Leahy, "Jesuits, Catholics, and Higher Education," 201; Maryland Province Society of Jesus, *A Plan for Renewal: A Community of Apostolic Men*, 2 vols. (Baltimore, 1969), 1:79–83.

28. Manchester, *Glory and the Dream*, 1055, 1125, 1131.

29. Ibid., 1110, 1101.

30. Ibid., 1128.

31. A.E.P. Wall, "Palm Sunday in the Inner City: 'People Are Deeply Ashamed,'" *Catholic Review*, April 12, 1968.

32. Shehan, *Blessing*, 240.

33. Manchester, *Glory and the Dream*, 1089, 1097, 1099; Helen Lefkowitz Horowitz, *Campus Life: Undergraduate Culture from the End of the Eighteenth Century to the Present* (Chicago, 1987), 223.

34. Pat Molloy, "Like the Old Cigar Store Indian, Loyola's Traditions Are Disappearing," *Greyhound*, October 24, 1967, 1.

35. Donald P. Gavin, *John Carroll University: A Century of Service* (Kent, Ohio, 1985), 403–4.

36. Minutes of the Academic Council, May 10, 1967, LCA, 3; William Davish to James Buckley, September 30, 1982, LCA.

37. "Town Hall Discusses School Policy: Students Seeking More Control," *Greyhound*, February 27, 1968, 1.

38. Joseph A. Sellinger, "Commentary on [the] Joint Statement on Rights and Freedoms of Students," *Alumnae Journal of Trinity College*, Spring 1968; conversation with Joseph Sellinger, July 7, 1982.

39. Dave Townsend to author, July 27, 1983, LCA.

40. Horowitz, *Campus Life*, 244.

41. Lowell E. Sunderland, "Gridders Earn Over 5 G's in Charity Mud Marathon," *Sun*, December 12, 1968; "Loyola Bows to Towson: Santa Leaves with $7,000," *Greyhound*, December 16, 1968, 2–3.

Chapter 21

1. Callcott, *Maryland and America*, 9–10, 88.

2. Conversations with Rhoda Dorsey, June 16, 1988; Steven Muller June 15, 1988. Hesburgh to author, May 4, 1988.

3. Sellinger to Edward Sponga, February 16, 1967, LCA.

4. Louis Fischer, "Academic Freedom and Tenure," in *Encyclopedia of Educational Research*, 5th ed., 4 vols., ed. Harold Mitzel (New York, 1982), 1:2.

5. [William G. Kelly], Revision of Rank and Tenure Policy, August 16, 1967, LCA, 10.

6. Minutes, Jesuit Education Asociation Commission on Colleges and Universities, March 27, 1967, 7–10. As late as 1970, some Jesuit administrators were still seeking an alternative to the generally accepted tenure system. See Robert I. Bradley, "A Proposed Revision of the Present Tenure System in Our Jesuit Colleges and Universities" (Washington, D.C.), October 5, 1970.

7. [Kelly], Revision, August 16, 1967, LCA, 1; Kearns, "Social Consciousness and Academic Freedom," 244.

8. William G. Kelly to Sellinger, March 11, 1969, LCA.

9. [William G. Kelly], Proposal: The Establishment of THE FEDERATED COLLEGES OF MARYLAND, with Loyola and Mount Saint Agnes Colleges as First Members, LCA.

10. Gerard A. Perseghin, "Two Colleges Studying Closer Ties," *Catholic Review*, September 13, 1968, B8.

11. Report to . . . Loyola College by an Evaluation Team . . . [of] the Middle States . . . after . . . a Visit . . . on November 16–19, 1969, LCA, 22; Report to . . . Mount Saint Agnes College by an Evaluation Team . . . [of] the Middles States . . . after . . . a Visit . . . on November 16–19, 1969, LCA, 17.

12. John Ford to F. Taylor Jones, February 9, 1970, LCA (copy).

13. Report to Loyola College by an Evaluation Team . . . after . . . a Visit . . . on November 16–19, 1969, LCA, 4, 5, 27.

14. "Layman Named Loyola Official," *Evening Sun*, May 30, 1969, 7A; conversation with Joseph Sellinger, July 7, 1982.

15. James L. Connor to Sellinger, December 11, 1969, as cited in Associated Professors of Loyola College . . . Board of Trustees, Records, 1961–1972 (Office of Provost), January 17, 1970.

16. Associated Professors of Loyola College . . . Board of Trustees, Records, 1961–1972 (Office of Provost), January 17, 1970.

17. Jencks and Reisman, *Academic Revolution*, 354.

18. Associated Professors of Loyola College . . . Board of Trustees, Records, 1961–1972 (Office of Provost), January 17, 1970.

19. FitzGerald, *Governance of Jesuit Colleges*, 205.

20. Neil G. McCluskey, "The New Catholic College," *America*, March 25, 1967, 417.

21. Leahy, "Jesuits, Catholics, and Higher Education," 242.

22. John J. McGrath, *Catholic Institutions in the United States: Canonical and Civil Law Status* (Washington, D.C., 1968), 8–9, 11–12, 14, 17, 18, 31, 34–35, 37. In 1963 authorities at all Jesuit schools agreed that their institutions were owned by the Society. See Manning M. Patillo, Jr., and Donald M. Mackenzie, *Church-Sponsored Higher Education in the United States* (Washington, D.C., 1966), 230–47.

23. J. A. Panuska to Daniel J. Altobello, November 23, 1971, LCA (copy).

24. Association of Jesuit Colleges and Universities (AJCU), Summary of Comments by the Presidents, at the January Board Meeting, on the Higher Education Report (Washington, D.C., March 24, 1971), 11, 14–15, 21; David O'Brien, "The Holy Cross Case," *Commonweal*, October 8, 1976, 648–49. This difficulty had been predicted several years earlier; see Andrew M. Greeley, "The Problem of Jesuit Education in the United States," *Jesuit Educational Quarterly* 29 (October 1966): 107, 110–12.

25. Ruth Cessna, *John McGrath: The Mask of Divestiture and Disaffiliation?* (San

Francisco, 1971), *LCA* (copy). For a summary of the opinions by institutional counsel, see Dexter L. Hanley to Board of Governors, AJCU, January 8, 1972, *LCA* (copy). For the opinion of Loyola's legal adviser, see Leonard to Sellinger, August 31, 1971, *LCA*. See also Joseph K. Drane, "Juridical Substructures of American Jesuit Educational Institutions," *Jesuit Educational Quarterly* 31 (October 1968), 79–85.

26. James L. Connor et al., *The Jesuit Apostolate of Education in the United States: An Overview* (Washington, D.C., 1974), 11.

27. Frederick Homann et al., Proposal for a Revised Curriculum in the Day Division, August 11, 1969, *LCA*, 1–2; idem, "The Interim Term: Its History and Modus Operandi" (n.d., c. August 1969), *LCA*, 1–2.

28. Minutes, Faculty Meeting, October 16, 1969, *LCA*; Stephen McNierney to the Academic Council, October 29, 1969, *LCA*; Minutes, Academic Council, November 4, 1969, *LCA*.

29. J. Grayson Grau, "The Progress of 4-1-4 at Loyola College, May 15, 1972," *LCA*; Committee on Undergraduate Studies, A Summary Report on 4-1-4 Attitudinal Survey, July 1973, *LCA*; Joseph Baker et al., A Summary Report on the Two Types of Curriculum, Spring 1978, *LCA*.

30. Muller, *Detroit*, 350–51; Gavin, *John Carroll*, 364–65, 404.

31. Minutes, Academic Council, September 11, 1969, *LCA*; College Statement on Campus Disruption, September 1969, *LCA*.

32. "Jewish-Christian Conference Set," *Catholic Review*, December 5, 1969, B8; Weldon Wallace, "New Christian Jewish Ties Urged," *Sun*, December 10, 1969; Joseph Gallagher, *The Pain and the Privilege: Diary of a City Priest* (Garden City, N.Y., 1983), 338; conversation with James O'Hara (1956), August 21, 1984.

33. Jencks and Reisman, *Academic Revolution*, 343.

34. Greeley, *Changing Catholic College*, 30.

35. Elizabeth Geen, Mount Saint Agnes College: Report of the President, 1970–1972, *LCA* (copy), 1–2; conversation with Elizabeth Geen, June 19, 1985.

36. Associated Professors of Loyola College . . . Board of Trustees, Records, 1961–1972, (Office of Provost), April 25, 1970.

37. Geen, Report, *LCA*, 2–3; Resolution of the Board of Trustees of Loyola College, August 21, 1970, *LCA*; conversation with Edward Donnelly, April 19, 1988. From 1964 to 1970, enrollments at Loyola fell from 847 to 801, or about 5.8 percent, but freshman registrations dropped from 270 to 229, or 15.2 percent; this latter figure is the more significant because it controlled total enrollments for the next four years.

38. Meeting of Ad Hoc Committee of the Board of Trustees, July 24, 1970, *LCA*.

39. Resolution of the Board of Trustees of Loyola College, August 21, 1970, *LCA*; Geen, Report, *LCA*, 2–3; conversations with Elizabeth Geen and Judith Schmelz, June 10, 1985.

40. Bruce Bortz interview of Joseph Sellinger, June 18, 1982, *LCA* (copy), 29; Geen, Report, *LCA*, 4, 11; Minutes, College Council, September 15, November 10, 1970, *LCA*; McNierney to Elizabeth Geen, September 16, 1970, *LCA*.

41. Bortz interview of Sellinger, June 18, 1982, *LCA* (copy), 30, 32; conversations with Elizabeth Geen and Judith Schmelz, June 10, 1985.

42. Conversation with Judith Schmelz, June 10, 1985.

43. Gilbert Sandler, "Change Came to Loyola in a Skirt," *Sun*, October 29, 1972, C1.

44. Joseph A. Sellinger, "Why Loyola Changed," January 11, 1972, *LCA*, 7. George A. Epstein, "Sellinger: It's Funny You Should Have Asked Me That," *Greyhound*, November 22, 1972 (insert), 2.

45. David Lightman, "Nursing Care Chronology," *Evening Sun,* April 15, 1975, C2.

46. Conversations with Steven Muller, June 15, 1988; Paul Kerschner, August 21, 1984. At the time of his appointment in 1972, Kerschner was an assistant professor at the University of Maryland School of Social Work and was a graduate of Georgetown, but he had not been personally acquainted with Father Sellinger before he was named the commission's staff director.

47. Joseph A. Sellinger, Address to the Medical and Chirurgical Faculty Seminar, c. October 19, 1971, *LCA,* 8–9; Commission to Governor Marvin Mandel, September 17, 1973, *LCA,* 3–4; Governor's Meeting, Press Conference, September 17, 1973, *LCA.*

48. Maryland State Retirement Systems to Loyola–Notre Dame Library, Inc., November 14, 1969 (copy), *LCA;* Sellinger to Robert Kirkwood, July 29, 1971, *AMSA.*

49. *Govanstown Courier* (Baltimore), May 1974; Leslie Freudenheim, "A Library That Won a Prize—But Works," *Evening Sun,* April 25, 1974; Denise Flynn, "Sr. Margaret Mary, Mrs. Knott Take Honors," *Lotre,* April 1973, 1; Georgia Bayard, "Unique Merger—First of Its Kind in U.S.," ibid., 4.

50. "To the Editors of the Joint Staff of *Twain,*" *Twain,* February 15, 1971, 1.

51. Marie Lerch, "An Unfortunate Decision," *Greyhound,* February 21, 1975, 6; Thomas Higgins, "A Perversion of Law," ibid., February 28, 1975, 7; Ed Gainor, "The Abortion Issue Regurgitated," ibid., March 14, 1975.

52. Pat Harlow, "Women Suffer from Sex Bias," *Greyhound,* February 14, 1975, 10; Janine Shertzer, "Girl's Lacrosse Team Goes over Kavanaugh's Head," ibid., May 2, 1975, 8; "Title IX Rule in Effect at Loyola," ibid., September 12, 1975.

53. James H. Jackson, "Lefty Reitz Retires as Loyola College A.D.," *Sun,* August 9, 1973.

Chapter 22

1. Calcott, *Maryland and America,* 10, 89–91; Joseph Arnold, "The Politics of the Baltimore Renaissance," in *Baltimore: A Living Renaissance,* ed. Leonora Heilig Nast et al. (Baltimore, 1982), 244–46; Laurence N. Krause, "William Donald Schaefer," *ibid.,* 238, 240–41.

2. William Donald Schaefer to author, August 24, 1988.

3. "Loyola Adds Apartments for 148," *Sun,* August 21, 1977, F11.

4. [William L. Kolb], *New Wine: A Report of the Commission on the Danforth Study of Campus Ministries* (St. Louis, Mo., 1969), 17–33, 51–61.

5. *Evening Sun,* July 16, 1974, A6.

6. Gerri Kobren, "The Eyes of the World Are Often Saved by Maryland," *Sunday Sun Magazine,* June 30, 1974, 5; conversations with Charles Graham (1962), June 7, 11, 1985.

7. Frederic Kelly, "Private Colleges Going in the Red," *Sun,* April 25, 1971, D1; Stephen E. Ambrose and Richard H. Immerman, *Milton S. Eisenhower: Educational Statesman* (Baltimore, 1983) 233–37.

8. Conversation with Paul Melanson, July 2, 1986.

9. Associated Professors of Loyola College . . . Board of Trustees, Records, 1973–1975 (Office of Provost), March 3, 1973.

10. Maryland Council for Higher Education, "Summary: A Report Concerning the Financial Condition of Private Higher Education in Maryland and the State's Rela-

tionship to these Institutions" (Annapolis, 1973), 1–2, 5, 9. Conversations with Marvin Mandel, November 20, 1985; Frank DeFillipo, November 6, 1985; Elizabeth Garroway, July 20, 1988.

11. Michael Wheatley, "City's Universities to Benefit Most in Mandel Plan," *Evening Sun*, March 9, 1971, C24.

12. Conversation with Joseph Sellinger, June 22, 1982.

13. Gavin, *John Carroll*, 361.

14. ACLU Suit, Transcript of Trial, *LCA*, 2:1342.

15. Associated Professors of Loyola College . . . Board of Trustees, Records, 1977–1978 (Office of Provost), March 8, 1977. See also: Minutes, College Council, *LCA*, October 10, 1974.

16. Callcott, *Maryland and America*, 78–80, 305; Charles F. Stein, *Origin and History of Howard County* (Baltimore, 1972), 146–48.

17. Conversation with Ron Biglin, August 13, 1984.

18. Brakeley, Jones Report, April 1975, Fund Raising, *LCA*, Appendix 3, 4.

19. Ibid., 5.

20. Ibid., ii, 2, 7.

21. Ibid., 17; Associated Professors of Loyola College . . . Board of Trustees, Records, 1973–1975 (Office of Provost), September 16, 1975.

22. Brakeley, Jones Report, April 1975, Fund Raising, *LCA*, 8, 17, 33.

23. Associated Professors of Loyola College . . . Board of Trustees, Records, 1973–1975 (Office of Provost), September 16, 1975; Decade of Decision II, 1975–1985, *LCA*, 1–2; conversation with Edward Donnelly, April 19, 1988.

24. Willa B. Player to McNierney, February 10, 1975, *LCA*.

25. "Appeal to Close Club Is Denied," *Sun*, October 1, 1969; "Judge Approves Use of Homes By Loyola," *News-American*, August 16, 1977; "Foes of Loyola Expansion Lose," *Sun*, May 12, 1978.

26. Barry Rascovar, "Sale Sign up on Old Loyola Complex," *Sun*, November 28, 1970, B5; "Revival in Baltimore," *Washington Post*, November 18, 1975; Ron Israel, "Center Stage," in Nast et al., *Baltimore: A Living Renaissance*, 168–69.

27. John Dorsey, "Center Stage: The Shape of a Theater to Come," *Sunday Sun*, June 1, 1975, D1; Peter Culman to Talton Ray, August 17, 1979, *LCA* (copy); Israel, "Center Stage," 169.

28. "Loyola Begins Minority Recruiting Program," *Afro-American* (Baltimore), November 29, 1977.

29. *Tilton v. Richardson* (1971), 403 U.S., 678, 682. To inform and guide its members, the Association of American Colleges distributed a pamphlet by the lawyer who was responsible for the legal research in the *Tilton* case and who later would represent Mount Saint Mary's in the *Roemer* case. See Charles H. Wilson, Jr., *Tilton v. Richardson: The Search for Sectarianism in Education* (Washington, D.C., 1971).

30. Lawrence Greenwald, Complaint, March 1972, *LCA* (copy), 3–4.

31. Conversation with Lawrence Greenwald, September 23, 1986.

32. ACLU Suit, Transcript of Trial, *LCA*, 1:1121–22; FitzGerald, *Governance of Jesuit Colleges*, 211.

33. ACLU Suit, Transcript of Trial, *LCA*, 1:1153, 1150.

34. Ibid., 2:1356.

35. Ibid., 1:1152.

36. Ibid., 1235.

37. Ibid., 2:1430–31, 1437–39, 1442.

38. Ibid., 1432.

39. Joseph H. Young, Findings of Fact, January 14, 1974, LCA (copy), 5.

40. ACLU Suit, Transcript of Trial, LCA, 2:1382–1463 (passim).

41. Ibid., 1468.

42. Ibid., 1477.

43. Conversation with Lawrence Greenwald, September 23, 1986.

44. Joseph H. Young, Opinion, *Roemer v. Board of Public Works*, LCA (copy), 6.

45. Arthur Bryan, Opinion, *Roemer v. Board of Public Works*, LCA (copy), 3–5.

46. Lawrence Greenwald, Stipulation between Appellants and Western Maryland College, Appellee, March 18, 1975, LCA (copy), 1–4.

47. Conversation with John C. Roemer III, September 14, 1985.

48. Leo Pfeffer, *Brief for National Coalition for Public Education and Religious Liberty Amicus Curiae* (n.p., May, 1975), 18–20; Charles M. Whelan, *Brief of Association of American Colleges . . ., Amici Curiae* (Washington, D.C., 1975), 3.

49. Robert H. Bork et al., *Brief for the United States as Amicus Curiae* (Washington, D.C., 1975), 2–3.

50. *Roemer v. Board of Public Works* (1976), 426 U.S., 750–59.

51. Ibid., 775.

52. ACLU Suit, Transcript of Trial, LCA, 1:1126.

53. "Statement by Rev. Joseph A. Sellinger, S.J., " June 21, 1976, LCA.

54. Charles H. Wilson to Sellinger, June 24, 1976, LCA.

55. John L. May to Sellinger, June 23, 1976, LCA.

56. Ross Jones to Sellinger, June 21, 1976, LCA.

57. H. Mebane Turner to Sellinger, June 22, 1976, LCA.

58. "State Aid to Higher Education," *Cincinnati Enquirer*, June 25, 1976; "Church and State . . . and the Court," *Washington Post*, June 25, 1976; "Ruling on Church College Aid," *Christian Science Monitor* (Boston, Mass.), June 23, 1976; "Gains and Risks Stem from School Decision," *State* (Columbia, S.C.), June 24, 1976; "It Is Aid to Education," *Post* (Frederick, Md.), June 23, 1976.

59. Conversation with Marvin Mandel, November 20, 1985.

60. Janine Shertzer, "Stephen McNierney, Teacher, Philosopher, Administrator," *Greyhound*, March 4, 1977, 2.

Chapter 23

1. Carleton Jones, "Loyola at 125: Keeping the Spirit Clean and the Ink Black," *Sunday Sun*, September 11, 1977, Trend 1.

2. Andrew M. Greeley, *American Catholics Since the Council: An Unauthorized Report* (Chicago, 1985). 75.

3. Jones, "Loyola at 125," 2.

4. Isaac Rehert, "Show Revives Maroger's 'Old Master's,'" *Sun*, February 23, 1978, B6.

5. Ray Truitt, "Scheye, Former Head of English Department, Fills Vacancy," *Greyhound*, September 15, 1978, 1.

6. Ibid., 1; conversation with Tom Scheye, July 8, 1982.

7. Bernard Weigman et al., Abstract of Proposal for Master of Engineering Science in Digital Systems, c. August, 1976, LCA, 1, 6–8.

8. "Presentation of Rev. Joseph A. Sellinger . . . before the State Board of Higher Education, Friday, June 3, 1977," LCA; Sellinger to Sheldon Knorr, June 21, 1977, LCA.

9. Michael Sagalnik, "Four College Heads Fight UMBC Plan," *Sun,* November 22, 1 1978.

10. Conversations with Rhoda Dorsey, June 16, 1988; Elizabeth Garroway, July 20, 1988.

11. Michael Rugby, "Zoning Board and Neighbors Squelch Loyola Grandstand," *Messenger* (Baltimore), August 17, 1979; Associated Professors of Loyola College . . . Board of Trustees, Records, March–December 1978 (Office of Provost), October 10, 1978.

12. Associated Professor of Loyola College . . . Board of Trustees, Records, January 1979–May 1981 (Office of Provost), January 9, 1979; "Loyola Cuts '79–'80 Tuition Hike to Fight Inflation," *Vantage* (Baltimore), January, 1979, 8.

13. "Mathias Hails Loyola, *Star* (Washington, D.C.), January 3, 1979.

14. Faculty Compensation Committee Report, c. January 5, 1979, LCA.

15. Robert K. Carr and Daniel K. Van Eyck, *Collective Bargaining Comes to the Campus* (Washington, D.C., 1973), 7, 25; Howard B. Means and Philip W. Semas, *Faculty Collective Bargaining* (Washington, D.C., 1976), 45–53; William B. Boyd, "The Impact of Collective Bargaining on University Governance," *Liberal Education* 58 (May 1972), 266–67.

16. Associated Professors of Loyola College . . . Board of Trustees, Records, January 1979–May 1981(Office of Provost), March 20, 1979.

17. Martin J. Finkelstein, *The American Academic Profession* (Columbus, Ohio, 1984), 137–38; conversation with Randall Donaldson, c. February 1979.

18. Sellinger to Kathleen Feeley, October 30, 1978, LCA.

19. Joseph P. O'Neill et al., "Cooperation and Quality: A Report to the Trustees of the College of Notre Dame and Loyola College," May 1982, LCA, 1, 14, 17.

20. Vesta Kimble, "Mayor Tours in Non-Political Visit," *Greyhound,* October 26, 1979, 1.

21. J. Paul Melanson to M. J. Brodie, December 10, 1979, LCA.

22. Antero Pietila, "Loyola Marshals Forces for Lights," *Sun,* March 8, 1980; Steven Muller to William Donald Schaefer, March 12, 1980 (copy), LCA.

23. "Draft of Fr. Sellinger's Remarks—Light Litigation Settlement _____ 1982," c. October 1982, LCA; "Proposals for Negotiations with Use of Field during Evening Hours," March 10, 1980, LCA.

24. Jeff Valentine, "Confrontations of Loyola, Its Neighbors, Taking Toll," *Evening Sun,* January 29, 1980.

25. [Thomas Scheye et al.], Loyola College Self-Study, 1979, LCA, 17–23, 31–34, 49–52.

26. Allan Kuuisto, Report to the Faculty, Administrators, Trustees, Students of Loyola College, 1979, LCA, 4, 6.

27. Ibid., 59, 10.

28. Ibid., 11–12.

29. Ibid., 16.

30. David Smith, "Butler Field Fate Still in Air," *Greyhound,* December 5, 1980, 1; Eileen Tehan, "Administration Reverses Decision on Butler Field," ibid., February 13, 1981, 1.

31. "The Anderson Alternative," *Greyhound,* October 31, 1980, 10.

32. Joseph A. Sellinger, 1985 Periodic Review Report of Loyola College [to the Middle States Association], April 15, 1985, LCA, B13, B15.

33. Department of Business Administration, AACSB Accreditation Proposal, Spring 1979, LCA, 1–4.

34. Conversation with Ray House, June 3, 1982.

35. Department of Business Administration, AACSB Accreditation Proposal, Spring 1979, *LCA*, 5, 11, 14, 28.

36. Thomas A. Bausch to Thomas Scheye, March 5, 1980, *LCA*.

37. Liz McMillen, "College Planners Proliferated during 1980s," *Chronicle of Higher Education*, January 27, 1988, 16.

38. Homestead II Report, Summer 1982, *LCA*, 5.

39. Ibid., 12–13; conversation with Tom Scheye, February 25, 1988.

40. Homestead II Report, Summer 1982, *LCA*, 7.

41. Conversation with Edward Donnelly, April 19, 1988.

42. Jencks and Reisman, *Academic Revolution*, 390.

43. Linda Taggart, "Knott Scholarship Program Underway, Seeks Fifty Youngsters," *Catholic Review*, October 2, 1981, 1.

44. Ramsey Flynn, "In the Name of the Father," *Baltimore Magazine*, March 1987, 48.

45. [Hollander, Cohen Associates], Summary Marketing/Opinion Survey: Prospective Students, Loyola College, May 18, 1983, *LCA*, 1–3.

46. Laura Somody, "Credit Proposal Stirs Controversary," *Greyhound*, May 18, 1981, 3.

47. Jack Breihan et al., "1981–1982: Committee on an Honors Program Report," *LCA*, 11.

48. Kathy Keeney, "Loyola Gets Half-Million Dollars NEH Grant," *Greyhound*, March 18, 1983, 4.

49. Shehan, *Blessing*, 220.

50. Kathy Keeney, "College Center Named after Trustee, *Greyhound*, October 29, 1982, 1.

51. David Simon, "Loyola Experiments with Life-Styles," *Sun*, August 30, 1983, D1.

52. Conversations with David Cordish, July 20, 1987; Tom Scheye, July 23, 1987; Joseph Sellinger, July 27, 1987.

53. Agreement between the Associated Professors of Loyola College . . . and the North Baltimore Neighborhood Coalition, c. December 10, 1986, *LCA*.

54. Conversations with Tom Scheye, July 23, 1987; Joseph Sellinger, July 27, 1987.

Select Bibliography

PRIMARY SOURCES

Archives

The minutes of the board of trustees provide the basic chronology from 1853 to 1986. Until 1947, the notations were little more than a record of some formal decisions. After 1947, the minutes began to include summaries of discussions. Since 1964, the trustees' minutes have become quite detailed.

The minister of the Jesuit community keeps a diary of house occurrences. Its title varies but generally is referred to as the house diary. Each diarist chooses what to include, and college activities are mentioned.

The prefect of studies or dean also kept a diary. These were not personal diaries but were kept to inform new deans on procedures and problems. A number of earlier volumes survive in the Loyola High School Archives. These were copied. At the college, the practice of deans keeping such diaries appears to have been discontinued after 1945.

There are two other formal sources of information about virtually any Jesuit community. These are the annual letters and the house history. They are dispatched periodically to the Jesuit general. In the nature of things, such reports tend to emphasize good news and achievement, but they also provide statistics and other information.

In the interest of brevity, only the names of the repositories used are listed:
Archdiocese of Baltimore
Cornell University Libraries
Enoch Pratt Free Library
Ferdinand Hamburger, Jr., Archives of the Johns Hopkins University
Georgetown University
Holy Cross College
Loyola College
Loyola High School
Maryland Province (Georgetown University)
Middle States Association, Philadelphia
Saint Ignatius Church

Interviews

Conversations with thirty-three alumni, especially from the 1920s through the early 1960s, are cited in the notes. Thirty-five other people, including Fathers Bunn, Beatty, and Sellinger and various officers of the administration, also provided useful information.

Newspapers and Magazines

Much of the tone of campus life and contemporaneous concerns was derived from the student newspaper, *Greyhound,* and yearbooks and variously titled publications for the alumni. These are cited when they are used for a direct quotation. Also utilized were:

The Baltimore *American* (the *News-American*)
The *Catholic Review*
The *Daily Record* (Baltimore)
The Baltimore *Evening Sun*
Journal of Saint Ignatius' Church
The Baltimore *Sun*
The Baltimore *Sunday Sun*
The *Woodstock Letters*

Government Publications

Journal of the Proceedings of the House of Delegates. Annapolis, 1853, 1888.
Journal of the Proceedings of the Senate. Annapolis, 1853, 1888.
Maryland Reports 137 (1921).
United States Supreme Court Reports 403 (1971); 426 (1976).

SECONDARY SOURCES

Books, Articles, Dissertations, and Theses

General Acounts

Ahlstrom, Sidney E. *A Religious History of the American People.* New Haven, 1972.

Dolan, Jay P. *The American Catholic Experience: A History from Colonial Times to the Present.* Garden City, N.Y., 1985.

Greeley, Andrew M. *American Catholics Since the Council: An Unauthorized Report.* Chicago, 1985.

Hennesey, James. *American Catholics: A History of the Roman Catholic Community in the United States.* New York, 1981.

Kaufmann, Christopher J. *Tradition and Transformation in Catholic Culture.* New York, 1988.

Manchester, William. *The Glory and the Dream: A Narrative History of America, 1932–1972.* Boston, 1973.

Merwick, Donna. *Boston Priests, 1848–1910.* Cambridge, 1973.

Nolan, Hugh I. *The Most Reverend Francis Patrick Kenrick, Third Bishop of Philadelphia, 1830–1851.* Philadelphia, 1948.

Perrett, Geoffrey. *Days of Sadness, Years of Triumph: The American People, 1939–1945.* Baltimore, 1973.

Spalding, Thomas W. *Martin John Spalding: American Churchman.* Washington, D.C., 1973.

Marylandiana

Baker, Jean H. *The Politics of Continuity: Maryland Political Parties from 1858 to 1870.* Baltimore, 1973.

Beirne, Francis F. *The Amiable Baltimoreans.* Baltimore, 1984.

Callcott, George H. *Maryland and America: 1940 to 1980.* Baltimore, 1985.

Callcott, Margaret Law. *The Negro In Maryland Politics, 1870–1912.* Baltimore, 1969.

Ellis, John Tracy. *The Life of James Cardinal Gibbons.* 2 vols. Milwaukee, 1952.

Hall, Clayton Colman, ed. *Baltimore: Its History and Its People.* 3 vols. New York, 1912.

Kirwin, Harry W. *The Inevitable Success.* Westminster, Md., 1962.

McCormick, Leo J. *Church-State Relationships in Education in Maryland.* Washington, D.C., 1942.

Manakee, Harold R. *Maryland during the Civil War.* Baltimore, 1961.

Marschall, John Peter. "Francis Patrick Kenrick, 1851–1863: The Baltimore Years." Ph.D. diss., Catholic University of America, 1965.

Nast, Leonora Heilig; Krause, Laurence, N.; and Monk, R. C., eds. *Baltimore: A Living Renaissance.* Baltimore, 1982.

Olson, Sherry H. *Baltimore: The Building of an American City.* Baltimore, 1980.

Owens, Hamilton. *Baltimore on the Chesapeake.* Garden City, N.Y., 1941.

Shehan, Lawrence, *A Blessing of Years: The Memoirs of Lawrence Cardinal Shehan.* Notre Dame, Ind., 1982.

Steiner, Bernard C. *History of Education in Maryland.* Washington, D.C., 1894.

Wagandt, Charles B. *The Mighty Revolution.* Baltimore, 1964.

Walsh, Richard, and Fox, William Lloyd, eds. *Maryland: A History, 1632–1974.* Baltimore, 1974.

Williams, Harold A. *The Baltimore Sun, 1837–1987.* Baltimore, 1987.

Jesuitiana

Clifford, Thomas P. "Ritual, Community, and Reform, the Catholic Experience in Baltimore: St. Ignatius' Parish, 1853–1880." Master's thesis, University of Maryland, 1986.

Connor, James L.; Padberg, John W.; and Tetlow, Joseph A. *The Jesuit Apostolate of Education in the United States: An Overview.* Washington, D.C., 1974.

Drane, Joseph K. "Juridical Substructures of American Jesuit Educational Institutions." *Jesuit Educational Quarterly* 31 (October 1968): 79–85.

Farrell, Allan P. *The Jesuit Code of Liberal Education.* Milwaukee, 1938.

FitzGerald, Paul A. *The Governance of Jesuit Colleges in the United States, 1920–1970.* Notre Dame, Ind., 1984.

Greeley, Andrew M. "The Problem of Jesuit Education in the United States." *Jesuit Educational Quarterly* 29 (October 1966): 104–20.

Grollmes, Eugene E., ed. *Guidelines for Jesuit Higher Education.* Denver, 1969.

LaFarge, John. *The Manner Is Ordinary.* New York, 1954.

Poetker, Albert H. "The Place of the Layman in Jesuit Schools." *Jesuit Educational Quarterly* 9 (June 1946): 12–19.

Ryan, John J. *Chronicle and Sketch of the Church of Saint Ignatius Loyola, Baltimore, 1856–1906.* Baltimore, 1907.

General Educational History

Ambrose, Stephen E., and Immerman, Richard H. *Milton Eisenhower: Educational Statesman.* Baltimore, 1983.

Burke, Colin B. *American Collegiate Populations: A Test of the Traditional View.* New York, 1982.

Erbacher, Sebastian Anthony. *Catholic Higher Education for Men in the United States, 1850–1866.* Washington, D.C., 1932.

Greeley, Andrew M. *The Changing Catholic College.* Chicago, 1967.

Hassenger, Robert, ed. *The Shape of Catholic Higher Education.* Chicago, 1967.

Horowitz, Helen Lefkowitz. *Campus Life: Undergraduate Culture from the End of the Eighteenth Century to the Present.* Chicago, 1987.

Jencks, Christopher, and Reisman, David. *The Academic Revolution.* Garden City, N.Y., 1968.

Leahy, William Patrick. "Jesuits, Catholics, and Higher Education in Twentieth-Century America." Ph.D. diss. Stanford University, 1986.

McGrath, John J. *Catholic Institutions in the United States: Canonical and Civil Law Status.* Washington, D.C., 1968.

Power, Edward J. *Catholic Higher Education in America: A History.* New York, 1972.

———. *A History of Catholic Higher Education in the United States.* Milwaukee, 1958.

Rudolph, Frederick, *The American College and University: A History.* New York, 1962.

Tewksbury, Donald G. *The Founding of American Colleges and Universities before the Civil War.* 1932. Reprint. New York, 1965.

Veysey, Lawrence. *The Emergence of the American University.* Chicago, 1970.

Institutional Histories

Anon. "History of Loyola College, 1852–1892." Loyola College Archives.

Brady, Charles A. *Canisius College: The First Hundred Years.* Buffalo, 1969.

Callcott, George H. *A History of the University of Maryland.* Baltimore, 1966.

Cameron, Mary David. *The College of Notre Dame, 1895–1945.* New York, 1947.

Dunigan, David B. *A History of Boston College.* Milwaukee, 1947.

Durkin, Joseph T. *Georgetown University: The Middle Years (1840–1900).* Washington, D.C., 1963.

Faherty, William B. *Better the Dream: St. Louis University and Community.* St. Louis, 1968.

French, John C. *A History of the University Founded by Johns Hopkins.* Baltimore, 1946.

Gannon, Robert I. *Up to the Present: The Story of Fordham.* Garden City, N.Y., 1967.

Gavin, Donald P. *John Carroll University: A Century of Service.* Kent, Ohio, 1985.

Hawkins, Hugh. *Between Harvard and America.* New York, 1972.

Klein, Christa R. "The Jesuits and Catholic Boyhood in Nineteenth-Century New York City: A Study of Saint John's College and the College of Saint Francis Xavier." Ph.D. diss., University of Pennsylvania, 1976.

Meagher, Walter J., and Grattan, William J. *The Spires of Fenwick.* New York, 1966.

Muller, Herman J. *The University of Detroit, 1877–1977: A Centennial History.* Detroit, 1976.

Ryan, Edmund Granville, "An Academic History of Woodstock College (1868–1944): The First Jesuit Seminary in North America." Ph.D. diss., Catholic University of America, 1964.

Ryan, John J. *Historical Sketch of Loyola College, Baltimore, 1852–1902.* N.p., n.d. [1903?].

Sweeney, Edward F. X. *The Story of the Mountain.* 2 vols. Emittsburg, Md., 1911.

Talbot, Francis X. *Jesuit Education in Philadelphia, Saint Joseph's College, 1851–1925.* Philadelphia, 1927.

Thompson, Mary Magdala. "A Brief History of Mount Saint Agnes College, 1890–1959." Master's thesis, Loyola College, 1959.

Index